SRI Internet Information $

Franklin F. Kuo, Series Edito.

INTERNET: MAILING LISTS

1993 Edition

Edited by Edward T. L. Hardie and Vivian Neou

D1307648

PTR Prentice Hall, Englewood Cliffs, New Jersey 07632

Acquisitions editor: *Mary Franz*
Cover design: *Bruce Kenselaar*
Buyer: *Mary Elizabeth McCartney*

©1993 by PTR Prentice-Hall, Inc.
A Simon & Schuster Company
Englewood Cliffs, New Jersey 07632

The publisher offers discounts on this book when ordered
in bulk quantities. For more information, contact:

> Corporate Sales Department
> PTR Prentice Hall
> 113 Sylvan Avenue
> Englewood Cliffs, New Jersey 07632
>
> Phone: 201-592-2863
> Fax: 201-592-2249

Many of the designations used by manufacturers and sellers to distinguish
their products are claimed as trademarks. Where those designations
appear in this book, and PTR Prentice Hall was aware of a trademark
claim, the designations have been printed in initial capital letters or all
capital letters.

Printed in the United States of America
10 9 8 7 6 5 4 3 2 1

ISBN   0-13-327941-3

Prentice-Hall International (UK) Limited, *London*
Prentice-Hall of Australia Pty. Limited, *Sydney*
Prentice-Hall Canada Inc., *Toronto*
Prentice-Hall Hispanoamericana, S.A., *Mexico*
Prentice-Hall of India Private Limited, *New Delhi*
Prentice-Hall of Japan, Inc., *Tokyo*
Simon & Schuster Asia Pte. Ltd., *Singapore*
Editora Prentice-Hall do Brasil, Ltda., *Rio de Janeiro*

Table of Contents

List of Figures

ACKNOWLEDGMENTS

SRI would like to extend our thanks to Rich Zellich who generously donated his time to maintain the "list of lists" for many years. We would also like to recognize the many people who maintain or moderate special interest group mailing lists. They embody the Internet tradition of information sharing, and help to make the Internet the rich informational resource it is today.

ACKNOWLEDGMENTS

THE SRI INTERNET INFORMATION SERIES

Electronic networks are a modern phenomenon; prior to the 19th century nothing existed which could even approximate the world-wide networks which seem so commonplace today. Telephone and fax services are now so expected, even banal, that few can imagine a world without them. The collection of computer networks known as the *Internet*, which has developed in the last twenty-five years, has not yet achieved that level of ubiquity, but it is rapidly approaching it.

An internet, loosely defined, is an interconnection of two or more networks. When we refer to *The Internet* in this series we refer to a specific collaboration of networks that allows users at disparate, heterogeneous computer networks to communicate with each other across organizational and geographical boundaries.

According to Dr. Vinton Cerf, the President of the Internet Society,

> The Internet is a global network of networks linked by means of the TCP/IP and other protocols. The system incorporates thousands of networks, hundreds of thousands of computers and millions of users in several dozen countries of the world. It is a grand collaboration involving private nets, public nets, government and industry sponsored nets whose operators cooperate to maintain the infrastructure.
>
> The Internet system is now poised for a rapid period of expansion during and beyond the final decade of the 20th Century. As networking, personal computing, workstations, mobile communication and distributed computing become more widespread and as information in digital form becomes a norm, the utility of systems like the Internet will rise dramatically.

The Internet is a dynamic system; its technology and protocol base is undergoing continuous change. A large community of network designers, users, and implementers are contributing to the knowledge-base of the Internet. Growth in network usage occurs so quickly as to be almost impossible to quantify, but indications are that usage has grown by at least 2000 per cent just since the beginning of this decade. The users of more than a million host machines now have some sort of access to interconnected electronic networks. For them, computer use no longer stops with their machine's capabilities or even with their organization's internal resources; their horizon is a vast, interconnected electronic world.

One of the biggest surprises to the creators of computer-based electronic networks has been the extent to which their creations have been used to connect people to people. Many networks were originally built to give people access to machine-based resources unavailable to them at their local sites, but increasingly networks have been used for access to information and human resources. Powerful mechanisms for enabling computers to share resources have become even more powerful methods for the users of those machines to share insights.

The books in the *SRI Internet Information Series* are intended as reference sources for users, implementors, designers, and students of the Internet and the protocols it uses. The *SRI Internet Information Series* is meant to be a guide both to understanding how to use certain networks for particular purposes and to understanding what our world will be like when these new resources have become as commonplace as the telephone is now.

1 INTRODUCTION

This volume of the Internet Information Series deals with mailing lists and interest groups, which provide one of the richest resources of the Internet; there are hundreds of lists covering almost every topic imaginable, allowing individuals with common interests to share their thoughts and discoveries. They are called mailing lists because they, like a church or other organization's mailing list, are built around a core group of people who are interested in information on a particular topic; the name does not, however, do justice to their many uses, as these lists are both far quicker and fully interactive.

Where a postal mailing list is usually controlled by a single entity for the distribution of information or instructions in a fairly top-down manner, electronic mailing lists are constructed so that any member (or commonly anyone knowing the name of the list) can send mail to the whole group. Electronic delivery methods are also far faster, and these enable the lists to be forums for discussions which take place in real time. (Some lists are limited to announcements or otherwise moderated, but most are free-form and allow for anyone to participate.) Because these lists are interactive and built around shared interests, participating in a mailing list is closer to being part of a conversation than being the passive recipient of an organization's mail. Through these lists users can seek help, discuss areas of common interest, or provide information unavailable through standard media.

By linking information, computer resources, and human insights, mailing lists can make the use of all three more timely and effective. While some mailing lists discuss technical matters, they are not, of course, like a disk stacker or co-processor; they don't increase effective use by maximizing the usefulness of hardware or software. They work because they make the resources of complex computing environments more human and less intimidating. Joining a mailing list can help naive users overcome any fear they may have of the complex world of electronic networks, and while following mystery writers or rock-and-roll bands may seem like a waste of time and resources to a cost-conscious system administrator, doing so helps make users aware and responsive to the resources of the net. Given the strength and size of those resources, list usage is very small overhead to pay.

1.1 Internet, BITNET and USENET

These three networks contain the bulk of traffic for special interest group mailing lists. The Internet is a network of networks throughout the world, that use the TCP/IP protocol suite and share a common name and address space. Like the Internet, BITNET is a worldwide network; its users can send mail to another user across the world just as easily as sending a message to a colleague down the hall. However, some parts of it are referred to by different names, which reflect administrative differences rather than technological ones. In Canada, the network using the NJE protocols and interconnected with BITNET is called NetNorth. In Europe, it is called the European Academic Research Network (EARN). BITNET supports mail, mailing lists, and a type of file transfer. It provides the LISTSERV mailing list function. It does not support remote login or general file transfer. It is administered in the U.S. by the Corporation for Research and Education Networking (CREN).

USENET is a worldwide network that provides the *news* broadcast service, which is rather like informational bulletin boards. USENET uses the UUCP (Unix to Unix Copy Program) protocol. The term *UUCP* is also used to refer to an affiliated network capable of sending electronic mail. The UUCP protocol was developed for Unix computers, but other types of computers can access the services via special software packages. There is no central administrative organization for USENET; normally sites wishing to join must find and attach to a site already connected.

1.2 Types of Mailing Lists

A mailing list's usefulness is partially dependant on the type of message filtering its owner has chosen. Lists which are not filtered in any way are called unmoderated lists and allow free form discussion. Since there is no restriction on the messages which are sent to the list, anyone can participate. This type of list is usually the most active as the interval between the time a message is sent and its receipt by the list members is usually a matter of minutes. However, the drawback is that these lists also often receive heavy traffic -- controversial messages to the list may result in a barrage of 10 or 20 replies in a matter of minutes. Additionally, these lists often receive messages which have little or nothing to do with the discussions on the list itself (such as "Please remove me from this list").

Moderated lists usually have a higher quality of traffic since messages which are sent to these lists are screened by the moderator before being passed on to the list's membership. The big drawback to this type of list is that it can be a fairly time-consuming task for the moderator, and there may be a longer turnaround time for messages to reach the list's membership. Since most moderators do not receive compensation for their efforts, this type of list is not as common as the unmoderated type.

Digestified lists are also popular. Messages which are sent to this type of list are gathered by the moderator, and then sent out as a group. This type of list is usually used for topics which receive heavy traffic. It helps to minimize network traffic by reducing the number of messages which subscribers receive. Digestified list messages typically have a table of contents at the beginning of each message to show what has been included in that message.

2 HOW TO JOIN A MAILING LIST

Messages to be added or removed from a mailing list should be sent to the list's maintainer, rather than to the membership of the entire mailing list. Sending this type of message to the entire list is a sure way of getting many complaints from a list's membership. There are different conventions for being added or deleted from a mailing list depending on whether the list is being solely maintained by a human, or whether the human is receiving help from an automated server.

If a person is taking care of the list, the convention is to send a message to *list*-REQUEST@host. For example, TCP-IP-REQUEST@NIC.DDN.MIL is the address to which requests for changes to the TCP-IP mailing list should be addressed. Lists which use an automated mail server will have the address *mailserver*[1]@host. In this case, a message is sent to the mail server's address with the appropriate command for being added or removed from the list. Section 3.1 describes the most commonly used automated mail servers.

If neither of the above conventions works for the list in which you are interested, try sending a message to the coordinator's address. Only as a last resort, should this type of message be sent to the list itself.

After your request is received and processed you will usually receive a message indicating that you have been sucessfully added to the list. You may also receive a description of a list, and guidelines for the use of the list. After that, you should begin to receive messages that are sent to the mailing list.

2.1 Guidelines for Using Mailing Lists

A mailing list's usefulness is directly tied to the quality of its members' participation. The following guidelines, which are based on the Usenet posting rules by Gene Spafford and Mark Horton, should help you make your participation on a list meaningful and embarrassment-free.

Before sending a message to a mailing list, make sure that it is appropriate for that list. Some mailing lists are intended for discussions and some for announcements or queries. It is not usually a good idea to carry on discussions in mailing lists that are designated

---

[1]*Mailserver* should be replaced with the name of the mail server -- such as LISTSERV or Majordomo

otherwise. It is never a good idea to carry on "meta-discussions" about whether a given discussion is appropriate. This type of traffic mushrooms until nobody can find messages that belong.

When you are replying to a message that has been sent to the list, consider whether your reply should be sent to the person who sent the original message, or the whole list. This is especially true if you are unhappy with what some user said. In most cases it is much better to send him or her mail directly; not to the entire list. For example, if someone sends a message like "please remove me from the list," there is no point in bogging down the list with even more mail just to let the person know that administrative requests shouldn't go to the whole list. If you feel compelled to reply to this type of message, only mail it to the sender - not to the whole list.

Do not send announcements regarding major news events -- by the time most people receive such items, they will long since have been informed by conventional media..

The "Subject" field of your mail message should give a reasonable summary of the contents of the message. This helps list members to sort and file mail messages. When you reply to a message, summarize it if appropriate. If your mail program allows you to include the old message in your reply consider using that facility, but be sure to remove parts of the old message that are irrelevant. When asking a question in a discussion list, request that people reply directly to you. After you have gathered the replies post a summary to the list.

If you have a standard signature you like to append to your messages, try to keep it concise, as people do not appreciate seeing lengthy signatures, nor paying the phone bills to repeatedly transmit them. Two or three lines are usually plenty. Sometimes it is also appropriate to add another line or two for addresses on other major networks where you can be reached (e.g., UUCP, BITNET). Long signatures are definitely frowned upon. Do not include drawings, pictures, maps, or other graphics in your signature. It is not the appropriate place for such material and is viewed as rude by other readers.

In preparing a message, be aware that people will be reading your message on many different types of machines. Cute pictures, and long lines which look fine on your system may be unrecognizable on another someone else's system. Your messages will be the most readable if you keep these things in mind while you are composing them:

1. Except for source code, keep your lines under 80 characters, and under 72 if possible. (most editors have a fill or format mode that will do this for you automatically)

2. Right justified text is almost always harder to read than leaving ragged right margins; do not justify your messages.

3. Most special control characters will not work on many systems. In fact, the space character is about the only one you can be sure will work consistently. Even tabs aren't always the same from machine to machine, and should be avoided. Many mail agents will strip or remap control characters.

4. Pictures and diagrams should not use embedded tabs.

5. Submissions in a single case (all upper or all lower) are difficult to read.

3 STARTING YOUR OWN LIST

If the topic you want is not listed here, you might consider starting your own list. To do this, all you need is some extra time, and a computer system that has network connectivity and can handle mailing lists. Most systems are able to handle this type of mail activity, but there are a few that cannot. To find out if your system can handle mailing lists, check with your system administrator. At the same time, ask your system administrator whether or not any automated mail service software is available to help with the maintenance of your list. If such software is available, it will make your task much easier. Section 3.1 describes some of the automated mail systems that are currently in use on the Internet.

Once you verified that you have the technical pieces in place for handling mailing lists, you must decide what you want from your list. Some issues that you should consider are: What should the scope of discussions on the list be? Do you want to moderate the list or allow free form discussion? Do you want to use a digest format? Do you want to keep archives of the messages that are sent to the list?

If you have time, you should consider keeping a "Frequently Asked Questions" (FAQ) list for your list. Much of the extraneous traffic on a mailing list comes from new list members who are asking questions that have already been asked and answered several times. By collecting these questions (and their answers) in a file which is made available to list members, you can reduce the amount of unnecessary traffic on your list.

After you have decided what you want from your list, write a mission statement for the list. This should include:

- A description of the topics that the list will cover.
- Policy guidelines for the types of messages that are appropriate for the list.
- If you plan to keep archives or a FAQ for your list, include information on where they will be and how to retrieve them.

This description will be used to announce the list to the Internet community, and should be sent to new list members. See figure 3 for a sample list description.

If you decide to provide your list in a digest format, there are numerous programs available on the Internet to help you do this. Two such programs are DIGEST and DLIST by Frank Wancho, which are available via anonymous FTP on Simtel20.Army.Mil. RFC 1153, *Digest Message Format*, describes a de facto standard for digest messages.

Now that you have decided what the list will look like, you need to set up the underlying mechanism to support it. If you are fortunate, your system will have an automated mailing list server such as listserv or majordomo. In this case, you should be able to get the instructions on the use of the system from your system adminstrator. If a server is not

List Name: CouchPotato@TV.COM

This is a mailing list for discussions regarding the art of watching television and associated topics. Members of this list must watch at least 50 hours of television each week; PBS does not count. Appropriate topics include:

- Video surfing
- Concurrently watching multiple TVs
- Late night TV shows

This is list not moderated so all messages sent to the list address are immediately forwarded to the list.

To join or be removed from the CouchPotato mailing list, send a message to CouchPotato-Request@TV.COM.

All messages to the list are being archived in pub/Couch/CouchPotato.nn.Z where nn stands for the year during which the messages were sent. The files are kept in a compressed format. There is also a FAQ for this list. It is kept in pub/Couch/FAQ. Archives and the FAQ are kept on FTP.TV.COM and are available via anonymous FTP.

List Coordinator:

I.M. Potato   1234 Couch St.
IMP@TV.COM   Family Room, NY

Figure 3-1: Sample List Description

available, the first step is to make a file that will contain the list of e-mail addresses for the people on your list. Consult the documentation on the mail system used on your computer (or ask your system administrator) to find out the format for the addresses. A list on a Unix system that uses the sendmail mail system would look like this:

```
user1@host1,
user2@host2,
localuser1,
localuser2
```

For ease of maintenance it is usually easier to place each entry on a separate line. After you set up the file (which initially will probably only have your address in it), ask your system administrator to place an entry in the master system mailing list that points to your file. In addition, have your administrator put a "-request" address in the list that points to your mailbox (or a file in which you can gather the messages).

If the mail system has a mechanism to allow error messages about bad addresses on the list to be sent to you (since you will be the list's maintainer) rather than the members of the list, have your system administrator set that up for you as well. This is particularly important as it greatly reduces a list's usefulness if most of the messages sent to it are error messages about bad addresses. This mechanism typically works by having an entry called owner-*LISTNAME* or *LISTNAME*-relay in the master system mailing list. The system will then send any error messages that are generated by the list to this address.

For example, if you wanted to set up a list for X-window users, you could create a file called *xwindow.dist* to hold the list of addresses for people that want to be on the list. After you create the file, have your system administrator put the entry *x-window-users* in the system mailing list and point it at your file. At the same time, have the administrator put in an entry, x-window-users-requests, that points to your mailbox. This way, requests to be added or deleted from the list will go to you rather than the list.

Once everything is in place, you are are ready to announce your list's existence to the Internet community. You can do this by sending a message containing your description to interest-groups-request@nisc.sri.com and to NEW-LIST@VM1.NODAK.EDU.

3.1 Automated List Management Systems

The task of maintaining a mailing list can be a cumbersome and time-consuming process. Fortunately, several automated list management systems have been created to make this task as pain-free as possible. Some of the most popular systems are described in the following sections.

3.1.1 LISTSERV

LISTSERV stands for *list server*, and was developed by Eric Thomas on the BITNET network. LISTSERV runs on IBM systems running the VM operating system. It provides a powerful mechanism for allowing lists to be maintained and archived with relatively little human intervention. A host which has a LISTSERV server will have the address *LISTSERV@HOST* to handle requests for changes to all the mailing lists that use the list server mechanism on that host.

Some of the commands which are available for lists that use this mechanism are:

Info	<topic|?>	Get detailed information files
List	<Detail|Short|Global>	Get a description of all lists
SUBscribe	listname <full_name>	Subscribe to a list
SIGNOFF	listname	Sign off from a list
SIGNOFF	* (NETWIDE	Sign off from all lists on all servers
REView	listname <options>	Review a list
STats	listname <options>	Review list statistics

Query	listname	Query personal distribution options
SET	listname options	Set personal distribution options
INDex	<filelist_name>	Obtain a list of LISTSERV files
GET	filename filetype	Obtain a file from LISTSERV
REGister	full_name|OFF	Tell LISTSERV about your name

To subscribe to a list that uses the LISTSERV mechanism, send a message to the LISTSERV address with the command *SUBSCRIBE MYLIST* in the body of the message. If the address listed is:

> AMERCATH on LISTSERV@UKCC

You would send a mail message to LISTSERV@UKCC with a message body containing:

> SUB AMERCATH

If you are on the Internet, you would also need to convert the BITNET hostname to an Internet hostname, so the address would become:

> LISTSERV%UKCC@CUNYVM.CUNY.EDU

If you want to get off a list that uses the LISTSERV mechanism, send a message containing the "SIGNOFF" command. For example, to be removed from the AMERCATH list, you would send a message to LISTSERV@UKCC containing:

> SIGNOFF AMERCATH

In recent years, mail servers which are similar to LISTSERV have been written for Unix. These servers are frequently referred to as *listserv* servers, with the word in lowercase letters. The most popular implentation was written by Anastasios C. Kotsikonas at Boston University. It is available via anonymous ftp in /pub/listserv on cs.bu.edu. There is a mailing list called unix-listserv@stormking.com that is served by listserv@stormking.com to discuss this version of listserv.

3.1.2 Majordomo

Majordomo is another system that handles routine administration of mailing lists. It was written by Brent Chapman, and is modeled after LISTSERV. Unlike the *listserv* server for Unix, the commands used with this system are not compatible with LISTSERV. The commands that are available with Majordomo are:

Command	Description
subscribe *list* [*address*]	Subscribe yourself to to *list*
unsubscribe *list* [*address*]	Unsubscribe yourself from *list*
which [*address*]	Find out which lists you are on

who [*address*]	Show the members of *list*
info [*address*]	Show the general introductory information for *list*
lists	Show the lists handled by this Majordomo server
help	Retrieve a help message
end	Stop processing commands

Majordomo is available via anonymous FTP in "pub/majordomo.tar.Z" on FTP.GreatCircle.COM. The mailing list Majordomo-Users@GreatCircle.COM is available for discussions about this package. Another list, List-Managers-Owner@GreatCircle.COM, is available for discussions about general issues related to mailing list maintenance.

4 THE LIST OF LISTS

This chapter contains the descriptions of over 800 Internet mailing lists. The descriptions were provided by the owners of the mailing lists. Most entries are in the format:

ListName@HomeHost

> Description of the list and suggested topic areas for submissions to the list.

> How to join the list and location of archives if they exist.

Some entries may list several addresses for postings to the list. In general, multiple addresses display formats for different networks such as BITNET or UUCP. If the hostname for an entry ends in ".BITNET", the address is for a system on BITNET. If no corresponding entry is listed for the Internet, the address can be converted for use in the Internet by changing the "@" in the address to a "%" and then adding the name of one of the gateways between BITNET and the Internet at the end of the address. One of the gateways between BITNET and the Internet is CUNYVM.CUNY.EDU. For example,

> 3COM-L@NUSVM.BITNET

would become

> 3COM-L%NUSVM.BITNET@CUNYVM.CUNY.EDU

SRI tries keep entries current. However, since information is provided by the list maintainers, some entries may be out of date.

386USERS@UDEL.EDU

> A moderated list for Intel 80386 topics, including hardware and software questions, reviews, rumors, etc. Open to owners, users, prospective users, and the merely curious.

> Archives are available via an electronic mail server. Details about its use can be obtained by sending a request to 386USERS-REQUEST@UDEL.EDU. All requests to be added to or deleted from this list, problems, questions, etc., should be sent to 386USERS-REQUEST@UDEL.EDU.

> List Maintainer: James Galvin <galvin@UDEL.EDU>
> List Moderator: Bill Davidsen <davidsen@CRDOS1.UUCP>

3COM-L%NUSVM.BITNET@CUNYVM.CUNY.EDU (Internet)
3COM-L on LISTSERV@NUSVM.BITNET

> This mailing list is to discuss 3Com products, such as 3+ Network, 3+Open LAN Manager, 3+Open TCP, 3+/3+Open Mail, NDIS, MultiConnect Repeater, LanScanner, 3Com Ethernet Cards etc.

> To subscribe, send the following command to one of the addresses above:

> SUBSCRIBE 3COM-L your_full_name.

> Archives of 3COM-L discussions can be listed by sending the command INDEX 3COM-L to LISTSERV@NUSVM.BITNET

Owner: Chandra Liem <CCECL@NUSVM.BITNET>

3D@BFMNY0.UU.NET
3D%BFMNY0@UUNET.UU.NET

An unmoderated list for discussing 3-D (Stereo) photography. Topics include tips, techniques, reviews, general information, war stories, and event announcements. Open to everyone interested in 3-D, including photographers, collectors, and those who want to know more about 3-D.

No formal archive facility is in place for 3D yet but all submissions will be archived privately and something may be set up later.

All requests to be added to or deleted from this list, problems, questions, etc., should be sent to 3D-REQUEST@BFMNY0.UU.NET.

Coordinator: Tom Neff <3D-REQUEST@BFMNY0.UU.NET> <tneff%bfmny0@UUNET.UU.NET>

4DOS on ListServ@IndyCMS
ListServ@IndyCMS.IUPUI.Edu

4DOS (4DOS command interpreter) is dedicated to discussion of the 4DOS command interpreter, or "DOS Shell," produced by JP Software Inc. 4DOS (the list) is completely independent of 4DOS (the command interpreter) and JP Software Inc (the manufacturer).

To subscribe to 4DOS send the following command SUB 4DOS yourfirstname yourlastname in the BODY or mail (or an interactive command on BITNET) to LISTSERV@INDYCMS.BITNET or LISTSERV@INDYCMS.IUPUI.EDU.

4DOS is owned and coordinated by an interested user (John B Harlan).

    List owner/coordinator: John B Harlan
                IJBH200@IndyVAX
                IJBH200@IndyVAX.IUPUI.Edu

78-L@cornellc.cit.cornell.edu

78-L is a discussion group devoted to music and recordings of the pre-LP era. The list is open to collectors and lovers of all kinds of music of this era, such as early jazz and blues, big bands, show music, vaudeville, classical, etc., as well as spoken word and other historical recordings. We also welcome discussion of recording history, discography, the collectors' market, and vintage phonographs. The group is not slanted toward any particular type of music or collector interest. Whether you're into cylinders or discs, vintage jazz or big bands, cranking up a victrola or playing your records through modern stereo equipment, we welcome your participation and hope that we can learn from each other and broaden our musical tastes. The common element is that what we listen to was recorded at (or near) 78 rpm.

The list is open and unmoderated. To subscribe, send mail to listserv@cornell.edu with the following text: 'SUB 78-L <your name>'.

If you have any questions about 78-L, contact the owner.

Owner: Doug Elliot <de3@cornellc.cit.cornell.edu>

90210@ferkel.ucsb.edu   [Last Update 8/92]

Purpose: Discussion of the Fox TV show, *Beverly Hills, 90210*.

Contact: 90210-request@ferkel.ucsb.edu (Jim Lick)

9370-L%HEARN.BITNET@MITVMA.MIT.EDU

Discussion of topics specific to the IBM 9370 family and the VM/IS packaging system, and the special opportunities/problems of those products.

To subscribe send the following command to LISTSERV@HEARN (non-BitNet users send mail to LISTSERV%HEARN.BITNET@MITVMA.MIT.EDU with the command in the message body): SUBSCRIBE 9370-L Your_Full_Name where Your_Full_Name is your real name, not your userid. To unsubscribe, send: UNSUBSCRIBE 9370-L

Coordinator: Rob van Hoboken <RCOPROB%HDETUD1@MITVMA.MIT.EDU>

9NOV89-L@DBOTUI11.BITNET   [Last Update 28 January-92]

Mailing list for whoever may attach a meaning to the date of 9.11.1989 (or 89-11-09, or 11/9/89). Unfortunately the people living in the German Democratic Republic will not be able to participate in this discussion, because they are not (yet?) on this network. The list name reflects the most important event in the recent German history, but it can't and shouldn't be seen isolated from what happened, and is now happening, in Poland, the USSR, and Hungary before. And yes, dear Joe Techno, all this will influence even such important things as our networks.

To subscribe, send a message to LISTSERV@DBOTUI11 (BitNet) or LISTSERV%DBOTUI11.BITNET@VM1.NODAK.EDU (Internet) with the following command in the body (text) of the message: SUB 9NOV89-L your_full_name where "your_full_name" is your real name, not your login Id. (Example: SUB 9NOV89-L Jane Doe)

Coordinator: Gerard Gschwind (GSCHWIND@DBOTUI11.bitnet)

A.Rice@HAMPVMS.BITNET (BITNET)

A list has been created for the discussion of the works of Anne Rice. The address is A.Rice@HAMPVMS.BITNET.

To subscribe, send a request to ngustas@HAMPVMS.BITNET.

Coordinator: GABRIELLE DE LIONCOURT <NGUSTAS%HAMPVMS.BITNET@VM1.NoDak.EDU>

AAI@ST-LOUIS-EMH2.ARMY.MIL

Digest for discussion of the Automated AUTODIN Interface system. The AAI system is a series of programs that interface a data processing installation (DPI) with an AUTODIN switching center. This digest will provide information to the user community and other personnel interested in the developments/enhancements and implementation thereof.

The AAI-Digests (and past AAI-Digest files contained in the Archive directory) are organized by Volume # and Issue #. Information was informally disseminated prior to the initiation of the AAI digest, and those newsletters stored in the aai account Archive directory can be requested by reference to month and year.

All requests to be added to or deleted from this list, problems, questions, etc., should be sent to AAI@ST-LOUIS-EMH2.ARMY.MIL.

Coordinator: Jo Ann M. Bohnenstiehl <jb1742@ST-LOUIS-EMH2.ARMY.MIL> Carol McDonald <carolmc@ST-LOUIS-EMH2.ARMY.MIL>

AAVLD-L on LISTSERV@UCDCVDLS.BITNET   [Last Update 9/92]

This list has been created to provide a forum for discussion between veterinary diagnostic laboratories and members of the AAVLD. Topics such as test standardization, fees, diagnostic information assistance, animal health surveillance, reports on conferences and symposia are especially welcomed. Discussions related to specific cases should be approached within the limits of diagnostic medicine and restrict discussions of therapy or treatments. The latter is discussed on another list, VETMED-L@UGA.BITNET

The list will be limited to members of the AAVLD.

Archives of AAVLD-L and related files are stored in the AAVLD-L FILELIST. To receive a list of files, send the command INDEX AAVLD-L to LISTSERV@UCDCVDLS.BITNET

To subscribe to the list, send the following command to LISTSERV@UCDCVDLS via interactive message or in the BODY of e-mail:

SUBSCRIBE AAVLD-L Your_Full_Name

eg. SUBSCRIBE AAVLD-L John Doe

List Owner: Jim Case DVM,Ph.D (JCASE@UCDCVDLS.BITNET)
James T. Case, Administrator   University of California
Information Systems   School of Veterinary Medicine
California Veterinary Diagnostic   P.O. Box 1770
  Laboratory System   Davis, CA 95617
jcase@ucdcvdls.bitnet   (916)752-4408

ACADV%NDSUVM1.BITNET@VM1.NODAK.EDU

ACADV is a private forum for those engaged in the delivery of academic advising services in higher education; it is primarily for professional advisors (those employed in the field of academic advising) and for faculty members who have academic advising responsibilities, rather than for computer support personnel.

Individuals in the field of academic advising may subscribe to the forum by sending the following message to LISTSERV@NDSUVM1 interactively: SUB ACADV your_full_name where "your_full_name" is your real name, not your login Id. (Example: SUB ACADV John R. Doe) Non-BitNet advisors can subscribe by sending the above command as the text/body of a message to LISTSERV%NDSUVM1.BITNET@VM1.NODAK.EDU.

Monthly notebooks are maintained and may be retrieved by any member of the forum by sending the command: INDEX ACADV

Coordinator: Dr. Harold L. Caldwell
<00HLCALDWELL%BSUVAX1.BITNET@VM1.NODAK.EDU>

ACSOFT-L%WUVMD.BITNET@CUNYVM.CUNY.EDU
ACSOFT-L@WUVMD

This list is for discussing all aspects of academic software development.

Some topics for discussion are:

- Courseware development
- Research tool development
- Institutional policies regarding development & use
- Development practices
- Available resources (including grant sources)
- Design techniques
- Faculty acceptance of courseware
- Role played by development in the faculty reward system
- Support policies
- Reviews

Types of academic software include:

- Simulations
- Authoring techniques
- Hypermedia
- Immersion learning environments
- Interactive learning
- Drills

To subscribe send an interactive message or mail to LISTSERV@WUVMD (LISTSRV%WUVMD.BITNET@CUNYVM.CUNY.EDU, for Internet users) containing SUB ACSOFT-L FirstName LastName.

Please do NOT send these commands to the list address ACSOFT-L@WUVMD. Doing so will cause your request to be broadcast to all subscribers and will not cause your name to be added to the list.

Comments and questions should be directed to:

ListOwner: Timothy Bergeron, C09615TB@WUVMD.BITNET
ListMaster: Steve Middlebrook, C94882SM@WUVMD.BITNET

ACTNOW-L on LISTSERV@BROWNVM.BITNET

College Activism/Information list.

To subscribe to this list, send the command,

SUBSCRIBE ACTNOW-L <myname> / <myschool> (for example, SUBSCRIBE ACTNOW-L John Q. Public / The University at Anytown)

to the LISTSERV machine at BrownVM. Be certain to send the command from the same account which you will normally be submitting articles from.

If you have questions about the list, please address them via electronic mail to one or more of the following network addresses:

ST710852@brownvm.brown.edu (ST701852@BROWNVM on BITNET)
atropos@drycas.club.cc.cmu.edu (atropos@DRYCAS on BITNET)

ADA-SW@WSMR-SIMTEL20.ARMY.MIL

A mailing list for those who in accessing and contributing software to the Ada Repository on SIMTEL20; it serves two purposes: to provide an information exchange medium between the repository users and to mail repository submissions to the Coordinator for inclusion in the archives.

Mail archives are kept on host WSMR-SIMTEL20.ARMY.MIL as TOPS20 mail files named yymm.n-TXT, where n starts with one and increments by one into another file as each file reached 150 disk pages. To conserve disk space, all the mail files in the archive, except for the current year, are individually compressed. The compressed files have the suffix -Z as part of the filetype field; they should be renamed to have the suffix .Z (uppercase Z) when transferred to a Unix system so the uncompress program will find them. The current month's mail is still kept in ADA-SW-ARCHIV.TXT. The archives are stored in directory: PD2:<ARCHIVES.ADA-SW> Archive files are available via ANONYMOUS FTP from WSMR-SIMTEL20.ARMY.MIL for those with TCP/IP access to the Internet.

The Ada Repository is divided into several subdirectories. These directories are organized by topic, and their names and a brief overview of their topics are contained in file PD:<ADA.GENERAL>DIRLIST.DOC. All requests to be added to or deleted from this list, problems, questions, etc., should be sent to ADA-SW-REQUEST@WSMR-SIMTEL20.ARMY.MIL.

Coordinator: Rick Conn <RCONN@WSMR-SIMTEL20.ARMY.MIL>

ADDICT-L on LISTSERV@KENTVM   [Last Updated 28-January-1992]
or LISTSERV@KENTVM.KENT.EDU

ADDICT-L is an electronic conference for mature discussion of the many types of addictions experienced by a large portion of society. The focus of this list is to provide an information exchange network for individuals interested in researching, educating or recovering from a variety of addictions. It is not the intent of this list to focus on one area of addiction, but rather to discuss the phenomena of addiction as it relates to areas of sexual, co-dependency, eating addiction, etc... Truly a list that many aspects could be discussed.

- -- All individuals with an interest in the topic area are welcome.
- -- Subscriptions of those interested will be added by the listowner
- -- Subscribers should look forward to educating themselves about addictions, and discussing relevant topics related to addiction and recovery.
- -- Intended as an information exchange network and discussion group

Possible Appropriate Subjects:

-- Discussion of etiology of addictions
-- Effects of addictions
-- Recovery from addiction and 12 Step Programs
-- Recent article publications relevant to addiction literature
-- Networking with others having related interests

Drug/Alcohol addiction has a way of becoming an easy topic of discussion. It is the intent of this list to broaden the awareness of addictions into a variety of other areas. There are Electronic lists devoted to drug/alcohol use for those interested only in that area

Subscription Procedure:

To subscribe from a bitnet account send an interactive or e-mail message addressed to LISTSERV@KENTVM. Internet users send mail to LISTSERV@KENTVM.KENT.EDU (In mail, leave the subject line blank and make the text of your message the following:

SUB ADDICT-L Yourfirstname Yourlastname

Questions can be addressed to listowner: David Delmonico Ddelmoni@kentvm.kent.edu

ADND-L%UTARLVM1.BITNET@CUNYVM.CUNY.EDU

Mailing list for discussing all aspects of the Dungeons & Dragons and Advanced Dungeons & Dragons games -- new spells, new monsters, etc...

To subscribe, send the following command to LISTSERV@UTARLVM1 via mail or interactive message: SUB ADND-L your_full_name where "your_full_name" is your real name, not your login Id. For example: SUB ADND-L Joan Doe Non-BitNet users can subscribe by sending the above command in the body of a message to LISTSERV%UTARLVM1.BITNET@CUNYVM.CUNY.EDU.

Also, the list is also peered at ADND-L@PUCC.

Coordinators: Faustino Cantu <FGC82B1%PANAM.BITNET@CUNYVM.CUNY.EDU>

adolph-a-carrot@ANDREW.CMU.EDU

Mailing list dedicated to the music of the Severed Heads and of bands on the Ralph label.

The Severed Heads are an Australian band that has been releasing music since 1980. Their recent albums have also been released in Europe and the USA. Ralph Records is a San Francisco label, and includes/has included the Residents, Tuxedomoon, Yello, Renaldo & The Loaf, Penn Jillette, Snakefinger, Fred Frith, Clubfoot Orchestra, Rhythm & Noise, MX 80 Sound, Eugene Chadbourne, & more. We also welcome discussion of Ralph's friends, such as the Longshoremen and the Blitzoids.

All requests to be added, dropped, etc., should be sent to adolph-a-carrot-request@andrew.cmu.edu

Coordinator: Yary Richard Phillip Hluchan <yh0a+@ANDREW.CMU.EDU>

ADV-ELO on LISTSERV@UTFSM.BITNET   [Last Update 11/92]

ADV-ELO is a list to discuss the latest advances in electronics.

Archives of ADV-ELO can be listed by sending the command INDEX to LISTSERV@UTFSM.

To subscribe, send the following command to LISTSERV@UTFSM via mail or interactive message. SUB ADV-ELO your full name Where "your full name" is your name. For example: SUB ADV-ELO Francisco Fernandez

Owner: Francisco Javier Fernandez (FFERNAND@UTFSM.BITNET)

ADV-ELI on LISTSERV@UTFSM.BITNET   [Last Update 11/92]

ADV-ELI is a list to discuss the latest advances in electric engineering.

Archives of ADV-ELI can be listed by sending the command INDEX to LISTSERV@UTFSM.BITNET

To subscribe, sent the following command to LISTSERV@UTFSM via mail or interactive message. SUB ADV-ELI your full name Where "your full name" is your name. For example: SUB ADV-ELI Francisco Fernandez

Owner: Francisco Javier Fernandez (FFERNAND@UTFSM.BITNET)

ADV-INFO on LISTSERV@UTFSM.BITNET   [Last Update 11/92]

ADV-INFO is a list to discuss the latest advances in computing.

Archives of ADV-INFO can be listed by sending the command INDEX to LISTSERV@UTFSM.

To subscribe, sent the following command to LISTSERV@UTFSM.BITNET via mail or interactive message.

SUB ADV-INFO your full name

Where "your full name" is your name. For example:

SUB ADV-INFO Francisco Fernandez

Owner: Francisco Javier Fernandez (FFERNAND@UTFSM.BITNET)

ADVANC-L on LISTSERV@IDBSU.BITNET

This list deals with the Geac Advance library system, which is used for online library catalogs, library circulation, book acquisitions, and journal control. All issues relating to the Advance hardware and software are relevant. To subscribe send mail to LISTSERV@IDBSU.BITNET with the body containing SUB ADVANC-L yourfirstname yourlastname

Owner:
Dan Lester   1910 University Dr. Bitnet: ALILESTE@IDBSU
Library   Boise, Idaho 83725 Internet:
Boise State University (208) 385-1234   ALILESTE@IDBSU.IDBSU.EDU

ADVISE-L%CANADA01.BITNET@CUNYVM.CUNY.EDU

Unmoderated mailing list intended for discussion among students who work part-time at the various university computer centers. It is particularly intended for people who work as student advisors or consultants, although others are welcome. Another use of the list is to get help from others on problems that might be encountered, or to let everyone know about new things such as new file servers, so that everyone can put the network to the best possible use.

Alternate paths/addresses: The list is served by 5 servers (ADVISE-L@UTORONTO, ADVISE-L@CANADA01, ADVISE-L@NCSUVM, ADVISE-L@UGA, and MD4F@CMUCCVMA) which are peer linked so that anything sent to one will be sent to the other two automatically. ADVISE-L@NCSUVM is probably the closest server to the CUNYVM Internet gateway.

To subscribe to the list:

From a VM site on BITNET do: TELL LISTSERV at CANADA01 SUBSCRIBE ADVISE-L Your_Full_Name where Your_Full_Name is your real name (not your userid).

From a VMS BITNET site use the SEND/REMOTE command.

If you are at a site not on bitnet or where you cannot send interactive messages you can send a message to LISTSERV%CANADA01.BITNET@CUNYVM.CUNY.EDU where the first non-header line consists of: SUBSCRIBE ADVISE-L Your_Full_Name

Please refer any questions to the Coordinator.

Coordinator: Scott Campbell <SCOTT%UTORONTO.BITNET@CUNYVM.CUNY.EDU>
<scott%utcs.toronto.edu@RELAY.CS.NET>

SCOTT@UTORONTO.BITNET

aeronautics@rascal.ics.utexas.edu

Purpose: The "aeronautics" mailing list is a moderated version of the sci.aeronautics newsgroup, and as such will deal with various technical aspects of aviation, such as human factors, airliner operations, avionics, and aerodynamics. It will be a one-way feed (sci.aeronautics -> mailing list), unless sufficient demand requires that it go in the opposite direction.

Contact: aeronautics-request@rascal.ics.utexas.edu

AFAS-L on LISTSERV@KENTVM   [Last Updated 6/92]
   or LISTSERV@KENTVM.KENT.EDU

Discussion of African American Studies and and Librarianship

AFAS-L is a computer conference among librarians and other interested people on topics relating to African American Experience and Librarianship. Topics can include peripheral issues such as race relations and multicultural diversity. Sample topics that could be discussed on this list include:

Information literacy and African Americans Pan African resources and core collections The impact of an afrocentric curriculum on society Subject headings for ethnic groups (controlled vocabulary) And many more...

To join AFAS-L, send e-mail to LISTSERV@KENTVM on BITNET or LISTSERV@KENTVM.KENT.EDU on the Internet with the following command in the BODY of the mail: SUB AFAS-L your full name

To send a message to AFAS-L, send your e-mail message to AFAS-L@KENTVM

This list is open but moderated. Anything intentionally posted to the list will appear on the list. The moderators will provide feedback on the appropriateness of a given posting, although anything that a subscriber thinks is appropriate is. Comments and suggestions on the functioning and moderating policy, however, should be posted directly to the moderators and will be considered carefully.

The moderators of AFAS-L are librarians in academic institutions:

Rochelle Redmond Ballard	fdballar@ucf1vm.Bitnet
Gladys Smiley Bell	gbell@kentvm.Bitnet
Gerald Holmes	gholmes@kentvm.Bitnet
Stanton Biddle	sfbbb@cunyvm.Bitnet
Michael Walker	mwalker@vcuvax.Bitnet
Carol Ritzen Kem	carolkem@nervm.Bitnet
Mark G. R. McManus	mmcmanus@s850.mwc.edu

AFRICA-L on LISTSERV@BRUFMG.BITNET   [Last Updated 27-March-1992]

A Pan-African forum for the discussion of the interests of African peoples (in Africa, and expatriate), and for those with an interest in the African continent and her peoples. Of special interest will be ways to help facilitate the flow of communications (electronic and other) to and from Africa. News, light-hearted discussions, and cultural and educational items are welcome.

To subscribe to AFRICA-L send the following message to LISTSERV@BRUFMG: (Note that this is a BITNET address)

   SUBSCRIBE AFRICA-L your name and your African interests
   SET AFRICA-L REPRO

   For example,   subscribe africa-l J. Smith Togo
                   set africa-l repro

To obtain a list of current subscribers, send the message "review africa-l" to

LISTSERV@BRUFMG.BITNET.

List Owner: Carlos Fernando Nogueira (CTEDTC09@BRUFPB)

AFRICANA on LISTSERV@WMVM1 or LISTSERV@wmvm1.cc.wm.edu [Last Update 11/92]

The purpose of AFRICANA LISTSERV is to provide an electronic forum for sharing and exchanging information on the various activities going on in the field of information technology in Africa. Interested parties are invited to post notices, questions, ideas and pertinent information on WHO is Doing WHAT, WHERE, HOW WHEN and even WHY anywhere on the continent of Africa.

We are interested in learning about successful, interactive linkages with institutions on the African continent. Tell us about your successes and failures, hardware, software, problems, solutions, on-going collaborative projects, policy and logistical issues, impending plans and so forth. Tell us about all applicable communication technologies that make it possible today for residents in Africa to interact with others around the world quickly.

One particularly vexing problem we are faced with is how to develop a viable infrastructure for accessing the new information technologies in African business and learning institutions. Some of you out there have or have had exciting experiences in linking parts of Africa with the global network. Let us hear from you!

Archives are stored in the AFRICANA FILELIST. To receive a list of available files, send the command INDEX AFRICANA to LISTSERV@WMVM1 or LISTSERV@wmvm1.cc.wm.edu.

To subscribe to AFRICANA, send the following command to LISTSERV@WMVM1 or LISTSERV@wmvm1.cc.wm.edu via mail text or interactive message: SUBSCRIBE AFRICANA firstname lastname For example, SUBSCRIBE AFRICANA Joan Doe

Owner: Paa-Bekoe Welbeck <PBWELB@WMVM1> or <pbwelb@wmvm1.cc.wm.edu>

AG-EXP-L%NDSUVM1.BITNET@CUNYVM.CUNY.EDU

Discusses the use of Expert Systems in Agricultural production and management. Primary emphasis is for practitioners, Extension personnel and Experiment Station researchers in the land grant system.

BITNET, EARN, or NetNorth subscribers can join by sending the Listserv SUB command with your name. For example, SEND LISTSERV@NDSUVM1 SUB AG-EXP-L Jon Doe or TELL LISTSERV AT NDSUVM1 SUB AG-EXP-L Jon Doe To be removed from the list, SEND LISTSERV@NDSUVM1 SIGNOFF AG-EXP-L or TELL LISTSERV AT NDSUVM1 SIGNOFF AG-EXP-L

Those without interactive access may send the Listserv Command portion of the above lines as the first TEXT line of a message. For example: SUB AG-EXP-L Jon Doe would be the only line in the body (text) of mail to LISTSERV@NDSUVM1.

Monthly public logs of mail to AG-EXP-L are kept on LISTSERV for a few months. For a list of files send the 'Index AG-EXP-L' command to LISTSERV%NDSUVM1.BITNET@CUNYVM.CUNY.EDU.

Coordinator: Sandy Sprafka <NU020746%NDSUVM1.BITNET@CUNYVM.CUNY.EDU>

AIBI-L on LISTSERV@UOTTAWA or LISTSERV@ACADVM1.UOTTAWA.CA

AIBI-L is the LISTSERV discussion forum of l'Association internationale bible et informatique).

AIBI-L is an on-going forum and meeting place for AIBI members and others who wish to join the discussion of issues related to the computerised-analysis of Biblical and related texts.

Possible subjects for discussion include (but are not limited to) computer-based interpretation of specific texts, methodological questions, preparation of the text for computerised analysis, software-design and programming, computer-based hermeneutics. Of particular interest will be a discussion of a new edition of the Biblia Hebraica, incorporating insights from computer-based analysis.

No formal membership in AIBI is necessary for participation in AIBI-L. The language of exchange will be English.

To subscribe to AIBI-L:

BITNET users
> send an interactive message: TELL LISTSERV AT UOTTAWA SUB AIBI-L your full name or send a mail message to LISTSERV@UOTTAWA in which the only line of the mail text (BODY) is: SUB AIBI-L your full name

for INTERNET users
> send a mail message to LISTSERV@ACADVM1.UOTTAWA.CA in which the only line of the mail text (BODY) is: SUB AIBI-L your full name

Moderator of AIBI-L: L. G. Bloomquist GBLOOMQ@ACADVM1.UOTTAWA.CA (Internet)
> @UOTTAWA (Bitnet)

Editor of AIBI Newsletter: R. F. Poswick CIBMARE@BUCLLN11 (Bitnet/Earn)

Postmaster at Ottawa: Tram Nguyen TRAMNG@ACADVM1.UOTTAWA.CA (Internet)
> @UOTTAWA (Bitnet)

AI-CHI <wiley!ai-chi@LLL-LCC.LLNL.GOV>

Unmoderated mailing list intended for discussion on the subjects related to AI applications to Human-Computer interface design. This could include user modeling, self-adaptive interfaces, intelligent user agents, multi-modal I/O (Natural Language, graphics, speech), intelligent user-interface management systems, intelligent on-line advising, task modelling, and any other related issues. Announcements of books, papers, conferences, new products, public domain software tools, etc. are also encouraged.

A limited archive of the most recent messages is available by request from wiley!ai-chi-request@LLL-LCC.LLNL.GOV.

All requests to be added to or deleted from this list, problems, questions, etc., should be sent to wiley!ai-chi-request@LLL-LCC.LLNL.GOV.

Coordinator: Dr. Sherman Tyler <wiley!sherman@LLL-LCC.LLNL.GOV>

AI-ED@SUN.COM

Discussions related to the application of artificial intelligence to education. This includes material on intelligent computer assisted instruction (ICAI) or intelligent tutoring systems (ITS), interactive encyclopedias, intelligent information retrieval for educational purposes, and psychological and cognitive science models of learning, problem solving, and teaching that can be applied to education. Issues related to teaching AI are welcome. Topics may also include evaluation of tutoring systems, commercialization of AI based instructional systems, description of actual use of an ITS in a classroom setting, user-modeling, intelligent user-interfaces, and the use of graphics or videodisk in ICAI. Announcements of books, papers, conferences, new products, public domain software tools, etc. are encouraged.

If there are several people at one site that are interested, users should try to form a local distribution system to lessen the load on SUN.COM.

Archives of messages are kept on host SUN.COM.

All requests to be added to or deleted from this list, problems, questions, etc., should be sent to AI-Ed-Request@SUN.COM.

Moderators: J.R. Prohaska <prohaska@SUN.COM>
Stuart Macmillan <smacmillan@SUN.COM>

AI-MEDICINE@VUSE.VANDERBILT.EDU ai-medicine is an unmoderated mailing list serving internet and bitnet domains since Sept. 1990. Current readership consists mainly of computer scientists and engineers with interest in biomedical and clinical research, and of physicians with interest in medical informatics.

AI in Medicine is a broad subject area which encompasses almost all research areas in artificial intelligence. For the purposes of this mailing list, AI in Medicine may be defined as "computed-based medical decision support" (or "computer-assisted medical decision making"). This definition may be expanded to include AI-based approaches to computer-assisted medical instruction. According to this definition, topics such as billing systems and hospital/medical office information retrieval systems clearly remain outside the scope of this forum.

There are some borderline topics which cannot readily be classified under AI in Medicine, yet have clear connections to both artificial intelligence and medical practice. Processing and interpretation of medical images and signals are among those subject areas, and the current readership of this list contains a substantial number of researchers working in these fields. These borderline subject areas will remain within the scope of the list, as long as the focus lies on the artificial intelligence aspects, and not the detailed engineering principles.

Who may join: any individual or organization with internet or bitnet mailing addresses may join.

Requests for subscription may be sent to: ai-medicine-request@vuse.vanderbilt.edu

List address for unmoderated distribution of messages: ai-medicine@vuse.vanderbilt.edu

List coordinator (Serdar Uckun, MD): serdar@vuse.vanderbilt.edu

AIDSNEWS%RUTVM1.BITNET@CUNYVM.CUNY.EDU

The AIDSNews Forum is used for the discussion of any issue relating to AIDS/ARC. AIDS Treatment News reports on experimental and alternative treatments, especially those available now. It collects information from medical journals, and from interviews with scientists, physicians and other health practitioners, and persons with AIDS or ARC; it does not recommend particular therapies, but seeks to increase the options available. The ethical and public-policy issues around AIDS treatment research will also be examined. AIDS Treatment News, Northern Lights Alternatives, and many other publications are also distributed to this list.

A library of files is also available. Send or mail the following command to LISTSERV@RUTVM1.BITNET for a current listing of available files: INDEX AIDSNEWS

Bitnet users may subscribe to the list by doing: TELL LISTSERV at RUTVM1 SUBSCRIBE AIDSNEWS Your_Full_Name where Your_Full_Name is your real name (not your userid). From a VMS BITNET site use the SEND/REMOTE command.

Users outside Bitnet should use the appropriate gateway to send mail to LISTSERV@RUTVM1.BITNET. The text of the message should be the single line: SUBSCRIBE AIDSNEWS Your_Full_Name

To protect privacy the subscriber list is kept confidential. If you have any problems subscribing to the list send mail to the Coordinator.

Coordinator: Michael Smith <MSMITH@CS.UMASS.EDU> <MSMITH@UMAECS.BITNET>

AIL-L@austin.onu.edu   [Last Updated 12-October-1991]

AIL-L is a list for the discussion of topics related to Artificial Intelligence and Law

To subscribe to AIL-L you should send a message to the internet address listserv@austin.onu.edu The body of the message should consist of:

subscribe AIL-L <your full name>

for example: subscribe ail-l Jane Doe

List Manager: David R. Warner, Jr. <WARNER@AUSTIN.ONU.EDU>

AIRCRAFT@GREARN.BITNET   [Last Updated 12-October-1991]

This list is a discussion forum about aircraft and helicopters, modern and old. Also info about air-shows and similar events can be exchanged through this list, offering to its subscribers a way of learning the latest news on this subject.

You can subscribe by sending the following command to LISTSERV@GREARN by mail/file/interactive message:

SUB AIRCRAFT Your_full_name

for example on an IBM VM system you could enter TELL LISTSERV AT GREARN SUB AIRCRAFT Susan Smith

Then, any mail can be distributed to the rest of subscribers by sending it to the address AIRCRAFT@GREARN.BITNET

Owner: Giorgos Kavallieratos <GIORGOS@GREARN.BITNET>

AIRLINE on LISTSERV@CUNYVM.BITNET   [Last update 11/92]
     or LISTSERVE@CUNYVM.CUNY.EDU

Airline has been established to enable those interested in Airlines and Civil Aircraft to discuss relevant topics. While prototype subjects are expected to be the main area of discourse, modelers are welcome as well. Discussion should generally be related to the prototypes whenever possible. Those seeking to join a list for military aircraft, non-commercial flying [pilots], or modelling, should contact the list owner for assistance in finding such lists.

To subscribe, you may send an interactive message (from BITNET sites which provide such a facility), or mail (with the command as the BODY of the mail - *NOT* in the subject field -) to:

                    LISTSERV@CUNYVM.BITNET or LISTSERV@CUNYVM.CUNY.EDU

The command should be in the form:

SUB AIRLINE full name

... where "full name" is your full (and correct) name.

To contribute to the list, send your mail messages to:

AIRLINE@CUNYVM or AIRLINE@CUNYVM.CUNY.EDU

Owner: Geert K. Marien <GKMQC@CUNYVM.CUNY.EDU GKMQC@CUNYVM.BITNET>

AIX-L%BUACCA.BITNET@MITVMA.MIT.EDU

This list is intended for the discussion of the AIX operating system, IBM's Unix solution for small and large computer systems. Initially, this list will be used for dissemination of information and technical details of AIX on all levels. It may be necessary to break this list down into machine types that AIX will run on.

To subscribe send the following command to LISTSERV@BUACCA (non-BitNet users send mail to LISTSERV%BUACCA.BITNET@MITVMA.MIT.EDU with the command in the message body): SUBSCRIBE AIX-L Your_Full_Name where Your_Full_Name is your real name, not your userid. To unsubscribe, send: UNSUBSCRIBE AIX-L

Moderator: Michael R. Gettes <CCMRG%BOSTONU.BITNET@MITVMA.MIT.EDU> CCMRG@BUACCA.BU.EDU

AIXNEWS on LISTSERV@PUCC.BITNET   [Last Updated 28-January-1992]
     or listserv@pucc.princeton.edu

Mailing list aixnews@pucc.bitnet (or aixnews@pucc.princeton.edu) has been created as a digested mail redistribution of the Usenet newsgroup comp.unix.aix, for sites that don't receive usenet news. About 90% of discussion focuses on the RS6000 platform. The remainder is mostly about PS2 AIX, with a rare posting about AIX/370. Expect about two digests per day, with twelve to fifteen articles each.

To subscribe:

Send e-mail to listserv@pucc.bitnet (or listserv@pucc.princeton.edu) In the body, put:

sub aixnews firstname lastname

(using your own first name and last name).

You cannot post directly to AIXNEWS. All postings should be sent to comp.unix.aix@cc.ysu.edu, where they'll be incorporated into the digest and forwarded to the usenet newsgroup.

Thanks to Michael Gettes (gettes@pucc) for setting up the bitnet end of the digest. He is also the coordinator for AIX-L@PUCC bitnet AIX discussion.

Doug Sewell, Tech Support, Computer Center, Youngstown State University
doug@ysu.edu doug@ysub.bitnet ...uunet!ysu.edu!doug

AJBS-L@NCSUVM.CC.NCSU.EDU   [Last Updated 12-October-1991]
AJBS-L@NCSUVM.BITNET

The Association of Japanese Business Studies (AJBS) is an international association of Japan scholars, students, government and business researchers, and executives interested in the Japanese economy and business systems. The AJBS is an independent academic association devoted to research and discussion of these topics. The AJBS-L is the association's communications network based at North Carolina State University, USA.

The objectives of AJBS are: to promote greater understanding of the Japanese business system; to foster high quality original research and study; to facilitate the dissemination of information; to advance knowledge of the field; and to promote the integration of Japanese studies with other academic disciplines.

To subscribe to AJBS-L send mail to LISTSERV@NCSUVM.BITNET or LISTSERV@NCSUVM.CC.NCSU.EDU with the body containing the command SUB AJBS-L yourfirstname yourlastname

For information request these files:

AJBS-L INTRO
CALLFOR PAPERS
ANNUAL MEETING
MAGS DBF

using the GET command. Eg. GET AJBS-L INTRO in the body of mail to LISTSERV@NCSUVM or LISTSERV@NCSUVM.CC.NCSU.EDU.

The list's address is: AJBS-L@NCSUVM.CC.NCSU.EDU
Contact: James W. Reese, AJBS Information Committee Chair,
R505040@UNIVSCVM.CSD.SCAROLINA.EDU

ALBION-L on LISTSERV@UCSBVM.BITNET

ALBION-L is an electronic discussion list for British and Irish history. All time-periods and fields are welcome.

To subscribe send e-mail to LISTSERV@UCSBVM.BITNET with the BODY of the mail (NOT the subject) containing the command:

SUBSCRIBE ALBION-L yourfirstname yourlastname

Owner: Questions about ALBION may be addressed to Joe Coohill at: 2120jtc@ucsbuxa.bitnet or gd03jtc@ucsbvm.bitnet

ALCOHOL ON LISTSERV@LMUACAD.BITNET [Last Updated 12-October-1991]

ALCOHOL is a list offering the BITNET Community a chance to voice their opinions about the abuse of Alcohol, Illegal and other commonly abused drugs. The list is open to anyone, but contributions from the psychological and medical professions are encouraged. Students are especially encouraged, as they may provide some fresh insight.

Archives of Alcohol may be obtained by sending the command

INDEX ALCOHOL to LISTSERV@LMUACAD.BITNET

To subscribe, send the following command via mail or interactive message to LISTSERV@LMUACAD.BITNET:

SUB ALCOHOL your-full-name

where "your-full-name" is your name For Example: SUB ALCOHOL JOHN DOE

OWNER: Phillip Charles Oliff <FXX1@LMUACAD.BITNET>

ALICEFAN on LISTSERV@WKUVX1.BITNET [Last Updated 28-January-1992]

This list (ALICEFAN) is an unmoderated list for discussions among fans of Alice Cooper. Virtually any topic relating to Alice Cooper is appropriate, including news, comments on his music, tour dates, etc.

To join ALICEFAN, send the following line in a mail message to LISTSERV@WKUVX1.BITNET:

SUBSCRIBE ALICEFAN "Your real name"

For example,

SUBSCRIBE ALICEFAN "Roderick Usher"

Submissions to the list should be sent to:

ALICEFAN@WKUVX1.BITNET

List owner: Hunter Goatley, goathunter@WKUVX1.BITNET

ALLIN1-L@CCVM.SUNYSB.EDU

Mailing list for ALL-IN-1 managers and users. For discussion of problems and suggestions relating to the installation, management and use of ALL-IN-1.

To join the list: VMS (jnet): $ SEND LISTSERV@SBCCVM SUB ALLIN1-L your full name VM (RSCS): TELL LISTSERV AT SBCCVM SUB ALLIN1-L your full name

Non-Bitnet users can send mail to LISTSERV@SBCCVM.BITNET or LISTSERV@CCVM.SUNYSB.EDU with an empty Subject: and message body: SUB ALLIN1-L your full name

Coordinator: Sanjay Kapur <SJKAPUR@CCMAIL.SUNYSB.EDU>

ALLMUSIC%AUVM.BITNET@VM1.NODAK.EDU

Mailing list is dedicated to the discussion of all forms of music, in all its aspects. It's founding is based on the understanding that most people who listen to and enjoy music do so from a variety of standpoints, and that a general, unlimited forum is desirable for both the integration and expansion of musical ideas, techniques, and understanding. Therefore, all topics having to do with music are welcome, including but not limited to: composition, performance, recording; research, critique, inquiry, advocacy, instrument design, ethnomusicology, psychacoustics, orchestration, jazz, classical, funk, plainchant, and anything else you can think of. If a topic is running that you have something to say about, or to question, jump in. If you have something entirely different in mind, start up another thread. Music is universal. With the advent of electronic communication, so are we.

To be added to or deleted from the list, send mail to the Coordinator.

Coordinator: Mike Karolchik <U6183%wvnvm.bitnet@vm1.nodak.edu>

AMALGAM@ibmvm.rus.uni-stuttgart.de

Mailing list for information about dental amalgam fillings and chronic mercury poisoning. It may be of interest for people who have "silver" dental fillings in their teeth.

BitNet users may subscribe by sending the following command to LISTSERV@ds0rus1i via mail or message: SUBscribe AMALGAM Your_full_name where "Your_full_name" is your real name, not your login Id. Non-BitNet users can join the list by sending the above command as the only line in the text/body of a message to LISTSERV@ibmvm.rus.uni-stuttgart.de

Coordinator: Siegfried Schmitt <UJ21@ibm3090.rz.uni-karlsruhe.dbp.de>, <UJ21@dkauni2>

AMERCATH on LISTSERV@UKCC [Last Updated 28-January-1992]
or LISTSERV@UKCC.UKY.EDU

Jefferson Community College - University of Kentucky announces an electronic discussion group for those interested in the history of American Catholicism, AMERCATH@UKCC. Access to AMERCATH is available internationally thus forming a global network of people who research and teach the history of American Catholicism. The use of the listserv AMERCATH is a major breakthrough in facilitating instant communication among faculty, students and researchers.

Appropriate messages for AMERCATH include: feedback on research; program proposals; calls for papers; meetings, media, and job announcements; information-gathering questions; syllabi and bibliographies; as well as any other issues pertinent to enhancing the study and teaching of the history of American Catholicsm.

While messages sent to AMERCATH are received by all subscribers, users may then contact specific individuals via BITNET or INTERNET to pursue particular projects, issues, and interests. To join this discussion group, you need access to the electronic mail facilities of BITNET or INTERNET. To subscribe to AMERCATH from BITNET send a message or mail to LISTSERV@UKCC. From the Internet send the mail to LISTSERV@UKCC.UKY.EDU. In the body of the mail (or message) include the command:

SUB AMERCATH Yourfirstname Yourlastname

Owner: If you have any questions or comments, please contact: Anne Kearney, Ph.D., Assistant Professor of History, Jefferson Community College - University of Kentucky, 109 East Broadway, Louisville, KY 40202, 502-584-0181 ext 353, BITNET: JCCANNEK@UKCC, INTERNET: JCCANNEK@UKCC.UKY.EDU

AMETHYST-USERS@WSMR-SIMTEL20.ARMY.MIL

This list is intended for people who use Amethyst, a software package of CP/M-80 programs: MINCE (an ersatz EMACS) and SCRIBBLE (an ersatz SCRIBE).

Mail archives are kept on host WSMR-SIMTEL20.ARMY.MIL as TOPS20 mail files named yymm.n-TXT, where n starts with one and increments by one into another file as each file reached 150 disk pages. To conserve disk space, all the mail files in the archive, except for the current year, are individually compressed. The compressed files have the suffix -Z as part of the filetype field; they should be renamed to have the suffix .Z (uppercase Z) when transfered to a Unix system so the uncompress program will find them. The current month's mail is still kept in AMETHYST-ARCHIV.TXT. The archives are stored in directory: PD2:<ARCHIVES.AMETHYST-USERS> Archive files are available via ANONYMOUS FTP from WSMR-SIMTEL20.ARMY.MIL for those with TCP/IP access to the Internet.

All requests to be added to or deleted from this list, problems, questions, etc., should be sent to AMETHYST-USERS-REQUEST@WSMR-SIMTEL20.ARMY.MIL.

Coordinator: Frank Wancho <WANCHO@WSMR-SIMTEL20.ARMY.MIL>

AMIGA-RELAY@UDEL.EDU

A direct (unmoderated) bi-directional gateway with the USENET comp.sys.amiga newsgroups tree for those people without access to USENET. All mail to AMIGA-RELAY is posted to comp.sys.amiga.

The list will not be archived, due to its high volume.

All requests to be added to or deleted from this list, problems, questions, etc., should be sent to AMIGA-RELAY-REQUEST@UDEL.EDU.

Coordinator: Mark Nelson <nelson@udel.edu>

AMLIT-L on LISTSERV@UMCVMB or LISTSERV@UMCVMB.MISSOURI.EDU

The American Literature Discussion List has been created for the discussion of topics and issues in the vast and diverse field of American Literature among a world-wide community interested in the subject. You can expect consultations, conferences, and an ongoing exchange of information among scholars and students of American Literature on this list. In addition, announcements of relevant conferences and calls for papers are welcome and encouraged.

To subscribe send a message to listserv@umcvmb or listserv@umcvmb.missouri.edu. In BODY of the message state: SUB AMLIT-L your full name eg. SUB AMLIT-L E. Allen Poe If you have any questions please contact the owner.

Owner: Michael O'Conner <ENGMO@UMCVMB.BITNET> or <ENGMO@UMCVMB.MISSOURI.EDU>

amnesty@VMS.CIS.PITT.EDU
AMNESTY%JHUVM.BITNET@VM1.NODAK.EDU

Mailing list to distribute Amnesty International's urgent action appeals, usually one per month. They are 1 or 2-page summaries of a specific case of human rights abuse, such as a small group of people who have been arrested without reason, or are being held secretly, or tortured, etc. They give the prisoners' names, why they were arrested, who to write to, and what they suggest you say. Amnesty International is concerned with human rights, not just amnesty. Sometimes they ask members to write letters requesting not freedom, but better or more just treatment. You don't have to be a member of, or endorse, Amnesty International to receive this list. Additional discussion or information from other organizations may be distributed.

To subscribe, send the following command to LISTSERV@JHUVM: SUBSCRIBE AMNESTY your_full_name where "your_full_name" is your real name, not your userid. To unsubscribe, send the command: UNSUBSCRIBE AMNESTY Non-BitNet users can [un]subscribe by sending one of the above commands in the text/body of a message to LISTSERV%JHUVM.BITNET@VM1.NODAK.EDU.

Coordinators: Jeff Carpenter <jjc@UNIX.CIS.PITT.EDU> <AMNESTY@VMS.CIS.PITT.EDU> Jim Jones <L64A0110%JHUVM.BITNET@VM1.NODAK.EDU>

AMP-L on LISTSERV@DEARN.BITNET

The Atomic- and Molecular-Physics List. A forum for scientists working on atoms and molecules. It is unmoderated. Experimental as well as theoretical topics are welcome. Discussion could also include software, instrumentation, new books, reviews and so on.

To subscribe to AMP-L, send the following command to LISTSERV@DEARN on BITNET/EARN in the BODY of e-mail or interactive message: SUBSCRIBE AMP-L your full name

For example: SUBSCRIBE AMP-L Sweeney Todd

Owner: Henrik Zawischa <F41ZAW@DHHDESY3.BITNET>

AMSSIS-L on LISTSERV@UAFSYSB

This list is intended to provide a forum for the discussion of topics relating to the American Management System Student Information System (AMSSIS). The topics discussed may be of a functional or technical nature.

You may subscribe to the AMSSIS-L list by sending RFC822 Mail to

LISTSERV@UAFSYSB on Bitnet or LISTSERV@uafsysb.uark.edu on Internet

In the BODY (text) of your mail include the command:

SUB AMSSIS-L firstname lastname eg. sub amssis-l Jane Doe

The LISTSERV server will take your address from the "From:" address of your mail. If you are on BITNET/EARN/NetNorth and can send interactive messages (eg. TELL on CMS or SEND on VMS with JNET) then you can send the SUB command as shown to LISTSERV at UAFSYSB interactively.

If you prefer, you may send mail to the Coordinator to be asked to be added to the list. However you subscribe, you should receive return mail with a confirmation and additional information.

You may leave the list at any time by sending a "SIGNOFF AMSSIS-L" command to LISTSERV@UAFSYSB. Please note that this command must NOT be sent to the list address (AMSSIS-L@UAFSYSB) but to the LISTSERV address (LISTSERV@UAFSYSB).

Coordinator: Allen Fields ALLENF@UAFSYSA.BITNET ALLENF@uafsya.uark.edu

ANCIEN-L on LISTSERV@ULKYVM or LISTSERV@ULKYVM.LOUISVILLE.EDU

ANCIEN-L is a forum for debate, discussion, and the exchange of information by students and scholars of the history of the Ancient Mediterranean. ANCIEN-L is ready to distribute newsletters from study groups, and to post announcements of meetings and calls for papers, short scholarly pieces, queries, and other items of interest.

The list currently does not maintain a FTP directory nor is archiving available. Hopefully, this will change in the near future.

ANCIEN-L is associated with the general discussion list HISTORY, and co-operates fully with other lists similarly associated.

To subscribe send a message to LISTSERV@ULKYVM on BITNET or LISTSERV@ULKYVM.LOUISVILLE.EDU. In BODY of the message state: SUB ANCIEN-L yourfirstname yourlastname

adding your full name; LISTSERV will accept both BITNET and Internet addresses. Postings should be made to ANCIEN-L@ULKYVM.

If you have any questions please contact the owner.

Owner:
James A. Cocks   BITNET: JACOCK01@ULKYVM
            Internet: JACOCK01@ULKYVM.LOUISVILLE.EDU

ANDREW-DEMOS@ANDREW.CMU.EDU

A mailing list to be used simply for demonstrations of the Andrew system software. You should not subscribe to it unless you expect to be reading it with the Andrew Message System, as messages will come to the list in full multi-media format. Indeed, we encourage people to post lots of neat animations, music, raster images, and the like to this list.

For more information about Andrew, see the list-of-lists entry for the "info-andrew" mailing list.

We expect to maintain an archive of this list in the future and make it available for anonymous FTP.

To be added to the list, send mail to ANDREW-DEMOS-REQUEST@ANDREW.CMU.EDU. To submit new items to the list, just send them to ANDREW-DEMOS@ANDREW.CMU.EDU.

Coordinator: Nathaniel Borenstein <nsb+@ANDREW.CMU.EDU>

ANEST-L on LISTSERV@UBVM   [Last Update 28-January-1992]
or LISTSERV@UBVM.CC.BUFFALO.EDU

This list was formed to serve as a vehicle for (1) discussion of topics related to anesthesiology and (2) collection of any information related to anesthesiology.

Archives of ANEST-L and related files are stored in the ANEST-L FILELIST. To receive a list of files send the command INDEX ANEST-L to LISTSERV@UBVM or LISTSERV@UBVM.CC.BUFFALO.EDU as the first line in the body of a mail message (not the Subject: line).

To subscribe to ANEST-L, send the command SUB ANEST-L yourfirstname yourlastname to LISTSERV@UBVM or LISTSERV@UBVM.CC.BUFFALO.EDU via a mail message (again, as the first line in the body of the mail, not the Subject: line).

For example: SUB ANEST-L John Doe

   Owner: Andrew M. Sopchak
      BITNET: sopchaka@snysyrv1
      Internet: sopchaka@vax.cs.hscsyr.edu
      Department of Anesthesiology
      SUNY Health Science Center
      750 East Adams Street
      Syracuse, NY 13210

ANIMAL-RIGHTS@CS.ODU.EDU

An unmoderated list for the discussion of Animal Rights. Peter Singer's book "Animal Liberation" proposes a "New Ethics for our Treatment of Animals" and many activist groups, such as PETA (People for the Ethical Treatment of Animals), regard this as the "Bible of the Animal Rights movement". Consumers and researches alike are facing new questions concerning the human animals' treatment of the rest of the animal kingdom. The purpose of this list is to provide students, researchers, and activists, a forum for discussing issues like:

Animal Rights	Animals in Laboratories	Ecology
Animal Liberation	Research using Animals	Environmental Protection
Consumer Product Testing	Hunting/Trapping/Fishing	Vegetarianism
Cruelty-free products	Animals in Entertainment	Vegan lifestyles
Vivasection/Dissection	Factory Farming	Christian Perspectives
Medical Testing	Fur	Other Perspecitives

Currently, no resources are available for archiving this list.

All requests to be added to or deleted from this list should be sent to Animal-Rights-Request@[XANTH.]CS.ODU.EDU (Internet) or Animal-Rights-Request@xanth.uucp (UUCP).

Coordinator: Chip Roberson <csrobe@CS.WM.EDU>

ANMI-L@RMCS.CRANFIELD.AC.UK

The purpose of this list is for the distribution of VT/ANSI ANIMATION files, and also the discussion of how these files can easily be created. Also to be included are Regis Graphics and Regis Animations files.

This list is being run manually and not through a LISTSERV. Contributions to the list will be moderated and sent out in batches once a week, if any have been recieved.

To subscribe to this list send a e-mail to :

ANIM-L@rmcs.cranfield.ac.uk (internet)

with the body of the message saying something like "add me to the list".

Owner: Tim Kimber <TJK@RMCS.CRANFIELD.AC.UK> or
<TJK@RMCS.CRAN.AC.UK::NSF.AC.UK> or <ST9047673@A.OXPOLY.AC.UK::NSF.AC.UK>

ANNEAL@CS.UCLA.EDU

Discussion of simulated annealing techniques and analysis, as well as other related issues (stochastic optimization, Boltzmann machines, metricity of NP-complete move spaces, etc). Membership is restricted to those doing active research in simulated annealing or related areas. Current membership is international, and about half of the members are published authors. The list itself is unmoderated.

Requests to be added to or deleted from the list, problems, questions, etc., should be sent to ANNEAL-REQUEST@CS.UCLA.EDU.

Coordinator: Daniel R. Greening <dgreen@CS.UCLA.EDU>

ANSAXNET <U47C2@WVNVM.WVNET.EDU>

ANSAXNET is a SIG (Special Interest Group) for scholars of the culture and history of England before 1100 C.E. Scholars interested in the later English Middle Ages and those interested in the early Medieval period throughout Europe are also encouraged to join the list. Members receive a directory of all our members in order to facilitate telecommunications, and a monthly electronic report to which they are encouraged to contribute announcements and information. This report often provides members with new information about the use of computers in some aspect of their disciplines, as well as news of more conventional developments in the field. We also have projects underway to encode databases which members may use in their own work. To this end, we are now working on the details of distributing to the membership a database of all manuscripts written or owned in England before 1100. We would be glad to add your name to our directory and thus to make you a member of ANSAXNET. Membership is free to everyone with access to a BITNET node.

Anyone who wants to be a member of ANSAXNET should send e-mail to the Coordinator, including a conventional mailing address and some information about your particular interests in early medieval cultural studies.

Coordinator: Patrick W. Conner <U47C2@WVNVM.WVNET.EDU>

ANTHRO-L%UBVM.BITNET@CUNYVM.CUNY.EDU

This list deals with discussions of various techniques and fields of research in Anthropology. Some suggested topics of discussion are:

- Computation in anthropology
- Graphics in archaeology
- What programs anthropologists are using at various places
- Where centers of computer interests are in anthropolgy
- Anglo-Saxon cemeteries
- Palaeodemography
- What individuals are doing, e.g. research, publication, computer info.
- Some spirited words on

- political economy
- Using anthropological assistance to describe the legal practices of American culture
- The development of Anglo-Saxon cemeteries
- The Northumberland landscape
- Use of Remote Sensing (resistivity and magnetometer) to locate and analyse village sites
- The population of

Anglo-Saxon England

To add yourself to the list, send the command SUBSCRIBE ANTHRO-L Your_Full_Name via mail to LISTSERV@UBVM.BITNET or LISTSERV%UBVM.BITNET@CUNYVM.CUNY.EDU (Internet) where Your_Full_Name is your real name (not your userid). To remove yourself from the list, send the command UNSUBSCRIBE ANTHRO-L

List Owner: Ezra Zubrow <APYEZRA%UBVMSD.BITNET@CUNYVM.CUNY.EDU>
APYEZRA@UBVMSD.BITNET (BitNet)
Coordinator: Patrick G. Salsbury <V291NHTP@UBVMSC.CC.BUFFALO.EDU>
V291NHTP%UBVMSD.BITNET@CUNYVM.CUNY.EDU
V291NHTP@UBVMSD.BITNET (BitNet)

ANU-NEWS@VM1.NODAK.EDU
ANU-NEWS@NDSUVM1

Discussion for administrators and users of the ANU-NEWS software for VAX/VMS systems. ANU-NEWS is a software system that allows VMS systems to act as Usenet nodes. Topics include bugs, fixes, integrating lists from other networks, and discussion of new features. Although the list is primarily for communication among ANU-NEWS administrators, users are also welcome.

To subscribe to this list BITNET/EARN/NetNorth Users may be able to send an interactive message to LISTSERV@NDSUVM1 (via SEND or TELL). For example: SEND LISTSERV@NDSUVM1 SUB ANU-NEWS Jane Doe (your first/last name) Or, you may send MAIL to LISTSERV@VM1.NoDak.EDU or LISTSERV@NDSUVM1 with the first line of the TEXT or BODY of mail being: SUB ANU-NEWS firstname lastname (e.g. SUB ANU-NEWS John Doe).

Coordinator: Tim Russell <russell@ZEUS.UNL.EDU> russell@UNOMA1 uunet!zeus.unl.edu!russell

aon@POLYSLO.CALPOLY.EDU

Mailing list for any discussions about or related to the music group The Art of Noise. The list is set up as a mail relay. The number of subscribers to the list is limited, so only those who feel they will have something to say should join.

All requests to be added to or deleted from this list, problems, questions, etc., should be sent to aon-request@POLYSLO.CALPOLY.EDU.

Coordinator: Cliff Tuel <ctuel@POLYSLO.CALPOLY.EDU>

apE-info@ferkel.ucsb.edu   [Last Update 8/92]

Purpose: Discussion of the scientific visualization software package apE.

Contact: apE-info-request@ferkel.ucsb.edu (Jim Lick)

APL-L%UNB.CA@VM1.NODAK.EDU

Mailing list for discussion of the APL language, its implementation, application and use. Contributions on teaching APL are particularly welcome.

To subscribe to this LISTSERV list send an E-mail message to your local LISTSERV (on BITNET/NetNorth/EARN) or to LISTSERV@UNB.CA containing the single line: SUBscribe APL-L your_full_name Non-BitNet users can send a message to LISTSERV%UNB.CA@VM1.NODAK.EDU with the SUB command as the only line in the message body.

Coordinator: David G. Macneil <DGM%UNB.CA@VM1.NODAK.EDU>
<T4327%UNB.CA@VM1.NODAK.EDU>

APOGEES%FRAIX11.BITNET@VM1.NODAK.EDU

Mailing list for the study of critical and strategic information management. The objective is to identify information of long-term value to an organization and to develop realistic methodologies and policies of management (data bases, ethics policy, education, supervisory systems...).

In APOGEES, we share the creation of business information supervising systems. We discuss methodologies suitable to the management and development of technological information through supervisory divisions.

People from all fields of sciences, management, information technology, computer science, and so on, are welcome including managers who are concerned with several critical items when making their business decisions.

BitNet users can subscribe by sending an application note to BAUMARD@FRAIX11 or by sending mail to LISTSERV@FRMOP11 with the body/text of the message: SUB APOGEES your_full_name where "your_full_name" is your real name, not your login Id. Internet users can subscribe by sending a message to LISTSERV%FRMOP11.BITNET@VM1.NODAK.EDU with the cody/text of the message containing the above command.

Coordinator: Philippe Baumard <BAUMARD%FRAIX11.BITNET@VM1.NODAK.EDU>

apollo@UMIX.CC.UMICH.EDU
{uunet,rutgers}!umix!apollo (UUCP)

Users of Apollo computers who are interested in sharing their experiences about Apollos. At least initially, the list will not be moderated or digested; if the volume is sufficient, this may change.

Mail to the list will be archived in some public place that will be announced at a later date.

All requests to be added to or deleted from this list, problems, questions, etc., should be sent to apollo-request@UMIX.CC.UMICH.EDU (or UUCP {uunet,rutgers}!umix!apollo-request).

Coordinator: Paul Killey <paul@UMIX.CC.UMICH.EDU> {uunet,rutgers}!umix!paul

APOLLO-L%UMRVMB.BITNET@VM1.NODAK.EDU

The purpose of this list is to provide an avenue for Apollo computer users to share comments, ideas, and problems (and possibly utilities), associated with the use of Apollo computers.

BitNet users can subscribe to the list by sending e-mail or a message to LISTSERV@UMRVMB with the body/text of the message containing the command: SUB APOLLO-L your_full_name where "your_full_name" is your real name, not your loginid. Non-BitNet users can subscribe by sending the above command in the body of a message to LISTSERV%UMRVMB.BITNET@VM1.NODAK.EDU.

Coordinator: Karl Lutzen <C0537%UMRVMB.BITNET@VM1.NODAK.EDU>

APPC-L on LISTSERV@AUVM.BitNet   [Last Update April 92]
or listserv@american.edu

APPC-L was formed to discussion IBM's Advanced Program-to-Program Communication (APPC) as well as associated topics such as LU 6.2 and CPI-C. Archives of APPC-L and related files, which will include examples of APPC programming, configuration files, and so forth, will be stored in the APPC-L FILELIST. To receive a list of files send the command INDEX APPC-L to LISTSERV@AUVM. These files will also be available from auvm.american.edu via ftp. APPC-L will be gateway'ed to the (soon to be created) bit.listserv.appc-l newsgroup, and posts can also be read there.

To subscribe to APPC-L, send the following command via either interactive BitNet message to LISTSERV@AUVM, or in the BODY of e-mail to LISTSERV@AUVM.BITNET or LISTSERV@AMERICAN.EDU

SUBSCRIBE APPC-L Your_name

For example: SUBSCRIBE APPC-L Jane Doe

Owner: Jim McIntosh <jim@american.edu>

ARIE-L on LISTSERV@IDBSU.BITNET Discussion of the RLG Ariel document transmission system

This list is for discussion of the usage of the Ariel document transmission system for the Internet developed by the Research Libraries Group. Although the group is oriented toward exchange of information among those already using the Ariel system, those considering adoption of the Ariel hardware and software may find it of interest.

NOTE: The list's name is ARIE-L. It is NOT the same as ARIEL, which is a discussion of a Spanish statistical package originating in Chile

To subscribe to ARIE-L send e-mail to LISTSERV@IDBSU.BITNET with the following command in the BODY of the mail:

SUB ARIE-L your full name Eg. SUB ARIE-L Danielle Webster

Owner: Dan Lester University Library Boise State University Boise, Idaho 83725
ALILESTE@IDBSU.BITNET

AQUA-L on LISTSERV@VM.UOGUELPH.CA

AQUA-L is an INTERNET list based at the University of Guelph. The purpose of the list is to promote discussion amongst individuals interested in the science, technology and business of rearing aquatic species. In the spirit of open discussion, membership in the list is public and unrestricted.

Potential topics include:

- Who's doing what and where?
- Problems and solutions rearing aquatic larvae.
- Diseases, parasites and pathology.
- Water quality.
- Recirculation technology and applications.
- Research aquatic systems design and operation.

- Commercial aquatic systems design and operation.
- Site selection and environmental impact.
- New species under culture.
- Genetics, sex reversal and hormonal manipulation.
- Computers in aquaculture.
- Public perceptions of aquaculture.
- Aqua-business ($$$$!).

Messages sent to the list should be of general interest although specific requests for information are quite welcome. It is hoped that this forum will provide a basis for rapid exchange of new ideas and provide an access for persons seeking information and advice.

To join in the Aquaculture Discussion List send an E-mail message to:
LISTSERV@VM.UOGUELPH.CA

with this line in the message body:

SUB AQUA-L your name

Note that "your name" means your proper name and not your userid. LISTSERV will extract your id from the message header. If you are unfamiliar with lists and LISTSERV send the following to receive an index of help information:

INDEX HELPINFO

You may cancel your subscription to AQUA-L at any time by sending:

SIGNOFF AQUA-L

Note that commands are sent to LISTSERV and not AQUA-L. If you send them to the list you will have the pleasure of knowing everyone subscribing is reading them.

List Owner: T. B. (Ted) White ZOOWHITE@VM.UOGUELPH.CA

Editor's note: I believe the BITNET style node name is UOGUELPH but some Canadian nodes are

going to Internet style addressing only. (from the header: Ted White
<ZOOWHITE%VM.UoGuelph.CA@VM1.NoDak.EDU>)

ARACHNET@acadvm1.uottawa.CA   [Last Updated 12-October-1991]

A Loose Association of Electronic Discussion Groups and Electronic Journals of Interest to Scholars.

There are more than 600 discussion groups, newsletters, digests and electronic journals devoted to topics of scholarly interest. As more scholars come on-line, the size of these groups, the diversity of material they have to offer, and their total number are all bound to increase. These groups could benefit from a loose confederation that would allow them to share resources easily without imposing any kind of restrictions on their manner of operation. Arachnet is such a confederation.

Arachnet is a ListServ list, Arachnet@Uottawa.BITNET or ARACHNET@ACADVM1. Uottawa.CA if you are on the Internet. All editors of discussion groups, newsletters, digests and electronic journals are invited to be members. On its file-server, Arachnet will contain a current list of its member groups, descriptions of each group, and lists of files they hold. As well as the current Directory of E-mail Based Conferences and Electronic Journals. Arachnet's fileserver will also hold various information files pertaining to the creation of e-serials.

The conversational component will be a means by which editors of new groups can receive help from their colleagues on questions of editorial policy and the social/ethical aspects of electronic conferencing. Arachnet is not intended to replace Lstown-L@INDYCMS which is a discussion list for listowners to discuss technical aspects of Listserv based discussion group management.

Arachnet will be an unedited list but will accept postings only from Arachnet subscribers. If you are an editor or owner of an existing or future e-mail based forum, you are cordially invited to join.

Please fill out the attached e-form and return it to one of the Editors listed below. Please follow the format below as closely as possible.

Owners:
  Michael Strangelove   Diane Kovacs
  Editor Contex-L   Editor LIBRES,Libref-L,Govdoc-L
  441495@Uottawa   dkovacs@kentvm
  441495@acadvm1.uottawa.CA   dkovacs@kentvm.kent.edu

Please fill in and mail to the editor (Please simply type over what is in parentheses)

  • Lastname, Firstname <e-mail address>
  • Address: (institutional and, if you wish, domestic, with telephone numbers).
  • Brief description of your ListServ and electronic discussion group activities, including the
    name and purpose of all lists which you have served in any editorial or organizational
    capacity. Also please note familiarity with any other BBS software (excluding ListServ, a
    knowledge of which is assumed here), regardless of the platform on which it runs. (100-500
    words).
  • List of files/Resources available from your List's Fileserver or FTP site:

ARCH-L on LISTSERV@DGOGWDG1.BITNET   [Last Updated 12-October-1991]

ARCH-L has been formed to facilitate discussions of archaeological problems, especially those concerned with research, excavations, etc. Also relevant conferences, job announcements, calls for papers, publications, bibliographies and the like should be publicized. It is hoped that the list will also serve as a central repository for public domain or shareware software related to archaeological studies.

If you have materials that you'd be willing to put on file, please contact one of the owners of the list.

If you're interested in joining the list, please send e-mail or interactive message to
LISTSERV@DGOGWDG1.BITNET:

SUBScribe ARCH-L Your full name

For example

SUBScribe ARCH-L Heinrich Schliemann

At present the list is unmoderated and will immediately distribute any incoming message to the list. Please note: only messages for distribution should be sent to ARCH-L; all commands (subscribe, signoff, review, etc.) should go to LISTSERV.

Owners are: s.p.q.rahtz@ecs.southampton.ac.uk Sebastian Rahtz
          fsiegmu@dgogwdg1   Frank Siegmund
          hsteenw1@dgogwdg1   Helge Steenweg

Archives@IndyCMS.IUPUI.Edu
Archives@IndyCMS.BITNET   [Last Updated 12-October-1991]

Archives (Archives & Archivists list) is for all persons involved and/or interested in archival theory and practice.

To subscribe to the "ARCHIVES" list send e-mail to ListServ@IndyCMS (BITNET) or ListServ@IndyCMS.IUPUI.Edu (Internet) with the following command in the body of the mail: SUB ARCHIVES yourfirstname yourlastname

List owner/coordinators: Donna B Harlan
          Harlan@IUBACS (CREN)
          Harlan@UCS.Indiana.Edu (Internet)

          John B Harlan
          IJBH200@IndyVAX (CREN)
          IJBH200@IndyVAX.IUPUI.Edu (Internet)

AREXX-L@UCF1VM.CC.UCF.EDU

In addition to REXXLIST, the VM/SP REXX discussion list, 3 other lists exist to discuss the REXX programming language. They are AREXX-L (for Amiga REXX users), TSO-REXX (for TSO), and PC-REXX (for Personal REXX) users.

Log files will be kept on a monthly basis.

BitNet users can subscribe by sending the following command to LISTSERV@UCF1VM: SUB AREXX-L Your_full_name where Your_full_name is your real name, not your userid; for example: SUB AREXX-L John Doe Non-BitNet users can subscribe by sending the SUB command as the text/body of a message to LISTSERV@UCF1VM.CC.UCF.EDU

Coordinator: UCF Postmaster <POSTMAST@UCF1VM.CC.UCF.EDU>

ARMS-L@BUACCA.BU.EDU (ARMS-L@BUACCA.BITNET)

The ARMS-L digest is for various and sundry comments and questions on policy issues related to peace, war, national security, weapons, the arms race, and the like.

Recent archives are available upon request from the moderator.

This list is handled by LISTSERV@BUACCA.BU.EDU (LISTSERV@BUACCA.BITNET), and administrative requests go to that address. Contributions to ARMS-L@BUACCA.BU.EDU (ARMS-L@BUACCA.BITNET).

To become a subscriber, send mail to LISTSERV@BUACCA.BU.EDU with the one line SUB ARMS-L first last where you replace "first" and "last" with your first and last name.

This list is gatewayed to the USENET list soc.politics.arms-d.

Moderator: GROSS@BCVMS.BITNET

ARPANET-BBOARDS@MC.LCS.MIT.EDU
ARPANET-BBOARDS@LCS.MIT.EDU

Redistribution address for all known BBoards on the ARPANET. The guidelines for postings are somewhat loose. The ostensible purpose of the list is to distribute: (a) emergency notices ("Southern California just slid into the Pacific, machines at ISI and UCSD will be down for a few days"), and (b) notices of "academic interest", such as seminar and symposium announcements. Advertisements and for-profit notices are not appropriate (the DoD would get upset, among other considerations). A touchy borderline case is job offerings. The practice has been to accept postings from universities (the research community) and the research oriented military installations (the people paying for our hardware) but to refuse postings from private companies. The (shaky) rationale behind this is that university and military job offerings are "research opportunities" as opposed to for-profit advertisements (ie, joining the army or a university is not the way to get rich).

Anyone is welcome to redistribute Arpanet-BBoards; it takes some of the (considerable) load off of MC's mailer. But please don't do it without sending a message to the -Request address first.

There are Archive copies of every message ever sent to the list but no guarantee is made that they will be online or available at any particular time. The current archive file, such as it is, can be found as "COMAIL;BBOARD ARCHIV" on MC.LCS.MIT.EDU.

All requests to be added to or deleted from this list, problems, questions, etc., should be sent to the Coordinators. Bitnet users may subscribe to the list by doing: TELL LISTSERV at RUTVM1 SUBSCRIBE ARPABBS Your_Full_Name where Your_Full_Name is your real name (not your userid). From a VMS BITNET site use the SEND/REMOTE command.

Coordinator: ARPANET-BBOARDS-REQUEST@MC.LCS.MIT.EDU
BitNet Coordinator: Michael Smith <MSMITH%UMASS.BITNET@CUNYVM.CUNY.EDU>

ars-magica@ocf.berkeley.edu   [Last Updated 12-October-1991]

This is a list for players of the Ars Magica roleplaying game. To get on the list, send mail to ars-magica-request@ocf.berkeley.edu. The mailing list itself is ars-magica@ocf.berkeley.edu. Archives are available via anonymous ftp from soda.berkeley.edu, or by mail. To find out how to use the mail-based archive server, send mail to ars-magica-archive@soda.berkeley.edu with the body of the mail being "help".

Moderators: Shannon Appel & Mark Phaedrus

ARTCRIT%YORKVM1.BITNET@VM1.NODAK.EDU

A discussion forum open to anyone interested in the visual arts. Topics will reflect the diversity of art critical discourse: ostmodernism, marxist and feminist theories, curatorial practices, funding and any issue which affects artists, critics and art viewers.

Subscribers are encouraged to contribute reviews to be distributed bi-weekly to the list in journal format. Reveiws should be sent to the Editor, Michele Macal GL253001@YUORION.

BitNet users may subscribe by sending the following command to LISTSERV@YORKVM1 via interactive message or e-mail:

SUB ARTCRIT your full name

where "your full name" is your name, not your login Id; For example: SUB ARTCRIT John Doe. Non-BitNet users can join the list by sending the above command as the only line in the text/body of a message to LISTSERV%YORKVM1.BITNET@VM1.NODAK.EDU.

Coordinator: Michele Macaluso <GL253001%YUORION.BITNET@VM1.NODAK.EDU>

ARTNET@UK.AC.NEWCASTLE   [Last Updated 12-October-1991]

The list is for anyone who has or who may have an interest in network; installation; project;

communication; temporary; ad-hoc; transient; mobile; time-based; formless; de-centred art. Potential members include artists, art-administrators, writers, theorists, students, teachers. The aim of the list is to encourage contributions from all who have dipped a toe into these waters and found them congenial, but who know not where to turn next. The idea is that alliances will be formed, projects launched, funding gained, technology utilised, ideas launched and wild speculation indulged in. I hope that art projects will be instigated via this list. It is within my desire for the list that it evolves.

The list encompasses:

*Projects	*New work	*Events
*Collaborations	*Funding	*Technology
*Shows	*Jobs	*Conferences
*Proposals	*Organisations	*Information
*Publications	*Education	*Wild speculation

ARTNET provides a forum for the discussion of ART that is concerned with: network; installation; project; communication; temporary; ad-hoc; transient; mobile; time-based; formless; de- centred. I call this PERIPATETIC art.

I define peripatetic art thus: The art or action of creative endeavour with lack of fixed base. There is no fixed centre which claims to have 'the knowledge'. All projects involve some aspect of lack of enclosure; the promotion of action without centre. Peripatetic art tends towards the transient, the time based, the mobile. Peripatetology is as much about receiving the action, the project, as it is about initiating it.

I am concerned with improving communication amongst those working in these and related areas. By its nature this kind of work often does not lend itself to easy documentation or definition. The concept mooted here, and encapsulated in the term 'peripatetic', has by its very nature a changeable agenda. I hope that in action we will create new ways of working alongside some very old human desires.

To subscribe to ARTNET send the command

subscribe artnet <firstname> <lastname>

in a mail message to MAILBASE@NEWCASTLE.AC.UK

To contact the list owner for help, advice, information, send mail to:
ARTNET-REQUEST@NEWCASTLE.AC.UK

If you need more information about MAILBASE you can send the commands:

send mailbase overview (for a general guide to Mailbase)

send mailbase userhelp (for a User Guide)

as a mail message to MAILBASE@NEWCASTLE.AC.UK (Janet UK.AC.NEWCASTLE)

ART-SUPPORT@NEWCASTLE.AC.UK   [Last Updated 12-October-1991]

Art-Support exists as a forum for the discussion of ART related matters. Potential members include artists, art-administrators, writers, theorists, students, teachers and others with an interest in art.

This list provides a general magazine type information exchange and discussion area. As in any specialist magazine there will be much of interest to subscribers and also some irrelevance.

Although not in any way subscription/geographically limited, the focus of the list is intended to be the UK art community. It is hoped that the list will stimulate the use of network resources. The idea is that alliances will be formed; projects launched; funding gained; technology utilised; ideas launched and wild speculation indulged in.

ART-SUPPORT is about ART, not technology. Any art or art related subject is acceptable.

The list encompasses:

*Projects	*New work	*Events
*Collaborations	*Funding	*Technology
*Shows	*Jobs	*Conferences
*Proposals	*Organisations	*Information
*Publications	*Education	*Wild speculation

To subscribe to ART-SUPPORT send the following mail command

subscribe art-support <firstname> <lastname>

to MAILBASE@NEWCASTLE.AC.UK

To contact the list owner for help, advice, information, send mail to:
ART-SUPPORT-REQUEST@NEWCASTLE.AC.UK (Janet UK.AC.NEWCASTLE).

If you need more information about MAILBASE you can issue the commands:

send mailbase overview (for a general guide to Mailbase)

send mailbase userhelp (for a User Guide)

as a mail message to MAILBASE@NEWCASTLE.AC.UK

ASHE-L on LISTSERV@UMCVMB

This list is for open communication concerning issues of higher education within the Association for the Study of Higher Education (ASHE).

To subscribe to the list send mail to LISTSERV@UMCVMB on BITNET with the body of the mail containing the command

SUB ASHE-L yourfirstname yourlastname

Coordinator: Irv Cockriel <EDRSR438%UMCVMB.BITNET@VM1.NoDak.EDU>

ASM370@UCF1VM.CC.UCF.EDU

Discussion of programming in IBM System/370 Assembly Language. This is primarily a working group designed to answer questions and help distribute programs; however, any theoretical (are there such things?) discussions are welcome too.

Log files will be kept on a monthly basis.

BitNet users can subscribe by sending the following command to LISTSERV@UCF1VM: SUB ASM370 Your_full_name where Your_full_name is your real name, not your userid; for example: SUB ASM370 John Doe Non-BitNet users can subscribe by sending the SUB command as the text/body of a message to LISTSERV@UCF1VM.CC.UCF.EDU

Coordinator: UCF Postmaster <POSTMAST@UCF1VM.CC.UCF.EDU>

ASMICRO-L@VME131.LSI.USP.ANSP.BR

This list is intended to be a forum for interchange of information regarding all aspects of the design and use of Application Specific Microprocessors.

Application Specific Microprocessors form a class of integrated circuits, composed of a microprocessor-type computing element and aditional circuitry on the same chip, and designed to satisfy the specific needs of a particular application. Please note that this list is not intended to be a place to discuss general purpose off-the-shelf microcomputers.

Subscription is open to the public and the list is not moderated. To subscribe or for general enquiries regarding the list, please send a mail message to

ASMICRO-REQUEST@VME131.LSI.USP.ANSP.BR or uunet!vme131!ASMICRO-REQUEST

All contributions are welcome. Postings to the list should be sent to

ASMICRO-L@VME131.LSI.USP.ANSP.BR or uunet!vme131!ASMICRO-L

When subscribing, please include your name and affiliation in the message (this is not required). This information will made available to all subscribers.

Owner:

Pedro Luis Prospero Sanchez   internet: pl@vme131.lsi.usp.ansp.br
University of Sao Paulo   uunet: uunet!vme131!pl
Dept. of Electrical Engineering
phone: (055)(11)211-4574 home: (055)(11)215-6492 fax: (055)(11)815-4272

ASSESS on LISTSERV@UKCC.UKY.EDU

The assessment discussion list (ASSESS@UKCC.UKY.EDU) has been established to provide for informal dialog on assessment issues and policies as well as information on current practices in higher education. The purpose is to provide a forum for the exchange of ideas, models, resources, and practical strategies on student assessment of learning and institutional effectiveness. Assessment practitioners, policy makers, and others interested in assessment are invited to join.

To subscribe to the assessment discussion list, send electronic mail to LISTSERV@UKCC.UKY.EDU with the following as the first line of text in the message body: SUBSCRIBE ASSESS Your Name Here

You will receive notification from the listserv that you have subscribed to the list. If you do not receive notification, please let us know!

If you want to send a message to everyone subscribed to the ASSESS list, send your message via electronic mail to ASSESS@UKCC.UKY.EDU

Note: Listserv commands such as SUBSCRIBE and UNSUBSCRIBE should be sent only to the listserv address LISTSERV@UKCC.UKY.EDU. If you send commands to ASSESS@UKCC.UKY.EDU, your text will be sent to all subscribers of the list and will not be executed.

Owner:
Thomas E. Kunselman
Information Specialist   INTERNET: VAATEK@UKCC.UKY.EDU
Office of the Assistant Chancellor   BITNET: VAATEK@UKCC
#7 Administration Building
University of Kentucky
Lexington, KY 40506-0032
Phone:(606) 257-1633

ASSMPC-L%USACHVM1.BITNET@VM1.NODAK.EDU

Mailing list for issues related to the PC Assembly languages (Intel 8086/88/286/386/...). There is an initial programming goal that the managers of this list wish to accomplish:

We are inviting all users to assist in the coding of projects. For instance, our first task will be a Resident Program Manager. We will use Turbo Assembler or MacroAssembler to develop the applications.

A second project will be an AV package to viruses, we already have programs for Jerusalem and Brain, these could be help for it.

The users of this list will receive mail with code contributions and discussions, and eventually the program source listing finished with the help of the participants. Then, the list will propose a new project to work on. Any and all code contributions, ideas, and anything else that will help in achieving this opening goal will be appreciated, discussed, reported and acknowledged for the list.

BitNet users can subscribe non-interactively by sending a message or mail to LISTSERV@USACHVM1.BITNET with the text/body of the message being: SUB ASSMPC-L your_full_name For example: SUB ASSMPC-L Jan Doe Non-BitNet users can subscribe by sending the above command in the text/body of a message to LISTSERV%USACHVM1.BITNET@VM1.NODAK.EDU. IBM BitNet users can subscribe interactively by doing: TELL LISTSERV AT USACHVM1 SUB ASSMPC-L your_full_name Or by: NOTE TO LISTSERV AT USACHVM1, with the following line: SUB ASSMPC-L your_full_name Please note that the link to Chile is connected at 18:00 hrs EDT; before that time interactive commands won't work.

All problems, questions, etc., should be sent to the Coordinators.

Coordinators:
    Luis Valdivia P.   <LVALDIVI%USACHVM1.BITNET@VM1.NODAK.EDU>
                         <LISTVIR%USACHVM1.BITNET@VM1.NODAK.EDU>
    Pedro Sepulveda J.   <PSEPULVE%USACHVM1.BITNET@VM1.NODAK.EDU>

Astronomy Events <koolish@BBN.COM>

A mailing list for astronomical events and meeting announcements (mostly in the Boston area). Items to be sent to the list are sent to koolish@BBN.COM for forwarding. An attempt is being made to keep it from becoming full of trivial messages, but new readers and valid input are welcome.

Coordinator: Dick Koolish <koolish@BBN.COM>

ATAVACHRON@MOREKYPR.BITNET   [Last Updated 28-January-1992]
ATAVACHRON@MOREKYPR.MOREHEAD-ST.EDU

ATAVACHRON is a discussion forum in digest format intended to exchange information and stimulate discussions on the works of guitarist Allan Holdsworth. The list is in a moderated digest format; all postings sent to ATAVACHRON will be compiled and distributed on an "as-needed" basis (typically 2-5 times weekly). As of 10/31/91, no archives will be offered, but may be in the future if demand exists.

To subscribe (or unsubscribe), send a short request via e-mail including your name and institutional or company affiliation and location to:

ATAVACHRON@MOREKYPR.BITNET -for Bitnet users or
ATAVACHRON@MOREKYPR.MOREHEAD-ST.EDU -for Internet users

For all other administrative issues, please send requests to:

PRESTON@MOREKYPR.BITNET

ATAVACHRON is NOT a LISTSERV list, so it is necessary to send subscription and signoff requests to ATAVACHRON@MOREKYPR.BITNET or ATAVACHRON@MOREKYPR.MOREHEAD-ST.EDU

Owner:

    Jeff Preston <preston@morekypr.bitnet>
    Morehead State University
    Morehead, Kentucky

AUDIO-L on LISTSERV@VMTECMEX

A listserv list providing a forum to discuss all topics related to audio, this includes theories, commercial equipment, applications, etc. The list runs unmoderated and it's located in AUDIO-L@VMTECMEX.BITNET

As in any listserv list, your commands should be sent to LISTSERV@VMTECMEX. To subscribe to the list send the following command to LISTSERV@VMTECMEX

SUB AUDIO-L yourfirstname yourlastname

in the text of a message or mail.

Coordinator: Alejandro Kurczyn S.

AUSTEN-L on LISTSERV@MCGILL1 or LISTSERV@vm1.mcgill.ca

A moderated digest for readers of Jane Austen. If you enjoy Jane Austen's novels and those of her contemporaries, such as Fanny Burney, Maria Edgeworth and Maria Wollstonecraft, you might want to exchange views with others on any aspect of her work and her time.

Moderator: Dr. Jacqueline Reid-Walsh,
　　　　　　Department of English,
　　　　　　McGill University,
　　　　　　853 Sherbrooke St. West
　　　　　　Montreal, Quebec, H3A 2T6

Subscription requests and contributions should be sent to: CCMW@MUSICA.MCGILL.CA

AUTISM on LISTSERV@SJUVM.BITNET

A list has been formed at St. John's University devoted to the Developmentally Disabled and called Autism. Its purpose is to provide a forum for those who are Developmentally Disabled, their teachers, and those interested in this area.

The list will provide a forum for the understanding and treatment of all types of Developmental Disability and to further Networking among those so handicapped to increase their interaction with the rest of society. Networking among the teachers of the Developmentally Disabled will be encouraged to share successful interventions.

To subscribe to the list, send the following command in the BODY of mail or an interactive message to LISTSERV@SJUVM.BITNET

SUB AUTISM firstname lastname

Owner: Bob Zenhausern, Ph.D.
　　　　St. John's University　　Bitnet: drz@sjuvm.bitnet
　　　　SB 15 Marillac　　　　　Phone: 718-990-6447
　　　　Jamaica, NY 11439　　　Fax:　718-990-6705

AUTO-L%TECHNION.BITNET@VM1.NODAK.EDU
AUTO-L@TECHNION.TECHNION.AC.IL
AUTO-L@TECHNION.BITNET

Mailing list to handle problems with Remote Autolog commands. To date, the list has been used for problems from users that have accounts at the Technion and work remotely through the Remote Server (VMAUTOLG) located at the Technion. The software for this Remote Server is be changed so as to be included as a local command for LISTSERV/LISTEARN sites that may want to use it. The list is not limited to the discussion of only this one package. Any other packages or software may be discussed. Please do not use this list for the discussion of any problems with using the GONE routine.

BitNet users may subscribe by sending the following command to LISTSERV@TECHNION via interactive message or e-mail: SUBSCRIBE AUTO-L your full name where "your full name" is your real name, not your login Id. Non-BitNet users can join the list by sending the above command as the only line in the text/body of a message to LISTSERV%TECHNION.BITNET@VM1.NODAK.EDU or LISTSERV@TECHNION.TECHNION.AC.IL.

Coordinator:
　　Robert (Al) Hartshorn <CCSM1AL%TECHNION.BITNET@VM1.NODAK.EDU>
　　　　　　　　　　　　<CCSM1AL@TECHNION.TECHNION.AC.IL>
　　　　　　　　　　　　<CCSM1AL@TECHNION.BITNET>

autox@autox.team.net

A mailing list for the discussion of autocrossing, which is a low-cost form of motorsports in which one car at a time competes against the clock. Courses are designed to emphasize the driver's car handling skill, rather than speed or power.

Subscription information: Send mail to autox-request@autox.team.net. Please include your geographical location and email address, as well as what sort of car, if any, you race.

The list is available in both standard and daily-digest forms.

Administrator: Mark Sirota (msirota@ee.rochester.edu)

AVIATION@MC.LCS.MIT.EDU

Aviation discusses topics of interest to pilots, including training systems, laws affecting availability or usability of airports, planes, and procedures, characteristics of aircraft and avionic products, comments on commercial aviation, such as safety and convenience issues, occasional advertisements for fly-ins or similar private pilot activities, historical notes, whatever else the readership wants. Aviation serves as an Internet gateway for the rec.aviation discussion on usenet. It is distributed in the form of a daily digest.

Due to disk space limitations, archives are only maintained for the previous few weeks of digests. They are maintained on the host MC.LCS.MIT.EDU in files named: AVIATN;DIGEST <number> Where <number> is the issue number of the digest.

All requests to be added to or deleted from this list, problems, questions, etc., should be sent to AVIATION-REQUEST@MC.LCS.MIT.EDU.

Coordinator: Christopher Maeda <cmaeda@CS.CMU.EDU>

AVIATION-THEORY@MC.LCS.MIT.EDU
aviation-theory-in@mc.lcs.mit.edu (USENET)

Mailing list dedicated to the more theoretical side of aerospace engineering. The intent is to conduct discussions on aerospace technology; also calls for papers, anouncements for seminars, etc., can be sent to the list. Although the list has its origin in the AVIATION digest, subjects related to aviation theory, like spaceflight technology, may be discussed as well. Topics open for discussion are:

Calls for papers Aerodynamics Aircraft structures Seminar anouncements Flight mechanics Aircraft materials Books to be published Stability and Control and others...

A mailing list for INTERNET and BITNET has been created already and we are looking for someone who would like to create the USENET group, so we can create digests from those messages.

All requests to be added to or deleted from this list, problems, questions, etc., should be sent to aviation-theory-request@MC.LCS.MIT.EDU.

Moderator: Rob A. Vingerhoeds <ROB%BGERUG51.BITNET@MITVMA.MIT.EDU>

Aware-L on LISTSERV@UKANVM.BITNET

The Authorware mailist was formed to offer a forum for discussion for developers that use the program Authorware Professional.

To subscribe to Aware-L send the following command to LISTSERV@UKANVM.BITNET in the BODY of a mail message:

SUBSCRIBE AWARE-L Your full name Eg. subscribe aware-l Norma Mailer

Owner: Donald W. Tracia (Tracia@UKANVM.BITNET)

BACKSTREETS@VIRGINIA.EDU
Backstreets@UVAARPA.VIRGINIA.EDU
BStreets@VIRGINIA (BitNet)
...!uunet!virginia!backstreets-heads (uucp)

Mailing list for fans of the music of Bruce Springsteen.

All requests to be added to or deleted from this list, problems, questions, etc., should be sent to Backstreets-Request@VIRGINIA.EDU or Backstreets-Request@UVAARPA.VIRGINIA.EDU (Internet), BS-Req@VIRGINIA (BitNet), or ...!uunet!virginia!backstreets-request (uucp).

Coordinator: Marc Rouleau <mer6g@VIRGINIA.EDU>

ballroom@athena.mit.edu

Unmoderated mailing list for the discussion of any aspect of Ballroom and Swing dancing. For instance: Places to dance, announcement of special events (e.g., inter-university competitions), exchange of information about clubs, ballroom dance music, discussion of dances, steps, etc.

Anyone may join; please send ALL of the following information to ballroom-request@athena.mit.edu: (1) Full name (2) Internet- compatible e-mail address (3) Affiliation, if any, with any ballroom dance organization or group (4) ZIP or postal code, and country if other than U.S. (5) Whether you have access to Netnews (Yes/No/Don't know/Yes but don't use).

Contact: ballroom-request@athena.mit.edu (Shahrukh Merchant c/o MIT Ballroom Dance Club)

BALT-L@UBVM.CC.BUFFALO.EDU
BALT-L on LISTSERV@UBVM.CC.BUFFALO.EDU

Baltic Republics news and development list

BALT-L is an online forum devoted to communications to, and about, the Baltic Republics of Lithuania, Latvia and Estonia. It aims to further networking with those countries, in two senses of that word: the technical one of establishing the basic links to permit electronic communications; and the softer definition of a network of people building up people-to-people contacts and working together on matters of common interest. A core aim of this list is to foster practical projects.

Subscription to this list is welcomed from anyone with skills or interests relevant to the Baltics, or who just wants to know whats going on.

We hope in particular to bring together

Participants living in the Baltic Republics. People around the world with origins in the Baltic Republics, or who have connections with those countries. Anyone with technical skills in electronic networking who may want to contribute to developing electronic links to the Baltic Republics. Anyone needing to research on developments in the Baltics. Anyone around the world with a need to contact, visit and/or work with College staff or students living and working in Lithuania, Latvia or Estonia.

Although English is likely to be the lingua franca, ALL languages of communication are WELCOME: but especially in Lithuanian, Latvian or Estonian.

To subscribe, send the following command to LISTSERV@UBVM.CC.BUFFALO.EDU via mail or interactive message:

SUB BALT-L your full name

where "your full name" is your name. (NOT your network userID). For example

SUB BALT-L Joan Doe

Archives of messages already sent through BALT-L can be obtained by interactive LDBASE or by sending an "INDEX BALT-L" command to LISTSERV@UBVM.CC.BUFFALO.EDU These files can then be retrieved by means of a "GET BALT-L filetype" command.

Owner (UKACRL):	Edis Bevan <AEB_BEVAN@UK.AC.OPEN.ACS.VAX>
Owner (UBVM):	Jean-Michel Thizy <jmyhg@acadvm1.uottawa.ca>
	<JMYHG@UOTTAWA.BITNET>

BALTUVA on LISTSERV@MCGILL1.BITNET or LISTSERV@VM1.MCGILL.CA

BALTUVA is a list focusing on issues and questions of concern to observant Jews. The name of the list is derived from "baal t'shuva" which is often used to refer to "newly religious" Jews. The list is not restricted to this group however - please feel free to post to the list ther whether or not you consider yourself to be a "baal t'shuva."

To subscribe send the following E-mail message to LISTSERV@VM1.MCGILL.CA in the BODY of mail (NOT the subject):

SUBSCRIBE BALTUVA Your Name

To receive more information concerning the list, send the following E-mail message to LISTSERV@VM1.MCGILL.CA (in the BODY of mail)

REVIEW BALTUVA

Owner: Claire Austin <CZCA@MUSICA.MCGILL.CA>

BANYAN-L%AKRONVM.BITNET@VM1.NODAK.EDU
BANYAN-L on LISTSERV@AKRONVM

BANYAN-L is a Listserv discussion list about any aspect of Banyan networks (marketed by Banyan Systems, Inc.).

To subscribe, send an interactive message or mail to LISTSERV@AKRONVM as follows:

SUBscribe BANYAN-L Your Name

Of particular interest is Banyan's VINES network.

BDGTPLAN%UVMVM.BITNET@VM1.NODAK.EDU Discussion of college and university budget and planning issues including, but not limited to: economic and enrollment forecasting, relationships with state governments, innovative approaches to integrating planning and budgeting, strategies for increasing participation, cost center analysis, use of financial databases for modelling and reporting, endowment spending policies, tuition pricing, resource reallocation, financial reporting to boards and legislators, etc.

BitNet users may subscribe by sending the following command to LISTSERV@UVMVM via interactive message or e-mail: SUBSCRIBE BDGTPLAN your full name where "your full name" is your real name, not your login Id. Non-BitNet users can join the list by sending the above command as the only line in the text/body of a message to LISTSERV%UVMVM.BITNET@VM1.NODAK.EDU.

Coordinator: Dayna Flath <DMF%UVMVM.BITNET@VM1.NODAK.EDU>

BEE-L%ALBNYVM1.BITNET@CUNYVM.CUNY.EDU BEE-L is for the discussion of research and information concerning the biology of bees. This includes honey bees and other bees (and maybe even wasps). We communicate about sociobiology, behavior, ecology, adaptation/evolution, genetics, taxonomy, physiology, pollination, and flower nectar and pollen production of bees.

To subscribe, send the following command to LISTSERV@ALBNYVM1 via mail or interactive message: SUB BEE-L your_full_name where "your_full_name" is your name. For example: SUB BEE-L Joan Doe Non-BitNet users can subscribe by sending the text: SUB BEE-L your_full_name in the body of a message to LISTSERV%ALBNYVM1.BITNET@CUNYVM.CUNY.EDU.

Coordinator: Mary Jo Orzech <MJO%BROCK1P.BITNET@CUNYVM.CUNY.EDU>

BELIEF-L on LISTSERV@BROWNVM

Personal Ideologies Discussion List

This list is designed to be a forum where personal ideologies can be discussed, examined, and analyzed. Topics for the list can range from "what is good" to "what happens after death" to "is there a god".

This list is designed to be open to members of ALL religious and political faiths or non-faiths; we do not discriminate based on religion, race, gender, sexual preference, handicap, et cetera.

The list is open for all discussion pertaining to ideological, religious, moral, and ethical topics. There are only four general rules:

1. Treat everyone's faith as if it were as sacred as your own. In fact, to be safe, treat their faiths BETTER than your own.
2. Excessively rude, obnoxious, or abusive posting will not be tolerated.
3. Personal attacks will NOT be tolerated. Take your fights to e-mail where they belong, NOT in public.
4. Due to the varied nature of computer systems, please take into account that not everyone has the time or disk space to read several thousand lines of BELIEF-L mail per day. If you have a large amount of material to send to the list, please do one or more of the following:
[a] Announce that you have something you'd like to discuss, and solicit opinions from from the list as to whether it would be o.k. to bring it up.
[b] Post in reasonably-sized "chunks" -- by my definition, in the range of 200 lines, once or twice a day at the most.
[c] If you will be reposting or crossposting material from another source, announce that you have it, and offer to send copies to interested parties.

The first "rule" is really a guideline. Proselytizing is OK, so long as you remember that you get what you dish out. With respect to the second rule, please remember that you are a professional, and professionals don't get abusive to others. If you violate the other rules, in the opinion of the List Owners, more than twice, you will be asked to stop. If you continue to be abusive, you will be removed from the list.

By signing on to this list, you acknowledge your right to critically respond to other's ideologies; you also acknowledge that your own ideologies can be critically responded to. You agree to abide by the rules of the list, insofar as they are listed above, and may be added to in the future as need be. You acknowledge the right of the list owners to have you removed from the list if you fail to abide by the rules. Further, you agree that this list and all material herein is PRIVATE PROPERTY, and will not engage in cross-list or cross-person posting without prior permission, which will only be obtained publicly on the list.

The opinions expressed on this list do not, unless explicitly stated, reflect the opinions of the United States, the universities or organizations of the members of this list, and are only the personal opinions of the list members. Any liability, expressed or implied, rests with the individual list members.

To subscribe to this list, send the command:

SUBSCRIBE BELIEF-L your_name

to LISTSERV@BROWNVM, where "your_name" is your full name (not your login Id). Non-BitNet users can subscribe by sending the above command in the text/body of a message to LISTSERV%BROWNVM.BITNET@VM1.NODAK.EDU.

Internet subscribers should go DIRECTLY to LISTSERV@BROWNVM.BROWN.EDU.

Coordinator: "David B. O'Donnell" <EL407006@brownvm.brown.edu>

BEN@cue.bc.ca

BEN is a newsletter distributed on e-mail, deals with botany and plant ecology of predominantly British Columbia, Canada and the Pacific Northwest (from California to Alaska) with broader references to planet Earth. Frequency: about once every two weeks.

Requests for subscription should be sent to the OWNER at the e-mail address below. This is NOT a listserv list.

Owner: Adolf Ceska <aceska@cue.bc.ca>

BGRASS-L on LISTSERV@UKCC.BITNET   [Last Updated 6/92]
    or LISTSERV@UKCC.UKY.EDU

The purpose of BGRASS-L is to be a forum for discussion of:

1. Issues related to the International Bluegrass Music Association (IBMA)
2. Bluegrass music in general, including but not limited to recordings, bands, individual performers, live performances, publications, business aspects, venues, history, you-name-it. Old-time music and early commercial country music are also acceptable topics.

Archives of traffic since 1 Feb. 1992 are available from the LISTSERVer; earlier by special arrangement.

To subscribe, send e-mail to: LISTSERV@UKCC or LISTSERV@UKCC.UKY.EDU with the following command in the BODY of the mail (NO subject:): SUB BGRASS-L your full name

To communicate, send e-mail to: BGRASS-L@UKCC or BGRASS-L@UKCC.UKY.EDU

For information, send e-mail to: UKA016@UKCC or UKA016@UKCC.UKY.EDU

Owner: Frank Godbey, University of Kentucky, Lexington, KY
BITNET: UKA016@UKCC.BITNET
Internet: UKA016@UKCC.UKY.EDU

bind@vangogh.cs.berkeley.edu

This list covers topics relating to BIND domain software. To join, send a message to bind-request@vangogh.cs.berkeley.edu.

BIRDEAST%ARIZVM1.BITNET@CORNELLC.CIT.CORNELL.EDU   [Last Updated 12-October-1991]
BIRDCHAT%ARIZVM1.BITNET@CORNELLC.CIT.CORNELL.EDU
BIRDCNTR%ARIZVM1.BITNET@CORNELLC.CIT.CORNELL.EDU
BIRDWEST%ARIZVM1.BITNET@CORNELLC.CIT.CORNELL.EDU

BIRDEAST, BIRDCHAT, BIRDCNTR, and BIRDWEST on LISTSERV@ARIZVM1

The National Birding Hotline Cooperative

We are pleased to announce that the National Birding Hotline Cooperative list on LISTSERV@ARIZVM1 has gone to a regional format. The three lists, which replace the former BIRD_RBA@ARIZVM1, provide a clearing-house for transcribed birding hotlines for three major areas of the country--East, West, and Central. The new lists are BIRDEAST, BIRDCNTR, and BIRDWEST.

Current subscribers to BIRD_RBA will be automatically shifted to all three of the new lists. New subscribers must choose which of the three regional lists best answers their needs. Of course, new subscribers may still subscribe to all three lists for full coverage.

Subscribers are invited to submit transcripts from their area of the country if it is not already represented. A current list of hotlines available from the National Birding Hotline Cooperative is appended.

Contributions to the lists are always welcome and should be sent in MAIL format to BIRDEAST, or BIRDWEST, or BIRDCNTR, all at ARIZVM1. Please note that these are not intended to be general chat lists. Contributions should either be transcripts of birding hotlines or, if a local hotline recording is not available to you, concise statements of species seen and the location of the sighting, along with any relevant information such as 'out of range,' 'out of normal time frame,' etc. If you are confused about which of the three lists to send your material to, contact either of the list owners first. Their Bitnet/Internet addresses are listed below.

You may subscribe to The National Birding Hotline Cooperative by sending an interactive SUBSCRIBE command or by including a SUBSCRIBE command as the ONLY line of a MAIL message to LISTSERV@ARIZVM1, as follows:

Interactive example from CMS:

```
TELL LISTSERV AT ARIZVM1 SUB BIRDEAST <Your full name>
```

or BIRDCNTR or BIRDWEST

MAIL example:

SUB BIRDEAST <Your full name> or BIRDCNTR or BIRDWEST

To cancel your subscription, issue the SIGNOFF command to LISTSERV@ARIZVM1:

SIGNOFF BIRDEAST or BIRDCNTR or BIRDWEST

Do NOT send SIGNOFF or other LISTSERV commands to BIRDEAST, BIRDCNTR, or BIRDWEST.

If you are on the Internet network, subscription messages should be sent to LISTSERV@ARIZVM1.BITNET and hotline transcripts should be mailed to BIRDEAST@ARIZVM1.BITNET (or CNTR or WEST, as the case may be). In some cases, Internet mailer programs will not know how to get to a local Internet/Bitnet gateway. If this appears to be a problem for you, send subscription messages to:

LISTSERV%ARIZVM1.BITNET@CORNELLC.CIT.CORNELL.EDU

and hotline transcripts to:

BIRDEAST%ARIZVM1.BITNET@CORNELLC.CIT.CORNELL.EDU or BIRDCNTR or BIRDWEST

The following states are currently represented with transcribed hotlines on the three regional lists:

BIRDEAST	Maine, New Jersey, Pennsylvania, Delaware, Maryland, District of Columbia, Virginia
BIRDCNTR	Ohio, Indiana, Michigan, Texas
BIRDWEST	New Mexico, Arizona, California

If you have any questions, problems, or suggestions please send a note to us at one of the addresses listed below:

Charles B. Williamson (Chuck)
Bitnet address   :   CHUCKW@ARIZEVAX2
Internet address :   CHUCKW%EVAX2@Arizona.edu
Snail mail   :   4425 E. Pima
                     Tucson, AZ 85712
Phones   :   602-323-2955 (voice + answering machine)
Bulletin board   :   602-881-4280 So. Arizona Birding BBS

Norman C. Saunders (Norm)
Bitnet address   :   NYS@NIHCU
Internet address :   NYS@CU.NIH.GOV
Snail mail   :   1261 Cavendish Drive
                     Colesville, MD 20905
Phones   :   202-272-5248 (o--Washington, DC)
                 :   301-989-9035 (h--Colesville, MD)
Bulletin board   :   301-989-9036 The Osprey's Nest Birders' BBS
                     (Colesville, MD -- PC Pursuitable)

BI-L%BINGVMB.BITNET@VM1.NODAK.EDU
BI-L on LISTSERV@BINGVMB

BI-L is a computer conference dedicated to discussing ways of assisting library users in effectively and efficiently exploiting the resources available in and through the libraries of the 1990s.

Contributors to the forum deal with the practical, theoretical, and technical aspects of what has been called Bibliographic Instruction, Library Use Instruction, Library Orientation, and several other names. We examine, explore, critique, appraise, and evaluate strategies, programs, and equipment that we have found to be valuable (or not) in working toward the goal of the self-sufficient library user.

To join BI-L, send the following e-mail message to LISTSERV@BINGVMB: SUBSCRIBE BI-L Your

Name. (Put your first and last name where it says "Your Name.")

To contribute to BI-L, send your e-mail message to BI-L@BINGVMB. ****NOTE that you send your message to the *list*, not to the list server.

For more information about BI-L contact

Martin Raish
Coordinator of Bibliographic Instruction
State University of New York at Binghamton
Box 6012
Binghamton, New York 13902-6012
(607) 777-4385 or MRAISH@BINGVMA
   (MRAISH%BINGVMA.BITNET@CUNYVM.CUNY.EDU)

BIBSOFT ON LISTSERV@INDYCMS.BITNET   [Last Update 9/92]
or LISTSERV@INDYCMS.IUPUI.EDU (134.68.1.1)

BIBSOFT is an international electronic forum for anyone interested in discussing software designed for personal bibliographic database management. BIBSOFT is not restricted to a particular software program or hardware platform.

BIBSOFT is for people trying to choose a program, librarians and others who consult with users, and people who conduct training in one or more programs

HOW TO JOIN AND SEND MESSAGES:

To subscribe, send the following message: SUBSCRIBE BIBSOFT First-name Last-name

To unsubscribe, send the following email message: UNSUBSCRIBE BIBSOFT

To stop BIBSOFT mail when you go on vacation, send the following message: SET BIBSOFT NOMAIL

To resume BIBSOFT email delivery, send the following email message: SET BIBSOFT MAIL

to: LISTSERV@INDYCMS.BITNET or to: LISTSERV@INDYCMS.IUPUI.EDU

To send a message to BIBSOFT, send an email message to: BIBSOFT@INDYCMS.BITNET or to: BIBSOFT@INDYCMS.IUPUI.EDU

BIBSOFT is not moderated! Any message you send is sent directly to the entire membership list. Please make sure your messages are intended for public consumption!

Neither the list owners nor Indiana University verify the accuracy of submitted messages or endorse the opinions expressed by authors of messages. Authors of BIBSOFT messages are considered to be solely responsible for their own comments.

If you have questions about the list or problems with its operation, send email to one of the list owners. Owners:

Jim Morgan <morganj@indyvax.bitnet>
         <morganj@indyvax.iupui.edu>
    Automation Librarian
    Ruth Lilly Medical Library
    Indiana University School of Medicine
    975 W. Walnut
    Indianapolis, IN 46202
    (317) 274-1408   FAX (317) 274-2088

Sue Stigleman <stigle@cs.unca.edu>
    Writer, consultant, and computer
    science major at University of
    North Carolina at Asheville
    PO Box 8074
    Asheville, NC 28814-8074
    (704) 251-9059

bicycles@BBN.COM

Mailing list for topics relating to bicycles including:

- Racing: How do I get started? What do I need for equiment? Why do they shave their legs anyway? Are there any big races coming to this area?
- Touring: Where are some great places to ride? Stories of some of your bike trips. What are some of the things I should take for an overnight trip?
- Commuting: What is the best way to get by major traffic roads?
- Plus: Equipment, Repairs, Good places to buy a bike, Cars vs Bicycles, Human Powered Vehicles, Fitness, Bike path construction, or anything else you might want to ask or talk about.

To be added to the list: bicycles-request@BBN.COM

Coordinator: Craig MacFarlane <cmacfarl@SOCRATES.BBN.COM>

BIG-LAN@SUVM.ACS.SYR.EDU
BIG-LAN@SUVM (BitNet)

Mailing list for discussion of issues in designing and operating Campus-Size Local Area Networks, especially complex ones utilizing multiple technologies and supporting multiple protocols. Topics include repeaters, bridges, routers and gateways; how to incorporate smaller Personal-Computer type LANs into the campus-wide LAN; how to unify the mail systems, etc. This is an ideal list in which to debate the relative merits of bridges vs. routers.

Archives are available through revised LISTSERV.

All requests to be added to or deleted from this list, problems, questions, etc., should be sent to BIG-LAN-REQUEST@SUVM.ACS.SYR.EDU or BIG-REQ@SUVM (BitNet). Those familiar with revised LISTSERV can subscribe thru LISTSERV@SUVM.ACS.SYR.EDU or LISTSERV@SUVM (BitNet).

Coordinator: John Wobus <JMWOBUS@SUVM.ACS.SYR.EDU> JMWOBUS@SUVM (BitNet)

BIGM-L on LISTSERV@VM.SAS.COM

This list is for users of BigmOuth and PowerLine voice mail PC cards, both products of Talking Technologies, Inc. It is intended as a mutual-aid/mutual-commiseration group.

To subscribe, send the following single line in the BODY of a mail message (not the subject) to LISTSERV@VM.SAS.COM:

SUB BIGM-L firstname lastname

To unsubscribe, send the following single line in a mail message to LISTSERV@VM.SAS.COM:

UNSUB BIGM-L

To get more information about using LISTSERV, send the following single line in the BODY of a mail message to LISTSERV@VM.SAS.COM:

INFO

Notebooks: yes public yearly Owner: snoddi@mvs.sas.com (Dale Ingold)

BILLING%HDETUD1.BITNET@CUNYVM.CUNY.EDU

LISTSERV distribution list for the topic of billing and chargeback of (computer) resources. This list is not dedicated to any one product or supplier, but discusses general issues as well as details pertaining to MVS and VM systems only. Also see the MICS-L list.

A monthly notebook will be provided for logging the discussion; this notebook can be obtained without being subscribed to the list. BILLING LOG8901 contains a summary of net mail during the last year on this subject.

You can subscribe to this list by sending a request to LISTSERV at HDETUD1: TELL LISTSERV AT HDETUD1 SUB BILLING your_full_name or by sending mail to

LISTSERV%HDETUD1.BITNET@CUNYVM.CUNY.EDU containing the line: SUB BILLING your_full_name

Coordinator: Rob van Hoboken <RCOPROB%HDETUD1.BITNET@CUNYVM.CUNY.EDU>

BIO-NAUT%IRLEARN.BITNET@VM1.NODAK.EDU
BIO-NAUT on LISTSERV@IRLEARN.BITNET

A mailing list for BIONAUTS has been established at IRLEARN The main purpose of the list is to facilitate communications between life scientists. This list will have three main functions.

1. It can be used to ask questions about networking addresses of scientists in the biological life sciences. e.g. I need to get in contact with some one at EMBL who should I send mail to.
2. If you have small databases of E-mail addresses related to your particular field of interest they can be uploaded onto BIO-NAUT for the benefit of others. Special interst groups welcome. e.g. Numerical taxonomists, Culture Collections, etc.
3. If you subscribe you will be asked to send one message to BIO-NAUT which gives a brief outline of who you are and your main interests. Instructions on the format of this MESSAGE will be sent to all subscribers individually.

To subscribe to the BIOSCI Bionauts distribution service at IRLEARN, send the following command as one line in the body of a mail message to LISTSERV@IRLEARN.BITNET saying just

SUBSCRIBE BIO-NAUT forename surname

Those of you who are directly on EARN or BITNET can also subscribe with an interactive message, e.g.

TELL LISTSERV AT IRLEARN SUB BIO-NAUT forename surname (on an IBM running VM/CMS) or SEND LISTSERV@IRLEARN SUB BIO-NAUT forename surname (on a VAX running VMS)

When you have done that, you will get an acknowledgement that you now belong to the distribution list. Once subscribed, you can send mail messages to

BIO-NAUT@IRLEARN.BITNET

and they will be AUTOMATICALLY redistributed to all the other subscribers. They (and you) can then reply to that address and everyone will see the answers.

Remember

The SUB command for subscribing goes to LISTSERV@IRLEARN.BITNET (LISTSERV%IRLEARN.BITNET@VM1.NODAK.EDU for Internet users) Your mail messages for others to see go to BIO-NAUT@IRLEARN.BITNET (BIO-NAUT%IRLEARN.BITNET@VM1.NODAK.EDU for Internet users) Moderator: Rob Harper <HARPER@CSC.FI>

BIO-SOFTWARE%NET.BIO.NET@VM1.NODAK.EDU
bio-soft@IRLEARN.UCD.IE Ireland EARN/BitNet
bio-soft@UK.AC.DARESBURY U.K. JANET
bio-software@BMC.UU.SE Sweden Internet
bio-software@NET.BIO.NET U.S.A. BitNet
bio-soft@NET.BIO.NET U.S.A. BitNet

The BIO-SOFTWARE newsgroup replaces three previous newsgroups on BIOSCI:

OLD BBOARD NAME	BITNET/EARN Name	USENET Newsgroup Name
CONTRIBUTED-SOFTWARE	SOFT-CON	bionet.software.contrib
PC-COMMUNICATIONS	SOFT-COM	bionet.software.pc.comm
PC-SOFTWARE	SOFT-PC	bionet.software.pc

NEW BBOARD NAME	BITNET/EARN Name	USENET Newsgroup Name

BIO-SOFTWARE   BIO-SOFT   bionet.software

The BIO-SOFTWARE newsgroup is not moderated. Questions, answers, and discussions are welcomed about software related to the biological sciences (or even about problems with other software that scientists might use in the course of their work such as word processors or communications software).

To subscribe to this newsgroup, please send your subscription request to one of the following addresses; if you previously received e-mail from any of the three superceded groups, then you should have been subscribed to BIO-SOFTWARE. If you have any questions or doubts about this, please contact the applicable BIOSCI address below:

Subscription Addresses	Location	Network
biosci%net.bio.net@VM1.NODAK.EDU		Internet
biosci@net.bio.net	U.S.A.	BitNet
biosci@irlearn.ucd.ie	Ireland	EARN/BitNet
biosci@uk.ac.daresbury	U.K.	JANET
biosci@bmc.uu.se	Sweden	Internet

Users on the BIONET DEC 2065 computer may subscribe (i.e., be shown all new messages at login) by entering DO BIO-SOFTWARE after the @ prompt.

Coordinator: Dave Kristofferson <Kristofferson%BIONET-20.BIO.NET@VM1.NODAK.EDU> kristofferson@BIONET-20.BIO.NET

BIOMCH-L%HEARN.BITNET@CUNYVM.CUNY.EDU

Mailing list for members of the International, European, American, Canadian and other Societies of Biomechanics, and for others with an interest in the general field of biomechanics and human or animal movement science. For the scope of this list, see, e.g., the Journal of Biomechanics (Pergamon Press), the Journal of Biomechanical Engineering (ASME), and Human Movement Science (North-Holland).

To subscribe to BIOMCH-L, send the following command to LISTSERV%HEARN.BITNET@CUNYVM.CUNY.EDU via mail text or interactive message: SUBSCRIBE BIOMCH-L Your_full_name For example: SUBSCRIBE BIOMCH-L Joan Doe

Coordinators: Anton J. van den Bogert <WWDONIC%HEITUE5.BITNET@CUNYVM.CUNY.EDU> Herman J. Woltring <WWTMHJW%HEITUE5.BITNET@CUNYVM.CUNY.EDU>

BIOMED-L%NDSUVM1.BITNET@VM1.NODAK.EDU

Mailing list for discussion on the topic of Biomedical Ethics. Since the field of medicine and medical technology are rapidly changing and the field is so broad, it is difficult to have clearly delineated rules as to what should and should not be discussed, but possible topics might include: Paternalism, Fetal Cell Transplant, The Right to Die, AIDS, Suicide, Patient Autonomy, Abortion, Drug Legalization, Euthanasia, Respirator Withdrawal, Transplants, Allocation of scarce resources and many others too numerous to list here. The discussions may be ethical, philosophical, religious, political, social or even, in some cases, personal. Open discussion, disagreement, and dissent is encouraged. Open flames are most certainly *not*.

To subscribe to BIOMED-L send the following command to LISTSERV@NDSUVM1: SUBSCRIBE BIOMED-L your_full_name where your_full_name is your real name, not your userid. Non-BitNet users can subscribe by sending the above command in the text/body of a message to LISTSERV%NDSUVM1.BITNET@VM1.NODAK.EDU.

Coordinator: Bill Sklar <86730%LAWRENCE.BITNET@VM1.NODAK.EDU>

BIOSPH-L%UBVM.BITNET@VM1.NODAK.EDU

This list replaces the now defunct list OZONE@ICNUCEVM. The new name reflects better the topics discussed. Anything relating to the biosphere, pollution, CO_2 effect, ecology, habitats, climate, etc., can be discussed. Basically anything that exerts an influence of some kind or another on the BioSphere.

New archives will be stored in a monthly notebook. Archives from the old Ozone List will eventually be transferred to the BIOSPH-L site. Even though there is no longer a connection to the owners of the old list, the idea is to continue on from the topics that were being discussed up to when it went dead.

To subscribe send the following command to LISTSERV@UBVM.BITNET: SUBSCRIBE BIOSPH-L Your_full_name To leave or signoff the list send: SIGNOFF BIOSPH-L Non-BitNet users can [un]subscribe by sending the commands in the body text of a message to LISTSERV%UBVMS.BITNET@VM1.NODAK.EDU.

Coordinator: Dave Phillips <V184GAVW%UBVMS.BITNET@VM1.NODAK.EDU>

BIOTECH%UMDC.BITNET@CUNYVM.CUNY.EDU
BIOTECH@UMDC.UMD.EDU

The Biotechnology mailing list is open for: software/hardware issues, announcements, submission of bulletins, exchange of ideas and data.

Previous bulletins are archived on BIOSERVE server disk. The server accepts commands from the Subject: line of a message. The request for information and previous bulletins can be sent to BIOSERVE%UMDC.BITNET@CUNYVM.CUNY.EDU or BIOSERVE@UMDC.UMD.EDU.

All requests to be added to or deleted from this list, problems, questions, etc., should be sent to BIOTECH%UMDC.BITNET@CUNYVM.CUNY.EDU or BIOTECH@UMDC.UMD.EDU.

Coordinator: Deba Patnaik <DEBA%UMDC.BITNET@CUNYVM.CUNY.EDU>

BISEXU-L@BROWNVM.BROWN.EDU
BISEXU-L@BROWNVM.BITNET

Mailing list for discussion of issues of bisexuality. Cordial and civilized exchange of relevant ideas, opinions and experiences between members of all orientations is encouraged - we do not discriminate on the basis of orientation, religion, gender, race, etc.

This list is not intended in the spirit of separatism from any other lists devoted to lesbian, gay and bisexual issues but as an additional resource for discussion of bisexual concerns in particular; by the same token, the existence of Bisexu-L should not imply in any way that other discussion lists are no longer appropriate forums for discussion of bisexuality.

The list of subscribers is confidential for purposes of personal privacy; excessively rude, obnoxious or abusive postings will not be tolerated.

BitNet users can subscribe by sending the following command to LISTSERV@BROWVM: SUBSCRIBE BISEXU-L your_full_name where "your_full_name" is your real name, not your login Id. Internet users can subscribe by sending the above command in the text/body of a message to LISTSERV@BROWNVM.BROWN.EDU.

Coordinator: Bill Sklar <86730%LAWRENCE.BITNET@VM1.NODAK.EDU>

BITNEWS%BITNIC.BITNET@CUNYVM.CUNY.EDU

BITNEWS is the official medium of the BitNet Network Information Center for distributing BitNet news and administrative developements.

BITNEWS archives are stored on LISTSERV at BITNIC and are created monthly, and are named in the format BITNEWS LOGyymm. To obtain a list of currently available files, the command is: INDEX BITNEWS The command to obtain a specific file is: GET BITNEWS file_name for example, GET BITNEWS LOG8710

To subscribe to the list, from a VM site on BitNet issue: TELL LISTSERV AT BITNIC SUBSCRIBE BITNEWS Your_Full_Name where Your_Full_Name is your real name (not your userid); from a VMS BITNET site use the SEND/REMOTE command. If you are at a site not on BitNet or where you cannot send interactive messages, you can send a message to

LISTSERV%BITNIC.BITNET@CUNYVM.CUNY.EDU, where the first non-header line consists of: SUBSCRIBE BITNEWS Your_Full_Name

Please note that there is no BITNEWS-REQUEST address. Questions, problems, etc., should be referred to the Editors.

Editors: Judith Molka <AKLOM%BITNIC.BITNET@CUNYVM.CUNY.EDU> Patricia Noeth <NOETH%BITNIC.BITNET@CUNYVM.CUNY.EDU>

BMDP-L%MCGILL1.BITNET@CORNELLC.CCS.CORNELL.EDU

Discussion group for users of BMDP software.

All requests to be added to or deleted from this list, problems, questions, etc., should be sent to one of the Coordinators.

Coordinators: Michael Walsh <CCMW%MCGILLA.BITNET@CORNELLC.CCS.CORNELL.EDU> CCMW@MUSICA.MCGILL.CA (BitNet) Sander Wasser <CCSW%MCGILLA.BITNET@CORNELLC.CCS.CORNELL.EDU> CCSW@MUSICA.MCGILL.CA (BitNet)

BNFNET-Lon LISTSERV@FINHUTC.BITNET

"BNFNET-MIRCEN" was established in 1990 by UNESCO's MIRCEN (Microbiological Resource Center) Network for Environmental, Applied Microbiological and Biotechnological Research for people who have a professional interest in biological nitrogen fixation (BNF). Members of BNFNET-MIRCEN primarily use computers to communicate with each other by electronic mail ("e-mail").

The aims of the Network are the following :

- to provide a forum for the exchange of information, experiences and scientific results on BNF
- to foster better communication and cooperation among MIRCENs and between MIRCENs and other organizations
- to encourage and help individuals to use e-mail for communications in BNF research

BNFNET-L is the name of the electronic mail distribution list for BNFNET-MIRCEN. Membership in BNFNET-L is open to any individual who have a professional interest in BNF. To become a member of BNFNET-MIRCEN and thereby be included in its mailing list BNFNET-L, send the following message.

SUBSCRIBE BNFNET-L <YOUR PERSONAL NAME> (e.g. SUBSCRIBE BNFNET-L Akiro Suzuki)

to the following e-mail address : LISTSERV@FINHUTC.BITNET

BNFNET-L can be used for any scientific purposes related to BNF, such as forum and exchange of information. Commercial advertisement is however strictly prohibited. The members of BNFNET-l have grouped themselves into the following 6 discussion groups :

* Legume-Rhizobium Group	* Free-living Fixers Group
* Nitrogen Fixing Trees Group	* Culture Collections Group
* Genetics/Biochemistry Group	* Computer Networking Group

On-going discussions (August-Sept 1990) concern members' research activities and world facilities for Rhizobium inoculant production. Members are encouraged to initiate discussions on topics of special interest to them. BNFNET-L also serves as an electronic newsletter and provides information on forthcoming conferences, recent publications and research profiles of organizations. Articles from the BNF BULLETIN, published by NifTAL MIRCEN (Hawaii), are also reproduced in BNFNET-L. Other activities are being planned.

BNFNET-MIRCEN currently provides two services:

- helps researchers to identify resources of culture collections
- identifies suitabble e-mail facilities for scientists who wish to join BNFNET-MIRCEN

For more information, please contact one of the following BNFNET-MIRCEN coordinators :

Eng-leong FOO   eng-leong_foo_@kom.komunity.se
     (MIRCEN-Stockholm)
Robert HARPER   harper@finfun.bitnet
     (Co-MIRCEN, Helsinki)

BONSAI on LISTSERV@WAYNEST1 or LISTSERV@CMS.CC.WAYNE.EDU   [Last Update 11/92]

This list has been setup to facilitate discussion of the art and craft of Bonsai and related art forms. Bonsai is the Oriental Art (Craft?) of minituarizing trees and plants into forms that mimic nature.

To subscribe, you may send an interactive message (from BITNET sites which provide such a facility), or mail (with the command as the body of the mail - *NOT* in the subject field -) to:

LISTSERV@WAYNEST1 or LISTSERV@CMS.CC.WAYNE.EDU

The command should be in the form:

SUB BONSAI full name

... where "full name" is your full (and correct) name.

To contribute to the list, send your mail messages to:

BONSAI@WAYNEST1 or BONSAI@CMS.CC.WAYNE.EDU

Owner: Daniel Cwiertniewicz DCWIERT@WAYNEST1 or dan@foghorn.pass.wayne.edu

BRAS-NET@CS.COLUMBIA.EDU   [Last updated 9/92]

BRAS-NET is a mailing list for Brazilians and is conducted in Portuguese. There is no specific subject orientation.

Requests to be added to or deleted from this list, problems, questions, etc., should be sent to bras-net-request@cs.columbia.edu.

Coordinator: Jay Marme'
Indiana University-Bloomington
Business/SPEA Library
jmarme@ucs.indiana.edu

BRASS@geomag.gly.fsu.edu   [Last Updated 12-October-1991]

A discussion group for people interested in brass musical performance and related topics, especially small musical ensembles of all kinds.

Requests to be added to or deleted from this list, problems, questions, etc., should be sent to brass-request@geomag.gly.fsu.edu.

Coordinator: Ted Zateslo <zateslo@geomag.gly.fsu.edu>

BRS-L%USCVM.BITNET@VM1.NODAK.EDU Mailing list for discussion of BRS/Search; a full-text retrieval system which runs on platforms including MS-DOS, XENIX, BSD 4.3 and AT&T System V UNIX, IBM VM/CMS and MVS/CICS, and Data General MV series machines. Most of the subscribers use BRS/Search for library applications but a substantial number of people have interest in litigation support and scientific/technical work.

Subscription requests, problems, or questions about BRS-L can be sent directly to the Coordinator or to POSTMAST%USCVM.BITNET@VM1.NODAK.EDU.

Coordinator: Karl P. Geiger <KARL%USCVM.BITNET@VM1.NODAK.EDU>

BRUNONIA on LISTSERV@BROWNVM or LISTSERV@BROWNVM.BROWN.EDU

BRUNONIA, encourages discussion among friends and alumni of Brown University of issues affecting the university and its students, faculty, staff, and alumni.

Topics may include (but will not be limited to) current events at Brown, trends in higher education, reactions to specific articles or letters in the _Brown Alumni Monthly_ and other media, questions about activities on campus, and updates on the activities of alumni as individuals and in reference to alumni organizations.

To subscribe to BRUNONIA send the following command via interactive message (BITNET) or via E-mail to LISTSERV@BROWNVM on BITNET or LISTSERV@BROWNVM.BROWN.EDU on the Internet:

SUB BRUNONIA yourfirstname yourlastname

List Owner:
Anne Diffily   (401) 863-2873
Brown Alumni Monthly   email: ADBAM@BROWNVM.BITNET
Box 1854   ADBAM@brownvm.brown.edu
Providence, RI 02912

BtL <ez000018@bullwinkle.ucdavis.edu>

"Between the Lines" or "BtL" is a mail group devoted entirely to Long Island's Debbie Gibson. The BtL moderators organize a "periodic" (usually monthly) newsletter issue that is sent out by e-mail to all BtL members. As well, the moderators attempt to keep BtL members informed of upcoming "events" such as concert appearances/shows, televised interviews, etc.

If people are interested in joining BtL and/or have questions concerning BtL, please send e-mail to the following address :

ez000018@bullwinkle.ucdavis.edu

We will give people further information upon receipt of e-mail.

BUDDHA-L on LISTSERV@ULKYVM.LOUISVILLE.EDU   [Last Updated 28-January-1992]
or LISTSERV@ULKYVM.BITNET

BUDDHA-L provides a means for those interested in Buddhist Studies to exchange information and views. It is hoped that the group will function as an open forum for scholarly discussion of topics relating to the history, literature and languages, fine arts, philosophy, and institutions of all forms of Buddhism. It may also serve as a forum for discussion of issues connected to the teaching of Buddhist studies at the university level, and as a place for posting notices of employment opportunities.

The primary purpose of this list is to provide a forum for serious academic discussion. It is open to all persons inside and outside the academic context who wish to engage in substantial discussion of topics relating to Buddhism and Buddhist studies. BUDDHA-L is not to be used for proselytizing for or against Buddhism in general, any particular form of Buddhism, or any other religion or philosophy, nor is it to be used as a forum for making unsubstantiable confessions of personal conviction.

The discussion on the list is to be moderated, not in order to suppress or censor controversies on any topic, but rather to limit irrelevant discussions and idle chatter, and to redirect or return messages sent to the list by accident. Content or style will never be altered by the moderator, whose only responsibility will be to forward all appropriate postings to the list.

If you wish to subscribe to BUDDHA-L, send an e-mail message to LISTSERV@ULKYVM.LOUISVILLE.EDU, or BITNET nodes can send to LISTSERV@ULKYVM. The message should contain only the following command (ie. in the body of the mail):

SUBSCRIBE BUDDHA-L <your first and last name>

Owner:
James A. Cocks

Senior Consultant Research/Instruction
University of Louisville
  Internet: JACOCK01@ULKYVM.LOUISVILLE.EDU
  Bitnet: JACOCK01@ULKYVM

BURC%TRBOUN.BITNET@VM1.NODAK.EDU

Bogazici University Alumni Group List. There is a non-LISTSERV list available here at TRBOUN. We invite all BOUNers (old/new/graduated). Its name is BURC coming from: Bogazici University - Robert College.

Since this is NOT an automatic subscription server, all the subscription requests should be sent to me including your: fullname, e-mail adres, year(s) of graduation from BU or RC and dept to DJAVI%TRBOUN.BITNET@VM1.NODAK.EDU

List Owner: Ferhat Djavidan <DJAVI%TRBOUN.BITNET@VM1.NODAK.EDU>

C-TREE <oha!ctree@UUNET.UU.NET>
          <alberta!oha!ctree@UUNET.UU.NET>

The C-Tree mailing list provides a forum for the discussion of FairCom's C-Tree, R-Tree, and D-Tree products. The list is not associated with FairCom. There are various subscribers using:

Hardware IBM PC, RT, some 68K, HP, VAX, PS/2, Altos
OS   DOS, QNX, Microport, SCO Xenix, Unix, HPUX, VMS, AIX, V.3
Applic'ns Accounting, educational, network server, real-time

All requests to be added to or deleted from this list, questions, comments, etc. should be sent to oha!ctree-request@UUNET.UU.NET or alberta!oha!ctree-request@UUNET.UU.NET.

  Coordinator: Tony Olekshy <tony@OHA.UUCP>
                 <oha!tony@UUNET.UU.NET>
                 <alberta!oha!tony@uunet.UU.NET>

C+Health on LISTSERV@IUBVM
  or LISTSERV@IUBVM.UCS.INDIANA.EDU   [Last Updated 12-October-1991]

C+Health is intended to promote sharing of information, experiences, concerns, and advice about computers and health. Anecdotal evidence, media reports, and some formal studies suggest that computer users are at risk from misuse and overuse of computers. Eyestrain, headache, carpal tunnel syndrome, and other apparently computer-related maladies are increasing. And, it would appear that colleges, universities, and other institutions have been slow to respond with education, training, office and lab design, furniture purchasing, and other programs that could make computing more healthful -- and productive.

We welcome questions and answers; article and book reviews; hardware, software, and furniture evaluations; approaches to influencing institutional policy; speculation; and humor. Medical, legal, technical, financial, aesthetic, and administrative viewpoints are encouraged. We hope that this forum will be of interest to end users, computing managers, epidemiologists, and policymakers.

Subscribers to this list may also wish to participate in EDUCOM's Project EASI: Equal Access to Software for Instruction, "dedicated to assisting higher education in developing computer support services for people with disabilities." EASI provides information and guidance on campus applications of adaptive computer technology. For information on EASI, contact Carmela Castorina, CSMICLC@UCLAMVS.BITNET.

In general, C+Health will focus on individual and institutional measures for "keeping healthy people healthy" as well as remedies for restoring temporarily disabled people to health. We suggest that computing issues related to those with permanent disabilities be referred to our dedicated colleagues at EASI. Although this distinction will not always be "easy," one goal of C+Health is to minimize the number of casualties in our increasingly computer-intensive campuses, offices, and homes.

This list will not be moderated, at least initially, so we encourage contributors to be succinct, to include relevant parts of messages to which they are responding, and to append their names, titles, and institutions to contributions. New users are welcome to send to the list a brief statement of their experiences and interests in this topic. Unless stated otherwise, it will be assumed that contributions represent individual opinion rather than institutional policy.

To subscribe to C+Health send mail with the following command to LISTSERV@IUBVM (from BITNET sites) or LISTSERV@IUBVM.UCS.INDIANA.EDU (from Internet sites).

Subscribe C+Health Full Name Institution

As list owners, we look forward to your contributions to C+Health:

Judy Smith, Data Analyst, Office of Data Administration and Information Resource Planning, University of Pennsylvania; SmithJ@a1.relay.upenn.edu.

Kimberly Updegrove, Lecturer, School of Nursing, University of Pennsylvania; kimu@dairp.upenn.edu.

C18-L%PSUVM.BITNET@VM1.NODAK.EDU

Mailing list for 18th-century discussion. It is open, unmoderated, and archived on a monthly basis. We hope to attract free-ranging discussion of topics of interest to students and scholars of the 18th century everywhere. What the list becomes is up to the contributors, of course, but we hope to see a wide range of functions - including calls for papers, notes & queries, arguments, friendly backchat, and so forth.

BitNet users may subscribe by sending the following command via interactive command or e-mail to LISTSERV@PSUVM: SUBSCRIBE C18-L Your full name where "Your full name" is your real name, not your login Id. Non-BitNet users can join the list by sending the above command as the only line in the text/body of a message to LISTSERV%PSUVM.BITNET@VM1.NODAK.EDU.

Coordinator: Kevin Berland <BCJ%PSUVM.BITNET@VM1.NODAK.EDU>

C370-L@NCSUVM.NCSU.EDU
C370-L@NCSUVM (BitNet)

Mailing list for discussion of the C programming language on 370-architecture machines. Products covered are IBM's new C/370 compiler (5688-040), the IBM C Program Offering (5713-AAH), Waterloo C, SAS/C, or any other such implementations.

To subscribe, send the following command to LISTSERV@NCSUVM (BitNet users) or LISTSERV@NCSUVM.NCSE.EDU (Internet users): SUBSCRIBE C370-L your_full_name where "your_full_name" is your real name, not your login Id.

Coordinator: Chuck Kesler <CHUCK@NCSUVM.NCSU.EDU> <CHUCK%NCSUVM.BITNET>

CADUCEUS@Beach.Gal.UTexas.EDU or @UTMBEACH.BITNET

CADUCEUS is a moderated discussion group organized for the members of the Association of Librarians in the History of the Health Sciences, and other individuals interested in medical history collections. The purpose is to provide a forum for the exchange of information about the administration of special collections in medical history. CADUCEUS is not on a Listserver. To subscribe, send a message to:

CADUCEUS@UTMBeach (Bitnet) or CADUCEUS@Beach.Gal.UTexas.Edu (Internet)

Moderator: Inci Bowman, Moody Medical Library The University of Texas Medical Branch Galveston, TX 77555-1035 Phone: 409/772-2397

CAMEL-L on LISTSERV@SAKFU00.BITNET   [Last Updated June 1992]

Camel-l (Camel forum discussion list) is a list in the field of Camel researches and studies. It is launched by the Camel Research Center at King Faisal University, Saudi Arabia.

To subscribe send an interactive message (TELL or SEND) or e-mail to LISTSERV@SAKFU00 on BITNET with the following command in the BODY:

SUB CAMEL-L firstname lastname

where firstname and lastname are your first and last name .

The temporary owner of this list is :

> Mustafa Ghazal (Devmtg12@Sakfu00.Bitnet)
> King Faisal University
> Computer Center
> P.O. Box 380
> Hofuf ,31982
> Saudi Arabia

camelot@castle.ed.ac.uk   [Last Updated Feb 92]

A mailing list on the subject of Arthurian legend and Grail Lore. The 'Matter of Britain', as it is known, in all its guises and all related subjects, discussed in an unmoderated mailing list.

Technical Details

There are two mailing addresses you will need to know.:

1) camelot-request@castle.ed.ac.uk If you wish to be added to or removed from the mailing list or if you want to report a bug or if you want info on the mailing list or any other such technical stuff, this is the address to use.

2) camelot@castle.ed.ac.uk This is for your articles and chat. It is unmoderated and unfiltered, so anything goes. This is the address you will post to mainly.

As well as this there is an FTP address with up to date archives and some GIF pictures and interesting articles. The address is: 129.215.56.11 (sapphire.epcc.ed.ac.uk) The login name is anonymous with your mail address as the password. Then cd pub/camelot and get the README to find the contents.

Owner: Chris Thornborrow <ct@castle.edinburgh.ac.uk>

CANADA-L on LISTSERV@VM1.MCGILL.CA   [Last Updated 28-January-1992]
or LISTSERV@MCGILL1.BITNET

Canada-L is a discussion forum for political, social, cultural and economic issues in Canada.

To subscribe to CANADA-L send a message or e-mail to LISTSERV@VM1.MCGILL.CA or LISTSERV@MCGILL1.BITNET with the body containing the command:

SUB CANADA-L yourfirstname yourlastname

Owner: Anastassia Khouri St-Pierre <ED22@MUSICA.McGill.CA>

CANDLE-L%UA1VM.BITNET@VM1.NODAK.EDU
CANDLE-L@UA1VM.UA.EDU

A forum for the discussion of Candle products. Topics could include installation, performance monitoring, or any other subject related to the use of Candle products on VM or MVS. These products include OMEGAMON, EPILOG, AF/REMOTE, CL/CONFERENCE 1000, CL/GATEWAY, CL/MENU, CL/SUPERSESSION and any other future products.

Archives of CANDLE-L can be listed by sending the command INDEX CANDLE-L to LISTSERV@UA1VM.

To subscribe to CANDLE-L, send the following command to LISTSERV@UA1VM via mail text or interactive message: SUBSCRIBE CANDLE-L your_full_name where "your_full_name" is your name. For example: SUBSCRIBE CANDLE-L Joe User Non-BitNet users should send the command in the text/body of a message to LISTSERV%UA1VM.BITNET@VM1.NODAK.EDU.

Coordinator: Darren Evans-Young <DARREN%UA1VM.BITNET@VM1.NODAK.EDU> <DARREN@UA1VM.UA.EDU>

CANINE-L on LISTSERV@PCCVM or LISTSERV@PSUVM.BITNET

The CANINE-L list has been created to discuss matters of interest to dog owners. A full statement of purpose, plus any applicable restrictions, will be automatically mailed to new subscribers.

Monthly notebooks will be kept at PCCVM.

To subscribe, send an interactive message or e-mail to LISTSERV@PCCVM.BITNET or LISTSERV@PSUVM.BITNET with the following text in the body:

SUB CANINE-L your-full-name

List Owner: W. K. (Bill) Gorman <34AEJ7D@CMUVM>

cards-request@tanstaafl.uchicago.edu

Purpose: For people interested in collection, speculation and investing in baseball, football, basketball, hockey and other trading cards and/or memoribilia. Discussion and want/sell lists are welcome. Open to anyone.

Membership must be requested and mail path verification is required before membership is granted.

> Contact: cards-request@tanstaafl.uchicago.edu
> List Maintainer: kean@tanstaafl.uchicago.edu (Keane Arase)

CARIBBEAN-ECONOMY@OAKLAND.BITNET   [Last Updated 28-January-1992]
CARIBBEAN-ECONOMY@VELA.ACS.OAKLAND.EDU

CARIBBEAN-ECONOMY is a discussion forum for the exchange of information and dialogue on the economies of the Caribbean Basin region.

All postings sent to CARIBBEAN-ECONOMY will be compiled and distributed several times weekly. Archives will be offered in due course, when the demand arises.

To SUBSCRIBE (or UNSUBSCRIBE) send a request to CARIBBEAN-ECONOMY-REQUEST@OAKLAND.BITNET or CARIBBEAN-ECONOMY-REQUEST@VELA.ACS.OAKLAND.EDU

Moderator:

> Addington Coppin <coppin@oakland.bitnet> (Moderator)
> Oakland University
> Rochester MI

CARR-L on LISTSERV@ULKYVM.BITNET   [Last Update 9/92]
or LISTSERV@ULKYVM.LOUISVILLE.EDU

CARR-L was started to facilitate communication between working journalists (any media), journalism educators, and news librarians and researchers.

The topic is focussed on the use of computers in journalism, not general journalism. Topics range from text processing and graphics to online database searching and computer communications and investigative reporting.

To subscribe to CARR-L, send the follwing command to LISTSERV@ULKYVM.BITNET via mail text or interactive message: SUBSCRIBE CARR-L your full name

For example: SUBSCRIBE CARR-L William A. White

Owners: Elliott Parker <3ZLUFUR@CMUVM.CSV.CMICH.EDU> Jim Cocks

<JACOCK01@ULKYVM.BITNET>

CASE-L%UCCVMA.BITNET@VM1.NODAK.EDU

Discussion of use of computer techniques in the systems development life cycle. Includes use of computers to aid in system analysis and design description (including graphical representation of functions), coding, and documentation. Emphasis is on *practical* applications, especially those of value to commercial firms and administrative type computer facilities (see the soft-eng list for more theoretical discusions).

Monthly archives will be kept; for access, contact the Coordinator.

BitNet users can subscribe by sending the following command to LISTSERV@UCCVMA via mail or interactive message: SUB CASE-L your_full_name where "your_full_name" is your real name, not your login Id. For example: SUB CASE-L Joan Doe Non-BitNet users can subscribe by sending the above command to LISTSERV%UCCVMA.BITNET@VM1.NODAK.EDU.

Coordinator: Richard Hintz <SPGRJH%UCCVMA.BITNET@VM1.NODAK.EDU>

CATALYST on LISTSERV@VTVM1.BITNET   [Last Updated 1/92]
or LISTSERV@VTVM1.CC.VT.EDU

CATALYST, a refereed print journal that has been serving community college educators for more than twenty years, will be distributed as an electronic journal in addition to its print version. Subscriptions to the electronic version of the journal are now available free of charge via BITNET and the Internet, according to Dr. Darrel A. Clowes, editor of the journal and a member of the faculty at Virginia Polytechnic Institute and State University.

The quarterly journal is published by the National Council on Community Services and Continuing Education, an affiliate council of the American Association of Community, Junior and Technical Colleges. The journal is being made available in its electronic form by the Scholarly Communications Project of Virginia Tech.

Initiated in 1971, CATALYST is the second oldest continuously published journal in the community college field. It publishes practitioner-oriented articles on practices in continuing/community education as delivered by community colleges, including papers on research in the field. CATALYST currently is distributed in print form to dues-paying members of the Council, as a benefit of their membership, and to libraries and other non-members at subscription prices of $20 per year in the U.S., $25 outside the U.S.

To subscribe to the electronic journal, send the command SUBSCRIBE CATALYST first name last name by electronic mail to the address LISTSERV@VTVM1 on BITNET and LISTSERV@VTVM1.CC.VT.EDU on the Internet. Electronic subscribers will receive instructions on how to order a list of available articles, how to retrieve the full text of those articles, and how to cancel their subscriptions.

Electronic subscribers, in addition to having access to past issues of the journal, will be sent the tables of contents of future issues as those issues are published; the subscribers then may order full text by electronic mail of any and all articles they wish to read. Currently, all articles from issue numbers 3 and 4 of volume 21 (1991) are available online. Consideration will be given to adding all articles from the remaining back issues to the archive.

For further information, contact Lon Savage, SAVAGE@VTVM1.BITNET or SAVAGE@VTVM1.CC.VT.EDU

Catholic-action <rfreeman@vpnet.chi.il.us>   [Last Updated 28-January-1992]

Catholic-action is a moderated list concerned with Catholic evangelism, church revitalization, and preservation of Catholic teachings, traditions, and values

Contact: rfreeman@vpnet.chi.il.us

CATV@quack.sac.ca.us   [Last Updated 12-October-1991]

For people interested in any topic having to do with cable television programming, technology, regulation, etc. Especially welcome are postings concerning 'cable tax' legislation, attempts to repeal syndex and ways to increase competition in local cable markets.

To sign up, send mail to catv-request@quack.sac.ca.us. The submission address is catv@quack.sac.ca.us.

Listowner: Nick Sayer mrapple@quack.sac.ca.us

Causerie on ListServ@UQuebec.BitNet   [Last Updated Feb 92]
or ListServ@UQuebec.CA

"Causerie" means talk or chat. And that is what this list is all about. Just for the fun of it.

Everyone is welcome though you should be aware of the fact that all the communication is in French. The rest of this announcement is in French.

Deben saber que la totalidad de los mensajes estan redactados en *** frances ***.

Pour jaser, parloter, palabrer: Causerie@UQuebec

En francais, un "Cafe Campus" pour discuter de choses et d'autres.

Causerie [kozri]. n.f. (1555; de causer). Causerie@UQuebec 1 Entretien familier. V. Conversation Causeries a batons rompus. "La lecon degenerait en causerie" (Gide). 2 Discours, conference sans pretention. Une causerie litteraire, scientifique. (Le Petit Robert 1)

Demarrage en fevrier 1992.

    concierge= UQPSGEN@UQSS.UQUEBEC.CA (Pierre Chenard)
    concierge= UQPSGEN@UQUEBEC   (Pierre Chenard)
    concierge= HAMEL@UQUEBEC   (Pierre J. Hamel)
    concierge= HAMEL@INRS-URB.UQUEBEC.CA (Pierre J. Hamel)

Pour s'abonner a ce nouveau repertoire comme pour tout autre,
il suffit d'envoyer a l'adresse: ListServ@UQuebec
            la commande: Sub Repertoire Prenom Nom
            par exemple: Sub Causerie Emile Durkheim

CBEHIGH ON LISTSERV@BLEKUL11.BITNET   [Last Update 9/92]
or LISTSERV@CC1.KULEUVEN.AC.BE (134.58.8.32)

CBEHIGH is an international electronic forum for anyone interested in discussing the use of computers as an educational tool in higher education.

Some examples of relevant topics for CBEHIGH: (These topics are just suggestions to indicate the scope).

    - who uses what as authoring tool
    - pro's and con's of different tools
    - own experience in the use of computers in higher education
    - pointers to specific articles or other sources of information
    - student administration and scoring
    - when to use what kind of course
    - guidelines to build a course
    - cost effective uses of computers in education
    - effectiveness of computers in education
    - special uses of computers in education
    - strategies for using computers in education
    - contrast the different learning theories as they apply to CBE

This mailing list can also be used to store files that have something to do with the topics mentioned above. If you have files that could be of interest to the readers of this list, please send them to Peter Arien (laaaa43@cc1.kuleuven.ac.be).

To retreive files, send the following message to LISTSERV@BLEKUL11.BITNET or LISTSERV@CC1.KULEUVEN.AC.BE :

INDEX CBEHIGH (to get an index of the CBEHIGH-files) GET filename filetype (to get a specific file)

HOW TO JOIN AND SEND MESSAGES:

The list is located at BLEKUL11.BITNET (CC1.KULEUVEN.AC.BE), so the commands described below should be sent to :

LISTSERV@BLEKUL11.BITNET or to LISTSERV@CC1.KULEUVEN.AC.BE

To subscribe, send the following message: SUBSCRIBE CBEHIGH First-name Last-name

To unsubscribe, send the following email message: UNSUBSCRIBE CBEHIGH

To send a message to CBEHIGH, send an email message to: CBEHIGH@BLEKUL11.BITNET or to: BIBSOFT@CC1.KULEUVEN.AC.BE

CBEHIGH is not moderated! Any message you send is sent directly to the entire membership list. Please make sure your messages are intended for public consumption!

Neither the list owners nor the University of Leuven verify the accuracy of submitted messages or endorse the opinions expressed by authors of messages. Authors of CBEHIGH messages are considered to be solely responsible for their own comments.

If you have questions about the list or problems with its operation, send email to one of the list owners.

Owners: * Peter Arien <laaaa43@blekul11.bitnet> <laaaa43@cc1.kuleuven.ac.be>

Computer Based Education University Computing Centre De Croylaan 52A B-3001 Leuven - Heverlee Belgium Fax : +32 16 207168

* Herman van Uytven <systhvu@blekul11.bitnet> * Wim Brems <laaaa05@blekul11.bitnet>

CCNET-L%UGA.BITNET@VM1.NODAK.EDU

Chinese Computing is a discussion group on technology relating to the use of Chinese on computers. It is intended to be a forum for both experts and regular users and to reach wherever computer networks can reach, from North America to the Far East. Although different people may have different definitions for Chinese computing, at it's current stage, the technology for Chinese word processing and desktop publishing software is in the greatest demand. Discussions will concentrate on this technology as implemented in both software and hardware.

The focus of the mailing list may change when other technologies become more important. There have been suggestions that Chinese programming languages may be a requirement when Chinese data base software gets more popular. The postings to this group may include: news of new software, hardware and technology, product reviews, comments, questions and answers.

The list is unmoderated, and archives are available from LISTSERV@UGA.

BitNet users may subscribe by sending the following command to LISTSERV@UGA: SUB CCNET-L Your_full_name where "Your_full_name" is your real name, not your login Id. Non-BitNet users can join the list by sending the above command as the only line in the text\/body of a message to LISTSERV%UGA.BITNET@VM1.NODAK.EDU.

Coordinator: Harold Pritchett <HAROLD%UGA.UGA.EDU@VM1.NODAK.EDU>

CDROM-L%UCCVMA.BITNET@VM1.NODAK.EDU

Mailing list for the discussion of hardware and software issues related to the design, production, and use of CD-ROM.

BitNet users may subscribe by sending the following command to LISTSERV at

Monthly archives are kept. UCCVMA via interactive message or e-mail: SUBSCRIBE CDROM-L Your full name where "Your full name" is your real name, not your login Id. Non-BitNet users can join the list by sending the above command as the only line in the text/body of a message to LISTSERV%UCCVMA.BITNET@VM1.NODAK.EDU.

Coordinator: Richard Hintz <OPSRJH%UCCVMA.BITNET@VM1.NODAK.EDU>

CDROMLAN on LISTSERV@IDBSU.BITNET
or LISTSERV@IDBSU.IDBSU.EDU

This list will provide an exchange of information on all types of CDROM products, whether they contain indexes, abstracts, full text, statistics, graphics, or other data. It will also cover all types of LAN environments (Banyan, Starlan, Ethernet, Novell, etc.) on all types of hardware (Mac, IBM, Unix, clones, etc.) Producers of hardware, LAN software, CDROM products, and integrated CDROM LAN systems will be encouraged to participate in the discussions and to answer questions about their products.

The list is owned by Dan Lester, Associate University Librarian at Boise State University, Boise, Idaho, USA. The list will be unmoderated.

To join the list, send an interactive message or mail message to LISTSERV@IDBSU with the text containing the command:

SUB CDROMLAN yourfirstname yourlastname

Owner:
Dan Lester   1910 University Dr. Bitnet: ALILESTE@IDBSU
Library   Boise, Idaho 83725 Internet:
Boise State University (208) 385-1234   ALILESTE@IDBSU.IDBSU.EDU

CELLULAR on Mail-Server@yngbld.gwinnett.com   [Last Updated 9/92]

The CELLULAR list is for the discussion of cellular telephoney and technology. This also includes technologies relating to the cellular industry such as microwave, RF, telco and more. Subjects could range from topics dealing with marketing ideas, test equipment, phones preferred for different reasons, system and site engineering and just about anything that was related to cellular.

All traffic will be archived and stored using the format CELLmmyy.ZIP. 'mm' will refer to the month, and 'yy' the year. These archives can be retrieved by sending a message to: Mail-Server@yngbld.gwinnett.com For help with the Mail-Server, put HELP in the message body. For an index to the files available, put INDEX in the message body. It is recommended that you send a HELP and INDEX request before attempting to retrieve files from the Mail-Server.

To subscribe to the CELLULAR mailing list, send a message to: Mail-Server@yngbld.gwinnett.com

In the body of the message put:

SUBSCRIBE CELLULAR

The default is NOECHOMAIL, which means when you send a message to be distributed, you will not receive an acknowledgement. If you want to get a response letting you know your message was received, put:

ECHOMAIL CELLULAR

in your subscription message as well.

To send a message to the mailing list for distribution, send it to:

CELLULAR@yngbld.gwinnett.com

Owner: Gregory S. Youngblood zeta@yngbld.gwinnett.com

CELLULAR-AUTOMATA@THINK.COM

Mailing-list for the exchange of information on all aspects of cellular automata and their applications. The list is gatewayed to/from the Usenet group comp.theory.cell-automata.

Archived messages will be kept at Think.COM in the files: mail/ca.archive*

There is a LISTSERV-maintained BitNet part of this list, CA-L@MITVMA. BitNet subscriptions can be managed in the usual way, e.g.: TELL LISTSERV AT MITVMA SUBSCRIBE CA-L your_full_name

BitNet Notebooks with monthly archives are available from MITVMA from 11/89. All other requests to be added to or deleted from this list, problems, questions, etc., should be sent to CELLULAR-AUTOMATA-REQUEST@THINK.COM.

Coordinator: Bruce Walker <bruce@THINK.COM>

CERRO-L on LISTSERV@AEARN.BITNET [Last Updated June 1992]
or LISTSERV@aearn.edvz.uni-linz.ac.at

CERRO-L is a list discussing issues of relevance to regional development and regional development research in Central Europe. CERRO-L discusses topics from a broad range of related disciplines: regional science, economic geography, regional and urban planning, environmental economics, regional sociology, policy analysis, regional political economy and institutions, etc. It is the intention of CERRO-L to stimulate and support regional research in and about the newly re-emerging region of "Central Europe" and to enhance contacts and discussion between researchers and scholars interested in these areas.

To subscribe to CERRO-L, send the following command to LISTSERV@AEARN via mail text or interactive message:

SUBSCRIBE CERRO-L your_full_name

where "your_full_name" is your name. For example:

SUBSCRIBE CERRO-L Joan Doe

Additional documents concerning regional development in Central Europe are also availabe through anonymous ftp to "ftp.wu-wien.ac.at" directory "pub/cerro".

Owner: Gunther Maier <cerro@awiwuw11> or <Gunther.Maier@wu-wien.ac.at>

CHAIRS-L@FAUVAX.BITNET or [Last Updated 28-January-1992]
CHAIRS-L@ACC.FAU.EDU

An unmoderated discussion list dealing with issues and problems that an academic chairperson faces daily. Discussion topics include the chairperson's role and power, faculty development, annual evaluation, tenure and promotion, budgetary problems, affirmative action, grievances, recruitment procedures, and personnel matters.

Membership is open free of charge to all interested individuals or organizations.

To subscribe, send Email to CHAIRS-REQUEST@ACC.FAU.EDU (BITNET-restricted users send to CHAIRS-REQUEST@FAUVAX) The sole content of the message BODY must be:

SUBSCRIBE CHAIRS-L John Q Public

To post a message to the list members, address it to:

CHAIRS-L@ACC.FAU.EDU or CHAIRS-L@FAUVAX

To unsubscribe, send to CHAIRS-REQUEST this command:

UNSUBSCRIBE CHAIRS-L

Questions and requests for information should be sent to the List Owner. Technical issues should be addressed to the List Manager.

> List Owner: M Yasar Iscan (Iscan@acc.fau.edu, Iscan@FauVax)
> List Manager: Ralph P Carpenter (Ralpho@acc.fau.edu, Ralpho@FauVax)

CHAUCER on LISTSERV@SIUCVMB.BITNET or LISTSERV@SIUCVMB.SIU.EDU [Last Update 11/92]

Some of your readers might be interested in a new list, CHAUCER@SIUCVMB (Internet: CHAUCER@siucvmb.siu.edu). This is an open-forum discussion list for Medieval English Literature.

To subscribe to CHAUCER send e-mail to LISTSERV@siucvmb.siu.edu or e-mail or message to LISTSERV@SIUCVMB.BITNET with the following command in the body:

SUB CHAUCER your full name

Owner: Jeff Taylor GR4302@SIUCVMB.BITNET

chaucer@unlinfo.unl.edu   [Last Update 11/92]

Chaucernet is an unedited discussion group devoted to the works of Geoffrey Chaucer and medieval English literature and culture in the period 1100-1500. The list is sponsored by the New Chaucer Society and is open to all who are interested in Chaucer.

To join, send the following command to listserv@unlinfo.unl.edu: subscribe chaucer <your name>

The address of the list is chaucer@unlinfo.unl.edu.

For more information, please contact Professor Bestul at the address below.

> Owner: Thomas Bestul Email: tbestul@crcvms.unl.edu
>   or tbestul@unlvax1.bitnet
> Department of English
> University of Nebraska-Lincoln
> Lincoln, NE 68588-0333

CHMINF-L on LISTSERV@IUBVM.BITNET

The Chemical Information Sources list is intended to serve as a discussion medium and information source for any topic related to chemistry and the sources used to find information about chemical compounds. News about existing reference sources, the appearance of new primary, secondary, or tertiary printed or machine-readable sources, pricing and availability, bibliographic instruction--all are fair topics for distribution as long as they have some link to chemistry.

To subscribe, send mail or a message to LISTSERV@IUBVM.BITNET which contains the following command in the body:

SUBSCRIBE CHMINF-L yourfirstname yourlastname

Owner: Gary Wiggins WIGGINS@IUBACS.BITNET or WIGGINS@UCS.INDIANA.EDU

Chemistry@osc.edu

The Computational Chemistry List is maintained by Ohio Supercomputer Center. This list is not restricted to particular computational chemistry software or methodology. Examples of topics discussed include: quantum chemistry, molecular mechanics/dynamics, molecular modeling, molecular graphics, etc.

To subscribe to the list, send a short note stating your name, affiliation and e-mail address to: CHEMISTRY-REQUEST@oscsunb.osc.edu or JKL@OHSTPY.BITNET.

To get more information about the list (rules for posting, accessing archives, etc.) send the following one-line message to OSCPOST@oscsunb.osc.edu or OSCPOST@OHSTPY.BITNET send help from chemistry The information will be automatically forwarded to you via e-mail.

Owner:
Mr. Jan Labanowski   Ohio Supercomputer Center
E-mail: jkl@osc.edu   1224 Kinnear Rd
    JKL@OHSTPY.BITNET   Columbus, OH 43212-1163, USA
Phone: 614-292-9279
FAX: 614-292-7168

CHESS-L%GREARN.BITNET@VM1.NODAK.EDU

Mailing list to offer to chess players inside the network a way to communicate, share ideas, and participate in tournaments which can be organised through the list.

BitNet users can subscribe by sending the following command to LISTSERV@GREARN: SUB CHESS-L your_full_name where "your_full_name" is your real name, not your login id. Non-BitNet users can subscribe by sending the above command in the body (text) of a message to LISTSERV%GREARN.BITNET@VM1.NODAK.EDU.

Coordinator: Giorgos Kavallieratos <NETSTU04%GREARN.BITNET@VM1.NODAK.EDU>

Child@Hampvms.Bitnet   [Last Update 28-January-1992]

A list on the subject of the Rights of Children and Adolescents. Moved to Y-Rights@SJUVM.BITNET

CHPOEM-L on LISTSERV@UBVM.BITNET or LISTSERV@UBVM.CC.BUFFALO.EDU

CHPOEM-L is an electronic mailing list devoted to sharing and discussing Chinese poems.

To subscribe to CHPOEM-L, send email to either LISTSERV@UBVM.BITNET or LISTSERV@UBVM.CC.BUFFALO.EDU. Leave the subject line blank. For the text of the message, enter the following line only (filling in your name as appropriate):

SUB CHPOEM-L Yourfirstname Yourlastname

Once you have subscribed to the list, you may send email to other subscribers by addressing it to either CHPOEM-L@UBVM.BITNET or CHPOEM-L@UBVM.CC.BUFFALO.EDU.

You can invoke many other useful LISTSERV functions by sending mail to the LISTSERV@UBVM.BITNET or LISTSERV@UBVM.CC.BUFFALO.EDU address, such as:

- By default, you will receive copies of any mail you send to the list. If you do not wish to receive copies of your own messages, send email with the message SET CHPOEM-L NOREPRO.

- The listserv program keeps automatic weekly archives of mail sent to the list. This allows new subscribers to catch up with previous postings. To get a list of the names of these archive files (called "filetypes" by listserv), send the message INDEX CHPOEM-L. Then, to get a copy of one of these "filetypes", send the message GET CHPOEM-L <filetype> (filling in the actual filetype, e.g.: GET CHPOEM-L LOG9111B).

- To unsubscribe from the list, send the message SIGNOFF CHPOEM-L.

UUENCODED GB/Big5 are used for posting.

For detailed conventions used for the list and technical info of Chinese computing, please FTP the CHPOEM-L Information File from ahkcus.org -192.55.187.25- in the directory ./gb/poem.

Additional Information

2. About messages posted in Chinese.

A number of coding schemes have been developed for using Chinese on computers. The two most common are GuoBiao (developed in mainland China) and Big5 (developed in Taiwan). Complicating matters further, there are different varieties of Big5 codes, the most common being ET Big5 (the code used by the Taiwanese program ETen, pronounced Yi3tian1) and HKU Big5 (the code used for programs developed at Hong Kong University).

There is a preference for GuoBiao (often abbreviated to GB) among CHPOEM-L subscribers, though files using other codes are welcome. Utilities are available for converting between GuoBiao and Big5, and between ET Big5 and HKU Big5; see below.

Chinese files sent to the list should be uuencoded. The uuencode command is included on most Unix-based systems; type "man uuencode" for instructions on its use, or ask your system administrator. PC versions of uuencode and uudecode are available via anonymous ftp from ahkcus.org [192.55.187.25] as uuduue20.zip in the src/pc directory. (Ask your system administrator for help using FTP.) For information about uuencode and the Mac, see the Mac help file mentioned below.

Note: Sometimes you may get an error message when uudecoding a file, indicating some kind of "short file" problem; garbage may then show up at the end of the decoded file. This is be- cause the mail system removes blank spaces from otherwise blank lines. When you uuencode a file, the next to last line is often just one blank space, which then disappears when you mail the file. When you try to uudecode the file, uudecode detects the missing space and announces the "short file" error. There are two ways to avoid this problem:

(1) Before mailing a uuencoded file, replace all spaces with an open-single-quote (') mark. (As far as uudecode is concerned, the ' mark and space are exactly equivalent.) If you receive a uuencoded file in the mail, but the sender neglected this step, simply type the ' mark in on the blank line above the "end" line, then uudecode the file.

(2) Ask your system administrator to install a more recent version of uuencode that uses ' instead of space. Source code for this is available via anonymous ftp from ahkcus.org in the src/unix directory.

To read a file written in Chinese, you will need a program that can interpret the Chinese code used in that file. Different programs are available for different hardware platforms.

PC users can get information about GuoBiao editors by sending email to LISTSERV@UGA.BITNET with the message GET PC HELP. HKU Big5 files can be viewed with shownews.exe or readnews.exe, available via anonymous ftp at ahkcus.org [192.55.187.25] in the src/pc/hku directory. (You will also need the chinese.16 font file from the same directory.) ET Big5 files must be read with the ETen operating system, which is commercial software selling for about US$80. However there is a utility, et2hku, to convert ET Big5 files to HKU Big5 files, which can then be read with shownews. (See below.)

Mac users can get information about both GuoBiao and Big5 software by sending email to LISTSERV@UGA.BITNET with the message GET MAC HELP.

X Windows users can use either cxterm or xhzview for both GuoBiao or Big5 files. For information about cxterm, send email to LISTSERV@UGA.BITNET with the message GET CXTERM HELP. For infor- mation about xhzview, send email to LISTSERV@UGA.BITNET with the message GET XHZVIEW HELP.

Note: Users may run into problems because different systems indicate line endings differently. Unix-based systems use linefeed (ASCII 10, ^J) to end a line, the Mac uses carriage return (ASCII 13, ^M), and PC systems use carriage-return/linefeed.

This usually can be solved by using an editor or automatically fixed though transferring process. If NOT, you can use the following methods:

+ MAC to UNIX convertion:

At unix prompt type, tr '\015' '\012' < Mac_file > Unix_file

+ MSDOS to UNIX conversion:

FTP folding.c from ahkcus.org:./src/unix. Folding removes carriage-returns and, if desired, adds linefeeds according to a specified linewidth. Simply compile the source code and excute it for 'how to use' message.

[...... this section is not complete]

3. Conversion Utilities.

To convert between GuoBiao and Big5 (et or hku) files, use hc ("Hanzi Converter"), available via anonymous ftp from ahkcus.org [192.55.187.25] in the src/unix directory. (There is another conversion utility available called b2g, but it seems to miss a large number of characters.) Since Big5 covers about 5,000 more characters than GuoBiao, it's likely there will be a few missing characters in Big5 to GuoBiao conversions.

To convert between ET Big5 and HKU Big5, use et2hku, available via anonymous ftp from cs.purdue.edu [128.10.2.1] in the pub/ygz/utils directory.

4. File naming conventions.

The names of files containing poems should indicate the poet and, if a non-GuoBiao Chinese file, the coding standard used (et, hku, etc.).

Since one goal of the list is to assemble a database of Chinese poems, there is a preference for using one uuencoded file per poem, and to number a poet's poems sequentially as they are posted to the list. For example, the first person to post a poem by Li Bai might name the file libai.001 (or, if an ET Big5 file, libai.001.et). The next person would call his or her file libai.002, and so forth.

Of course latecomers or those with short memories will not know how many poems by a given poet have already been posted to the list. In that case, add your name or id after the poet's name and start your own numbering system. For example, if your computer id were nw1, and you wanted to post a Li Bai poem but didn't know the number of the last Li Bai poem posted, you should name yours libai_nw1.001.

Indexes of poems previously sent to the list will be distributed periodically.

If you want to post a large number of files at once (say, more than three or four poems), we suggest you use the tar file archiving program. Unix users can get instructions for tar by typing "man tar" at their system prompt, or by consulting their system administrators. There is a PC version of tar available via anonymous ftp at procyon.cis.ksu.edu [129.130.10.80] in the pub/PC/UnixLike directory.

Try to use as reliable a source as possible when typing poems, and identify it in your message. As a general rule, try to use the following format:

```
line 1:  AUTHOR TITLE   ; (Poet's name, a space, then title of poem)
line 2:  <blank line>   ; (Leave a blank line before starting text)
line 3:  ...text...     ; (Text of poem)
   ...        ....
```

Add your name and/or email id at the end, if you wish.

5. Still confused?

If you have any questions, can't get software working, or whatever, try sending mail to the list. Someone is likely to know the answer, or at least offer sympathy.

[Much of this information was gathered from Tony Lim's CCNET-L "Frequently Asked Questions" message (lin@tasman.cc.utas.edu.au).]

CHRISTIA%FINHUTC.BITNET@MITVMA.MIT.EDU

Mailing list for discussions on practical Christian life.

Contributions sent to this list are automatically archived. You can obtain a list of the available archive files by sending an "INDEX CHRISTIA" command to LISTSERV@FINHUTC. These files can then be retrieved by means of a "GET CHRISTIA filetype" command, or using the database search facilities of LISTSERV. Send an "INFO DATABASE" command for more information on the latter.

To subscribe to CHRISTIA, send the command: SUB CHRISTIA your_full_name to LISTSERV@FINHUTC e.g. SUB CHRISTIA "William H. E. Day" To have your name removed from the CHRISTIA subscriber list, send: SIGNOFF CHRISTIA Commands can be sent to LISTSERV@FINHUTC either as interactive messages or in e-mail (one command per line in the body of the e-mail message).

CIRCPLUS on LISTSERV@IDBSU.BITNET

The list Circplus has moved from an internet-only operation at UNC to a new status and home at idbsu. Circplus deals with issues related to circulation control in libraries, including circulation, shelving, reserve room or reserve desk operations, stacks maintenance, and so on. It is Circplus@idbsu.BITNET but to subscribe send mail to LISTSERV@IDBSU with the body containing the command: SUB CIRCPLUS yourfirstname yourlastname

Owner: Dan Lester 1910 University Dr. Bitnet: ALILESTE@IDBSU Library Boise, Idaho 83725 Internet:

CIRCUITS-L@UWPLATT.EDU

PURPOSE: This list was created to discuss all aspects of the introductory course in circuit analysis for electrical engineering undergraduates. The discussion will focus upon sharing thoughts, ideas, and teaching strategies focused upon the introductory circuits course for electrical engineering majors. Participants include faculty, students, and other interested individuals. Discussion is concentrated on the introductory circuits course, other topics are not permitted. Topics include but are not limited to:

1. Teaching approaches.
2. Classroom techniques.
3. Laboratory skills/tools.
4. Design methods.
5. Theory and practice of circuit analysis.
6. Simulators and simulations.
7. Role played by circuits course development in the faculty reward system.
8. E_mail? Another teaching tool? Student access?
9. Authoring new teaching approaches; reporting efforts; available journals and practices.
10. Integrating design into the introductory circuits course.
11. Integrating research into the introductory circuits course.
12. Solving assigned problems.
13. Textbook reviews.

SUBSCRIBE: Note Carefully! To subscribe to CIRCUITS-L send an e_mail message to

CIRCUITS-REQUEST@UWPLATT.EDU

This message MUST contain the following information:

1. Name
2. e_mail address
3. Home Phone, Business Phone, FAX (including area code)
4. U.S. Postal address (including ZIP code)

For Example:

SUBSCRIBE CIRCUITS-L
JOHN SMITH
SMITH@HIS.NETWORK.ADDRESS
555-555-5555,555-555-4444,NA (NA - not applicable)
STREET

CITY STATE ZIP

LIST OWNER: Name : Paul E. Gray e_mail : GRAY@UWPLATT.EDU : GRAY@UWPLATT.BITNET

cisco@SPOT.COLORADO.EDU

Mailing list for discussion of the network products from cisco Systems, Inc; primarily the AGS gateway, but also the ASM terminal multiplexor and any other relavent products. Discussions about operation, problems, features, topology, configuration, protocols, routing, loading, serving, etc are all encouraged. Other topics include vendor relations, new product announcements, availability of fixes and new features, and discusion of new requirements and desirables.

Archives are available via anonymous ftp from SPOT.COLORADO.EDU in the subdirectory "cisco".

All requests to be added to or deleted from this list, questions, comments, etc., should be sent to cisco-request@SPOT.COLORADO.EDU. The list is "slightly" moderated in that you must be validated to send mail to the list. Sending in a request will get you validated, as will reasonable attempts to send reasonable messages to the list. Once you are validated, your messages will be redirected to the whole list without interference.

Coordinator: David Wood <dcmwood@SPOT.COLORADO.EDU>

clarissa@ferkel.ucsb.edu   [Last Update 8/92]

Purpose: Discussion of the Nickelodeon TV show *Clarissa Explains It All.*

Contact: clarissa-request@ferkel.ucsb.edu (Jim Lick)

CLASS-L%SBCCVM.BITNET@CUNYVM.CUNY.EDU

Mailing list and file server for researchers in classification, clustering, phylogenetic estimation, and related areas of data analysis. CLASS-L provides facilities to:

- Enable researchers to mail messages automatically to all subscribers
- Provide researchers with announcements, newsletters, and information about classification and clustering.

The Coordinators are inviting officials of professional classification societies to own (and to be responsible for) files which would be maintained by the SBCCVM file server. Any CLASS-L subscriber can retrieve these files by issuing appropriate LISTSERV commands. Alternatively, a CLASS-L subscriber can arrange to receive automatically copies (or announcements) of files updated by particular societies. We hope officials of the Member Societies of the International Federation of Classification Societies will eventually participate in this project as file owners. Officials from other societies (e.g. Psychometric Society, Willi Hennig Society, International Association of Pattern Recognition Societies) may also be interested in participating.

To subscribe to CLASS-L, send the command: SUB CLASS-L your_full_name to LISTSERV@SBCCVM e.g. SUB CLASS-L "William H. E. Day" To have your name removed from the CLASS-L subscriber list, send: SIGNOFF CLASS-L Commands can be sent to LISTSERV@SBCCVM either as interactive messages or in e-mail (one command per line in the body of the e-mail message).

Coordinators: Bill Day <whday%MUN.BITNET@CUNYVM.CUNY.EDU> Jim Rohlf <rohlf%SBBIOVM.BITNET@CUNYVM.CUNYDU>

CLASSICS@uwavm.u.washington.edu or CLASSICS@UWAVM.BITNET

An unmoderated list for discussing ancient Greek and Latin subjects. This list is open to everyone interested in Classics, and prospective members are warmly welcomed. The discussions assume a background in ancient Greek and/or Latin. The CLASSICS list is neither run by nor directly affiliated with the University of Washington Classics Department.

All requests to be added to this list should be sent to listserv@uwavm.bitnet or listserv@uwavm.u.washington.edu with the one-line message:

SUBSCRIBE CLASSICS your-full-name

To unsubscribe, send: UNSUBSCRIBE CLASSICS

Coordinator: Linda Wright <lwright@u.washington.edu>

CLASSM-L@BROWNVM.BROWN.EDU CLASSM-L@BROWNVM.BITNET

[Last Updated 12-October-1991]

The Classical Music List was created to discuss classical music of all kinds. All topics and periods are welcome, from Gregorian Chants to George Crumb.

To subscribe to CLASSM-L, send a mail message to:

Internet: LISTSERV@brownvm.brown.edu BITNET: LISTSERV@BROWNVM

with the text:

SUB CLASSM-L <First Name> <Last Name>

Owner: Catherine "Pumpkin" Yang Internet: cyang@brownvm.brown.edu BITNET: CYANG@BROWNVM

clay=xldev@cs.cmu.edu

There is now an Excel Developers Mailing List on the internet. Our reason for existence is to serve as a forum on the internet for people who are doing, or want to do, sophisticated things with Microsoft Excel, such as executive informations systems, numerical simulations, financial forecasts, or stock analysis programs. We want to encourage exploration of Excel's nooks and crannies (Hey! Undocumented: FOO.BAR macro works on arrays!), and as much as possible, avoid the well-worn paths (How do I insert rows?). While we do expect some degree of sophistication from our posters, new or casual Excel users are welcome to read the list.

For those with netnews access, one way to look at the list is as a sort of high-S/N, Excel-directed complement to comp.apps.spreadsheets. Some cross-posting is likely. Traffic to date has been light.

To subscribe, you *must* send mail to <clay=xldev-add@cs.cmu.edu>. Non-internet (e.g. uucp, BITNET) subscribers should make sure that the "From:" field of their subscription message has an internet form. CompuServe users needn't bother, since CIS automatically converts their addresses. Feel free to forward this announcement to interested parties or groups.

SUBSCRIBE TO LIST: clay=xldev-add@cs.cmu.edu OTHER ADMINISTRATIVE REQUESTS: clay=xldev-request@cs.cmu.edu TO POST: clay=xldev@cs.cmu.edu

Owner: Clay Bridges clay+@cs.cmu.edu Excel Developers List Administrator

CLAYART on LISTSERV@UKCC or LISTSERV@UKCC.uky.edu

[Last Update 8/92]

The focus of CLAYART is to provide a forum for discussion of issues of interest to those in the fields of ceramic arts/pottery. Appropriate postings include:

* aesthetic issues/concerns
* exhibition opportunities
* conference information
* book reviews
* grant information
* technical information
* workshops/seminars
* job listings

This is a LISTSERV managed list, so normal subscription requests apply. To subscribe send mail to LISTSERV@UKCC (or on the Internet to LISTSERV@UKCC.uky.edu) with the body of the mail containing the command: SUB CLAYART Yourfirstname Yourlastname

Owner:

Joe Molinaro   id: ARTMOLIN@EKU.BITNET
Assistant Professor/Art   phone: (606) 622-1634
Eastern Kentucky University
Richmond, Kentucky 40475

CLP.X@XEROX.COM

Unmoderated, direct-redistribution mailing list devoted to discussion of the following topics (among others):

* Concurrent logic programming languages
  - Problematic constructs
  - Comparisons between languages
* Concurrent constraint programming languages
  - Constraint solvers, including those for discrete constraint satisfaction
  - Language issues
* Semantics, proof techniques and program transformations
  - Partial evaluation
  - Meta interpretation
  - Embedded languages

* Parallel Prolog systems
  - Restricted And-parallel
  - Or-parallel Prolog
* Implementations
  - Announcement of software packages
  - Reports on performance
  - Issues in implementation
* Programming techniques and idioms, applications
  - Open systems and distributed computation
  - Small demonstration programs
* Seminars, conferences, trip reports etc. related to the above

All messages will be archived and can be obtained on request from the list coordinator.

All requests to be added to or deleted from this list, problems, questions, etc., should be sent to CLP-REQUEST.X@XEROX.COM or to jlevy.PA@XEROX.COM.

Coordinator: Jacob Levy <jlevy.PA@XEROX.COM>

CLTHOPT on LISTSERV@ETSUADMN.BITNET or LISTSERV@ETSUADMN.ETSU.EDU

CLTHOPT is an online discussion list for clothing optional living. This is is open to discussing skinny-dipping, visiting nude beaches, or resorts, and top-free issues for women. This is not a sexual discussion list. If anything, we hope to dispell the myth that nudity is always equated with sex. Subscriptions to this list are open to all.

To subscribe, send the following command to LISTSERV@ETSUADMN via mail or interactive message:

SUB CLTHOPT your full name

where "your full name" is your name. For example:

SUB CLTHOPT Joan Doe

Owner: John Hendry <HENDRY@ETSUADMN>

CLUB-USM on LISTSERV@UTFSM.BITNET

General Information about Universidad Tecnica Federico Santa Maria. It is meant to cover all aspects of student life in the University. Mainly intended for students,graduates, teachers and everybody related to the University. Subscriptions are wellcome. All Chilean subscriptions are screened, international ones, are accepted as is.

The prefered language is Spanish, though English is accepted.

Archives of LISTNAME and related files are stored in CLUB-USM FILELIST. To receive a list of files send the command INDEX CLUB-USM to LISTSERV@UTFSM.BITNET

To subscribe to CLUB-USM, send the following command to LISTSERV@UTFSM via mail text or interactive message: SUBSCRIBE CLUB-USM Your_full_name. For example: SUBSCRIBE

CLUB-USM Joe Shmoe

Owner: Douglas Sargent <POSTMAST@UTFSM.BITNET>

CLU-SW <mcvax!cs.utu.fi!clu-sw@SEISMO.CSS.GOV>

Mailing list for exchange of CLU software and for technical discussion of related topics. This list is identical to the USENET mailing list 'mail.clu'.

All requests to be added to or deleted from this list, problems, questions, etc., should be sent to <mcvax!cs.utu.fi!clu-sw-request@SEISMO.CSS.GOV>.

Coordinator: Matti Jokinen <mcvax!cs.utu.fi!jokinen@SEISMO.CSS.GOV>

CMSUG-L%UTARLVM1.BITNET@MITVMA.MIT.EDU

This list unmoderated discussion for topics that relate to CMS; any related question is encouraged. The list is intended for the beginner as well as experienced CMS users.

To subscribe to the list from a VM site on BITNET do: TELL LISTSERV at UTARLVM1 SUBSCRIBE CMSUG-L Your_Full_Name where Your_Full_Name is your real name (not your userid). Use the command TELL LISTSERV HELP for more information. From a VMS BITNET site use the SEND/REMOTE command. If you are at a site not on BitNet or where you cannot send interactive messages, send a message to LISTSERV%UTARLVM1.BITNET@MITVMA.MIT.EDU where the first non-header line consists of: SUBSCRIBE CMSUG-L Your_Full_Name To remove yourself from the list, send: TELL LISTSERV at UTARLVM1 UNSUBSCRIBE CMSUG-L or send a message to LISTSERV%UTARLVM1.BITNET@MITVMA.MIT.EDU with: UNSUBSCRIBE CMSUG-L

Coordinator: Gary Samek <C133GES%UTARLVM1.BITNET@MITVMA.MIT.EDU>

CMU-TEK-TCP@CS.CMU.EDU

Mailing list for the discussion of the CMU-TEK TCP/IP package for VAX/VMS.

Archives are not currently aviailable.

All requests to be added to or deleted from this list, problems, questions, etc., should be sent to CMU-TEK-TCP-REQUEST@CS.CMU.EDU.

Coordinator: Dale Moore <Dale.Moore@PS1.CS.CMU.EDU>

CNEDUC-L@tamvm1.tamu.edu

This list deals with Computer Networking, not the LAN type but the reach out and touch communications type of networking. Mainly will be used for K-12 educational arena.

Coordinator: Richard Lee Holbert <X075RT@tamvm1.tamu.edu>

CNSF-L on LISTSERV@UBVM or LISTSERV@UBVM.CC.BUFFALO.EDU

This list was formed to serve as a vehicle for the distribution of information regarding activities and events at the Cornell National Supercomputing Facility (CNSF).

Archives of CNSF-L and related files are stored in the CNSF-L FILELIST. To receive a list of files send the command INDEX CNSF-L to LISTSERV@UBVM or LISTSERV@UBVM.CC.BUFFALO.EDU as the first line in the BODY of a mail message (not the Subject: line).

To subscribe to CNSF-L, send the command SUB CNSF-L your name to LISTSERV@UBVM or LISTSERV@UBVM.CC.BUFFALO.EDU via a mail message (again, as the first line in the BODY of the mail, not the Subject: line).

For example: SUB CNSF-L John Doe

Owner: Tom Britt <BRITTT@SNYSYRV1.BITNET>

CoCo%PUCC.BITNET@CUNYVM.CUNY.EDU

CoCo@PUCC.PRINCETON.EDU

Discussion related to the Tandy Color Computer (any model), OS-9 Operating System, and any other topics relating to the "CoCo", as this computer is affectionately known.

To access COCO files on LISTSERV@PUCC, include the following line at the top of the message body: SUBSCRIBE COCO Your Full Name This command may also be issued by means of the TELL or MSG commands.

BITNET users can subscribe to the list via ListServ, which takes care of the list processing and distribution. Simply issue a TELL command or MAIL message to LISTSERV@PUCC with the command: SUB COCO Your Real Name.

Internet users wishing to be on the list should send mail to the Coordinator; UUCP users, PLEASE NOTE: a nearby ARPA or BITNET node is needed to get things through to you reliably, so please send a path in the form: zeus!yourcomp!yourid@SUN.COM All Internet and BitNet nodes can be reached, but PUCC's UUCP gateway is unreliable, so this will improve things.

Coordinator: Paul Campbel <PECAMPBE%MTUS5.BITNET@CUNYVM.CUNY.EDU>

COHERENT on LISTSERV@INDYCMS.BITNET

Coherent (Coherent Operating System list) is a public discussion and distribution list dedicated to the Coherent operating system produced by the Mark Williams Company. Coherent (the list) is completely independent of Coherent (the operating system) and Mark Williams Company (the manufacturer).

There is a bidirectional gateway to the Usenet newsgroup, comp.os.coherent.

To subscribe, send request to: ListServ@IndyCMS (CREN) ListServ@IndyCMS.IUPUI.Edu (Internet) Using the following message text: Sub Coherent Your_full_name

List owners/coordinators: Phillip G Corporon
                           F3PB88@IrishMVS (CREN)
                           F3PB88@IrishMVS.CC.ND.Edu (Internet)

                           John B Harlan
                           IJBH200@IndyVAX (CREN)
                           IJBH200@IndyVAX.IUPUI.Edu (Internet)

COM-ALG%NDSUVM1.BITNET@VM1.NODAK.EDU

Mailing list for discussion, inquiry, and the dissemination of information by professionals in the field of commutative algebra.

Archives of COM-ALG and related files are stored in COM-ALG FILELIST. To receive a list of files send the command INDEX COM-ALG to LISTSERV@NDSUVM1.

To subscribe to COM-ALG send the following command to LISTSERV@NDSUVM1 via mailtext or interactive message: SUBSCRIBE COM-ALG Your_full_name For example: SUBSCRIBE COM-ALG Emmy Noether Non-BitNet users can subscribe by sending the command in a message to LISTSERV%NDSUVM1.BITNET@VM1.NODAK.EDU.

Coordinator: Joseph P. Brennan <NU160025%NDSUVM1.BITNET@VM1.NODAK.EDU> <nubrenna@PLAINS.NODAK.EDU>

COMMCOLL@UKCC.UKY.EDU   [Last Updated 12-October-1991]
COMMCOLL@UKCC.BITNET

Jefferson Community College - University of Kentucky announces an electronic discussion group for faculty, staff and administration at two-year institutions, COMMCOLL@UKCC.

Access to COMMCOLL is available internationally thus forming a global network of two-year college educators who recognize the importance of teaching in communicating knowledge to the next generation.

The use of COMMCOLL is a a major breakthrough in facilitating instant communication among faculty, administrators, and staff at two-year institutions.

Appropriate messages for COMMCOLL include: polls; information-gathering questions; feedback on one's research; program proposals and development; calls for papers; meetings, media, and job announcements; consultation with other faculties discussing problems and solutions facing campuses around the world; as well as any other issues pertinent to creating and enhancing teaching effectiveness in two-year institutions.

While messages sent to COMMCOLL are received by all subscribers, users may then contact specific individuals via BITNET to pursue particular projects, issues, and interests. Since computer systems differ, please be sure to include your userid and node at the end of each posting.

To subscribe to the COMMCOLL list send e-mail to LISTSERV@UKCC (on BITNET) or LISTSERV@UKCC.UKY.EDU with the following command in the text (or body) of the mail:

SUB COMMCOLL yourfirstname yourlastname

If you have any questions or comments, please contact:

Anne Kearney, Ph.D.
Assistant Professor of History
Jefferson Community College - University of Kentucky
109 East Broadway
Louisville, KY 40202
BITNET: JCCANNEK@UKCC
INTERNET: JCCANNEK@UKCC.UKY.EDU

commune-list@STEALTH.ACF.NYU.EDU

Mailing list for discussion of the COMMUNE protocol, a TELNET replacement.

All requests to be added to or deleted from this list, problems, questions, etc., should be sent to commune-request@STEALTH.ACF.NYU.EDU.

Coordinator: Dan Bernstein <brnstnd@STEALTH.ACF.NYU.EDU>

comp-academic-freedom-talk on LISTSERV@eff.org   [Last Updated 12-October-1991]
   comp-academic-freedom-batch on LISTSERV@eff.org
   comp-academic-freedom-news on LISTSERV@eff.org

Computers and Academic Freedom Mailing Lists

Purpose: To discuss questions such as: How should general principles of academic freedom (such as freedom of expression, freedom to read, due process, and privacy) be applied to university computers and networks? How are these principles actually being applied? How can the principles of academic freedom as applied to computers and networks be defended?

There are three versions of the mailing list.

comp-academic-freedom-talk - you'll received dozens of e-mail notes every day.

comp-academic-freedom-batch - about once a day, you'll receive a compilation of the day's notes.

comp-academic-freedom-news - about once a week you'll receive a compilation of the best notes of the
               week.
To join a version of the list, send mail to listserv@eff.org. Include the line "add <name-of-version>". (Other commands are "delete <name-of-version>" and "help"). NOTE: This is NOT the same LISTSERV that is being used on BITNET sites.

In any case, after you join the list you can send e-mail to the list by addressing it to caf-talk@eff.org.

Alternatively, if you may be able to read the mailing lists as newsgroups. Look for alt.comp.acad-freedom.talk and alt.comp.acad-freedom.news.

The best notes from each month are available via anonymous ftp from eff.org as files "pub/academic/news/July", etc. Also, see file "pub/academic/README".

Owner: Carl Kadie -- kadie@eff.org or kadie@cs.uiuc.edu

COMP-CEN%UCCVMA.BITNET@VM1.NODAK.EDU
COMP-CEN on LISTSERV@UCCVMA

This is a list for discussion about the day to day activities of operating and planning mid to large sized computer centers.

Scope is wide, but could include:
1. Is it worth it to migrate from wide, fanfold paper to cut sheet or COM or fiche?
2. How to pick a hot site/chiller/UPS/generator.
3. Samples of evaluation criteria for hardware and software.
4. In general, how to do more with less.

List is open, but target audience consists of hands-on technical managers and planners.

To subscribe,

TELL LISTSERV@UCCVMA SUBscribe COMP-CEN Firstname Lastname

or send mail with the SUB... in the first line of text to LISTSERV%UCCVMA.BITNET@VM1.NODAK.EDU

List ownter: Rich Hintz <opsrjh@uccvma.bitnet@vm1.nodak.edu>

comp-privacy@pica.army.mil   [Last Update 11/92]

The computer Privacy Digest is an Internet mailing list dedicated to the discussion of how technology impacts privacy. All too often technology is way ahead of the law and society as it presents us with new devices and applications. Technology can enhance and detract from privacy.

This list is gatewayed into the moderated USENET newsgroup comp.society.privacy. In lot of ways it is a subsection of the risks digest concentrating on the risks of technology on privacy.

Submissions go to: comp-privacy@pica.army.mil and administrative requests go to comp-privacy-request@pica.army.mil.

Moderator: Dennis G. Rears
MILNET: drears@pica.army.mil
UUCP: ...!uunet!cor5.pica.army.mil!drears
INTERNET: drears@pilot.njin.net USPS: Box 210, Wharton, NJ 07885

COMP-SCI <JO%ILNCRD.BITNET@CUNYVM.CUNY.EDU>

A Bitnet newsletter on computer science in Israel.

To subscribe, send a message to LISTSERV%TAUNIVM.BITNET@CUNYVM.CUNY.EDU with the body of the letter containing the command: SUB COMP-SCI Your_Full_Name where Your_Full_Name; is your title, first name and last name.

Coordinator: Joseph van Zwaren de Zwarenstein <JO%ILNCRD.BITNET@CUNYVM.CUNY.EDU>

Comp-Soc@LIMBO.INTUITIVE.COM

The Computers And Society mailing list was created to provide a forum for discussion of various issues related to the impact of technology and information on society. Among the issues being discussed are:

Computers and social responsibility
Dealing with information overload
The classed society in the information age

Public perceptions of computers
The value of information
Dangers and advantages of reliance on machines
Risks of technological dependence
and other related topics

All requests to be added to or deleted from this list, problems, questions, etc., should be sent to the Coordinator.

Coordinator: Dave Taylor <taylor@LIMBO.INTUITIVE.COM> {uunet!}{decwrl,apple}!limbo!taylor

COMPOS01%ULKYVX.BITNET@CUNYVM.CUNY.EDU

The Composition Digest is a moderated weekly newsgroup for the study of computers and writing, specifically writing instruction in computer-based classrooms. It is intended to be a forum for writing professionals (those who must use computers for their writing) and computing professionals (those who design the hardware and software that writers depend upon) to meet and discuss issues relevant to both fields, but notes are also welcome from novice computer writers. There is interest in articles pertaining to, but not limited by, the following topics:

Human/Factors research and writing environments
Text editor design
Natural Language adjuncts to writing instruction
Writing without paper
Psychological effects of computer writing/instruction
Composition theory applied to computer-based instruction
Anecdotal accounts of computer writing experiences
Using the NET in the classroom
Computer-based conferences
Public domain software for the classroom
Reviews of writing and editing packages
Conference announcements and proceedings
Telecommunications and its effects on language
Computers and the soft sciences
Computers and hearing impaired students
Computers and learning disabled students
Computers and basic writers
Computers and humanists
Computers and writing professionals

All requests to be added to or deleted from this list, problems, questions, etc., should be sent to COMPOS01%ULKYVX.BITNET@CUNYVM.CUNY.EDU.

COMTEN-L on LISTSERV@UCSBVM.BITNET   [Last Update 9/92]

This List is a forum for the discussion of software, hardware, LAN/WAN attachments, workstations, problems, etc. In short, anything at all to do with networking. It's called COMTEN-L because I'd like to see if there's enough interest in NCR boxes for us to do a little of our own self-help and design. NCR has their so-called value added products, which make the network generations quite interesting compared to a vanilla NCP. For now, just about any communications topic is fair game.

To subscribe, send the following command to LISTSERV@UCSBVM.BITNET via mail or interactive message:

SUB COMTEN-L your full name

where "your full name" is your name. For example:

SUB COMTEN-L Joan Doe

Owner: Dwight M. McCann <DWIGHT@UCSBVM.BITNET>

concrete-blonde@ferkel.ucsb.edu [Last Update 8/92]

Purpose: Discussion of the musical group Concrete Blonde.

Contact: concrete-blonde-request@ferkel.ucsb.edu (Robert Earl)

CONFOCAL%UBVM.BITNET@VM1.NODAK.EDU

Mailing list dealing with all aspects of confocal microscopy and confocal microscope design.

BitNet users can subscribe by sending the following command to LISTSERV@UBVM in an interactive message or the text/body of mail: SUB CONFOCAL your_full_name where Your_full_name is your real name, not your login Id. Non-BitNet users can send the above command to LISTSERV%UBVM.BITNET@VM1.NODAK.EDU in the text/body of a message.

Coordinator: Robert G. Summers <ANARGS%UBVMS.BITNET@VM1.NODAK.EDU>

CONS-L%MCGILL1.BITNET@CORNELLC.CCS.CORNELL.EDU

This group provides a forum for university computing centre consultants to discuss such issues as problem tracking, resource management, training, and consulting strategies.

All requests to be added to or deleted from this list, problems, questions, etc., should be sent to one of the Coordinators.

Coordinators: Michael Walsh <CCMW%MCGILLA.BITNET@CORNELLC.CCS.CORNELL.EDU>
CCMW@MUSICA.MCGILL.CA (BitNet)
Sander Wasser <CCSW%MCGILLA.BITNET@CORNELLC.CCS.CORNELL.EDU>
CCSW@MUSICA.MCGILL.CA (BitNet)

CONSIM-L on LISTSERV@UALTAVM (LISTSERV@VM.UCS.UALBERTA.CA)

CONSIM-L provides an unmoderated environment for discussion of historical conflict simulation games, particularly the games published in Strategy and Tactics and Command magazines, but also including boxed games from such publishers as The Avalon Hill Game Company, Victory Games, and Game Designers Workshop.

The explicit purpose of CONSIM-L is to provide a platform for discussion of recently published games, but discussion can range over the general topics of conflict simulation design, military history, tactics and strategy, game collecting, convention and club announcements, or any other topic related to conflict simulation games. As is the case on all unmoderated lists, the discussion and topics are only limited by the participation and interest of its subscribers. Subscribers are welcome to take an active role by posting and/or an inactive role by monitoring the list. Although not necessary for participation, it shall be assumed that all subscribers are basically familiar with board wargames.

To subscribe to CONSIM-L, please send mail or file to LISTSERV@UALTAVM or listserv@vm.ucs.ualberta.ca and place in the body of the text the line

SUB CONSIM-L <your name>.

This list does not support any archive functions.

Contents on LISTSERV@Uottawa (BITNET)
or LISTSERV@Acadvm1.Uottawa.Ca (Internet)

This list will simply announce new and recent publications of relevance to Religious Studies and related disciplines. It will post the table of contents, prices, and when available, abstracts of both books and journals. These postings will be logged in notebooks for searching and, in future, made available as a TELNET accessible and searchable database.

The Wilfrid Laurier University Press is the first to make this information available to the CONTENTS list. I hope to soon convince the AAR and SBL presses to join in asap. The rest should come running soon enough.

The list will not be conversational. Frequency of postings will depend on the number of cooperating publishers. If the load gets heavy postings will be grouped together accounding to some extremely esoteric classification system. There is the possibility that down the road, CONTENTS will also serve to distribute reviews from IOUDAIOS, RELIGION and other lists, if such a service is deemed useful.

To subscribe to CONTENTS send the following email message to Listserv@Uottawa or Listserv@Acadvm1.Uottawa.Ca

SUB CONTENTS your name

Contact the list coordinator, Michael Strangelove, for more information or if you experience difficulties in attempting to subscribe.

Michael Strangelove University of Ottawa <441495@Uottawa> <441495@Acadvm1.Uottawa.Ca>

CONTEX-L on LISTSERV@UOTTAWA

CONTEX-L is an academic special interest group (also known as a Listserv List) for all who are interested in the cross-disciplinary analysis of ancient texts. This list provides a forum for the scholarly, informal and polite discussion of the social worlds behind and within the texts of antiquity, including those of the Hebrew bible, early Christianity, Rabbinic Judaism and all the literature associated with the Graeco-Roman world.

Any discussion which involves cross (inter/multi) disciplinary modeling and analysis and attempts to move beyond *intuitive* historical criticism is considered valid. Such methodologies include and encompass social-scientific criticism, feminist hermeneutics, sociological exegesis, social history, political science, psychohistory, and anthropology (social, cultural, symbolic linguistic...).

To subscribe send mail or an interactive message to LISTSERV@UOTTAWA on BITNET with the text containing the command sub CONTEX-L firstname lastname where firstname lastname is your own name (do not include id).

Any queries concerning CONTEX-l should be send to Michael Strangelove <441495@ACADVM1.UOTTAWA.CA> University of Ottawa

com-priv@psi.com

This is a mailing list devoted to discussing the commercialization of the Internet.

Back issues can be ftp'd from

com-priv uu.psi.com:/archive/com-priv/

Requests to join go to com-priv-request@uu.psi.com.

CORPORA@X400.HD.UIB.NO

The CORPORA list is open for information and questions about text corpora such as availability, aspects of compiling and using corpora, software, tagging, parsing, bibliography, etc.

To join the list send a message to CORPORA-REQUEST@X400.HD.UIB.NO asking to be added to the CORPORA list and including your e-mail address.

To contribute to the list send e-mail to CORPORA@X400.HD.UIB.NO

List administrator: Knut Hofland Norwegian Computing Centre for the Humanities, Harald Haarfagres gt. 31, N-5007 Bergen, Norway

Phone +47 5 212954/5/6 Fax: +47 5 322656 E-mail: knut@x400.hd.uib.no

CORRYFEE on SARASERV@HASARA11.BITNET

CORRYFEE Online Information Service of the Faculty of Economics and Econometrics University of

Amsterdam the Netherlands

In 1991 the Faculty of Economics of the University of Amsterdam, the Netherlands will start an experiment with the electronic mailing system CORRYFEE. This mailing system is intended to serve as an information distribution system for researchers in the fields of Economics, Econometrics and Management. If you have an electronic mailbox connected to a major network it is possible to subscribe, free of charge, to our mailing system CORRYFEE. If you are a bitnet user you can subscribe automatically by just sending an electronic mail to the bitnet address

The first line of this electronic mail should contain the following text SUBSCRIBE CORRYFEE full name

An example: SUBSCRIBE CORRYFEE Lao Tze

If the format of your electronic mail is correct you will be acknowledged for your subscription to CORRYFEE. Users of other networks, like Internet, UUNET, JANET, JUNET can sent their requests for subscription to the bitnet address CORRYFEE@HASARA11. Any information that might be of interest to you will than automatically be forwarded to your electronic mailbox. If you should have any information that might be of value to other subscribers of the CORRYFEE or you want to raise a question to the other subscribers, please send an electronic mail to bitnet

CORRYFEE@HASARA11

and your electronic mail will, after monitoring, be distributed to the subscribers of CORRYFEE. In case you should want further information concerning CORRYFEE please contact

```
Hans M. Amman                      Hans van Ophem
Department of Macroeconomics       Department of Econometrics
University of Amsterdam            University of Amsterdam
Jodenbreestraat 23, room 3347      Jodenbreestraat 23, room 3191
1011 NH Amsterdam-NL               1011 NH Amsterdam-NL
telephone +31-20-5254203/4193      telephone +31-20-5254222
telefax   +31-20-5252491           telefax   +31-20-5252491
bitnet    amman@hasara5            bitnet    a6079001@hasara11
Internet  amman@sara.nl            internet  a6079001@vml.sara.nl
```

CP on LISTSERV@opus.hpl.hp.com   [Last Updated 9/92]

The CP listserv hosts a roundtable discussion of all aspects of carnivorous plants - cultivation, ecology, protection, etc. The CP archive contains lists of plants available from both members and commercial sources. Information on archived files can be listed by sending the command: "INDEX CP" to listserv@opus.hpl.hp.com.

To subscribe, send a mail message consisting of the text: SUBSCRIBE CP your full name to the address: listserv@opus.hpl.hp.com

For example: SUBSCRIBE CP Joan Doe

Owner: Rick Walker <walker@hpl-cutt.hpl.hp.com>

CPE-LIST@UNCVM1.OIT.UNC.EDU   [Last Updated 12-October-1991]

Computer Performance Evaluation Interested Parties List

CPE-LIST is an electronic conference designed to foster communication concerning performance evaluation issues involved in the use large-scale computing engines.

Please share your constructive solutions to problems, issues, and thoughts about performance-related topics.

While intended as a forum for users of large-scale IBM or near-blue equipment other foci are welcome. The list can always be subdivided along more spcific lines.

Subscription is open to anyone interested.

You may subscribe to CPE-LIST by sending a subscribe command by interactive message or by e-mail. To subscribe by interactive message, send the command: SUB CPE-LIST YourFirstname YourLastname to LISTSERV@UNCVM1.BITNET. or to LISTSERV@UNCVM1.OIT.UNC.EDU. For example:

IBM VM CMS users would enter tell listserv at uncvm1 sub CPE-LIST YourFirstname YourLastname
VAX VMS users would enter send listserv@uncvm1 sub CPE-LIST YourFirstname YourLastname

You may also subscribe by sending an e-mail message to LISTSERV@UNCVM1.BITNET or if your account is on the internet send to LISTSERV@UNCVM1.OIT.UNC.ED, with the following command as the text of the message.

SUB CPE-LIST YourFirstname YourLastname

This, the 'SUB ...,' must be part of the message; the subject line is ignored.

Additional information in the form of a list of commands for the list server can be obtained by sending the message HELP to the list server (LISTSERV@uncvm1 etc) NOT to the list (CPE-LIST@uncvm1 etc).

More detailed information is available by sending an information request message to the list server. Use one of the following formats:

INFO ? for a list of topics

INFO topic where "topic" is one of the following: GENintro REFcard NEWs KEYwords

Remember two simple rules-of-thumb:

If it's a command (SUBscribe, Help, Info, UNSUBscribe, etc), send it to the list server (LISTSERV@uncvm1...).

If it's a message for general distribution to the members of the list, send it to the list (CPE-LIST@uncvm1...).

The list is supported by the University of North Carolina Office of Information Technology. Our thanks to their management and staff for permission to use their VM system for the list and for assistance in setting it up.

The list is sponsored by the Information Services Division of the University of North Carolina Hospitals.

```
Owner:
  Lyman A. Ripperton III        Lyman@unchmvs.unch.unc.edu
  Technical Services Manager           voice 919/966-3969
  Information Services Division          fax 919/966-2110
  The University of North Carolina Hospitals
  Chapel Hill, NC 27514
```

CPSR on LISTSERV@GWUVM.GWU.EDU   [Last Updated 9/92]
or LISTSERV@GWUVM.BITNET

Computer Professionals for Social Responsibility (CPSR) has set up a list server to (1) archive CPSR-related materials and make them available on request, and (2) disseminate relatively official, short, CPSR-related announcements (e.g., press releases, conference announcements, and project updates). It is accessible via Internet and Bitnet e-mail. Mail traffic will be light; the list is set up so that only the CPSR Board and staff can post to it. Because it is self-subscribing, it easily makes material available to a wide audience.

We encourage you to subscribe to the list server and publicize it widely, to anyone interested in CPSR's areas of work.

To subscribe, send mail to:

listserv@gwuvm.gwu.edu (Internet) OR listserv@gwuvm (Bitnet)

With the following command in the BODY of the mail:

SUBSCRIBE CPSR yourfirstname yourlastname

You will get a message that confirms your subscription. The message also explains how to use the list server to request archived materials (including an index of everything in CPSR's archive), and how to request more information about the list server.

Please continue to send any CPSR queries to cpsr@csli.stanford.edu.

If you have a problem with the list server, please contact the administrator, Paul Hyland (phyland@gwuvm.gwu.edu or phyland@gwuvm).

CREWRT-L@UMCVMB.MISSOURI.EDU   [Last Updated 12-October-1991]

Creative Writing Pedagogy for Teachers and Students

This list was created as a place to discuss how and why creative writing is being taught at colleges and universities, including the role it plays in the curriculum, the history of creative writing programs, the shape and flavor of creative writing courses, and the influence it has or should have on students' lives. Any teacher who has ever taught a creative writing course (poetry or fiction) and any student who has ever taken such a course should feel welcome to participate.

The list is open and unmoderated, so discussion can range as far and wide as members want, from ethereal theory to classroom strategies and anything remotely tangential to either. However, this list is not intended to be a place for sharing creative work. Not that such sharing is in any way forbidden, but there are other lists designed for that purpose.

To subscribe, send an interactive message or mail to LISTSERV@UMCVMB or LISTSERV@UMCVMB.MISSOURI.EDU and include the command:

SUB CREWRT-L Your Name

Owner: Eric Crump LCERIC@UMCVMB.BITNET or LCERIC@UMCVMB.MISSOURI.EDU

CRICKET on LISTSERV@NDSUVM1   [Last Updated 28-January-1992]
or LISTSERV@vm1.nodak.edu

Cricket is an online magazine featuring the scoresheets of first class matches and iteneraries of the tours. The scoresheets will be as complete as the contributors send them. This mailing list is an edited list and all the contributions will be directed to the moderator. If and when rec.sport.cricket.scores is formed, this list and the newsgroup will be gatewayed so that archives of the newsgroups are available at NDSUVM1.

The following commands are for persons from BITNET sites. If you are from an internet site follow the procedure: from internet sites

From BITNET Sites: Archives of cricket back issues can be listed by sending the command INDEX CRICKET to LISTSERV@NDSUVM1.

To subscribe, send the following command to LISTSERV@NDSUVM1 via mail or interactive message:

SUB CRICKET your_full_name

where "your_full_name" is your name. For example:

SUB CRICKET Joan Doe

From Internet Sites: Archives of cricket back issues can be listed by sending the mail to listserv@vm1.nodak.edu

The message body should have the line

INDEX CRICKET

or you may try /FILES80 CRICKET to get an experimental "narrower" listing.

To subscribe, send the following command to LISTSERV@vm1.nodak.edu via mail :

SUB CRICKET your_full_name

where "your_full_name" is your name. For example:

SUB CRICKET Joan Doe

Owner: K. Sankara Rao <ksrao@power.eee.ndsu.nodak.edu>

CROMED-L@AEARN.BITNET   [Last Updated 12-October-1991]

The intention of this list is to inform an international community on current events in Croatia, particularly in the sphere of medicine. Our intention is also to establish E-mail as a tool for easier organization of gathering medical and humanitarian help.

Wherever you live and whatever you do, you could help the people from Croatia not only by material help, but also with your advises and your knowledge. As you know, we have suddenly found ourselves in the winds of war and terror with ambition neither to kill, nor to hurt anyone. With your help we will be closer to our aim to win the war by the weapon of common sense.

Either you are so generous and want to help us or you are only interested in current events in Croatia, please make a subscription to this list by sending the following command to LISTSERV@AEARN.BITNET SUB CROMED-L your full name

8. maja 42, 41000 YU-Zagreb	Ministry of Health
E-Mail:	Republic of Croatia
whocro@uni-zg.ac.mail.yu	Office for Cooperation between
Phone: +38 41 430 621	World Health Organization
Fax: +38 41 431 067	and the Republic of Croatia

CRTNET%PSUVM.BITNET@CUNYVM.CUNY.EDU

Communication Research and Theory NETwork. Discusses all aspects of human communication.

BitNet users may subscribe by sending this interactive message command to LISTSERV@PSUVM: SUBSCRIBE CRTNET your-full-name Others may subscribe by sending mail to T3B%PSUVM.BITNET@CUNYVM.CUNY.EDU.

Moderator: Tom Benson <T3B%PSUVM.BITNET@CUNYVM.CUNY.EDU>

cryonics <kqb@whscad1.att.com>

Purpose: Cryonic suspension is an experimental procedure whereby patients who can no longer be kept alive with today's medical abilities are preserved at low temperatures for treatment in the future. This list is a forum for topics related to cryonics, which include biochemistry of memory, low temperature biology, legal status of cryonics and cryonically suspended people, nanotechnology and cell repair machines, philosophy of identity, mass media coverage of cryonics, new research and publications, conferences, and local cryonics group meetings.

Contact: ...att!whscad1!kqb -or- kqb@whscad1.att.com (Kevin Q. Brown)

CSEMLIST%HASARA11.BITNET@VM1.NODAK.EDU

Mailing list run by the journal of Computer Science in Economics and Management Science; it is intended to serve as an information distribution system for researchers in the field of Computer Science in Economics and Management.

BitNet users can subscribe by sending electronic mail to SARASERV@HASARA11 with the text (body) of the message containing the line: SUBSCRIBE CSEMLIST your_full_name (Ex: SUBSCRIBE CSEMLIST Lao Tze) Non-BitNet users can subscribe by sending a similar message to A601HANS%HASARA11.BITNET@VM1.NODAK.EDU.

Moderator: Hans M. Amman <A601HANS%HASARA11.BITNET@VM1.NODAK.EDU>
<A608HANS%HASARA11.BITNET@VM1.NODAK.EDU>

CSNET-FORUM@SH.CS.NET

A digest-style mailing list devoted to topics of interest to the CSNET community. The CSNET staff contributes informal announcements, up-to-the-minute news, and special features. The CSNET-FORUM is sent to CSNET liaisons and to local mailing lists and bulletin boards on CSNET hosts. New issues appear several times a year.

All requests to be added to or deleted from this list, problems, questions, etc., should be sent to CSNET-FORUM-REQUEST@SH.CS.NET or CIC@SH.CS.NET.

Coordinator: Charlotte Mooers <CSNET-FORUM-REQUEST@SH.CS.NET>

CSP-L%TREARN.BITNET@VM1.NODAK.EDU

Mailing list to discuss the problems about the maintenance, installation and administration of CSP (Cross System Product); it is not a User Group. Mostly technical issues will be discussed.

Requests to be added to or deleted from the list, problems, questions, etc., should be sent to the Coordinator.

Coordinator: Esra Delen <ESRA%TREARN.BITNET@VM1.NODAK.EDU>

CTI-Complit@durham.ac.uk   [Last Updated 12-October-1991]

CTI-complit is an open discussion group for anyone who is interested in computer literacy in higher education and related issues. Founder members of the list were delegates to the Computer Literacy Workshop held at the University of Durham (in the UK) last December.

To subscribe, address your mail to:

mailbase@newcastle.ac.uk

with the following in the body:

SUB CTI-COMPLIT (first name last name)

At the Workshop speakers from selected universities and representing different strategies for computer literacy described their programmes. The Universities of Queen's Belfast, Bradford, Durham, Exeter and Stirling presented their programmes. The latter half of the Workshop addressed some issues connected with teaching computer literacy in universities. The issues included the influence of teaching in schools on undergraduate skills, funding sources for computer literacy programmes, changing methods of teaching and learning and the role of the CTI centres in relation to computer literacy. The intention of the mailbase list is to carry on discussion of the issues raised during the Workshop. You are welcome to subscribe to CTI-complit if you would like to participate in our discussions.

You may be interested to know also that the Proceedings from the Workshop have just been published by CTISS. A copy of the paper given by every speaker is included in the document. Called Computer Literacy for every Graduate Strategies and Challenges for the early Nineteen-nineties, it is available, price 8.00 Pounds Sterling, from CTISS Publications, University of Oxford, 13 BAnbury Road, Oxford, OX2 6NN; UK. Telephone 0865 273273.

List Owner:
Audrey McCartan
Computer Literacy Programme
University of Durham, UK
091 374 3943
Audrey.McCartan@durham.ac.uk

CTI-L on LISTSERV@IRLEARN.UCD.IE

CTI-L is an unmoderated list to facilitate the discussion of issues in the use of computers in teaching. The list is intended to promote discussion on how computers can be used in learning and teaching via the following:

CTI Computers in Teaching Initiative CAT Computer Aided Teaching CBT Computer Based Training CAL Computer Aided Learning CBL Computer Based Learning TBT Technology Based Training

To subscribe, send a message to LISTSERV@IRLEARN.UCD.IE with the following line of text in the BODY:

SUB CTI-L Your_full_name

where Your_full_name is your firstname lastname .

List co-ordinator: Claron O'Reilly <CLARON@IRLEARN.UCD.IE>

ctt-Digest on LISTSERV@SHSU.BITNET or LISTSERV@SHSU.edu

ctt-Digest is a (most probably) multi-part daily digest of activity on the comp.text.tex newsgroup. ctt-Digest is *not* intended to include:

1. posts to comp.text.tex originating on INFO-TeX, nor
2. those periodicals included on TeX-Pubs (i.e, Texhax Digest, UKTeX Digest, TeXMaG, the "Frequently Asked Questions" and "FAQ Supplement" posts from comp.text.tex, and TUG's "TeX and TUG News"). When these periodicals are removed, it is noted at the end of that issue.

Daily digests are designed to keep distribution parts under 42k in size to accommodate as many mailers as possible. Efforts are made to keep each comp.text.tex post in whole between parts (although certain size constraints may preclude this as a universal rule). In general, each day's distribution has been between 1 and 3 parts, but the number of parts will vary directly with comp.text.tex activity, as well as how spontaneously our news feed keeps up with traffic to SHSU. The ctt-Digest distribution is automatically processed and forwarded to subscribers at approximately 0200 Central Standard/ Daylight Time (US).

The address <ctt-Digest@SHSU.edu> is restricted with respect to posting as it is purely a redistribution list. The posting address via mail to access comp.text.tex remains INFO-TeX@SHSU.BITNET (INFO-TeX@SHSU.edu), although posts to INFO-TeX will not appear in ctt-Digest.

If you would like to subscribe to ctt-Digest, please include the command: SUBSCRIBE ctt-Digest "Your Real Name in Quotes" in the body of a mail message to LISTSERV@SHSU.BITNET (LISTSERV@SHSU.edu). Please note that this LISTSERV does *not* support interactive messages.

If you have any questions or comments about this new service (or any of our TeX-related services), please contact me directly.

George D. Greenwade, Ph.D.   Bitnet: BED_GDG@SHSU
Department of Economics and Business Analysis   THEnet: SHSU::BED_GDG
College of Business Administration   Voice: (409) 294-1266
P. O. Box 2118   FAX: (409) 294-3612
Sam Houston State University   Internet: bed_gdg@SHSU.edu
Huntsville, TX 77341   bed_gdg%SHSU.decnet@relay.the.net

CUBE-LOVERS@AI.AI.MIT.EDU

The Rubik's Cube mailing-list. Much of the information in the Scientific American article was presented in Cube-Lovers first; also many mathematical discussions have taken place as well as the development of a cube notation and various transformations used to solve it. Recently this list has been very quiet.

Messages are archived in the MIT-AI files ALAN;CUBE MAIL(0 1 2 ...) with the most recent messages in ALAN;CUBE MAIL

All requests to be added to or deleted from this list, problems, questions, etc., should be sent to CUBE-LOVERS-REQUEST@AI.AI.MIT.EDU.

Coordinator: Alan Bawden <ALAN@AI.AI.MIT.EDU>

CUPLE-L on LISTSERV@UBVM.BITNET or LISTSERV@UBVM.CC.BUFFALO.EDU

This list was formed to serve as a vehicle for (1) discussion of topics related to the Comprehensive Unified Physics Learning Environment (CUPLE) software for PC compatible computers and (2) collection of any information related to this software.

Archives of CUPLE-L and related files are stored in the CUPLE-L FILELIST. To receive a list of files send the command INDEX CUPLE-L to LISTSERV@UBVM.BITNET or LISTSERV@UBVM.CC.BUFFALO.EDU as the first line in the body of a mail message (NOT the Subject: line).

To subscribe to CUPLE-L, send the command SUB CUPLE-L your full name to LISTSERV@UBVM.BITNET or LISTSERV@UBVM.CC.BUFFALO.EDU via a mail message (again, as the first line in the body of the mail, not the Subject: line).

For example: SUB CUPLE-L John Doe

Owner: Jack_Wilson@mts.rpi.edu

cussnet on listserv@stat.com   [Last Update 11/92]

Computer Users in the Social Sciences (CUSS) is a discussion group devoted to issues of interest to social workers, counselors, and human service workers of all disciplines. The discussion frequently involves computer applications in treatment, agency administration, and research. Students, faculty, community based professionals, and just good 'ole plain folks join in the disucssion. Software, hardware, and ethical issues associated with their use in the human service generate lively and informative discussions. Please join us.

To join the list, send email to "listserv@stat.com" The first line of text should be: *subscribe cussnet*

To remove yourself from the list, send email to "listserv@stat.com" The first line of text should be: *unsubscribe cussnet*

Any problems should be directed to cussnet-request@stat.com

Moderator: Bill Allbritten, Ph.D. (Director, Counseling and Testing Center, Murray State University, Murray, KY. 42071)

CUMREC-L%NDSUVM1.BITNET@CUNYVM.CUNY.EDU

The list is intended for anyone involved with computer use in college and university administration, especially for non-technical administrators; it is named after the annual conference. Topics include, but are not limited to:

- Purchase of administrative software from vendors--advice from some campuses that may not be on a vendors list of *showcases*
- General purpose software and hardware purchase--not nuts and bolts, but some general sharing of ideas
- You've decided to write a major administrative system from scratch-- will someone share something with you so you don't need to re-invent the wheel?
- The CUMREC conference itself--sharing information, keeping in touch with people we've met at past conferences.
- Just about anything that a CUMREC paper could be written on.

To subscribe to the list, send mail to the Coordinator if you can't use LISTSERV commands or do: TELL LISTSERV at NDSUVM1 SUB CUMREC-L your_full_name from any system that will let you use TELL or send the command:: SUB CUMREC-L your name as the only text in a message to

LISTSERV@NDSUVM1.

Note: this list has the option SEND=PRIVATE which means that only people who are current subscribers can send to the list. This is not intended to discourage participation, but to encourage subscription and to help avoid some types of mailer loops. If you want to send something to the list, simply subscribe to the list first by following the above instructions.

Coordinator: Joe Moore <SMWJ17%SDNET.BITNET@CUNYVM.CUNY.EDU> <CC19%SDSUMUS.BITNET@CUNYVM.CUNY.EDU>

CVNET%YORKVM1.BITNET@CUNYVM.CUNY.EDU

The Color and Vision Network; the purpose is to make people in vision research and in color research who utilize e-mail communication known to each other. Mass mailing can also be easily done, so announcements supplied to CVNET@YORKVM1 get distributed to the subscriber list. Another activity is the compilation of a key word list that describes the activities of those listed.

All requests to be added to or deleted from this list, problems, questions, etc., should be sent to CVNET%YORKVM1.BITNET@CUNYVM.CUNY.EDU.

Coordinator: Peter K. Kaiser <pkaiser%YORKVM1.BITNET@CUNYVM.CUNY.EDU>

CW-MAIL%TECMTYVM.BITNET@VM1.NODAK.EDU

Mailing list for discussion of campus-wide electronic mail systems. The recent developments in computer networking have created the need for unified E-mail systems, capable of handling mail-type communications among users on many different kinds of computers (mainframes, superminis, minis, personal computers), working for the same organization. This communication can be within the organization or directed to other users on the different networks (BitNet, Internet, etc.). This list strives to provide a forum for developers of such systems. Topics to be discussed are how to carry out such an effort, experiences in the implementation, recommended policies, hardware issues, etc. It is aimed primarily (but not limited to) developers of university campus-wide e-mail systems.

In an effort to assure a productive environment, subscription will be filtered by the list Coordinators, who may require additional information before a subscription request is accepted (curious bystanders clogging up the network are not desired). The list itself is unmoderated. Monthly notebooks are kept.

BitNet users may subscribe by sending the following command to LISTSERV@TECMTYVM via interactive message or mail: SUBSCRIBE CW-EMAIL Your full name where "Your full name" is your real name, not your login Id. Non-BitNet users can join the list by sending the above command as the only line in the text/body of a message to LISTSERV%TECMTYVM.BITNET@VM1.NODAK.EDU.

Coordinator: Juan M. Courcoul <POSTMAST%TECMTYVM.BITNET@VM1.NODAK.EDU> <POSTMAST%TECMTYSM.BITNET@VM1.NODAK.EDU>

CWIS-L%WUVMD.BITNET@VM1.NODAK.EDU Mailing list for discussing the creation and implimentation of campus-wide information systems. The term CWIS includes systems which make information and services publicly available on campus via kiosks, interactive computing systems and/or campus networks. Services routinely include directory information, calendars, bulletin boards, databases and library information.

BitNet users may subscribe by sending the following command to LISTSERV@WUVMD via interactive message or mail: SUB CWIS-L Your full name where "your full name" is your real name, not your login Id. Non-BitNet users can join the list by sending the above command as the only line in the text\/body of a message to LISTSERV%WUVMD.BITNET@VM1.NODAK.EDU.

Comments, questions, etc., should be directed to the Coordinator.

Coordinator: Steve Middlebrook <C94882SM%WUVMD.BITNET@VM1.NODAK.EDU>

Cyber-L%Bitnic.BITNET@CUNYVM.CUNY.EDU

Network digest for people who support and/or install Control Data (CDC) systems. In general, any topic which may be of general interest to people who support and/or install CDC systems is relevant to the digest, including:

- Problem reports and solutions, including information from the support system, SOLVER.
- Requests for help concerning problems on CDC systems.
- Announcements and reviews of new products or upgrades to products, including CDC supplied as well as site supplied products.
- Installation experiences/problems encountered when installing products: things to watch out for; things to avoid.

All requests to be added to or deleted from this list, problems, questions, etc., should be sent to Info%Bitnic.BITNET@CUNYVM.CUNY.EDU.

Coordinator: <Info%Bitnic.BITNET@CUNYVM.CUNY.EDU>

CYBSYS-L@BINGVAXU.CC.BINGHAMTON.EDU
CYBSYS-L%BINGVMB.BITNET@CUNYVM.CUNY.EDU
CYBSYS-L@BINGVMB.BITNET

The Cybernetics and Systems mailing list is an open list serving those working in or just interested in the interdisciplinary fields of Systems Science, Cybernetics, and related fields (e.g. General Systems Theory, Complex Systems Theory, Dynamic Systems Theory, Computer Modeling and Simulation, Network Theory, Self-Organizing Systems Theory, Information Theory, Fuzzy Set Theory). The list is coordinated by members of the Systems Science department of the Watson School at SUNY-Binghamton, and is affiliated with the International Society for the Systems Sciences (ISSS) and the American Society for Cybernetics (ASC).

To subscribe, send the following command to LISTSERV@BINGVMB via mail or interactive message: SUB CYBSYS-L your_full_name where "your_full_name" is your name. For example: SUB CYBSYS-L Joan Doe Non-BitNet users can subscribe by sending the text: SUB CYBSYS-L your_full_name in the body of a message to LISTSERV@BINGVAXU.CC.BINGHAMTON.EDU or LISTSERV%BINGVMB.BITNET@CUNYVM.CUNY.EDU. To unsubscribe send the following command: UNSUB CYBSYS-L

Coordinator: Cliff Joslyn <vu0112@BINGVAXU.CC.BINGHAMTON.EDU>

D-ORAL-L on LISTSERV@NIHLIST or LISTSERV@LIST.NIH.GOV   [Last Update 11/92]

The Oral Microbiology/Immunology Interest Group is an international forum for discussions of problems facing scientists and clinicians that deal with human and mammalian oral microbiota. Microbiology discussions include the prevalence of, and diseases caused by oral microbiota, physiology and genetics of virulence factors, host response to pathogens and virulence factors, autoimmune oral diseases, and the effects of aging on immune response. This forum will also serve as a conduit between members of professional societies that have Oral Microbiology and Immunology interest Sections including the NIDR, IADR/AADR, ASM, FEMS, AAAS and other groups. Announcement of coming events and public pre-meeting organizational communications are encouraged.

To subscribe to D-ORAL-L, send the following command to LISTSERV@NIHLIST (or LISTSERV@LIST.NIH.GOV) via mail text or interactive message:

SUBSCRIBE D-ORAL-L your full name For example: SUBSCRIBE D-ORAL-L Jane Doe

   Owners: Dr. John Spitznagel <jks@giskard.uthscsa.edu>
          Cynthia Walczak   <caz@cu.nih.gov>

DANCE-L%HEARN.BITNET@CUNYVM.CUNY.EDU
DANCE-L on LISTSERV@HEARN

The purpose of DANCE-L is to create a global electronic forum and medium for information exchange between all who are interested in folkdance and traditional dance.

This list hopes to contribute to a better contact between dancers, dancing masters, choreographers, dance documentalists, choreologists, organizers of folkloristic festivals and performances, dance and folklore organizations, publishers of dance books, records, videotapes.

The information in this list should concentrate on: addresses of the above-mentioned groups, terminology, bibliographies, discographies, facts on historic and social backgrounds of folkdance, dance and choreography descriptions, costumes, announcements and reports of performances and festivals.

The list participants will be stimulated to actively engage and share responsibility in a number of projects:

- to establish an INTERNATIONAL FOLKDANCE DATABASE, by using a standard exchange record format, with the dance name as the main entry.
- to establish a FOLKDANCE DOCUMENTATION DATABASE, also by using a standard exchange record format, with book or article title as the main entry.
- to establish a MULTILINGUAL FOLKDANCE TERMINOLOGY DATABASE,also by using a standard exchange record format, with the English term as the main entry.

To subscribe to DANCE-L send a message or MAIL to one of the addresses above: SUB DANCE-L your full name eg. SUB DANCE-L Ginger Rogers

Description of List

DASP-L on LISTSERV@CSEARN.BITNET

This is to annonce an electronic mailing list for the discussion of digital acoustic signal processing and related subjects. Topics include:

- Digital Signal Processing Techniques in Time and Frequency Domain,
- Advanced Spectral Analysis Methods,
- Applications of Neural Networks in Acoustics,
- Efficient Computational algorithms.

To subscribe, send e-mail or tell to LISTSERV@CSEARN.BITNET with the following command in the body or text:

subscribe DASP-L your_first_name your_surname

Coordinator: Frantisek Kadlec BITNET, EARN : FKADLEC@CSEARN Czech Technical University Prague, Czechoslovakia

DB2-L%AUVM.BITNET@VM1.NODAK.EDU

This list is intended to serve those interested in discussions of IBM's DB2 Data Base Product and any associated topics such as SQL and QMF.

Archives of DB2-L back issues can be listed by sending the command INDEX DB2-L to LISTSERV@AUVM.

To subscribe, send the following command to LISTSERV@AUVM: SUB DB2-L your_full_name where "your_full_name" is your name, not your login Id. For example: SUB DB2-L Joan Doe Non-BitNet users can subscribe by sending the above command in the text/body of a message to LISTSERV%AUVM.BITNET@VM1.NODAK.EDU.

Coordinator: Patty Burke <PBURKE%AUVM.BITNET@VM1.NODAK.EDU>

DBASE-L%TECMTYVM.BITNET@VM1.NODAK.EDU
DBASE-L@TECMTYVM.MTY.ITESM.MX
DBASE-L@TECMTYVM.BITNET

Mailing list dedicated to the use of the dBase language for manipulating databases. Emphasis will be given on comments of how to build and maintain working systems using any of the dialects of these languages (Clipper, Fox, dbase II, III, IV, etc). Users of the list are encouraged to participate on topics such as: transaction processing, system implementation on networks, concurrency, library construction, modular design, function design, etc. All the above topics will be treated under the light of the dBase language, so the focus will be on implementing algorithms using this language.

BitNet users can subscribe by issuing the following command: TELL LISTSERV AT TECMTYVM SUBSCRIBE DBASE-L Your_full_name Example: TELL LISTSERV AT TECMTYVM SUBSCRIBE DBASE-L Mary Doe or the equivalent for sending messages, if your operating system is not VM/SP. Non-BitNet users can join by sending a message to LISTSERV@TECMTYVM.MTY.ITESM.MX with the one-line command "SUBSCRIBE DBASE-L Your_full_name" in the body/text (*NOT* in the Subject: field).

Owner: Agustin Gonzalez Tuchmann <PL155880%TECMTYVM.BITNET@VM1.NODAK.EDU> <PL1559.0@TECMTYVM.BITNET> <PL155990@TECMTYVM.MTY9ITESM.MX>

DDTs-Users@BigBird.BU.EDU [Last Update 11/92]

The DDTs-Users mailing list is for discussions of issues related to the DDTs defect tracking sofware from QualTrak, including (but not limited to) software, methods, mechanisms, techniques, general usage tips, policies, bugs, and bug workarounds. It is intended primarily for DDTs administrators, but that does not necessarily preclude other topics.

To join the DDTs-Users mailing list, send the command

subscribe ddts-users

in the body of a message to "Majordomo@BigBird.BU.EDU". If you want to subscribe something other than the account the mail is coming from, then append that address to the "subscribe" command; for example, to subscribe "my-other-address":

subscribe ddts-users my-other-address@your.domain.net

The list is an open list; anyone may subscribe. I would like to discourage subscribing subsidiary redistribution points, because that makes administering the mailing list harder, but I do not forbid it. There is not yet either an FAQ list or a "digestified" version of the mailing list.

Submissions should be sent to "DDTs-Users@BigBird.BU.EDU". That address is a direct mail reflector; all messages sent to that address are immediately forwarded to every member of the mailing list, including the submitter. The mailing list is unmoderated.

All messages to the list are being archived, but no method has yet been provided for retrieving these archives.

If you encounter a problem subscribing or submitting messages to the mailing list, you may send e-mail to the mailing list manager. Include detailed information on what the problem is. If you get an error message, include that.

List Manager: Joe Wells <jbw@cs.bu.edu>

DEAD-FLAMES@VIRGINIA.EDU
Dead-Flames@UVAARPA.VIRGINIA.EDU
D-Flames@VIRGINIA (BitNet)
...!uunet!virginia!dead-flames (uucp)

Digest for fans of Grateful Dead music. The list is bidirectionally gatewayed with the USENET newsgroup rec.music.gdead. A digest is created and distributed at least once per day, more often if traffic warrants.

All requests to be added to or deleted from this list, problems, questions, etc., should be sent to Dead-Flames-Request@VIRGINIA.EDU or Dead-Flames-Request@UVAARPA.VIRGINIA.EDU (Internet), DF-Req@Virginia (BitNet), or ...!uunet!virginia!dead-flames-request (uucp).

Coordinator: Marc Rouleau <mer6g@VIRGINIA.EDU>

DEAD-HEADS@VIRGINIA.EDU
>   Dead-Heads@UVAARPA.VIRGINIA.EDU@* D-Heads@VIRGINIA (BitNet)
>   ...!uunet!virginia!dead-heads (uucp)

>   Mailing list for Grateful Dead music fans who don't have time to read Dead-Flames but want to hear about upcoming shows, ticket availability, ride-sharing, etc.

>   All requests to be added to or deleted from this list, problems, questions, etc., should be sent to Dead-Heads-Request@VIRGINIA.EDU or Dead-Heads-Request@UVAARPA.VIRGINIA.EDU (Internet), DH-Req@VIRGINIA (BitNet), or ...!uunet!virginia!dead-heads-request (uucp).

>   Coordinator: Marc Rouleau <mer6g@VIRGINIA.EDU>

dead-runners-society@utxvm.cc.utexas.edu   [Last Update 28-January-1992]
>   dead-runners-society@utxvm.bitnet

>   The Dead Runners Society, formerly on a private account, has moved to a listserv at the University of Texas.

>   The Dead Runners Society is a discussion group for runners of all levels and interests, from nature-lovers to competitors. We discuss everything from meditation to marathon training, and we tend to share the belief that there is something about running that goes beyond just the exercise or sport of it!

>   If you would like to subscribe or re-subscribe to the DRS, please send the command:

>   SUB DRS Your Name

>   to:

>   listserv@utxvm.cc.utexas.edu (Internet) or listserv@utxvm (BITNET)

>   This is a 'closed' list, which means that listserv will not accept your subscription right away, but will forward it to the list owner, who then will add you to the list.

>   The mail from this group also comes out in digest form, so that members who don't like getting a lot of mail can receive it in a daily dose. If you want the digest version then send a note to the list owner once you are added to the list.

>   Carpe Viam (Seize the Road),

>   Listowner: Chris Conn sascmc@unx.sas.com Austin, TX

decmcc@ralph.rtpnc.epa.gov   [Last Updated 28-January-92]
>   vmsnet.networks.management.decmcc (newsgroup)

>   The charter of this group is talking about anything to do with network management using the DEC Enterprise Management Architecture product-set named DECmcc. The newsgroup and the mailing list are gatewayed so that you can take your pick of how to participate. If you wish to subscribe to the mailing list, you can do so by sending a 1-line mail message to listserv@ralph.rtpnc.epa.gov. The body of the message should contain only the single line

>   subscribe decmcc FirstName SurName (Optional Additional Comments)

>   Note: To include special characters in your comments, please put "'" (single quote/apostrophe) on each end of the string. Your mail address is captured from the header of your registration request.

>   To receive more info about the listserver and how to talk to it, send a 1-line mail message to listserv@ralph.rtpnc.epa.gov with the body containing the single line

>   help

>   The subject field is ignored by the listserver when addressing it with requests.

>   After subscribing, to post to the mailing list send your messages to

decmcc@ralph.rtpnc.epa.gov

If you have the vmsnet.* distribution available on news, I would recommend that you follow the group there. The mailing list is primarily intended for those who don't have access to the vmsnet newsgroups.

Bob Boyd <rbn@ralph.rtpnc.epa.gov> 919-541-4441

DECNEWS on LISTSERV@UBVM   [Last Updated 1/92]
        or LISTSERV@UBVM.CC.BUFFALO.EDU

DECNEWS is a new list for people interested in receiving a monthly electronic newsletter from Digital Equipment Corporation's Education/Science Business Unit. The newsletter's purpose is to provide a single, compact source of information about Digital to users in educational institutions and research organizations. Content includes brief announcements of new products, new third-party applications available on Digital platforms, special programs and services for education users (e.g. TEI), resources, and new installations or innovations from Digital's education/science customers.

Items will be brief, and pointers will be given on how to obtain more background information over the network if interested. The conference is a moderated list, and only the monthly newsletter will be posted, plus an occasional special announcement. Readers' responses will be directed to the newsletter's editor.

Archives of DECNEWS and related files are stored in the DECNEWS FILELIST. To receive a list of files send the command INDEX DECNEWS to LISTSERV@UBVM or LISTSERV@UBVM.CC.BUFFALO.EDU as the first line in the body of a mail message (NOT the Subject: line).

To subscribe to DECNEWS, send the command SUB DECNEWS your name to LISTSERV@UBVM or LISTSERV@UBVM.CC.BUFFALO.EDU via a mail message (again, as the first line in the body of the mail, NOT the Subject).

For example: SUB DECNEWS Joe Shmoe

DECNEWS is also gatewayed into the bit.listserv.decnews news group of USENET News so if you have access to news reading software, you should read this list there to reduce unnecessary network traffic.

Owner: Mary Hoffmann <hoffmann@mr4dec.enet.dec.com>

DECRDB-L@CCVM.SUNYSB.EDU   [Last Updated 12-October-1991]

A list named DECRDB-L@SBCCVM has been started for those interested in Digital Equipment Corporation's Relational Database products.

This purpose of this list is to discuss any issue related to Rdb or any associated software and competing products. This may include but is not limited to any problems/solutions/hints/suggestions/useful programs/etc. Although this is list is intended as a user forum, Individuals from DEC and other Relational Database vendors are also welcome and are encouraged to become members and participate in the discussion. The only restriction is that imposed by BITNET: Advertisements are not permitted.

To join the list, send a mail message to LISTSERV@SBCCVM.BITNET or LISTSERV@CCVM.SUNYSB.EDU with the text containing the command:

SUB DECRDB-L yourfirstname yourlastname

Owner: Sanjay Kapur |Internet: Sanjay.Kapur@sunysb.edu Systems Staff, Computing Services, |Bitnet: SKAPUR@USB State University of New York, |SPAN/HEPnet: 44132::SKAPUR Stony Brook, NY 11794-2400 |Phone:(516)632-8029, FAX:(516)632-8046

DEOS-L on LISTSERV@PSUVM.BITNET   [Last Updated 12-October-1991]
        or LISTSERV@PSUVM.PSU.EDU

The American Center for the Study of Distance Education at Pennsylvania State University have now decided to open DEOS-L, an international discussion forum for distance education.

Initially, the intention is to facilitate discussion of some of the issues presented in DEOSNEWS. We hope to promote communication among distance educators, and to disseminate information and requests about distance education around the world.

DEOS-L will be open for everyone who wants to subscribe, and all subscribers may post information to the list. However, to enhance the quality of DEOS-L, we have decided to review the notes posted.

To subscribe to DEOS-L, just post the following command to LISTSERV@PSUVM or LISTSERV@PSUVM.PSU.EDU: SUBSCRIBE DEOS-L Your Full Name

The following are the titles of the first articles posted in DEOSNEWS:

#1   The American Center for Study of Distance Education
#2   GO MEEC! A Goal Oriented Method for Establishment of an Electronic College
#3   Audio-Conferencing in Graduate Education: A Case Study
#4   Abstracts from the American Journal of Distance Education 1987
#5   The ICDL Database for Distance Education
#6   Bibliography on Computer Mediated Communication in Distance Education
#7   Computer-Assisted Language Learning at a Distance: An International Survey
#8   Abstracts from the American Journal of Distance Education 1988
#9   China's Network of Radio and Television Universities
#10 Computer-Mediated Communication and Distance Education Around the world
#11 New Accessions List 1991, No. 2.
#12 Abstracts from the American Journal of Distance Education 1989
#13 Interview with Reidar Roll, Secretary General of the International Council for Distance Education
#14 Innovative Computer Conferencing Courses
#15 Features of Distance Education in Finland
#16 Abstracts from the American Journal of Distance Education 1990

To subscribe to DEOSNEWS, just post the following command to LISTSERV@PSUVM or LISTSERV@PSUVM.PSU.EDU: SUBSCRIBE DEOSNEWS Your Full Name"

DERYNI-L on MAIL-SERVER@mintir.new-orleans.la.us   [Last Update 9/92]

DERYNI-L is a mailing list for fans of Katherine Kurtz' novels set in the Deryni universe, along with her other works.

This list is a return of the list I had started before experiencing major hardware problems with the system forcing me to close the site for some time. Now that we've returned with new hardware and in a new domain, along with an automated mail-server, it's time to re-start the list.

To subscribe to DERYNI-L, send the following command to MAIL-SERVER@mintir.new-orleans.la.us:

SUBSCRIBE DERYNI-L

Owner: Edward J. Branley <elendil@mintir.new-orleans.la.us>

DERRIDA@CFRVM.BITNET   [Last Updated 12-October-1991]

A list devoted to a discussion of Jacques Derrida and deconstruction. To subscribe, send a one line message to listserv@cfrvm.bitnet

subscribe derrida your full name

If I can be of any assistance, please contact me.

Owner: David L Erben dqfacaa@cfrvm.bitnet

dqfacaa@cfrvm.cfr.usf.edu

DEVEL-L@AUVM [Last Updated 12-October-1991]
DEVEL-L@AUVM.AMERICAN.EDU

A public discussion list for all persons interested in technology transfer in international development. The list is sponsored by Volunteers in Technical Assistance (VITA), a private, nonprofit, voluntary organization for humanitarian assistance established in 1959. Subscribers discuss their shared interests in the list's subject, which can include current news, new books, computers and communications in development, other new technologies, personal experiences, entrepreneurship, relations between technology and the amelioration of poverty in Third World countries, projects, organizations, and educational programs, but need not be restricted to these topics. Subscribers automatically receive VITA's monthly newsletter.

To subscribe, send mail text or interactive message to LISTSERV@AUVM or LISTSERV@AUVM.AUVM.EDU that reads as follows: SUB DEVEL-L <your full name> You may leave the list at any time by sending a "SIGNOFF DEVEL-L" command to LISTSERV@AUVM. To post a message to all subscribers, use the address DEVEL-L@AUVM.

For editorial correspondence on the newsletter or messages to VITA, use the address VITA@GMUVAX; please don't use it for other purposes.

Coordinator: R. R. Ronkin, VITA Volunteer, VITA@GMUVAX.

DIABETIC on LISTSERV@PCCVM

A forum for the open discussion of diabetic concerns by the people directly involved - the diabetic patient. I take this move because my wife is also a diabetic with advanced complications. I feel that an open forum for those most affected that is free from criticism is sorely needed.

To subscribe to this list send a message or MAIL to LISTSERV@PCCVM on BITNET with the content containing the command:

SUBSCRIBE DIABETIC your full name

```
R N Hathhorn, VM Systems Support    |  Portland Community College
Computer Services Department         |  P. O. Box 19000
Sylvania Campus:  CCB27c             |  12000 S. W. 49th Ave.
(503) 244-6111  ext. 4705            |  Portland Oregon  97219
SYSMAINT@PCCVM.Bitnet
```

DIARRHOE on LISTSERV@SEARN or LISTSERV@SEARN.SUNET.SE

DIARRHOE is a mailing list for information exchange and discussions on all aspects related to diseases, disorders, and chemicals which cause diarrhoea in humans and animals.

To become a member send mail (or message on BITNET) to listserv@searn (bitnet) or listserv@searn.sunet.se (internet) with the following command in the BODY: SUBSCRIBE DIARRHOE your full name

To send messages to all other members of the group: address your message to: diarrhoe@searn (bitnet) or diarrhoe@searn.sunet.se (internet)

Owner: Eng-leong Foo Karolinska Institute, Stockholm, Sweden Unesco Microbial Resources Center & Dept of Bacteriology email: eng-leong_foo_mircen-ki%micforum@mica.mic.ki.se

dibug@avogadro.barnard.columbia.edu

A mailing list has been started for users of Biosym Technologies, Inc. software. This includes the following products:

InsightII: visualization and manipulation of biological macromolecules
Discover: molecular mechanics, molecular dynamics, E. minimization

Dmol: LDF quantum chemistry calculations
Homology: protein model-building tool
Delphi: electrostatic-field calculations on biological macromolecules
Polymer: calculations on polymer chains

This list is not run by Biosym; however, several of their in-house people subscribe, and may contribute from time to time.

To subscribe (or, later, to unsubscribe, if you wish!) send electronic mail containing your full name and affiliation to: dibug-request@avogadro.barnard.columbia.edu

If you wish some path other than what appears on the "From:" line to be your offical dibug address, say so in the body of your epistle. Once I get it and add you, I'll send you the Official Introduction, receipt of which will indicate that I hear you and you hear me.

To post to the list, send mail to: dibug@avogadro.barnard.columbia.edu

Oh, yes: this list is undigested and unmoderated. In fact, it is barely coordinated! However, I have agreed to take on that onorous task. If you have reason to believe that email isn't getting through, you can write to me personally as shenkinb@avogadro.barnard.columbia.edu (first choice), or shenkin@cunixf.cc.columbia.edu (second choice), or as shenkin@cunixf.BITNET (way down on the list).

Finally a disclaimer. DIBUG stands for "Discover Insight Biosym Users' Group." Any resemblance to any other term commonly in use among the computationally literate is purely coincidental. :-)

Owner:

Peter S. Shenkin, Department of Chemistry
Barnard College, New York, NY 10027
(212)854-1418
shenkin@avogadro.barnard.columbia.edu   shenkin@cunixf.BITNET

digital-games-submissions@DIGITAL-GAMES.INTUITIVE.COM

Digest devoted to computer and video game reviews, with interested in just about any games that run on computers, including IBM PC, Atari, Amiga, Macintosh, Apple II and Unix computers, as well as video games for the Nintendo, Sega, NEC, Atari, and so on. It also covers games for the portable market (e.g. the Atari Lynx and Nintendo GameBoy).

This is a *REVIEWS ONLY* mailing list, with all submissions edited to fit into a common and consistent format. Discussion of the relative merits of different gaming computers, technical discussion of resolution required to display 3D graphics, and general flaming and hostility will be left to the many different forums appropriate for that type of discussion.

To subscribe to the digest, send your request to digital-games-request@Digital-Games.Intuitive.Com.

Coordinator: Dave Taylor <taylor@LIMBO.INTUITIVE.COM>
<limbo!taylor%limbo.intuitive.com@VM1.NODAK.EDU>

DIPL-L@MITVMA   [Last Update 9/92]
DIPL-L@mitvma.mit.edu

Mailing list dedicated to the game Diplomacy as played via electronic mail, especially via the Diplomacy Adjudicator (the judge)

BITNET users can subscribe by sending the message SUBSCRIBE DIPL-L your_full_name to LISTSERV@MITVMA.BITNET

Internet users send SUBSCRIBE DIPL-L your_full_name in the BODY of a mail message to LISTSERV@mitvma.mit.edu

For more information about the judge, send the message *help* to the judge. (judge@u.washington.edu)

Owner: Nicholas Fitzpatrick nick@sunburn.waterloo.edu
nick@sunburn.uwaterloo.ca

Direct-L on LISTSERV@uafsysb
or LISTSERV@uafsysb.uark.edu

The DIRECT-L list was formed to provide a forum for discussions of the software program MacroMind Director for the Macintosh. Possible discussion topics include but are not limited to:

Programming in Lingo
Hardware configurations
Use with other software packages
Video sources, techniques, methods
Kiosk development
Device drivers

This will be an unmoderated list with archives. Archives of DIRECT-L will be stored in the DIRECT-L FILELIST. To receive a list of files send the command INDEX DIRECT-L to LISTSERV@UAFSYSB

To subscribe to DIRECT-L, send the following command to LISTSERV@UAFSYSB via mail text or interactive message:

SUBSCRIBE DIRECT-L Your_full_name

where "Your_full_name" is your name. For example:

SUBSCRIBE DIRECT-L Rita Someone

Owner: CB Lih <CBLIH@UAFSYSB>

DISARM-L%ALBNYVM1.BITNET@CORNELLC.CCS.CORNELL.EDU

DISARM-L provides discussions of military and political strategy, technology, sociology, and popular peace activism involved in accelerating disarmament of nuclear, conventional ,chemical and biological weapons. Also discussion of other destabilizing actions such as suprpower intervention and exploitation of the 3rd world. Soviet, WTO, European, Asiatic and Latin American participants welcomed! Also see DISARM-D for a monthly-Digest form of the list.

Those with interactive BITNET communication can subscribe and also access the monthly logs by issuing the command: TELL LISTSERV@ALBNYVM1 INDEX DISARM-L and the command: TELL LISTSERV@ALBNYVM1 GET DISARM-L LOGyymm Those without interactive BitNet access should send requests to the Moderator by E-mail.

Moderator: Donald Parsons <DFP10%ALBNYVM1.BITNET@CORNELLC.CCS.CORNELL.EDU>

DISARM-D%ALBNYVM1.BITNET@CORNELLC.CCS.CORNELL.EDU

The list that stores and distributes the monthly digests. Interactive users can obtain these directly as disarm-d logyymm. Also see DISARM-L for an immediate-redistribution (mailing list) form of the Digest.

Those with interactive BITNET communication can subscribe and also access the monthly logs by issuing the command: TELL LISTSERV@ALBNYVM1 INDEX DISARM-D and the command: TELL LISTSERV@ALBNYVM1 GET DISARM-D LOGyymm Those without interactive BitNet access should send requests to the Moderator by E-mail.

Moderator: Donald Parsons <DFP10%ALBNYVM1.BITNET@CORNELLC.CCS.CORNELL.EDU>

DISASTER RESEARCH <myers_mf@CUBLDR.COLORADO.EDU>
<myers_mf%CUBLDR@COLORADO> (BitNet)

The Disaster Research Center at the University of Delaware moderates an electronic teleconference entitled DISASTER RESEARCH. The teleconference is designed to enable sociologists and other scholars to exchange information and share expertise in areas of common research interest. The discussion groups take on a sociological approach, as they look at human social behavior within organizations and communities during times of disaster. Sub-areas include:

- Interactive newsletter: latest developments in disaster research field.
- Hotline: notification network to dispatch teams to large-scale community emergencies, and for coordination between research units.
- Bulletin board: upcoming reports & publications, conferences, new database releases, resources for visitors.
- Research: discussion groups, messages from visiting faculty, inter-library communication to track fugitive disaster-related literature.
- Education: interdisciplinary liaison with scholars primarily involved in other fields, contact with professionals in corporate and government offices work in emergency management.

The actual messages are transmitted via a special distributed server called GRAND (GRAND@UDACSVM) with peers located worldwide. The system operates 24 hours per day and contributions may be made via RFC822 mail, PUNCH format, class M. Copies of previous postings are available on request from the server.

All requests to be added to or deleted from this list, problems, questions, etc., should be sent to the Coordinators.

Coordinators: Mary Fran Myers <myers_mf@CUBLDR.COLORADO.EDU>
David Butler <myers_mf%CUBLDR@COLORADO> (BitNet)

DISC-L on listserv@sendit.nodak.edu

DISCOVERY COMMUNICATIONS ON-LINE LISTINGS

Discovery Communications has establised a "listserv" to make available advanced listings and curriculum material for educational programming on The Discovery Channel and The Learning Channel.

The listserv originates from SENDIT, NoDak's K-12 Telcom Network, and sends listings automatically via the Internet to list subscribers. These listings may be re-posted on educational computer networks as long as educators are _NOT_ charged for access.

Subscribing to this listserv is FREE and only requires access to Internet and an Internet address. The procedure for subscribing to this listserv is as follows: (The listserv below is NOT the same as the BITNET version by Eric Thomas) - send e-mail to:

listserv@sendit.nodak.edu

- the "subject" line can be left blank

- the body of the message should consist of the following:

subscribe disc-l YourFirstName YourLastName set disc-l mail ack

NOTE: l is a lower case L

- in a few minutes you should receive an e-mail message confirming that you have subscribed

- if you want a help file, send e-mail to:

listserv@sendit.nodak.edu

the message should contain only the word "help"

Owner: Gleason Sackmann sackman@sendit.NoDak.edu

DISSPLA%TAUNIVM.BITNET@VM1.NODAK.EDU

Mailing list for news and information exchange concerning DISSPLA. DISSPLA (Display Integrated Software System and Plotting LAnguage) is a high-level FORTRAN graphics subroutine library designed for programmers in engineering, science and business. The list is intended for users and maintainers of DISSPLA. Topics include programming hints, bugs and fixes, implementation on various operating systems and I/O devices.

To subscribe to the list send the command: SUB DISSPLA your_full_name (where your_full_name is your real name, not your userid/logonid) to LISTSERV@TAUNIVM.Bitnet either in an interactive message (TELL/SEND) or as the only line of text in the BODY of mail. Non-BitNet users can join by sending the SUB command in the text/body of a message to LISTSERV%TAUNIVM.BITNET@VM1.NODAK.EDU.

Coordinator: Zvika Bar-Deroma <AER7101%TECHNION.BITNET@VM1.NODAK.EDU>

DISTOBJ@HPLB.HPL.HP.COM
DISTOBJ@HPL.HP.CO.UK

An unmoderated list for discussing large scale distributed object systems.

If you are interested in joining the mailing list, please send mail using any of the addresses below. To help introduce each other, it would be nice if you could include something about what your interests are, and maybe something about what areas you are working in.

    Internet domain address: distobj-request@hplb.hpl.hp.com
    Old style arpa address: distobj-request%hplb@hplabs.hp.com
    USA usenet address: ...!hplabs!hplb!distobj-request
    UK usenet address: ...!mcvax!ukc!distobj-request@hpl.co.uk

Coordinator: Harry Barman <hjb@hplb.hpl.hp.com>

DITTO-L@AWIIMC12.BITNET   [Last Update 9/92]
DITTO-L@AWIIMC12.IMC.UniVie.AC.AT

Data Interfile Transfer, Testing and Operations Utility

DITTO-L is an international electronic forum for anyone interested in discussing the use of the IBM Data Interfile Transfer, Testing, and Operations utility (DITTO for VSE & VM, MVS/DITTO).

To subscribe send the command SUB DITTO-L full name in one of the following ways: a) from BITNET as interactive message to your nearest backbone LISTSERV or LISTSERV@AWIIMC12 b) from BITNET, Internet and connected networks in the BODY of a mail with your preferred mailbox in the From:-field to 1) your preferred backbone LISTSERV 2) LISTSERV@AWIIMC12 (BITNET) LISTSERV@AWIIMC12.IMC.UniVie.AC.AT (Internet) 3) DITTO-L-request@AWIIMC12.IMC.UniVie.AC.AT

DIVERS-L on LISTSERV@PSUVM.BITNET   [Last Update 9/92]
or LISTSERV@PSUVM.PSU.EDU

Link up all persons with diversity concerns for exchange of information. We are interested in persons of all backgrounds, including African American, Asian Pacific American, Hispanic/Latino American, Alaskan Native/American Indian...Caucasian American, Foreign (nonimigrant), including genders. In terms of particular academic needs, we would like to have representative ethnic inputs into various academic programs.

While the founders of the list are in the architectural area, they intend the list to be general. Specific uses could be in terms of studio design problems, lecturers, exhibits, etc. We would hope that we could enrich our studies in this way rather than focusing on any particular group. We believe that every culture in America has something of value to contribute to the whole of American culture.

To subscribe to the DIVERS-L list send e-mail to LISTSERV@PSUVM on BITNET or LISTSERV@PSUVM.PSU.EDU with the BODY of the mail containing the command:

SUB DIVERS-L your full name

Eg. SUB DIVERS-L Eldridge Franklin

Owner: Howard Lawrence <HRL@PSUARCH.BITNET>

DJ-L%NDSUVM1.BITNET@VM1.NODAK.EDU

Mailing list for campus radio DJ's, station managers, etc., to discuss various topics concerning college radio today, including federal and campus regulations, station policy discussions, equipment reviews, etc. (but not MUSIC reviews, there is a separate list for that).

BitNet users may subscribe to the list by sending the following command to LISTSERV@NDSUVM1: SUB DJ-L Your full name where "Your full name" is your real name, not your login Id. Not-BitNet users can join by sending the above command as the only line in the text/body of a message to LISTSERV@VM1.NODAK.EDU.

Coordinator: Andrew Tabar <ARTABAR%MTUS5.BITNET@VM1.NODAK.EDU>

DKB-L on LISTSERV@TREARN.BITNET DKB Ray Tracer
DKBGUI on LISTSERV@TREARN.BITNET DKB Graphical User Interface
DKBPORT on LISTSERV@TREARN.BITNET DKB Ray Tracer Porting

This list concentrates on the DKB Ray Tracer that is developped by David Buck. We also intend to archive the various versions of this software and art work created with this package.

To join, issue: SUB DKB-L Firstname Lastname to LISTSERV@TREARN

Greetings.. Now that our general-purpose DKB-L is working well, I'd like to announce two more discussion lists, DKBGUI and DKBPORT@TREARN.BITNET

DKBGUI is designated to work on a graphical interface for DKB, and DKBPORT is concerned about porting DKB Ray Tracer to other platforms.

to join either, send: SUB listname Your_Full_Name (where "listname" is either DKBGUI or DKBPORT)

to LISTSERV@TREARN.BITNET in the body of a mail message. You may put more than one command in your mail file, for example to subscribe to both lists. Put these commands on separate lines in your mail message.

Mailings for the list must go to either DKBGUI@TREARN.BITNET or, DKBPORT@TREARN.BITNET.

Regards, -turgut <TURGUT@TREARN.BITNET>

Donosy (przemek@ndcvx.cc.nd.edu)

A mailing list for distribution of a news bulletin from Poland. It is a volunteer effort, sent 5 days a week from Warsaw, summarizing the events there. It is also translated into English here, and I maintain the English edition mailing list as well.

DOROTHYL on LISTSERV@KENTVM   [Last Updated 12-October-1991]
or LISTSERV@KENTVM.KENT.EDU

DOROTHYL is a discussion and idea list for lovers of the mystery genre. It was concocted by a group of women librarians at a July 1991 Washington, D.C. meeting of the Association of Research Libraries and named in in honor of one of the great women mystery writers of the century. Agatha Christie and Josephine Tey were strong contenders, but Dorothy L. Sayers had a LISTSERV-blessed middle initial. Although there was serious discussion about limiting DOROTHY to women particpants and it would be entertaining to identify impostors (no doubt men would sneak on with anonymous ID@node, to join in DOROTHY's energizing discussion), the organizers opted for the widest possible number of serious participants.

Tenets of DOROTHYL:

  -Everyone is welcome.

-Those who wish to adopt the name of a mystery character, may use
that name in postings.
-The participants WILL have fun.

Some suitable subjects for posting are:

- Announcements of forthcoming books and previews.
- Reviews, criticisms, comments, and appreciations of mysteries (books, plays, films).
- Great mystery bookshops.
- Awards. It can take a long time to learn which are the annual prizewinners. DOROTHYL may consider posting these as files.
- Mysterious events. Mystery travels, mystery walks in cities, mysteries of life.
- Ideas for happenings, perhaps an evening of mystery readings at ALA or ARL or MLA?
- An electronic mystery, with clues (apples, perhaps red ones of the Macintosh variety?), villains (the mailer-Daemon?), red herrings (byte-marks?), heroines, detectives -- the potential is as unlimited as the world of networking.

At the outset, the list will be un-moderated (self-monitored).

Everyone who joins ought to consider contacting her (his) favorite mystery author and inviting her (him) to join this list. Since many mystery writers are academics, this could be a very fruitful and exciting chase.

Subscription Instructions:

To subscribe from a Bitnet account send an interactive or e-mail message addressed to Listserv@kentvm. From the Internet send mail to listserv@kentvm.kent.edu.

If you send e-mail leave the subject line blank. The text of the message must be:

Sub DOROTHYL Yourfirstname Yourlastname

If you have questions please contact the owners. If you need to know how to send e-mail or interactive messages contact your local computer services people for assistance with your local system.

Yours for networked thrills, the Owners:

Harriet Vane (Harriet@e-math.ams.com) Kinky X.Y.Z Friedman (Tey@e-math.ams.com)

dosip-list@terminus.umd.edu MD-DOS/IP Package

Welcome to the MD-DOS/IP Mailing List! Thanks to the continuing efforts of Tracy Logan of Lafayette there is now an official place for users and administrators to discuss their successes and failures using the University of Maryland and IBM's MD-DOS/IP package.

I am one of the developers of DOS/IP and will be the administrator of this mailing list. It will be unmoderated. To send mail to the list, use the following id: dosip-list@terminus.umd.edu and requests to be added to the list should be addressed to: dosip-request@terminus.umd.edu.

If you anticipate many users at your site being interested in being part of this list, please arrange for a local mail reflector / exploder.

All articles posted on this list are being archived here at Maryland. The archive is available via anonymous ftp from terminus.umd.edu and is in the file dosip-list in the anonymous root directory.

The developers of DOS/IP here at the University of Maryland will be reading this list and may address concerns here as suits their individual ability and inclination.

List Owner: Billy E. Taylor, Jr. (301) 403-4611 Comp Sci Ctr, U of MD billy@terminus.umd edu College Pk, MD 20842

DRUGABUS@UMAB.UMD.EDU
DRUGABUS@UMAB.BITNET

DRUGABUS%UMAB.BITNET@VM1.NODAK.EDU

A forum for issues related to community drug abuse education and the epidemiology and study of drug abuse. It is run by the Office of Substance Abuse Studies at the University of Maryland at Baltimore.

VM BitNet users can subscribe with the command: TELL LISTSERV AT UMAB SUBSCRIBE DRUGABUS your name Other BitNet and Internet users ca subscribe by sending a request to the Coordinator or directly to the list address.

> Coordinator: Treat Tschirgi <TTSCHIRG@UMAB.UMD.EDU>
>   <TTSCHIRG@UMAB.BITNET>
>   <TTSCHIRG%UMAB.BITNET@VM1.NODAK.EDU>

DSA-LGB@midway.uchicago.edu   [Last Updated 12-October-1991]

Contact: DSA-LGB-request@midway.uchicago.edu

DSA-LGB is a mailing list for members of the Lesbian/ Gay/Bisexual Commission of the Democratic Socialists of America, and for other people interested in discussing connections between sexual identity and the democratic socialist movement in the U.S. and other nations. The list is neither archived nor moderated.

DTP-L on LISTSERV@YALEVM.BITNET

Many users throughout internet, bitnet & elsewhere have expressed an interest in starting a digest to exchange information on desktop publishing in general, and on the subtleties and complexities of specific programs, including, but not limited to, Quark Xpress, Aldus PageMaker and FreeHand, Adobe Illustrator, Ventura Publisher, Framemaker, Interleaf, and Fontographer. Please note that these would not be system level discussions; they would deal more at the user-level. Also, technical discussions of PostScript for its own sake (and not how it related to these programs) would be covered in the PostScript forums and digests.

Caveats aside, every user of these and other programs has discovered some excellent work-arounds, irritating problems, or elegant solutions. These could be shared for the benefit of all. I have also set up contacts with Quark, and I'm receiving quick shipment of Zappers and other software to be available to list members and the net_community at large. Hopefully similiar agreements can be made with other publishers.

Some emphasis will be placed on use of service bureaus and medium- to high-resolution output devices (Linotronics, Agfas, Varitypers, etc.) without becoming overly technical.

The list organizers (myself and Jeff Wasilko of RIT) also have conventional typesetting backgrounds, and we manage service bureaus at our schools.

The list is called DTP-L. To subscribe, execute the CMS command: tell listserv@yalevm subscribe DTP-L firstname middleinit lastname

Or send a mail to listserv@yalevm (or listserv@yalevm.ycc.yale.edu) which contains as its first & only line (substitute your name for firstname, etc.):

subscribe dtp-l firstname middleinit lastname

Because this is a digest, items of interest should NOT be sent to the listserver for efficiency's sake. Send submissions to:

glenn_fleishman@yccatsmtp.ycc.yale.edu or to jjwcmp@ultb.isc.rit.edu

These submissions will be edited & compiled. When collected items reach 30K they will be distributed through the listserver mechanism to all subscribers.

If you cannot subscribe through conventional means, please contact Glenn Fleishman at the above address. Put "subscription" in the subject field of the memo.

Owners: Jeff Wasilko, Rochester Institute of Technology Communications Dept.
Glenn Fleishman, Yale University Printing Service

DTK-L@SHSU.BITNET

DTK-L is a list to provide an unmoderated environment where issues, questions, comments, ideas, and uses of Digital's DECTalk can be discussed.

The explicit purpose of DTK-L is to provide timely interchange between subscribers, to provide a forum where interesting questions can be addressed within the context of interactive exchange between many individuals, to discuss the evolution and application of DECTalk. The discussions of DTK-L will be archived for reference. As is the case on all unmoderated lists, the discussion and topics are only limited by the participation and interest of its subscribers. Subscribers are welcome to take an active role by posting to DTK-L or an inactive role by monitoring the list.

To subscribe to DTK-L, please send a MAIL message to: LISTSERV@SHSU.BITNET The body of this MAIL message should be one line and contain the words: SUBSCRIBE DTK-L

LISTSERV@SHSU.BITNET is not supported by the conventional interactive VM-based LISTSERV, but is instead entirely MAIL oriented.

Questions regarding this announcement should be addressed to the List Owner: James Horn <HORN@SHSU.BITNET>

DYLANDOG@IGECUNIV.BITNET
DYLANDOG@IGECUNIV.CISI.UNIGE.IT

[Last Update 9/92]

A net fan Club dedicated to the famous (in Italy) horror comic Dylan Dog.

This list will also deal with the world of Horror fiction in general. You can send Infos, poems, stories, all that you like, but it must deal with Horror (so don't send the evening news!).

WARNING: the list should be in Italian, but it will accept mail in any language it is written. For any question, idea, etc. contact the listowner:

Davide Bianchini DAVIDE@IGECUNIV.BITNET

DYNA-L on LISTSERV@TAMVM1.BITNET

Discussion list about the mainframe spreadsheet DYNAPLAN, by Dynasoft Corp. Subscription is Open.

Owner:
Chris Barnes   x045cb@tamvm1   (BITNET)
(409) 845-8300   x045cb@tamvm1.tamu.edu (Internet)

DynSys-L%UNC.BITNET@CUNYVM.CUNY.EDU

The Dynamical System is a mailing list for the exchange of information among people working in ergodic theory and dynamical systems. Almost all kinds of contributions are welcome, especially:

Announcements of meetings	Conference reports
Abstracts	Illuminating comments
Open problems	Historical remarks
News items	Reviews
Address changes	Bibliographies
Examples	Work planned or in progress
Questions	Anecdotes, jokes, puzzles.

The list will be maintained by a list-server facility called NEWSERV, which acts as a userid at the BitNet node UNCVM1. To be added to or deleted from this list, see the following directions, or send a message to one of the Coordinators.

BitNet users can use the ADD command to add their name to a list:

For users at remote IBM/VM sites the following format is used: TELL NEWSERV AT UNCVM1 ADD DYNSYS-L username

At UTSO use the VMSG command send to userid NEWSERV, node UNCVM1, and a message of ADD DYNSYS-L username.

VAX/VMS sites running jnet version 2 use the ADD command like this: SEND NEWSERV@UNCVM1 ADD DYNSYS-L username

BitNet users with other environments can contact their local user services group for assistance. Users without interactive messaging capability, or non-BitNet users can send a request to ULTIMA@UNCVM1 (ULTIMA%UNC.BITNET@CUNYVM.CUNY.EDU) or to one of the list Coordinators to have their names added to the list.

The DROP command is used to remove a name from a list:

For remote IBM/VM sites, the DROP command is used like this: TELL NEWSERV AT UNCVM1 DROP DYNSYS-L

At UTSO use the VMSG command send to userid NEWSERV, node UNCVM1, and a message of DROP DYNSYS-L.

VAX/VMS sites with jnet version 2 can use this command: SEND NEWSERV@UNCVM1 DROP DYNSYS-L

> Coordinators: Karl Petersen <UNCKEP%UNC.BITNET@CUNYVM.CUNY.EDU>
> Doug Lind <lind@ENTROPY.MS.WASHINGTON.EDU>

E-EUROPE on LISTSERV@NCSUVM.BITNET   [Last Update 28-January-1992]
or LISTSERV@NCSUVM.CC.NCSU.EDU

E-EUROPE is the new electronic communications network for doing business in Eastern Europe countries (including the countries of the former Soviet Union). Its purpose is to help these countries in their transition to market economies. It will link business persons in Western Europe-Asia-North America with those in Eastern Europe.

E-EUROPE allows transmission of electronic mail and files worldwide (via Bitnet, Internet, Junet, Compuserve, MCI Mail, etc.). Subscription is free and open to anyone who can access a BITNET or INTERNET electronic address. While the E-EUROPE is located on a mainframe computer, anyone with a personal computer and modem may gain access.

E-EUROPE provides information exchange via e-mail and also provides document/file transfers between E-EUROPE subscribers. A subscriber is anyone who has requested an E-EUROPE subscription by sending a message to the communications management software (called LISTSERV) located on the mainframe computer at North Carolina State University, USA. A subscriber also has the option of concealing their name and node address from public scrutiny.

A. Present Activities of E-EUROPE

> 1. E-mail Once a user subscribes to E-EUROPE, (s)he may send mail to the list for distribution to all its members. All members of the mailing list will receive a copy of each piece of mail sent to the list. All of the mail that is received and redistributed by the list is cataloged and stored in a database that can be searched or retrieved by individuals with access to E-EUROPE.
> In order to prevent "rapid-fire" random e-mail transmissions, all messages are relayed to the E-EUROPE editor for a once-daily (maximum) batch mail release. In addition, each subscriber may disable the automatic E-EUROPE e-mail transmission to their site and download logfiles of each month's traffic.
> 2. E-EUROPE Filelist Datafiles will be available for downloading to subscribers. The objective is to develop a clearinghouse of information on doing business with Eastern European countries.

3. Potential/Future Activities

    a) electronic business newsletter
    b) electronic user directories
    c) bibliographies of current business research
    d) seeking interested parties for business activities (exports,
      imports, or direct investment)
    e) job bank

B. Subscription and File Downloads: To subscribe to E-EUROPE send E-mail to LISTSERV@NCSUVM or LISTSERV@NCSUVM.CC.NCSU.EDU with the body containing the command

SUB E-EUROPE yourfirstname yourlastname

To download a file, send E-mail to the LISTSERV using the GET command. E.g. GET filename filetype E-EUROPE

For example, GET E-EUROPE INTRO E-EUROPE

Direct any questions to the list editor:
James W. Reese, E-EUROPE Editor
Associate Professor of Economics
University of South Carolina, Spartanburg
Spartanburg, SC 29303 USA
Tel/Fax: 803-472-4527
R505040@UNIVSCVM   (BITNET)
or R505040@UNIVSCVM.CSD.SCAROLINA.EDU   (INTERNET)

E-HUG on LISTSERV@DARTCMS1.BITNET

The list E-HUG@DARTCMS1 provides for distribution of the Electronic Hebrew Users Newsletter. The newsletter is the successor to the print publication, "Hebrew Users Group Newsletter" which was edited by Jack Love, and emanated from the Berkeley Hillel Foundation through 1989.

This incarnation is electronic-only, and is mandated, like the original, to cover all things relating to use of Hebrew, Yiddish, Judesmo, and Aramaic on computers. It is released as time permits and information demands, currently every 1-2 weeks. This newsletter is dedicated to the proposition that computers, to be useful, must be usable to people working in all languages, at the convenience of those users. In that spirit, we print all questions pertaining to use of the Hebrew alphabet on computers and answer all those that we can. We encourage discussion on all levels of computer facility--from new users looking for software or Hebrew-related resources (educational, graphic, or otherwise), to discussions by developers on how the software should work (when it works :-)). We also do our best to report on new software (or updates) of interest and to serve as a general news source to the field.

The list is maintained via LISTSERV and subscription may be obtained by the usual mechanism of sending the command SUB E-HUG yourfirstname yourlastname to LISTSERV@DARTCMS1.

Questions may be directed to the list owner, Ari Davidow <well!ari@apple.com>. Archives may be obtained from LISTSERV@DARTCMS1 using the SEND command and currently consist of E-HUG 91-00001 to E-HUG 91-00011.

EARLYM-L@AEARN.BITNET or   [Last Updated 12-October-1991]
EARLYM-L@AEARN.EDVZ.UNI-LINZ.AC.AT

EARLYM-L and the newsgroup rec.music.early are linked. They were created to provide a forum for exchange of news and views about

    1. Medieval, renaissance and baroque music (sacred and secular - both 'art' and 'folk')
      derived as part of European culture, its researchers, performers, instruments,

instrument-makers, festivals, concerts and societies, records, song texts and translations, machine-readable notations of (early) music;

2. Authenticity in music of (these and) later periods, e.g. classical and romantic.

To subscribe to EARLYM-L, send the command: SUB EARLYM-L your_full_name to LISTSERV@AEARN e.g. SUB EARLYM-L "Tylman Susato" To have your name removed from the EARLYM-L subscriber list, send: SIGNOFF EARLYM-L To obtain a listing of all files and archives available send: INDEX EARLYM-L

Commands can be sent to LISTSERV@AEARN either as interactive messages or in e-mail (one command per line in the body of the e-mail message).

Coordinator: Gerhard Gonter <GONTER@AWIWUW11.BITNET> or <gonter@awiwuw11.wu-wien.ac.at>

EBCBBUL%HDETUD1.BITNET@VM1.NODAK.EDU

EBCBBUL is short for EBCB BULletin board, a facet of the European Bank of Computer Programs in Biotechnology (EBCB). EBCB is a non-profit making organization mainly funded by the European Community (EC). The main goal of EBCB is to stimulate and facilitate the use of computers in biotechnological training and research in Europe. EBCBBUL will not only promote user/user communication, but will also provide users with up to date information (e.g. about courses/congresses).

Items accepted for the bulletin board will be distributed via electronic mail (e-mail) to all participants and will also be retained for future reference.

EBCBBUL is public, and anyone with access to EARN can participate. Before you gain access to EBCBBUL through EARN or a related system, however, you must issue one of the following commands:

For EARN nodes operating with VM/CMS systems type the following: TELL LISTSERV AT HDETUD1 SUBSCRIBE EBCBBUL (followed by your name)

For EARN nodes operating with VAX/VMS systems type the following: SEND LISTSERV @ HDETUD1 SUBSCRIBE EBCBBUL (followed by your name)

On other systems send mail to LISTSERV@HDETUD1 (or LISTSERV@HDETUD1.TUDELFT.NL, or for Internet users LISTSERV%HDETUD1.BITNET@VM1.NODAK.EDU) with the body/text of the mail containing the command: SUB EBCBBUL yourfirstname yourlastname

As soon as your request for access has been accepted, you will receive, by e-mail, confirmation of this fact. Because of limitations imposed by e-mail (traffic volume etc.) this may take several hours. After that you will be able to search EBCBBUL using LDBASE or LSVTALK (these are programmes, available within the EARN node, that make interactive searching possible).

Coordinator: Arie Braat <RCSTBRA%HDETUD1.TUDELFT.NL@VM1.NODAK.EDU>
<RCSTBRA@HDETUD1.TUDELFT.NL>
<EBCBBUL%HDETUD1.BITNET>

EC on LISTSERV@IndyCMS.BITNET   [Last Updated 28-January-1992]
or LISTSERV@IndyCMS.IUPUI.Edu

EC (European Community) is dedicated to discussion of the European Community, and is open to all interested persons.

To subscribe send mail to LISTSERV@INDYCMS.BITNET or on the Internet to LISTSERV@IndyCMS.IUPUI.EDU with the following command in the body:

SUB EC yourfirstname yourlastname

List owner/coordinator: John B Harlan IJBH200@IndyVAX (CREN) IJBH200@IndyVAX.IUPUI.Edu (Internet)

ecixfiles@igc.org

The Energy and Climate Information Exchange File Distribution Service

The Energy and Climate Information Exchange (ECIX) is a project of EcoNet aimed at educating the environmental community and the general public on the potential of energy efficiency and renewable energy to reduce the use of fossil fuels and their contribution to climate change.

ECIX now offers as a public service the distribution of files pertaining to energy and climate change. We accept files electronically submitted by those who wish to share information, advertise the existence of the files, and electronically mail files to those who request them.

As an information provider, your shared files will reach a large audience. We advertise our list of available files on EcoNet, several Internet newsgroups, and several LISTSERV distribution lists. EcoNet is a member of an international association of networks, so your information will potentially reach people in over 90 countries. In addition, we maintain a list of those requesting your files so that you can determine what type of demand there is for your information.

As an information subscriber, you will regularly receive an updated list of available files. Each list contains a brief description of the files, enabling you to select those of interest to you. You send us a list of your choices; we send you the files. It's that simple.

To submit files: Send us your file (of publishable quality please) electronically. Please include with your submission: * your name * the organization, if any, with which you are affiliated * a title for your file, indicating it's content * how long you wish us to advertise the file

To subscribe: Please send us an electronic message indicating: * your name * the organization, if any, with which you are affiliated * your reason for interest * whether you wish to be a regular subscriber, or would like to receive the most recent file list only.

Note to Internet-users: Files are also available in the ftp directory at igc.org, internet address 192.82.108.1. Use standard anonymous ftp login.

Submissions and request for subscriptions should be sent to:
EcoNet/PeaceNet/APC:............................cdp:ecixfiles
Internet, FidoNet:..........................ecixfiles@igc.org
BITNet:....................................ecixfiles@igc.org
.............................-OR- ecixfiles%igc.org@stanford
UUCP:.....................................uunet!cdp!ecixfiles

ECIX is brought to you by:

* Lelani Arris, ECIX Project Direct............larris@igc.org
* Tom Gray, ECIX Energy Issues Facilitator......tgray@igc.org
* Dan Yurman, ECIX Climate Digest Editor.......ecixdy@igc.org
* Eva Henin, ECIX Volunteer.................ecixfiles@igc.org

ECIX is an EcoNet project funded by a grant from the Joyce Mertz- Gilmore Foundation with added support from the Energy Foundation.

ECONOMY@TECMTYVM.MTY.ITESM.MX
ECONOMY@TECMTYVM.BITNET

The economy and economic problems of Less Developed Countries (LDCs) have become real laboratories for both the economic discipline, and economic policy measures. This discussion list is aimed at analyzing economic problems, theories, policies, social conditions, political settings, etc., of LDCs and their relationship with the industrial world.

BitNet users can join by issuing the following command: TELL LISTSERV AT TECMTYVM SUBSCRIBE ECONOMY Your_full_name Example: TELL LISTSERV AT TECMTYVM

SUBSCRIBE ECONOMY Jane Doe or the equivalent for sending messages, if your operating system is not VM/SP. Non-BitNet users can join by sending a message to LISTSERV@TECMTYVM.MTY.ITESM.MX with the one-line command "SUBSCRIBE ECONOMY Your_full_name" in the body/text (*NOT* in the Subject: field).

Coordinator: Alejandro Ibarra <5343TBIT@TECMTYVM.MTY.ITESM.MX> <5343TBIT@TECMTYVM.BITNET>

ectl@snowhite.cis.uoguelph.ca   [Last Updated 12-October-1991]

Electronic Communal Temporal Lobe (ECTL) is a communication mechanism for those doing research (or are simply interested in) computer speech interfaces.

For more information or to be added to the list send mail to the owner at ectl-request@snowhite.cis.uoguelph.ca .

Moderator: David Leip; University of Guelph, Canada. <david@snowhite.cis.uoguelph.ca>

EDI-L%UCCVMA.BITNET@VM1.NODAK.EDU

Mailing list for discussion of Electronic Data Interchange issues. The list will discuss electronic transmission and receipt of business documentation including purchase orders, invoices, payment, academic transcripts, standardized test scores. ANSI X12 and international EDIFACT standards will also be discussed.

Monthly archives will be maintained; contact the Coordinator for access information.

BitNet users can subscribe by sending the following command to LISTSERV@UCCVMA via mail or interactive message: SUB EDI-L your_full_name where "your_full_name" is your name. For example: SUB EDI-L Joan Doe Non-BitNet subscribers can join by sending the above command to LISTSERV%UCCVMA.BITNET@VM1.NODAK.EDU.

Coordinator: Richard Hintz <SPGRJH%UCCVMA.BITNET@VM1.NODAK.EDU>

EDISTA on LISTSERV@USACHVM1.BITNET   [Last Updated 28-January-1992]

The University Distance Program (UNIDIS) at the University of Santiago (Chile), has started a discussion list to serve as a forum on distance education, EDISTA@USACHVM1.BITNET

New research findings, UNIDIS activities and announcements, and discussions on distance education will be the main topics of the list.

To sign up on the list, send a mail message with the content of the message in the form of:

SUBSCRIBE EDISTA "your_full_name"

To the following Bitnet address:

LISTSERV at USACHVM1.BITNET

To send Contribution to the list via mail, use the following bitnet address:

EDISTA@USACHVM1.BITNET

These contributions will then be sent to everyone on the list.

To sign off of the list, send a message in the form of:

SIGNOFF EDISTA

to: LISTSERV@USACHVM1.BITNET

```
        U  N  I  D  I  S       TEL. OFICINA : +56 +2 6813125
   (UNIVERSIDAD A DISTANCIA)   FAX          : +56 +2 6811422
                               TELEX        : 441674 USACH  CZ
PROF. JORGE URBINA FUENTES     E-MAIL       : UNIDIS@USACHVM1.BITNET
          VICERRECTORIA DE DOCENCIA Y EXTENSION
```

UNIVERSIDAD DE SANTIAGO DE CHILE

EdLaw on LISTSERV@UKCC or LISTSERV@UKCC.uky.edu

EdLaw is designed for those who teach and practice law concerning public education, private education, and colleges and universities. It is intended to be an exchange of information on legislation and litigation and their various components. It should not be viewed as legal advice in any form, but rather as a conversation among those knowledgeable in the field.

Archives of EdLaw are stored in the EdLaw FILELIST. To receive a list of files send the command INDEX EdLaw to LISTSERV@UKCC.

To subscribe to EdLaw, send the following command to LISTSERV@UKCC via mail text (in the BODY of the mail) or interactive message:

SUBSCRIBE EdLaw your full name

For example: SUBSCRIBE EdLaw Joe Shmoe

Owner: Virginia Davis-Nordin <NORDIN@ukcc.uky.edu>

EDNET on listserv@nic.umass.edu   [Last Update 11/92]

Ednet is a Massachusetts and 5-college area list for those interested in exploring the educational potential of the Internet. Discussion ranges from K12 to adult higher education. Though somewhat provincial, those engaged in teaching and research who wish to begin or extend their work through the Internet are welcome. University alumni, particularly those of the School of Education, might find this an excellent way to maintain ties and educational interests. The list is independent and has no official connection to any school or department.

To subscribe, email to: listserv@nic.umass.edu

First line in Body: Subscribe Ednet (Your Name)

For further information email: pgsmith@ucsvax.ucs.umass.edu

EDPOLYAN%ASUACAD.BITNET@VM1.NODAK.EDU

The "Education Policy Analysis ListServ" is intended to be a place where people will discuss, ask questions, give answers and make their work and ideas available to their colleagues around the country. We will make some special efforts to contribute to the list, such things as the contents of the major policy analysis journals, abstracts of particularly important papers and studies, job announcements, meeting announcements, and the like. We also intend to place papers - completed or in draft form - in an archive that will be readily available to all members of the list. If you have a paper to contribute, write to either of the Coordinators, and they will provide instructions on sending it so it can be placed in the archives.

BitNet users may subscribe by intereactive message or e-mail by sending the following command to LISTSERV at ASUACAD: SUBSCRIBE EDPOLYAN Your name and your institution where "Your name..." is your real name (and institutional affiliation), NOT your login Id. Non-BitNet users can join the list by sending the above command as the only line in the text/body of a message to LISTSERV%ASUACAD.BITNET@VM1.NODAK.EDU.

Coordinators: Gene Glass <ATGVG%ASUACAD.BITNET@VM1.NODAK.EDU>
Dewayne Matthews <AGD2M%ASUACAD.BITNET@VM1.NODAK.EDU>

EDSTAT-L on LISTSERV@NCSUVM.BITNET   [Last Updated 28-January-1992]
or LISTSERV@ncsuvm.cc.ncsu.edu

The purpose of this list is to provide a forum for comments, techniques and philosophies of teaching statistics. The primary focus is that of college level statistics education, both undergraduate and graduate studies.

Statistical literacy has become a social imperative if we are to share a responsible, thoughtful citizenry.

As people involved or interested in the instruction of statistics, we have a precious asset in our collective knowledge.

This list exists because WE CAN LEARN FROM EACH OTHER:

- What techniques are we using in statistical instruction?
- What strategies should we use to prepare our students for the future?
- What part do/should computers play in instruction? (are computers a new tool or a new subject for students?)
- What assets can we share among ourselves? (public-domain software programs, datasets, etc.)

There are many individuals working in these areas, each with knowledge valuable to the others. This list attempts to bring together every teacher, student, researcher, and specialist interested in improving statistical instruction.

You are encouraged to:

- Submit summaries of or commentary on published articles and books which address problems or solutions in teaching statistics
- Share the results of your experiments with teaching statistics
- Ask thought-provoking questions about the future of statistics education and the environments in which it takes place.
- Recruit interested parties to this list, regardless of their status in education, industry or government.

Subscribing to EDSTAT-L

BITNET USERS: Send the following command as the first line of a mail file to LISTSERV@NCSUVM SUBSCRIBE EDSTAT-L Your_full_name

IBM VM users in BITNET may add themselves to the mailing list with
this command:
    TELL LISTSERV AT NCSUVM SUBSCRIBE EDSTAT-L Your_full_name

VAX/VMS users in BITNET can subscribe in a similar way:
    SEND LISTSERV@NCSUVM SUBSCRIBE EDSTAT-L Your_full_name

INTERNET USERS: Send the following command as the first line of a mail file to LISTSERV@ncsuvm.cc.ncsu.edu SUBSCRIBE EDSTAT-L Your_full_name

Owner: Tim Arnold
    Internet address: arnold@stat.ncsu.edu
    Bitnet address: ARNOLD@NCSUSTAT
    North Carolina State University
    Department of Statistics BOX 8203
    Raleigh, NC 27695
    (919) 515-3426/(919) 515-2584

EDTECH%OHSTVMA.BITNET@VM1.NODAK.EDU

This list was conceived to bring together students, faculty, and "interested others" in the field of educational technology to share ideas and information. Some topics we have in mind include:

- A discussion of articles, books, and blurbs you've found stimulating and worthwhile
- Information about course offerings and edtech graduate program requirements at your school
- Notable educational hardware and software, as well as junk one should avoid
- Current dissertations and research projects in edtech
- What's been keeping you up at all hours? Perhaps another one of us could help.

A list of the archived files of previous EDTECH discussions can be received by sending the command: INDEX EDTECH to LISTSERV@OHSTVMA. You can then request a specific month's discussion by sending the command: SENDME Filename Filetype For example: TELL LISTSERV@OHSTVMA SENDME EDTECH LOG8905 (would send the May log)

To subscribe, send the following command to LISTSERV@OHSTVMA via mail or interactive message: TELL LISTSERV@OHSTVMA SUB EDTECH your_full_name Or SUB EDTECH your_full_name where "your_full_name" is your name. (Example: SUB EDTECH Joan Doe) Non-BitNet users can subscribe by sending the text: SUB EDTECH your_full_name in the body of a message to LISTSERV%OHSTVMA.BITNET@VM1.NODAK.EDU.

If you have any questions or comments about the EDTECH mailing list, please send them to one of the Owners/Coordinators.

Coordinators: Vickie Banks   <21602VB%MSU.BITNET@VM1.NODAK.EDU>
               Mark Rosenberg <21602MR%MSU.BITNET@VM1.NODAK.EDU>
               Dr. Joe Byers   <20506JLB%MSU.BITNET@VM1.NODAK.EDU>
               Josie Csete   <21602JMC%MSU.BITNET@VM1.NODAK.EDU>

EDUCOM-W%educom.bitnet@cunyvm.cuny.edu

EDUCOM-W is an unmoderated list to facilitate discussion of issues in technology and education that are of interest to women. The list is intended to promote discussion of how EDUCOM can help address those issues in its services to members. To subscribe, send a message to LISTSERV@BITNIC with the following line of text:

SUB EDUCOM-W Your_full_name

where Your_full_name is your name, not your login ID. The list coordinator is Sue Ellen Anderson, Anderson@EDUCOM.Bitnet

EGRET-L on LISTSERV@DARTCMS1   [Last Update 9/92]
    or LISTSERV@DARTCMS1.DARTMOUTH.EDU

EGRET-L is a moderated listserver for the discussion of topics relating to the epidemiological software package EGRET. It is hoped that this forum will be used to enhance the use of EGRET by the exchange of tips, shortcuts, news and information about problems among the users of this package. It is especially de desirable that EGRET-L be used as a resource for new and experienced users to turn to for help when problems are encountered or when they come up with novel applications of the software.

Egret-l will not be a medium for flame wars, or for non-Egret related topics.

Archives of EGRET-L can be listed by sending the command:

INDEX EGRET-L to LISTSERV@DARTCMS1.DARTMOUTH.EDU or
LISTSERV@DARTCMS1.BITNET

To subscribe, send the following command to LISTSERV@DARTCMS1.DARTMOUTH.EDU or
LISTSERV@DARTCMS1.BITNET in the BODY of mail or interactive message:

SUB EGRET-L your full name

where "your full name" is your name. For example:

SUB EGRET-L Joan Doe

Owner: Stephen P. Baker <SBAKER@UMASSMED.UMMED.EDU or
SBAKER@UMASSMED.BITNET>

ELEASAI on LISTSERV@ARIZVM1.BITNET or LISTSERV@ARIZVM1.CCIT.ARIZONA.EDU

ELEASAI is a LISTSERV conference on research in library and information science. It concerns current research in progress or in planning stages, methodological and statistical issues, funding for research, computing as a research tool, broad trends in scientific research as they affect library and information science, and similar research-oriented topics. ELEASAI's address is ELEASAI@ARIZVM1.

It is a companion conference to JESSE, which focuses on teaching and educational concerns in library and information science. JESSE concerns curricula, educational methodologies and issues, courses in development, resources, computing as a teaching tool, broad trends in education as they affect library and information science education, and similar education- oriented topics. JESSE's address is JESSE@ARIZVM1.BITNET

To subscribe to ELEASAI, send the following command to LISTSERV@ARIZVM1 on BITNET or LISTSERV@ARIZVM1.CCIT.ARIZONA.EDU in the BODY of mail text or interactive message:

SUBSCRIBE ELEASAI Your_full_name.

For example: SUBSCRIBE LISTNAME Joe Shmoe

Owners: Gretchen Whitney (GWHITNEY@ARIZVMS) Charley Seavey (DOCMAPS@ARIZVMS)

ELENCHUS on LISTSERV@UOTTAWA.BITNET or LISTSERV@ACADVM1.UOTTAWA.CA Christian Thought and Literature in Late Antiquity

ELENCHUS is devoted to discussions of the thought and literature of Christianity during the period 100 to 500 a.d. (c.e.).

This will include discussions of patristics, gnosticism, asceticism, monasticism, archeology, the Nag Hammadi and Manichaean corpora, the canon of Scripture and the early translations of the Scriptures (into, among other languages, Latin, Syriac, Coptic), the history of exegesis (including the appropriation by Christians of the texts of Judaism and other religious, philosophical, or ideological groupings), as well as historical and theological developments from the time of the Apologists to the fall of the Western Empire.

LANGUAGES: The languages of discussion will be English or French. Submissions in either language are welcomed, and patience and understanding on the part of all are encouraged!

TO SUBSCRIBE TO ELENCHUS: If you are on BITNET: send an interactive message to LISTSERV@UOTTAWA as follows (CMS form shown): TELL LISTSERV AT UOTTAWA SUB ELENCHUS your full name or send a mail message to the same address with the following text: SUB ELENCHUS your full name in the BODY of the mail.

If you are on INTERNET or related network send a mail message to LISTSERV@ACADVM1.UOTTAWA.CA with the following text in the BODY of the e-mail: SUB ELENCHUS your full name

Owner: L. Gregory Bloomquist Saint Paul University / University of Ottawa BITNET: GBLOOMQ@UOTTAWA Internet: GBLOOMQ@ACADVM1.UOTTAWA.CA S-Mail: 223 Main St., Ottawa, Ontario, K1S 1C4 CANADA Voice: (613) 782-3027 / 236-1393 FAX: (613) 567-2959 / 782-3005

ELLHNIKA on LISTSERV@DHDURZ1.BITNET

Thanks to the friendly support of DANTE and especially of Joachim Lammarsch a discussion list on Greek TeX (cf. "CALL FOR STANDARDIZATION OF GREEK TeX AND CREATION OF A GREEK TeX GROUP") has been opened, at

ELLHNIKA@DHDURZ1

You can subscribe by sending the usual

SUBSCRIBE ELLHNIKA yourfirstname yourlastname

to LISTSERV@DHDURZ1. Please note that messages to the list should be send to the list adress ELLHNIKA@DHDURZ1 and not to the LISTSERV.

Languages of the list are English and Greek (Modern please!!) It would be appreciated if you use Silvio Levy's transliteration for Greek, as long as no other transliteration has been fixed. If you have to use a different one, please precise the corres- pondences at top of the message.

The list is intended for linguists of any origin having to typeset ancient Greek, as well as for people using Greek as their everyday's language. It is quite a dilemma for me to encourage

- the former to participate in English and discuss the TeXnical problems of ancient Greek
- the latter to participate in Greek and in this way get used to the transliterated expression of the language; as I said in the "CALL", a certain effort must be taken to bypass the handicap of having a different alphabet, this list should serve as a starting point inside the TeX world.

So there are two languages and two directions to take. Let's find a compromise based on the spirit of cooperation! (and if a scholar decides to learn Modern Greek for breaking this Gordian knot, I guarantee him that he won't be dissapointed!).

YOU ARE INVITED TO JOIN US IN THE DISCUSSION ON GREEK TeX

Owner: Yannis Haralambous <YANNIS@FRCITL81.BITNET>

EMEDCH-L on LISTSERV@USCVM.BITNET

EMEDCH-L is devoted to promoting discussion centered around the studies of the period of Chinese history between the Han and the Tang dynasties (3rd through 6th centuries A.D.). Membership is unrestricted.

To subscribe, send a mail message to LISTSERV@USCVM.BITNET with the body of the mail containing the line: SUB EMEDCH-L yourfirstname yourlastname

EMULPC-L%USACHVM1.BITNET@VM1.NODAK.EDU

Mailing list for issues related to the PC Emulation software and hardware (PC3270, IRMA, PCOX, Extra, Graph-Tek APA, GWSP, Yterm, Smarterm and others). Any and all contributions, ideas, and knowledge in the area of emulation software, will be be appreciated, discussed, reported and learned for the list.

BitNet users can subscribe to the list by sending mail to LISTSERV@USACHVM1 with the body or text of the mail having the line: SUB EMULPC-L your full name where "your full name" is your real name, not your login Id. Non-BitNet users can join by sending the above command in the text/body of a message to LISTSERV%USACHVM1.BITNET@VM1.NODAK.EDU.

Coordinator: Pedro Sepulveda J. <PSEPULVE%USACHVM1.BITNET@VM1.NODAK.EDU>

EMUSIC-D%AUVM.BITNET@CUNYVM.CUNY.EDU
EMUSIC-L%AUVM.BITNET@CUNYVM.CUNY.EDU

EMUSIC is a complementary pair of lists (EMUSIC-L for undigested mail, EMUSIC-D for the moderately edited digest) devoted to the discussion of Electronic Music. Topics of interest include (but are not limited to): synthesis methods, algorithmic composition, psychoacoustics, timbral research, instrument design, MIDI troubleshooting, new tricks for old machines, musique concrete, pedagogic methods, performance techniques, reviews of current and historical musical and technical trends, announcements of events, papers, homegrown sounds and software.

The EMUSIC-D FILELIST contains the archive of the discussions to date as well as data files, programs and other materials of interest to the Elec- tronic Music community.

To add yourself to the list, send the command: SUBSCRIBE EMUSIC-L Your_Full_Name (for undigested mail) or SUBSCRIBE EMUSIC-D Your_Full_Name (for digested mail) via mail to LISTSERV@AUVM.BITNET or LISTSERV%AUVM.BITNET@CUNYVM.CUNY.EDU where Your_Full_Name is your real name (not your userid). To remove yourself from the list send the command: SIGNOFF EMUSIC-L or SIGNOFF EMUSIC-D

Moderator: Eric Harnden <EHARNDEN%AUVM.BITNET@CUNYVM.CUNY.EDU>

ENERGY-L <JO%ILNCRD.BITNET@CUNYVM.CUNY.EDU>

A Bitnet newsletter on energy research in Israel.

To subscribe, send a message to LISTSERV%TAUNIVM.BITNET@CUNYVM.CUNY.EDU with the body of the letter containing the command: SUB ENERGY-L Your_Full_Name where Your_Full_Name; is your title, first name and last name.

Coordinator: Joseph van Zwaren de Zwarenstein <JO%ILNCRD.BITNET@CUNYVM.CUNY.EDU>

ENGLISH%CANADA01.BITNET@CUNYVM.CUNY.EDU

This forum is primarily for faculty in English Departments in Canada who are using mainframes for teaching and research and who may be using microcomputers as well; secondarily it is for English faculty anywhere who have access to BITNET.

All requests to be added to or deleted from this list, problems, questions, etc., should be sent to the Coordinator or the administrator of LISTSERV@CANADA01.

Coordinator: Marshall Gilliland <GILLILAN%SASK.BITNET@CUNYVM.CUNY.EDU>
(UUCP) alberta!sask!marshall

ENVBEH-L@GRAF.POLY.EDU
ENVBEH-L%POLYGRAF.BITNET@MITVMA.MIT.EDU
ENVBEH-L@POLYGRAF (BitNet)

Mailing list on Environmental Behavior: Environment, Design, and Human Behavior. ENVBEH-L is a discussion on a variety of topics concerning the relations of people and their physical environments, including architectural and interior design and human behavior, environmental stress (pollution, catastrophe) and behavior, human response to built and natural settings, etc.

BITNET subscribers can join by sending the Listserv SUB command with your name. For example: SEND LISTSERV@POLYGRAF SUB ENVBEH-L Jon Doe or TELL LISTSERV AT POLYGRAF SUB ENVBEH-L Jon Doe To be removed from the list, SEND LISTSERV@POLYGRAF SIGNOFF ENVBEH-L or TELL LISTSERV AT POLYGRAF SIGNOFF ENVBEH-L

Those without interactive access may send the Listserv Command portion of the above lines as the first TEXT line of a message. For example: SUB ENVBEH-L Jon Doe would be the only line in the body of a message to LISTSERV%POLYGRAF.BITNET@MITVMA.MIT.EDU. As a last resort, send mail to one of the Coordinators.

Coordinators: Richard Wener <????%POLYGRAF.BITNET@MITVMA.MIT.EDU> Tony Monteiro <MONTEIRO%POLYGRAF.BITNET@MITVMA.MIT.EDU>

ENVST-L on LISTSERV@BROWNVM.BITNET

The purpose of this list is to exchange information about Environmental Studies (ES) programs, generally -- about course designs, successful student projects, important information sources, etc. We invite all who have a serious interest in ES at the undergraduate and graduate levels. Some topics that might be of interest are: the balance between science/social science/humanities in our degrees; the role of project classes and individual applied projects in our programs; our relations with more traditional departments and disciplines; and even exciting new ideas that we would like to refine.

Entries to this list will be restricted to items of general interest. This list will not be used for personal exchanges or dialogues.

To subscribe to this list, send the following command in the body of a message or mail to LISTSERV@BROWNVM.BITNET SUB ENVST-L yourfirstname yourlastname

You will receive acknowledgement from listserv together with a more detailed description of the list.

Owner: Sandra Baptista <ST802218@BROWNVM>

EOCHR@QueensU.CA

The purpose of the Eastern Orthodox Christian discussion group is to give a fo r um for discussion and exchange of ideas by members of the various Eastern and Oriental Orthodox churches around the world, as well as any other people who are seriously interested in Eastern Orthodox Christianity and the concerns of the Orthodox. It exists for polite, open, tolerant, and truly pan-Orthodox discussions of any topics related to the Orthodox faith, to the corporate life of the various national Orthodox churches, and/or to the individual lives of Orthodox Christians. Please let Orthodox Christians know of its existence. For subscription, just send the owner your full name and e-mail address.

Owner: Dragic V.Vukomanovic <Dragic.Vukomanovic@QueensU.CA>

EQUINE-D on LISTSERV@PCCVM.BITNET   [Last Updated June 1992]

The Rec.Equestrian Digest is a redistribution of articles from the USENET rec.equestrian newsgroup for persons without USENET access. Distribution is in digest format as described in RFC 1153 by Frank Wancho. The list is currently running in read-only mode; no subscriber postings are permitted. EQUINE-D originated as an outgrowth of, and companion list to, EQUINE-L.

At present no archives are maintained.

Subscriptions to EQUINE-D are open.

To subscribe to this list, send a mail/note message to LISTSERV@PCCVM with a blank subject line and the following one-line command in the BODY of the mail:

SUBSCRIBE EQUINE-D your full name

For example: SUBSCRIBE EQUINE-D Hermann Schwartz

BITNET VM systems may use the interactive command:

TELL LISTSERV at PCCVM SUBSCRIBE EQUINE-D your full name

Non-IBM systems may use their equivalent interactive message command.

Identity of subscribers is confidential. REVIEW is not available.

Owner: W. K. (Bill) Gorman <34AEJ7D@CMUVM.BITNET> or
<34AEJ7D@CMUVM.CSV.CMICH.EDU>

EQUINE-L on LISTSERV@PCCVM.BITNET or LISTSERV@PSUVM.BITNET

EQUINE-L is a list for the discussion of all phases of horse ownership, management, use and related concerns for all horse breeds, both hot and cold blood.

You may subscribe via either mail or interactive message. NOTE: MAIL is the recommended method for subscription requests.

To subscribe send MAIL to <LISTSERV@PCCVM.BITNET or LISTSERV@PSUVM.BITNET> with the following message:

SUB EQUINE-L your-full-name

You will receive an acknowledgement from the listserv together with a more detailed description of the list and its scope.

Owner: W. K. (Bill) Gorman <34AEJ7D@CMUVM.BITNET>

ermis on listserv@vlsi.bu.edu

A discussion list for people of Hellenic descent is available for subscription: ermis@vlsi.bu.edu

To subscribe send email to listserv@vlsi.bu.edu with the following lines in the body of the message:

subscribe <your name>
help

ESPORA-L@UKANVM.BITNET   [Last Updated 28-January-1992]

We are pleased to announce the establishment of a list for Spanish and Portuguese Historical Studies. Subscriptions should be made to LISTSERV AT UKANVM with the command

SUB ESPORA-L yourfirstname yourlastname

adding your full name; LISTSERV will accept both BITNET and INTERNET addresses. Postings should be made to ESPORA-L@UKANVM. The owners would appreciate it if subscribers would send them BY E-MAIL a short biographical resume for inclusion in a directory of members: send to either LHNELSON@UKANVM or RCLEMENT@UKANVM.

Our FTP directory is presently empty. If subscribers have materials they believe worth including, please contact either of the list owners. This site will operate in co-operation with ra.msstate.edu and the contents of its directories will form part of a union catalogue with ra.msstate and other co-operating sites.

The following is a formal statement of purpose. We would like to welcome our colleagues to ESPORA-L and express our hope that it will prove a benefit to us all.

Owners:
Richard Clement   RCLEMENT@UKANVM
Lynn H. Nelson   LHNELSON@UKANVM
The University of Kansas

STATEMENT OF PURPOSE

ESPORA-L is a forum for debate, discussion, and the exchange of information by students and scholars of the history of the Iberian Peninsula from the earliest times to the present. Although the command language of ESPORA-L is English, postings in Portuguese, Spanish, and Catalan are welcome, and list members are encouraged to communicate in whichever language they are most comfortable. ESPORA-L is ready to distribute newsletters from study groups, and to post announcements of meetings and calls for papers, short scholarly pieces, queries, and other items of interest.

The lists maintains a directory at the FTP site kuhub.cc.ukans.edu (CD DUA9 [malin.espora]), for the collection and preservation of materials of use for its members.

ESPORA-L is associated with the general discussion list HISTORY, and co-operates fully with other lists similarly associated.

ESPER-L%TREARN.BITNET@CUNYVM.CUNY.EDU

A list on the Esperanto Language.

To subscribe, send the following command to LISTSERV@TREARN via mail or interactive message: SUB ESPER-L your_full_name where "your_full_name" is your name. For example: SUB ESPER-L Joan Doe Non-BitNet users can subscribe by sending the text: SUB ESPER-L your_full_name in the body of a message to LISTSERV%TREARN.BITNET@CUNYVM.CUNY.EDU.

Coordinator: Turgut Kalfaoglu <TURGUT%TREARN.BITNET@CUNYVM.CUNY.EDU>

ESPERANTO@LLL-CRG.LLNL.GOV@Index(Esperanto)

A forum for people interested in the neutral international language Esperanto. Discussions about the language itself, the Esperanto movement, publications, and news are encouraged. Of course, discussion in Esperanto is especially encouraged, although English translations may be advisable when the material is of interest to beginners or non-Esperantists.

This list is identical to the USENET mailing list 'mail.esperanto'. The forwarding addresses were installed on LLL-CRG-LLNL.GOV by Andy Beals; ESPERANTO forwards to the "real" mail.esperanto address trwrb!trwspp!spp2!esperanto and ESPERANTO-REQUEST forwards to the Coordinator (trwrb!trwspp!spp2!urban).

All requests to be added to or deleted from this list, problems, questions, etc., should be sent to ESPERANTO-REQUEST@LLL-CRG.LLNL.GOV.

Coordinator: Mike Urban <ESPERANTO-REQUEST@LLL-CRG.LLNL.GOV>

ETHCSE-L@UTKVM1.UTK.EDU [Last Updated 12-October-1991]

ETHCSE-L is an unmoderated, unarchived list which deals with ethical issues of interest to professional software engineers. The list is intended to provide the opportunity for software engineers and those interested in software engineering to discuss ethical concerns of the discipline. As the discipline is rapidly advancing new ethical issues arise in the practice of software engineering.

The group might be expected to discuss things like the move by some state governments toward licensing software engineers, establishing a code of ethics, or articulating a set of principles which guide professional practice. The list can also be used as a place to announce conferences, and publications and issue call for papers.

To subscribe, send an interactive message or mail to LISTSERV@UTKVM1 or mail to LISTSERV@UTKVM1.UTK.EDU with the body containing the command

SUBscribe ETHCSE-L First_name Last_name

List Owner: Don Gotterbarn I01GBARN@ETSU.BITNET

ETHICS-L%MARIST.BITNET@CUNYVM.CUNY.EDU

Discussions of ethics in computing usually generate more heat than light. This list could do a lot toward generating more light if we do more than trade war stories and opinions of the "I'm right and you're NOT" variety. Of course we can't get any work done without some war stories, since they furnish food for thought. But we shouldn't stop there. Given our experiences, we ought to be able to delineate the basic issues and hot areas in computer ethics. Some current ones have to do with:

- ownership of information (both data and program files)
- what happens when systems programs fail? Is anyone responsible for damage done? Or is the responsibility only for the necessary fix?
- responsibility for program failures (Is the company responsible? the programmer? the lead programmer? the project manager?) Who's responsible for the "fix"?
- how much privacy is reasonable (there are all kinds of levels here; data bases, systems, LANs, networks, etc.)

BitNet users can add themselves to the list by issuing the following command to LISTSERV@MARIST.BITNET: SUBSCRIBE ETHICS-L your_full_name where your_full_name is your real name (not your userid). BitNet users can unsubscribe with the command: UNSUBSCRIBE ETHICS-L

All other requests to be added to or deleted from this list, problems, questions, etc., should be sent to the Moderators.

Moderators: Jane Robinett <JROBINET%POLYTECH.BITNET@CUNYVM.CUNY.EDU>
Matthew J. Miner <MINER%POLYGRAF.BITNET@CUNYVM.CUNY.EDU>
Harry Williams <HARRY%MARIST.BITNET@CUNYVM.CUNY.EDU>

ETHNOHIS on LISTSERV@hearn or LISTSERV@nic.surfnet.nl [Last Update 11/92]

ETHNOHIS - GENERAL ETHNOLOGY AND HISTORY DISCUSSION LIST

ETHNOHIS is an online discussion list on the intersection of two disciplines: ethnology and history, and on topics touching both upon ethnology and history. Interested researchers are encouraged to discuss relevant themes, e.g. 'the anthropology of museums', 'ethnographical collections', 'missionary photography', methodological issues, or all topics covered by journals such as *Gradhiva* and *History and*

Anthropology. We hope to stimulate a general discussion between the various approaches in this interdisciplinary field.

To subscribe to ETHNOHIS, send the following command to LISTSERV@HEARN or to LISTSERV@nic.surfnet.nl, via e-mail or interactive message:

SUB ETHNOHIS Your full name

where "Your full name" is your name. For example:

SUB ETHNOHIS Jim Down

Owner: Fred Melssen <u211610@hnykun11.urc.kun.nl> <u211610@hnykun11.urc.kun.nl>

ETHOLOGY%FINHUTC.BITNET@CUNYVM.CUNY.EDU

An unmoderated mailing list for the discussion of animal behaviour and behavioural ecology. Possible topics could be e.g. new or controversial theories, new research methods, and equipment. Announcements of books, papers, conferences, new software for behavioural analysis etc., are also encouraged.

BitNet, EARN, and NetNorth users may subscribe by sending a command via an interactive message: TELL LISTSERV AT FINHUTC SUB ETHOLOGY John Doe or SEND LISTSERV@FINHUTC SUB ETHOLOGY John Doe If you are at a non-BitNet site, or where you cannot send interactive messages, you can send mail to LISTSERV%FINHUTC.BITNET@CUNYVM.CUNY.EDU where the first non-header line consists of: SUBSCRIBE ETHOLOGY Your full name

Coordinator: Jarmo Saarikko <SAARIKKO%FINHUTC.BITNET@CUNYVM.CUNY.EDU>

EUEARN-L on LISTSERV@UBVM.BITNET [Last Updated 28-January-1992]

EUEARN-L is a list devoted to discussion of computers, computer communications and electronic developments in Eastern Europe. It is an attempt to help the new networks in these areas with technical and social advice, and to foster their development.

It hopes to smooth the integration of computer networks in Eastern Europe into the world networking system. Eastern Europe is defined roughtly as that area between the Baltic and Adriatic/Mediterranean sees, and between the borders of Byelorussia/Ukraine and France/ Switzerland.

It is a counterpart to such lists as PLEARN (Polish computing)and SUEARN (Soviet). Earn is the European Academic Research Network. The list is to be a mixture of technical and conversational. The principal language will be English but there will be no objection to the use of languages native to the countries concerned. Where possible, and if the messages are of general rather than individual interest, English summaries should be provided.

The list is unmoderated for the time being. The list manager is as below. EUEARN-L is is based at University of Buffalo. Subscriptions should be send to LISTSERV@UBVM.BITNET with the following command in the body of the mail: SUB EUEARN-L yourfirstname yourlastname

Owner:
Jan George Frajkor <gfrajkor@ccs.carleton.ca>
School of Journalism
Carleton University, Ottawa, Canada
613 788-7404   fax:613 788-5604

EV on LISTSERV@sjsuvm1.sjsu.edu

The EV Electric Vehicle Discussion Mailing List is intended to provide a forum to discuss the current state of the art and future direction of electric vehicles. It is not intended to discuss either EV appropriateness or comparisons with other transportation primary drive modes such as the venerable internal combustion engine. Those "discussions" are best relegated to the appropriate usenet newsgroup.

An electric vehicle is any vehicle which uses an electric motor as the primary or sole motive force. The energy storage device used to drive said motor can use any technology including, but not limited to, solar electric, electric battery, internal combustion engine coupled with a electric generator, or any combination of these. Production electric vehicles are currently available. Internal combustion engine vehicles can be converted to electric. There exist a number of companies who perform this conversion. There is also a number of manufacturers of equipment allowing you to do-it-yourself.

To subscribe, send the following command to LISTSERV@SJSUVM1 (bitnet) or LISTSERV@SJSUVM1.SJSU.EDU (in the BODY of e-mail):

SUBSCRIBE EV firstname lastname

After subscribing, messages may be sent to the list by sending to: EV@SJSUVM1 (bitnet) or ev@sjsuvm1.sjsu.edu.

Owner: Clyde R. Visser, KD6GWN <cvisser@ucrmath.ucr.edu>

EXPER-L%TREARN.BITNET@VM1.NODAK.EDU

The Coordinator is in the process of preparing a paper on "Security in Computer Networks". To accomplish this task there is a need to gather information about past Viral Experiences on Networks. If your system has experienced such an attack (like CHRISTMA EXEC or other kinds of hacking) please send it to this list. Later all the information will be compiled and used in the paper. The names of the people who submitted to the list will never be used in the paper. All the Coordinator is interested in is what kind of an attack, done where, and what harm it caused.

Also if there is anyone who thinks they can help in determining a way to compile such experiences please write to the Coordinator directly.

BitNet users may subscribe by sending the following command via interactive message or e-mail to LISTSERV@TREARN: SUB EXPER-L Your full name where "Your full name" is your real name, not your login Id. Non-BitNet users can join the list by sending the above command as the only line in the text/body of a message to LISTSERV%TREARN.BITNET@VM1.NODAK.EDU.

Coordinator: Esra Delen - NAD <ESRA%TREARN.BITNET@VM1.NODAK.EDU>

explorer@castle.ed.ac.uk

This list is intended as a forum for discussion on any aspects of the Explorer Modular Visualisation Environment (MVE).

IRIS Explorer is an application creation system developed by SiliconGraphics that provides visualisation and analysis functionality for computational scientists, engineers and other scientists. The Explorer GUI allows users to build custom applications without having to write any traditonal code.

For general administration, send your requests to be added, removed, have your address changed or whatever to : explorer-request@castle.ed.ac.uk.

If you wish to contribute to the 'users list', then when you subscribe to the list, please send some details on what you are using, or intend using Explorer for, and any contact information that you wish to give others.

For general discussion, send your e-mail to the address : explorer@castle.ed.ac.uk,

and this will be forwarded to all other subscribers.

Owner: Gordon Cameron <gordonc@epcc.ed.ac.uk>

express-users@cme.nist.gov

The purpose of the "express-users" mailing list is to facilitate the sharing of information among users of the EXPRESS information modeling language.

Sample subjects include:

1. EXPRESS information sources (where to find things, how to download information, etc.) We hope eventually to include some such information in this introductory posting.
2. Information modeling techniques and sample models built in EXPRESS.
3. Sample applications of EXPRESS (we need as many as possible!).
4. The EXPRESS-I instantiation language, and the EXPRESS-G graphical form of EXPRESS.
5. EXPRESS tools, both those that exist and requirements for new tools (translators, editors, validation tools, EXPRESS-G editors, database implementations, etc.)
6. Discussions of the EXPRESS metamodel, for example: The STEP Semantic Unification Metamodel (SUMM), Dr. Stanley Su's work at the University of Florida, and Michael Yinger's EXPRESSWARE work at TSC.
7. The relationship of EXPRESS to other modeling languages and methodologies (IDEF1X, NIAM, OSAM*, ERM, etc.)
8. We hope that the Users' Group will be able to contribute to the development of EXPRESS, both by contributing actual effort and by bringing relevant work to the attention of the community.
9. How to organize/mobilize the EXPRESS User Group activities; how to spread the word about EXPRESS to the rest of the world.

The mailing list is a simple mail exploder, which means that mail sent to the submission address is automatically sent to all subscribers. Please keep this in mind when posting.

Addresses: Administrative ([un]subscription requests, etc.): express-users-request@cme.nist.gov

Submissions: express-users@cme.nist.gov Please do not send administrative items to the submission address.

Owners: express-users-request@cme.nist.gov
Steve Clark
Charlie Lindahl
Mailing list administrators

eyemov-l@spcvxa.bitnet   [Last Updated 28-January-1992]
eyemov-l@spcvxa.spc.edu

Subscribers are investigators representing a range of research interests in eye movements.

There are two addresses for your use. The first address allows immediate distribution of your message to all subscribers on the latest version of the distribution list. The second address allows subscribers to join or leave the list or modify e-mail addresses.

If you wish to send a message to all subscribers, use the address

eyemov-l@spcvxa.bitnet or eyemov-l@spcvxa.spc.edu

For requests to join or leave the list, use the address

eyemov-r@spcvxa.bitnet or eyemov-r@spcvxa.spc.edu

A subscription request sent to eyemov-r will appear in my personal mail only. I will send an acknowledgement to you when the change is made.

Owner:

Dennis Carmody   carmody_d@spcvxa.spc.edu
Saint Peter's College
Jersey City, New Jersey 07306 USA

FACSER-L%WVNVM.BITNET@MITVMA.MIT.EDU

FACilities and SERvices is a LISTSERV for the exchange of ideas related to college and university facilities and services, including:

Physical plant operations

Security and public safety
Transportation and parking
Telephone
Mail service
Environmental health and safety
Capital planning
Facilities utilization

To subscribe send the following command to LISTSERV@WVNVM (non-BitNet users send mail to LISTSERV%WVNVM.BITNET@MITVMA.MIT.EDU with the command in the message body): SUBSCRIBE FACSER-L Your_Full_Name where Your_Full_Name is your real name, not your userid. To unsubscribe, send: UNSUBSCRIBE FACSER-L

Coordinator: Roman Olynyk <VM0BA9%WVNVM.BITNET@MITVMA.MIT.EDU>

FACXCH-L@PSUVM.PSU.EDU   [Last Updated 12-October-1991]

FACXCH-L@PSUVM is a list for faculty members in art, architecture, and both visual and basic design. If you are interested in making a faculty exchange then post your interest to this list. While initially established for programs at Pennsylvania State University, the list may be used by others in the fields of art, architecture, and design.

To subscribe to the list send e-mail to LISTSERV@PSUVM.BITNET (or LISTSERV@psuvm.psu.edu on the Internet) with the command: SUB FACXCH-L yourfirstname yourlastname

To obtain a list of files in the archives send LISTSERV@PSUVM the command INDEX FACXCH-L

Owner: Howard Ray Lawrence HRL@PSUARCH.BITNET

FAMLYSCI%UKCC.BITNET@VM1.NODAK.EDU

Mailing list for researchers and scholars whose work focusses on family science, marriage and family therapy, family sociology, and the behavioral science aspects of family medicine. The purpose of the list is to enhance communication among family scientists and to support research programs; it is a service provided by the Department of Family Studies at the University of Kentucky.

To join the mailing list, send a request to the Coordinator.

Coordinator: Greg Brock <GWBROCK%UKCC.BITNET@VM1.NODAK.EDU>

FASTBS-L%UALTAVM.BITNET@CUNYVM.CUNY.EDU

News and information list for those who are, or intend to, be involved with FASTBUS, a standardised modular 32-bit wide data-bus system for data aquisition, data processing and control, used mainly by the High Energy Nuclear Physics community. FASTBUS is an international standard, recognised by the IEC, ANSI and IEEE (STD 960-1986) and is freely available for use by any profit or non-profit organisation.

For BitNet users, to Subscribe: SEND LISTSERV@UALTAVM SUBSCRIBE FASTBS-L Your Full Name

To Unsubscribe: SEND LISTSERV@UALTAVM UNSUBSCRIBE FASTBS-L

Internet users can put the SUBSCRIBE or UNSUBSCRIBE command ("SUBSCRIBE FASTBS-L Your Full Name" or "UNSUBSCRIBE FASTBS-L") in the body of a message (the Subject: field may be left blank) and send it to LISTSERV%UALTAVM.BITNET@CUNYVM.CUNY.EDU.

Coordinator: Robert G. Skegg <ROSK%TRIUMFCL.BITNET@CUNYVM.CUNY.EDU>

FAU-L@FAUVAX.BITNET   [Last Updated 28-January-1992]
FAU-L@ACC.FAU.EDU

Florida Atlantic University Interest Group Discussion List

FAU-L is an unmoderated discussion list dealing with issues, concerns and news related to Florida Atlantic University, its alumni, students, faculty, visitors, and friends. The discussion list intends to exchange ideas, answer questions and share experiences between and among members.

FAU is located in Boca Raton, Florida, halfway between the Cities of West Palm Beach and Ft. Lauderdale. It is 2 miles from the beach. FAU is one of the 9 state universities having both undergraduate and graduate programs in liberal arts and sciences as well as engineering, business, urban and regional planning, and education.

This discussion list is open to all interested individuals or organizations. There are no archives as of yet (August 1991).

To subscribe send mail to FAU-REQUEST@FAUVAX on BITNET; Internet users send to FAU-REQUEST@ACC.FAU.EDU with the request in the message body:

SUBSCRIBE FAU-L Your_full_name

To unsubscribe, send:

UNSUBSCRIBE FAU-L

All questions, requests for information, etc., should be sent to the List Owner.

List Owner: M. Yasar Iscan (ISCAN@FAUVAX, Iscan@acc.fau.edu)
List Manager: Ralph P Carpenter (RALPHO@FAUVAX, Ralpho@acc.fau.edu)

FedTax-L@SHSU.BITNET   [Last Updated 12-October-1991]

FedTax-L is a list supported by Sam Houston State University of Huntsville, Texas, to provide a generally unmoderated environment for the discussion of federal taxation issues from both a practical and academic viewpoint. The discussions are intended to include latest trends, regulatory actions, and, of course, a lively exchange of ideas and concerns.

The explicit purpose of FedTax-L is to provide quick and timely interchange between subscribers, to provide a forum where support may be available for interesting questions which may not be addressed locally (or may desire a "second opinion"), and to discuss current and potential taxation issues. It is also the hope of the owner of the list to develop databases of at least late breaking tax matters for access to all subscribers. Archives of FedTax-L postings will be available for reference. As is the case on all unmoderated lists, the discussion and topics are only limited by the participation and interest of its subscribers. Subscribers are welcome to take an active role by posting to FedTax-L or an inactive role by monitoring the list.

This group is now gatewayed to the usenet group misc.taxes.

To subscribe to FedTax-L, please send a MAIL message to: LISTSERV@SHSU.BITNET. The body of this MAIL message should be one line and contain the words: SUBSCRIBE FedTax-L

Please note that LISTSERV@SHSU.BITNET is MAIL-oriented only -- interactive commands send to this address will not be recognized.

Questions regarding this announcement should be addressed to the list owner at any of the addresses listed below.

```
Owner:
   Taylor S. Klett, J.D., CPA          Bitnet:    KLETT@SHSU
   Sam Houston State University        THEnet:    SHSU::KLETT
   P. O. Box 2027       Internet: klett%shsu.decnet@relay.the.net
   Huntsville, TX 77341                Voice: (409) 294-1015
```

FDDI@List.Kean.EDU

Fiber Distributed Data Interface list

FDDI: This mailing list is to discuss Fiber Distributed Data Interface technology.

To subscribe to the list,   send to FDDI-subscribe@List.Kean.EDU
To reach a List Administrator, send to Admin@List.Kean.EDU
For generic help,   send to Help@List.Kean.EDU

fiction-writers%studguppy@LANL.GOV

The Fiction Writers Group exists for two purposes:

To give people interested in writing fiction professionally a support group of peers for where information can be shared and discussions of the task of writing can be carried on.

To create an environment where Works In Progress can be passed around and criticized so that the author can find the weak spots and polish the manuscript into a salable work.

The group has handled mostly Science Fiction, Fantasy, and related genres, but is not restricted to them. Membership is open to anyone who has in interest in writing fiction regardless of previous experience or published/unpublished status. Members must be prepared to regularly contribute either by critiquing the work of others or presenting work for critique.

All requests to be added to or deleted from this list, problems, questions, etc., should be sent to writers-request%studguppy@LANL.GOV

Moderator: Doug Roberts <roberts%studguppy@LANL.GOV>

FIGI-L <ZMLEB%SCFVM.BITNET@CUNYVM.CUNY.EDU>

The FORTH Interest Groups International List (FIGI-L) is dedicated to any and all things connected directly or indirectly with the FORTH computer language. The list is not restricted to technical, professional levels; novice FORTH'ers are encouraged to take part. Also there is no particular implementation, machine, or product emphasiszed. Submissions are requested to keep in mind the issue of portablility of any specific source code. Follow a recognized standard when possible like Forth 79, Forth 83, or FigForth. Any submissions, letters, source listings, etc. will be resent to all subscribers. Copyrighted material, of course, cannot be resent by this list. Public Domain code only! Furthermore, Bitnet prohibits commercial distribution or advertising.

The list is maintained on a LISTSEV at SCFVM.

List submissions, as well as all requests to be added to or deleted from this list, problems, questions, etc., should be sent to ZMLEB%SCFVM.BITNET@CUNYVM.CUNY.EDU.

Coordinator: Lee Brotzman <ZMLEB%SCFVM.BITNET@CUNYVM.CUNY.EDU>

FILM-L%VMTECMEX.BITNET@VM1.NODAK.EDU

Mailing list to serve as a crossroad of different points of view about cinema: The film as art, entertainment, busines, or communications media. Also to serve as a source for help of amateur film makers on any format. This includes reviews about new equipment, techniques, et cetera. The contribution of everybody interested in any way, or area of specialization, from the moviegoer to the expert in a field is encouraged.

BitNetusers may subscribe by sending the following command to LISTSERV@VMTECMEX: SUBSCRIBE FILM-L your_full_name where "your_full_name" is your real name, not your login Id. Non-BitNet users may subscribe by sending the above command in the text/body of a message to LISTSERV%VMTECMEX.BITNET@VM1.NODAK.EDU.

Coordinator: Alejandro Kurczyn S. <499229%VMTECMEX.BITNET@VM1.NODAK.EDU>

FINAID-L on LISTSERV@PSUVM.BITNET
     or LISTSERV@PSUVM.PSU.EDU

FINAID-L on LISTSERV@PSUVM - Administration of Student Financial Aid

FINAID-L IS: designed to provide subscribers with an interactive, informational network. Administrative questions, concerns, comments, problems and problem resolution can be shared with others in the student financial aid community. The concept is to discuss financial aid-related matters and to share expertise, experiences and knowledge with other university student financial aid administrators and related personnel.

FINAID-L IS: a mechanism for student financial aid information exchange. Appropriate topics include, but are not limited to, the use of professional judgment, interpretation and potential impact of federal regulations (e.g. Reauthorization), student financial aid automation and institutional policies and regulations. The posting of financial aid-related position vacancies is permitted.

FINAID-L IS NOT: a medium through which to apply for financial aid or to solicit for private business matters regardless of their relation to financial aid.

To subscribe to the list, send the following command to LISTSERV@PSUVM or LISTSERV@PSUVM.PSU.EDU in the BODY of e-mail or a BITNET interactive message:

SUB FINAID-L your full name

For example: SUB FINAID-L Joseph Aid Administrator

Archives of FINAID-L can be accessed by sending the command INDEX FINAID-L to LISTSERV@PSUVM.

Owner: Robert E. Quinn, Director of Computer Services, Office of Student Aid, The Pennsylvania State University <REQ1@PSUADMIN.BITNET>

FINEART%ecs.umass.edu@RELAY.CS.NET

The FINEART Forum is dedicated to International collaboration between artists and scientists. It is subsidized by the International Society for the Arts, Science, and Technology (ISAST), 2020 Milvia, Berkeley, CA 94704. The purpose of this bulletin board is to disseminate information regarding the use of computers in the Fine Arts. Topics to be included are:

Computers used in the design of works of art
Computers used to fabricate works of art
Computers used within works of art
Computers used to analyse works of art
Computers used to criticize art
Computers used to distribute art

General areas of interest include:

Art & AI	Interactive Video
Computer Aided Fabrication	Sensory Environments
Computer Animation	Shape Grammars
Design Rule Systems	Style Simulation
Image Rendering	Picture Networks
Image Synthesis	Paint Systems

Send submissions & requests for list membership to:
Internet: FINEART%ecs.umass.csnet@RELAY.CS.NET
BITNET submissions: FINEART@umaecs
BITNET subscriptions: LISTSERV@RUTVM1   (U.S.)
               LISTSERV@EB0UB011 (Europe)
CSNET: FINEART@ecs.umass.edu
MCI-mail: FAST
PHONE: (413) 545-1902

Moderator: Ray Lauzzana <lauzzana%ecs.umass.edu@RELAY.CS.NET>

firearms}@TUT.CIS.OHIO-STATE.EDU
firearms@cs.cmu.edu
cbosgd!osu-cis!firearms (UUCP)

This mailing list has been created to provide an environment in which sportsmen can discuss issues of concern to them. Topics include but are not limited to hunting, firearms safety, legal issues, reloading tips, maintenance suggestions, target shooting, and dissemination of general info. The list is NOT intended to discuss the merits of gun control.

Archives are maintained by the moderator. As of 1 Jul 85, the list is 4 months old, having 11 back issues comprising approximately 160K of text.

All requests to be added to or deleted from this list, problems, questions, etc., should be sent to firearms-request@cs.cmu.edu.

Moderator: Karl Kleinpaste <Karl_Kleinpaste@N2.SP.CS.CMU.EDU>

firearms-politics@cs.cmu.edu

Mailing list for the purpose of political discussion, announcements, and coordination in the area of firearms legislation and general talk about 2nd Amendment rights and current trends. Companion mailing list to firearms@cs.cmu.edu, which is restricted to technical discussion.

All requests to be added to or deleted from this list, problems, questions, etc., should be sent to firearms-politics-request@cs.cmu.edu

Moderator: Karl Kleinpaste <Karl_Kleinpaste@N2.SP.CS.CMU.EDU>

Firewalls@GreatCircle.COM   [Last Update 11/92]

This is a list for discussions of issues involved with setting up and maintaining Internet security firewall systems. All messages sent to the list are immediately forwarded to the list. There is digestified version of the list is available as "Firewalls-Digest@GreatCircle.COM". The digestified version has exactly the same messages as the direct version; the messages are simply bundled into digests daily (or more frequently, if traffic warrants). Both lists are unmoderated.

To join the Firewalls mailing list, send the command

subscribe firewalls

in the body of a message to "Majordomo@GreatCircle.COM". If you want to subscribe something other than the account the mail is coming from, such as a local redistribution list, then append that address to the "subscribe" command; for example, to subscribe "local-firewalls":

subscribe firewalls local-firewalls@your.domain.net

To subscribe to the digestified version, substitute "firewalls-digest" for "firewalls" in the examples above.

All messages to the list are being archived. A copy of the archive is available by anonymous FTP from host FTP.GreatCircle.COM, directory "pub/archive", compressed file "firewalls.Z". The copy of the archive available by anonymous FTP is updated every night at midnight local time (0700 GMT in the summer, 0800 GMT in the winter).

For further information, contact:

Brent Chapman   Great Circle Associates
Brent@GreatCircle.COM   1057 West Dana Street
+1 415 962 0841   Mountain View, CA 94041

FIST@hamp.hampshire.edu

This list is for discussion of feminism and science and technology. This will be an unmoderated list. If you are a scientist and a feminist or if you are a feminist and interested in science and technology this list is for you. The idea of this list is to discuss critiques of science and move beyond these critiques into the realm of how to create a feminist science? What do we need to pay attention to? How does one do this and get tenure? How do we teach science?

To get on this list, send a message to FIST-request@hamp.hampshire.edu. Send all adminstrivia there too (getting off the list, changing addresses, etc.) Please include a paragraph introducing yourself and what you do.

Please be patient with the list subscription requests.

To send a message to the whole list, send to FIST@hamp.hampshire.edu

List owner: Michelle Murrain, School of Natural Science
Hampshire College Amherst, MA 01002
mmurrain@hamp.hampshire.edu

FIT-L on LISTSERV@ETSUADMN.BITNET

FIT-L is a discussion list for exchanging ideas, tips -- any type of information about wellness, exercise, and diet.

To subscribe, send the following command to LISTSERV@ETSUADMN.BITNET in the BODY of mail or interactive message :

SUB FIT-L your full name

where "your full name" is your name. For example:

SUB FIT-L Jon Doe

Owner: Chris Jones <JONES@ETSUADMN.BITNET>

FLEXWORK on LISTSERV@PSUHMC.BITNET

FLEXWORK (Flexible Work Environment List) is a list to discuss how people are handling flexible work situations. Telecommuting, work-sharing and flex-time are some examples.

Archives of FLEXWORK back issues can be listed by sending the command INDEX FLEXWORK to LISTSERV@PSUHMC.BITNET

To subscribe, send the following command to LISTSERV@PSUHMC.BITNET in the BODY of the mail or message:

SUB FLEXWORK your full name

where "your full name" is your name. For example:

SUB FLEXWORK Joan Doe

Owner: MHOLCOMB@PSUHMC.BITNET Maria Holcomb

flight-sim@grove.iup.edu   [Last Update 28-January-1992]

An unmoderated list for flight simulation topics, including hardware and software questions, product reviews, rumors, etc. While most discussion is expected to center around Microsoft Flight Simulator and its add-ons, it is not restricted to any particular product or class of products.

Archives of list traffic and flight simulation files are available via anonymous ftp from acorn.grove.iup.edu.

All requests to be added to or deleted from this list should be sent to flight-sim-request@grove.iup.edu as should problems or questions relating to list operation.

Co-ordinator: Mark J Strawcutter <mjstraw@grove.iup.edu>

Folk_Music@nysernet.org

New American Folk Music discussion List

Folk_music is a moderated discussion list dealing with the music of the recent wave of american singer/songwriters. List traffic consists of tour schedules, reviews, album release info and other information on artists like Shawn Colvin, Mary-Chapin Carpenter, David Wilcox, Nanci Griffith, Darden Smith, Maura O'Connell, Don Henry, and others.

Membership to this discussion list is open free of charge to all interested individuals or organizations.

There are no archives as of yet.

To subscribe, send mail to <listserv@nysernet.org> with this request

SUBSCRIBE FOLK_MUSIC Your Fullname

To unsubscribe, send:

UNSUBSCRIBE FOLK_MUSIC

To post a message, send it to:

folk_music@nysernet.org

We also will maintain files for FTP at nysernet.org. To access these files via anonymous FTP logon as GUEST giving your user-id@your.local.host as a password. Files and subdirectories are contained within the directory /FOLK_MUSIC. These may not be available until July.

All questions, requests for information, etc., should be sent to the moderator.

List Moderator: Alan Rowoth <alanr@nysernet.org>

FOODWINE on LISTSERV@CMUVM or LISTSERV@CMUVM.CSV.CMICH.EDU   [Last Update 11/92]

FOODWINE is designed to facilitate discussion among those seriously interested in the academic study of food and its' accompaniments.

The list takes a broad approach to the study of food and its accompaniments, from a variety of disciplines, such as marketing, communications, hospitality, consumer affairs, hotel and catering management. People in fields with marginal interests in the subject, such as cultural anthropology and sociology, and all others with a serious interest in the subject are also invited.

To subscribe to FOODWINE, send the following command to LISTSERV@CMUVM via mail text or interactive message: SUBSCRIBE FOODWINE your full name

where "your full name" is your name. For example, SUBSCRIBE FOODWINE Joe Shmoe

Owners: Musa Knickerbocker <32HYFEV@CMUVM>
   or 32HYFEV@CMUVM.CSV.CMICH.EDU
   Elliott Parker <3ZLUFUR@CMUVM>
   or 3ZLUFUR@CMUVM.CSV.CMICH.EDU

foNETiks <r34334%UQAM.BITNET@CUNYVM.CUNY.EDU>

Special interest group for the phonetic sciences called "foNETiks". It will publish information of current interest to researchers and students interested in speech production and speech perception, speech disorders, automatic speech recognition and speech synthesis. We would like to see contributions on signal analysis software used in speech research, current research in the phonetic sciences, meetings, questions, etc. The newsletter can be obtained by sending a simple request to R34334@UQAM on the BITNET network. foNETiks is also available from Psychnet <EPSYNET%UHUPVM1.BITNET@CUNYVM.CUNY.EDU>.

All requests to be added to or deleted from this list, problems, questions, etc., should be sent to the Coordinator.

Coordinator: Eric Keller <r34334%UQAM.BITNET@CUNYVM.CUNY.EDU>

FORENS-L@FAUVAX.BITNET (BITNET) [Last Updated 12-October-1991]
FORENS-L@ACC.FAU.EDU (Internet)

Forens-L is an unmoderated discussion list dealing with forensic aspects of anthropology, biology, chemistry, odontology, pathology, psychology, serology, toxicology, criminalistics, and expert witnessing and presentation of evidence in court.

Membership to this discussion list is open free of charge to all interested individuals or organizations.

To subscribe, send mail to FORENS-REQUEST@ACC.FAU.EDU (BITNET-restricted users send to FORENS-REQUEST@FAUVAX) with this request in the message body:

SUBSCRIBE FORENS-L Your Real Name

To unsubscribe, send:

UNSUBSCRIBE FORENS-L

To post a message, send it to:

FORENS-L@ACC.FAU.EDU or FORENS-L@FAUVAX

All questions, requests for information, etc., should be sent to the List Owners. Technical issues should be addressed to the List Manager.

List Owners: M. Yasar Iscan (Iscan@acc.fau.edu, Iscan@FauVax)
  Ronald K. Wright (RKW@MedExam.FtL.FL.US)
List Manager: Ralph P Carpenter (Ralpho@acc.fau.edu, Ralpho@FauVax)

FRAC-L%GITVM1.BITNET@CUNYVM.CUNY.EDU

Mailing list dedicated to the computergraphical generation of fractal images.

In conjunction with the list, an archive of programs submitted by users will be maintained. Mr. Homer Smith of "Art Matrix" in Ithaca, New York, has donated a program library, which will soon be available from LISTSERV at GITVM1.

To add yourself to the list, send the command SUBSCRIBE FRAC-L Your_Full_Name via mail to LISTSERV@GITVM1.BITNET or to LISTSERV%GITVM1.BITNET@CUNYVM.CUNY.EDU (Internet) where Your_Full_Name is your real name (not your userid). To remove yourself from the list, send the command UNSUBSCRIBE FRAC-L

All other problems, questions, etc., should be sent to the Coordinator.

Coordinator: David D. Lester <CC100DL%GITVM1@CUNYVM.CUNY.EDU>

FRANZ-FRIENDS@BERKELEY.EDU

Discusses the Franz Lisp Language, both the public domain version and the versions from Franz Inc.

A sub-list, FRANZ-COMPOSERS@BERKELEY.EDU, is composed of people who are in charge of maintaining Franz LISP. The sub-list is used for sending bug fixes.

The archive of old messages is kept on MIT-MC, in the file: LSPMAI; FRANZL FORUM

All requests to be added to or deleted from this list, problems, questions, etc., should be sent to FRANZ-FRIENDS-REQUEST@BERKELEY.EDU.

Coordinator: Charley Cox (cox@BERKELEY.EDU)

FREE-L on LISTSERV@INDYCMS or LISTSERV@INDYCMS.IUPUI.EDU [Last Update 11/92]

FREE-L is an electronic conference for the free exchange of information regarding the issues of fathers' rights. These issues arise in the context of divorce, custody disputes, and visitation and child-support arrangements.

FREE-L is sponsored by FREE, the Fathers' Rights and Equality Exchange, and was set up by FREE's Indiana Area Coordinator, Dale Marmaduke. Dale can be reached via email at:

ITOG400@INDYCMS.IUPUI.EDU

Anyone with an interest in this subject is welcome to subscribe and take part in the discussion. We look forward to this being an interesting, animated, and educational discussion group.

SUBSCRIPTION PROCEDURE:

To subscribe from a bitnet account send an interactive or e-mail message addressed to LISTSERV@INDYCMS . Internet users send mail to LISTSERV@INDYCMS.IUPUI.EDU. (In mail, leave the subject line blank and make the text of your message the following:

SUB FREE-L Yourfirstname Yourlastname

Questions can be addressed to either Dale, or Anne Mitchell [free@gw.home.vix.com].

Owner: Dale Marmaduke ITOG400@INDYCMS.IUPUI.EDU

FREEMACS

Mailing list for Freemacs, the PD (actually copylefted) programmable editor for the IBM-PC and Z-100.

To sign up, send a mail message to LISTSERV at CLVM (LISTSERV%CLVM.BITNET@CUNYVM.CUNY.EDU). If you are on bitnet, you can send a direct message. The list server command, whether sent by mail or BitNet "direct message", should be "SUBSCRIBE FREEMACS human name". Example: TELL LISTSERV AT CLVM SUBSCRIBE FREEMACS John Q. Public or in the body of a netmail message: SUBSCRIBE FREEMACS John Q. Public The help command will return a help screen via direct message or mail.

Cordinator: Russell Nelson <BH01%CLUTX.BITNET@CUNYVM.CUNY.EDU>

FRONTIER on LISTSERV@DARTCMS1.BITNET   [Last Update April 1992]
or LISTSERV@DARTCMS1.DARTMOUTH.EDU

This list is for the exchange of information for Userland's Frontier, a scripting environment for the Macintosh under System 7. Users are encouraged to share any technical information and interesting scripts they have and post technical questions. Postings from America Online CompuServe, and AppleLink will be gatewayed to this list. This list is unmoderated.

To subscribe to the list, send mail to LISTSERV@DARTCMS1.BITNET or LISTSERV@DARTCMS1.DARTMOUTH.EDU with the contents (of the BODY of the mail):

SUB FRONTIER your full name Eg. SUB FRONTIER J. Appleseed

The list owner is Andy Williams <andy.j.williams@dartmouth.edu>

fsp-discussion@Germany.EU.net   [Last Update 11/92]

Contact: listmaster@Germany.EU.net

Purpose: Discussion of the new FSP protocol. FSP is a set of programs that implements a public-access archive similar to an anonymous-FTP archive. The difference is that FSP is connection-less and virtually state-less. This list is open for everybody.

Coordinator: Ingo Dressler <archive-admin@Germany.EU.net>

fusion@ZORCH.SF-BAY.ORG
fusion%zorch@AMES.ARC.NASA.GOV
fusion%zorch.sf-bay.org@RELAY.CS.NET

The "Fusion" list is for discussion of nuclear fusion.

Contributions sent to this list are automatically archived. BitNet users can obtain a list of the available archive files by sending an "INDEX FUSION" command to LISTSERV@NDSUVM1. These files can then be retrieved by means of a "GET FUSION filetype" command, or using the database search facilities of LISTSERV. Send an "INFO DATABASE" command for more information on the latter.

You may also obtain copies of the list notebooks via anonymous FTP to VM1.NoDak.EDU (192.33.18.30), userid ANONYMOUS, any password. Once validated do a CD LISTARCH and DIR FUSION.* to see the notebooks available. The file system is NOT hierarchical so you must do a CD ANONYMOUS if you want to return to the "root".

BitNet users may subscribe to FUSION by sending the command: SUB FUSION Your_full_name (eg. SUB FUSION Jane Doe) to LISTSERV@NDSUVM1 (or LISTSERV@VM1.NODAK.EDU). The command may be in the BODY or TEXT of the mail (NOT the subject) or be sent interactively (via TELL or SEND) to LISTSERV on BITNET/EARN/NetNorth.

Non-BitNet users can join the list by sending their reqeust to fusion-request@ZORCH.SF-Bay.ORG.

Coordinator: Scott Hazen Mueller <scott@ZORCH.SF-BAY.ORG>
<scott%zorch@AMES.ARC.NASA.GOV> <scott%zorch.sf-bay.org@RELAY.CS.NET>

fuzzy-ramblings@ferkel.ucsb.edu   [Last Update 8/92]

Purpose: Discussion of the musical group Fuzzbox.

Contact: fuzzy-ramblings-request@ferkel.ucsb.edu (Robert Earl)

FWAKE-L%IRLEARN.BITNET@CUNYVM.CUNY.EDU

A forum for a broad discussion about James Joyce's FINNEGANS WAKE. The James Joyce Institute of Ireland's Finnegans Wake Study Group has been doing their best to get the jokes in Finnegans Wake for the past decade or so. The Study Group thinks it is time for such groups to pool their findings.

There are plans to start a second associated service to share page-by-page, line-by-line notes to the text of FINNEGANS WAKE in a fixed format analogous to that of Roland McHugh's ANNOTATIONS. The Coordinator is working on a program to vet the mail from such a service.

All requests to be added to or deleted from the mailing list, or to have files distributed, should be sent to the Coordinator.

Coordinator: Michael O'Kelly <MOKELLY%IRLEARN.BITNET@CUNYVM.CUNY.EDU>

GAELIC-L%IRLEARN.BITNET@VM1.NODAK.EDU

An open, multi-disciplinary, discussion list set up to facilitate exchange of news, views, and information in Irish/Scots Gaelic.

To subscribe send a message or mail to one of:

        LISTSERV%IRLEARN.BITNET@VM1.NODAK.EDU   Internet (US)
        LISTSERV@IRLEARN.UCD.IE   Internet (via MX)
        LISTSERV@IRLEARN   BitNet/EARN/NetNorth
        LISTSERV@EARN.IRLEARN   JANET
    with the BODY or TEXT being:
    SUB GAELIC-L yourfirstname yourlastname

Coordinator: Marion Gunn <MGUNN%IRLEARN.BITNET@VM1.NODAK.EDU>

GAMES-L@BROWNVM.BROWN.EDU   [Last Updated 12-October-1991]

Mailing list dedicated to the discussion of computer games. Games played on any type of system are covered.

BitNet users can add themselves to the list by issuing the following command to LISTSERV@BROWNVM, @DHDURZ1, @LEHIIBM1, @GREARN, @KRSNUCC1, or

@UTARLVM1: SUBSCRIBE GAMES-L your_full_name where your_full_name is your real name (not your userid). BitNet users can delete themselves from the list with the command: UNSUBSCRIBE GAMES-L

Non-BitNet users should [un]subscribe by sending mail to LISTSERV@BROWNVM.BROWN.EDU with the above commands in the message body.

All other requests, problems, questions, etc., should be sent to the Moderator.

Moderator: Spyros Bartsocas <SCB@BROWNVM.BROWN.EDU>

GARDENS on LISTSERV@UKCC [Last Updated 28-January-1992]
or LISTSERV@UKCC.UKY.EDU

The purpose of Gardens & Gardening is to promote and exchange information about home gardening. Everyone is welcome to participate, especially the novice gardener. Topics will include vegetable gardens, herbs, flowers, ornamental gardening, container gardening, and so on.

Since this is such a broad topic, we may, at a later date, divide the list into various groups, such as indoor and outdoor gardening.

If you wish to subscribe to GARDENS, send an e-mail message to LISTSERV@UKCC.UKY.EDU, or BITNET nodes can send to LISTSERV@UKCC. The message should contain only the following command (ie. in the body of the mail):

SUBSCRIBE GARDENS yourfirstname yourlastname

Owner: Crovo@UKCC (Bob Crovo)
          Editor@UKCC (Marguerite Floyd)
Notebooks: yes public weekly

GATED-PEOPLE@DEVVAX.TN.CORNELL.EDU

This list is for discussion of Cornell's GateDaemon software product (aka gated). Gated is a Unix daemon supportting multiple routing protocols, including RIP, EGP and BGP. Topics include capabilities, bug reports and fixes, requests for help and announcements of new releases.

Uncompressed archives are available by anonymous FTP from DEVVAX.TN.CORNELL.EDU in the directory pub/lists/gated-people. Archives are also available from the archive server, GATED-PEOPLE-ARCHIVE@DEVVAX.TN.CORNELL.EDU. For instructions on the use of the archive server, send mail with a subject line of "help".

All requests to be added to or deleted from this list, problems, questions, etc., should be sent to GATED-PEOPLE-REQUEST@DEVVAX.TN.CORNELL.EDU.

Coordinator: Jeffrey C Honig <JCH@DEVVAX.TN.CORNELL.EDU>

GayNet@ATHENA.MIT.EDU

A mailing list about lesbian and gay concerns on college campuses including, but not limited to, outreach programs, political action, AIDS education, dealing with school administrations, social programs, and just finding out what other support and social groups are doing. Items of general lesbian/gay interest are also welcome. The list is not moderated; messages are sent in digest format.

Archives are being kept, but are not easily available. Contact gaynet-request@ATHENA.MIT.EDU for more info.

Requests to be added or deleted from this list, problems, questions, etc., should be sent to gaynet-request@ATHENA.MIT.EDU.

Coordinator: Mark Rosenstein <mar@MIT.EDU>

Genetics@IndyCMS.IUPUI.EDU (Internet) [LastUpdated 12-October-1991]
Geneteics@IndyCMS.BITNET (BITNET)

Genetics is dedicated to the discussion of clinical human genetics. Its focus is on the diagnosis, management and counseling of conditions of known or possible genetic origin, and the clinical application of genetic technologies in obstetrics, pediatrics and medicine.

Genetics is open to all persons interested in clinical human genetics, including health care providers (clinicians, nurses, and other health professionals) and consumers (interested laypeople).

Genetics is owned and coordinated by a Board-certified Clinical Geneticist (Luis Fernando Escobar, MD) and an interested layperson (John B Harlan).

Available by free subscription from ListServ@IndyCMS (CREN) ListServ@IndyCMS.IUPUI.Edu (Internet). To subscribe send mail to either of those LISTSERV addresses with the following command in the body (text) of the mail: SUB GENETICS yourfirstname yourlastname

List owners/coordinators:

>   Editorial: Luis Fernando Escobar MD
>   IZED100@IndyVAX (CREN)
>   IZED100@IndyVAX.IUPUI.Edu (Internet)

>   Administrative: John B Harlan
>   IJBH200@IndyVAX (CREN)
>   IJBH200@IndyVAX.IUPUI.Edu (Internet)

GEODESIC%UBVM.BITNET@MITVMA.MIT.EDU

This list is for the discussion of Buckminster "Bucky" Fuller, his works and his philosophies on Life, the Universe, and Everything (NOT The Douglas Adams book!). For those of you who don't know, Bucky is the person who invented the Geodesic Dome, which is what we all played on as children in the playground (the domes with all the triangles, remember?). Another example of geodesic architecture is the giant white sphere at Disney World's "Epcot Center". Of course, Bucky did a LOT more than just invent the Geodesic Dome! He invented other means of housing people cheaply, efficiently, COMFORTABLY, and basically anywhere in the world! (Yes, even ON the oceans!) So if you're interested in discussing Bucky, learning more about him, or finding out about 8500 ft. high pyramidal cities that float in the ocean and house 1,000,000 people comfortably (2000 sq ft. apartments with 1000 sq ft. extra patio/garden space), or 1+ mile diameter spherical cities that FLOAT IN THE AIR *WITHOUT POWER*, then sign up on the list!

To sign up, send a mail message to LISTSERV%UBVM.BITNET@MITVMA.MIT.EDU with the line SUBSCRIBE GEODESIC Your Real Name as the body of the letter.

Coordinator: Patrick G. Salsbury <V291NHTP@UBVMSC.CC.BUFFALO.EDU>
V291NHTP@UBVMSD.BITNET

GEOGRAPH%FINHUTC.BITNET@CUNYVM.CUNY.EDU
GEOGRAPH on LISTSERV@FINHUTC

GEOGRAPH - a global mailing list for geography has been opened for general or topical discussions about geographical issues at the node FINHUTC by a group of young university geographers in Helsinki, Finland.

Subscription to this list is welcomed from anyone with skills and/or interests relevant to the field of geography.

To subscribe, send the following command to LISTSERV@FINHUTC, via mail or interactive message (Internet users send mail only, to the address:
LISTSERV%FINHUTC.BITNET@CUNYVM.CUNY.EDU):

SUBscribe GEOGRAPH <your_full_name>

example: SUBscribe GEOGRAPH John Smith

IMPORTANT: Send the subscription command to LISTSERV@FINHUTC and NOT to GEOGRAPH@FINHUTC !!

Contributions to the discussion list must be sent to GEOGRAPH@FINHUTC.

More information about the GEOGRAPH list may be obtained from:

PKOKKONE@FINUHA	Pellervo Kokkonen
PYYHTIA@FINUHA	Mervi Pyyhtia

In technical questions, please refer to the listserver HELP system by sending the command HELP to LISTSERV@FINHUTC or your nearest listserver. (For more specific informations, use the command HELP <topic>)

GO-L%SMCVAX.BITNET@VM1.NODAK.EDU (Internet)
GO-L on MAILSERV@SMCVAX (BITNET)

GO-L, a list for game players interested in the game of GO is now available for public use. The list is sponsored by Saint Michael's College in Winooski, Vermont. The list is intended to serve as a discussion point for GO-related topics, and as a meeting place for EMAIL games between list members.

In contrast to the majority of BITNET lists, this one is supported by a DEC uVAX 3400 running the MAILSERV program for VAX/VMS. Consequently, commands used to access the list are slightly different than those used by LISTSERV. MAILSERV supports the following commands, among others:

HELP   - Ask for the HELP file.
SUBSCRIBE - Subscribe to a list.
LISTS   - List all mailing lists for a MAILSERVer.

MAILSERV accepts only mail messages; not interactive SENDs or TELLs. Be sure to send only a mail message with your commands in the body of the message. Don't type any other text into the message; it won't work!

As an example, to subscribe to the GO-L list, send a mail message to

MAILSERV%SMCVAX.BITNET@VM1.NODAK.EDU

and in the body of the message just put the command

SUBSCRIBE GO-L

Notice that you don't need to give a subscription name; MAILSERV gets it From your address. List owner: <GOODWIN%SMCVAX.BITNET@VM1.NODAK.EDU>

golden@hobbes.ucsd.edu   [Last Update 9/92]

A mailing list for Golden Retriever enthusiasts. Suitable topics include questions and answers regarding the Golden Retriever breed in general, news bits, article summaries, discussions of particular lines and breeders, shows, activities (CCI, therapy dogs, guide dogs), training techniques, bragging, summaries of local GR club activities or newsletters, other items which might be considered too Golden-introverted for rec.pets.dogs, cooperation on a breed specific FAQ for r.p.d, etc.

This list is NOT a substitute for rec.pets.dogs - please post items of general interest to that newsgroup. Should list traffic warrant, this list may be converted from message-at-a-time to digest format. Messages sent to the list should not be reposted without permission of the author.

To subscribe, send a message to "listserv@hobbes.ucsd.edu" with the line "subscribe golden firstname lastname" in the message body, where <firstname lastname> is your own name. The list server will deduce your email address. Once subscribed, send messages to the list at "golden@hobbes.ucsd.edu", and send administrative requests to the listserver "listserv@hobbes.ucsd.edu" or to "golden-request@hobbes.ucsd.edu"

Coordinator: Wade Blomgren <wade@hobbes.ucsd.edu>

Golf-L on LISTSERV@ubvm.bitnet   [Last Update 9/92]
or LISTSERV@ubvm.cc.buffalo.edu

The Golf-L discussion list was formed to give golfers and those interested in golf a place to discuss all forms of golf and all topics related to golf. Some topics may be current tournaments, etc.

To subscribe to Golf-L, send the following command to LISTSERV@UBVM via mail text or interactive messaging: SUBSCRIBE GOLF-L your name. For example: SUBSCRIBE GOLF-L John Doe

Owner: Chris Tanski captanski33@snycorva.bitnet cttx@vax5.cit.cornell.edu

GOULDBUGS@cs.utah.edu   [Last Updated 12-October-1991]

A mailing list for reporting bugs and problems with the GOULD UTX/32 (UNIX) operating system and software.

All requests to be added to or deleted from this list, problems, questions, etc., should be sent to gouldbugs-request@BRL.MIL.

There is a BitNet sub-distribution list, GOULDBUG@CLVM; BitNet subscribers can join by sending the SUB command with your name. For example, SEND LISTSERV@CLVM SUB GOULDBUG Jon Doe To be removed from the list, SEND LISTSERV@CLVM SIGNOFF. To make contributions to the list, BitNet subscribers should send mail to the Internet list name, NOT to the BITNET list name.

Coordinator: Howard Walter <howard@BRL.MIL>

GovDoc-L%PSUVM.BITNET@VM1.NODAK.EDU

Mailing list with a focus is specifically on issues of information dissemination through Federal Depository Libraries. Issues to be discussed include: electronic dissemination policies of the Government Printing Office(GPO), the 1990 Census, access to Federal documents (Freedom of Information Act issues), automation of document collections in libraries (Marcive v. OCLC tapes; database consideration; retrospective conversion; etc.), document end user education and legislation related to depository libraries. United Nations, State and Foreign Government documents can be included for discussion.

The list is moderated but uncensored. It is edited with the intention of producing a digest at the end of the year.

BitNet users may subscribe by sending the following command via mail or an interactive message to LISTSERV@PSUVM: SUB GovDoc-L Your full name where "Your full name" is your real name, not your login Id. Non-BitNet users can join the list be sending the above command as the only line in the text/body of a message to LISTSERV%PSUVM.BITNET@VM1.NODAK.EDU.

Coordinators: Diane Kovacs <KOVACSD%BKNLVMS.BITNET@VM1.NODAK.EDU> Michael J. Kovacs <KOVACS%BKNLVMS.BITNET@VM1.NODAK.EDU>

grad-adv@listserv.acs.unc.edu

This list has three major goals at the onset:
1. to put folks who advise undergraduates about graduate school in touch with their peers and with graduate schools. Being on the list will provide this service.
2. to create of a catalog of accessable catalogs (using Art St. George's Library catalog catalog as a model) to facilitate electronic access to graduate school information. I will gather information here unless there is another volunteer out there.
3. to identify useful and/or neccessary information that would be used in a graduate school information database with an eye toward network standard tags and a single engine queriable distributed database of graduate school information (probably SQL for example) that would allow students and advisors to search several catalogs maintained at different universities.

Point three is very blue sky for the moment, but if we keep it in mind, the technology exists and the end is actually achievable. Other points will, I'm sure, arise.

To add yourself to grad-adv, send a MAIL message of: subscribe grad-adv to listserv@listserv.acs.unc.edu

To remove yourself from grad-adv, send a MAIL message of: unsubscribe grad-adv to listserv@listserv.acs.unc.edu

Mail to be distributed to grad-adv should be sent to: grad-adv@listserv.acs.unc.edu

To learn more about our UNIX-based listserv and mail archiver send a MAIL message of: help to listserv@listserv.acs.unc.edu

GRANOLA%GITVM1.BITNET@CUNYVM.CUNY.EDU
GRANOLA on LISTSERV@GITVM1

The GRANOLA list is a forum for discussion of vegetarian-relevant issues. Topics include but are not limited to the following: exchange of really cool recipes, discussion of the various types of vegetarianism, nutrition information, a supportive atmosphere, animal rights issues, cookbook reccomenda- tions, tips on surviving as a vegetarian while on a college meal plan, herbal remedies, ideas/support for those wanting to shift to a vegetarian diet, etc. This list does not discriminate on the basis of gender, sexual orientation. race, religion, nationality, eating preferences (the list is open to all: lacto-ovo-vegetarians, vegans, macrobiotics, people who are not vegetarian, etc). Respect for the ideals and practices of others is appreciated.

To subscribe to GRANOLA use LISTSERV interactives or send mail to LISTSERV%GITVM1.BITNET@CUNYVM.CUNY.EDU with the text: SUB GRANOLA (your full name)

To send mail to the list, the address is GRANOLA%GITVM1.BITNET@CUNYVM.CUNY.EDU

Note that a default setting of the list is such that you do not receive copies of the letters that you send to GRANOLA - if you wish to change the option for your account after you subscribe, then TELL LISTSERV AT GITVM1 SET GRANOLA REPRO (or send mail to LISTSERV@GITVM1.BITNET with the command SET GRANOLA REPRO).

Feel free to send any questions or comments to the owners/moderators of GRANOLA:

Geri Weitzman ST702355%BROWNVM.BITNET@CUNYVM.CUNY.EDU
Carole Mah ST701852%BROWNVM.BITNET@CUNYVM.CUNY.EDU

GRAPHIX on LISTSERV@UTFSM.Bitnet

This list is for discussion of Graphics Formats, Documents, and Many Archives relatives with Graphics, all oriented to PC/PS and "COMPATIBLEs" users.

To subscribe to the list send e-mail to LISTSERV@UTFSM.BITNET with the BODY of the mail containing the command

SUB GRAPHICS your full name

Problems, question and contribucions send to GRAPHIX list.

Owner: Hernan Lobos *Mitzio* HLOBOS@UTFSM.Bitnet

GraphUK%graphics.computer-science.manchester.ac.uk@NSS.CS.UCL.AC.UK

Discussion of all aspects of computer graphics.

Moderators: Terry Hewitt Toby Howard
<THOWARD%graphics.computer-science.manchester.ac.uk@NSS.CS.UCL.AC.UK>

Green on ListServ@IndyCMS (BITNET/CREN)

or ListServ@IndyCMS.IUPUI.Edu (Internet)

Green is dedicated to the study of Green movements worldwide and their influence on public opinion and public policy. The scope of the list's discussion is global: all Green movements, at every level, are of interest to this list.

Of special interest to the list is the emerging Green movement in the US -- how it is being organized by various competing elements, how it is being influenced by other Green movements worldwide (especially European), how it is interacting with those movements, and how it is influencing American public opinion and public policy on the local, state, regional and national level.

It is emphasized that the purpose of Green is the *study* of Green movements. Green is *not* a tool for organizing or promoting those movements. In keeping with policies defining the appropriate use of academic networks (which often include prohibitions on explicit political activism), adherence to the stated purpose of this list is strictly monitored and enforced.

Green is open to all persons interested in the study of Green movements worldwide. To subscribe send mail to LISTSERV@IndyCMS on BITNET or LISTSERV@IndyCMS.IUPUI.EDU with the body containing SUB GREEN yourfirstname yourlastname

> List owner/editor/coordinator: John B Harlan
> IJBH200@IndyVAX (CREN)
> IJBH200@IndyVAX.IUPUI.Edu (Internet)

GreenOrg on ListServ@IndyCMS.BITNET

GreenOrg (Green organizations) is dedicated to discussion of strategic and tactical issues facing Green organizations worldwide.

GreenOrg joins the Green (Green movements) list, dedicated to the study of Green movements worldwide and their influence on public opinion and public policy. The scope of the Green list's discussion is global: all Green movements, at every level, are of interest to the Green list.

To subscribe to the GREENORG list send e-mail to LISTSERV@INDYVAX on BITNET with the following command in the BODY of the mail:

SUB GREENORG yourfirstname yourlastname

List owner/coordinator: John B Harlan JBHarlan@IndyVAX JBHarlan@IndyVAX.IUPUI.Edu

GRiD@STALLER.SPT.TEK.COM (Internet)
tektronix!tekcrl!staller!GRiD (UUCP)

AGOG (A GRiD Owners' Group) mailing list. This list is primarily for hobbyist-types who have purchased used GRiD Compass computers.

All requests to be added to or deleted from this list, problems, questions, etc., should be sent to jans@TEKCRL.TEK.COM or tektronix!tekcrl!jans (UUCP).

Coordinator: Jan Steinman <jans%STALLER.SPT.TEK.COM@RELAY.CS.NET>

GSDSP@OCF.Berkeley.edu   [Last Updated 28-January-1992]

The GS/DSP Discussion List serves as an unmoderated forum for discussion of GS/DSP co-processor board for the Apple II family of computers currently being developed by Pete Snowberg. This list is for the discemination of information about the GS/DSP and the discussion of possible applications for the GS/DSP.

Messages sent to this list are not reviewed by the list owner and are automatically forwarded to everyone on the list. If you want to send private messages to each other or to Pete this is not the way to do it. If you would like to send a private message to Pete Snowberg you can reach him at:

pets@abacus.com

Messages are not verified and the authors of the messages are solely responsible for their content.

List coordinator:

If you want to unsubscribe, change address, contact me at the following address:

gsdsp-request@ocf.berkeley.edu

To post submissions to everyone on the mailing list you can send it to:

GSDSP@OCF.Berkeley.edu

When you send your message to the above address, everybody on the list gets it! This is where you send your submissions to the mailing list. If you want to be removed from the mailing list do not send it here but send it to the list coordinator address (gsdsp-request@ocf.berkeley.edu).

One more note on this mailing list. This list is being run out of the Open Computing Facility at UC Berkeley. This is a cluster of 18 Apollo Domain DN3500 workstations run by a completely student staff. This cluster is not the most stable one in the world but mail here generally is. (Note: I said GENERALLY.) From time to time this cluster might disappear off of the net and your submission might not make it through. But these occurrences should be even less frequent now with the addition of another network gateway. So if your submission to the list bounce, try again later and the list should be back up.

Archives:

From time to time there will be informational postings from Pete or other developers about their products related to the GS/DSP, these messages will be archived and if you want send a message to the list coordinator and he will forward to you the requested file.

Archive Listing:

This will be listing which files are availble. Currently we only have two files, the GS/DSP Preliminary Press Info that was posted to comp.sys.apple2, this one and a long question and answer post by Pete Snowberg about the DSP board.

Coordinator: Terry Yeung <terryy@ocf.berkeley.edu>

gug-sysadmin@vlsivie.tuwien.ac.at   [Last Updated 28-January-1992]

The list is for rumors, bugfixes, and workarounds concerning the CAD-Tool genesil and related tools. Primary members of the list are associated with the Eurochip project, but other interested parties are welcome. Requests to join the list should be sent to gug-sysadmins-requiest@vlsivie.tuwien.ac.at

Coordinator: Chytil Georg

gwmon@SH.CS.NET

Originally created as a list to discuss the development of a monitoring suite for gateways, currently expanded to a discussion group for issues related to monitoring and managing networks and internetworks.

Archives are currently available by anonymous FTP from LBL-RTSG(??).LLNL.GOV

All requests to be added to or deleted from this list, problems, questions, etc., should be sent to gwmon-request@SH.CS.NET.

Coordinator: Craig Partridge <craig@LOKI.BBN.COM>

HAMLICEN@VMD.CSO.UIUC.EDU (Internet)
HAMLICEN@UIUCVMD.BITNET (BITNET)

Mailing list for discussion of Licensing matters of Ham Radio. This is a splinter group from the USENET newsgroup "rec.ham-radio" and the digest "INFO-HAMS@WSMR-SIMTEL20.ARMY.MIL" to separate the high traffic of the licensing discussions.

To subscribe to the list, send mail to the Coordinator.

Coordinator: Philip Howard <PHIL%UIUCVMD.BITNET@CUNYVM.CUNY.EDU>

HAM-UNIV@VMD.CSO.UIUC.EDU
    HAM-UNIV@UIUCVMD (BitNet)
    HAM-UNIV%UIUCVMD.BITNET@VM1.NODAK.EDU
    HAM-UNIV%VMD.CSO.UIUC.EDU@VM1.NODAK.EDU

Mailing list for an exchange of information between and/or about College and University based Amateur Radio Clubs. Duplication of material from other ham radio mailing lists or news groups should not be made unless it is of special interest to this category of clubs.

Anyone who is interested in College and University Ham Radio Clubs may subscribe and participate. It is not necessary to be a student or a member of a club, or even a ham radio operator. I do ask if you have the information, to supply it with your subscription request so that others can be more informed. I'd like to know your call sign and club affiliation (and office if you are an officer).

BitNet users may subscribe by sending the command: SUB HAM-UNIV firstname lastname callsign - clubname to LISTSERV@UIUCVMD or LISTSERV@VMD.CSO.UIUC.EDU by either BITNET interactive message or by electronic mail with the command as the only line in the message text/body. To unsubscribe send the command: UNSUB HAM-UNIV If you are on UUCP and the address listserv@vmd.cso.uiuc.edu fails, try uiucuxc!vmd!listserv instead. Non-BitNet users can join by sending the above SUB command to LISTSERV%UIUCVMD.BITNET@VM1.NODAK.EDU.

Coordinator: Phil Howard <PHIL@VMD.CSO.UIUC.EDU>
                       <phil@UIUCVMD> (BitNet)

HANDHELDS@CSL.SRI.COM

Mailing list for those who are interested in handheld computers or programmable calculators. The mailing list can be used to distribute or request programs. Messages are not moderated at this time.

There are special addresses for archive submissions and retrievals:

    ARCHIVE-SERVER@CSL.SRI.COM   - Electronic server for archives
    ARCHIVE-MANAGEMENT@CSL.SRI.COM - Address for submissions to archives

The archive server is similar to that used at other sites. If you send an empty message with HELP on the Subject: line, it will provide a message about its usage. If you wish to see what is contained in the archives, send a Subject: line with INDEX HANDHELDS.

Currently, all the messages for the handhelds mailing list are contained on host CSL.SRI.COM in file HANDHELDS.TXT. Additionally, two programs are available for the HP41C.

All requests to be added to or deleted from this list, problems, questions, etc., should be sent to HANDHELDS-REQUEST@CSL.SRI.COM.

Coordinator: David Edwards <DLE@CSL.SRI.COM>

hart@vtcc1.cc.vt.edu

There was discussion recently on the J.-M. Jarre mailing list of starting a mailing list for devotees of Mike Oldfield and his music. For now, the address for this list is hart@vtcc1.cc.vt.edu

The list will initially be available only in digest form. To subscribe, send mail with the word "sub" in the subject line to the above address; you may include your first posting in the main body of this message if you wish.

Owner: "Heath (703)552-3177" <HART@VTMATH.BITNET>

HDESK-L@WVNVM.WVNET.EDU
    HDESK-L@WVNVM (BitNet)

Mailing list for the discussion of Help Desks. Staff and management of Help Desks are encouraged to exchange experiences with the startup and operation of Help Desks at their sites, as well as their experiences with problem-tracking software.

BitNet users may subscribe by sending the following command in a message to LISTSERV@WVNVM: SUBSCRIBE HDESK-L Your full name where "Your full name" is your real name, not your login Id. Non-BitNet users can join the list by sending the above command as the only line in the text/body of a message to LISTSERV@WVNVM.WVNET.EDU or LISTSERV%WVNVM.BITNET@VM1.NODAK.EDU.

> Coordinator: Roman J. Olynyk <U0BA9@WVNVM.WVNET.EDU>
> <U0BA9@WVNVM.BITNET>

HEADER-PEOPLE@MC.LCS.MIT.EDU

Interest specifically in the format of message headers and related issues such as inter-network mail formats/standards, etc.

Recent messages are filed in MIT-MC (MC.LCS.MIT.EDU) file KSC;HEADER MINS, while older archives are in KSC;HEADER MINS00 through MINS15. These files are accessible over the Internet via FTP.

All requests to be added to or deleted from this list, problems, questions, etc., should be sent to HEADER-PEOPLE-REQUEST@MC.LCS.MIT.EDU.

Coordinator: Pandora B. Berman <CENT@AI.AI.MIT.EDU>

Heath-People@MC.LCS.MIT.EDU

Discussion of the construction, use, and modification of Heath and/or Zenith terminals, computers, and related products.

The archives of old messages are kept on MC.LCS.MIT.EDU, in files:

```
COMAIL;HEATH MAIL1   -Oldest Mail
COMAIL;HEATH MAIL2   -Next oldest
   etc.          -Up to 8 as of 26 August 86
COMAIL;HEATH MAIL    -Incoming mail is being added to this one
```

These files are each stored in reverse time order (i.e. newer messages come first in the file, older messages are later); each file is between approx. 100K and 150K characters. Copies of these files are available via FTP with no login needed; some are off-line - if you get an error, send a request to the administrative address below and they can be put on-line briefly.

All requests to be added to deleted deleted from this list, problems, questions, etc., should be sent to HEATH-PEOPLE-REQUEST@MC.LCS.MIT.EDU.

Coordinator: Michael A. Patton <MAP@AI.AI.MIT.EDU>

HELPNET%NDSUVM1.BITNET@VM1.NODAK.EDU

HELPNET is intended as a working list for those interested in the roles global computer networks might play in times of disasters such as earthquakes, hurricanes, etc.

Archives are kept for this list. Send LISTSERV the commands INDEX HELPNET and INFO DATABASE for more information (Note: The commands are sent to LISTSERV@NDSUVM1 (BitNet) or LISTSERV@VM1.NODAK.EDU and NOT to the list). They are also available via ANONYMOUS FTP to VM1.NODAK.EDU (134.129.111.1). Enter CD HELPNET after connecting.

Anyone may subscribe to the HELPNET list; however, the list is set up so that only subscribers may send mail to the list (to avoid accidental SUBSCRIBE commands). You may subscribe to HELPNET by sending mail to LISTSERV@NDSUVM1 (BitNet) or LISTSERV@VM1.NODAK.EDU with the body/text of the message containing the command: SUB HELPNET your_full_name where "your_full_name" is your real name, not your loginid. If BitNet users wish to be able to send messages to the list but read it through some other means (eg. GRAND), then ALSO include the command: SET HELPNET NOMAIL which will allow you to contribute but not send you redundant mail.

Coordinator: Marty Hoag <NU021172@VM1.NODAK.EDU>

HELP-NET on LISTSERV@TEMPLEVM.Bitnet

HELPSERV has evolved. Helpserv and all its component files have been integrated (finally!) into LISTSERV at TEMPLEVM. In addition, there has been the addition of a mailing list, and a NAME CHANGE.

Help-Net is a discussion list for the purposes of solving user problems with utilities and software related to the Internet and Bitnet networks. In addition, LISTSERV at TEMPLEVM maintains a set of low-level help files intended to help the beginning user acclimatize himself to the network systems.

Both novice and experienced users are encouraged to join the discussion list, either to ask questions, or to answer them. Questions on almost any network topic are encouraged, however there are a few ground rules we ask that you observe.

1. Please do not post where can I find this game, or that specific gif file, etc. There are several lists that deal specifically with those topics. The question, Where would I find a list that could tell me where to get ??? on the other hand is quite acceptable.
2. Please do not post any messages that relate to the illegal traffic of copyrighted material.
3. Feel free to redistribute the help files freely. We do ask that you identify the source of any materials.
4. We gratefully accept both topics for additional Help sheets, and submissions to be placed on the server. For more information about submitting, get the file SUBMIT INFO from the server. See below for instructions.

Below are some brief instructions on how to access the HELP-NET list.

1. Signing on to the list. Send the following command to LISTSERV at TEMPLEVM, as either an interactive message or the body of a mail message:

SUB HELP-NET (Your Name)

2. Getting a file from the list. Send the following command to LISTSERV at TEMPLEVM:

GET HELP-NET FILELIST

Choose which files you want and send a get command for each of those files. If you have a problem, ask the list. It's what we are here for. Please note that you must be a list subscriber to access files.

3. Posting a message on the list. - Send your mail message to HELP-NET at TEMPLEVM. Your mail will be forwarded to all list members, and you will be replied to.

I thank everyone for their support and interest and hope that I and the HELP-NET will continue to be of service to everyone in the network community. If you have any questions regarding Help-Net, please direct them to V4078 at TEMPLEVM. Again, thank you for your support.

Jeff Linder   Bitnet: V5057U at TEMPLEVM
Temple University   Internet: JEFF@MONET.OCIS.TEMPLE.EDU
Computer Services
Mainframe Consultant

HESSE-L on LISTSERV@UCSBVM.BITNET

This international discussion group is devoted to the study of the life and literary works of Hermann Hesse, the Swiss- German Nobel-Prize winner of 1946.

The List is edited and published electronically by Gunther Gottschalk of the University of California at Santa Barbara and will include discussion items, pre-publication announcements, texts, interpretations, analyses, critiques, reviews, bibliographies on Hesse and his contemporaries. The principal languages of the list will be English and German, but contributions in other languages are welcome. The list is intended to establish better contacts among readers of Hesse and related authors and to contribute to the discussion of his life and his works.

In the near future, archives of HESSE-L and related files will be stored in the HESSE-L filelist. It is hoped to attract a number of prepublication manuscripts and other materials released by their authors, by journals, or by the holder of the rights to Hesse's works, Suhrkamp Verlag. Part of the year the List will be run by its owner through the facilities of the J.W. Goethe University in Frankfurt. To receive a list of files send the command INDEX HESSE-L in the BODY of mail or a message to LISTSERV@UCSBVM on BITNET.

To subscribe to HESSE-L, send the following command to LISTSERV@UCSBVM via mail text (in the body) or interactive message: SUBSCRIBE HESSE-L your full name

For example: SUBSCRIBE HESSE-L Plinio Designori

> Owner: Gunther Gottschalk <hcf2hess@ucsbvm.bitnet>
> (G.H.Gottschalk, Ger/Or/Slav. Dept, UC Santa Barbara, CA 93106)
> (E-mail: gs01gott@hcfmail.ucsb.edu - Phone/Fax: 805-893-2374)

HISLAW-L on LISTSERV@ULKYVM   [Last Updated June 1992]
or LISTSERV@ULKYVM.LOUISVILLE.EDU

HISLAW-L is a forum for debate, discussion, and the exchange of information by students and scholars of the history of the Law (Feudal, Common, Canon). HISLAW-L is ready to distribute newsletters from study groups, and to post announcements of meetings and calls for papers, short scholarly pieces, queries, and other items of interest.

The list currently does not maintain a FTP directory nor is archiving available. Hopefully, this will change in the near future.

HISLAW-L is associated with the general discussion list HISTORY, and co-operates fully with other lists similarly associated.

To subscribe send a message to LISTSERV@ULKYVM or LISTSERV@ULKYVM.LOUISVILLE.EDU. In BODY of the message state: SUB HISLAW-L yourfirstname yourlastname

adding your full name; LISTSERV will accept both BITNET and Internet addresses. Postings should be made to HISLAW-L@ULKYVM.

If you have any questions please contact the owner.

Owner: James A. Cocks BITNET: JACOCK01@ULKYVM Internet: JACOCK01@ULKYVM.LOUISVILLE.EDU

HISTEC-L@UKANVM.BITNET   [Last Updated 28-January-1992]

HISTEC-L@UKANVM is a list for the study of the History of Evangelical Christianity. Subscription requests should be sent to BAYS@UKANVM. I will attempt to act upon them as quickly as possible. Postings should be made to HISTEC-L@UKANVM. LISTSERV@UKANVM will accept both BITNET and INTERNET mailings. I would appreciate subscribers' sending me by e-mail (at BAYS@UKANVM) a short biographical resume for inclusion in a members' directory.

Our FTP directory is presently empty. Subscribers who have materials they believe worth including should contact me by e-mail. This site will operate in co-operation with ra.msstate.edu and the contents of its directories will form part of a union catalogue with ra.msstate and other co-operating sites.

To subscribe, please send your request and a short biographical note to the owner:

Daniel H. Bays

(BAYS@UKANVM)
The University of Kansas

HISTEC-L is a non-sectarian forum for discussion, debate, and the exchange of information by students and scholars of the history of evangelical Christianity. It is not a medium for proselytizing, and the advocacy or disparagement of any faith or sect are not welcome. Requests for SUBscription pass through the list owner, and SEND and REVIEW commands are restricted to list members. The command language of HISTEC-L is English, but postings in other languages are accepted. HISTEC-L is ready to distribute newsletters from study groups, and to post announcements of meetings and calls for papers, short scholarly pieces, queries, and other items of interest.

HISTEC-L maintains a directory at the FTP site kuhub.cc.ukans.edu (CD DUA9 [malin.histec]), for the collection and preservation of materials of use to its members.

HISTEC-L is associated with the general discussion list HISTORY, and co-operates fully with other lists similarly associated.

HIT%UFRJ.BITNET@CUNYVM.CUNY.EDU (Internet)
HIT on LISTSERV@UFRJ (BITNET)

The Highly Imaginative Technology - Science Fiction List

Have you ever wondered how software can start paranoic? Did your last SciFi book described a new kind of energy-plant? Can networks create a new revolution in the world? Is the NeXt the model for your next computer?

HIT is a discussion list about Technology that can/can't be developed in the near/far future. Based on Science Fiction and nowadays discoveries, we plan to discuss how to develop and which are the consequences of new and imaginative technology.

Suggested topics are: Artificial Reality, Software Psychiatry, new developments in science, space stations, High Energy Physics, etc. Multi-disciplinary ideas are wellcome (as Software Psychiatry).

To subscribe to HIT, send the following command to LISTSERV@UFRJ via mail text or interactive message (Internet Users, mail only, to the address LISTSERV%UFRJ.BITNET@CUNYVM.CUNY.EDU):

SUBSCRIBE HIT Your_full_name.

For example: SUBSCRIBE HIT Joe Smith

List owner:Geraldo Xexeo XEXEO@VXCERN.DECNET.CERN.CH

HL-7@VIRGINIA.EDU   [Last Updated 12-October-1991]

HL-7 is an electronic conference designed to foster communication concerning technical, operational, and business issues involved in the use of the HL-7 interface protocol. It is also intended as a forum for the HL-7 Working Group members who are participating in the specification of the interface protocol.

Health Level Seven is an application protocol for electronic data exchange in health care environments. It is called level seven because the protocol assumes the underlying network support of levels one through six of the Open Systems Interconnection (OSI) network model of the International Standards Organization (ISO). The HL-7 standard is specified at the seventh level, which is the application level.

This HL-7 (Health Level Seven) Conference is *not* an offical part of the HL-7 Working Group and Executive Committee. Official inquiries concerning HL-7 (Health Level Seven) should be sent directly to: Health Level Seven, P.O. Box 66111, Chicago, IL 60666-9998, fax: (708) 616-9099. In accordance with current CREN regulations, commercial activity (such as the selling of software) will be prohibited. Subscription to this conference is open to *anyone* interested.

You may subscribe by sending an e-mail message to:

HL-7-REQUEST@VIRGINIA.EDU

if your account is on the internet, with the following request as the text of the message.

SUB HL-7 YourFirstname YourLastname

This, the 'SUB ...,' must be part of the message; the subject line will be ignored.

Remember two simple rules-of-thumb:

If it's a request (SUBscribe, UNSUBscribe), send it to the list requester (HL-7-REQUEST@VIRGINIA.EDU).

If it's a message for general distribution to the members of the list, send it to the list (HL-7@VIRGINIA.EDU).

The list is supported by the University of Virginia Medical Center Computing. Our thanks to their management and staff for permission to use their system for the list and for assistance in setting it up. The list is sponsored by the University of Virginia Health Sciences Center. Questions may be directed to David John Marotta.

Owner:

David John Marotta	Internet: djm5g@virginia.edu
Senior Computer Systems Enginerr	Bitnet: djm5g@virginia
Strategic Planning Group	IBM US Mail: USUVARG8
Health Science Center	voice: (804) 982-3718
The University of Virginia	messages: (804) 924-5261
Charlottesville, VA 22903	fax: (804) 296-7209
(804) 295-2471	

HOCKEY-D on LISTSERV@MAINE (BITNET)   [Last Updated 28-January-1992]
or LISTSERV@MAINE.MAINE.EDU

This list is a mechanism for periodically distributing a compendium of postings made to HOCKEY-L for those folks interested in the information on HOCKEY-L, but wish to limit the number of arriving E-Mail files, and do not wish to participate in the discussions.

The HOCKEY-L list is for the discussion of collegiate ice hockey, including scores, team info, schedules, etc. allowing fans to become more involved and knowledgeable about the game.

The list resides at the University of Maine System MAINE.MAINE.EDU cpu. When the owner posts a digest to the list, LISTSERV distributes a copy to everyone subscribed. An archive of the digest is also created on a disk of LISTSERV. Each digest posting is a separate file on that disk.

HOCKEY-D does not accept postings; it merely distributes a periodic collection of postings from another list, HOCKEY-L. Subscription information for HOCKEY-D or HOCKEY-L may be requested from Wayne Smith at WTS@MAINE.MAINE.EDU.

Send a request to sign off the list or ask for an archived file to LISTSERV@MAINE.MAINE.EDU as described below.

Questions, comments and problems may be sent to the HOCKEY-D list owner Wayne Smith at WTS@MAINE.MAINE.EDU.

The opinions expressed on HOCKEY-D are those of the posters and not of the University of Maine System nor of the list owner.

How to Subscribe to HOCKEY-D

As with any LISTSERV list, send mail to

LISTSERV@MAINE (bitnet/cren) or LISTSERV@MAINE.MAINE.EDU (Internet)

The *body* of the mail should contain:

SUBSCRIBE HOCKEY-D your full name

HOCKEY-L@MAINE.MAINE.EDU

College_Hockey discussion list.

This list is for the discussion of collegiate ice hockey, including scores, team info, schedules, etc. allowing fans to become more involved and knowledgeable about the game.

Owner: WTS@MAINE (Wayne T. Smith)

homebrew%hpfcmr@HPLABS.HP.COM
hplabs!hpfcmr!homebrew (UUCP)

The Homebrew Mailing List is primarily for the discussion of the making and tasting of beer, ale, and mead. Related issues, such as breweries, books, judging, commercial beers, beer festivals, etc, are also discussed. Wine-making talk is also welcome, but non-homeade-wine talk is not.

Archives are now available from Mthvax.CS.Miami.EDU via the netlib program and anonymous ftp; please use anonymous ftp if you can, if not send mail to netlib@Mthvax.CS.Miami.EDU with subject index for a top level index and help file.

All requests to be added to or deleted from this list, problems, questions, etc., should be sent to homebrew-request%hpfcmr@HPLABS.HP.COM (or UUCP hplabs!hpfcmr!homebrew-request).

Coordinator: Rob Gardner <rdg%hpfcmr@HPLABS.HP.COM>

HONDA@MSCRC.SUNYSB.EDU

Mailing list for discussion of Honda and Acura automobiles.

Send requests to join to:

HONDA-REQUEST@MSRC.SUNYSB.EDU

Send submissions to:

HONDA@MSRC.SUNYSB.EDU

Coordinator: Rob Malouf RMALOUF@MSRC.SUNYSB.EDU

HONORS on LISTSERV@GWUVM.BITNET   [Last Updated 9/92]

The HONORS discussion forum delivers news of NCHC conferences and events. It provides a place for members of different Honors program to meet and talk. It is also a place for Honors directors, facutly and students to post questions and to discuss issues of Honors education.

The HONORS discussion is disctributed by a standard LISTSERV program. To join the discussion, send electronic mail to LISTSERV@GWUVM with the single line:

SUB HONORS your name

To remove yourself from the discussion, send electronic mail to LISTSERV@GWUVM containing the single line:

UNSUB HONORS

Should you have any problems or questions about the operations of the HONORS electronic discussion, please contact the HONORS owner.

Owner: Honors Newsletter Editor <HNREDIT@GWUVM.BITNET>

HOPOS-L on LISTSERV@UKCC.Bitnet or LISTSERV@UKCC.UKY.EDU HOPOS-L, the History of Philosophy of Science Discussion List, has been established in conjunction with the new History of Philosophy of Science Working Group (HOPOS) as a forum for the exchange of information, ideas, queries, job notices, course syllabi, conference announcements, and other news of interest to scholars working in areas related to HOPOS's main focus. The discussion list will also be used to distribute occasional HOPOS newsletters.

The topical focus of HOPOS-L is intended to be quite broad, covering all periods in the history of the philosophy of science, from antiquity to the twentieth century, extending to related areas of investigation in the history of logic, mathematics, and the natural and social sciences, and including, as well, diverse methodologies, ranging from more internalist, history of ideas approaches to more externalist, social and institutional history.

This is a LISTSERV managed list, so normal subscription requests apply. To subscribe, send mail to LISTSERV@UKCC or on the Internet to LISTSERV@UKCC.UKY.EDU with the body containing the command

SUB HOPOS-L Yourfirstname Yourlastname

Questions, comments, or suggestions concerning HOPOS-L should be directed, offlist, to the owner.

Owner: Don Howard einphil@ukcc.uky.edu Department of Philosophy University of Kentucky Lexington, Kentucky 40506-0027 606.257.4376 (Office) 606.258.1073 (FAX)

HOSPEX@PLEARN.BITNET

HOSPEX@PLEARN was created to provide those interested in being a host to foreign visitors a way to satisfy their interests. For those interested in finding a host when they are traveling in difference countries, this new database will satisfy this interest.

To subscribe just send mail stating that you want to join to HOSPEX@PLEARN. This will be automatically forwarded to one of the owners. Of course issuing standard 'SUB HOSPEX your full name' to LISTSERV@PLEARN will do as well. You'll be sent a form to be filled and returned. This subsribtion procedure is manual, so it may take few days sometimes.

We are looking for lots of users outside the U.S. to subscribe (and U.S. users too, but now there are many more U.S. users than an other nation).

Eventually, those who subscribe will be asked to send us a form which describes something about yourself, the type of accommodations you have, languages you speak, restrictions you want, etc. When a file exists with this information on you, those traveling can look through all the files for the countries in which they will be traveling to find a host that seems interesting them. So, this information you must eventually send to one of HOSPEX owners is important.

HOSPEX-L on LISTSERV@PLEARN.BITNET   [Last Update 11/92]

The list is devoted to hospitality exchange (homestays) discussions. It also serves as a broadcast channel for members of HospEx database. Please note that HOSPEX-L is different from HOSPEX@PLEARN as the latter serves as a homestay exchange database only. HOSPEX-L is archived monthly.

To subscribe to HOSPEX-L send e-mail to listserv@plearn.bitnet with the BODY of the mail containing the listserv command:

SUB HOSPEX-L Yourfirstname Yourlastname

To subscribe to HOSPEX, use following command instead:

SUB HOSPEX Yourfirstname Yourlastname

For more information write to hospex@appli.mimuw.edu.pl

List owner: Wojtek Sylwestrzak wojsyl@appli.mimuw.edu.pl

HSPNET-L on LISTSERV@ALBNYDH2

HSPNET-L provides consultation, a monthly digest, and a data base of hospital networks. It emphasizes restoration and extension of consulting for rural hospitals by connection to major medical centers. All aspects (hardware, software, staff training, confidentiality of patient data, etc) will be covered. Particular attention will be paid to existing networks both in USA and abroad.

Transmission of both text and medical image data will be considered via both land- lines and satellite. The cost-effectiveness of such distance-consulting will be reviewed in the light of declining rural hospital acute-care capabilities, and the economic benefits of keeping the patient in the rural area.

> Owner= DFP10@ALBNYVM1 (Donald F. Parsons MD)
> Editor= DFP10@ALBNYVM1 (Donald F. Parsons MD)
> Donald F. Parsons MD, Wadsworth Center, New York State Dept.Health, Empire
> State Plaza, Albany, NY 12201. (518) 474-7047, FAX (518) 474-8590.

HP-28%NDSUVM1.BITNET@VM1.NODAK.EDU

Mailing list for users/owners of HP-28C and HP-28S calculators, ranging from "everyday-type" questions/discussion to more advanced and technical-type support. The list will be for open discussion, posting of programs (see footnote) technical support, advancements, and problem solving. Things you may want to share/talk about:

> Bugs in the HP-28
> Nifty programs
> Uses of SYSEVAL
> Modifying Hardware (although not recommended)
> Accesories/Hardware
> Other HP clubs and organizations
> Machine Language Programming
> New Models!??
> Making your 28C more like a 28S
> Music and Graphics processing (not great, but neat)
> More uses of SYSEVAL... etc.
> And questions regarding any of the above....

If you would like to join this list issue the following command: TELL LISTSERV AT NDSUVM1 SUB HP-28 your_full_name If on VMS: SEND LISTSERV@NDSUVM1 SUB HP-28 your_full_name Non-BitNet users can send e-mail to LISTSERV%NDSUVM1.BITNET@VM1.NODAK.EDU with the first line of the TEXT or BODY of the mail being: SUB HP-28 your_full_name

> Coordinator: Eric J. Zmyslowski <GRIK%MTUS5.BITNET@VM1.NoDak.EDU>

HPMINI-L%UAFSYSB.BITNET@VM1.NODAK.EDU

Mailing list to address hardware and software issues, as they relate to the Hewlett Packard 9000 series (9000/825, 9000/835, 9000/840, etc). Initially, the operating system will be limited to HP/UX.

To subscribe to the list send the message: SUB HPMINI-L your_real_name (where "your_real_name" is your name, not your userid) to LISTSERV@UAFSYSB.BITNET in the text/body of a message or in the text of an interactive command like TELL or SEND (if available). Non-BItNet users can send the command in the body of a message to LISTSERV%UAFSYSB.BITNET@ VM1.NODAK.EDU.

> Coordinator: Christopher Corke <CC06067%UAFSYSB.BITNET@VM1.NODAK.EDU>
> ccc1@uafhp.UUCP

HR-L@VMS.CIS.PITT.EDU

Mailing list for discussions relating to human rights issues. The list is currently unmoderated.

There are currently no archives, but hopefully there will be in the future.

All requests to be added to or deleted from this list, problems, questions, etc., should be sent to HR-L-REQUEST@VMS.CIS.PITT.EDU.

> Coordinator: Jeff Carpenter <HR-L-REQUEST@VMS.CIS.PITT.EDU>

<JJC@VMS.CIS.PITT.EDU>
<JJC@UNIX.CIS.PITT.EDU>

Human-Genome-Program@genbank.bio.net

The National Institute of Health's Human Genome Program is planning to start a newsgroup for the disucussion of genome-related issues. Information on how to subscribe follows.

The HUMAN-GENOME-PROGRAM newsgroup can be received anywhere in the world via USENET under the USENET name bionet.molbio.genome-program.

For those who need to receive messages by regular electronic mail instead of through USENET news software, there are four distribution points for the HUMAN-GENOME-PROGRAM newsgroup depending upon your geographical and network locations:

1. If you reside in the Americas, to subscribe to the HUMAN-GENOME-PROGRAM bulletin board, please send a message to the Internet address
biosci@genbank.bio.net
This address also serves American BITNET users.
2. If you use the European Academic Research Network (EARN) and live in Continental Europe or Ireland, you can subscribe automatically to the newsgroup by sending a message containing the line
SUBSCRIBE GNOME+PR your_personal_name
to the address
LISTSERV@IRLEARN
(for example, SUBSCRIBE GNOME+PR Chris Smith). The Subject line of the message should be left blank.
3. If you reside in the United Kingdom, please send your subscription request to
biosci@uk.ac.daresbury
4. If you reside in Scandinavia (or in Continental Europe and have Internet access), please send your subscription to
biosci@bmc.uu.se

If you do not fall into any of the above categories you may contact whichever of the above sites is most convenient.

Once you have chosen your distribution point, you may post messages by sending to the bulletin board address at that site. Note below the shorter addresses used for BITNET/EARN/JANET sites.

Location	Posting address
Americas / Internet format:	human-genome-program@genbank.bio.net
Americas / BITNET format:	gnome-pr@genbank.bio.net
Ireland / EARN format:	gnome-pr@irlearn.ucd.ie
U.K. / JANET format:	gnome-pr@uk.ac.daresbury
Sweden / Internet format:	human-genome-program@bmc.uu.se

USENET news software users may post messages on their local computer to bionet.molbio.genome-program (set distribution to "world") and let the software handle distribution details.

From: JP2@nihcu.bitnet, Jane Peterson, National Center for Human Genome Research

HUMAN-NETS@RED.RUTGERS.EDU

Mailing list originally consisting of the combined memberships of INFO-PCNET, HOME-SAT, and TELETEXT mailing lists. Human-Nets has discussed many topics, all of them related in some way to the theme of a world-wide computer and telecommunications network usually called WorldNet. The topics have ranged very widely, from something like tutorials, to state of the art discussions, to rampant speculation about technology and its impact. The list is extremely large, making it necessary to batch messages sent to the list and distributing them once each day during off peak periods to avoid overloading the system.

The permanent archives contain all of the material distributed to the list. Due to size, this archive is broken down into several different files, stored in reverse temporal order. The files are currently stored on Internet host RU-BLUE in files RHYTHM:<PLEASANT.HUMAN-NETS>HUMNET.* (where "*" is a wild-card).

All requests to be added to or deleted from this list, problems, questions, etc., should be sent to HUMAN-NETS-REQUEST@ARAMIS.RUTGERS.EDU.

Moderator: Charles McGrew <MCGREW@RED.RUTGERS.EDU>

HUMANIST%UTOREPAS.BITNET@CORNELLC.CCS.CORNELL.EDU

HUMANIST is an international electronic discussion group for computing Humanists and for those who support the application of computers to scholarship in the humanities. It currently consists of nearly 300 members in 13 countries in North America, Europe, and the Near East. Relevant topics are technical questions about hardware and software, specific problems in humanistic scholarship, and both the administrative difficulties and philosophical issues arising from the application of computing to the humanities; calls for papers, bibliographies, and reports of lasting interest are also welcome.

Interested individuals should send a note together with a brief biography to the Coordinator in the following format:

*Family-name, Given-names <e-mail address>

Title, mailing address(es), telephone number(s).

Body of biography. This should not be a c.v. and need not be very detailed but should cover the full range of your professional activities and interests, both present and past. Mention other things at your discretion. Biographies vary considerably in length, though few are less than 100 words or more than 500.

Coordinator: Willard McCarty
<MCCARTY%UTOREPAS.BITNET@CORNELLC.CCS.CORNELL.EDU>

HUMBIO-L@ACC.FAU.EDU   [Last Updated 12-October-1991]
HUMBIO-L@FAUVAX

Human Biology Interest Group Discussion List

Humbio-L is an unmoderated discussion list dealing with biological anthropology, adaptation, environmental stress, biological race, growth, genetics, paleoanthropology, skeletal biology, forensic anthropology, paleodemography, paleopathology, primate biology & behavior.

This discussion list is open to all interested individuals or organizations.

To subscribe send mail to HUMBIO-REQUEST@FAUVAX (Internet users send to HUMBIO-REQUEST@ACC.FAU.EDU) with the request in the message body:

SUBSCRIBE HUMBIO-L Your_full_name

To unsubscribe, send:

UNSUBSCRIBE HUMBIO-L

All questions, requests for information, etc., should be sent to the List Owner.

List Owner: M.Y. Iscan (ISCAN@FAUVAX, Iscan@acc.fau.edu)
List Manager: Ralph P Carpenter (RALPHO@FAUVAX, Ralpho@acc.fau.edu)

HUNGARY on LISTSERV@UCSBVM

An electronic discussion group on Hungarian issues is now open to scholars and students from all disciplines. Although the working language of the group is English, contributions in other languages will be accepted and posted. However, they may not be understood by a significant proportion of the membership.

Electronic mail connections have already been established with three Hungarian universities: Budapest Technical University, Budapest University of Economic Sciences, and Eotvos Lorand University.

The group and list server addresses of the new group, based at the University of California, Santa Barbara, are:

> hungary@ucsbvm.bitnet   For mail to broadcast to the list ONLY
> listserv@ucsbvm.bitnet   For commands or to subscribe

To subscribe to the discussion group, send an e-mail message, without any subject, to the list server address, listserv@ucsbvm.bitnet, containing the single line:

subscribe hungary "your name"

with your own name, not your e-mail address, inserted in place of the phrase "your name," without quotes.

Once you have subscribed, any messages which you want to circulate to the group should be sent to the group address, hungary@ucsbvm.bitnet.

The list is moderated, and will be edited by:

Eric Dahlin hcf2hung@ucsbuxa.bitnet

HY-PEOPLE@ORVILLE.ARC.NASA.GOV

Mailing list for the discussion of hyperchannel networks within the context of an IP network.

All requests to be added to or deleted from this list, problems, questions, etc., should be sent to HY-PEOPLE-REQUEST@ORVILLE.ARC.NASA.GOV.

Coordinator: John Lekashman <lekash@ORVILLE.ARC.NASA.GOV>

HYPBAR-L on LISTSERV@TECHNION (LISTSERV@TECHNION.TECHNION.AC.IL)

HYPBAR-L provides an unmoderated environment where issues, questions, comments, ideas, and procedures can be discussed. In a broad sense, this includes virtually anything dealing with medicine in relation to diving and HyperBaric Medicine.

The explicit purpose of HYPBAR-L is to provide timely interchange between subscribers, to provide a forum where interesting questions can be addressed within the context of interactive exchange between many individuals, to discuss the evolution and application of HyperBaric and Diving Medicine, to announce professional meetings, calls for papers, and any additional information that would be of interest.

As is the case on all unmoderated lists, the discussion and topics are only limited by the participation and interest of its subscribers. Subscribers are welcome to take an active role by posting and/or an inactive role by monitoring the list. Although not necessary for participation, it shall be assumed that all subscribers are basically familiar with the medical jargon that is used on this list.

To subscribe to HYPBAR-L, please send mail or file to LISTSERV@TECHNION or listserv@technion.technion.ac.il and place in the body of the text the line

SUB HYPBAR-L <your name>.

This list does not support nor is supported by any medical group or medical installation. This list was created due to requests by several individuals within the medical community located in different countries.

Coordinator: Robert Al Hartshorn <AL%VMSA.technion.ac.il@VM1.NoDak.EDU>

We have the hyperami mailing list. For informal product discussion and mutual assistance concerning:

AmigaVision	InterActor
CanDo	PILOT
DeluxeVideo III	ShowMaker
Director 2	TACL
Foundation	Thinker
Hyperbook	VIVA

If you'd like to join us to discuss your hypermedia projects on the Amiga and ask questions about how to get them working better, send a mail request to hyperami's new home, the OIT listserver, like so: mail listserv@archive.oit.unc.edu and give a one-line message (it can be the subject) asking subscribe hyperami and you're on.

(You can also ask the listserver for "help" if you want more info; same idea, a one-line request. For now there's no "index" listing for hyperami, though.)

This list is separate from the Usenet newsgroup comp.sys.amiga.multimedia (by request of the listmembers) but material from the list may occasionally be presented to the newsgroup.

HYPERCRD@PURCCVM.BITNET   [Last Updated 12-October-1991]

Mailing list to discuss anything and everything about HyperCard for Apple Macintosh microcomputers. The list is open and unmoderated.

To join, send email to LISTSERV@PURCCVM.BITNET. Ignore the "Subject:" line, and send a one-line message as follows:

SUBSCRIBE HYPERCRD Your_Name

where "Your_Name" is how you would like to be known to the list.

For further information about this list, contact its "owner," George D. Allen, <allenge@ecn.purdue.edu>, phone (317) 494-3796, Dept. of Audilogy & Speech Sciences, Purdue University, West Lafayette, IN 47907.

I-BBoard@SPCVXA.SPC.EDU
I-BBOARD@SPCVXA.BITNET (Bitnet)

Discussion of the BBoard package. BBoard is a VMS utility to link mail, delivered by Jnet, and VAX Notes, an electronic conferencing system from Digital Equipment Corp. BBoard's primary purpose is to reduce the number of LISTSERV or mailing list subscribers at a node so that only one user (BBOARD) is subscribed. The messages from each mailing list will then be posted in a separate Notes conference.

There is no automated archive retrieval facility. However, requests for archived material may be sent to the I-BBReq address below.

Requests to be added to or deleted from this list, problems, questions, etc., should be sent to I-BBReq@SPCVXA.SPC.EDU (Internet) or I-BBREQ@SPCVXA.BITNET (BitNet).

Coordinator: Benjamin Cohen <BEN@SPCVXA.SPC.EDU>
<BEN%SPCVXA.BITNET@VM1.NODAK.EDU>
<BEN@SPCVXA> (BitNet)

I-Finger%SPCVXA.BITNET@CUNYVM.CUNY.EDU

Discussion of the Finger program and related utilities. Finger is a utility which performs username lookup, WHOIS functions, and system status functions. This list is hosted on the system where VMS Finger and RSTS/E Finger are maintained, so initial discussions will probably center around these versions. However, discussions about any Finger variant or similar utilities are welcomed.

There is no automated archive retrieval facility, however requests for archived material may be sent to the I-FinReq/I-FINREQ address below.

Requests to be added to or deleted from this list, problems, questions, etc., should be sent to I-FinReq%SPCVXA.BITNET@CUNYVM.CUNY.EDU (Internet) or I-FINREQ@SPCVXA.BITNET (BitNet)

Coordinator: Terry Kennedy <terry%SPCVXA.BITNET@CUNYVM.CUNY.EDU>

I-PASCAL on LISTSERV@UTFSM.BITNET

A bi-directional gateway exists between info-pascal (internet) and comp.lang.pascal (usenet); all messages sent to one list are automatically forwarded to the other list.

Mailing list archives are available by anonymous ftp from wsmr-simtel20.army.mil. The old archives are stored in compressed form by month in:

PD2:<ARCHIVES.PASCAL>yymm.1-TXT.Z (where yymm means Year and Month)

Starting with PD2:<ARCHIVES.PASCAL>8404.1-TXT.Z and the newest (current month's) archives are in:

PD2:<ARCHIVES.PASCAL>PASCAL-ARCHIV.TXT

Feel free to ask questions, start new discussions, etc. Please send all messages regarding list maintenance to the address given below, but address "ordinary" messages to info-pascal@brl.mil.

For Subcription the BITNET users To I-PASCAL@UTFSM.BITNET, send the following command in the BODY of e-mail or the text of an interactive message to LISTSERV@UTFSM.BITNET

SUB I-PASCAL your full name

BITNET Owner: Hernan Lobos *Mitzio* HLOBOS@UTFSM.Bitnet

IAMEX-L on LISTSERV@TECMTYVM (BITNET)
or LISTSERV@TECMTYVM.MTY.ITESM.MX (INTERNET)

I am glad to inform you that we just opened a list of artificial intelligence, with the purpose to change ideas from Latinoamerica and the rest of the world, this list will look general topics (medicine, mechanical engineering, games, electronics, administration, etc), we will show applications, discussions, ideas of AI in this areas. We will be glad if you decide to join us. Some information of the list:

Artificial Intelligence list of ITESM.

Artificial Intelligence is a very powerful tool, and still very new. Some Thoughts about this topic are very dissapointed, the reason of it, it is that AI is a unknown area for most of the people, or it seems to them that artificial intelligence is more theorical than practical. The purpose of this list is to present to the people, there is a practical use for this science, and its technics are very useful for the understanding of the knowledge. Letting knowing to the people how we are developing this area in Mexico, and other countries. This will be done in the following way:

1) Answering questions (doubts about a topic from a class, project,etc)
2) Presenting and discussion of interviews from experts
3) Presenting and discussion projects around the world
4) Sending out a periodical general information about a topic
5) Sending out information about simposiums, meetings, bibliography, etc.

This project is administrated by the AI Invetigation Center in Instituto Tecnologico y de Estudios Superiores de Monterrey (ITESM) in Monterrey, N.L.

The people who are interesting about subscribing this list must fill these requirements:

1: Be a student, investigator, profesor who are interesting and have
   some knowledge of this area
2: Must fill the registration form, please ask for it to owners.

To Be Added to the List Please Contact one of the Owners:

PL500368@TECMTYVM.BITNET (Juana Maria Gomez Puertos)
PL157961@TECMTYVM.BITNET (Fernando Careaga Sanchez)

IB@proteus.qc.ca   [Last Update 9/92]

Purpose: To provide a forum for teachers, IB coordinators and administrators involved with the International Baccalaureate Diploma Program. Discussion of all aspects of the IB program is welcome. Send subscription requests to <ib-request@proteus.qc.ca>.

Contact: hreha@vax2.concordia.ca (Dr. Steve Hreha)

IBM-NETS%BITNIC.BITNET@CUNYVM.CUNY.EDU (Internet)
Ibm-Nets@BITNIC (Bitnet)

IBM-Nets is a forum for any discussions relating to IBM mainframes and networking. It is an immediate redistribution list with no filtering or digesting. Examples:

TCP/IP and VM or MVS	Pronet
Wisconsin Wiscnet	SNA
Spartacus Knet	Vnet
X.25	Bitnet NJE protocols
Ethernet	

or anything else that is related to IBM mainframes and networking

The system server Database@Bitnic.Bitnet contains a 6 month archive of all IBM-Nets transactions. In order to learn more on how to access these archives via the Internet, send a valid piece of RFC822 mail to Database%BITNIC.BITNET@CUNYVM.CUNY.EDU with the first nonblank lines reading as follows:

HELP
HELP ARPANET
HELP DESIGN

Note: If your mail header does not contain a proper "From:' or "Reply-To:" field, in addition to being fully domain qualified (RFC920), your mail will not be processed.

All requests to be added to or deleted from this list, problems, questions, etc., should be sent to:

Internet: Hank%BITNIC.BITNET@CUNYVM.CUNY.EDU
Bitnet: Hank@BITNIC

Be sure to specify IBM-Nets

Coordinator: Henry Nussbacher <Hank@BITNIC>
<Hank%BITNIC.BITNET@CUNYVM.CUNY.EDU>

IBM-SRD on LISTSERV@NDSUVM1 or
LISTSERV@vm1.nodak.edu

IBM-SRD is a discussion list for things relating to the IBM Screen Reader Product.

The IBM Screen reader is a hardware/software combination that enables a blind user to navigate around the screen when a speech synthesizer is attatched to the computer. What I hope to establish is a user's forum to discuss aspects of the use and programming of Screen Reader.

The list can be subscribed to by sending mail to LISTSERV@NDSUVM1 on BITNET (or LISTSERV@vm1.nodak.edu) with the TEXT of the mail saying: SUB IBM-SRD yourfirstname yourlastname

There will also be an archive site at ndsuvm1 of Screen Reader materials - essentially source code in Screen Reader's Profile Access Language which is the mechanism one uses to teach Screen Reader about different application programs. For e-mail access send mail to LISTSERV@NDSUVM1 (or

LISTSERV@vm1.nodak.edu) with the commands

    INDEX IBM-SRD
    GET SRD-0001 README

in the text (body) of the message. (Be sure to send these to LISTSERV and NOT to the list).

You may also use FTP to connect to vm1.nodak.edu (134.129.111.1) using userid anonymous and any password. Enter CD IBM-SRD and DIR to see what files are available.

    List Owner: Brett G. Person <NU079509@NDSUVM1.BITNET>
                              <NU079509@vm1.nodak.edu>

IBMTCP-L@CUNYVM.CUNY.EDU

IBMTCP-L is intended for discussion of the IBM TCP/IP For VM program offering (5798-FAL). It is also for discussion of the IBM DACU (7170), 8232 LAN Channel Station, 9370 Ethernet adapter and other similar hardware, as they relate to the IBM product, as well as the PC/IP portion of the product.

To subscribe to the list, from a VM site on BITNET issue: TELL LISTSERV AT CUNYVM SUBSCRIBE IBMTCP-L Your_Full_Name where Your_Full_Name is your real name (not your userid). From a VMS BITNET site use the SEND/REMOTE command.

If you are at a site not on Bitnet or where you cannot send interactive messages, you can send a message to LISTSERV@CUNYVM.CUNY.EDU, where the first non-header line consists of: SUBSCRIBE IBMTCP-L Your_Full_Name

IBMTCP-L archives are stored at LISTSERV@CUNYVM.CUNY.EDU. Logs are created monthly, and are named in the format IBMTCP-L LOGyymm. As of October 1987, these logs were available:

    IBMTCP-L LOG8707   2054 lines
    IBMTCP-L LOG8708   1903 lines
    IBMTCP-L LOG8709   633 lines
    IBMTCP-L LOG8710   3839 lines

To obtain a list of currently available files, the command is: INDEX IBMTCP-L

The command to obtain a specific file is: GET IBMTCP-L file_name

for example, GET IBMTCP-L LOG8710

Please note that there is no IBMTCP-L-REQUEST address. Requests should be sent directly to LISTSERV@CUNYVM.CUNY.EDU as described above. Note also that CUNYVM.CUNY.EDU is node CUNYVM on Bitnet. Questions should be referred to the Coordinator.

    Coordinator: Steven Polinsky <SMPCU@CUNYVM.CUNY.EDU>

Icon-Group@ARIZONA.EDU

Discussion of topics related to the Icon programming language (a high-level, general-purpose programming language that emphasizes string and structure processing). Such topics include: Programming Techniques, Theoretical Aspects, Icon in relation to other languages, Applications of Icon, Implementation Issues, Porting Icon, Bugs.

N.B.: The Icon programming language has no particular relationship to icons such as those used in window systems.

All requests to be added to or deleted from this list, problems, questions, etc., should be sent to Icon-Group-Request@ARIZONA.EDU. Questions about obtaining Icon should be sent to Icon-Project@ARIZONA.EDU.

    Coordinator: Bill Mitchell <whm@ARIZONA.EDU>

ICU-L on LISTSERV@UBVM (LISTSERV@UBVM.CC.BUFFALO.EDU)

This list was formed to serve as a vehicle for (1) discussion of topics and articles related to computing in education and (2) delivery of the ICU Newsletter which is a joint publication of Iowa State University and Digital Equipment Corporation.

Archives of ICU-L and related files are stored in the ICU-L FILELIST. To receive a list of files send the command 'INDEX ICU-L' (without the ' ') to LISTSERV@UBVM or LISTSERV@UBVM.CC.BUFFALO.EDU as the first line in the body of a mail message (not the Subject: line).

To subscribe to LISTNAME, send the command 'SUB ICU-L your name' (without the ' ') to LISTSERV@UBVM or LISTSERV@UBVM.CC.BUFFALO.EDU via a mail message (again, as the first line in the body of the mail, not the Subject: line).

For example: SUB ICU-L Joe Shmoe

> Owner: Jim Gerland <LISTMGR@UBVM>
> Jim Gerland <LISTMGR@UBVM.CC.BUFFALO.EDU

IDFORUM on LISTSERV@YORKVM1

IDFORUM provides a global electronic meeting place for all involved in industrial design. Practicing designers, design educators and design students are invited to subscribe. Subscribers will receive Voice of Industrial Design (VOID), a newsletter complied by industrial design students.

To subscribe to this list send a mail/note to LISTSERV@YORKVM1

VM systems may use the interactive command: TELL LISTSERV at YORKVM1 SUBSCRIBE IDFORUM your-full-name

VAX systems: SEND LISTSERV@YORKVM1 SUBSCRIBE IDFORUM your-full-name

Please direct enquiries to the

> List Owner: Maurice Barnwell
> GL250267@Venus.Yorku.CA

> Veronica Timm
> VM/CMS and AS/400 Technical Support
> York University
> Toronto, Canada.

IDMS-L%UGA.BITNET@VM1.NODAK.EDU

A forum for users of Cullinet software. Cullinet system software and application software operate on several platforms. IDMS/R is the data base management software for mainframes; IDMS/SQL (aka Enterprise DB) operates on VAX. Goldengate, Infogate, and IDMS/Architect are examples of micro-computer software. Appropriate discussion topics include (but are not limited to): installation/migration issues, "How To" questions, and any other concerns/problems encountered by users of Cullinet software.

To subscribe to IDMS-L, send the command: SUB IDMS-L your_full_name to LISTSERV@UGA e.g. SUB IDMS-L "William H. E. Day" To have your name removed from the IDMS-L subscriber list, send: SIGNOFF IDMS-L Commands can be sent to LISTSERV@UGA either as interactive messages or in e-mail (one command per line in the body of the e-mail message). Subscription problems or questions may be directed to the List Coordinator).

Coordinator: James F. Bradshaw <JAMES%CLEMSON.BITNET@VM1.NODAK.EDU>

IDX3000@SUVM.ACS.SYR.EDU
IDX3000@SUVM (BitNet)

Mailing list for discussion of the IDX-3000 Data PBX (manufactured by M/A-COM Linkabit). Topics include good news and bad.

Archives are available through revised LISTSERV.

All requests to be added to or deleted from this list, problems, questions, etc., should be sent to IDX-REQ@SUVM.ACS.SYR.EDU or IDX-REQ@SUVM (BitNet). Those familiar with revised LISTSERV can subscribe thru LISTSERV@SUVM.ACS.SYR.EDU or LISTSERV@SUVM (BitNet).

> Coordinator: John Wobus <JMWOBUS@SUVM.ACS.SYR.EDU>
> JMWOBUS@SUVM (BitNet)

IEEE-L on LISTSERV@BINGVMB.BITNET [Last Updated 12-October-1991]
LISTSERV@BINGVMB.CC.BINGHAMTON.EDU

The purpose of this list is to serve as a forum for all IEEE student branch officers and members. Practicing engineers and interested non-engineers are also invited to join.

Suggested topics for discussion include (but are not limited to): activities and fundraisers, discussion of curriculum at your institution, or whatever issues are important to EE's.

To subscribe to IEEE-L, send the following command to LISTSERV@BINGVMB via mail text or interactive message:

SUBSCRIBE IEEE-L your_full_name

> Listowners: Paul D. Kroculick (TJW0465 @ BINGTJW.BITNET)
> Chas Elliott
> Thomas J. Watson School of Engineering IEEE Student Branch

IEEE on LISTSERV@USACHVM1.BITNET [Last Updated 28-January-1992]

The purpose of this list is to serve as a forum for all IEEE student branch officers and members. Practicing engineers and interested non-engineers are also invited to join.

The LANGUAGE FOR THIS LIST IS "SPANISH", but other languages will be acepted too.

This a moderated mailing list for events and meeting announcements (related to electrical, electronic & computer engineering)

The posting to this list may include: New of new software, hardware & technology, product reviews, comments, questions & answers....

To subscribe to IEEE, send the following command to LISTSERV@USACHVM1 on BITNET via mail text or interactive message:

SUBSCRIBE IEEE your_full_name

Listowner: Eric A. Soto-Lavin <IEEESB@USACHVM1.BITNET> This list was created in march (1991).

IFIP-DIALUP@ics.uci.edu [Last Updated 1/92]

The <ifip-dialup@ics.uci.edu> mailing list was set up to support an ad hoc open task group of volunteers to work under the aegis of IFIP Working Group 6.5 in the Pre-Standards Development Mode, rather than in the Post-Standards Profiling or Implementation Agreements Mode, or in the IETF/IAB Standards Development Mode. It does however draw on the concepts, traditions and expertise of all of these other standards activities.

The purpose of this list is to discuss the issues related to provision of "local loop" PSTN dialup service for mail transfers between X.400/X.500 service host systems (MTA, MS, UA) and to develop draft specifications for experimental implementation of such a service.

It is intended and expected that one or more openly available experimental implementations will be forthcoming after specifications are completed, and before any formal standards work is initiated.

Although the ad hoc DIALUP Task Group is open to anyone, it is not intended to be a news group with a broad mission to educate. The list was established to foster serious work by experts in the field. New members are expected to do their homework before entering the discussion.

IFIP-DIALUP is not distributed to any USENET newsgroup. It is only served by an INTERNET mailing list exploder at ICS.UCI.EDU.

Archives of ifip-dialup are available from an automatic server at ICS.UCI.EDU. For more information, send a request for archive information to ifip-dialup-request@ics.uci.edu.

IFIP-DIALUP is NOT a LISTSERV mailing list. Administration is manual. To subscribe, send your request to <ifip-dialup-request@ics.uci.edu>. DO NOT SEND subscription requests to the main discussion list.

Include your Full Name and be sure that your subscription netmail address is in a CC of your request message. This CC address will help to verify that the address you supply is valid as received by the list administration agent, especially if it transits any gateways.

```
Owner:         "IFIP WG 6.5 Chair - Einar Stefferud" <stef@nma.com>
Requests:      "Administrivia" <ifip-dialup-request@ics.uci.edu>
Contributions: "IFIP-DIALUP Contribution" <ifip-dialup@ics.uci.edu>
```

IFIP-GTWY@UCS.UCI.EDU

Mailing list for the IFIP 6.5 Task Group on Gateways (gateways and interworking between X.400 and non-X.400 MHS environments and between 1984 and 1988 X.400 conformant systems). Participation is open to anyone with something to contribute.

For those with Internet access, the archives are maintained on host ICS.UCI.EDU in directory mhs, file ifip-gtwy; it can be accessed via ANONYMOUS FTP.

All requests to be added to or deleted from this list, problems, questions, etc., should be sent to <IFIP-GTWY-REQUEST@ICS.UCI.EDU>.

Tssk Group Chair/List Maintainer: Tim Kehres <Kehres@TIS.LLNL.GOV>

IFPHEN-L%WSUVM1.BITNET@CUNYVM.CUNY.EDU

Discussion group on Interfacial Phenomena (Group 1c, American Institute of Chemical Engineers). Meetings, articles, software, theories, materials, methods, tools, etc., are discussed.

To subscribe to the list:

From a VM site on BITNET do: TELL LISTSERV at WSUVM1 SUBSCRIBE IFPHEN-L Your_Full_Name where Your_Full_Name is your real name (not your userid). From a VMS BITNET site use the SEND/REMOTE command.

If you are at a site not on bitnet or where you cannot send interactive messages you can send a message to LISTSERV%WSUVM1.BITNET@CUNYVM.CUNY.EDU where the first non-header line consists of: SUBSCRIBE IFPHEN-L Your_Full_Name

```
Coordinator: Richard L. Zollars <SCEF0002%WSUVMS1.BITNET@CUNYVM.CUNY.EDU>
             SCEF0002@WSUVMS1  (BitNet)
```

ILAS-NET on LISTSERV@TECHNION.TECHNION.AC.IL
or LISTSERV@TECHNION.BITNET

ILAS - The International Linear Algebra Society - was constituted during the Combinatorial Matrix Analysis Conference in Victoria, May 1987. The general goal of ILAS is to encourage activities in linear algebra.

ILAS aims to encourage and support existing groups and individuals active in organizing meetings and publications in all aspects of linear algebra. Our purpose is international co-ordination, to assist the development of linear algebra. We welcome activities in all applications of linear algebra and we desire a proper share for theoretical matrix analysis and abstract linear algebra.

Among others, ILAS operates ILAS-NET, an electronic news service. We transmit announcements of ILAS activities and circulate other notices of interest to linear algebraists. Announcements for ILAS-NET or request to be on the mailing list for ILAS-NET, should be sent to Danny Hershkowitz (E-mail address: mar23aa@technion.bitnet). Subscription to ILAS-NET is independent of membership in ILAS and is free.

To subscribe to ILAS-NET, send the following command to LISTSERV@TECHNION (or LISTSERV AT TECHNION.TECHNION.AC.IL) in the BODY (text) of MAIL or in an interactive message: SUBSCRIBE ILAS-NET Your_full_name For example: SUBSCRIBE ILAS-NET Joe Shmoe

Archives of ILAS-NET are kept. Send the command INDEX ILAS-NET to LISTSERV@TECHNION.TECHNION.AC.IL.

You can also use anonymous FTP to host 132.68.1.6 at directory MAT to retrieve ILAS-NET notebooks.

Owner : Danny Hershkowitz <mar23aa@technion.BITNET>
<mar23aa@technion.technion.ac.il>

IMAGE-L@TREARN.BITNET   [Last Updated 12-October-1991]

This list deals mainly in image processing and related issues, focusing on video compression for multimedia applications, image processing applications, o bject isolation, linear predictive systems, motion detection, motion video compression.

To subscribe the list send a command or mail to LISTSERV@TREARN.BITNET with the following command in the body: SUB IMAGE-L Yourfirstname Yourlastname

To Submit to the list, mail your contribution to: IMAGE-L@TREARN.BITNET

Owner: Yusuf Ozturk <BILYOZ@TREARN.BITNET>

immune@weber.ucsd.edu

Purpose: A support group for people with immune-system breakdowns (and their symptoms) such as Chronic Fatigue Syndrome, Lupus, Candida, Hypoglycemia, Multiple Allergies, Learning Disabilities, etc, and their SO's, medical caretakers, etc. We have over 80 members and average 1-4 postings per week. The group is unmoderated and open to anyone anywhere in the world (no arguments about whether or not these disabilities exist).

Contact: immune-request@weber.ucsd.edu (internet) or: cnorman@ucsd.edu (bitnet) (both go to me, Cyndi Norman) Those on the bitnet can receive the list but may have to post by sending messages to me.

IMAGEN-L%UOGUELPH.BITNET@VM1.NODAK.EDU

Mailing list for discussion of the various features of the Imagen XP series of printers. Topics of interest include techniques used to create host-based print-spooling and accounting software, TCP/IP and UDP interfaces to the printer via it's LAN attachment and production of Postscript output. Hopefully this list will eventually serve as a repository for user-contributed spooling/accounting software should there be sufficient interest.

IMAGEN-L is archived monthly; to obtain a list of available files send the following command as the only line in the text/body of an e-mail message to LISTSERV@UOGUELPH: INDEX IMAGEN-L

BitNet users may subscribe by sending the following command to LISTSERV at OUGUELPH via interactive message or e-mail: SUB IMAGEN-L Your full name where "Your full name" is your real name, not your login Id. Non-BitNet users can join the list by sending the above command as the only line in the text/body of a message to LISTSERV%OUGUELPH.BITNET@VM1.NODAK.EDU.

Coordinator: Steve Howie <SCOTTY%UOGUELPH.BITNET@VM1.NODAK.EDU>
<scotty@COMMHUB.UOGUELPH.CA>

INCLEN-L@MCMVM1.CIS.MCMASTER.CA

The purpose of this list is to provide units of the International Clinical Epidemiology Network presently connected by electronic mail, with a vehicle for questions and comments to an "expert" in different aspects of clinical epidemiology.

To subscribe to this list send a mail/note message to CLIFTONJ@MCMASTER or CLIFTONJ@SSCVAX.CIS.MCMASTER.CA requesting a subscription to list INCLEN-L giving your full name and title.

INDIA-L%UTARLVM1.BITNET@VM1.NODAK.EDU

Mailing list for discussion of anything that is of interest to people of the Indian subcontinent. The list includes distributions of the Usenet Newsgroup soc.culture.indian.

Archives of INDIA-L and related files are stored in the INDIA-L FILELIST. To receive a list of files, send the following command to LISTSERV@UTARLVM1 via mail or interactive message: INDEX INDIA-L

BitNet users may subscribe by sending the following command to LISTSERV@UTARLVM1 via mail or interactive message: SUBSCRIBE INDIA-L Your full name where "Your full name" is your real name, not your login Id. Non-BitNet users can join the list by sending the above command as the only line in the text/body of a message to LISTSERV%UTARLVM1.BITNET@VM1.NODAK.EDU.

Coordinator: K. Vaninadha Rao <KVRAO%BGSUOPIE.BITNET@VM1.NODAK.EDU>

indigo@athena.mit.edu

Topics relating to the Indigo Girls. The submission address is: indigo@athena.mit.edu and the administrative address (for [un]subscription requests, etc.) is: indigo-request@athena.mit.edu.

INDOLOGY on LISTSERV@LIVERPOOL.AC.UK

The INDOLOGY list is chiefly aimed at academics interested in the study of classical India. The group might be expected to discuss topics such as the history of linguistics, Indo-european philology and grammar, issues of character set encoding, the location of citations, and the exchange of e-texts.

To subscribe, please send the following line as the body of a mail item

SUB INDOLOGY your_first_name your_second_name

to LISTSERV @ LIVERPOOL.AC.UK

Note: This was formerly a private list based at ucl.ac.uk

List owners:
D.WUJASTYK @ UCL.AC.UK   Dominik Wujastyk
QQ43 @ LIVERPOOL.AC.UK   Chris Wooff

INFO-1100@TUT.CIS.OHIO-STATE.EDU

This discussion list focuses on the Xerox/Envos Lisp environment and the associated protocols. Its purpose is to stimulate communication and sharing between computer science research groups that use or are interested in the environment. The list may be used for messages such as announcements of available lispusers packages or for queries such as "Does anybody know of a PUP file server implementation for the Sinclair ZX-80?" or to warn others of Interlisp-D and Medley bugs and/or suggest workarounds or to solicit help or discussion.

Xerox PARC, SIS, and Envos people are included in the distribution to facilitate communication about new developments, bugs, performance issues, etc.. Additionally, Info-1100 is automatically forwarded to AISupport.pasa@Xerox.com, where bugs are noted and acted upon if appropriate. Xerox AIS and Envos employees will not respond in Info-1100 unless the reply is of general interest or silence would mislead the readership. This mailing list is also distributed as the usenet newsgroup comp.sys.xerox.

A historical note describing the name: The Lisp environment was originally implemented on Xerox' 1100-series workstations, and the user base is primarily still on 1108's, 1109's, and 1186's.

Requests to be added to or deleted from this list, problems, questions, etc. should be sent to Info-1100-Request@TUT.CIS.OHIO-STATE.EDU.

Coordinator: Arun Welch <welch@TUT.CIS.OHIO-STATE.EDU>

INFO-68K@BERKELEY.EDU

Mailing list for users of OS's capable of running on small 68000 systems, primarily CP/M-68K. Related systems (OS/9-68K, etc.) and topics welcome.

Mail archives are kept on host WSMR-SIMTEL20.ARMY.MIL as TOPS20 mail files named yymm.n-TXT, where n starts with one and increments by one into another file as each file reached 150 disk pages. To conserve disk space, all the mail files in the archive, except for the current year, are individually compressed. The compressed files have the suffix -Z as part of the filetype field; they should be renamed to have the suffix .Z (uppercase Z) when transfered to a Unix system so the uncompress program will find them. The current month's mail is still kept in 68K-ARCHIV.TXT. The archives are stored in directory: PD2:<ARCHIVES.68K> Archive files are available via ANONYMOUS FTP from WSMR-SIMTEL20.ARMY.MIL for those with TCP/IP access to the Internet.

All requests to be added to or deleted from this list, problems, questions, etc., should be sent to Info-68K-Request@BERKELEY.EDU.

Coordinator: Mike Meyer <mwm@BERKELEY.EDU>

info-ada@AJPO.SEI.CMU.EDU

Mailing list for announcements, questions and discussions of a technical nature, requests for information, and just about anything else having to do with the Ada programming language (ANSI/MIL-STD-1815A-1983).

Messages are collected and automatically digested on a daily basis for mail distribution via WSMR-SIMTEL20.ARMY.MIL. Individual messages are bidirectionally gatewayed with the USENET newsgroup comp.lang.ada. The list is redistributed for BITNet, EARN, and NetNorth via the peered lists INFO-ADA@NDSUVM1 and INFO-ADA@FINHUTC on BITNet and EARN; both sites run Eric Thomas's LISTSERV.

Archives of messages can be found on host AJPO.SEI.CMU.EDU in the files ~ftp/public/infoada/* (the path name is case-sensitive), and are available to DDN users via anonymous FTP.

All Internet requests to be added to or deleted from this list, problems, etc., should be sent to info-ada-request@AJPO.SEI.CMU.EDU. BITNet, EARN, and NetNorth users can subscribe by sending the SUB command with your name; for example: SEND LISTSERV@host SUB INFO-APP your_full_name or TELL LISTSERV AT host SUB INFO-APP your_full_name To be removed from the list, SEND LISTSERV@host SIGNOFF INFO-APP or TELL LISTSERV AT host SIGNOFF INFO-APP where "host" is NDSUVM1 or FINHUTC and "your_full_name" is your name (NOT your net address).

Coordinator: Karl A. Nyberg <Karl@GREBYN.COM>

info-alliant@MCS.ANL.GOV   [Last Updated 12-October-1991]

An unmoderated mailing list for the discussion of Alliant computer systems. Software, programming techniques, and bugs are more than welcome.

All requests to be added to or deleted from this list, problems, etc., should be sent to info-alliant-request@MCS.ANL.GOV

Coordinator: Gene Rackow <rackow@MCS.ANL.GOV>

Info-Andrew@ANDREW.CMU.EDU

An informal mailing list intended for general discussion by recipients of the Andrew distribution (and implementors of Andrew). Andrew, a joint project of Carnegie Mellon University & IBM, is a prototype computing environment for academic and research use under the UNIX operating system. There are four main parts to Andrew:

- The Andrew File System (AFS), a large-scale distributed central file system.
- The Andrew Toolkit (ATK), a toolkit for building complex graphical user interface programs in a window-manager independent way (currently runs on X11 and the old Andrew window manager)
- The Andrew Message System (AMS), a multi-media mail and bulletin board system compatible with non-multi-media systems
- The Andrew application programs, a suite of programs that use the ATK to provide various useful features.

Topics can include (but are not limited to):

- hints about using/building Andrew
- discussions about desired features, changes, etc.
- comments about the Andrew distribution (e.g., "it stinks", "it's great")
- questions about the availability/existence of other parts of Andrew

The mailing list is available in both Andrew multi-media format (if you have the AMS up and running) and plain-text format. By default you will be sent plain-text versions of the posts, but you can request a change in which version you receive by sending mail to the -Request address. When sending a message to this list, you should feel free to include any multi-media images (rasters, animations, etc.) which might help to express you question, comment, etc. Such images will automatically be stripped out and replaced by "A picture appeared here" before being redistributed to the plain-text recipients.

All requests to be added to or deleted from this list, problems, questions, etc., should be sent to Info-Andrew-Request@ANDREW.CMU.EDU. NOTE: All subscription requests will also be added to the Info-Andrew-Bugs distribution list unless specifically requested not to.

Coordinator: Adam Stoller <ghoti+@ANDREW.CMU.EDU>

Info-Andrew-Bugs@ANDREW.CMU.EDU

Mailing list for reporting bugs/problems with the Andrew distribution. (See Info-Andrew entry for more detailed description on what "Andrew" is). Official responses to queries and bug reports will be posted to this mailing list. Topics include:

- problems discovered in building the distribution
- problems discovered in running parts of the distribution
- questions about difficulties encountered (even if you're not sure they're bugs)

When sending a message to this list, you should feel free to include any multi-media images (rasters, animations, etc.), that might help to clarify a bug report. Such images will automatically be stripped out and replaced by "A picture appeared here" before being redistributed to the plain-text recipients.

The list will be moderated, so that all bugs can be tracked and referenced with patch files. We expect that posts will go out to the subscribers about once a week, summarizing those reports which have been fixed and those still being looked into.

All requests to be added to or deleted from this list, problems, questions, etc., should be sent to Info-Andrew-Bugs-Request@ANDREW.CMU.EDU. NOTE: All subscription requests will also be added to the Info-Andrew distribution list unless specifically requested not to.

Coordinator: Adam Stoller <ghoti+@ANDREW.CMU.EDU>

INFO-APPLE@BRL.MIL

APPLE II series user's mailing list.

Mail archives are kept on host WSMR-SIMTEL20.ARMY.MIL as TOPS20 mail files named yymm.n-TXT, where n starts with one and increments by one into another file as each file reached 150 disk pages. To conserve disk space, all the mail files in the archive, except for the current year, are individually compressed. The compressed files have the suffix -Z as part of the filetype field; they should be renamed to have the suffix .Z (uppercase Z) when transfered to a Unix system so the uncompress program will find them. The current month's mail is still kept in APPLE-ARCHIV.TXT. The archives are stored in directory: PD2:<ARCHIVES.APPLE> Archive files are available via ANONYMOUS FTP from WSMR-SIMTEL20.ARMY.MIL for those with TCP/IP access to the Internet.

All requests to be added to or deleted from this list, problems, questions, etc., should be sent to Info-Apple-Request@BRL.MIL.

INFO-APP@NDSUVM1 is the BITNET/NetNorth/EARN Redistribution for the Internet list. BITNET, EARN, or NetNorth subscribers can join by sending the SUB command with your name; for example: SEND LISTSERV@NDSUVM1 SUB INFO-APP Jon Doe or TELL LISTSERV AT NDSUVM1 SUB INFO-APP Jon Doe To be removed from the list, SEND LISTSERV@NDSUVM1 SIGNOFF INFO-APP or TELL LISTSERV AT NDSUVM1 SIGNOFF INFO-APP To MAKE CONTRIBUTIONS to the list, BitNet, EARN, and Netnorth users should send mail to the Internet list name: Info-Apple@BRL.MIL, NOT to the BITNET list name!

Moderators: Brint Cooper <abc@BRL.MIL>
Bill Mermagen, Jr. <wm@BRL.MIL>

INFO-APPLETALK@ANDREW.CMU.EDU

List to facilitate communication between Applebus hardware and software developers and other interested parties. Applebus is Apple's networking scheme, which is used for connecting personal computers and other devices (laser printers, file servers, gateways to to other networks, etc.).

Archives are available on LANCASTER.ANDREW.CMU.EDU (IP address 128.2.13.21) in directory pub/info-appletalk.

All requests to be added to or deleted from this list, problems, questions, etc., should be sent to INFO-APPLETALK-REQUEST@ANDREW.CMU.EDU

Moderator: Tom Holodnik <tjh+@ANDREW.CMU.EDU>

Info-AS400@Joiner.BITNET
or Info-AS400@Joiner.COM

This is a "how-to" discussion on IBM AS/400 architecture, systems, and software. It is for the discussion of most topics, including hardware, systems and applications programming, networking, and connectivity. IBM and third-party solutions may be discussed.

The list is primarily aimed at system administrators, managers, and programmers. Because this is an Internet/BITNET list, the use of AS/400 systems in research and education, and in the context of cooperative interational networks, is certain to be of interest.

It is hoped that beginners will turn to the list for answers to their questions, and that more experienced participants will provide gentle answers.

These topics should be avoided, as they will get in the way of our discussions of how to solve real problems with the systems we have: (1) the merits of IBM AS/400 products relative to their competitors, (2) product announcements, and (3) IBM bashing. (Other topics may be added to this list in the future.)

Owner: Info-AS400-Request@Joiner.COM (IBM AS/400 Discussion Coordinator)
Arnold@Joiner.COM (Stephen L. Arnold)

Notebooks: No

Notes:

1. This list is unmoderated. Submissions to Info-AS400@Joiner (Info-AS400@Joiner.COM) are immediately forwarded to the list.
2. This is not a LISTSERV list and requests for list changes are handled manually by the coordinator. Send requests to update the list to Info-AS400-Request@Joiner.COM. The list is a PMDF distribution list hosted on a VAX system running VMS.
3. Contributions sent to this list are manually archived. Requests for old postings will be answered by the coordinator. Send such requests to Info-AS400-Request@Joiner.COM. If there is sufficient demand for automatic subscription and archive service, I'll explore ways to provide it.

INFO-ATARI <INFO-ATARI8@NAUCSE.CSE.NAU.EDU>   [Last Updated 12-October-1991]
<INFO-ATARI16@NAUCSE.CSE.NAU.EDU>

Discussions of 8- and 16-bit Atari computers and related topics. Commercial messages and advertisements are not permitted.

LISTSERV provides access to files for everyone who can send mail, independent of their location. On Bitnet messages should be sent to your nearest LISTSERV (the one from which you receive the info-atari digests); if your address is not on Bitnet, an address for file servers is given below. All mail sent to LISTSERV contains command lines. LISTSERV will respond by return mail. No subject is necessary in such mail. For more information send the command INFO

The list_name for 16-bit Ataris is INFO-A16. The list_name for 8-bit Ataris is INFO-A8. These list names are used by Bitnet addressees for subscribing and unsubscribing and by everyone for obtaining back copies of news digests. The list_names for programs stored in the archives are PROG-A16 and PROG-A8.

You can obtain copies of files from LISTSERV by sending a message in the specified format. To obtain a list of files in the file server, the command is INDEX list_name The command to obtain a specific file is GET list_name file_name for example, GET INFO-A16 87-00076 If you want to learn more, send the message HELP

If you are on Bitnet you may add or remove yourself from the distribution list. The command to join the list is SUBSCRIBE list_name User_name The command to remove yourself from the list is UNSUBSCRIBE list_name

If you are on Internet (or gatewayed to it), your mail concerning 16-bit Atari information should be addressed to LISTSERV%CANADA01.BITNET@CUNYVM.CUNY.EDU. Mail concerning 8-bit Atari information should be addressed to LISTSERV%TCSVM.BITNET@WISCVM.WISC.EDU.

Administrative messages should be sent to
info-atari8-request@SCORE.STANFORD.EDU or
info-atari16-request@SCORE.STANFORD.EDU.

Moderators:
  (Un)Subscribing problems:
    Harry Williams <harry%MARIST.BITNET@CUNYVM.CUNY.EDU>
  16-bit digest archives:
    Peter Jasper-Fayer <sofpjf@UOGUELPH.BITNET@CUNYVM.CUNY.EDU>
  16-bit program archives:
    Richard Werezak <carson@MCMASTER.BITNET@CUNYVM.CUNY.EDU>
  8-bit archives:
    John Voigt <sysbjav@TCSVM.BITNET@CUNYVM.CUNY.EDU>
  8-bit program archives:

Arnold de Leon <adeleon@HMCVAX.BITNET@CUNYVM.CUNY.EDU>.

INFO-C@RESEARCH.ATT.COM

INFO-C is gatewayed with the comp.lang.c newsgroup on USENET. Its purpose is to carry on discussions about C programming and the C programming language.

BitNet, EARN, or NetNorth subscribers can join by sending the SUB command to NDSUVM1 with your name. For example: SEND LISTSERV@NDSUVM1 SUB INFO-C Your_Full_Name or TELL LISTSERV AT NDSUVM1 SUB INFO-C Your_Full_Name where Your_Full_Name is your real name, not your userid. To be removed from the list, send the SIGNOFF command: SEND LISTSERV@NDSUVM1 SIGNOFF INFO-C or TELL LISTSERV AT NDSUVM1 SIGNOFF INFO-C

Requests by Internet users to be added to or deleted from this list, as well as problems, questions, etc., should be sent to info-c-request@RESEARCH.ATT.COM.

Coordinator: Mark Plotnick <info-c-request@RESEARCH.ATT.COM>

Info-CCMD@CUNIXF.CC.COLUMBIA.EDU

Mailing list dealing with the CCMD package (TOPS-20 COMND% JSYS emulation written in C). Currently, CCMD runs under Berkeley 4.x Unix, System V, and MS-DOS. We'd like to see some other ports come along too. If there is anyone currently working on porting CCMD to something not mentioned above, or would like to work on porting CCMD to another OS, we'd like to hear about it (VMS comes to mind).

CCMD source code is available via ANONYMOUS FTP from CUNIXF.CC.COLUMBIA.EDU Files are in directory ccmd.

All requests to be added to or deleted from this list, problems, questions, etc., should be sent to Info-CCMD-Request@CUNIXF.CC.COLUMBIA.EDU.

Coordinator: Fuat Baran <fuat@columbia.edu>

INFO-CELERITY@DOLPHIN.BU.EDU

Discussions pertaining to superminicomputer systems manufactured by Celerity.

Archives are available upon request to INFO-CELERITY-REQUEST@DOLPHIN.BU.EDU.

All requests to be added to or deleted from this list, problems, questions, etc., should be sent to INFO-CELERITY-REQUEST@DOLPHIN.BU.EDU.

Coordinator: Glenn Bresnahan <glenn@DOLPHIN.BU.EDU>

INFO-CONVEX@PEMRAC.SPACE.SWRI.EDU   [Last Updated 12-October-1991]

Mailing list for sharing ideas, questions, bug fixes, and so forth concerning any aspect of the hardware and software products produced by Convex Corp. Initially, this group will not be moderated.

All requests to be added to or deleted from this list, problems, questions, etc., should be sent to info-convex-request@PEMRAC.SPACE.SWRI.EDU.

Coordinator: karen@pemrac.space.swri.edu (Karen Birkelbach)

INFO-CPM@WSMR-SIMTEL20.ARMY.MIL

Information and discussion on both 8 and 16-bit versions of the CP/M microcomputer operating system.

Mail archives are kept on host WSMR-SIMTEL20.ARMY.MIL as TOPS20 mail files named yymm.n-TXT, where n starts with one and increments by one into another file as each file reached 150 disk pages. To conserve disk space, all the mail files in the archive, except for the current year, are individually compressed. The compressed files have the suffix -Z as part of the filetype field; they should be renamed to have the suffix .Z (uppercase Z) when transfered to a Unix system so the uncompress program will find them. The current month's mail is still kept in CPM-ARCHIV.TXT. The archives are stored in directory: PD2:<ARCHIVES.CPM> Archive files are available via ANONYMOUS FTP FROM WSMR-SIMTEL20.ARMY.MIL for those with TCP/IP access to the Internet.

Over 80 megabytes of public domain software (most of it CP/M) are kept in five program archives. For a description of these archives, request a copy of the "archive blurb" from INFO-CPM-REQUEST@WSMR-SIMTEL20.ARMY.MIL.

All requests to be added to or deleted from this list, problems, questions, etc., should be sent to INFO-CPM-REQUEST@WSMR-SIMTEL20.ARMY.MIL.

Coordinator: Keith Petersen <W8SDZ@WSMR-SIMTEL20.ARMY.MIL>

info-databasix@blx-a.prime.com   [Last Updated 28-January-1992]

Info-databasix is an unmoderated mailing list for the discussion of all software products from Databasix Information Systems.

Applications like:

- ADLIB database (not the music pc card)
- ADCIRC public library application
- OPAC database application

Topics can include (but are not limited to):

- Hints about using and designing applications
- Discussions about desired features, changes etc.
- Problems, bugs etc.
- Questions about all related subjects

To subscribe to the list send a mail message to: listserver@blx-a.prime.com The message should contain one line with: sub info-databasix "your full name"

Contributions to the list should be sent to: info-databasix@blx-a.prime.com

Archives are not available yet.

Coordinator: Ronald van der Meer <ronald@dcs.prime.com>

INFO-DEC-MICRO@ANDREW.CMU.EDU

A forum for users to ask questions and share answers about various topics concerning DEC Microcomputers (i.e. Rainbow 100, MicroVax, Professional 350/380).

All requests to be added to or deleted from this list, problems, questions, etc., should be sent to Info-DEC-Micro-Request@ANDREW.CMU.EDU.

Coordinator: Rob Locke <rl1b+@ANDREW.CMU.EDU>
                  <RALII@DRYCAS.CLUB.CC.CMU.EDU>

INFO-DSEE@APOLLO.COM

Discussion of DSEE, a software engineering environment from Apollo in wide-spread use by tens of thousands of programmers, on projects up to 5,000,000 lines of code.

DSEE elegantly and efficiently solves many common problems -- how to work on multiple versions of a program at a time, how to tell when someone has made a change you need to know about, how to develop software for multiple target machines, how to KNOW the right version of each source file was used, etc.

If all this sounds like hype, join the mailing list, and listen to users.

At least initially, the list will not be moderated or digested; if the volume is sufficient, this may change. Mail to the list will be archived in some public place that will be announced at a later date.

All requests to be added to or deleted from this list, problems, questions, etc., should be sent to info-dsee-request@apollo.com.

Coordinator: David Lubkin <lubkin@APOLLO.COM>

INFO-ENCORE@UB.D.UMN.EDU

Mailing list for users of the Encore MultiMax computers and Encore Annex terminal servers.

All requests to be added or deleted from this list, problems, questions, etc., should be sent to INFO-ENCORE-REQUEST@UB.D.UMN.EDU.

Moderator: Dan Burrows <dburrows@CS-GW.D.UMN.EDU>

info-frame@AEROSPACE.AERO.ORG

Mailing list for System Frameworks. This group is designed to provide information for software tool developers that are responsible for integrating heterogenous software products. This can include in-house and vendor supplied. Usually, the integration of the products is designed to provide an environment that makes using the tools easier. The basic issue is to build a 'framework' around the tools that provides a common and consistent view of the system. The framework is not limited to homogeneous environments, but also can span heterogeneous systems. Companies like EDA and government sponsored projects like EIS are trying to tackle this problem. This group can be viewed as a forum for users and developers to voice their opinions on this subject. Frameworks are common in the area of CAD/CAE, CASE and office automation; but they are not limited to only these areas. Topics open for discussion are:

Process Control/Flow	Data Transfer Languages	Tool Portability
Tool encapsulation	Data Management	Network Computing
User Interface	Object Programming	Anything Else

All requests to be added to or deleted from this list, problems, questions, etc., should be sent to info-frame-request@AEROSPACE.AERO.ORG.

Moderator: Louis McDonald <louis@AEROSPACE.AERO.ORG>

INFO-FUTURES@World.STD.COM

Digest to provide a speculative forum for analyzing current and likely events in technology as they will affect our near future in computing and related areas. In broad terms, topics of interest include developments in both computing research and industry which are likely to affect our decision making, particularly decisions we are probably grappling with right this minute. Technologies can change so rapidly that simply forecasting for needs within any organization one or two years in advance can be extremely difficult, frequently we are forced to provide foundations that effectively lock us into a technology for longer periods of time. It is hoped the information this list provides can help both the practitioner and researcher determine where best to expend resources.

All requests to be added to or deleted from this list, problems, questions, etc., should be sent to INFO-FUTURES-REQUEST@WORLD.STD.COM

Moderator: Barry Shein <bzs@WORLD.STD.COM>

INFO-GCG%UTORONTO.BITNET@VM1.NODAK.EDU

Mailing list covering topics in computer aided molecular biology and of particular interest to users and managers of the "Genetics Computer Group" software from the University of Wisconsin.

BitNet users can subscribe by sending the following command to LISTSERV@ UTORONTO: SUBscribe INFO-GCG your_full_name where your_full_name is your real name, not your loginid. Non-BitNet users can subscribe by sending the above command in the body of a message to LISTSERV%UTORONTO.BITNET@VM1.NODAK.EDU.

Coordinator: John Cargill <CARGILL%UTOROCI.BITNET@VM1.NODAK.EDU>

<SYSJOHN%UTOROCI.BITNET@VM1.NODAK.EDU>

info-gnu-msdos@wugate.wustl.edu

The GNUISH MsDos Development Group

The Free Software Foundation (FSF) is not directly interested in integrating or maintaining ports of GNU software to MS-DOS, because of limited resources. These activities take time away from finishing a complete standalone GNU, which FSF and many in the GNU Project considers much more important.

There is a mailing list to discuss these MsDos ports of GNU software. It is called info-gnu-msdos@wugate.wustl.edu. It is managed by an experimental Unix-based listserv program. Send the command:

add info-gnu-msdos to: listserv@wugate.wustl.edu

to become subscribed to the list. Send a message containing only 'help' to get more information about the listserv. Do not send these commands to info-gnu-msdos. They should go to the listserv address.

The list is not moderated, not digestified, and open to subscription by anyone. Problems with the mailing list should be directed to:

info-gnu-msdos-request@wugate.wustl.edu

To get more information about the GNUISH project, look at the file on wuarchive.wustl.edu (128.252.135.4) in the mirrors/msdos/gnuish directory called '00msdos.gnu'.

```
david@wubios.wustl.edu          ^    Mr. David J. Camp
david%wubios@wugate.wustl.edu   < * >  +1 314 382 0584
...!uunet!wugate!wubios!david    v    "God loves material things."
```

INFO-GRAPHICS@ADS.COM

Discussion of Graphics hardware, software, and any topic related to graphics. Basically a free-wheeling exchange of information, much like INFO-CPM.

All requests to be added to or deleted from this list, problems, questions, etc., should be sent to INFO-GRAPHICS-REQUEST@ADS.COM.

Coordinator: Andy Cromarty <andy@ADS.COM>

INFO-HAMS@WSMR-SIMTEL20.ARMY.MIL

A mailing list for Amateur Radio (not CB) operators. INFO-HAMS is gatewayed to/from Usenet's rec.ham-radio so Usenet people will get it there.

Mail archives are kept on host WSMR-SIMTEL20.ARMY.MIL as TOPS20 mail files named yymm.n-TXT, where n starts with one and increments by one into another file as each file reached 150 disk pages. To conserve disk space, all the mail files in the archive, except for the current year, are individually compressed. The compressed files have the suffix -Z as part of the filetype field; they should be renamed to have the suffix .Z (uppercase Z) when transfered to a Unix system so the uncompress program will find them. The current month's mail is still kept in HAMS-ARCHIV.TXT. The archives are stored in directory: PD2:<ARCHIVES.HAMS> Archive files are available via ANONYMOUS FTP for those with TCP/IP access to the Internet.

Phil Howard KA9WGN <PHIL%UIUCVMD.BITNET@CUNYVM.CUNY.EDU> also archives the INFO-HAMS mailing list on BITNET node UIUCVMD using the LISTSERV mailing list server (subscriptions disabled for this). Users on BITNET may request files to be sent to them by sending commands, either by interactive message or in the message body by mail, to the address LISTSERV@UIUCVMD. The command to see the current online list of files is: INDEX INFOHAMS (Note there is no dash "-"). To obtain volume 88 issue 73, send the command: GET INFOHAMS 88-00073 INFO-HAMS is a digested mailing list, and each digest is available separately from LISTSERV@UIUCVMD.

All Internet requests to be added to or deleted from this list, problems, questions, etc., should be sent to INFO-HAMS-REQUEST@WSMR-SIMTEL20.ARMY.MIL.

Coordinator: Keith Petersen <W8SDZ@WSMR-SIMTEL20.ARMY.MIL>

INFO-HIGH-AUDIO@CSD4.csd.uwm.edu

This list is for the exchange of subjective comments about high end audio equipment and modifications performed to high end pieces. Techniques used to modify equipment especially, but not limited to, vacuum tube electronics are exchanged. Some comments may be subjective or intuitive and may not yet have a measurable basis. Other topics of discussion include turntables, arms and cartridges; preamplifiers, headamps and cartridge matching; speakers, amplifiers and matching; placement of speakers, and room treatments. Any comments that prevent an open exchange of ideas and techniques are not encouraged.

Archives of projects will be maintained on CSD4.csd.uwm.edu and available via anonymous FTP.

All requests to be added to or deleted from this list, problems, questions, etc., should be sent to INFO-HIGH-AUDIO-REQUEST@CSD4.csd.uwm.edu

Cordinator: Thomas Krueger <tjk@CSD4.csd.uwm.edu>

INFO-HZ100@TOPS20.RADC.AF.MIL

INFO-HZ100 is a forum for discussion concerning topics related to the Zenith Z-100 (Heath H-100) family of professional desktop computers. Messages are forwarded for immediate redistribution to the main list. Distribution is limited to one central mailbox per site.

Periodically, useful knowledge and items generated from the list and other random sources will be edited into a newsletter for distribution to both network and non-network interested groups. Any comments, suggestions, help, knowledge, software, ideas, etc., would be greatly appreciated.

The INFO-HZ100 PD Library of software is available in directory PD2:<HZ100> on host WSMR-SIMTEL20.ARMY.MIL.

All requests to be added to or deleted from this list, problems, questions, etc., should be sent to INFO-HZ100-REQUEST@TOPS20.RADC.AF.MIL

There is a BitNet sub-distribution list, INF-Z100@CLVM; BitNet subscribers can join by sending the SUB command with your name. For example, SEND LISTSERV@CLVM SUB INF-Z100 Jon Doe To be removed from the list, SEND LISTSERV@CLVM SIGNOFF. To make contributions to the list, BitNet subscribers should send mail to the Internet list name, NOT to the BITNET list name.

Coordinator: Gern <GERN@TOPS20.RADC.AF.MIL>

Info-IBMPC@WSMR-SIMTEL20.ARMY.MIL

Info-IBMPC is a forum for technical discussion of the IBM Personal Computer and compatible micro-computers, providing a way for interested members of the Internet community to compare notes, ask questions, and share insights of a technical nature about these machines. While it is not primarily a consumer's guide to the IBM PC, the digest may also be useful for that purpose.

Messages are collected, edited into digests and distributed as the volume of mail dictates (generally twice a week). All messages regarding hardware for IBM PCs, PC and compatibles and software are welcomed; messages on other topics will not be run. In addition, two topics are taboo and are routinely edited out: (1) self promotion of products for sale, and (2) anything about copy protection.

An archive of back issues and a program library are available to those with FTP access (essentially anyone on the Internet). Digests are archived at WSMR-SIMTEL20.ARMY.MIL in PD2:<ARCHIVES.IBMPC> in <YYMM.1-TXT> format. Digests from September 1982 through the current issue are available by ANONYMOUS FTP login.

A library of free software in binary and source code form is maintained at SIMTEL20 in directory

PD1:<MSDOS> and PD2:<MSDOS2>. A list of all MS-DOS programs available from WSMR-SIMTEL20.ARMY.MIL is contained in PD1:<MSDOS>FILES.IDX. Donations of source code are welcomed. Donated programs must be truly free and public domain, with no fee or contribution required or requested, and no license agreement. To donate a program to the library, send a description of the program along with a copy of the source code to INFO-IBMPC-REQUEST@WSMR-SIMTEL20.ARMY.MIL.

Files may be FTP'ed by logging in to the SIMTEL20 FTP server with username ANONYMOUS, password GUEST. (Although GUEST is a perfectly good password, a password of <YOUR-NAME@YOUR-HOST> is preferred.) For those subscribers without Internet FTP access, a file transfer mechanism has been set up with RPIECS.bitnet. For more details, send a message to <LISTSERV@RPIECS.bitnet> with the first line of 'HELP' or ask the editor for the Simtel-Bitnet FTP help file. Requested files are mailed to those users with a VALID Internet return address.

WSMR-SIMTEL20.ARMY.MIL can be accessed using LISTSERV commands from BITNET and those users without Internet FTP access via LISTSERV@NDSUVM1, LISTSERV@RPIECS, LISTSERV@FINTUVM and in Europe from EARN TRICKLE servers. Send commands to LISTSERV or TRICKLE@<host-name> (example: TRICKLE@TREARN). The following TRICKLE servers are presently available: AWIWUW11 (Austria), BANUFS11 (Belgium), DKTC11 (Denmark), DB0FUB11 (Germany), IMIPOLI (Italy), EB0UB011 (Spain) TAUNIVM (Israel) and TREARN (Turkey).

All requests to be added to or deleted from this list, problems, questions, etc., should be sent to INFO-IBMPC-REQUEST@WSMR-SIMTEL20.ARMY.MIL.

BITNET users must join the INFO-IBMPC distribution list through the BITNET LISTSERV mechanism. There are IBMPC-L BITNET sub-distribution lists at the following BITNET hosts: BNANDP11, UTORONTO, CEARN, DEARN, EB0UB011, FINHUTC, HEARN, VTVM1, POLYGRAF, $$INFOPC@RICEVM1, TAMVM1, TAUNIVM, UBVM, UGA, and VTVM2. BitNet subscribers can join by sending a SUB command to the nearest LISTSERV node or to <LISTSERV@POLYGRAF.bitnet>. For example: SEND LISTSERV@CEARN SUB IBMPC-L Jon Doe To be removed from the list substitute the keyword "SIGNOFF" for "SUB". To make contributions to the list, BITNET subscribers should send mail to <INFO-IBMPC@WSMR-SIMTEL20.ARMY.MIL> and NOT to the BITNET list name.

For those users on USENET, the Digest is available from newsfeed comp.sys.ibm.pc.digest. Since the current editor does not have a USENET feed, please include <INFO-IBMPC@WSMR-SIMTEL20.ARMY.MIL> as a CC: address on all messages sent to USENET.

On BITNET, the archives can be obtained from DATABASE@BITNIC.BITNET and the program library can be obtained from CCUC@UMCVMB.BITNET. The WSMR-SIMTEL20.ARMY.MIL FTP server may also be reached via <LISTSERV%RPICICGE.BITNET@CUNYVM.CUNY.EDU>. For more details, send a message to the above addresses with the first line of 'HELP'.

Editor: Gregory Hicks <GHICKS@WSMR-SIMTEL20.ARMY.MIL>

Former Editors: Billy Brackenridge <BRACKENRIDGE@C.ISI.EDU>
       Richard Gillmann <GILLMANN@C.ISI.EDU>
       Eliot Moore <Elmo@C.ISI.EDU>
       Phyllis O'Neil

INFO-IBMRT@POLYA.STANFORD.EDU

INFO-IBMRT is for discussion of the IBM RT Computer and related topics. If traffic warrants, this list may be split into multiple lists (e.g. AIX, UNIX, hardware, et cetera), but for the time being, it will be one list. Messages are manually screened to weed out list-maintenance requests and then individually remailed.

Archives are kept on host POLYA.STANFORD.EDU in directory ~ftp/rt. Archives are available via anonymous FTP from Internet sites only; please DON'T do file transfers weekdays between 9am and 5pm (Pacific Time).

All requests to be added to or deleted from this list, problems, questions, etc., should be sent to INFO-IBMRT-REQUEST@POLYA.STANFORD.EDU.

Moderator: James Wilson <jwilson@POLYA.STANFORD.EDU>

INFO-IDL@SEI.CMU.EDU

Discussion of issues relating to IDL (the Interface Description Language) and IDL-like technologies.

All requests to be added to or deleted from this list, problems, questions, etc., should be sent to INFO-IDL-REQUEST@SEI.CMU.EDU.

Coordinator: Don Stone (ds@SEI.CMU.EDU)

INFO-IRIS@BRL.MIL

Mailing list focusing on Silicon Graphics Iris workstations and software. It's purpose is to stimulate communication and sharing between computer science research groups that are using or are interested in these machines.

An archive of messages is kept on host VGR.BRL.MIL in file: <INFO-IRIS>INFO-IRIS.TXT For sites with FTP access, the file can be retrieved with user "anonymous" and any password. Public domain software for the Iris submitted by Info-Iris readers is kept in directory <INFO-IRIS>; file <INFO-IRIS>DIR is an annotated list of the files found there.

Requests to be added to or deleted from this list, problems, questions, etc. should be sent to Info-Iris-Request@BRL.MIL. Contributors who wish never to see error messages from the mailer should specify this address as the return-path of their messages.

Coordinator: Chuck Kennedy <kermit@BRL.MIL>

INFO-KERMIT@WATSUN.CC.COLUMBIA.EDU

Kermit is a file transfer protocol developed at Columbia University in New York City, USA, for use primarily between micros and mainframes over asynchronous serial connections, dialed or direct, over public data networks, etc. Kermit programs that implement this protocol can transfer textual as well as binary files over both 7-bit and 8-bit communication links, singly or in groups. As of this writing (May 1989), Kermit programs are available for nearly 350 different computers and operating systems. The Info-Kermit mailing list is a digest intended for people who maintain or install Kermit at their sites, or who are (thinking about) working on a new implementation, or who have bugs and/or fixes to report, or who are interested in discussing the protocol, and also for Kermit users. The digest is available on Internet, CSNET, MAILNET, BITNET, EARN, USENET, CCNET, DEC EASYNET, and any other network gatewayed to the Internet.

Info-Kermit archives are collected in kermit/e/imail.*, one file (paginaged and indexed) per volume, generally 2 volumes per year. Other Kermit files are also available via both Internet and BitNet/EARN and by mail order.

All requests to be added to or deleted from this list, problems, questions, etc., should be sent to Info-Kermit-Request@WATSON.CC.COLUMBIA.EDU or to KERMIT@CUVMA.BITNET. You may also subscribe to Info-Kermit automatically via LISTSERV. To do this, send e-mail to LISTSERV@CUVMB.BITNET, containing the message text: SUBSCRIBE I-KERMIT your name To remove yourself from the Info-Kermit LISTSERV distribution list, send a message to LISTSERV@CUVMA.BITNET with the message text: UNSUBSCRIBE I-KERMIT

To make contributions to the list, BITNET subscribers should send mail to the Internet list name, NOT to the BITNET list name.

Moderator: Christine M. Gianone <CMG@WATSUN.CC.COLUMBIA.EDU>

KERMIT@CUVMA.BITNET

info-labview@pica.army.mil

Info-LabVIEW is an internet mailing list for the discussion of the use of National Instruments' LabVIEW package for the Apple Macintosh.

LabVIEW is a graphical software system for developing high-performance scientific and engineering applications. LabVIEW acquires data from IEEE-488 (GPIB), RS-232/422 and modular (VXI or CAMAC) instruments and plug-in data acquisition boards.

LabVIEW programs, called "virtual instruments" (VIs), are created using icons, instead of conventional, text-based code. A VI consists of a front panel and a block diagram. The front panel (with knobs, switches, graphs, and so on) is the user interface. The block diagram, which is the executable code, consists of icons that operate on data connected by wires that pass data between them. [I swiped this description from National Instruments' promotional blurbs]

The list is being run as a simple redistribution of all submitted messages.

To post to the list, send your mail to <info-labview@pica.army.mil>. All administrative issues should go to <info-labview-request@pica.army.mil>.

FTP archives are on caesar.pica.army.mil [129.139.160.200], /pub/labview.

Coordinator: Tom Coradeschi <tcora@pica.army.mil>

INFO-LAW@BRL.MIL

Interest in computers and law. Mail gets distributed after first being manually screened. Process may involve returning to author for clarification and/or other sanitization.

Archived messages are kept on SRI-CSL at:
newest messages: <INFO-LAW>ARCHIVE.TXT
older messages: <INFO-LAW>ARCHIVE.001
         <INFO-LAW>ARCHIVE.002
         <INFO-LAW>ARCHIVE.003

All requests to be added to or deleted from this list, problems, questions, etc., should be sent to INFO-LAW-REQUEST@BRL.MIL.

Coordinator: Mike Muuss <INFO-LAW-REQUEST@BRL.MIL>

INFO-M2@UCF1VM.CC.UCF.EDU

A discussion list for the Modula-2 programming language. Modula-2 is a language by Niklaus Wirth which extends the Pascal foundation by providing an updated statement syntax (generalized LOOP, EXIT, RETURN, no GOTO), separate compilation with a module (compilation unit) broken into specification and implementation parts with importing and exporting of objects, controlled machine level access, and concurrent programming and coroutines. Modula-2 has most of the power of Ada but is small enough that excellent full implementations exist for CP/M 80.

Contributions may be sent to INFO-M2@ucf1vm.Bitnet (from the US) or to INFO-M2@db0tui11.Bitnet (from Europe); these are both entry points for the same list.

Currrent messages are archived on host WSMR.SIMTEL20.ARMY.MIL in file <ARCHIVES.MODULA-2>MODULA-2-ARCHIV.TXT Older messages are in file <ARCHIVES.MODULA-2>MODULA-2.ARCHIV.ymmdd SIMTEL20 supports ANONYMOUS login for those with FTP access to the Internet.

Log files will be kept on a monthly basis.

BitNet users can subscribe by sending the following command to LISTSERV@UCF1VM: SUB INFO-M2 Your_full_name where Your_full_name is your real name, not your userid; for example: SUB

INFO-M2 John Doe Non-BitNet users can subscribe by sending the SUB command as the text/body of a message to LISTSERV@UCF1VM.CC.UCF.EDU

Coordinator: UCF Postmaster <POSTMAST@UCF1VM.CC.UCF.EDU>

Thomas Habernoll <habernol%DB0TUI11.BITNET@CUNYVM.CUNY.EDU>

INFO-MAC@SUMEX-AIM.STANFORD.EDU

Network interest group for the Apple Macintosh computer. This list is SUMEX's contribution to the community of research and instructional developers and users of the Macintosh; all submissions of messages and programs in this spirit are welcome.

For those sites with FTP access to SUMEX-AIM, archives for INFO-MAC are kept under {SUMEX-AIM}/info-mac/digest/infomacvM-NNN, where M is the volume number and NNN is the digest number. These numbers have little to no bearing on reality.

Programs submitted to the bulletin board, along with documentation files and other references are also stored in the info-mac directory. With FTP access as user "anonymous" and any password, you can bring these files over to your host and download them to your Macintosh. "Usenet" and some of the other networks that copy info-mac will see sources redistributed at the time they are mentioned in the digest distributions.

Messages to INFO-MAC@SUMEX-AIM.STANFORD.EDU are scanned to filter out any list requests, questions previously answered, pure speculation or opinion, or message obviously not in line with the stated purpose of the list.

All requests to be added to or deleted from this list, problems, questions, etc., should be sent to INFO-MAC-REQUEST@SUMEX-AIM.STANFORD.EDU. Due to the size of this list, INFO-MAC only sends to relays, i.e. addresses such as INFOMAC@yoursite.whatever which then distribute it locally. Please check with your local gurus to gain access your local relay.

Moderators: Bill Lipa <Info-Mac-Request@SUMEX-AIM.STANFORD.EDU>
Jon Pugh <Info-Mac-Request@SUMEX-AIM.STANFORD.EDU>

INFO-MACH@CS.CMU.EDU

This mailing list exists for the purpose of discussing issues related to the Mach operating system. Mach is a UNIX BSD4.3 compatible operating system based on a message passing architecture that incorporates such features as multiprocessor support, lightweight tasking, external pagers, and a machine independent vm system. Mach is being developed at Carnegie Mellon University.

All requests to be added to or deleted from this list, problems, questions, etc., should be sent to INFO-MACH-REQUEST@CS.CMU.EDU.

Coordinator: Doug Orr <Doug.Orr@CS.CMU.EDU>

INFO-MICRO@WSMR-SIMTEL20.ARMY.MIL

Information/discussion list on the general interest topic of microcomputers.

Questions/discussions on a particular Operating System, such as CP/M, should be addressed to the specific list if one already exists (such as INFO-CPM@WSMR-SIMTEL20.ARMY.MIL for this example).

Mail archives are kept on host WSMR-SIMTEL20.ARMY.MIL as TOPS20 mail files named yymm.n-TXT, where n starts with one and increments by one into another file as each file reached 150 disk pages. To conserve disk space, all the mail files in the archive, except for the current year, are individually compressed. The compressed files have the suffix -Z as part of the filetype field; they should be renamed to have the suffix .Z (uppercase Z) when transfered to a Unix system so the uncompress program will find them. The current month's mail is still kept in INFO-MICRO-ARCHIV.TXT. The archives are stored in directory:

PD2:<ARCHIVES.INFO-MICRO> Archive files are available via ANONYMOUS FTP for those with TCP/IP access to the Internet.

Many megabytes of public domain software are kept in the program archives. For a description of these archives, request a copy of the "archive blurb" from INFO-MICRO-REQUEST@WSMR-SIMTEL20.ARMY.MIL. All correspondence and program archives described here are available to Internet users via FTP with user-name ANONYMOUS.

All requests to be added to or deleted from this list, problems, questions, etc., should be sent to INFO-MICRO-REQUEST@WSMR-SIMTEL20.ARMY.MIL.

Coordinator: Keith Petersen <W8SDZ@WSMR-SIMTEL20.ARMY.MIL>

INFO-MINIX@UDEL.EDU

Mailing list for the discussion of the Minix Operating System, a Version 7 Unix clone written for IBM Compatible PCs and Atari STs by Andy Tanenbaum (minix@VU44.UUCP or minix@CS.VU.NL). The list is gatewayed to the BitNet list MINIX-L@NDSUVM1 and the USENET newsgroup comp.os.minix. Currently, all list distribution is handled from the BitNet listserver, which is also on the Internet as VM1.NODAK.EDU.

Archives are kept on VM1.NODAK.EDU in the directory "listserv" in files: MINIX-L.LOGyymmw where "yy" is the year, "mm" is the numeric month and "w" is an alphabetic character from A to E indicating what week of the month. Several months of log files are kept online, the number depending on available disk space. Archives are also available from a number of other sources, including a mail server. You can obtain information on these sites by sending mail to LISTSERV@VM1.NODAK.EDU with text/body: GET MINIX INFO MINIX and you will be sent the "Minix Information Sheet", which also contains other general information on MINIX, such as what versions exist and how to order them from Prentice-Hall and a list of machines it is known to work with.

To subscribe to the list, send the following command to LISTSERV@VM1.NODAK.EDU in the text/body of a message: SIGNUP MINIX-L Your_Full_Name where "Your_Full_Name" is your real name, not your login Id.

All other requests, questions, problems, etc., should be sent to INFO-MINIX-REQUEST@UDEL.EDU.

Coordinator: Glen Overby <minix%plains.nodak.edu@VM1.NODAK.EDU>

Info-MM@COLUMBIA.EDU BUG-MM@COLUMBIA.EDU

The Info-MM/Bug-MM mailing lists are a way for Columbia-MM maintainers and sites running MM to communicate, distribute patches, get bug reports, send comments, suggestions, enhancements, etc.

Columbia-MM is a UNIX mail manager program based on the TOPS-20 MM program running on Digital Equipment Corporation DEC20 systems. Columbia-MM is written in C using the CCMD (TOPS-20 COMND Jsys in C) package developed at Columbia University, and thus has command/keyword/filename completion (on ESC or TAB), context sensitive help on "?", command history and command line editing.

MM is compatible with various other mail programs, and has hooks for adding more in the future. MM has support for several mail file formats: "mtxt" which is the MM-20 format on DEC20's, "mbox" used by UNIX mail(1), and "babyl" the format of Gnuemacs rmail mode. Support for mh(1), pop (post office protocol), and usenet news are planned for the future.

Sources are available via ANONYMOUS FTP from CUNIXF.CC.COLUMBIA.EDU [128.59.40.130] in the mm directory.

All requests to be added to or deleted from the mailing lists should be sent to Info-MM-Request@COLUMBIA.EDU.

Coordinator: Fuat Baran <fuat@columbia.edu>

INFO-MODEMS@WSMR-SIMTEL20.ARMY.MIL

Info-Modems is a discussion group of special interest to modem users. The list is gatewayed to/from Usenet newsgroup comp.dcom.modems.

Mail archives are kept on host WSMR-SIMTEL20.ARMY.MIL as TOPS20 mail files named yymm.n-TXT, where n starts with one and increments by one into another file as each file reached 150 disk pages. To conserve disk space, all the mail files in the archive, except for the current year, are individually compressed. The compressed files have the suffix -Z as part of the filetype field; they should be renamed to have the suffix .Z (uppercase Z) when transfered to a Unix system so the uncompress program will find them. The current month's mail is still kept in MODEMS-ARCHIV.TXT. The archives are stored in directory: PD2:<ARCHIVES.MODEMS> Archive files are available via ANONYMOUS FTP for those with TCP/IP access to the Internet.

All requests to be added to or deleted from this list, problems, questions, etc., should be sent to Info-Modems-Request@WSMR-SIMTEL20.ARMY.MIL.

Coordinator: Keith Petersen <W8SDZ@WSMR-SIMTEL20.ARMY.MIL>

INFO-NETS@THINK.COM

Mailing list for general discussion of networks, focusing on inter-network connectivity. Questions about connections to particular sites are very common, as are discussions of new networks in the US and abroad.

New archives are maintained on THINK.COM, and can be accessed via anonymous ftp as mail/info-nets.archives*. Archives cannot be mailed, but they are available on BITNIC for Bitnet users. Old archives are not currently available, but if demand warrants it may be possible to retrieve them.

All non-BitNet requests to be added to or deleted from this list, problems, questions, etc., should be sent to INFO-NETS-REQUEST@THINK.COM. Multiple users at a given site should create a local distribution list and request that the local alias be added to the list, in order to reduce the load on the THINK.COM mailer.

There is a BitNet sub-distribution list, INFONETS@BITNIC; BitNet subscribers can join by sending the SUB command with your name. For example, SEND LISTSERV@BITNIC SUB INFONETS Jon Doe To be removed from the list, SEND LISTSERV@BITNIC SIGNOFF To make contributions to the list, BitNet subscribers should send mail to the Internet list name, NOT to the BITNET list name.

Coordinator: Robert L. Krawitz <rlk@THINK.COM>

info-oda+@ANDREW.CMU.EDU

This is a mailing list for discussions about the ISO standard 8613 "Office Document Architecture" (also known as the CCITT standard "Open Document Architecture". Messages pertaining to the meaning of the standard, extensions to it, implementations of it and demonstrations of it are appropriate. Also appropriate are discussions of other multimedia document representations, such as DSSSL.

No archives are kept.

Requests for additions, deletions and changes should be sent to info-oda-request+@ANDREW.CMU.EDU.

Coordinator: Mark Sherman <mss+@ANDREW.CMU.EDU>

INFO-PASCAL@BRL.MIL

This list is intended for people who are interested in the programming language Pascal. Discussions of any Pascal implementation (from mainframe to micro) are welcome.

Mail archives are kept on host WSMR-SIMTEL20.ARMY.MIL as TOPS20 mail files named yymm.n-TXT, where n starts with one and increments by one into another file as each file reached 150 disk pages. To conserve disk space, all the mail files in the archive, except for the current year, are individually compressed. The compressed files have the suffix -Z as part of the filetype field; they should be renamed to have the suffix .Z (uppercase Z) when transfered to a Unix system so the uncompress program will find them. The current month's mail is still kept in PASCAL-ARCHIV.TXT. The archives are stored in directory: PD2:<ARCHIVES.PASCAL> Archive files are available via ANONYMOUS FTP from WSMR-SIMTEL20.ARMY.MIL for those with TCP/IP access to the Internet.

All requests to be added to or deleted from this list, problems, questions, etc., should be sent to INFO-PASCAL-REQUEST@BRL.MIL.

Info-PCNet@AI.AI.MIT.EDU

This list was started in the 1970's to discuss and begin implementing a network of personal computers to extend the advantages of net-mail to the large community of personal computer users. A nearly complete specification for the protocol layers and all protocols needed for mail and file transferm has been written. A few partial implementations have been done and one complete one. Recently the list has not been very active, although some discussion does occur.

The archive of old messages is kept on AI.AI.MIT.EDU, in the file PCNET;INFPCN ARCHIV There is also extensive documentation and partial code which has been migrated to backup tapes.

All requests to be added to or deleted from this list, problems, questions, etc., should be sent to Info-PCNet-Request@AI.AI.MIT.EDU.

Coordinator: Michael A. Patton <MAP@AI.AI.MIT.EDU>

info-pdp11@TRANSARC.COM   [Last Updated 12-October-1991]

INFO-PDP11 is an unmoderated mailing list for discussion of any and all issues relating to Digital's PDP-11 series minicomputers and their operating systems.

All requests to be added to or deleted from this list, problems, questions, etc., should be sent to info-pdp11-request@TRANSARC.COM.

Coordinator: Pat Barron <pat@TRANSARC.COM>

INFO-PRIME@Blx-A.Prime.COM   [Last Updated 27-March-1992]

Info-Prime is a public, unmoderated mailing list for discussion of all aspects of computing on Prime supplied hardware and software.

Though this list is now located at a node within .Prime.COM, that is the ONLY relationship with Prime Computer, Inc. this list has. NOTHING distributed by this list is official, unless otherwise stated.

Submissions to the list should be addressed to: Info-Prime@Blx-A.Prime.COM

All requests to be added to or removed from the list are handled by an automated process reachable at: ListServer@Blx-A.Prime.COM. Send mail to that address with on the subject line or in the message-body 'subscribe info-prime' or 'unsubscribe info-prime' . Send 'help' to receive a list of other available commands.

Archives of this list, as well as other information and programs for Prime machines (mostly Primos), are available from the following sites:

- prime.nysaes.cornell.edu FTP to this site and login with userid ANONYMOUS and pasword GUEST.

- Turbo.Kean.edu Mail 'index' to Service@Turbo.Kean.edu for a list of available files.

- Blx-A.Prime.COM Mail 'index' to ListServer@Blx-A.Prime.COM for a list of available files.

Coordinator of the list is: Toni van de Wiel <Toni@Blx-S.Prime.COM>

INFO-PRINTERS@EDDIE.MIT.EDU

Information on printers.

No recent archives exist. Will some volunteer donate space for archives?

All requests to be added to or deleted from this list, problems, questions, etc., should be sent to INFO-PRINTERS-REQUEST@EDDIE.MIT.EDU.

Coordinator: Jon Solomon <jsol@EDDIE.MIT.EDU>

info-prograph@grove.iup.edu　　　　　　　　　　　　　　[Last Updated 12-October-1991]

Users of the Macintosh programming language Prograph now have their own Internet list! To subscribe to this list, send an Email message to info-prograph-request@grove.iup.edu

We aren't using any automated subscription process, so no special syntax is required. Just say you want to subscribe, and I'll add your name to the list. Prograph, for those who have not seen it before, is an icon-based object-oriented programming language, published by TGS Systems, Halifax, Nova Scotia. My only connection with TGS is that I own Prograph, and am beta-testing the 2.5 version, and that they have subscribed to the list. Prograph includes an application "shell", which makes it easy to quickly generate prototypes of your application. Unlike other application generators, such as Serius Developer or AppMaker, Prograph is a complete and self-contained programming language, with full access to the Mac Toolbox (including System 7 calls). The versatile Interpreter lets you quickly test and debug your code, actually allowing you to add new code *while your app is running*! Once you have your application debugged, the Compiler lets you turn it into a standalone, double-clickable Mac application, which you are free to distribute as you see fit (no licensing fees are required).

INFO-PYRAMID@MIMSY.UMD.EDU

List for the discussion of Pyramid (the manufacturer, not the shape) computers.

All requests to be added to or deleted from this list, problems, questions, etc., should be sent to INFO-PYRAMID-REQUEST@MIMSY.UMD.EDU.

[On CSNet and UseNet, "MARYLAND" is known as "umcp-cs".]

Coordinator: Mark Weiser <mark@MIMSY.UMD.EDU>.

Info+Ref@IndyCMS.IUPUI.Edu　　　　　　　　　　　　　[Last Updated 12-October-1991]
Info+Ref@IndyCMS.BITNET

Info+Ref (Information + Referral list) is for anyone involved and/or interested in the provision of Information and Referral services. Information and Referral providers, reference librarians, and other information professionals are encouraged to subscribe.

To subscribe to Info+Ref send e-mail to ListServ@IndyCMS (BITNET) or ListServ(IndyCMS.IUPUI.EDU (Internet) with the body containing the command SUB INFO+REF yourfirstname yourlastname

　　List owner/coordinator: John B Harlan
　　　　　　　　IJBH200@IndyVAX (CREN)
　　　　　　　　IJBH200@IndyVAX.IUPUI.Edu (Internet)

Info-Solbourne@acsu.Buffalo.EDU

Discussions about Solbourne computers, multiprocessor Sun-4 compatible workstations and servers. This is a mail reflector.

Archives are available to Internet hosts from urth.acsu.buffalo.edu (128.205.7.9), using FTP with the anonymous login convention in pub/info-solbourne. . . .

All requests to be added to or deleted from this list, problems, questions, etc., should be sent to info-solbourne-request@acsu.buffalo.edu.

Coordinator: Paul Graham <pjg@acsu.buffalo.edu>

INFO-SPERRY-5000@WSMR-SIMTEL20.ARMY.MIL

A forum in support of the Unisys 5000/80; it is intended to allow the free exchange of ideas and suggestions related to the care and feeding of the 5000/80. The list is open only to registered host administrators of Sperry 5000/80 Internet hosts.

The mail is also archived on host WSMR-SIMTEL20.ARMY.MIL in directory: PD2:<ARCHIVES.SPERRY-5000>.

All requests to be added to or deleted from this list, problems, questions, etc., should be sent to INFO-SPERRY-5000-REQUEST@WSMR-SIMTEL20.ARMY.MIL.

Coordinator: Frank Wancho <WANCHO@WSMR-SIMTEL20.ARMY.MIL>

INFO-TAHOE@CSD1.MILW.WISC.EDU
ihnp4!uwmcsd1!info-tahoe (UUCP)

Discussions pertaining to the Tahoe type of CPU. These include the CCI Power 6/32, the Harris HCX/7, and the Sperry 7000 series computers.

Archives are available to Internet hosts from CSD1.MILW.WISC.EDU (192.12.221.1), using FTP with the Anonymous login convention.

All requests to be added to or deleted from this list, problems, questions, etc., should be sent to INFO-TAHOE-REQUEST@CSD1.MILW.WISC.EDU or ihnp4!uwmcsd1!info-tahoe-request.

Coordinator: Jim Lowe <james@CSD4.MILW.WISC.EDU>

INFO-TeX@SHSU.Bitnet

INFO-TeX is a list to provide an unmoderated environment for the discussion of the TeX document processing system. The discussions are intended to include all related aspects and extensions of TeX on all operating platforms, including LaTeX, AMSTeX, BibTeX, METAFONT, and others based on or consistent with the logic and structure of TeX.

The explicit purpose of INFO-TeX is to provide quick and timely interchange between subscribers, to provide a forum where support may be available for interesting questions which cannot be addressed locally, and to discuss the evolution of TeX and its related products. Subscribers are welcome to take an active role by posting to INFO-TeX or an inactive role by monitoring the list. Archives of INFO-TeX will be available for reference via MAIL from FILESERV@SHSU.

To subscribe to INFO-TeX, please send a MAIL message to: LISTSERV@SHSU.BITNET The body of this MAIL message should be one line and contain the words: SUBSCRIBE INFO-TeX

INFO-TeX is supported by MAIL-oriented LISTSERV@SHSU only. This is NOT the same as the common LISTSERV on VM systems!

Owner: George D. Greenwade <BED_GDG@SHSU.BITNET>

INFO-TI-EXPLORER@SUMEX-AIM.STANFORD.EDU
BUG-TI-EXPLORER@SUMEX-AIM.STANFORD.EDU

Mailing lists to facilitate information exchange among DARPA sponsored projects using TI Explorers. INFO-TI-EXPLORER will be used for general information distribution, such as operational questions, or announcing new generally available packages or tools. BUG-TI-EXPLORER will be used to report problems with Explorer software, as well as fixes. These lists signify no commitment from Texas Instruments or Stanford University.

All requests to be added to or deleted from this list, problems, questions, etc., should be sent to INFO-TI-EXPLORER-REQUEST@SUMEX-AIM.STANFORD.EDU or BUG-TI-EXPLORER-REQUEST@SUMEX-AIM.STANFORD.EDU, respectively.

Coordinator: Richard Acuff <ACUFF@SUMEX-AIM.STANFORD.EDU>

INFO-TMODEM@WSMR-SIMTEL20.ARMY.MIL

BUG-TMODEM@WSMR-SIMTEL20.ARMY.MIL

The INFO-TMODEM list is a means for the maintainer of the TMODEM program to send notices to users of TMODEM. Users of TMODEM send bug reports and feature requests to BUG-TMODEM@WSMR-SIMTEL20.ARMY.MIL.

TMODEM is a new TOPS-20 implementation of the Christensen Protocol, with all the latest features, such as:

- o wildcard file transfers in the style of MODEM7 (YMODEM batch is coming)
- o the YMODEM implementation of the K option with a new algorithm
  to return to K mode after falling back to "normal" mode
- o extensive built-in HELP for all commands and options.

TMODEM is an amalgamation of the old TOPS-20 MODEM program, originally written by Bill Westfield while he was at SRI and now at Stanford, major pieces of the TOPS-20 TELNET program, currently maintained by Mark Crispin, and some pieces of code stolen from TTLINK and KERMIT-20 by Frank da Cruz at Columbia University.

The archives for replaced mailing list INFO-MODEMXX are frozen on host WSMR-SIMTEL20.ARMY.MIL as TOPS20 mail files named yymm.n-TXT, where n starts with one and increments by one into another file as each file reached 150 disk pages. To conserve disk space, all the mail files in the archive, except for the current year, are individually compressed. The compressed files have the suffix -Z as part of the filetype field; they should be renamed to have the suffix .Z (uppercase Z) when transfered to a Unix system so the uncompress program will find them. The current month's mail is still kept in MODEMXX-ARCHIV.TXT. The archives are stored in directory: PD2:<ARCHIVES.MODEMXX> Archive files are available via ANONYMOUS FTP from WSMR-SIMTEL20.ARMY.MIL for those with TCP/IP access to the Internet.

A new set of archives for INFO-TMODEM is on host WSMR-SIMTEL20.ARMY.MIL as TOPS20 mail files named yymm.n-TXT, where n starts with one and increments by one into another file as each file reached 150 disk pages. To conserve disk space, all the mail files in the archive, except for the current year, are individually compressed. The compressed files have the suffix -Z as part of the filetype field; they should be renamed to have the suffix .Z (uppercase Z) when transfered to a Unix system so the uncompress program will find them. The current month's mail is still kept in TMODEM-ARCHIV.TXT. The archives are stored in directory: PD2:<ARCHIVES.TMODEM> Archive files are available via ANONYMOUS FTP from WSMR-SIMTEL20.ARMY.MIL for those with TCP/IP access to the Internet.

All requests to be added to or deleted from this list, problems, questions, etc., should be sent to INFO-TMODEM-REQUEST@WSMR-SIMTEL20.ARMY.MIL.

Coordinator: Frank J. Wancho <WANCHO@WSMR-SIMTEL20.ARMY.MIL>

INFO-TPU@SHSU.BITNET

INFO-TPU is a list to provide an unmoderated environment where issues, questions, comments, ideas, and uses of Digital's TPU (Text Processing Utility) language can be discussed.

The explicit purpose of INFO-TPU is to provide timely interchange between subscribers, to provide a forum where interesting questions can be addressed within the context of interactive exchange between many individuals, to discuss the evolution and application of TPU. The discussions of INFO-TPU will be archived and available for reference. Additionally, it is hoped that INFO-TPU will be able to serve as a repository for interesting TPU applications placed in the public domain. As is the case on all unmoderated lists, the discussion and topics are only limited by the participation and interest of its subscribers. Subscribers are welcome to take an active role by posting to INFO-TPU or an inactive role by monitoring the list.

To subscribe to INFO-TPU, please send a MAIL message to: LISTSERV@SHSU.BITNET The body of this MAIL message should be one line and contain the words: SUBSCRIBE INFO-TPU

LISTSERV@SHSU.BITNET is not supported by the conventional interactive VM-based LISTSERV, but is instead entirely MAIL oriented.

Questions regarding this announcement should be addressed to the list owner, Ken Selvia <UCS_KAS@SHSU.BITNET>

INFO-UNIX@BRL.MIL

INFO-UNIX is intended for Question/Answer discussion, where "novice" system administrators can pose questions. Also, much of the discussion of UNIX on small (micro) computers may be moved from INFO-MICRO, INFO-CPM, etc., into INFO-UNIX. Hopefully, enough people who know some answers will subscribe so that the list serves a purpose; some overlap is expected with the UNIX-WIZARDS list.

All requests to be added to or deleted from this list, problems, questions, etc., should be sent to INFO-UNIX-REQUEST@BRL.MIL

Moderator: Mike Muuss <mike@BRL.MIL>

Info-VM@uunet.uu.net The Info-VM Mailing List, for discussion of Kyle Jones' View Mail mode for GNU Emacs (VM-Mode).

SUBSCRIPTION REQUESTS should be mailed to Info-VM-Request@UUNET.UU.NET. Submissions are gleefully accepted at Info-VM@UUNET.UU.NET.

The latest release version of VM is still 4.41, available via anonymous ftp from tut.cis.ohio-state.edu in /pub/gnu/vm/.

The current beta version is 5.15(beta), available via anonymous ftp from abcfd20.larc.nasa.gov in /pub/.

By the way, Kyle is currently without Net access. He has a working mailbox at <kyle@xanth.cs.odu.edu>, but I don't know how frequently he checks it.

INFO-V@PESCADERO.STANFORD.EDU

Interest group for the V distributed operating system (V-System), developed by the Distributed Systems Group of Stanford University. The purpose of this list is to stimulate communication and sharing among individuals and groups that are using or are interested in the V-System.

Messages will be sent to the list as submitted; depending on the volume of mail, content, etc., messages may be collected and digested in the future. There is no current archive.

All requests to be added to or deleted from this list, problems, questions, etc., should be sent to INFO-V-REQUEST@PESCADERO.STANFORD.EDU.

Coordinator: Keith A. Lantz <LANTZ@GREGORIO.STANFORD.EDU>

INFO-VAX@SRI.COM

INFO-VAX is a discussion of the Digital Equipment Corporation VAX series of computers. Typically the material is question-and-answer, where someone wants information on some program or bug/feature. Both UNIX and VAX/VMS operating systems are discussed, however, the list is primarily about VAX/VMS. This list is gatewayed to the usenet group COMP.OS.VMS.

Archived messages are kept at CRVAX.SRI.COM in the files [ANONYMOUS.INFO-VAX]INFO-VAX-ARCHIVE.yymmdd For a list of the Archive files send a mail message to INFO-VAX-REQUEST@SRI.COM with the subject DIRECTORY.

All requests to be added to or deleted from this list, problems, questions, etc., should be sent to INFO-VAX-REQUEST@SRI.COM. Internet subscribers can join by sending a mail message with a subject of ADD. To be removed from the list the subject should be REMOVE.

There is a BitNet sub-distribution list, INFO-VAX@UGA; BitNet subscribers can join by sending the SUB command with your name.and with your name. For example, SEND LISTSERV@UGA SUB INFO-VAX Jon Doe To be removed from the list, SEND LISTSERV@UGA SIGNOFF. To make contributions to the list, BitNet subscribers should send mail to the Internet list name, NOT to the BITNET list name.

Coordinator: Ramon Curiel <Ray@SRI.COM>

INFO-VLSI@THINK.COM

Mailing list for the exchange of information on all aspects of integrated circuit (IC) design. The list is gatewayed to/from the Usenet group comp.lsi.

Archived messages are kept at Think.COM in the files: mail/info-vlsi.archive*

There is a LISTSERV-maintained BitNet part of this list, VLSI-L@MITVMA. BitNet subscriptions can be managed in the usual way, e.g.: TELL LISTSERV AT MITVMA SUBSCRIBE VLSI-L your_full_name Notebooks with monthly archives are available from MITVMA from 11/89. All other requests to be added to or deleted from this list, problems, questions, etc., should be sent to INFO-VLSI-REQUEST@THINK.COM.

All requests to be added to or deleted from this list, problems, questions, etc., should be sent to INFO-VLSI-REQUEST@THINK.COM.

Coordinator: Bruce Walker <bruce@THINK.COM>

INFO-XENIX310@WSMR-SIMTEL20.ARMY.MIL

Mailing list devoted to discussing the problems, capabilities, incompatibilities, successes, failures, or whatever, with Xenix on the Intel 310s. The list is primarily aimed at systems administrators and others who are responsible for making these machines useful in the workplace. Particular interests are successful ports of existing software to the 310 and procedures to simplify systems administration.

Mail archives are kept on host WSMR-SIMTEL20.ARMY.MIL as TOPS20 mail files named yymm.n-TXT, where n starts with one and increments by one into another file as each file reached 150 disk pages. To conserve disk space, all the mail files in the archive, except for the current year, are individually compressed. The compressed files have the suffix -Z as part of the filetype field; they should be renamed to have the suffix .Z (uppercase Z) when transfered to a Unix system so the uncompress program will find them. The current month's mail is still kept in XENIX310-ARCHIV.TXT. The archives are stored in directory: PD2:<ARCHIVES.XENIX310> Archive files are available via ANONYMOUS FTP from WSMR-SIMTEL20.ARMY.MIL for those with TCP/IP access to the Internet.

All requests to be added to or deleted from this list, problems, questions, etc., should be sent to INFO-XENIX310-REQUEST@WSMR-SIMTEL20.ARMY.MIL.

Coordinator: John Mitchener <JMITCHENER@WSMR-SIMTEL20.ARMY.MIL>

INFO-XMODEM@WSMR-SIMTEL20.ARMY.MIL

Discussion group for XMODEM Christensen protocol file transfer programs. The group is concerned with development, upgrades and bug-fixes. The list name was changed from INFO-MODEM7 to INFO-XMODEM in August, 1986.

Mail archives are kept on host WSMR-SIMTEL20.ARMY.MIL as TOPS20 mail files named yymm.n-TXT, where n starts with one and increments by one into another file as each file reached 150 disk pages. To conserve disk space, all the mail files in the archive, except for the current year, are individually compressed. The compressed files have the suffix -Z as part of the filetype field; they should be renamed to have the suffix .Z (uppercase Z) when transfered to a Unix system so the uncompress program will find them. The current month's mail is still kept in XMODEM-ARCHIV.TXT. The archives are stored in directory: PD2:<ARCHIVES.XMODEM> Archive files are available via ANONYMOUS FTP from WSMR-SIMTEL20.ARMY.MIL for those with TCP/IP access to the Internet.

All requests to be added to or deleted from this list, problems, questions, etc., should be sent to INFO-XMODEM-REQUEST@WSMR-SIMTEL20.ARMY.MIL.

Coordinator: Keith Petersen <W8SDZ@WSMR-SIMTEL20.ARMY.MIL>

Info-ZIP@WSMR-SIMTEL20.ARMY.MIL

Info-ZIP@WSMR-SIMTEL20.Army.Mil, has been created for the developers of ZIP-releated programs for mainframe use. This will help the present work with UNZIP for Unix, as well as possible future work on a ZIP maker.

If you wish to be added to the list, please send email to Info-ZIP-Request@WSMR-SIMTEL20.Army.Mil. Please be aware, however, that this group will be exchanging uuencoded tar archives and sections of source code. These are very likely to be 40K to 60K in size. The programs distributed will be "under construction", not finished products. Many many not work correctly or may not work at all on some systems.

> Info-ZIP mailing list maintainer: Keith Petersen
> Internet: w8sdz@WSMR-SIMTEL20.Army.Mil
> BITNET: w8sdz@NDSUVM1
> Uucp: {ames,decwrl,rutgers,ucbvax,uunet}!wsmr-simtel20.army.mil!w8sdz

INFOCD@CISCO.NOSC.MIL

The INFOCD mailing list is for the exchange of subjective comments about the Compact Audio Disc medium and related hardware. Topics of discussion may include CD reviews, players, portables, import CD's, etc.

All requests to be added to or deleted from this list, problems, questions, etc, should be sent to CDREQUEST@CISCO.NOSC.MIL

Coordinator: Michael Pawka <MIKE@CISCO.NOSC.MIL>

informix-list@rmy.emory.edu

An unmoderated list for the discussion of Informix software and related subjects. Topics include all Informix offerings, from C-ISAM to WingZ, plus third-party products. Membership is open to anyone, including end-users, vendors and employees of Informix Software, Inc. An optional gateway service of Informix-related articles from comp.databases is offered. Not affiliated with Informix Software, Inc.

Contact informix-list-request@rmy.emory.edu for instructions on subscribing to the list.

Coordinator: Walt Hultgren <walt@rmy.emory.edu>

INGRES-L%HDETUD1.BITNET@VM1.NODAK.EDU

Mailing list for discussion of all relevant aspects of the INGRES RDBMS. A secondary purpose is to function as a medium for communication between the users of Ingres at the universities of Delft and Rotterdam; such messages may be in Dutch, but should begin with a warning that they are intended for these users only.

Discussion may include any topic related to the subject, such as problems in implementing, tuning or using the product in any environment (MS/DOS, UNIX, VMS, CMS, MVS or a combination of any of these), conversion to new versions (such as from Version-5 to Version-6), announcements of conferences, etc.

BitNet users may subscribe by sending the following command: TELL LISTSERV AT HDETUD1 SUBSCRIBE INGRES-L your_full_name (where "your_full_name" is your real name, not your login Id) or the equivalent in VMS, UNIX or whichever Operating System your account uses, or send the same message (SUBSCRIBE etc.) in the BODY or TEXT of mail to LISTSERV@HDETUD1.BITNET. Non-BitNet users can join by sending the SUBSCRIBE command to LISTSERV%HDETUD1.BITNET@VM1.NODAK.EDU.

Coordinator: Jan Snoek <RCIVJAN%HDETUD1.TUDELFT.NL@VM1.NODAK.EDU>
<RCIVJAN@HDETUD1>
<SYS2ILE@HDETUD1>

INGRAFX on LISTSERV@PSUVM

INGRAFX is a listserv devoted to the interdisciplinary areas of cartography, information graphics and scientific visualization. As owner of the list, I would like to invite all those who have an interest in the broad range of images known as "graphics" (maps, photographs, drawings and information or quantitative graphics) to consider signing up.

Please do not take these requirements too formally! Ideally, the discussion will be uninhibited and free-flowing.

Candidate topics for discussion might be; the relation of maps to graphics as a whole (are they different kinds of representation?); the philosophy of graphic representation (what theories are there of graphic representations, and how does a graphic "represent" segments of the world); how can we use graphics in education; to what extent does "graphicacy" matter in today's world; what is the relationship between academic or scientific graphics, and graphics in the popular media; can we or should we accrue rules for "good" graphics; are there graphic variables or elements that are basic to all graphics, and can these be used in animation?

In general our aim is for an informal discussion which is cross-disciplinary, and about graphics.

How to Join in

Curious to see what's going on so far? Why not sign up now?

Sign up in the usual way for LISTSERVs, i.e., send mail to LISTSERV@PSUVM on BITNET or LISTSERV@PSUVM.PSU.EDU on Internet with the following command in the TEXT: SUB INGRAFX your firstname and last name

Once you are a subscriber you can retrieve any files that have been archived on the listserv, including the monthly discussion logs, and other files of interest. To see what is there, either TELL or send a email note to LISTSERV AT PSUVM or LISTSERV AT PSUVM.PSU.EDU with the command INDEX INGRAFX . Once you have decided on a file you can retrieve it by using the GET command. E.g., TELL LISTSERV AT PSUVM GET 'File name', or GET 'Another file'.

Post by sending email to ingrafx@psuvm.

Owner: "Jeremy Crampton" <ELE@PSUVM> or <ele@psuvm.psu.edu>

Future Discussions on the List

As a geographer/cartographer, I am particularly interested in getting fellow cartographers to join in the debate. Especially students. However, one of the goals of the list is to broaden cartographic debate to include consideration of the many forms and roles of graphics in today's highly visual world.

To this end, the list will be interdisciplinary. It will seek to include people from the worlds of information graphics (see the work by Edward Tufte for one position on this), scientific visualization, and the media (_USA Today_ style graphics?...)

To my knowledge there does not yet exist such an interdisciplinary forum for the discussion of graphics as a whole.

I would also like to have people share their graphics. This can be done by compressing and converting a file to binary form. I do not encourage posting of these files to the list, but those people interested in swapping graphics should describe what they have, and what they'd like to see, on the INGRAFX list.

Transactions could then take place over private email, with a list of available graphics being held in our archives.

Reviews, either of software, books or articles on graphics, are also especially encouraged. If you have been asked to write one and can't wait to see it in "print," send it to INGRAFX (retaining your copyright).

We aim to create an informal environment for the discussion of all issues related to graphics. This might also include discussion of ideas you are working on for future articles, or research projects announcements of job openings, interesting graphics you have discovered, or just general commentary with a graphic flavor.

jeremy   ele@psuvm.psu.edu

INMYLIFE@WKUVX1.BITNET

Beatles era popular culture.

Topics will include but not be restricted to history, politics, culture, music, literature, collectibles, comic books, comix, counter culture, drugs, Vietnam (and the war), Cold War, etc. between 1962 (the first Beatle hit record in England) and 1974 (US out of Vietnam).

Interested parties should send a one line command SUB INMYLIFE firstname lastname to LISTSERV@WKUVX1.BITNET.

Owner: Matt Gore <goremh@WKUVX1.BITNET>

INT-LAW on LISTSERV@UMINN1.BITNET   [Last Updated 28-January-1992] or
LISTSERV@VM1.SPCS.UMN.EDU

INT-LAW (Foreign and International Law Librarians) is a list on BITNET for librarians and others interested in exchanging information related to foreign, comparative and international legal materials and issues.

Selected topics in the six months since INT-LAW began include the READEX CD-ROM Index to United Nations documents, databases containing information on foreign and international law, the "European Court Reports", sources of information on careers in international law, GATT panel reports, the "National Trade Data Bank" CD-ROM, etc. INT-LAW came up on April 31, 1991.

There are approximately 185 subscribers to INT-LAW at present, mainly from the U.S.. Other countries represented include Canada, Mexico, and Germany. To subscribe to INT-LAW, send the following message to LISTSERV@UMINN1.BITNET or LISTSERV@VM1.SPCS.UMN.EDU (Internet address) Subscribe INT-LAW Firstname Lastname.

Send any questions, comments, etc. to the moderators of the list: Lyonette Louis-Jacques (L-LOUI@UMINN1) or Mila Rush (M-RUSH@UMINN1). Mila Rush is the listowner.

INTEREST-GROUPS LIST

See entry in this file for "LIST OF MAILING LISTS".

interfaces-p-m@crim.ca

This mailing list, focussed on user-system interfaces and related topics, is intended to foster discussion among researchers and practitioners from universities, government and industry who are working on user interface research, design, and implementation.

Relevant topics include:

- business and legal issues, such as patents, licensing, copyright, commercialization and standardization
- lessons learned
- user interface studies
- user interface courses offered at CRIM (Centre de recherche informatique de Montreal; Computer research institute of Montreal)
- new user interface software and hardware available at CRIM's software engineering laboratories

- presentations of user interface tools organized by CRIM
- presentations of relevant software organized by other companies
- any other pertinent information

We foresee, as well, exchanges between participants concerning the research and development of user interfaces.

The interfaces-p-m list is moderated by Julian Lebensold. Submissions may be in either English or in French.

To request to be added to or dropped from the list, please send mail to:

interfaces-p-m-request@crim.ca

Please include the words "ADD" or "REMOVE" in your subject line.

Other administrative matters or questions should also be addressed to:

interfaces-p-m-request@crim.ca

INTUDM-L on LISTSERV@UTEPA.Bitnet
INTUDM-L on LISTSERV@UTEPVM.EP.UTEXAS.EDU

Discuss, conduct and promote interdisciplinary research on the use of intuition in decision making.

As archives accumulate they will be stored monthly in INTUDM-L LOGyymm and indexed in INTUDM-L FILELIST. To receive a list of files send the command INDEX INTUDM-L to LISTSERV@UTEPA.

To subscribe to INTUDM-L, send the following command to LISTSERV@UTEPA via mail text or interactive message:

SUBscribe INTUDM-L Your_full_name. For example: SUBSCRIBE INTUDM-L Joe Student.

Listowner: Weton H. Agor <HY00@UTEP.BITNET>

IOOB-L%UGA.BITNET@CUNYVM.CUNY.EDU

Discussion of topics in the fields of Industrial/Organizational Psychology and Organization Behavior.

To subscribe to the list: From a VM/CMS site on BITNET issue the command: TELL LISTSERV AT UGA SUB IOOB-L yourname where "yourname" is your real name (not your userid). From a VAX/VMS site on BITNET issue the command: SEND LISTSERV@UGA SUB IOOB-L yourname Non-BitNet users can subscribe by sending a message to LISTSERV%UGA.BITNET@CUNYVM.CUNY.EDU containing the one line: SUB IOOB-L yourname

Coordinator: John L. Cofer <COFER%UTKVX.BITNET@CUNYVM.CUNY.EDU>

IOUDAIOS%YORKVM1.BITNET@CUNYVM.CUNY.EDU
IOUDAIOS on LISTSERV@YORKVM1

IOUDAIOS (Greek for "Jew") is an electronic seminar devoted to the exploration of first-century Judaism; its special interest is in the writings of Philo of Alexandria and Flavius Josephus. The list began as an informal discussion of two papers by Robert A. Kraft (Pennsylvania) but quickly blossomed into an international forum, with participants in North America, Europe, Australia, and The Middle East.

The Philonic and Josephan corpora are extensive enough that they invite all sorts of analysis -- from literary, historical, and philosophical perspectives, to name a few. There is also considerable interest, among participants, in the social realities that lie behind these texts. Prospective members are warmly welcomed. (The discussion assumes a significant background in first-century Judaism and also the ability to read Greek.)

To subscribe to this list send a mail/note message to LISTSERV@YORKVM1 (LISTSERV%YORKVM.BITNET@CUNYVM.CUNY.EDU for Internet users) with the one-line message: SUBSCRIBE IOUDAIOS your-full-name

Coordinator: Veronica Timm <VERONICA%YORKVM1.Bitnet@CUNYVM.CUNY.EDU>

IPCT-L on LISTSERV@GUVM or LISTSERV@GUVM.GEORGETOWN.EDU

The Interpersonal Computing and Technology List (IPCT-L) was created by the Center for Teaching and Technology (CTT) at the Academic Computer Center, Georgetown University. A special effort will be made to promote an international forum for pedagogical issues important to higher education involving teaching with technology, and especially with connectivity and networking.

A goal is to create a forum for the discussion of computing and other technology that can be used to promote learning. Topics for discussion may involve teaching and training; collaboration; partnerships among learners, faculty or teachers, and other interested persons in the educational community; and research that reflect these interests. The decade of the 1980s was characterized by the _personal_ computer, and development of individual product- ivity. The focus of the IPCT-L, as we move toward the 21st century, is that _interpersonal_ computing and technology will tie persons together throughout the world -- to share ideas and solve problems.

Besides creating a forum for the topics of interest noted above, another interest of the CTT is to publish a scholarly, refereed international journal. To that end, the IPCT-L will develop a subscription list and act as a resource to develop the community necessary to review articles and recommend editorial policies as these publishing goals move forward.

To subscribe send the following in an interactive command (TELL or SEND) or in the BODY of mail (NOT the Subject:) to LISTSERV@GUVM on Bitnet, or LISTSERV@GUVM.GEORGETOWN.EDU on Internet:

SUBSCRIBE IPCT-L yourfirstname yourlastname

Example: SUBSCRIBE IPCT-L John Doe

Owner: Zane Berge <BERGE@GUVAX.BITNET> or
            <BERGE@GUVAX.GEORGETOWN.EDU>

IPE-ISA-L@mach1.wlu.ca

A LISTSERV discussion group to facilitate the business and interests of members of the IPE section of the ISA.

IPE-ISA-L is an electronic discussion list that will allow persons around the world interested in International Political Economy to discuss matters of mutual concern. IPE-ISA-L is an unmoderated and open list. This means that all messages posted to the list will be automatically redistributed around the world.

Possible topics for discussion on the list might include any of the following:

1. IPE section business re: regional and national meetings.
2. Substantive discussion over topics such as NAFTA, regional trading blocs, trade regimes, international debt, long cycles, historical world systems, EEC, currency and market crises, democracy and governance in Latin and South America, Africa and Asia, commodity negotiations.
3. Comment and contributions on curriculum questions; suggested texts, new articles of common interest for course-related adoption.
4. Circulation of draft articles for comment and discussion.
5. Personal exchanges in the effort to develop a greater sense of community among IPE section colleagues.

To join IPE-ISA-L send the following message:

Mail to: listserv@mach1.wlu.ca Sub IPE-ISA-L <your name>

If you have any questions, please free to contact:

Lev S. Gonick
Department of Political Science
Wilfrid Laurier University
Waterloo, Ontario N2L 3C5
CANADA
Ph: 519 884-1970 ext. 2860
Fax: 519 570-1419
Internet: lgonick6@mach1.wlu.ca

iPSC <ipsclist@TCGOULD.TN.CORNELL.EDU>

Mailing list to allow iPSC/1 and iPSC/2 users and systems administrators from different installations to communicate easily and directly.

Local aliases for this mailing list are to be handled by the local systems administrators, since most sites already have local user mailing lists. What is desired to accomplish is to link all these iPSC user lists together. The first thing needed is an administrator list and the user list will hopefully follow. If you are a system administrator for Intel Hypercube(s) you are invited to send the following information to ipsclist@TCGOULD.TN.CORNELL.EDU:

- systems, iPSC/1's or iPSC/2's
- administrator's e-mail address OR alias
- institution
- user alias list (might want this separate from existing
           user list, a good idea)
- suggestions, opinions, ideas....

PLEASE! Systems Administrators Only.

Coordinator: Dave Fielding <fielding@TCGOULD.TN.CORNELL.EDU>
cornell!batcomputer!fielding (UUCP)

IRLIST <IR-L%UCCVMA.BITNET@VM1.NODAK.EDU>

IRList is open to discussion of any topic (vaguely) related to Information Retrieval. Certainly, any material relating to ACM SIGIR (the Special Interest Group on Information Retrieval of the Association for Computing Machinery) is of interest. The field has close ties to artificial intelligence, database management, information and library science, linguistics, etc. A partial list of suitable topics is:

Information Management/Processing/Science/Technology

AI Applications to IR	Hardware aids for IR
Abstracting	Hypertext and Hypermedia
CD-ROM/CD-I/...	Indexing/Classification
Citations	Information Display/Presentation
Cognitive Psychology	Information Retrieval Applications
Communications Networks	Information Theory
Computational Linguistics	Knowledge Representation
Computer Science	Language Understanding
Cybernetics	Library Science
Data Abstraction	Message Handling
Dictionary analysis	Natural Languages, NL Processing
Document Representations	Optical disc technology and applications
Electronic Books	Pattern Recognition, Matching
Evidential Reasoning	Probabilistic Techniques
Expert Systems in IR	Speech Analysis
Expert Systems use of IR	Statistical Techniques

| Full-Text Retrieval | Thesaurus construction |
| Fuzzy Set Theory | |

Contributions may be anything from tutorials to rampant speculation. In particular, the following are sought:

Abstracts of Papers, Reports, Dissertations	Address Changes
Bibliographies	Conference Reports
Descriptions of Projects/Laboratories	Half-Baked Ideas
Humorous, Enlightening Anecdotes	Histories
Questions	Requests
Seminar Announcements/Summaries	Research Overviews
Work Planned or in Progress	

The only real boundaries to the discussion are defined by the topics of other mailing lists. Please do not send communications to both this list and AIList or the Prolog list, except in special cases. The Moderator tries not to overlap much with NL-KR, except when both lists receive materials from contributors or from some bulletin board or researchers.

There is no objection to distributing material that is destined for conference proceedings or any other publication. The Coordinator is involved in SIGIR Forum and, unless submittors request otherwise, may include submissions in whole or in part in future paper versions of the FORUM. Indeed, this is one form of solicitation for FORUM contributions! Both IRLList and the FORUM are unrefereed, and opinions are always those of the author and not of any organization unless there are other indications. Copies of list items should credit the original author, not necessarily the IRLList.

The IRLIST Archives will be set up for anonymous FTP, and the address will be announced in future issues.

To subscribe send the following command to LISTSERV@UCCVMA.BITNET: SUB IR-L your_full_name where "your_full_name" is your real name, not your login Id. Non-BitNet users can join by sending the above command as the only line in the text/body of a message to LISTSERV%UCCVMA.BITNET@VM1.NODAK.EDU.

Moderator: IRLUR%UCCMVSA.BITNET@VM1.NODAK.EDU
Editorial Staff: Clifford Lynch <lynch@POSTGRES.BERKELEY.EDU>
              <calur@UCCMVSA.BITNET>
     Mary Engle   <engle@CMSA.BERKELEY.EDU>
              <meeur@UCCMVSA.BITNET>
     Nancy Gusack   <ncgur@UCCMVSA.BITNET>

ISLAM-L on LISTSERV@ULKYVM or LISTSERV@ULKYVM.LOUISVILLE.EDU

ISLAM-L is a non-sectarian forum for discussion, debate, and the exchange of information by students and scholars of the history of Islam. ISLAM-L is not to be used for proselytizing for or against Islam in general, any particular form of Islam, or any other religion or philosophy.

ISLAM-L is ready to distribute newsletters from study groups, and to post announcements of meetings and calls for papers, short scholarly pieces, queries, and other items of interest.

The list currently does not maintain a FTP directory nor is archiving available. Hopefully, this will change in the near future.

ISLAM-L is associated with the general discussion list HISTORY, and co-operates fully with other lists similarly associated.

Requests for SUBscription pass through the list owner, and SEND and REVIEW commands are restricted to list members. The command language of ISLAM-L is English, but postings in other languages are accepted. ISLAM-L is ready to distribute newsletters from study groups, and to post announcements of meetings and calls for papers, short scholarly pieces, queries, and other items of interest.

To subscribe send a message to LISTSERV@ULKYVM or LISTSERV@ULKYVM.LOUISVILLE.EDU. In BODY of the message state: SUB ISLAM-L yourfirstname yourlastname

adding your full name; LISTSERV will accept both BITNET and Internet addresses. Postings should be made to ISLAM-L@ULKYVM.

If you have any questions please contact the owner.

Owner: James A. Cocks BITNET: JACOCK01@ULKYVM Internet: JACOCK01@ULKYVM.LOUISVILLE.EDU

isdn@teknologi.agderforskning.no

An Internet ISDN mailing-list is now in operation with address: isdn@teknologi.agderforskning.no and request-adress: isdn-request@teknologi.agderforskning.no

(Coordinator: Per.Sigmond@teknologi.agderforskning.no)

The (preliminary) topics of the list are "all aspects specific to ISDN (protocols, services, applications etc.) for both data and voice".

An archive of the list will soon be available. This will be announced later through the list.

Per Sigmond	Tel.: +47-41-42555
Agderforskning Teknologi	Fax: +47-41-40696
Televeien 1	Priv: +47-41-44371
4890 Grimstad, Norway	

ISO@NIC.DDN.MIL

Discussion group focusing on the ISO protocol stack. The list naturally has some overlap with the ISODE list; contributors are urged to use the appropriate list based on their topic of discussion.

All requests to be added to or deleted from this list, problems, questions, etc., should be sent to ISO-REQUEST@NIC.DDN.MIL.

Coordinator: ISO-REQUEST@NIC.DDN.MIL.

ISO10646%JHUVM.BITNET@VM1.NODAK.EDU
ISO10646 on LISTSERV@JHUVM

Purpose:

To serve as a clearing house for information on and discussion of multi-byte coded-character-set issues.

The ISO 10646 draft and Unicode draft standards represent two different approaches to encoding the world's characters into a multi-byte code.

Background:

People are looking at multi-byte codes as a way to solve many of the problems we are experiencing with single-byte, 7-bit and 8-bit codes. Although most of us do not need all 191 of the characters in the ISO 8859-1 character set (repertoire), we frequently need characters outside of this set; for example, bullets or nice quotation marks for professional looking documents, symbols for mathematics and science, etc. The reason for developing multi-byte codes is that processing ONE multi-byte code appears easier than several single-byte codes.

As of March, 1990, two coding schemes have emerged. The International Organization for Standardization (ISO) Subcommittee 2, Working Group 2 (SC2/WG2) has developed the ISO 10646 Multi-Octet Code. It is now a "draft proposed" standard (two levels removed from being an international standard). The ISO working group has been working on this project for the last 6 years and it has been subject to unusually wide review for a proposed standard. The other draft standard is the result of the work of a consortium of U.S. companies, mostly from the west coast. It is called Unicode. Both of these draft standards enable the worlds communication (newspapers and magazines) and business characters, ideographs, and symbols to be encoded for storage and communication between computers. However, each uses a different approach to making the inevitable tradeoffs.

Mechanics:

To subscribe send mail to LISTSERV%JHUVM.BITNET@VM1.NODAK.EDU with the BODY or TEXT of the mail containing the command: SUB ISO10646 yourfirstname yourlastname

Contributions to the LIST go to ISO10646%JHUVM.BITNET@VM1.NODAK.EDU

> Owner: Edwin F. Hart BITNET: HART@APLVM
>   INTERNET: HART%APLVM.BITNET@VM1.NODAK.EDU

ISODE@NIC.DDN.MIL

Discussion group focusing on the ISO Development Environment, an openly available implementation of some of the higher-level protocols adopted by international organizations (ISO, CCITT, ECMA). These implementations are hosted on top of TCP/IP using the method discussed in RFC983. Appropriate topics are:

- Questions about how to use ISODE (and announcements of ports to other target environments)
- Discussion of ISODE as a part of a TCP/IP to ISO migration strategy
- Exchange of ideas regarding ISO-based applications running in a native TCP/IP environment
- Debate regarding where ISODE should go next

The list naturally has some overlap with the TCP-IP list, the ISO list, and so on; contributors are urged to use the appropriate list based on their topic of discussion.

All requests to be added to or deleted from this list, problems, questions, etc., should be sent to ISODE-REQUEST@NIC.DDN.MIL.

Coordinator: ISODE-REQUEST@NIC.DDN.MIL.

ITALIC-L on LISTSERV@IRLEARN

ITALIC-L stands for the Irish Tex And Latex Interest Conference. (but will also include GML and SGML interest) Subscription is open to all and Peter Flynn and myself will moderate the list (in a very loose way).

To subscribe send mail or a message to LISTSERV@IRLEARN on EARN/BITNET with the body of the mail or message containing:

SUB ITALIC-L yourfirstname yoursecondname

Brendan Dixon <BDIXON@IRLEARN> (Contributed by Mike Norris)

IVCF-L%UBMV.BITNET@CUNYVM.CUNY.EDU
IVCF-L on LISTSERV@UBVM

This list is originated from the State University of New York at Buffalo and is intended for discussion related to InterVarsity Christian Fellowship, a multi-denominational Christian group. Welcome is discussion from Members, Staff, and all people affiliated with Inter-Varsity, or those wanting more information. This list, while not a moderated list, will be edited if innapropriate material is sent to it. Welcome to IVCF-L!

To subscribe to IVCF-L send mail to LISTSERV@UBVM with the body/text containing the command sub ivcf-l yourfirstname yourlastname

OWNER: V067PXNR@UBVMS (Mark E. Keating)

J-FOOD-L%JPNKNU10.BITNET@CUNYVM.CUNY.EDU
J-FOOD-L on LISTSERV@JPNKNU10

This list, created at Kinki university in Japan, is for people interested in the Japanese food and culture.

If you wish to subscribe to the list issue the following (FOR BITNET)

TELL LISTSERV AT JPNKNU10 SUB J-FOOD-L <your full name>

or send mail to LISTSERV%JPNKNU10.BITNET@CUNYVM.CUNY.EDU with the following in the text/body:

SUB J-FOOD-L <your full name>

jamie@vax5.cit.cornell.edu   [Last Updated 28-January-1992]

Mailing list for the discussion of Jamie Notarthomas, an up-and-coming acoustic guitarist/singer/songwriter in the northeast. The list was implemented very recently, so membership and traffic is a bit low, but picking up. Currently, it's unmoderated, set up for mail reflection, and postings are kept for one month.

Requests to be added or deleted, or for information, should be sent to <jamie-request@vax5.cit.cornell.edu>

Owner: Jeffrey Anbinder <bory@cornella.cit.cornell.edu>

janes-addiction@ms.uky.edu

To subscribe, or to get information about the list, send to:

janes-addiction-request@ms.uky.edu -or- janes-addiction-request@ukma.bitnet -or-uunet!ukma!janes-addiction-request

This group is for discussing anything relating to the musical group Jane's Addiction.

Owner: Joel Abbott, DoD#272 -> abbott@ms.uky.edu, abbott@ukma.bitnet, or uunet!ukma!abbott

JANET%GWUVM.BITNET@CUNYVM.CUNY.EDU
JANET on LISTSERV@GWUVM

The Janet list is a discussion list for users of the Waterloo Janet network Software for IBM machines. Any user/administrator of Janet is encouraged to join this list.

To subscribe: TELL LISTSERV AT GWUVM SUB JANET your_full_name or send mail to LISTSERV@GWUVM with the command SUB JANET your_full_name in the body/text of the mail.

Please note that this command is sent to the LISTSERV and not to the list.

Coordinator: Jonathan M. Lang <JMLANG%GWUVM.BITNET@VM1.NODAK.EDU>

JANITOR@UKANVM.CC.UKANS.EDU   [Last Updated 12-October-1991]

A distribution list dedicated to the discussion of any topic of interest to those engaged in the cleaning of Public Buildings. Expected topics might include staffing guidelines, levels of cleanliness, appropriate equipment, new discoveries in cleaning chemicals, environmental concerns, employee relations, training concepts and methods, time and motion studies as related to cleaning task times, and employee safety. Subscription is open to all, but those involved with "Keywords" such as "Custodians", "Maids", "Janitors", "Environmental Services", "Sanitary Engineer", "Housekeeping" and other related nouns will find this list most beneficial!

This forum welcomes new users of electronic communications; those of us with some expertise will gladly assist newcomers. The list is configured so that REPLY goes to the entire list in an effort to stimulate discussion and facilitate the exchange of information.

Subscriptions should be sent to Bitnet: <LISTSERV@UKANVM.BITNET> or Internet: <LISTSERV@UKANVM.CC.UKANS.EDU> with the BODY or text of the mail containing the line SUB JANITORS yourfirstname yourlastname

Owner: For additional information or assistance in subscribing, send e-mail to: Phil Endacott <ENDACOTT@UKANVAX.BITNET> OR <ENDACOTT@kuhub.cc.ukans.edu>

jays@hivnet.ubc.ca   [Last Updated 9/92]

This is a mailing list for fans of the Toronto Blue Jays baseball team. Scores and highlights of games, player transactions, draft picks, and status of rival teams will be discussed on this group.

This list is not archived.

To join:

Please send all requests to jays-request@hivnet.ubc.ca or to phill@hivnet.ubc.ca

Coordinator: Phill St-Louis (phill@hivnet.ubc.ca or stlouis@unixg.ubc.ca)

JESSE on LISTSERV@ARIZVM1.BITNET or LISTSERV@ARIZVM1.CCIT.ARIZONA.EDU

JESSE is a LISTSERV conference which focuses on teaching and educational concerns in library and information science. JESSE concerns curricula, educational methodologies and issues, courses in development, resources, computing as a teaching tool, broad trends in education as they affect library and information science education, and similar education- oriented topics. JESSE's address is JESSE@ARIZVM1 on BITNET.

It is a companion conference to ELEASAI , which focuses on research in library and information science. It concerns current research in progress or in planning stages, methodological and statistical issues, funding for research, computing as a research tool, broad trends in scientific research as they affect library and information science, and similar research-oriented topics. ELEASAI's address is ELEASAI@ARIZVM1.BITNET

To subscribe to JESSE, send the following command to LISTSERV@ARIZVM1 on BITNET or LISTSERV@ARIZVM1.CCIT.ARIZONA.EDU in the BODY of mail or interactive message:

SUBSCRIBE JESSE Your_full_name.

For example: SUBSCRIBE LISTNAME Joe Shmoe

Owners: Gretchen Whitney (GWHITNEY@ARIZVMS) Charley Seavey (DOCMAPS@ARIZVMS)

JNET-L%BITNIC.BITNET@CUNYVM.CUNY.EDU

A forum for discussing Jnet running under VAX VMS. Some possible topics include VMSmail, Interactive Messages (SEND), file transfers (SEND /FILE, RECEIVE), POSTMASTER, hints about hooks into Jan_Lib:BitLib.OLB. Related topics might include RSCS emulations (non-Jnet), GMAIL (a VMS utility for BITNET-to-Internet communications), conversion of non-VMS tools (VM, NOS, UNIX, etc.) to VMS, file servers (KERMSERV), list servers, etc.

Coordinator: INFO%BITNIC.BITNET@CUNYVM.CUNY.EDU

JOB-LIST on LISTSERV@FRORS12

* Job offers from EARN Institute members

The EARN Association announces this list for posting job offers at institutions that are full EARN members. The list is open for subscription but it is a moderated list so that messages to the list will be reviewed to make sure they conform to the following rules:

- Mail to the list should be job offers from full EARN institute members.

- The mail should be signed by a person from the institution in question and it should contain a source from which further information (e.g. the full announcement) can be requested.

- The volume of the mail should be no more than one standard screen (20 lines).

- Only posts where applications from other countries are welcome should be posted on this list. Purely national recruitment should be handled by the national EARN association or network.

The list is only for posting announcements. Further communication should NOT be done via the list.

Owner: DECK@FRORS12 (Hans Deckers)

JOBPLACE on LISTSERV@UKCC or LISTSERV@UKCC.UKY.EDU

JobPlace (Self Directed Job Search Techniques and Job Placement Issues)

Please Note: 0 This is not a place to list or look for job openings

0 This list is unmoderated but archived

0 This list is of particular interest to job search trainers, career educators, researchers looking at job search/labor market/job placement issues and private practice practitioners who believe in the Self Directed Job Search philosophy.

0 Flames will not be tolerated

Purpose: The purpose of JobPlace is to provide job search trainers, career educators, researchers, private practitioners and other interested constituents a computerized network to ask questions, share information, discuss ideas, observations, research data, techniques and current issues relating to self directed job search training and job placement.

There are no restrictins on subject material other than it should relate to self directed job search techniques and/or job placement strategies. Topics may include but are not limited to:

- Tools, practical techniques, theories, paradigms on self directed job search
- Creative job placement strategies
- Recent research, books, articles, programs on job search and/or job placement
- Outplacement
- Employer Job Development
- Job Search strategies that serve special populations of job seekers, for example, the chronically unemployed, students, ex-offenders, handicapped, non U.S.citizens
- Anecdotes, humor about the job search process
- Update on current workshops, conferences, seminars on the job search and job placement issues
- Research on how people get jobs

This is a LISTSERV managed list, so normal subscription requests apply. To subscribe send mail to LISTSERV@UKCC.BITNET or on the Internet to LISTSERV@UKCC.UKY.EDU with the body containing the command SUB JOBPLACE Yourfirstname Yourlastname

Owner:
Drema Howard   DKHOWA01@UKCC
Associate Director   DKHOWA01@UKCC.UKY.EDU
UK Career Center   (606) 257-3395

JOURNET%QUCDN.BITNET@VM1.NODAK.EDU
JOURNET@QUCDN.QUEENSU.CA

Mailing list for discussion of topics of interest to journalists and journalism educators.

Anyone wishing to write longer contributions (about three screens) for inclusion in a proposed monthly electronic digest should send them directly to the Coordinator for editing and compiling.

BitNet users may subscribe by sending the following command to LISTSERV@QUCDN in the text/body of an e-mail message: Subscribe JOURNET your full name where "your full name" is your real name, not your login Id. Non-BitNet users can join the list by sending the above command as the only line in the text/body of a message to JOURNET%QUCDN.BITNET@VM1.NODAK.EDU or JOURNET@QUCDN.QUEENSU.CA.

Coordinator: George Frajkor <FRAJKOR%CARLETON.CA@VM1.NODAK.EDU>

jpop@ferkel.ucsb.edu   [Last Update 8/92]

Purpose: Discussion of Japanese popular music.

Contact: jpop-request@ferkel.ucsb.edu (Jim Lick)

JTE-L on LISTSERV@VTVM1 or LISTSERV@VTVM1.CC.VT.EDU

ELECTRONIC JOURNAL OF TECHNOLOGY EDUCATION

The JOURNAL OF TECHNOLOGY EDUCATION, launched three years ago as a refereed scholarly print journal, has initiated simultaneous publication of an electronic edition with its first issue of 1992. The text of the journal's articles are offered in ASCII format, while a single graphic illustration of one of the articles is available as a separate Postscript file.

To become an electronic subscriber of the JTE, send the following e-mail message (in the BODY of the mail) to LISTSERV@VTVM1 (Bitnet) or to LISTSERV@VTVM1.CC.VT.EDU (Internet): SUBSCRIBE JTE-L firstname lastname

Subscribers will receive information about how to access articles and how to remove their names from the electronic subscription list.

For further information, contact Mark Sanders, Technology Education, 144 Smyth Hall, Virginia Tech, Blacksburg, VA 24061-0432; telephone: 703/231-8173. E-mail to: MSANDERS@VTVM1.CC.VT.EDU (Internet) or MSANDERS@VTVM1 (Bitnet).

JTIT-L@PSUVM.PSU.EDU   [Last Updated 12-October-1991]
JTIT-L@PSUVM.BITNET

JTIT-L is a discussion forum for teachers of Japanese as well as for media professionals to exchange ideas and information. Discussion topics among others will include theory and practice of second/foreign language, computer aided language programs, interactive video programs, distance education with satellite dishes. JTIT-L also intends to provide a comprehensive database for teachers of Japanese and media professionals involved in Japanese programs. In the future, the databse will comprise of Japanese language programs in Japan and other countries, information on conferences and job opportunities, book review/bibliography, scholarship/grant information, and information about Japanese software and hardware.

Archives of JTIT-L can be listed by sending the command INDEX JTIT-L to LISTSERV@PSUVM, or LISTSERV@PSUVM.PSU.EDU

To subscribe, Bitnet users should send the following command to LISTSERV@PSUVM via mail or interactive message. Internet users should send the same command to LISTSERV@PSUVM.PSU.EDU via mail:

SUB JTIT-L your_full_name

where "your_full_name" is your name. For example:

SUB JTIT-L Nihon Taro

Owner: Hideo Tomita (tomita@Vax001.Kenyon.Edu>

JuggleN on LISTSERV@INDYCMS.BITNET
or LISTSERV@INDYCMS.IUPUI.EDU

This is a first-cousin to the wildly-popular JUGGLING list. This is devoted to the discussion and development of JUGGLING syntax, computer simulation of juggling, and computer analysis of juggling.

Subscription is automatic. Logs are accumulated weekly. No weekly distribution of logs is available as it is with the JUGGLING list (new feature of the JUGGLING list).

Send your subscription queries to: LISTSERV@INDYCMS.BITNET or LISTSERV@INDYCMS.IUPUI.EDU with the body of the mail containing the command:

SUB JUGGLEN yourfirstname yourlastname

The list is unmoderated.

> Owner:
> Phil Paxton
> IPWP400@INDYCMS.BITNET or
> IPWP400@INDYCMS.IUPUI.EDU

jump-in-the-river@PRESTO.IG.COM
> jitr@PRESTO.IG.COM
> {apple,ames,rutgers}!bionet!ig!jitr (UUCP)

Jump-In-The-River is a list for discussion of the music and recordings of Sinead O'Connor, and related matters such as lyrics, tour information, and the like. The list is unmoderated and is open to all. It is currently set up to remail single messages and is not a digest. Archives have been kept since the list's inception in March 1990; contact the request address for information (they are not yet available by direct FTP).

All requests to be added, dropped, or for more information should be sent to jump-in-the-river-request@PRESTO.IG.COM -or- {apple,ames,rutgers}!bionet!ig!jump-in-the-river-request (uucp)

Coordinator: Michael C. Berch <mcb@PRESTO.IG.COM>

KIDSNET@VMS.CIS.PITT.EDU
> KIDSNET@PITTVMS.BITNET (BitNet)
> pitt!vms.cis.pitt.edu!kidsnet UUCP)

Mailing list formed to provide a global network for the use of children and teachers in grades K-12. It is intended to provide a focus for technological development and for resolving the problems of language, standards, etc. that inevitably arise in international communications.

All requests to be added to or deleted from this list, problems, questions, etc., should be sent to KIDSNET-REQUEST@VMS.CIS.PITT.EDU or to JOINKIDS@PITTVMS.BITNET (BitNet).

Coordinator: Bob Carlitz <carlitz@VMS.CIS.PITT.EDU>

KILLER%UMASS.BITNET@CUNYVM.CUNY.EDU

This mailing list/notesfile is dedicated to the playing of all forms of Live-Role-Playing games. Assassin, Killer, K.A.O.S, RECON, DELOS, and any sort of game where one is is doing any sort of role playing in a real live-real time (i.e. YOU, not a paper character); setting is what this discussion covers. This is intended as a forum for discussion of scenarios, rules suggestions, "no kidding there we were" stories, comments on legal aspects, and anything else that a reader would like to talk about if it deals with live role-playing.

All requests to be added or deleted from this list, questions, problems, etc., should be sent to CEREBUS%UMASS.BITNET@CUNYVM.CUNY.EDU.

Coordinator: David Kovar <dk1z#@ANDREW.CMU.EDU>

KISSARMY on LISTSERV@WKUVX1   [Last Update 28-January-1992]

KISSARMY is a discussion list for fans of the rock group KISS. Any topic of interest to KISS fans is appropriate, from news about the groups activities to discussions about opinions on albums, etc.

To subscribe, send a mail message whose body consists of the line to LISTSERV@WKUVX1.BITNET:

SUBSCRIBE KISSARMY "your full name"

where "your full name" is your name. For example:

SUBSCRIBE KISSARMY "Joe Smith"

Please note that the LISTSERV at WKUVX1 is NOT a real IBM LISTSERV; interactive commands are not supported.

> Owner: Hunter Goatley <goathunter@WKUVX1.BITNET>
> VMS Systems Programmer, Western Kentucky University
> 502-745-5251

KLARINET on LISTSERV@VCCSCENT.BITNET   [Last Update 9/92]

KLARINET is an online network featuring news, information, research and teaching items of interest, and other related information concerning clarinet players, teachers, students, and enthusiasts. This network will provide a place to share such information with dialogues amongst participants, research papers, lists of performances, old and new repertoire, makers, etc.

Archives of KLARINET can be listed by sending the command INDEX KLARINET to LISTSERV@VCCSCENT via mail or interactive message.

To subscribe to KLARINET send the following command in the BODY of e-mail or a message to LISTSERV@VCCSCENT on BITNET:

SUB KLARINET your full name

where "your full name" is your name. For example:

SUB KLARINET John Doe

Owner: Jim Fay <NVFAYXJ@VCCSCENT.BITNET>
Cap Bromley <NVBROMH@VCCSCENT.BITNET>

L-HCAP%NDSUVM1.BITNET@CUNYVM.CUNY.EDU
...!psuvax1!NDSUVM1.BITNET!L-HCAP (UUCP)
L-HCAP@NDSUVM1 (BITNET, EARN, NetNorth)

Discussion group for technology for the handicapped; mailing list set up at North Dakota State University for discussing computer and other technology for people with any kind of handicap, plus meetings, conferences, funding agencies, and so forth. Some discussion areas might be:

- Computer hardware and software
- Adaptive devices that makes computers accessable to people no matter the type of handicap
- Literature that discusses various issues addressed in 1 & 2 above
- Meetings and conferences
- Funding agencies and their interests, local and federal
- Suppliers of adaptive hardware and software
- What type(s) of hardware and software is needed for various types of handicap
- Learning disabilities and how can computers help

All requests to be added to or deleted from this list, problems, questions, etc., should be sent to the Coordinator.

> Coordinator: Bob Puyear <NU025213%NDSUVM1.BITNET@CUNYVM.CUNY.EDU>
> ...!psuvax1!NDSUVM1.BITNET!L-HCAP   (UUCP)
> L-HCAP@NDSUVM1   (BITNET, EARN, NetNorth)

LABMGR on LISTSERV@UKCC.BITNET or LISTSERV@UKCC.UKY.EDU

LABMGR has been started to provide a forum for discussion of issues concerning the management of microcomputer labs in academic settings. Issues for discussion may include: security of both hardware and software, networking, hardware and software in a networked environment, and information acess within microlabs in libraries (including OPACS over the Internet, CD-ROMs in labs, etc.)

This is a Listserv managed list, so normal subscription instructions apply. To subscribe send e-mail to LISTSERV@UKCC or on the Internet to LISTSERV@UKCC.uky.edu with the BODY of the mail consisting of the following: (the command MUST be in the BODY, NOT the subject) SUB LABMGR Yourfirstname Yourlastname

Owner: Mary Molinaro (MOLINARO@ukcc.uky.edu)
    Head of Library Computing Facilities
    University of Kentucky
    213 King-South
    Lexington, KY 40506-0039
     (606)257-6199

LACROS-L%VILLVM.BITNET@VM1.NODAK.EDU

Men's Lacrosse information list. Information such as scores and standings will be posted as they are received. Also, any discussion about Lacrosse is encouraged. The Coordinator will try to bring up topics of interest: new rules or coaching changes or anything else which effects the Lacrosse world.

BitNet users can subscribe to this list by sending the following command to LISTSERV@VILLVM via an interactive message (TELL or SEND) or in the text/body of Mail. SUB LACROS-L your_full_name where "your_full_name" is your real name, not your login Id. Non-BitNet users can subscribe by sending the above command in the message text/body of a message to LISTSERV%VILLVM.BITNET@VM1.NODAK.EDU.

Coordinator: Alec Plotkin <185422285%VUVAXCOM.BITNET@VM1.NODAK.EDU>

LACTACID on LISTSERV@SEARN.BITNET
or LISTSERV@SEARN.SUNET.SE

Purpose of List : This is a mailing List for discussion and information exchange on all aspects related to the biology and uses of lactic acid bacteria; e.g.

- in human beings and animals (e.g. in new-borns, oral cavity, vaginal tract, etc)
- in fermented foods (cheese, pickles, sauerkraut, etc)
- in animal feeds (ensilage)
- in the production of polysaccharides and others (e.g. dextran).

To become a member :

address your message to: listserv@searn (bitnet)
or listserv@searn.sunet.se (internet) with the following contents SUBSCRIBE LACTACID your full name
Eg. SUBSCRIBE LACTACID Eng-leong Foo

To send messages to all other members of the group:

address your message to: lactacid@searn   (bitnet)
or   lactacid@searn.sunet.se (internet)

Listowner: Eng-leong Foo
        (UNESCO Microbial Resources Center
        Karolinska Institute, Stockholm, Sweden)
        eng-leong_foo_mircen-ki%micforum@mica.mic.ki.se

LANMAN-L on LISTSERV@NIHLIST or LISTSERV@LIST.NIH.GOV   [Last Update 11/92] The
LANMAN-L list has been created for the discussion of Microsoft LAN Manager and its variants,

including (but not limited to): LAN Manager for Unix, DEC Pathworks, and IBM LAN Server.

To subscribe to LANMAN-l, send the following command to LISTSERV@NIHLIST (or LISTSERV@LIST.NIH.GOV) via mail text or interactive message: SUBSCRIBE LANMAN-L Your full name For example: SUBSCRIBE LANMAN-L Joe Schmoe

> Owner: Chris Ohlandt <CJO@helix.nih.gov>
> Division of Computer Research and Technology
> National Institutes of Health
> cjo@helix.nih.gov
> (301)402-1974

LANTRA-L%FINHUTC.BITNET@CUNYVM.CUNY.EDU

A forum for all aspects of translation and interpreting of natural languages including, but not restricted to, computer aids for translation and interpreting. All translators, interpreters, educators, and other people who are interested in this fascinating subject are welcome. Topics which can be discussed are:

- computer aided translation
- terminology
- lexicography
- intercultural communication
- sociolinguistics
- psycholingusistics
- professional ethics for interpreters and translators
- education and training of interpreters and translators etc.

To add or remove yourself from the list, send a message to LISTSERV%FINHUTC.BITNET@CUNYVM.CUNY.EDU. The Sender of the message you send must be the name (E-mail address) you want to add or remove from the list. The text body of the message should be: SUBSCRIBE LANTRA-L your_full_name or: SIGNOFF LANTRA-L where your_full_name is your normal name, not your E-mail address.

Coordinator: Helge Niska <HNISKA%QZCOM.BITNET@CUNYVM.CUNY.EDU>

LASMED-L <JO%ILNCRD.BITNET@CUNYVM.CUNY.EDU>

A Bitnet newsletter on lasers in medicine.

To subscribe, send a message to LISTSERV%TAUNIVM.BITNET@CUNYVM.CUNY.EDU with the body of the letter containing the command: SUB LASMED-L Your_Full_Name where Your_Full_Name; is your title, first name and last name.

Coordinator: Joseph van Zwaren de Zwarenstein <JO%ILNCRD.BITNET@CUNYVM.CUNY.EDU>

LAWSCH-L%AUVM.BITNET@VM1.NODAK.EDU

A forum to discuss matters of concern which affect all law students; it is also designed to allow for interaction between students and law schools to lessen the gap between them. The list is based at American University Law School.

BitNet users can subscribe by sending an interactive message or e-mail to LISTSERV@AUVM with the following command in the body/text: SUB LAWSCH-L your_full_name where "your_full_name" is your real name, not your login Id. Not-BitNet users can subscribe by sending the above command in the text/body of a message to LISTSERV%AUVM.BITNET@VM1.NODAK.EDU.

Coordinator: Ed Kania <EKANIA%AUVM.BITNET@VM1.NODAK.EDU>

LDBASE-L on LISTSERV@UKANVM.BITNET or LISTSERV@UKANVM.CC.UKANS.EDU

A discussion list created to provide a forum for the indepth investigation of the power of the Listserve

Database Search facility. Discussion topics will include proper code syntax, construction of "skeleton" code batch-jobs to allow for rapid modification for specific SEARCH projects, logical sequence and development of SEARCH plans resulting in successful, efficient SEARCHES, and any other topic directly related to conducting SEARCHES of the vast knowledge base residing on the Listserve's throughout the world. This forum welcomes new users of electronic communications; those of us with some expertise will gladly assist newcomers. The list is configured so that REPLY goes to the entire list in an effort to stimulate discussion and facilitate the exchange of information.

Subscriptions should be sent to:

Bitnet: <LISTSERV@UKANVM.BITNET> or Internet: <LISTSERV@UKANVM.CC.UKANS.EDU>

with the BODY or text of the mail containing the line: SUB LDBASE-L yourfirstname yourlastname

Owner: For additional information or assistance in subscribing, send e-mail to: Phil Endacott <ENDACOTT@UKANVAX.BITNET> OR <ENDACOTT@kuhub.cc.ukans.edu>

Learning@sea.east.sun.com   [Last Update 11/92]

The Learning List: A Resource for Helping our Children Learn

Purpose: The Learning List was founded on Friday, 13 November 1992, as an electronic forum for discussing child-centered learning. It is intended to provide a meeting place in cyberspace in which to advance our understanding of the processes of learning, and to share personal experiences and practical suggestions to help in the great adventure we share with our children.

Philosophy: Our philosophy is that humans as a species have an innate ability to learn, and that current methods of "teaching", "education" and "schooling" serve primarily to thwart or diminish that ability. We seek to learn how we can best reaffirm and enhance that ability in ourselves and, above all else, in our children.

As our spiritual and religious backgrounds are varied, we affirm that we will agree to disagree on these issues. In particular, we will not attempt to convince others of the rightness of our particular ethical or moral stand, whether it is motivated by religion, personal belief or societal standards. Such discussions should be conducted elsewhere.

We find inspiration in the writings of such people as John Holt, and in the ongoing dialogue in such periodicals as Growing Without Schooling.

Submissions and Subscriptions: Members of the list are considered subscribers of a service that is currently offered free of charge. All subscribers are urged to submit articles and letters, and to join in ongoing discussion.

Although individual submissions will NOT be censored for content by the moderator, all subscribers are requested to observe the statements of purpose and philosophhy in their writing. Anyone who regularly flouts these standards will be asked to leave the List.

Submissions: Learning@sea.east.Sun.COM
Subscriptions: Learning-Request@sea.east.Sun.COM
Moderator: Rowan Hawthorne <rowan@sea.east.Sun.COM>

legs <wyle@inf.ethz.ch>

Legs is an informal, anonymous list for sharing images, discussion about womens' legs.

To subscribe to legs, send a request to one of:

internet: wyle@inf.ethz.ch
uucp: uunet!chx400!ethz!wyle
bitnet: WYLE@CZHETH5A

Owner: Mitchell Wyle <WYLE@CZHETH5A>

Legs on LISTSERV@UTFSM.BITNET   [Last Updated 28-January-1992]

Discusion sobre piernas de Mujeres.

The purpose of this list is to serve as a forum for all student lovers of Women's legs.

The LANGUAGE for this list is "SPANISH", but other languages will be acepted too.

The posting to this list may include: GIF , .GL , comments , etc

To subscribe to LEGS, send the following command to LISTSERV@UTFSM on BITNET via mail text or interactive message:

SUBSCRIBE LEGS your_full_name

ListOwner: Hernan Lobos *Mitzio* <I5HLOBOS@UTFSM.BITNET>

LEXX-L on LISTSERV@IRISHVMA

The LEXX-L list has been created to discuss IBM's LEXX Live Parsing Editor for VM. Its mailing address is LEXX-L@IRISHVMA; it's administered by LISTSERV@IRISHVMA. For those on Internet, I'd recommend using LEXX-L%IRISHVMA.BITNET@UICVM.UIC.EDU until IRISHVMA gets an Internet address of its own.

Monthly notebooks will be kept at IRISHVMA.

To subscribe, send an interactive message or e-mail to LISTSERV@IRISHVMA.BITNET or LISTSERV%IRISHVMA.BITNET@UICVM.UIC.EDU with the message line (in the text/body): subscribe lexx-l firstname lastname

Owner: Nick Laflamme <NLAFLAMM@IRISHVMA>

LIBADMIN on LISTSERV@UMAB

A discussion of library administration and management

LIBADMIN is an electronic mailing list dealing with issues of library administration and management. The list is intended to serve as a vehicle of communication to enhance and promote discussion among library administrators and managers. The goal of LIBADMIN, then, is to provide a sort of electronic brainstorming session. The University of Maryland serves as host to the listserver.

LIBADMIN is an open list. Any messages posted to LIBADMIN will automatically be sent to all subscribers. The list organizers will monitor topics on the list and may make suggestions, for example, as to appropriateness of topics for LIBADMIN, but the organizers will not serve as moderators or editors. It is assumed participants on this list will cooperate in submitting messages related to issues of library management.

TO SUBSCRIBE TO LIBADMIN Send the following message to LISTSERV@UMAB on BITNET:

SUBSCRIBE LIBADMIN Jane Smith

Put your name in place of Jane's. Please note that this command must NOT be sent to the list address but to the listserver address (LISTSERV@UMAB).

HOW TO SEND A MESSAGE TO LIBADMIN Send an electronic message addressed to LIBADMIN@UMAB on BITNET in the same way you might send an electronic message to a person. The listserver at Maryland will accept your mail and distribute it to everyone subscribed to LIBADMIN.

The organizers of LIBADMIN would be happy to assist you with subscription problems or answer any other questions you may have about LIBADMIN. Please contact us personally.

OWNERS:

Pamela Bluh   John Culshaw
Thurgood Marshall Law Library   James P. Magill Library

University of Maryland
(301) 328-7400
pbluh@umab on bitnet

Haverford College
(215) 896-1170
j_culshaw@hvrford on bitnet
j_culshaw@acc.haverford.edu

LIBERNET@DARTMOUTH.EDU

An electronic mailing list/discussion group/magazine for libertarians, classical liberals, objectivists, and anybody else interested in a free market/social tolerance approach to political issues.

All requests to be added to or deleted from this list should be sent to LIBERNET-REQUEST@DARTMOUTH.EDU.

Coordinators: Barry Fagin <fagin@ELEAZAR.DARTMOUTH.EDU>
June Genis <GA.JRG@FORSYTHE.STANFORD.EDU>

Libmastr on LISTSERV@Uottawa (Bitnet)   [Last Updated 28-January-1992]
or LISTSERV@Acadvm1.Uottawa.Ca (Internet)

This Listserv list is designed to provide an informal forum for users of the Library Master bibliographic and textual database management system. Libmastr will facilitate the exchange of user tips, index frequently asked questions and maintain a fileserver for archiving databases of academic interest, as well as customized database structures, style sheets, format files, sort order files, and import parameter files.

The list is open to automatic subscription by sending the following e-mail message to Listserv@Uottawa or Listserv@Acadvm1.Uottawa.Ca :

Sub Libmastr your name

This service is provided free of charge to the virtual community in cooperation with Balboa Software and Harry Hahne, the author of Library Master.

Contact the list owner, Michael Strangelove, for more information or if you experience difficulties in attempting to subscribe.

Owner:

Michael Strangelove
University of Ottawa
<441495@Uottawa>
<441495@Acadvm1.Uottawa.Ca>

Library on ListServ@IndyCMS or ListServ@IndyCMS.IUPUI.Edu

Library (Libraries & Librarians) is dedicated to *general* news and information of interest to libraries, their employees and users.

Library seeks to complement and supplement preexisting specialized library-related lists.

Library is owned and coordinated by a retired professional archivist and librarian (Donna B Harlan) and an interested layperson and former library paraprofessional (John B Harlan). It is a mother and son project :-)

To subscribe to "Library" send e-mail to LISTSERV@INDYCMS on BITNET or ListServ@IndyCMS.IUPUI.EDU on the Internet with the following command in the BODY of the mail:

sub library yourfirstname yourlastname

List owner/coordinators:

Editorial: Donna B Harlan
Harlan@IUBACS (CREN)
Harlan@UCS.Indiana.Edu (Internet)

Administrative: John B Harlan
IJBH200@IndyVAX (CREN)
IJBH200@IndyVAX.IUPUI.Edu (Internet)

LibRef-L on LISTSERV@KENTVM

This list is a discussion of the changing environment of library reference services and activities. Topics include traditional reference services, patron expectations, staff training, as well the impact of CD-ROM and online searching on reference service.

This forum will serve as a professional networking and information source. We will share ideas, solutions and experiences.

This list is run from the LISTSERV at Kent State University and moderated by the Reference Librarians at Kent State University Libraries. The Internet address of the LISTSERV is LISTSERV@kentvm.kent.edu.

You may subscribe to this list by sending a subscribe command by interactive message or by e-mail. To subscribe by interactive message, send the command:

"SUB LIBREF-L yourfirstname yourlastname"

to LISTSERV@KENTVM. For example:

IBM VM CMS users would enter

tell listserv at kentvm "sub Libref-L A. Librarian"

VAX VMS users would enter

send listserv@kentvm "sub Libref-L A. Librarian"

You may also subscribe by send mail to LISTSERV@KENTVM with the command "SUB LIBREF-L your name" in the body of the mail item.

Please do NOT send these commands to the list address LIBREF-L@KENTVM. Doing so will cause your request to be broadcast to all subscribers and will not cause your name to be added to the list.

Owners:
Diane Kovacs	dkovacs@kentvm
Laura Bartolo	lbartolo@kentvm
Gladys Bell	gbell@kentvm
Mary DuMont	mdumont@kentvm
Julie McDaniel	jmcdanie@kentvm
Carolyn Radcliff	cradclif@kentvm
Kara Robinson	krobinso@kentvm
Barbara Schloman	bschloma@kentvm

LIBRES on LISTSERV@KENTVM or LISTSERV@KENTVM.KENT.EDU

LIBRES is an electronic conference designed to foster library and information science research and support the development of our knowledge base.

This forum will serve as a professional networking and information source. We will share ideas, solutions and experiences.

LIBRES will include discussions of research in progress, reviews of research, queries and responses from participants, and conference announcements. LIBRES will be distributed weekly as editorial staffing allows. All editors are volunteers on the LIBRES Project.

Subscription is open to anyone interested. All participants will be asked to submit a biography form before being added to the list. Completed biographies will be available on the LIBRES fileserver and via anonymous ftp from ksuvxa.kent.edu for review by LIBRES participants in order to facilitate identifying others with similar research interests.

You may subscribe to LIBRES by sending a subscribe command by interactive message or by e-mail. To subscribe by interactive message, send the command: SUB LIBRES YourFirstname YourLastname to LISTSERV@KENTVM. For example:

IBM VM CMS users would enter tell listserv at kentvm sub LIBRES YourFirstname YourLastname VAX VMS users would enter send listserv@kentvm sub LIBRES YourFirstname YourLastname

You may also subscribe by sending an e-mail message to LISTSERV@KENTVM or if your account is on the internet send to LISTSERV@KENTVM.KENT.EDU, with the following command as the text of the message.

SUB LIBRES YourFirstname YourLastname

You must leave the subject line *empty* and please don't include any extra text as a machine will read this not a human (at first)

EDITORS@KENTVM or EDITORS@KENTVM.KENT.EDU is the address to which to send submissions and questions about the LIBRES Conference

The Co-Editors are
Diane Kovacs	dkovacs@kentvm	dkovacs@kentvm.kent.edu
Tom Froehlich	tfroehli@kentvm	tfroehli@kentvm.kent.edu
Julie McDaniel	jmcdanie@kentvm	jmcdanie@kentvm.kent.edu
Amey Park	apark@kentvm	apark@kentvm.kent.edu
Barbara Schloman	bschloma@kentvm	bschloma@kentvm.kent.edu
Ellen Detlefsen	ellen@pittvms	ellen@idis.lis.pitt.edu
Rosemary Dumont	rdumont@kentvm	rdumont@kentvm.kent.edu

life-talking@ferkel.ucsb.edu   [Last Update 8/92]

Purpose: Discussion of the musical group Life Talking.

Contact: life-talking-request@ferkel.ucsb.edu (Jim Lick)

LINES-L on LISTSERV@NDSUVM1.BITNET   [Last Update 9/92] or LISTSERV@vm1.nodak.edu

LINES-L will serve as a vehicle for topics related to the enhancement of "LifeLines Genealogical Database and Report Generator". LifeLines is an experimental, second-generation Genealogical system.

LINES-L is for the exchange of information, reports, programming hints, ideas and also an electronic newsletter about the LifeLines Genealogy program which works on the Operating Systems: UNIX (Sun3/4) and Xenix386. Dr. Thomas T. Wetmore IV is the author of LifeLines Database.

TO SUBSCRIBE TO LINES-L

Send the e-mail to Listserv@Vm1.NoDak.Edu or LISTSERV@NDSUVM1.BITNET with the following command in the BODY of the mail (NOT the subject):

SUB LINES-L your full name Eg. SUB LINES-L Cliff Manis

After you SUBSCRIBE, if you want to send a message to all subscribed to the list by sending mail to any ONE of the following addresses: LINES-L@vm1.nodak.edu or lines-l@vm1.nodak.edu or LINES-L@NDSUVM1 on BITNET

Any piece of mail sent to one of these special user-ids would then be automatically distributed by the list server to each and every person on the list.

When you SUB to the list, please send the SUB command msg to: LISTSERV@vm1.nodak.edu or LISTSERV@NDSUVM1 and NOT to the list.

List Owner: Cliff Manis < cmanis@csoftec.csf.com >

LINGUIST@UNIWA.UWA.OZ.AU

A new list has been formed, which will serve as a place of discussion for those issues which concern the academic discipline of linguistics and related fields. The list is international in orientation, and hopes to provide a forum for the community of linguists as they exist in different countries. Though the list is moderated, and all submissions are subject to editorial discretion, it has no areal, ideological or theoretical bent, and discussion of any linguistic subfield are welcomed. Membership of the list is open to all.

To subscribe to this list, please send a message to LINGUIST-REQUEST@UNIWA.UWA.OZ.AU containing as its first and only line the following: SUBSCRIBE LINGUIST

Any other questions may be directed to: LINGUIST-EDITORS@UNIWA.UWA.OZ.AU

LIST OF MAILING LISTS

Mailing-list for "List of lists" update notices.

To keep people up to date on the large number of such lists, there is a mailing-list for list-of-lists update notices. Copies of the list itself are not sent to the world at large, but for those internet users who seriously intend to copy the updated versions when updated, a brief notice will be sent when a new version is available.

An electronic mail server is available to copy the list to those who lack the IP internet. Send a message to mail-server@nisc.sri.com with a line "send netinfo/interest-groups" in the message body. For more information, use the line "send HELP" (Caps Matter).

To get on the list (or to submit updates to existing mailing-lists or add new ones), send requests to interest-groups-request@nisc.sri.com.

ListOwnL%INDYCMS.BITNET@VM1.NODAK.EDU
ListOwnL on LISTSERV@INDYCMS

ListOwnL is a discussion list for owners/editors/coordinators of ListServ-based discussion and distribution lists. ListServ managers and other interested persons (especially other computing center staff) are encouraged to join.

To subscribe, request to: ListServ@IndyCMS Using the following text: Sub ListOwnL Your_full_name / Your_listname

Example: Sub ListOwnL John B Harlan / ListOwnL List Owner: John B. Harlan BITNET: JBHTech@IrishMVS Internet: JBHTech@IrishMVS.CC.ND.Edu

List-Managers@GreatCircle.COM   [Last Update 11/92]

This is a mailing list for discussions of issues related to managing Internet mailing lists, including (but not limited to) software, methods, mechanisms, techniques, and policies.

All messages sent to that address are immediately forwarded to the list. There is digestified version of the list is available as "List-Managers-Digest@GreatCircle.COM". The digestified version has exactly the same messages as the direct version; the messages are simply bundled into digests daily (or more frequently, if traffic warrants). Both lists are unmoderated.

To join the List-Managers mailing list, send the command

subscribe list-managers

in the body of a message to "Majordomo@GreatCircle.COM". If you want to subscribe something other than the account the mail is coming from, such as a local redistribution list, then append that address to the "subscribe" command; for example, to subscribe "local-list-managers":

subscribe list-managers local-list-managers@your.domain.net

To subscribe to the digestified version, substitute "list-managers-digest" for "list-managers" in the examples above.

All messages to the list are being archived. A copy of the archive is available by anonymous FTP from host FTP.GreatCircle.COM, directory "pub/archive", compressed file "list-managers.Z". The copy of the archive available by anonymous FTP is updated every night at midnight local time (0700 GMT in the summer, 0800 GMT in the winter).

If email to you bounces for more than 24 hours, I'll probably simply drop you from the list; you'll have to resubscribe when you get the problem fixed, and retrieve the archives to find out what you missed.

For further information, contact:

Brent Chapman   Great Circle Associates
Brent@GreatCircle.COM   1057 West Dana Street
+1 415 962 0841

LITERA-L on LISTSERV@TECMTYVM (BITNET)
or LISTSERV@TECMTYVM.MTY.ITESM.MX (INTERNET)

The purpose of this list is to have a medium for exchanging ideas about literature and related topics, like: linguistics, semantics, philology, etc.... and moreover, allow users to share their literary creations and receive a constructive criticism of it to improve their writing style.

What about your favorite authors or translations of their works? Also, the list, attempts some exchanging between english and spanish literature, Vgr.: common grounds, opinions about authors, works, literary styles....and additionally about translations of english to spanish and viceversa.

Any opinion, discussion or questions bordering on these topics are welcome and encouraged.

To subscribe, send the following command to LISTSERV@TECMTYVM (if on BITNET) or LISTSERV@TECMTYVM.MTY.ITESM.MX (if on INTERNET), either by interactive message (only for BITNET subscribers) or in the body of a E-mail letter:

SUBSCRIBE LITERA-L your_full_name

The list-owners are:
PL157961@TECMTYVM (Fernando Careaga Sanchez).
PL247526@TECMTYVM (Claudia Puertos Gonzalez).

This is a PRIVATE list in attempt to prevent naive or malicious "noise" and to protect the seriousness of criticism; so, if you want to have more information about the contents of this list please send a personal request to PL157961@TECMTYVM (BITNET) or either PL157961@TECMTYVM.MTY.ITESM, al157961@mtecv2.mty.itesm.mx (INTERNET).

LITERARYLITERARY@UCF1VM.CC.UCF.EDU   [Last Updated June 1992]

Mailing list for any lover of literature. Discussions will include favorite authors, favorite works, literary styles, criticisms, etc. (in fact, basically anything you can think of regarding literature, unless postings become too numerous). Postings from scholars as well as interested parties are welcome.

Log files will be kept on a monthly basis.

BitNet users can subscribe by sending the following command to LISTSERV@UCF1VM: SUB LITERARY Your_full_name where Your_full_name is your real name, not your userid; for example: SUB LITERARY John Doe Non-BitNet users can subscribe by sending the SUB command as the text/body of a message to LISTSERV@UCF1VM.cc.ucf.edu

Coordinator: UCF Postmaster <POSTMAST@UCF1VM.CC.UCF.EDU>

LITURGY on MAILBASE@MAILBASE.AC.UK

LITURGY provides an academic forum for discussion of all aspects of Christian liturgy. The list does not confine itself to any one historical period, geographical area or Christian tradition. Therefore contributions are welcome from all historical and theological fields. We also welcome discussion from those involved in other disciplines such as literary analysis, comparative religions and sociology of religion.

The list is unmoderated with all messages to the list being archived and can be retrieved by sending the following command to MAILBASE@MAILBASE.AC.UK

INDEX LITURGY

To subscribe to LITURGY send the following command via e-mail to MAILBASE@MAILBASE.AC.UK

SUBSCRIBE LITURGY your_full_name

For example:

SUBSCRIBE LITURGY Joan Smith

Owner: Michael Fraser <m.a.fraser@durham.ac.uk>

LM_NET on LISTSERV@SUVM.BITNET or LISTSERV@SUVM.ACS.SYR.EDU

For all school library media people--a new listserv called LM_NET (library media network) has just been set up to serve the school library media community world-wide. This list is operated by Mike Eisenberg, Syracuse University, AASL, and Peter Milbury, a library media specialist in Chico California.

Conversation on this list will focus on the topics of interest to the school library media community, including the latest on school library media services, operations, and activities. It is a list for practitioners helping practitioners, sharing ideas, solving problems, telling each other about new publications and up-coming conferences, asking for assistance or information, and linking schools through their library media centers.

To join send an email to either:

Peter Milbury PMILBUR@ATL.CALSTATE.EDU or Mike Eisenberg MIKE@SUVM.ACS.SYR.EDU (MIKE@SUVM.BITNET)

It's important to include your full userid/address, your firstname lastname.

LN on LISTSERV@FRMOP11.Bitnet

Bulletin Electronique LN

Le bulletin electronique LN a pour but de favoriser la circulation d'informations a travers la communaute "Informatique Linguistique": appels a communication, annonces de conferences ou seminaires, requetes specifiques concernant logiciels, corpus et donnees diverses, descriptions d'activites et de projets, discussions sur des sujets techniques, etc. Le bulletin est principalement francophone, mais de nombreuses informations sont retransmises sous leur forme originale en anglais. Il constitue un forum pour les chercheurs travaillant sur le Francais mais n'est en aucun cas restreint a ce seul champ d'etude.

Le bulletin est parraine par l'Association for Computational Linguistics (ACL) et l'Association for Computers and the Humanities (ACH). Ce double parrainage reflete l'interet croissant des linguistes informaticiens pour, a cote de domaines plus traditionnels, des domaines tels que la lexicographie informatique, l'etude et l'utilisation de corpus, les modeles statistiques, etc., qui sont depuis longtemps centraux dans l'ACH.

Le bulletin comporte a l'heure actuelle pres de 400 abonnes dans 25 pays. Il est edite par Jean Veronis (GRTC-CNRS, France) et Pierre Zweigenbaum (DIAM-INSERM, France).

Vous pouvez vous abonner au bulletin en envoyant un message compose de la seule ligne suivante a LISTSERV@FRMOP11.BITNET:

SUBSCRIBE LN Prenom Nom

Vous pouvez transmettre des informations pour diffusion dans le bulletin en envoyant un message a LN@FRMOP11.BITNET.

En cas de probleme, adressez-vous directement aux editeurs:

Jean Veronis VERONIS@VASSAR.BITNET

Pierre Zweigenbaum ZWEIG@FRSIM51.BITNET

LN Electronic List

LN is an international electronic distribution list for computational linguists. Its goal is to disseminate calls for papers, conference and seminar announcements, requests for software, corpora, and various data, project descriptions, discussions on technical topics, etc. The list is primarily French-speaking, but many items are circulated in English. It provides a forum for scholars working on French, but it is by no means restricted to this field.

The list is sponsored by the Association for Computational Linguistics (ACL) and the Association for Computers and the Humanities (ACH). This joint sponsorship reflects the fact that in addition to more traditional concerns, computational linguists have a growing interest in areas such as computational lexicography, study and use of corpora, statistical models, etc., which have been traditionally central to ACH.

Currently the list consists of about 400 members in 25 countries. It is moderated by Jean Veronis (GRTC-CNRS, France) and Pierre Zweigenbaum (DIAM-INSERM, France).

To join LN, send a message to LISTSERV@FRMOP11.BITNET, containing only the following line:

SUBSCRIBE LN your name

Send messages to be transmitted on the list to LN@FRMOP11.BITNET. In case of problems, send a message to one of the editors:

Jean Veronis	Pierre Zweigenbaum
VERONIS@VASSAR.BITNET	ZWEIG@FRSIM51.BITNET

lojban-list@snark.thyrsus.com

This list is for exchange of information, ideas, comments, and text about the artificial language Lojban (also called Loglan) - reference Scientific American, June 1960. This language has been recently completed after 35 years work, and is spoken by a few people, and growing steadily. Its original purpose was as a tool in testing the Sapir-Whorf hypothesis of linguistics. Other applications, including language education, machine translation, artificial intelligence, an international language, etc. have surfaced and gained adherents.

For information about Lojban, send a snail address to: -- lojbab = Bob LeChevalier, President, The Logical Language Group, Inc. 2904 Beau Lane, Fairfax VA 22031-1303 USA 703-385-0273 lojbab@snark.thyrsus.com

since there is little on-line published material yet. Use the above address for lojban-list. Send administrative requests to subscribe to lojban-list-request@snark.thyrsus.com

The list is not formally moderated, though Bob LeChevalier and John Cowan (cowan@snark.thyrsus.com) tend to lead discussions. List maintenance is by Cowan and by snark-machine-host Eric Raymond, but these should be contacted through lojban-list-request per the above.

Love-Hounds@EDDIE.MIT.EDU

This is a mailing list for the discussion of Kate Bush's music (and any other artistic music or anything else for that matter).

All requests to be added to or deleted from this list, problems, questions, etc., should be sent to

Love-Hounds-Request@EDDIE.MIT.EDU.

Coordinator: Doug Alan <nessus@EDDIE.MIT.EDU>

LSTERN-L%FRMOP11.BITNET@CUNYVM.CUNY.EDU
　　LSTERN-L on LISTSERV@FRMOP11

A new list has been created to discuss the issues related to the LISTEARN server. Anyone wishing may subscribe to it by sending:

SUB LSTERN-L Your_full_name to one of the addresses above.

The messages that you would like to see distributed to the list should go to the list address (LSTERN-L) and not to the server address.

LSTIAF-L on LISTSERV@TAUNIVM.BITNET　　　　　　　　　　[Last Updated 28-January-1992]

This list will attempt to define and formalise the LISTEARN Interactive Access Facility development. Topics will include: Commands and options to be added, bug reports, User Interface Development, TCP/IP interfacing, and more.

Interactive Access Facility is a method for user interfaces to communicate with a ListEARN server in a structured method using interactive messages.

To subscribe, send the following command to LISTSERV@TAUNIVM

SUB LSTIAF-L Myname Mylastname

Messages may be posted by mailing your submission to LSTIAF-L@TAUNIVM

Owner: Turgut Kalfaoglu <TURGUT@FRORS12.BITNET>

LWUsers%NDSUVM1.BITNET@CUNYVM.CUNY.EDU
　　LWUsers on LISTSERV@NDSUVM1

LWUsers is an e-mail list to be used as a forum for technical discussions among users and developers of the LANWatch Local Area Network Analyzer for the IBM PC from FTP Software, Inc. While LANWatch has its roots in the MIT Netwatch program, it is different and the list is intended to focus on LANWatch.

To subscribe, send the following command to LISTSERV@vm1.nodak.edu or LISTSERV@NDSUVM1.Bitnet in the BODY or TEXT of mail:

SUB LWUSERS your_full_name

where "your_full_name" is your name. For example:

SUB LWUSERS Im A. Packet

Subscription is open to anyone, but list contributions are set up as "Private" which means that a user address MUST be on the list of subscribers in order to contribute. This is ONLY done to cut down on stray "noise". Anyone may subscribe to the list. If you read the list on some other medium or want to contribute from a different mail address you may still do so. Just subscribe as usual then send the command "set lwusers nomail" to LISTSERV to prevent it from sending you mail at that address.

Once subscribed you may send contributions to LWUSERS@vm1.nodak.edu or LWUSERS@NDSUVM1 on BITNET. You should use the address corresponding to the LISTSERV address you used to subscribe.

Contributions sent to this list are automatically archived. You can obtain a list of the available archive files by sending an "INDEX LWUSERS" to LISTSERV@vm1.nodak.edu or LISTSERV@NDSUVM1.Bitnet. You may also access these archives via anonymous FTP on the Internet from host VM1.NoDak.EDU (CD LISTARCH and DIR LWUSERS.*).

Owner: Marty Hoag <nu021172@vm1.nodak.edu> <nu021172@NDSUVM1.Bitnet>

machi386@cs.cmu.edu

> A group for discussion of Mach 2.5 and 3.0 on Intel 386/486 architectures. Unmoderated.
>
> Coordinator: machi386-request@cs.cmu.edu

MACPROG@WUVMD.WUSTL.EDU   [Last Updated 12-October-1991]

> Hosted by Washington University, the MACPROG list is the Internet answer to the excellent Usenet programming forum. Hopefully the easier access of an Internet-based list will promote even better communication between Macintosh developers of commercial, in-house, and shareware software. In addition, this list will move some of the more technical topics out from lists devoted to user-oriented issues.
>
> I will be moderating the list remotely from Wayne State University. I'm not a Mac programming expert per se. But I am one of those sadistic indiviuals who, convinced life alone wasn't handing me enough problems, decided to take up Mac programming for the sheer fun of it. Luckily I found a job where they'd pay me to have fun (actually I'm a System's Analyst but they give me in-house programming time for good behavior).
>
> The list will be moderated in a digest format (Info-mac style). I'll collect submissions into one digest and crank one out every day or two as traffic dictates. If the initial membership is any indication, this list should have heavy traffic. 30 people have subscribed already, with 40 more inquiries, without even having officially announced the list.
>
> The focus of MacProg will be to discuss mainstream language coding techniques. What's a mainstream language? C & Pascal principally, although other languages like LISP, Prologue, Fortran, Basic, HyperTalk, and application scripting are certainly welcome. Besides Q&A, I'd like to have other features running. For example, I'd like participants to report errors in documentation from Apple or other sources. There's been times when I've felt like terminating execution of my program with a 16lb., chrome-plated sledge hammer, simply because of an error I was getting caused by errant specifications from Apple. Also I'd like participants to offer quick reviews on books they've read, seminars they've attended, or interactive courses they've used which have been particularly good or bad. Since no one can ever know everything about Mac programming, and since system compatibility is a constantly moving target, sources of programming information are important for beginners and experts alike.
>
> So, if you think you'd like to use this informative service for Macintosh developers send mail to LISTSERV@WUVMD.WUSTL.EDU or LISTSERV@WUVMD.BITNET with the following command in the BODY of the mail: SUBSCRIBE MACPROG your name
>
> Special thanks to Eric Oberle of Washington University for setting this all up on his mainframe. But what do you mean when you say I have to pay the electric bill?
>
> Owner and Moderator: Bill Brandt <WBRANDT@WAYNEST1.BITNET>

mac-security@eclectic.com

> A mailing list for people interested in Macintosh security. This can be used to:
>
> - Discuss existing security problems in various Macintosh applications.
> - Discuss security applications, hardware, and solutions.
> - Discuss potential problems and their solutions.
> - Announcements of new Macintosh viruses and virus control software. (Discussion of viruses in depth should be carried out on virus specific mailing lists.)
> - Just about anything else related to Macintosh security and access control.

With the arrival of System 7.0 and its wealth of information sharing facilities, Macintosh security has entered a new era. Originally you only had to worry about someone getting into your Macintosh via the keyboard, or stealing it outright. Now it's much easier to browse through information on someone else's Macintosh over the network.

If you're interested in joining the list, please send a message to:

mac-security-request@eclectic.com

Contributions to the list should go to:

mac-security@eclectic.com

At present, the list is unmoderated and will immediately distribute any incoming messages to the list. If conditions change, the list will change to a moderated list, a digest, or some other form. Also, we can look into making it a newsgroup at some point but I'd like to start it in this form and see what develops.

Owner:
David C. Kovar
Consultant   ARPA: kovar@eclectic.com
Eclectic Associates   AppleLink: ECLECTIC
Ma Bell: 617-643-3373   MacNET: DKovar

MACRO32 on LISTSERV@WKUVX1.BITNET

MACRO32 is dedicated to a discussion of VAX/VMS systems programming using MACRO-32, the VAX assembly language. This list is currently unmoderated. All topics relating to VMS systems programming are welcome, from MACRO-32 syntax problems to VMS internals questions.

This list was created to complement the discussions on INFO-VAX, which tends to be oriented toward management more than systems programming.

To subscribe to MACRO32, send a mail message containing the following command to LISTSERV@WKUVX1.bitnet:

SUBSCRIBE MACRO32

List owner: Hunter Goatley <goathunter@WKUVX1.bitnet>

MacTurk%TRBOUN.BITNET@CUNYVM.CUNY.EDU
MacTurk@TRBOUN

As you can easily understand from the name, it is related to MacIntosh'es. The only addition is Turk. The list will deal on Academic Computing on MacIntosh Environment in Turkey (which is derived from the Workshop under the same name, on May 14-16, Istanbul, Bogazici University).

This is not a LISTSERV/LISTEARN list! There is no automatic subscription available at the moment! Subscription requests should be sent to me at djavi%trboun.bitnet@cunyvm.cuny.edu. Postings should be sent to:

MacTurk@TRBOUN

in mail format. Only class M (that is MAIL) files will be accepted.

List Owner: Ferhat Djavidan <djavi%trboun.bitnet@cunyvm.cuny.edu>

MAIL-MEN@usl.com

Mail-men is a moderated discussion group about men's issues and is open to everyone. The intent is to create an atmosphere of openess and understanding for discussions about being male in today's world. Flames are best sent elsewhere. Since men can't truly be free until women are, feminism is generally viewed as a good thing on this list. The list is digested as a kindness to various mail systems.

All requests to be added to or deleted from this list, problems, questions, etc., should be sent to mail-men-request@ATTUNIX.ATT.COM.

Moderator: Marcel-Franck Simon <mingus@usl.com>

Mail-Zilog <cbmvax!mail-zilog@SEISMO.CSS.GOV>

A self-help group to provide communications among Zilog users. Topics include problems with Zeus, fixes, portability problems, availability of ported software and exchange of programs on Zilog compatible media. Open to both end users and systems houses, but all should be able to cope with the phrase Zilog Brain Damage with some degree of equanimity.

All requests to be added to or deleted from this list, problems, questions, etc., should be sent to cbmvax!mail-zilog@SEISMO.CSS.GOV or UUCP {ihnp4|seismo|caip}!cbmvax!mail-zilog-request.

Coordinator: George Robbins <cbmvax!grr@SEISMO.CSS.GOV>

mail.interleaf <leaf%TEKSCE.SCE.TEK.COM@RELAY.CS.NET>

Discussions on all aspects related to the Interleaf publishing environment, including (but not restricted to) the Interleaf language, user environment, implementations on new platforms, user written enhancements, and filters, bug reports and workarounds.

On addressing users at Interleaf:

Note that we have a registered domain in the uucp zone, and you can find us in the uucp maps. "user@ILEAF.COM" is equivalent to "ileaf!user@EDDIE.MIT.EDU" (10 Canal Park), and "user@HQ.ILEAF.COM" is equivalent to "leafusa!user@UUNET.UU.NET" (25 First Street). Note that, at least in the hq.ileaf.com subdomain, you can mail to most users at Interleaf via a first initial + last name alias (for example, I am reachable as "sfreedman@hq.ileaf.com"). Finally, using explicit uucp paths inside Interleaf is unnecessary, since the alias files on our gateways should resolve the user anyway. '

All requests to be added to or deleted from this list, problems, questions, etc., should be sent to leaf-request%TEKSCE.SCE.TEK.COM@RELAY.CS.NET or ...tektronix!teksce!tekgen!leaf-request.

MAIL.YIDDISH <dave@LSUC.ON.CA>

Mailing list for discussion of Yiddish language, literature and culture; a familiarity with Yiddish language is required. Some of the discussion is carried on in transliterated Yiddish. (Note: this is not a mailing list for discussion of Judaism or Jewish culture in general; those reside elsewhere.)

Archives are Located on host LSUC.ON.CA;for access contact the Moderator.

Requests to be added to or deleted from the list, problems, questions, etc., should be sent to the Moderator.

Moderator: David Sherman <dave@LSUC.ON.CA>
lsuc!dave%lsuc.uucp@GPU.UTCS.UTORONTO.CA

mailjc@GRIAN.CPS.ALTADENA.CA.US
ames!elroy!grian!mailjc@CIT-VAX.CALTECH.EDU
mailjc@CITPHOBO.BITNET

To provide a non-hostile environment for discussion among christians. Non-christians may join the list and "listen-in", but full blown debates between Christians and non-Christians are best carried out in soc.religion.christian or talk.religion newsgroups (those are Usenet groups).

All requests to be added to or deleted from this list, problems, questions, etc., should be sent to mailjc-request@GRIAN.CPS.ALTADENA.CA.US,
ames!elroy!grian!mailjc-request@CIT-VAX.CALTECH.EDU, or
mailjc-request@CITPHOBO.BITNET.

Coordinator: Liz Allen-Mitchell <liz@GRIAN.CPS.ALTADENA.CA.US>

Majordomo-Users@GreatCircle.COM   [Last Update 11/92]

Discussions concerning the use of, problems with and enhancements to the Majordomo mailing list maintenance package.

manchester@irss.njit.edu
...!uunet!irss.njit.edu!manchester

Purpose: This list is primarily a forum where people interested in bands representative of the "Manchester" sound can get together for discussion. Examples of bands being discussed here include the Stone Roses, Happy Mondays, Inspiral Carpets, the Charlatans, 808 State, Northside, etc. The definition of the Manchester sound is vague at best: use your best judgement when trying to determine if a group falls under the aegis of Manchester.

Both list and weekly digest formats are available.

Contact: manchester-request@irss.njit.edu -or- uunet!irss.njit.edu!manchester-request (Eric Ng)

mardi-gras@mintir.new-orleans.la.us   [Last Updated 9/92]

This list (mardi_gras) is an unmoderated list dealing with the celebration of Mardi Gras (also known as carnival, Fat Tuesday, etc.) Emphasis will be on the New Orleans carnival celebration: parades, customs, traditions, etc., but any submissions dealing with carnival in other cities/countries are welcome.

To join this list, send a request with the text: SUBSCRIBE MARDI-GRAS

to mail-server@mintir.new-orleans.la.us

Submissions to the list should be sent to: mardi_gras@mintir.new-orleans.la.us

Owner: Edward J. Branley <elendil@mintir.new-orleans.la.us>

MARINE-L@UOGUELPH.CA   [Last Updated 12-October-1991]

MARINE-L is an open Forum for the discussion and development of Marine-related Studies, and Semester-at-Sea/Education-at-Sea programs, including the development of e-mail connectivity at sea. Interest areas include:

    Marine electronic communications/networking/maintenance;
    Coastal/Marine Database;
    Marine Parks and Coastal National Parks;
    General coastal and marine ecosystems;
    Marine zoology and biology;
    Aquaculture;
    Ocean environmental sciences;
    Ocean and atmospheric sciences;
    Marine sciences research stations and marine museums;
    Maritime academies and sail-training;
    Marine engineering and ship design, shipbuilding, and shipyard management;
    Fisheries science;
    Stellar navigation;
    Satellite oceanography;
    Blue-water sailing and ship maintenance;
    History of Sea Education;
    Traditional navigation methods around the world;
    Co-operative links between Sea-Education programs;
    Ocean racing;
    Marine/maritime publishing and publications;
    Submersible design;
    Shipping movements;
    Ocean research, funding, grants and awards;
    Oceania and maritime anthropology;
    International shipboard/port relations;
    Intercultural communications;

Ocean resources management and ocean industries;
Weather information transmission and information storage/retrieval;
Ham and marine radio communications.

Within this broadbased Marine Studies format, it is the direction of the Forum to co-develop a multi-campus international program and to charter/purchase a large oceangoing vessel (tall-ship) to sail the Oceans, offering academics, researchers and students a diverse program of ongoing Marine Studies, together with the opportunity to visit international ports, attend foreign campus programs, both in conjunction with brief visits to ports, and full-credit courses during prolonged visits/full semester programs etc.

Further, through the Marine-L format, we will discuss the needs for shipboard LAN communications, plus ship-to-MARINE-L e-mail connectivity, general ship-to-mainland and international communications services, and the development of video telecourses for presentation via satellite, around the planet. It is hoped that broad cooperation will enable this program to be able to offer a truly international selection of credit courses for a wide group of campuses, academics, researchers and students.

To join in the Marine Studies List send an E-mail message to:

LISTSERV@UOGUELPH.CA (or LISTSERV@UOGUELPH.BITNET)

with this line in the message body:

SUB MARINE-L your name

Note that "your name" means your proper name and not your userid. LISTSERV@UOGUELPH will extract your userid from the message header.

If you are unfamiliar with lists and LISTSERV send the following to receive an index of help information:

INDEX HELPINFO

You may cancel your subscription to MARINE-L at any time by sending:

SIGNOFF MARINE-L

Note that commands are sent to LISTSERV and not MARINE-L. If you send them to the list you will have the pleasure of knowing everyone subscribing is reading them.

Owners are: Melcir Erskine-Richmond <USERNTCP@SFU.BITNET>
          Ted White <ZOOWHITE@VM.UOGUELPH.CA>

MARKET-L@UCF1VM.CC.UCF.EDU   [Last Updated June 1992]

Mailing list open to any marketing academics or practitioners of marketing who want to discuss marketing related topics.

Log files will be kept on a monthly basis.

BitNet users can subscribe by sending the following command to LISTSERV@UCF1VM: SUB MARKET-L Your_full_name where Your_full_name is your real name, not your userid; for example: SUB MARKET-L John Doe Non-BitNet users can subscribe by sending the SUB command as the text/body of a message to LISTSERV@UCF1VM.CC.UCF.EDU

Coordinator: UCF Postmaster <POSTMAST@UCF1VM.CC.UCF.EDU>

martial-arts@DRAGON.CSO.UIUC.EDU

uunet!uiucuxc!dragon.cso.uiuc.edu!martial-arts (uucp)

Mailing list for discussion of the martial arts.

Archives are kept on DRAGON.CSO.UIUC.EDU for Internet people. The file of current messages is 'martial-arts/archives' and is available thru ANONYMOUS login or through the martial-arts-request address for those without FTP access. Previous years' messages are kept in similar files, named 'martial-arts/archives.<year>'.

All requests to be added to or deleted from this list, problems, questions, etc., should be sent to martial-arts-request@DRAGON.CSO.UIUC.EDU.

Coordinator: Steven Miller <smiller@DRAGON.CSO.UIUC.EDU>

MASONIC <PTREI@ASGARD.BBN.COM>

Discussion of Freemasonry, its affiliated bodies, and other (non-university) fraternal and sororal organizations. This list is moderated, but is open to all.

Requests to be added to or deleted from the list, problems, questions, etc., should be sent to the Coordinator.

Coordinator: Peter Trei <PTREI@ASGARD.BBN.COM>

MATERI-L <JO%ILNCRD.BITNET@CUNYVM.CUNY.EDU>

A Bitnet newsletter on material sciences in Israel.

To subscribe, send a message to LISTSERV%TAUNIVM.BITNET@CUNYVM.CUNY.EDU with the body of the letter containing the command: SUB MATERI-L Your_Full_Name where Your_Full_Name; is your title, first name and last name.

Coordinator: Joseph van Zwaren de Zwarenstein <JO%ILNCRD.BITNET@CUNYVM.CUNY.EDU>

MBA-L%MARIST.BITNET@MITVMA.MIT.EDU

The MBA-L student curriculum discussion mailing list is for any information or news about MBA programs, their administration, problems, issues, questions, etc.; it is intended for administrators, faculty, and MBA students.

To subscribe send the following command to LISTSERV@MARIST (non-BitNet users send mail to LISTSERV%MARIST.BITNET@MITVMA.MIT.EDU): SUBSCRIBE MBA-L Your_Full_Name To unsubscribe, send: UNSUBSCRIBE MBA-L where Your_Full_Name is your real name, not your userid.

Coordinator: Bob Comerford <KGW101%URIMVS.BITNET@MITVMA.MIT.EDU>

MBU-L on LISTSERV at TTUVM1.BITNET

MBU stands for MegaByte University; this is intended as a forum for planning "electronic universities" of the future.

Coordinator:Jay Marme'
Indiana University-Bloomington
Business/SPEA Library
jmarme@ucs.indiana.edu

MCLR on LISTSERV@MSU

You are invited to actively participate, dialogue and exchange research ideas dealing with Latinos (Mexican, Mexican American, Chicano; Puerto Rican; Cuban or other Latino), living in the United States, via the Midwest Consortium for Latino Research List Service--MCLR-L.

Whether you wish to ask questions or share your wealth of knowledge on Latinos in the Midwest with other MCLR-L subscribers, MCLR-L can be the impetus for conducting collaborative and comparative research which can be used to develop culturally relevant public policy that is beneficial to Latinos.

To subscribe to MCLR-L use an interactive message (TELL or SEND) or send mail to LISTSERV@MSU.BITNET with the following command

SUB MCLR-L your full name

in the body or text (NOT in the subject) of the message or mail.

The Midwest Consortium for Latino Research (MCLR) is committed to the proliferation of research on and by Latinos in the Midwest. MCLR is dedicated to producing a viable Latino research agenda and increasing the intellectual pool of Latino faculty, staff and students in Midwestern institutions of higher education. MCLR has two intrinsically related goals: first, to address the multitude of economic, educational, political and social issues confronting Midwestern Latino communities; and, second, to promote Latino scholarship.

The mission of MCLR is to facilitate the provision of opportunities leading to:

* A receptive enviroment to support the development and production of research on and by Latinos, including assistance for funding;

* A network for the development of Latino scholars, as well as to contribute to the identification, recruitment and retention of more Latino faculty at member institutions;

* A network of Latino students at the graduate and undergraduate levels for the development of future generations of Latino professionals;

* A source of information on Latinos in the form of databases, archives, library collections and publications;

* A link to a range of institutions of higher education in the Midwest which share a committment to the development of Latino scholarship;

* A link to the major Latino community organizations and leadership in the Midwest to ensure the application of new knowledge to address the problems and concerns of the population; and,

* A link to national level consortia and Latino scholar networks which share the mission of the Consortium.

If you have any questions or comments about MCLR, the list, etc., please send them to MCLRIMOD@MSU or write to:

Ramiro Gonzales ramirog@msu on bitnet

MDS32-L%INDYCMS.BITNET@VM1.NODAK.EDU

MDS32-L is a LISTSERV list for discussion of creative ideas and techniques using MDS32, Menu Design System from Ergodic, Inc., for VAX/VMS systems.

MDS32-L originates on the list server at Indiana University - Purdue University at Indianapolis; LISTSERV@INDYCMS.BITNET, where you may subscribe to the list by issuing the following command via interactive message or mail: SUBscribe MDS32-L Your_name where Your_name is your full name,not your user Id. Non-BitNet users can subscribe by sending the command in the text/body of a message to LISTSERV%INDYCMS.BITNET@VM1.NODAK.EDU.

Coordinator: Holly Lee Stowe <IHLS400%INDYCMS.BITNET@VM1.NODAK.EDU>

MECH-L%UTARLVM1.BITNET@CUNYVM.CUNY.EDU

Mailing list for discussion of any topics pertinent to the Mechanical Engineering communities such as meeting announcements, software evaluation, composite material research and others. MECH-L welcomes any suggestions and comments and encourages faculty/students in ME-related areas (such Aerospace and Civil) to join the list.

To subscribe, send the following command to LISTSERV@UTARLVM1 via mail or interactive message: SUB MECH-L your_full_name where "your_full_name" is your name. For example: SUB MECH-L Joan Doe Non-BitNet users can subscribe by sending the text: SUB MECH-L your_full_name in the body of a message to LISTSERV%UTARLVM1.BITNET@CUNYVM.CUNY.EDU.

Coordinator: S. Nomura <B470SSN%UTARLVM1.BITNET@CUNYVM.CUNY.EDU>

MEDCONS%FINHUTC.BITNET@VM1.NODAK.EDU

This list is not intended for non-professionals or patients, which still are welcome to follow the activity on the list. It is intended for Physicians and investigators in the medical field to allow medical consulting on a voluntary basis. The final responsibility for the care of patients is always that of the personal Physician exclusively.

Short descriptions of cases "hard to solve" in the form anamnesis status and laboratory findings - question: what bothered the patient - followed by the diagnosis and cure are encouraged. Real bedside problem solving could also be enlightened by short descriptions of the most exotic and puzzling cases the colleagues have encountered.

Absolute anonymity for the patients is required. Please favour Latin and professional terminology to make it easier to keep laymen from obstructing the list. Contributions from the field of so called alternative medicine are obsolete, and will not be redistributed to the subscribers.

BitNet users can subscribe by sending the following command to LISTSERV@FINHUTC: SUBSCRIBE MEDCONS Your_full_name where "Your_full_name" is your real name, not your login Id. Non-BitNet users can join by sending the above command in the text/body of a message to LISTSERV%FINHUTC.BITNET@VM1.NODAK.EDU.

Coordinator: Dr. Mikael Peder <PEDER%FINUH.BITNET@VM1.NODAK.EDU>
<PEDER@FINUH.BITNET>
<PEDER@CC.HELSINKI.FI>

MEDIA-L%BINGVMA.BITNET@MITVMA.MIT.EDU

Mailing list for people in the media services profession who would like to share information or ask questions about educational communications and technology issues.

To subscribe send the following command to LISTSERV@BINGVMB (non-BitNet users send mail to LISTSERV%BINGVMB.BITNET@MITVMA.MIT.EDU) SUBSCRIBE MEDIA-L your_full_name To unsubscribe, send UNSUBSCRIBE MEDIA-L

Coordinator: Jim Blake <AS0JEB%BINGVMA.BITNET@MITVMA.MIT.EDU>

MEDIEV-L on LISTSERV@UKANVM.BITNET or LISTSERV@UKANVM.CC.UKANS.EDU

An unmoderated discussion list for scholars and students of the Middle Ages, which, for our present purposes, comprise the period A.D 283 - 1500. Although announcements are in English, subscribers are encouraged to use the language in which they feel most comfortable.

Subscribers are reminded that discussion lists are intended to facilitate discussion rather than provide services. The benefits that participants derive from a list depends entirely upon what they are willing to contribute.

To subscribe:

e-mail LISTSERV AT UKANVM on BITNET or LISTSERV@UKANVM.CC.UKANS.EDU on the Internet with the BODY of the mail containing the command:

SUB MEDIEV-L your name

e.g., SUB MEDIEV-L John Doe

MEDIEV-L discussions are not archived, but UKANVM History Lists maintains an anonymous/guest FTP site named MALIN.

To reach MALIN:

FTP KUHUB.CC.UKANS.EDU Userid: ANONYMOUS Password YOURUSERID CD DUA9:[MALIN] DIR

Updated catalogues named MALIN.CAT are periodically posted. MALIN invites the submission of materials that UKANVM History List subscribers consider appropriate for MALIN to maintain, and is happy, within the limits of its capacity, to serve as a repository for newsletters and similar materials. MALIN works cooperatively with FTP ra.msstate.edu.

MEDIEV-L@UKANVM is affiliated with the international HISTORY network and cooperates actively with all other lists similarly affiliated.

If you encounter any difficulties, contact:

Jeff Gardner JGARDNER@UKANVM.BITNET or JGARDNER@UKANVM.CC.UKANS.EDU Lynn Nelson LHNELSON@UKANVM.BITNET or LHNELSON@UKANVM.CC.UKANS.EDU

MEDINF-L%DEARN.BITNET@CUNYVM.CUNY.EDU

Mailing list for people working in medical data processing/medical informatics.

For those in BITNET and subscribed to the list its content can be made availabe by: TELL LISTSERV AT DEARN REVIEW MEDINF-L. General information about LISTSERV can be obtained with TELL LISTSERV at DEARN INFO.

All requests to be added to or deleted from this list, problems, questions, etc., should be sent to PL_REI%DHVMHH1.BITNET@CUNYVM.CUNY.EDU or REICHERTZ@SUMEX.STANFORD.EDU. For BITNET users direct subscription is possible by: TELL LISTSERV@DEARN SUBSCRIBE MEDINF-L <full name>, and signing off may be done by TELL LISTSERV@DEARN SIGNOFF MEDINF-L.

MEDLIB-L on LISTSERV@UBVM
MEDLIB-L on LISTSERV@UBVM.CC.BUFFALO.EDU

MEDLIB-L is a forum for librarians in the health sciences. Discussion will include practical and theoretical issues in both the public and technical service areas. This list may be used to exchange ideas, questions, concerns and announcements of particular interest to health sciences librarians.

To subscribe to the list send a message or mail to LISTSERV@UBVM on BITNET or LISTSERV@UBVM.CC.BUFFALO.EDU on the Internet with the text or body of the message containing the command

SUB MEDLIB-L yourfirstname yourlastname

Owner: HSLSTART@UBVM (Nancy Start)
Notebook: Yes, public, monthly
Subscription: Open

MEDNETS%NDSUVM1.BITNET@VM1.NODAK.EDU

A forum to discuss medical telecommunication networks in the areas of clinical practice, medical research, and administration. The list is intended to be used for ongoing discussions, information searches, contact searches, surveys, and so on.

Contributions sent to this list are automatically archived. You may obtain a list of the available archive files by sending the command "INDEX MEDNETS" to LISTSERV@VM1.NODAK.EDU or LISTSERV@NDSUVM1 on BITNET. These files can then be retrieved by means of a "GET MEDNETS LOGyymmw" command, or by using the database search facilities of LISTSERV. Send an "INFO DATABASE" command to LISTSERV@VM1.NODAK.EDU for more information on DATABASE searches.

You may also access these archives via anonymous FTP on the Internet. FTP to host VM1.NODAK.EDU (134.129.111.1) with any password. After you are connected enter CD MEDNETS to access the archives (our file system is NOT hierarchical so to go back to the "root" you would enter CD ANONYMOUS.

BitNet users may subscribe by sending a message or e-mail to LISTSERV@NDSUVM1 with the following line in the text/body: SUB MEDNETS your full name where "your full name" is your real name, not your login Id. Non-BitNet users can join the list by sending the above command as the only line in the text/body of a message to LISTSERV@VM1.NODAK.EDU or to LISTSERV%NDSUVM1.BITNET@VM1.NODAK.EDU.

Coordinator: Marty Hoag <NU021172@VM1.NODAK.EDU>
              <NU021172%NDSUVM1.BITNET@VM1.NODAK.EDU>
              <NU021172@NDSUVM1>

MEDNEWS%ASUACAD.BITNET@CUNYVM.CUNY.EDU

The MEDNEWS LISTSERV list is for distribution of the Health Info-Com Network medical newsletter. It is distributed weekly and contains the latest MMWR from the Center for Disease Control, weekly AIDS Statistics, FDA bulletins, medical news from the United Nations, and other assorted medical news items. Submissions for the newsletter are welcomed; please contact the Editor if you have any questions or newsletter submissions.

To subscribe send the following command to LISTSERV@ASUACAD (non-BitNet users send mail to LISTSERV%ASUACAD.BITNET@CUNYVM.CUNY.EDU with the command in the message body): SUBSCRIBE MEDNEWS Your_Full_Name where Your_Full_Name is your real name, not your userid. To unsubscribe, send: UNSUBSCRIBE MEDNEWS

Editor: David Dodell <ATW1H%ASUACAD.BITNET@CUNYVM.CUNY.EDU>

MEDSTU-L on LISTSERV@UNMVM

The University of New Mexico is pleased to announce that effective immediately, we are hosting a new Listserv discussion list for medical students worldwide. The name of the new list is MEDSTU-L and initially, the list will be unmoderated with subscriptions open. Due to a present limitation on disk storage, notebooks will be kept for a period of 30 days.

The impetus for this list was mail I sent out several weeks ago soliciting medical students with e-mail accounts to exchange mail with medical students here. As a result of that solicitation, I found that while there are many medical students with e-mail accounts, most of them are unaware of others with e-mail accounts. Thus, this list. While it is an open list and therefore there is no way of verifying the subscription request, the two list owners respectfully request that the list be limited to students in medical schools.

To subscribe to the list send e-mail to LISTSERV@UNMVM and in the body of the message say SUB MEDSTU-L your_first_name your_last_name

If you have any questions, please let us know.

Owners:
  Art St. George STGEORGE@UNMB or STGEORGE@BOOTES.UNM.EDU
  David Goldstein DGOLDST@UNMB or DGOLDST@BOOTES.UNM.EDU

Art St. George, Ph.D.
Executive Network Services Officer
University of New Mexico

High-Tech Access: Soft Touch Access
stgeorge@unmb (BITNET)   (505) 277-8046 VOICE
stgeorge@bootes.unm.edu (Internet)   (505) 277-8101 FAX

MELLON-L@VM1.YORKU.CA   [Last Updated 12-October-1991]

MELLON-L is an unmoderated list for anyone holding a Mellon Fellowship or interested in Mellon related happenings. MELLON-L postings include publicizing local Mellon conferences, requests for aid from Mellon Fellows, distribution of information about the fellowships, and conversation on issues of concern to Mellons (e.g. teaching in the humanities, personal life and academia, applying for jobs). In short, MELLON-L will continue the discussions which began at the Mellon Conferences at Bryn Mawr.

To subscribe to this list send a mail/note message to LISTSERV@YORKVM1 or LISTSERV@VM1.YORKU.CA with the one-line message:

SUBSCRIBE MELLON-L your-full-name

VM systems may use: TELL LISTSERV at YORKVM1 SUBSCRIBE MELLON-L your-full-name

Owner: GL250264@YUORION Robert Stainton

melrose-place@ferkel.ucsb.edu   [Last Update 8/92]

Purpose: Discussion of the Fox TV show *Melrose Place*.

Contact: melrose-place-request@ferkel.ucsb.edu (Jim Lick)

MENDELE on LISTSERV@YALEVM or LISTSERV@YALEVM.YCC.YALE.EDU

The purpose of this list is to promote a friendly atmosphere for the discussion of Yiddish literature and language. Submissions are acceptable in Yiddish or English. The list is moderated.

It is a joint venture of Trinity College and the Classics Department of Yale University.

Please address questions to: nmiller@trincc (Bitnet) nmiller@vax1.trincoll.edu (Internet)

To subscribe, send the following command to LISTSERV@YALEVM (or for Internet subscribers to LISTSERV@YALEVM.YCC.YALE.EDU) in the BODY of mail or in an interactive message:

SUB MENDELE your_full_name

where "your_full_name" is your name. For example:

SUB MENDELE Yisroel Yoshua Singer

  Owner: Norman Miller <NMILLER@TRINCC>
  Owner: Victor Bers <VBERS@YALEVM>

MEXICO-L@TECMTYVM.MTY.ITESM.MX
MEXICO-L@TECMTYVM.BITNET

Mexico is a large and diversified country, with many different customs, subcultures, etc., as well as cities, places to go and things to do when visiting. However, many of the wonderful things that this beautiful country has to offer are unknown to most people in other parts of the world. The purpose of this list is to present to the world as many of these attractions as possible. Anybody interested in knowing more about Mexico is invited to join.

BitNet users can join by issuing the following command: TELL LISTSERV AT TECMTYVM SUBSCRIBE MEXICO-L Your_full_name or the equivalent for sending messages, if your operating system is not VM/SP. Example: TELL LISTSERV AT TECMTYVM SUBSCRIBE MEXICO-L David Doe Non-BitNet users can join by sending a message to LISTSERV@TECMTYVM.MTY.ITESM.MX, with the one-line command "SUBSCRIBE MEXICO-L Your_full_name" in the body/text (*NOT* in the Subject: field).

Coordinator: Guillermo Rosas Madrigal <PL335466@TECMTYVM.MTY.ITESM.MX>
<PL335466@TECMTYVM.BITNET>

MH-USERS@ICS.UCI.EDU

MH-Users is a discussion group which focuses on the UCI version of the Rand Message Handling (MH) system; it is a list is for the MH user community at large. MH runs on a number of versions of UNIX (4.xBSD, v7, xenix) on top of a number of mail transport systems (MMDF-{I,II}, SendMail, stand-alone (with UUCP support)); for information on getting an MH distribution, contact Bug-MH@ICS.UCI.EDU. Appropriate topics are:

- questions about how to use MH
- tips on MH usage
- exchange of MH shell scripts

As a general rule, messages submitted to MH-Users should *NOT* be submitted to MH-Workers (a list with a different charter).

All requests to be added to or deleted from this list, along with problems, questions and suggestions, should be sent to MH-Users-Request@ICS.UCI.EDU.

Coordinator: John L. Romine (JLR3) <Bug-MH@ICS.UCI.EDU>

MH-WORKERS@ICS.UCI.EDU

MH-Workers is a discussion group which focuses on the UCI version of the Rand Message Handling (MH) system; it is a list is for MH maintainers and experts. MH runs on a number of versions of UNIX (4.xBSD, v7, xenix) on top of a number of mail transport systems (MMDF-{I,II}, SendMail, stand-alone (with UUCP support)); for information on getting an MH distribution, contact Bug-MH@ICS.UCI.EDU. Appropriate topics are:

- questions on how to configure MH
- tips on MH configuration
- exchange of MH bug reports (and fixes)

As a general rule, messages submitted to MH-Workers should *NOT* be submitted to MH-Users (a list with a different charter).

All requests to be added to or deleted from this list, along with problems, questions and suggestions, should be sent to MH-Workers-Request@ICS.UCI.EDU.

Coordinator: John L. Romine (JLR3) <Bug-MH@ICS.UCI.EDU>

MHSnews@ICS.UCI.EDU
mhsnews@SINTEF.NO (from Europe)
s=mhsnews; o=sintef; prmd=uninett; admd= ; c=no;

This conference/mailing list is open to anyone who is seriously interested in implementing the CCITT X.400 (MHS) message handling protocols. The conference/mailing list can discuss such things as how to understand and interpret the MHS recommendations, how to map existing mail systems and mail network features onto the MHS structure etc.

MHS gateway discussions can be found in IFIP-GTWY@TIS.LLNL.GOV.

To minimize international communications costs, distribution lists are being maintained in Europe and North America. European users should contribute messages to mhsnews@SINTEF.NO (s=mhsnews; o=sintef; prmd=uninett; admd= ; c=no;) and North American users should send messages to MHSnews@ICS.UCI.EDU. Messages sent to either list will be forwarded to subscribers to the other lists.

BITNET and NORTHNET subscribers will be served by a LISTSERV facility at BYU in the USA. EARN subscribers can be served from BYU, but we would prefer EARN to be served by some site in Europe, if it can be arranged.

USENET "subscribers" will be served by a Moderated feed to USENET with "inet" distribution. "Followup" contributions from USENET subscribers will be fed by the moderator into MHSnews@ICS.UCI.EDU.

To subscribe to the conference: European users: Send a message to mhsnews-request@SINTEF.NO s=mhsnews-request; o=sintef; prmd=uninett; admd= ; c=no; North American users: Send a message to mhsnews-request@ICS.UCI.EDU

Coordinators: Tim Kehres <kehres@TIS.LLNL.GOV>

Alf Hansen <alf-hansen@vax.runit.unit.uninett>

MICS-L%HDETUD1.BITNET@CUNYVM.CUNY.EDU

Technically-oriented LISTSERV distribution list on the topic of Morino's MVS Information Control System. Also see the BILLING list.

You can subscribe to this list by sending a request to LISTSERV at HDETUD1: TELL LISTSERV AT HDETUD1 SUB MICS-L your_full_name or by sending mail to LISTSERV%HDETUD1.BITNET@CUNYVM.CUNY.EDU containing the line: SUB MICS-L your_full_name

Coordinator: Rob van Hoboken <RCOPROB%HDETUD1.BITNET@CUNYVM.CUNY.EDU>

MIDEUR-L%UBVM.BITNET@VM1.NODAK.EDU

Mailing list for discussion of Middle European politics, etc.

An unmoderated list concerning the history, culture, politics and current affairs of those countries lying between the Mediterranean/ Adriatic and the Baltic Seas, and between the German/Austrian borders and the Soviet Union. The emphasis is particularly on the nationalities policies of these countries, their economic development, their possible union or disunion, and their place in a united Europe. Cross-posting with lists concerning West Europe/ Germany and the USSR is encouraged where the topics bear directly on Middle Europe.

It is presumed that the bulk of the discussions will be on serious current or past events, treated in a scholarly manner. However, there is no set policy and personal observations, advice-seeking, and gossip are not ruled out.

BitNet users may subscribe by sending the following command to LISTSERV@UBVM via interactive message or e-mail: SUB MIDEUR-L Your full name where "Your full name" is your real name, not your login Id. Non-BitNet users can join by sending the above command as the only line in the text/body of a message to LISTSERV%UBVM.BITNET@VM1.NODAK.EDU.

Coordinator: Jan George Frajkor <NEWSTV1@CARLETON.CA>

military@ATT.ATT.COM

Mailing list for discussions of military technology and related matters. The list is gatewayed bi-directionally with the Usenet newsgroup "sci.military", which is moderated; it is distributed in the form of a daily digest.

All requests to be added to or deleted from this list, problems, questions, etc., should be sent to military-request@ATT.ATT.COM.

Moderator: Bill Thacker <military@ATT.ATT.COM> <military@CBNEWS.ATT.COM>

Milton-L@URVAX.URICH.EDU   [Last Updated 12-October-1991]
Milton-L@URVAX.BITNET

Milton-L is a moderated electronic digest for scholars, students, and others interested in the life and work of John Milton. As participation grows Milton-L will also serve as a repository for information on the current state of Milton scholarship (proposals and projects, bibliographies, and conferences).

To subscribe, please send a brief note to Milton-request@URVAX (or to Milton-request@urvax.urich.edu for Internet addresses). Any questions regarding Milton-L may be sent to the list moderator, Kevin Creamer at Milton-request@URVAX.

List Owner: Kevin J.T. Creamer (CREAMER@URVAX.BITNET) (Creamer@urvax.urich.edu)

MIND-L@Asylum.SF.CA.US   [Last Update 9/92]

The Mind-l mailing list is a forum devoted to discussions on the use, construction, and future potential of mind machines. Mind machines are electronic devices or methods that non-invasively alter human consciousness. Other topics of discussion can include: meditation, accelerated learning, hypnosis, float tanks, nootropics and other methods of altering consciousness . A strong emphasis is placed on the scientific study of these methods as well as the construction of mind machines devices.

To subscribe to this list send a mail/note message to MIND-L-REQUEST@ASYLUM.SF.CA.US with your email address.

Note that MIND-L started out life on a LISTSERV but is now a regular mailing list hosted on a UNIX system.

MIND-L has an anonymous FTP area containing archives and related material located on asylum.sf.ca.us in /pub/mind-l.

LIST OWNER: John Romkey <romkey@asylum.sf.ca.us>

MINISTRY-L%GACVAX1.BITNET@VM1.NODAK.EDU

An open forum for the discussion of concerns and experiences of people who are planning a career in religious ministry, or for those considering such a move. All denominations are welcome (at least!), and a variety of personal backgrounds would probably be helpful. What is intended here, if it will work, is a discussion of the issues one faces as one approaches the question of the ministry as a career.

BitNet users can subscribe by sending the following command to MAILSERV@GACVAX1 as mail text/body: SUBSCRIBE MINISTRY-L Your_full_name. where Your_full_name is your real name, not your loginid; for example: SUBSCRIBE MINISTRY-L Joe Shmoe Interactive commands will not function; THIS IS NOT A LISTSERV. Non-BitNet users can subscribe by sending the above command in the text/body of a message to MAILSERV%GACVAX1.BITNET@VM1.NODAK.EDU.

Coordinator: Charles Piehl <UNDERHILL%GACVAX1.BITNET@VM1.NODAK.EDU>

MISC on LISTSERV@TREARN.BITNET

The MISC@TREARN list is for all kinds of information, requests, problems or searches NOT related to computers. This list is for all people directly and especially indirectly related to computers.

This list is for discussing subjects that contain everything else than computers. If you want to get some help from someone from another country but don't know anybody there this list is for that! Or you may want to get advice on how to fix your dripping faucet. Or if you want to know if there is a special make-up product sold in France you can ask this to the list.

MISC is operational now. Review, Subscription and Submission is OPEN. Confirmation is yearly. To subscribe to the list send the following command to LISTSERV@TREARN on BITNET (NOT to MISC@TREARN) either with an interactive command (TELL, SEND) OR in the BODY of e-mail (NOT the subject):

SUB MISC your name

The owner is Esra Delen (ESRA@TREARN.BITNET).

MISG-L@psuvm.psu.edu   [Last Updated 12-October-1991]

Misg-Net is a mailing list (MISG-L) of those who are interested in Malaysian affairs and are reachable by electronic mail.

Note : Most discussions are in Bahasa Malaysia (Malay Language)

To be a member of MISG-NET, please send the following info.

(1) E-mail to axh113@psuvm.psu.edu or mmz103@psuvm.psu.edu

(2) Your name, major, current university, and some other info about you...

MISG-NET Maintainer:
Azmi Hashim

<AXH113@psuvm.psu.edu>
Md. Mahfudz Md. Zan
<mmz103@psuvm.psu.edu>

MLA-L%IUBVM.BITNET@VM1.NODAK.EDU

Mail distribution service for the Music Library Association; this is being done on a trial basis. It is intended that the list be used for various activities of MLA that can benefit by wide-scale distribution (such as announcements of deadlines for NOTES and the Newsletter, news items, general inquiries about MLA activities, etc.). The list could also be used for reference inquiries and other topics of interest to the music library community.

The list will initially be limited to mail distribution. No archives will be maintained and no file/document server capability will be utilized (these additional features may be considered at a later time).

BitNet users can subscribe in several ways: For IBM (VM/CMS) systems TELL LISTSERV AT IUBVM SUBSCRIBE MLA-L <your name> For VAX (VMS) systems SEND LISTSERV@IUBVM SUBSCRIBE <your name> Send a mail message to LISTSERV at IUBVM which consists of one line (in the BODY or TEXT of the message): SUBSCRIBE MLA-L <your name> Non-BitNet users can also subscribe by sending the above message to LISTSERV%IUBVM.BITNET@VM1.NODAK.EDU. If all else fails, send mail to the Coordinator.

Coordinator: A. Ralph Papakhian <PAPAKHI%IUBVM.BITNET@VM1.NODAK.EDU> Executive Secretary, Music Library Association

MMDF2@SH.CS.NET

A mailing list for people who implement, install or maintain the MMDF2 mailer on UNIX hosts. MMDF2 is widely used in many environments, including the Internet and CSNET's PhoneNet.

All requests to be added to or deleted from this list, problems, questions, etc., should be sent to MMDF2-REQUEST@SH.CS.NET or to CIC@SH.CS.NET.

Coordinators: David Herron <david@TWG.COM>

MMEDIA-L on LISTSERV@VMTECMEX

The Multimedia discussion list has been opened in order to provide a forum to discuss this growing field in education and training. It is a listserv list located at MMEDIA-L@VMTECMEX, please send your commands to LISTSERV@ VMTECMEX.

To subscrive to MMEDIA-L send mail to LISTSERV@VMTECMEX.BITNET with the following command in the body or text of the mail:

SUB MMEDIA-L yourfirstname yourlastname

The list runs unmoderated with monthly logs available.

Owner: Alejandro Kurczyn S. <499229@VMTECMEX>

MMM-PEOPLE@ISI.EDU

Discussion group for those active or interested in multimedia mail. The intent is to use this list mainly for discussion of the developing multimedia mail procedures and protocols.

The mail sent to MMM-PEOPLE is kept on host VENERA.ISI.EDU in file mmm/mmm-people.mail. The distribution list is kept in file mmm/mmm-people.list. One may copy these public access files via FTP using the username ANONYMOUS and password GUEST.

All requests to be added to or deleted from this list, problems, questions, etc., should be sent to MMM-PEOPLE-REQUEST@ISI.EDU or contact Ann Westine, "WESTINE@ISI.EDU".

ModBrits on LISTSERV@KentVM   [Last Updated 1/92]

or LISTSERV@KentVM.kent.edu

ModBrits, is the international computer discussion group for scholars, teachers, and students of Modern British and Irish literature (1895-1955) and those who share their interests.

ModBrits offers a medium for announcements and bulletins, notes and queries, scholarly papers. But ModBrits also offers spontaneous and informal conversation on its subject(s).

Members can submit formal newsletters and announcements, calls for papers, employment announcements, and notices of work in progress and of public events for electronic distribution. They can also send short reviews of scholarly books, remarks about videotape and film resources, abstracts of news reports, and even draft articles for comment by other members. Reports from Britain and Ireland about developments related to the subject matter of ModBrits are welcome. Queries and notes about fine or grand points are expected to generate some of the conversation on ModBrits.

Lengthier electronic texts such as conference papers, articles, or theses submitted by ModBrits members may be made available for on-line retrieval on an individual basis. Quite possibly, computerized (electronic) texts of works by Conrad, Joyce, Lawrence, Woolf, and others will also be archived. Other forms of electronic information may also become available, such as concordances, sample journals, publishers' catalogues, and bibliographical resources. An e-mail directory of ModBritians will be accessible to all members, to facilitate the electronic distribution of seminar papers prior to a conference (for example) and to encourage private correspondence and collaboration.

E-mail inquiries about the discussion group should be sent directly to ModBrits@KentVM.Kent.Edu. (The appended '.Kent.Edu' is necessary only for those desiring access through INTERNET; BITNET users may omit this part of the 'address' or 'domain'.) Failing that, contact Editing@KentVM (the e-mail address of the Center for Conrad Studies, Institute for Bibliography & Editing, Kent State University, Kent, Ohio 44242, USA).

MODLSHOP on LISTSERV@irishvma (BITNET)   [Last Updated 1/92]
          or LISTSERV@vma.cc.nd.edu (Internet)

The mailing list MODLSHOP has been created to discuss the Macintosh modeling package ModelShop. The application, produced by San Francisco-based MacroMind-Paracomp, is used primarily to quickly create three-dimensional models, produce low-quality rendered views, and generate animated "walk-thrus" or "fly-bys" of models.

This mailing list exists to discuss techniques, problems, "undocumented features", and other user concerns with ModelShop. I (listowner) frequently call MM-P's customer support line with bug reports and questions, and they have expressed some interest in monitoring and possibly contributing to this list in the future.

The list was created in January 1992.

To subscribe via BITNET, send the following command to LISTSERV@IRISHVMA via mail or interactive message:

SUB MODLSHOP your_full_name

where "your_full_name" is your name. For example:

SUB MODLSHOP Sanjay Singal

To subscribe via Internet, send the same one-line message to LISTSERV@VMA.CC.ND.EDU in the BODY of the mail (NOT the subject).

To submit messages to the list, send e-mail to MODLSHOP@VMA.CC.ND.EDU or MODLSHOP@IRISHVMA. If you are unfamiliar with mailing lists, please save these instructions for future reference. Please address any concerns or questions regarding the operation of the list to me directly.

Owner: Mike W. Miller <MWMILLER@IRISHVMA> or <Mike.W.Miller.40@nd.edu>

MOPOLY-L on LISTSERV@UMCVMB.BITNET   [Last Updated 28-January-1992]
or LISTSERV@UMCVMB.MISSOURI.EDU

A new discussion list, MOPOLY-L has been established at UMCVMB for the topic of Missouri Political Issues.

The discussion on this list will be pretty much up to those who participate. Topics I can think of include any Missouri state-wide issue, whether candidates for office or other issues. With the current revenue shortage and it's effect on education, that may well be a popular topic.

Also, there may be some local issues that have wide interest, again, it's up to the participants.

This is a LISTSERV managed list, so normal subscription requests apply. To subscribe send mail to LISTSERV@UMCVMB.BITNET or on the Internet to LISTSERV@UMCVMB.MISSOURI.EDU with the body containing the command SUB MOPOLY-L yourfirstname yourlastname

> Owner:
> Len Rugen   C4322LR@UMVMA.BITNET
> Sr. Systems Programmer   C4322LR@UMVMA.UMSYSTEM.EDU
> University of Missouri System   (314) 882-9237

moto.chassis@OCE.ORST.EDU

Mailing list devoted to the theory and practice of motorcycle chassis design and construction.

Requests to be added to or deleted from the list, problems, questions, etc., should be sent to moto.chassis-request@OCE.ORST.EDU.

Coordinator: Paul O'Neill <pvo@OCE.ORST.EDU> <pvo3366@SAPPHIRE.OCE.ORST.EDU>

MOUNT-L on LISTSERV@TRMETU

MOUNT-L is meant for the discussion and communication amoung mountaineers.

To subscribe to MOUNT_L send mail or interactive message to LISTSERV@TRMETU on BITNET with the TEXT or BODY of the message containing the command:

SUB MOUNT-L yourfirstname yourlastname

> Loopcheck=Full   Title='MOUNT-L'
> Review= Public   Subscription= Open
> Notify= No   Reply-to= List,Respect
> Ack = Msg   Files=Yes
> Validate= Store only   Stats= Normal,Private
> x-Tags= Comment   Formcheck= Yes
> Notebook= Yes,A,Monthly,Public Mail-via= Distribute
> Errors-to= Owner   Formcheck= Yes

> Owner= TURAN@TRMETU (Metin TURAN) on BITNET

> Metin TURAN   MWSC
> Middle East Technical University   Middle East Technical University
> Computer Center, Student Advisor   Mountaineering and Winter Sports Club
> 06531 ANKARA   TURKEY   06531 Ankara   TURKEY
> Voice:(4) 2237100 / 2086   Voice:(4) 2237100 / 2052
> Bitnet:TURAN@TRMETU   Bitnet:MOUNT@TRMETU

MsgGroup Interest in electronic mail, message formats, message systems, and the sociological implications of the above.

This list ceased its operation during the summer of 1986 after almost 11 continuous years of operation, but the record has been kept intact for anyone who cares to poke and search for the nuggets that are hidden therein.

Achives are kept on host WSMR-SIMTEL20.ARMY.MIL in Twenex Mail files PD2:<ARCHIVES.MSGGROUP>xxx.*, where xxx.* is a specific file name with (in most cases) 100 messages per file -- MSGGROUP.* indicates a message file, and SURVEY.* indicates a message containing a list/index of the messages in a specific number range.

Archives Coordinator: Frank J. Wancho <WANCHO@WSMR-SIMTEL20.ARMY.MIL>

MSMAIL-L on LISTSERV@YALEVM.BITNET or LISTSERV@YaleVM.YCC.Yale.EDU

MSMAIL-L is a Listserv list for the purpose of discussing Microsoft mail.

To subscribe send an interactive message (BITNET only) or e-mail to LISTSERV@YALEVM on BITNET or LISTSERV@yalevm.ycc.yale.edu with the following command in the BODY:

SUB MSMAIL-L yourfirstname yourlastname Eg. sub msmail-l Bill Gates

Owner: Peter Furmonavicius <PETER@YALEVM.BITNET> <PETER@YaleVM.YCC.Yale.EDU>

MSSQL-L on LISTSERV@DUKEFSB
MSSQL-L on LISTSERV@DUKEFSB.AC.DUKE.EDU

A list dealing with Microsoft's SQL Server for OS/2. This is the only discussion group for MS SQL Server that I'm aware of on any network (other then Microsoft's own). If you are aware of any other lists, please let me know.

Also, if you know of another user or discussion group that would find this topic of interest, please forward this note to them. Please pardon any multiple mailings.

When subscribing, please address your subscriptions to: ListServ@Dukefsb.Bitnet (BITNET) or ListServ@DUKEfsb.AC.DUKE.EDU (Internet).

The list name is: MSSQL-L

When sending mail please send it to: MSSQL-L@DUKEfsb.BITNET (BITNET) or MSSQL-L@Dukefsb.AC.DUKE.EDU (Internet).

> Owner:
> Brian Eder
> Eder@dukefsb.bitnet
> Duke Univ.

mst3k <rsk@gynko.circ.upenn.edu>   [Last Updated 28-January-1992]

Purpose: MST3K is a moderated mailing list for fans of the television show "Mystery Science Theater 3000", which is shown on the Comedy Channel (available on various cable networks in North America). Requests to be added/deleted and submissions for the list itself should be sent to the address above; please include "mst3k" somewhere on the "Subject:" line of each message to ensure that it is filed correctly. Archives of the list are maintained, but are not FTP'able yet.

Contact: rsk@gynko.circ.upenn.edu (Rich Kulawiec)

mug@MERIDIAN.COM

Mailing list for users of Meridian Software Systems's Ada compilers.

Requests to be added to or deleted from the list, problems, questions, etc., should be sent to mug-request@MERIDIAN.COM.

> Coordinators: Jerry N. Sweet <jns@ARRAKIS.MERIDIAN.COM>
> Meridian support staff <support@MERIDIAN.COM>

Multicast@Arizona.EDU [Last Update 9/92]

The multicast mailing list has been set up for discussion of multicast and broadcast issues in an OSI network environment. In the current CCITT recommendations and ISO standards, there is little or no mention of multicast capability. However, there is work in this area in other environments.

The goal of this mailing list is to facilitate discussion on the following topics:

- what can we learn from existing multicast and broadcast work in other environments (local area networks, TCP/IP Internets, XTP, ST-II, etc.)

- what can we do to facilitate quality international standards (ISO and CCITT, especially) for multicast data transmission

To subscribe to the multicast mailing list, send a message to Multicast-Request@Arizona.EDU with your full name and preferred electronic mail address. Archives of the list and a database of contributed documents are also available on Arizona.EDU.

List Maintainer: Joel Snyder (Multicast-Request@Arizona.EDU)

MUS@TMC.EDU
   masscomp@SOMA.BCM.TMC.EDU

Masscomp Users Society (MUS) mailing list; people who are interested in the Masscomp line of computers are invited to join.

All requests to be added to or deleted from this list, problems, questions, etc., should be sent to mus-request@TMC.EDU.

Coordinator: Stan Barber <sob@BCM.TMC.EDU>

MUSEUM-L on LISTSERV@UNMVM.BITNET [Last Updated 12-October-1991]

Museum-L is a general interest dicussion list for museum professionals and others interested in museum related issues.

It is hoped that an open discussion by those who work in exhibits, education, collection, or curatorial positions can foster an understanding among those who work in museums. It is also hoped that the discussion can share ideas and information regarding new methods of interpreting information for visitors, both high tech and low tech.

To subscribe, send a one line message to LISTSERV@UNMVM.BITNET:

subscribe MUSEUM-L Your_Full_Name

If I can be of further assistance, please feel free to contact me.

Owner: john chadwick chadwick@unmb (bitnet) chadwick@bootes.unm.edu (internet)

music-research%prg.oxford.ac.uk@NSS.CS.UCL.AC.UK

The Music-Research electronic mail redistribution list was established after a suggestion made at a meeting in Oxford in July 1986, to provide an effective and fast means of bringing together musicologists, music analysts, computer scientists, and others working on applications of computers in music research. Initially, the list was established for people whose chief interests concern computers and their applications to

   - music representation systems
   - information retrieval systems for musical scores
   - music printing
   - music analysis
   - musicology and ethnomusicology
   - tertiary music education
   - databases of musical information

The following areas are NOT the principal concern of this list, although overlapping subjects may well be interesting:

- primary and secondary education
- sound generation techniques
- composition

This group is gatewayed to the USENET group "comp.music", but postings to comp.music are not included in the digest.

On-line archives are not yet available, but copies will be mailed on request by Brad Rubenstein <bradr@INGRES.BERKELEY.EDU>.

All requests to be added to or deleted from this list, problems, questions, etc., should be sent to music-research-request%prg.oxford.ac.uk@NSS.CS.UCL.AC.UK or UUCP ...!ukc!ox-prg!music-research-request.

> Coordinator: Stephen Page <sdpage%sevax.prg.oxford.ac.uk@NSS.CS.UCL.AC.UK>
> US Redistributor: Brad Rubenstein <bradr@bartok.sun.com>
>   {most US backbones}!sun!bartok!bradr (UUCP)

mutex@stolaf.edu

Mutex a mailing list for the discussion of MuTeX and MusicTeX related issues.

To be added to the list send mail to:

Owner: mutex-request@stolaf.edu

MVSTCPIP@VM.USC.EDU
MMVSTCPIP@USCVM.BITNET

Mailing list for discussion of MVS TCP/IP implementations. The MVSTCPIP list is open to discussion of any MVS TCP/IP implementations, however, discussion specific to the IBM MVS TCP/IP product occurs mostly on IBMTCP-L@CUNYVM.CUNY.EDU.

BitNet users should subscribe themselves by sending the following command to LISTSERV@USCVM.BITNET or LISTSERV@VM.USC.EDU: SUBSCRIBE MVSTCPIP Your_Full_Name where "Your_Full_Name" is your real name, not your login Id. To unsubscribe, send the command: UNSUBSCRIBE MVSTCPIP Non-BitNet users can subscribe or unsubscribe by sending one of the above commands to LISTSERV@VM.USC.EDU in the text/body of the message.

Problems accessing the list may be addressed to the Coordinator.

Coordinator: Leonard D. Woren <LDW@MVSA.USC.EDU> <LDW@USCMVSA.BITNET>

NA@SCORE.STANFORD.EDU

Numerical Analysis mailing-list.

Moderator: Gene Golub <GOLUB@SCORE.STANFORD.EDU>

NAC@VM1.NODAK.EDU
NAC@NDSUVM1.BITNET

The "NAC" list is a BITNET/NetNorth/EARN Redistribution list for Usenet Newsgroup news.announce.conferences. "news.announce.conferences" is used to post calls for papers and conference announcements. Contributions should be submitted to mcmi!news-announce-conferences@uunet.uu.net, news-announce-conferences@mcmi.uucp, NAC@VM1.NODAK.EDU.,or NAC@NDSUVM1.BITNET (the list is MODERATED. Submissions to NAC@NDSUVM1 (NAC@VM1.NODAK.EDU) will be forwarded to the Moderator).

Contributions sent to the list are automatically archived. You can obtain a list of the available archive files by sending an "INDEX NAC" command to LISTSERV@NDSUVM1 or

LISTSERV@VM1.NODAK.EDU. These files can then be retrieved by means of a "GET NAC filetype" command, or using the database search facilities of LISTSERV. Send an "INFO DATABASE" command for more information on the latter. The command may be in the BODY or TEXT of the mail, NOT the subject, or may be sent interactively via TELL or SEND on BitNet/EARN/NetNorth.

You may also obtain copies of the list notebooks via anonymous FTP to VM1.NODAK.EDU (192.33.18.30), userid ANONYMOUS, any password. Once validated do a CD LISTARCH and DIR NAC.* to see the notebooks available. The file system is NOT hierarchical so you must do a CD ANONYMOUS if you want to return to the "root".

You may subscribe to NAC by sending the command: SUB NAC Your_full_name (eg. SUB NAC Jane Doe) to LISTSERV@NDSUVM1 or LISTSERV@VM1.NODAK.EDU.

Moderator: Dennis Page mcmi!denny@uunet.uu.net

NACUBO%CTSTATEU.BITNET@VM1.NODAK.EDU

Mailing list for discussion of any topics dealt with by college business, finance and administrative professionals. This is an informal discussion group sponsored by NACUBO's Communications Committee, designed to test and generate interest in electronic networking.

To subscribe to the mailing list, send a message to NACUBO%CTSTATEU.BITNET@VM1.NODAK.EDU.

Coordinator: Janet Chayes <CHAYES%CTSTATEU.BITNET@VM1.NODAK.EDU>

NAMEDROPPERS@NIC.DDN.MIL

The NAMEDROPPERS mailing list is to be used for discussion of the concepts, principles, design, and implementation of the domain style names. The main focus of this group is the review of documents describing domain style names. This is a list for participants in a discussion, not observers. Everyone on the list is expected to contribute from time to time.

Archives can be found on SRI's Internet CD-ROM. They are also available via anonymous ftp on NIC.DDN.MIL and ftp.nisc.sri.com. New members may wish to copy and read these archives before joining the discussion.

All requests to be added to or deleted from this list, problems, questions, etc., should be sent to NAMEDROPPERS-REQUEST@NIC.DDN.MIL.

Coordinator: Hostmaster@NIC.DDN.MIL

Nanny-Users@XHMEIA.CALTECH.EDU

Mailing list for people using the Nanny package written for VAX using VMS.

All requests to be added to or deleted from this list, problems, questions, etc., should be sent to Nanny-Users-Request@XHMEIA.Caltech.Edu.

Coordinator: Perfect Tommy <zar@IAGO.CALTECH.EDU>

nearnet@NIC.NEAR.NET

Mailing list for general discussion of NEARnet, the New England Academic and Research Network, its services, growth, policies, etc. This list is open to anyone interested in learning more about NEARnet.

Archives are available via anonymous ftp from NIC.NEAR.NET in the subdirectory "mail-archives".

All requests to be added to or deleted from this list, questions, comments, etc., should be sent to nearnet-request@NIC.NEAR.NET.

Coordinator: NEARnet Staff <nearnet-staff@NIC.NEAR.NET>

nearnet-tech@NIC.NEAR.NET

Mailing list for technical discussion about NEARnet, the New England Academic and Research Network. This list reaches technical contacts at all NEARnet member sites and is open to anyone interested in participating in or learning more about the technical and operational aspects of NEARnet.

Archives are available via anonymous ftp from NIC.NEAR.NET in the subdirectory "mail-archives".

All requests to be added to or deleted from this list, questions, comments, etc., should be sent to nearnet-tech-request@NIC.NEAR.NET.

Coordinator: NEARnet Staff <nearnet-staff@NIC.NEAR.NET>

Nerdnosh@scruz.ucsc.EDU   [Last Update 9/92]

Purpose: Begun as a breakfast club for local nerds and writers in Santa Cruz, CA, US, it has expanded into an international forum about where, how, and why we live where we do. Think of it as a universal camp town meeting in M F K Fisher shades and Jack Kerouac tones. Frivolous, friendly, and informative, in roughly that order.

Contact: nerdnosh-request@scruz.ucsc.EDU (Tim Bowden)

netblazer-users@telebit.com   [Last Updated 12-October-1991]

Contact: netblazer-users-request@telebit.com

Purpose: To provide an unmoderated forum for discussions among users of Telebit NetBlazer products. Topics include known problems and workarounds, features discussions, and configuration advice.

NetMonth

NetMonth is a network service publication distributed free of charge to students and professionals in BITNET and other networks. This magazine and it's companion file, BITNET SERVERS, are the work of the Yale Computer Center BITNET Services Library (BITLIB) staff. The BITLIB is a local online help facility designed to inform Yale network users about what services are available to them through BITNET, and provide instructions and utilities for their proper use. In publishing NetMonth the BITLIB staff members hope to share the fruits of their labor with institutions outside of Yale in order to promote a productive and enjoyable networking environment for everyone. The BITLIB system is now distributed to more than thirty educational institutions worldwide.

BITNET SERVERS is BITNET's most complete and up-to-date list of servers and services. It is sent to NetMonth subscribers at the same time as the magazine.

Subscribing to NetMonth and BITNET SERVERS:

VM users in BITNET may add themselves to the mailing list with this command: TELL LISTSERV AT MARIST SUBSCRIBE NETMONTH Your_full_name VAX/VMS users in BITNET can subscribe in a similar way: SEND LISTSERV@MARIST SUBSCRIBE NETMONTH Your_full_name If you cannot send messages in this way, you can send the following command as the first line of a mail file to LISTSERV@MARIST: SUBSCRIBE NETMONTH Your_full_name

Internet users may use this method, but must address the mail to: LISTSERV%MARIST.BITNET@CUNYVM.CUNY.EDU

A subscriber can delete him/herself from the mailing list by sending LISTSERV@MARIST the command UNSUBSCRIBE NETMONTH.

Coordinator: Chris Condon <BITLIB%YALEVM.BITNET@CUNYVM.CUNY.EDU> BITLIB@YALEVM (BitNet)

NETSCOUT%VMTECMEX.BITNET@CUNYVM.CUNY.EDU

A forum for the general user of the BitNet and/or the Internet to discuss and exchange information about Servers, FTP sites, Filelists, lists, tools and any related aspects:

Are you trying to find that WIZMO EXEC on a forgotten Listserv? Where were those great utilities to transfer files from PC to Mac? Do you want to know the latest FTP directories? Where is the NutWorks list?

This is the place to ask.

To subscribe to the list send the following command in the text/body of mail to LISTSERV@VMTECMEX (BitNet) or LISTSERV%VMTECMEX.BITNET@CUNYVM.CUNY.EDU (Internet): SUB NETSCOUT your full name where "your full name" is your real name, not your login Id.

Coordinator: Alejandro Kurczyn S. <499229%VMTECMEX.BITNET@CUNYVM.CUNY.EDU>

NVAS-L on LISTSERV@CUVMC.BITNET   [Last Update 9/92]

NVAS-L was formed to provide a forum for discussing issues related to IBM's NetView Access Services session manager. Any matter relating to the modification, support, maintenance and/or use of NVAS is welcome.

Archives of NVAS-L back issues may be listed by sending the command INDEX NVAS-L to LISTSERV@CUVMC.

To subscribe, send the following command to LISTSERV@CUVMC.BITNET in the BODY of e-mail or in an interactive message:

SUB NVAS-L your full name

where 'your full name' is your name. For example:

SUB NVAS-L Algernon Windburn

Owner: Terrence Ford <TFOCU@CUVMC.BITNET>

NEURON@@cattell.psych.upenn.edu   [Last Update 11/92]

NEURON is a list (in digest form) dealing with all aspects of neural networks (and any type of network or neuromorphic system), especially:

NATURAL SYSTEMS	Software Simulations
Neurobiology	Hardware
Neuroscience	Digital
ARTIFICIAL SYSTEMS	Analog
Neural Networks	Optical
Algorithms	Cellular Automatons

Some key words which may stir up some further interest include:

Hebbian Systems	Widrow-Hoff Algorithm
Perceptron	Threshold Logic
Holography	Content Addressable Memories
Lyapunov Stability Criterion	Navier-Stokes Equation
Annealing	Spin Glasses
Locally Couples Systems	Globally Coupled Systems
Dynamical Systems	(Adaptive) Control Theory
Back-Propagation	Generalized Delta Rule
Pattern Recognition	Vision Systems
Parallel Distributed Processing	Connectionism

Any contribution in these areas is accepted. Any of the following are reasonable:

Abstracts	Reviews
Lab Descriptions	Research Overviews
Work Planned or in Progress	Half-Baked Ideas

Conference Announcements	Conference Reports
Bibliographies	History Connectionism
Puzzles and Unsolved Problems	Anecdotes, Jokes, and Poems
Queries and Requests	Address Changes (Bindings)

Archived files/messages will be sent to individuals on request.

All requests to be added to or deleted from this list, problems, questions, etc., should be sent to neuron-request@cattell.psych.upenn.edu

Moderator: Peter Marvit <marvit@cattell.psych.upenn.edu>

NEWEDU-L on LISTSERV@USCVM.BITNET   [Last Updated 12-October-1991]
or LISTSERV@VM.USC.EDU

This list is dedicated to experimenting with and exploring the way we educate. We ask: what are the new paradigms in education and how can they be implemented.

For instance:

- How is technology changing the way we view education?
- What effects will cooperative/collaborative strategies have on teaching and learning?
- Does the so-called "information age" change the way we view our responsibilities as educators?
- Artificial intelligence research is changing our view of how we know things. How does this affect education?
- How can we reduce dependency in education and foster independent learning?

There are many individuals working in these areas, each with a conviction that education will change. This list attempts to bring together every teacher, student, researcher, librarian, multimedia expert and information specialist interested in educational change -- Kindergarten through post-graduate.

You are encouraged to:

- Submit summaries of or commentary on published articles and books which explore the frontiers of teaching and learning.
- Submit in-progress papers or abstracts of those papers for comment.
- Share the results of your experiments with teaching and learning.
- Ask thought-provoking questions about the future of education and the environments in which it takes place.
- Recruit interested parties to this listserv, regardless of their status in education, industry or government.

Subscribing to NEWEDU-L:

IBM VM users in BITNET may add themselves to the mailing list with this command: TELL LISTSERV AT USCVM SUBSCRIBE NEWEDU-L Your_full_name

VAX/VMS users in BITNET can subscribe in a similar way: SEND LISTSERV@USCVM SUBSCRIBE NEWEDU-L Your_full_name

If you cannot send messages in this way, you can send the following command as the first line of text in a mail item to LISTSERV@USCVM: SUBSCRIBE NEWEDU-L Your_full_name

Internet users may use this method, but must address the mail to: LISTSERV@vm.usc.edu

A subscriber can delete him/herself from the mailing list by sending LISTSERV@USCVM (or listserv@vm.usc.edu) the command: SIGNOFF NEWEDU-L

Moderators: Greg Swan
        Paul Privateer
    Internet address: NPADMIN@mc.maricopa.edu
    Bitnet address: NPADMIN@MC

NEW-LIST@VM1.NODAK.EDU
    NEW-LIST@NDSUVM1.BITNET

The "NEW-LIST" list has been established as a central address to post announcements of new public mailing lists. In addition, "NEW-LIST" might be used as a final verification before establishing a list (to check for existing lists on the same topic, etc.). However, be sure to check sources such as the Internet List-of-Lists (SIGLIST or INTEREST-GROUPS list), LISTSERV GROUPS, Usenet News newusers lists, and the LISTS database on the major LISTSERVs (we have the LISTS database on NDSUVM1).

It is not our intent to replace the various lists of lists that are available. We want to provide a clearinghouse to feed list announcements to all those maintaining the lists and others who are interested.

You may subscribe to the NEW-LIST list by sending RFC822 Mail to LISTSERV@VM1.NoDak.EDU on Internet or LISTSERV@NDSUVM1 on BitNet. In the BODY (text) of your mail include the command: SUB NEW-LIST firstname lastname eg. sub new-list Jane Doe The LISTSERV server will take your address from the "From:" address of your mail. If you are on BITNET/EARN/NetNorth and can send interactive messages (eg. TELL on CMS or SEND on VMS with JNET) then you can send the SUB command as shown to LISTSERV at NDSUVM1 interactively.

If you prefer, you may send mail to the Coordinator to be asked to be added to the list. However you subscribe, you should receive return mail with a confirmation and additional information.

    Coordinator: Marty Hoag <INFO@VM1.NODAK.EDU> <INFO@NDSUVM1.BITNET>

NeWS-makers@BRILLIG.UMD.EDU
    ...!mimsy!NeWS-makers (uucp)

Mailing list for the discussion of NeWS: the Network/extensible Window System. NeWS, originally called SunDew, was written primarily by James Gosling, at Sun Microsystems, who is well known for his Unix Emacs. NeWS is an extensible multitasking window system environment, consisting of a network based display server that is controlled and programmed in PostScript, Adobe's page description language. NeWS was designed to be a portable, device independent window system development platform that runs on a wide range of hardware, in a distributed heterogeneous environment.

The archives are available via anonymous FTP from BRILLIG.UMD.EDU, in the file "news-makers.archive".

All requests to be added to or deleted from this list, problems, questions, etc., should be sent to NeWS-makers-request@BRILLIG.UMD.EDU.

    Coordinator: don@BRILLIG.UMD.EDU

NeXT-L%BROWNVM.BITNET@MITVMA.MIT.EDU

Mailing list for discussion of the NeXT Computer.

To subscribe, send a message to LISTSERV AT BROWNVM: SUBSCRIBE NEXT-L Your Full Name Non-BitNet users send a message to LISTSERV%BROWNVM.BITNET@MITVMA.MIT.EDU.

    Coordinator: Atul Butte <ATUL%BROWNVM.BITNET@MITVMA.MIT.EDU>

next-managers@stolaf.edu   [Last Updated 28-January-1992]

This list is intended to be a quick-turnaround trouble shooting aid for those who administer and manage NeXT systems. Its primary purpose is to provide the NeXT manager with a quick source of information for system management problems that are of a time-critical nature. Its secondary purpose is to disseminate time-critical or security- related information.

To be added to the list send mail to the owner (below).

    Owner: next-managers-request@stolaf.edu

    NEXT-MANAGERS POLICY

This is a summary of the next-managers charter and rules. Failure to adhere to these guidelines may result in severe chastisement by the list maintainer and other list participants or your being removed from the next-managers mailing list.

1: This list is NOT moderated! Every message that is sent to the list next-managers@stolaf.edu will be passed on to every member of the list

2: Requests to have addresses added or removed from the list should NOT be sent to the entire list. Instead, they should be mailed to: next-managers-request@stolaf.edu

3: This list is intended to be a quick-turnaround trouble shooting aid for those who administer and manage NeXT systems. Its primary purpose is to provide the NeXT manager with a quick source of information for system management problems that are of a time-critical nature. Its secondary purpose is to disseminate time-critical or security- related information.

4: Answers to questions are to be mailed back to the questioner and are NOT to be sent to the entire list. The person who originally asked the question has the responsibility of summarizing the answers and sending the entire summary back to the list. If everyone follows this, one problem will only generate two or possibly three messages on the list. The summary message should contain the keyword "SUMMARY" in the subject line.

5: Corrections to compiled answers should be addressed only to the person who first asked the question; this person (the writer of the original question) is then responsible for distributing the corrected information to the list.

6: Discussions on ANY topic are very strongly discouraged.

7: If it is not specifically related to NeXT system management, then it does NOT belong on this list.

8: PLEASE PLEASE PLEASE...Think before you send a message! Ask yourself is this really appropriate? have you checked in the reference manuals? have you checked NextAnswers? have you checked the Digital Librarian? have you checked in the online man pages? have you checked the Frequently Asked Questions (FAQ) list? have you checked the next-managers archive? before mailing to the next-managers list. There are enough other newsgroups, mailing lists and other resources around to cover the marginal topics.

9: Do NOT send message from "root" or from "me"; send them from your own personal account.

10: Do not send messages with NeXT attachments; please use straight-text only.

11: next-managers is currently archived on "ftp.stolaf.edu" in ~ftp/pub/next-managers.

NeXTstep on LISTSERV@IndyCMS.BITNET or LISTSERV@IndyCMS.IUPUI.Edu

NeXTstep (NeXTstep operating environment) is dedicated to discussion of the NeXTstep operating environment produced by NeXT Computer, Inc. NeXTstep (the list) is completely independent of NeXTstep (the operating environment) and NeXT Computer, Inc. (the manufacturer).

NeXTstep (the list) is owned and coordinated by a computing professional (Phillip Gross Corporon) and an interested layperson (John B Harlan).

NeXTstep (the list) is bidirectionally gatewayed to the INET newsgroup, comp.soft-sys.nextstep.

To subscribe to the NeXTstep e-mail list send mail to LISTSERV@IndyCMS.BITNET or LISTSERV@IndyCMS.IUPUI.Edu the the following command in the BODY of the mail:

SUB NEXTSTEP yourfirstname yourlastname

List owners/coordinators: Phillip Gross Corporon
                                phil@CSE.ND.Edu
                                F3PB88@IrishMVS
                                F3PB88@IrishMVS.CC.ND.Edu

John B Harlan
JBHarlan@IndyVAX
JBHarlan@IndyVAX.IUPUI.Edu

NIHONGO@MITVMA.MIT.EDU

For discussion of the Japanese language, including both spoken and written forms. Also see the entry for the INFO-JAPAN mailing list. The list is also cross-posted to sci.lang.japan on UUCP netnews.

The complete archives are publicly accessible by FTP from host MIT-MC, which uses the ITS operating system. Case is not significant, but the space after "NIHON" is. The archives are in: COMAIL;NIHON GO

BitNet users can join by sending the following command to LISTSERV@MITVMA:

SUBSCRIBE NIHONGO Your_full_name

For example: SUBSCRIBE NIHONGO John Doe

Non-BitNet users can join by putting the above command in the text/body of a message to LISTSERV%MITVMA.BITNET@CUNYVM.CUNY.EDU.

Coordinator: Steve Strassmann <straz@MEDIA-LAB.MEDIA.MIT.EDU>

nis@cerf.net   [Last Update 11/92]

Network Information Services Announcements List

CERFnet has established a mailing list to serve network information service providers and end users. In a nutshell, the nis@cerf.net list will be a group effort (in true Internet style) to concentrate network information services (nis) announcements onto one list for everyone's use. A few dozen individuals around the Internet will each be monitoring a specific source (mailing list, news group, list serve) and sending the information to CERFnet. We will serve as the moderator, forwarding pertinent submissions to the entire readership of the list, omitting duplicates.

In this way, individuals can receive regular nis information even if they choose not to read discussion lists. This should prove especially valuable for end users in specific disciplines who are not in the networking business, but are using the network as tool and a resource.

Advantages:

* everyone doesn't have to read every mailing list to stay current
* volume will stay low (it won't be a discussion list)
* pointers will be provided for more info and discussion

What you can do:

* To subscribe: send mail to listserv@cerf.net with the following command in the body of message: subscribe <your mailing address> nis (Note the difference in format from other LISTSERV servers)

* to volunteer to monitor a source: send mail to nis@cerf.net

* to submit an item of interest for the list to the moderator, comments, suggestions, helpful hints, etc. send mail to nis@cerf.net

Contact:

Susan Calcari   (619) 455-3900
Director, Network Information Services   FAX: (619) 455-3990
CERFnet   P.O. Box 85608
calcaris@cerf.net   San Diego, CA. 92186-9784

nl-kr@cs.rpi.edu

NL-KR is open to discussion of any topic related to the natural language (both understanding and generation) and knowledge representation, both as subfields of AI. The Moderator's interests are primarily in:

Knowledge Representation   Natural Language Understanding
Discourse Understanding   Philosophy of Language
Plan Recognition   Computational Linguistics

Contributions are also welcome on topics such as:

Cognitive Psychology (as related to NL/KR)
Human Perception (same)
Linguistics
Machine Translation
Computer and Information Science (as may be used to implement various
Logic Programming (same)   NL systems)

Contributions may be anything from tutorials to speculation. In particular, the following are sought:

Puzzles and Unsolved Problems   Anecdotes, Jokes, and Poems
Abstracts   Reviews
Lab Descriptions   Research Overviews
Work Planned or in Progress   Half-Baked Ideas
Conference Announcements   Conference Reports
Bibliographies   History of NL/KR
Queries and Requests   Address Changes (Bindings)

This list is in some sense a spin-off of the AIList, and as such, a certain amount of overlap is expected. The primary concentration of this list should be NL and KR, that is, natural language (be it understanding, generation, recognition, parsing, semantics, pragmatics, etc.) and how we should represent knowledge (aquisition, access, completeness, etc. are all valid issues). Topics deemed to be outside the general scope of this list will be forwarded to AIList (or other more appropriate list) or rejected. Readers are warned not to submit any information that is export-controlled or classified.

All requests to be added to or deleted from this list, problems, questions, etc., should be sent to NL-KR-REQUEST@cs.rpi.edu.

Moderator: Christopher Welty weltyc@cs.rpi.edu

NNEWS on LISTSERV@NDSUVM1.BITNET or LISTSERV@vm1.NoDak.edu

Network News is an online newsletter focusing on library and information resources on the Internet. It updates the information found in A Guide to Internet/Bitnet.

Send subscription requests/cancellations to either:

listserv@ndsuvm1.bitnet (BITNET) or listserv@vm1.nodak.edu (Internet)

In the BODY of the message type:

subscribe nnews firstname lastname (to subscribe)

for example: subscribe nnews Melvyl Dewey

or unsubscribe nnews (to cancel subscription)

Back issues of the newsletter and the latest version of A Guide to Internet/Bitnet are available in the archive. Send the following command to get a list of what's available:

index nnews

Owner: Dana Noonan <noonan@msus1.msus.edu>

NNMVS-L on LISTSERV@USCVM LISTSERV@VM.USC.EDU

NNMVS-L is an unmoderated list for discussion of the MVS/TSO NNTP News Reader (NNMVS).

To subscribe to NNMVS-L, send the following command to LISTSERV@USCVM or LISTSERV@VM.USC.EDU in the body of an email message or via BITNET interactive message:

SUBSCRIBE NNMVS-L Your Full Name

For example: SUBSCRIBE NNMVS-L John Doe

Contributions sent to this list are automatically archived. You can obtain a list of the available archive files by sending an "INDEX NNMVS-L" command to LISTSERV@USCVM. These files can then be retrieved by means of a "GET NNMVS-L filetype" command, or using the database search facilities of LISTSERV. Send an "INFO DATABASE" command for more information on the latter.

Instructions on how to obtain the NNMVS software for your site are included in the welcome message that you will receive upon being subscribed to the list.

The author of NNMVS is: Steve Bacher (Batchman) Draper Laboratory Internet: seb@draper.com Cambridge, MA, USA

The list administrator for NNMVS-L is: Leonard D. Woren University of Southern California LDW@USCMVSA.BITNET LDW@MVSA.USC.EDU

NORTHSTAR-USERS@WSMR-SIMTEL20.ARMY.MIL

Discussion group for Northstar microcomputer users.

Mail archives are kept on host WSMR-SIMTEL20.ARMY.MIL as TOPS20 mail files named yymm.n-TXT, where n starts with one and increments by one into another file as each file reached 150 disk pages. To conserve disk space, all the mail files in the archive, except for the current year, are individually compressed. The compressed files have the suffix -Z as part of the filetype field; they should be renamed to have the suffix .Z (uppercase Z) when transfered to a Unix system so the uncompress program will find them. The current month's mail is still kept in NORTHSTAR-ARCHIV.TXT. The archives are stored in directory: PD2:<ARCHIVES.NORTHSTAR> Archive files are available via ANONYMOUS FTP from WSMR-SIMTEL20.ARMY.MIL for those with TCP/IP access to the Internet.

All requests to be added to or deleted from this list, problems, questions, etc., should be sent to NORTHSTAR-USERS-REQUEST@WSMR-SIMTEL20.ARMY.MIL.

Coordinator: Frank J. Wancho <WANCHO@WSMR-SIMTEL20.ARMY.MIL>

NOVELL@SUVM.ACS.SYR.EDU   [Last Update 8/92]
NOVELL@SUVM.BITNET

This list is for those in higher education who use the Novell Netware (c) Network Operating System (NOS). The list is especially good for folks in multi-vendor environments. We focus on questions and helpful hints about hardware, software and administration of Novell Networks in Higher Ed. Since the list focuses on support we try to keep *FLAMES* to a minimum (Flames can be sent to BIG-LAN@SUVM).

To join or leave the list, contact the Coordinator.

   NOVELADM@SUVM.ACS.SYR.EDU or noveladm@suvm.bitnet
   Contact person is Dr. Bruce Riddle or Don Hanley

NP-FORUM@UMUC.UMD.EDU   [Last Updated 12-October-1991]
NP-FORUM@UMUC.BITNET

"New Pathways to a Degree" is the Annenberg/CPB funded initiative to help colleges use technologies to open degree programs to new students and new academic resources. NP-FORUM is an open discussion list for individuals interested in New Pathways.

To subscribe, send the following command to LISTSERV@UMUC via mail or interactive message:

SUB NP-FORUM your_full_name

where "your_full_name" is your name. For example:

SUB NP-FORUM Joan Doe

Owner: Michael Strait <Strait@UMUC>

NP-NEWS@UMUC.UMD.EDU   [Last Updated 12-October-1991]
NP-NEWS@UMUC.BITNET

The information made available to you through NP-NEWS is information on "New Pathways to a Degree," the Annenberg/CPB funded initiative to help colleges use technologies to open degree programs to new students and new academic resources.

NP-NEWS is an online archive, and a once-a-month email message (like this one) which lets you know what's new in the archive and how you can gain access to it, and passes along to you other items of interest.

To subscribe, send the following command to LISTSERV@UMUC via mail or interactive message:

SUB NP-NEWS your_full_name

where "your_full_name" is your name. For example:

SUB NP-NEWS Joan Doe

Owner: Michael Strait <Strait@UMUC>

nren-discuss@psi.com   [Last Updated 12 Mar 91]

An open mailing list to discuss the NREN (National Research and Education Network). It is a high energy and volume redistribution mailing list.

Send email to nren-discuss-request@psi.com to be added.

NT-GREEK@VIRGINIA.EDU   [Last Updated 12-October-1991]
NT-GREEK@VIRGINIA.BITNET

NT-GREEK is an electronic conference designed to foster communication concerning the scholarly study of the Greek New Testament. Anyone interested in New Testament Studies is invited to subscribe, but the list will assume at least a working knowledge of Biblical Greek.

Subscription to this conference is open to anyone interested.

You may subscribe by sending an e-mail message to

NT-GREEK-REQUEST@VIRGINIA.EDU NTGRKREQ@VIRGINIA.BITNET

with the following request as the text of the message.

SUB NT-GREEK YourFirstname YourLastname

This, the 'SUB ...,' must be part of the message; the subject line will be ignored.

Remember two simple rules-of-thumb:

If it's a request (SUBscribe, UNSUBscribe), send it to the list requester:
NT-GREEK-REQUEST@VIRGINIA.EDU (Internet) NTGRKREQ@VIRGINIA.BITNET (Bitnet)

If it's a message for general distribution to the members of the list, send it to the list:
NT-GREEK@VIRGINIA.EDU (Internet) NT-GREEK@VIRGINIA.BITNET (Bitnet)

The list is supported by the University of Virginia. Our thanks to their management and staff for permission to use their system for the list and for assistance in setting it up. The opinions expressed do not reflect those of the University.

The list is sponsored by the the Center for Christian Study, an independent Christian ministry at the University of Virginia. The Center for Christian Study has been dedicated to providing quality Christian Education since its inception in 1976. The main purposes of the Center are to maintain a caring University outreach ministry and to encourage Chrisitians (and others) to think serious about the Christian faith. If you wish more information about the Center for Christian Study please write:

The Center for Christian Study
128 Chancellor Street
Charlottesville, VA 22903
(804) 295-2471

Questions about this conference may be directed to David John Marotta:
David John Marotta, Medical Center Computing, Stacey Hall
Univ of Virginia (804) 982-3718 wrk INTERNET: djm5g@virginia.edu
Box 512 Med Cntr (804) 924-5261 msg BITNET: djm5g@virginia
C'ville VA 22908 (804) 296-7209 fax IBM US: usuvarg8

NUTWORKS%TCSVM.BITNET@VM!.NODAK.EDU
NUTWORKS@TCSVM (BITNET)

Subscribe via standard LISTSERV commands.

All back issues are available from LISTSERV@TCSVM.BITNET via the "get" command (GET NUTWORKS ISSUE025, for example). Non-BitNet users can send the GET command to LISTSERV%TCSVM.BITNET@VM1.NODAK.EDU in the text/body of a message.

Moderator: Joe Desbonnet (phydesbonnet@vax1.ucg.ie)

NYSO-L on LISTSERV@UBVM or LISTSERV@UBVM.CC.BUFFALO.EDU

The NYSO-L list was formed to serve as a vehicle for (1) discussion of topics related to the New York State/Ontario chapter of the Music Library Asssociation and (2) collection of any information pertaining to the same organization.

Archives of NYSO-L and related files are stored in the NYSO-L filelist. To receive a list of files send the command INDEX NYSO-L to LISTSERV@UBVM or LISTSERV@UBVM.CC.BUFFALO.EDU as the first line in the BODY of a mail message (not the Subject: line).

To subscribe to NYSO-L, send the command SUB NYSO-L your name to LISTSERV@UBVM or LISTSERV@UBVM.CC.BUFFALO.EDU (again, as the first line in the BODY of the mail, not the Subject: line).

For example: SUB NYSO-L Jane Doe

Owner: Rick McRae <mmlrick@ubvm> <mmlrick@ubvm.cc.buffalo.edu>

obed@reepicheep.gcn.uoknor.edu   [Last Update 9/92] This group discusses all issues related to training dogs, particularly for AKC and UKC obedience trials. Canine good citizenship, temperment testing and therapy dog training are also discussed as well as less formal issues.

For group subscription, send mail to obedreq@reepicheep.gcn.uoknor.edu

Coordinator:Mike Richman richman@reepicheep.gcn.uoknor.edu

OIL-GAS@PAVNET.NSHOR.NCOAST.ORG   [Last Updated 12-October-1991]

SUBSCRIPTION CONTACT: nshore!pavnet!oil-gas-request OR oil-gas-request@pavnet.nshore.ncoast.org (Please use SUBSCRIBE or UNSUBSCRIBE as the subject)

INFORMATION CONTACT: nshore!pavnet!oil-gas-info OR oil-gas-info@pavnet.nshore.ncoast.org

PURPOSE: An electronic newsletter for the serious oil and gas investor. Discusses current oil and gas industry issues, problems, events, and opportunites. Includes day-by-day oil prices. Published monthly, with periodic "Extra" updates or additional coverage.

OPERA-L%BRFAPESP.BITNET@VM1.NODAK.EDU

Are you one of the happy few who knows that Wagner called his Leitmotive Grundthemae? Or you can't tell a leitmotiv from a pretzel, and yet you love all sorts of operas? Do you think that Mozart wrote "Il Barbiere di Siviglia" and Rossini "Le Nozze di Figaro", because you were told that "Figaro ca', Figaro... " is by Rossini? Or are you an expert on Caron de Beaumarchais' contributions to everything - from philosophy to poetry to the American revolution - and to the music of Mozart? Do you unabashedly love Beethoven's "Fidelio"? (You must be a real opera buff, if you do...) And Alban Berg's "Wozzeck"? And Benjamin Britten's "Peter Pears", sorry, "Peter Grimes"? (Now you smile contently; *you* know what the joke is about !)

Do you just love opera? Then enlist yourself in our list!

Send mail to MAILSERV%BRFAPESP.BITNET@VM1.NODAK.EDU containing the command SUBSCRIBE OPERA-L

List Coordinator:

Francisco Antonio de M. A. DORIA; e-mail: Doria@suwatson.bitnet Doria@suwatson.stanford.edu

OPERS-L on LISTSERV@AKRONVM
or LISTSERV@VM1.CC.UAKRON.EDU

This is a discussion group about MAINFRAME Computer Operations for computer operators, lead operators and supervisors, etc. Some of the possible topics (but not limited to):

- Operator Training (or lack of - as is too often the case in some installations).
- Tips on operating the various computer systems and I/O gear. Those helps and hints that could be shared by veteran operators to aid new operators in their learning process. Those hints that are not in the documentation to make an operators job a little easier!
- Software packages available to help day to day computer operations such as job scheduling, disk and tape management etc.
- Problems caused by working night shift, weekends and holidays.
- Education and career advancement issues.
- Overcoming boredom - many operators get locked in to the same old same old day after day.
- War stories about hardware and software problems. What products to avoid under certain conditions.
- Health concerns - Eye strain and related VDT concerns. Carpel tunnel problems.
- Pros and cons on shift rotation vs. permanent shifts.
- An 'I told you so' column - how many times does management say how to operations staff is going to do something and the operators try to give their input (which is rarely heard!).
- Humor - Funny stories about those instances where you just gotta laugh. You got to have a sense of humor to be in our line of work!

To subscribe, send an interactive message or mail to LISTSERV@AKRONVM as follows:

SUBscribe OPERS-L Your Name

Owners: Tom Evert, O1EVERT@AKRONVM Gary Sponseller, SPONSELL@AKRONVM

OPT-PROC on LISTSERV@TAUNIVM   [Last Updated 28-January-1992]
or listserv@vm.tau.ac.il

The OPT-PROC mailing list is a moderated mailing list, and is involved with optical computing, optical information processing and holography.

To join OPT-PROC send the message

SUBSCRIBE OPT-PROC your-everyday-name

to LISTSERV@TAUNIVM.bitnet or listserv@vm.tau.ac.il (those are two forms of the same address).

Moderator: Shelly Glaser 972 3 545 0060 <GLAS@TAUNIVM.BITNET> or <GLAS@vm.tau.ac.il>

OPTICOMP on LISTSERV@TAUNIVM.bitnet   [Last Updated 12-January-1992]

Name changed to OPT-PROC

OPTICS-L <JO%ILNCRD.BITNET@CUNYVM.CUNY.EDU>

A Bitnet newsletter on optics and lasers in Israel.

To subscribe, send a message to LISTSERV%TAUNIVM.BITNET@CUNYVM.CUNY.EDU with the body of the letter containing the command: SUB OPTICS-L Your_Full_Name where Your_Full_Name; is your title, first name and last name.

Coordinator: Joseph van Zwaren de Zwarenstein <JO%ILNCRD.BITNET@CUNYVM.CUNY.EDU>

OPTICS@TOE.TOWSON.EDU

OPTICS is an open list devoted to the interchange of ideas, discussions and meeting announcements in the field of optics. You are welcome to send any newsworthy item to OPTICS@TOWSONVX or OPTICS@TOE.TOWSON.EDU and it will be forwarded to the mailing list. For example, If you will be giving a lecture (colloquium), organizing a scientific meeting in some optic related discipline or if you would just like to comment in some specific area of

The schedule of the National Capital Section of the Optical Society of America will post its meeting schedule on the list in addition to sending mailings to the membership.

The schedule of the National Capital Section of the Optical Society of America will post its meeting schedule on the list in addition to sending mailings to the membership.

To add your name to the list send a mail message to MAILSERV@TOWSONVX or MAILSERV@TOE.TOWSON.EDU with the command

SUBSCRIBE OPTICS

To remove your name from the list, send a mail message to MAILSERV@TOWSONVX or MAILSERV@TOE.TOWSON.EDU with the command

UNSUBSCRIBE OPTICS

This list is *NOT* LISTSERV-based.

ORACLE@IUVAX.CS.INDIANA.EDU

The Usenet Oracle is available to answer all your questions. Send mail to oracle@iuvax.cs.indiana.edu with the word "help" in the subject line for complete details.

There is a distribution list for compilations of the Oracle's best answers (The Usenet Oracularities, also posted to the Usenet newsgroup rec.humor). Send mail to oracle-request@iuvax.cs.indiana.edu to get on this list.

Oracle Priesthood: oracle-people@iuvax.cs.indiana.edu
Oracularities Moderator: Steve Kinzler <kinzler@iuvax.cs.indiana.edu>

ORACLE-L%SBCCVM.BITNET@CUNYVM.CUNY.EDU
ORACLE-L on LISTSERV@SBCCVM

This is the ORACLE database mailing list.

This list is for discussion of all issues relevant to the ORACLE database management system. ORACLE is a registered trademark of ORACLE corporation.

We are in the process of obtaining ORACLE for our Campus VAXes and wanted to find out more about ORACLE. Since no mailing list existed for the discussion of ORACLE, this list was created. If some other list does exist for the discussion of ORACLE, or if someone from inside ORACLE objects to this list, please send me a note.

To subscribe to this list, send a message to LISTSERV@SBCCVM on BITNET.

SEND LISTSERV@SBCCVM SUBSCRIBE ORACLE-L your full name

or

TELL LISTSERV AT SBCCVM SUBSCRIBE ORACLE-L your full name

On the internet, send a mail message to LISTSERV@CCVM.SUNYSB.EDU to subscribe.

The message should contain the following text:

SUBSCRIBE ORACLE-L your full name

ORCHIDS%SCU.BITNET@CUNYVM.CUNY.EDU

ORCHIDS on MAILSERV@SCU.BITNET This unmoderated list was created to share and discuss information and experiences of orchid growers. The discussions will include, but not be restricted to:

-Discussion of types grown
-Cultivation techniques of certain types
-Orchid Society events
-Helpful orchid tips to assist growers
-Scientific, biological issues relating to orchid growth
-Seeding and propagating techniques
-hybrids and hybridizing
-Anything that would be of interest to orchid growers

To subscribe to the list:

Send a mail message (MAIL only) to MAILSERV%SCU.BITNET@CUNYVM.CUNY.EDU The first line of the message should include the TEXT line:

SUBSCRIBE ORCHIDS

A short introduction and some instructions will be sent to you as a confirmation of the addition of your name to the list.

Coordinator : Willis Dair <DAIR@SCU.BITNET> <DAIR%SCU.BITNET@CUNYVM.CUNY.EDU>

ORCS-L on LISTSERV@OSUVM1.bitnet

ORCS-L is a list to discuss the topics at the interface of Operations Research/Management Science and Computer Science. This list will serve as a "bulletin board" for researchers, practitioners, and graduate students working in OR/CS interface. This list may be used to ask specific questions for references, or to initiate discussion on a topic. Other appropriate uses may include announcements of conferences, software, special issues of journals, books, availability of technical reports/working papers, etc.

Please subscribe to this list to keep current with the topics in this area. Also, the level of activity is totally dependent on the list members' contributions. You are invited to post relevant messages to the list.

To subscribe to ORCS-L, send the following command to LISTSERV@OSUVM1 via mail text (BODY) or interactive message:

SUBSCRIBE ORCS-L your full name

To post a message to the list, send the message to: ORCS-L@OSUVM1 Please note that (at least initially) this is not a moderated list. Anything you send ORCS-L@OSUVM1 will be broadcast (unedited) to subscribers.

List Owner: Ramesh Sharda <MGMTRSH@OSUVM1>

ORGCHE-L on LISTSERV%RPICICGE.BITNET@CUNYVM.CUNY.EDU

Organic Chemistry mailing list. To facilitate the interchange of ideas, information, computer programs, papers, to announce opportunities for doing collaborative efforts (teaching and/or research activities) between specialists in Organic Chemistry and related areas.

To subscribe to the list send mail with the following line to LISTSERV%RPICICGE.BITNET@CUNYVM.CUNY.EDU:

SUBS ORGCHE-L Your_Real_Name

If you do not receive mail confirming your subscription, contact MSMITH%AMHERST.BITNET@CUNYVM.CUNY.EDU and he will add your name to the list.

Coordinator: Asuncion Valles <D3QOAVC0%EB0UB011.BITNET@CUNYVM.CUNY.EDU>

ORIGAMI@CS.UTEXAS.EDU

This unmoderated mailing list is for discussion of all facets of origami, the Japanese art of paper folding. Topics include bibliographies, folding techniques, display ideas, descriptions of new folds, creativity, materials, organizations, computer representations of folds, etc.

Archives available on request to origami-request@CS.UTEXAS.EDU.

All requests to be added to or deleted from this list, problems, questions, etc., should be sent to origami-request@CS.UTEXAS.EDU

Coordinater: Brad Blumenthal (brad@CS.UTEXAS.EDU)

Orthodox on ListServ@IndyCMS   [Last Updated 28-January-1992]
or ListServ@IndyCMS.IUPUI.Edu

Orthodox (Orthodox Christianity list) is dedicated to the thoughtful exchange of information regarding Orthodox Christianity worldwide, especially its impact upon and resurgence within Russia and her neighbors.

Orthodox is a moderated list with no gateways to any other ListServ lists or Usenet newsgroups. Orthodox is archived. To receive a list of files available, send the command INDEX ORTHODOX to the ListServ CREN or Internet address below.

To subscribe to Orthodox send e-mail to LISTSERV@IndyCMS on BITNET or LISTSERV@IndyCMS.IUPUI.edu on the Internet with the body of the mail containing the command: SUB ORTHODOX yourfirstname yourlastname

List owner/coordinator: John B Harlan IJBH200@IndyVAX (CREN) IJBH200@IndyVAX.IUPUI.Edu (Internet)

OS2-L on LISTSERV@FRORS12.BITNET

This non-edited list is dedicated to issues regarding OS/2, including but not limited to user queries, Workplace, programming, OS/2 2.0 and other related issues. Since FRORS12 has fast connections to the European core, you can expect fast delivery of posted queries.

How to subscribe:

This list is running on a ListEARN 1.3 server, and the command to issue to subscribe to this list is:

SUB OS2-L myfirstname mylastname

Substitute your name in the above command. You can send this command in the BODY of a mail message, or via interactive message to: LISTSERV@FRORS12 (and NOT to the list!).

Once you receive confirmation, you can post to the list by mailing your contribution to: OS2-L@FRORS12.BITNET

To signoff from the list, send SIGNOFF OS2-L to LISTSERV@FRORS12.

OS2 on LISTSERV@BLEKUL11   [Last Updated 12-October-1991]
or LISTSERV@cc1.kuleuven.ac.be

The OS2 list was formed to provide a forum for discussions of the operating systems OS/2 for IBM Compatible PCs. Possible discussion topics include but are not limited to:

> The base operating system in all its flavors and versions
> Hardware configurations and possible conflicts
> Use with software packages, existing OS/2 softwares
> Communications: LAN, SNA, ASYNC, TCP/IP, ...
> Database Manager and other SQL Servers
> Device drivers

OS2 is a weekly digest, called the OS/2 Discussion Forum, with roughly 1000 lines of Q&A each week, including articles picked up at the various comp.os.os2.* newsgroups on USEnet. OS-2 had up to now 700+ direct subscriptions, besides several redistribution points and NETNEWS gateways. OS2 always was a moderated list with archives. Archives of OS2 (before called OS-2), even the older ones (before today) with the old OS-2 name, will be stored in the OS2 FILELIST. To receive a list of files send the command INDEX OS2 to LISTSERV@cc1.kuleuven.ac.be a.k.a. LISTSERV@BLEKUL11 (a LISTEARN file distribution vm machine)

To subscribe to OS2, send the following command to LISTSERV@BLEKUL11 or LISTSERV@cc1.kuleuven.ac.be via mail text or interactive message:

SUBSCRIBE OS2 Your_full_name

where "Your_full_name" is your name. For example:

SUBSCRIBE OS2 Bill Gates

Moderator: OS2MOD@cc1.kuleuven.ac.be OS2MOD@BLEKUL11

OT-HEBREW on OT-HEBREW-REQUEST@VIRGINIA.EDU (Internet)   [Last Updated 12-October-1991]
OTHEBREW on OTHEBREQ@VIRGINIA.BITNET (Bitnet)

OT-HEBREW (Old Testament Hebrew Studies) Conference

OT-HEBREW is an electronic conference designed to foster communication concerning the scholarly study of the Hebrew Old Testament. Anyone interested in Old Testament Studies is invited to subscribe, but the list will assume at least a working knowledge of Biblical Hebrew and Aramaic.

Subscription to this conference is open to anyone interested.

You may subscribe by sending an e-mail message to

OT-HEBREW-REQUEST@VIRGINIA.EDU if you are on the Internet, or
OTHEBREQ@VIRGINIA.BITNET if you are on Bitnet

with the following request as the text of the message.

SUB OT-HEBREW YourFirstname YourLastname

This, the 'SUB ...,' must be part of the message; the subject line will be ignored.

Remember two simple rules-of-thumb:

If it's a request (SUBscribe, UNSUBscribe), send it to the list requester:
OT-HEBREW-REQUEST@VIRGINIA.EDU (Internet) OT-HEBREQ@VIRGINIA.BITNET (Bitnet)

If it's a message for general distribution to the members of the list, send it to the list:
OT-HEBREW@VIRGINIA.EDU (Internet) OTHEBREW@VIRGINIA.BITNET (Bitnet)

The list is supported by the University of Virginia. Our thanks to their management and staff for permission to use their system for the list and for assistance in setting it up. The opinions expressed do not reflect those of the University.

The list is sponsored by the the Center for Christian Study, an independent Christian ministry at the University of Virginia. The Center for Christian Study has been dedicated to providing quality Christian Education since its inception in 1976. The main purposes of the Center are to maintain a caring University outreach ministry and to encourage Chrisitians (and others) to think serious about the Christian faith. If you wish more information about the Center for Christian Study please write:

```
The Center for Christian Study
128 Chancellor Street
Charlottesville, VA 22903
(804) 295-2471
```

Questions about this conference may be directed to David John Marotta:

```
David John Marotta, Medical Center Computing, Stacey Hall
Univ of Virginia (804) 982-3718 wrk INTERNET: djm5g@virginia.edu
Box 512 Med Cntr (804) 924-5261 msg  BITNET: djm5g@virginia
C'ville VA 22908 (804) 296-7209 fax  IBM US: usuvarg8
```

P4200@COMET.CIT.CORNELL.EDU [Last Updated 12-October-1991]

For discussions about Proteon network products

Uncompressed archives, begun on November 21st, 1986, are available as individual files by anonymous FTP from COMET.CIT.CORNELL.EDU. The current archives are listed in file "pub/lists/p4200/Contents".

All requests to be added to or deleted from this list, problems, questions, etc., should be sent to P4200-REQUEST@COMET.CIT.CORNELL.EDU.

Coordinator: Scott Brim <SWB@COMET.CIT.CORNELL.EDU>

INFO-PROTEON@UXC.CSO.UIUC.EDU has been merged with P4200

PACIFIC on LISTSERV@BRUFPB.BITNET

The Forum for and about the Pacific Ocean and Islands

A forum for and about the Pacific Ocean and islands (Pacific Basic), the Pacific coastlines and hinterlands of those nations who border the edge of the Pacific (Pacific Rim), ie. Asia, Australia, North & South America - For those living within these areas, and by others who are interested in the Pacific Basic and Rim.

Ways to increase (electronic) communications with, and interaction between Pacific peoples will be of special interest, as will news, exchanges of informal interests and ideas, cultural and educational sharings, economic, and other material concerns, and activities, both lighthearted and serious.

To subscribe, send the following message to listserv@BRUFPB (Bitnet):

subscribe pacific Your Name Your Interests set pacific repro (so you will receive a copy of your own postings)

eg. subscribe pacific John Doe oceanography set pacific repro

To get a list of current subscribers, and their interests, if provided, send the message "review pacific" to listserv@BRUFPB.BITNET.

List owner: CTEDTC09@BRUFPB.BITNET (Carlos Fernando Nogueira)

PACKET-RADIO@WSMR-SIMTEL20.ARMY.MIL
{ames,decwrl,harvard,rutgers,ucbvax,uunet}!wsmr-simtel20.army.mil!packet-radio (UUCP)

The packet-radio mailing list is intended to provide a forum where people can exchange ideas about packet radio, and discuss projects they are working on. This list is gatewayed to/from Usenet's rec.ham-radio.packet.

List archives are available via ANONYMOUS FTP from WSMR-SIMTEL20.ARMY.MIL in files:

> PD2:<ARCHIVES.PACKET>PACKET-ARCHIV.TXT current messages
> PD2:<ARCHIVES.PACKET>yymm.n-TXT   older messages

All requests to be added to or deleted from this list, problems, questions, etc., should be sent to PACKET-RADIO-REQUEST@WSMR-SIMTEL20.ARMY.MIL.

Coordinator: Keith Petersen <W8SDZ@WSMR-SIMTEL20.ARMY.MIL>

PACS-L%UHUPVM1.BITNET@VM1.NODAK.EDU

The University Libraries and the Information Technology Division of the University of Houston have established this list that deals with all computer systems that libraries make available to their patrons, including CD-ROM databases, computer-assisted instruction (CAI and ICAI) programs, expert systems, hypermedia programs, library microcomputer facilities, locally-mounted databases, online catalogs, and remote end-user search systems. The list is open for general subscription.

Archives of PACS-L are stored in the PACS-L FILELIST. To receive a list of files send the command INDEX LISTNAME to LISTSERV@UHUPVM1.

To subscribe to PACS-L, send the following command to LISTSERV@UHUPVM1.BitNet via mail text or interactive message: SUBSCRIBE PACS-L Your_full_name For example: SUBSCRIBE PACS-L Jane Doe Non-BitNet Internet users can join by sending the above command in the text or body of a message to LISTSERV%UHUPVM1.BITNET@VM1.NODAK.EDU.

> Coordinator: Charles Bailey <LIB3%UHUPVM1.BITNET@VM1.NODAK.EDU>
> Owner: LIBPACS@UHUPVM1.BitNet

PAGAN@DRYCAS.CLUB.CC.CMU.EDU
    PAGAN@DRYCAS (BitNet)

Mailing list created as an offshoot of PSI-L to discuss the religions, philosophy, etc., of Paganism.

Requests to be added to or deleted from the list, problems, questions, etc., should be sent to PAGAN-REQUEST@DRYCAS.CLUB.CC.CMU.EDU (Internet) or PAGAN-REQUEST@DRYCAS (BitNet).

> Coordinator: Stacey Greenstein <UTHER@DRYCAS.CLUB.CC.CMU.EDU>
>   <UTHER@DRYCAS> (BitNet)

PAGE-L@UCF1VM.CC.UCF.EDU

Mailing list for IBM 3812 and IBM 3820 Page Printer discussions, problems, and tips. Questions about these devices are also sometimes covered by other lists (e.g., SCRIPT-L, GDDM, Info-Printers).

Log files will be kept on a monthly basis.

BitNet users can subscribe by sending the following command to LISTSERV@UCF1VM: SUB PAGE-L Your_full_name where Your_full_name is your real name, not your userid; for example: SUB PAGE-L John Doe Non-BitNet users can subscribe by sending the SUB command as the text/body of a message to LISTSERV@UCF1VM.CC.UCF.EDU

> Coordinator: UCF Postmaster <POSTMAST@UCF1VM.CC.UCF.EDU>

PAGEMAKR@INDYCMS.IUPUI.EDU
    PAGEMAKR%INDYCMS.BITNET@VM1.NODAK.EDU
    PAGEMAKR@INDYCMS (BitNet)

Mailing list for PageMaker users to share their ideas and problems with. The list is for desktop publishers who use PageMaker in either the MAC or PC environment. Since the program runs exactly the same in both settings, all PageMaker users are invited to subscribe.

BitNet users may subscribe by sending the following command in a message to LISTSERV@INDYCMS: SUBSCRIBE PAGEMAKR Your full name where "Your full name" is your real name, not your login Id. Non-BitNet users can join the list by sending the above command as the only line in the text/body of a message to LISTSERV@INDYCMS.IUPUI.EDU or LISTSERV%INDYCMS.BITNET@VM1.NODAK.EDU.

Coordinator: Cindy Stone <stonec@GOLD.UCS.INDIANA.EDU> <STONEC%IUBACS.BITNET@VM1.NODAK.EDU> <stonec@IUGOLD> (Bitnet)

PAKISTAN@ASUVM.INRE.ASU.EDU   [Last Updated 12-October-1991]
PAKISTAN@ASUACAD.BITNET

A new list "PAKISTAN" has been established on listserv server at Arizona State University. It is intended to be used mainly for exchanging news about Pakistan.

There are a number of editors who will bring all contributions from list members togeather and publish a newsletter with frequency of at most one per day.

The object is to provide information regarding/concerning Pakistan. The services include:

1. Radio Pakistan News
2. News Clips from Pakistani Newpapers
3. News about Pakistan from other sources (Digest)
4. Exchange rates of Pakistani Ruppee (updated fortnightly)
5. Radio Pakistan Frequency Chart & Timings (updated fortnightly)
6. Info on Filing Income Tax Return in the light of Pakistan-United States Tax Treaty
7. Info on Travel Agents dealing with travel arrangements to Pakistan
8. Articles, news briefs, miscellaneous info etc

Please Note: The list is being test run right now. First Official Issue will be on August 14, 1991 (Independence Day of Pakistan)

Subscription to list is open to public through the server called LISTSERV. In order to subscribe to list PAKISTAN, please send following command in E-mail (or bitnet users may also send an on-line interactive message) to "LISTSERV@ASUACAD.BITNET" or its internet address "LISTSERV@ASUVM.INRE.ASU.EDU" with the following command as the first line of text (body)

SUB PAKISTAN your_first_name Your_Last_name

e.g. in my case it will be SUB PAKISTAN Nauman K. Mysorewala

More information about signing-off and other services will be automatically mailed to you incase you successfully subscribe to the list.

  Owners and Editors:
   Nauman K. Mysorewala (Coordinator) AUNSM@ASUACAD.BITNET
                   AUNSM@Asuvm.Inre.Asu.EDU
   Javed Iqbal   (Editor)
   Asim Mughal   (Editor)

PALS-L on LISTSERV@KNUTH.MTSU.EDU

PALS-L is an international computer conference that deals will all aspects of the MSUS/Unisys/PALS Library Automation application, and the Unisys 1100/2200 series computers it runs on. Hopefully, through this conference, PALS users can share experiences, report problems, discuss solutions, plan future enhancements, gossip, commiserate, and just generally have a grand old time. PALS-L is unmoderated, and is open to everyone interested in PALS.

To subscribe to the PALS-L list, send e-mail to LISTSERV@KNUTH.MTSU.EDU with no subject line, and the command: SUBSCRIBE PALS-L yourfirstname yourlastname as the body of the mail message.

To post to the list, send e-mail to PALS-L@KNUTH.MTSU.EDU.

To get PALS-L to bounce a copy of your posting back to you send an e-mail message with the command: SET MAIL ACK to LISTSERV@KNUTH.MTSU.EDU

MTSU is working on an interactive connection to the internet. Consequently, you might not get a response back to your subscription request for a few hours.

Owner: David Robinson robinson@mtsu.edu Middle Tennessee State University Murfreesboro, Tennessee 37132

PARA-DAP%IRLEARN.BITNET@VM1.NODAK.EDU

Mailing list for discussion of parallel and distributed processing, parallel methodologies, visualisation and related topics. Special emphasis on regular topologies, homogeneous systems, SIMD architectures. Information sub-network for AMT DAP users (an SIMD machine).

The PARA-DAP list has been set up to cater for the needs of researchers, software and hardware developers in the field of parallel/concurrent/distributed processing. Additionally it serves as a medium for users of the AMT DAP but is not restricted to this machine. Contributions to the list are invited from all persons involved in parallel processing.

Archives are kept monthly and can be obtained directly from the subscription address.

BitNet users may subscribe by sending the following command via interactive message or e-mail to LISTSERV@IRLEARN: SUBSCRIBE PARA_DAP your_full_name where "your_full_name" is your real name, not your login Id. Non-BitNet users can join by sending the above command as the only line in the text/body of a message to LISTSERV%IRLEARN.BITNET@VM1.NODAK.EDU.

Queries, suggestions or complaints should be directed to the Coordinator.

Coordinator: Rotan Hanrahan <HANRAH88%IRLEARN.BITNET@VM1.NODAK.EDU>

PARAPSYCH <PSI-L%RPICICGE@VM1.NODAK.EDU>

A forum for discussing experiences, questions, ideas, or research having to do with parapsychology (e.g. ESP, out-of-body experiences, dream experiments, and altered states of consciousness). We are especially interested in hearing about personal experiences, and considering why and how these different phenomena happen, the connections between them, how to bring them about, and what psychological or philosophical implications they have.

To subscribe, send a message to LISTSERV%RPICICGE@VM1.NODAK.EDU containing the text: SUB PSI-L your_real_name

Editor: Lusi Ngai <LUKQC.CUNYVM.CUNY.EDU>

PB-FX@PUCING.PUC.CL   [Last Updated 12-October-1991]
PB-FX@PUCING.BITNET

The purpose of this list is to discuss and to exchange information on subjects related to Calculators and microcomputers Casio (models PB and FX). If you want to enter the list, just send your request to the owner or to listserv@pucing.bitnet or the listserv@pucing.puc.cl

SUB PB-FX Full name

List languages are Spanish and English

List owner : Italo@pucing.puc.cl

PBP-L on LISTSERV@ETSUADMN.BITNET or LISTSERV@ETSUADMN.ETSU.EDU

PBP-L is an online discussion list for play-by-play sportscasters for all sports. If you are a student studying sportscasting for radio or tv, or a veteran broadcaster, this list is for you.

Subscriptions to this list are open to all.

To subscribe, send the following command to LISTSERV@ETSUADMN or LISTSERV@ETSUADMN.ETSU.EDU in the BODY of mail:

SUB PBP-L your full name

where "your full name" is your name. For example:

SUB PBP-L Joan Doe

Owner: John Hendry <HENDRY@ETSUADMN>

PC-REXX@UCF1VM.CC.UCF.EDU

In addition to REXXLIST, the existing VM/SP REXX discussion list, 3 other lists exist to discuss the REXX programming language. They are AREXX-L (for Amiga REXX users), TSO-REXX (for TSO), and PC-REXX (for Personal REXX) users.

Log files will be kept on a monthly basis.

BitNet users can subscribe by sending the following command to LISTSERV@UCF1VM: SUB PC-REXX Your_full_name where Your_full_name is your real name, not your userid; for example: SUB PC-REXX John Doe Non-BitNet users can subscribe by sending the SUB command as the text/body of a message to LISTSERV@UCF1VM.CC.UCF.EDU

Coordinator: UCF Postmaster <POSTMAST@UCF1VM.CC.UCF.EDU>

PCARAB-L on LISTSERV@SAKFU00.BITNET   [Last Updated 12-October-1991]

I have the pleasure to inform you that a new group list called PCARAB-L has been started in our node. This list discusses various researches and problems related to personal computer arabization tools such as Nafitha, Musaad Alarabi, Sakhr ..etcs, or any new researches in arabization. The subscribtion to this list is open for public.

CMS users on BITNET/EARN/etc. can issue the following interactive command to subscribe :

TELL LISTSERV AT SAKFU00 SUB PCARAB-L firstname lastname

Others may subscribe by sending mail to LISTSERV@SAKFU00.BITNET with the BODY of the mail containing the command

SUB PCARAB-L firstname lastname

For more info send a mail to the list owner : DEVYAZ69@SAKFU00.BITNET (Yasser Ahmed Zaki)

PCGEOS-LIST@CSD.MOT.COM   [Last Updated 28-January-1992]

An unmoderated list for users of PC/GEOS products, including GeoWorks Ensemble, GeoWorks Pro, GeoWorks POS, and third party products. Topics include general information, tips, techniques, applications, experiences, etc.

New subscribers will automatically receive digests of all previous messages from the List, at least until such time that it becomes unwieldy to do so.

To subscribe or unsubscribe to the pcgeos-list, send a request to pcgeos-list-request@csd.mot.com. At present, requests are handled by a human operator. No particular format for request is required, but please make sure that your full name is included somewhere in the message or header.

Administrative messages other than subscription and unsubscription should be sent to pcgeos-list-owner@csd.mot.com.

Coordinator: Brian Smithson <brian@csd.mot.com>

PCIP@UDEL.EDU

Discussion group for the various sets of TCP/IP implementations for personal computers. Bugs are reported here and help bringing up a new environmnent may be forthcoming from members of this list. In the past, discussions have included the MIT package, the Stanford TCP modifications and work at Wisconsin and Maryland.

Archives are available via an electronic mail server. Details about its use can be obtained by sending a request to PCIP-REQUEST@UDEL.EDU.

All requests to be added to or deleted from this list, problems, questions, etc., should be sent to PCIP-REQUEST@UDEL.EDU.

List Maintainer: James Galvin <galvin@UDEL.EDU>

PCORPS-L on LISTSERV@CMUVM or LISTSERV@CMUVM.CSV.CMICH.EDU   [Last Update 11/92]

PCORPS-L is for current, returned, and potential volunteers to discuss the "Peace Corps experience" and related subjects of interest to volunteers serving outside their home country. The emphasis is on the U. S. Peace Corps, but participation is actively sought from other international volunteer organizations, both in the U. S. and abroad. Although U. S. Peace Corps staff are invited to participate, this list is not an official distribution channel and does not necessarily reflect official policy.

To subscribe to PCORPS-L, send the following command to LISTSERV@CMUVM via mail text or interactive message or e-mail to LISTSERV@CMUVM.CSV.CMICH.EDU SUBSCRIBE PCORPS-L firstname lastname where firstname and lastname are your real name (not computer ID). For example: sub pcorps-l Joan Doe

Owner: Elliott Parker <3ZLUFUR@CMUVM> or <3ZLUFUR@CMUVM.CSV.CMICH.EDU>

PCSUPT-L%YALEVM.BITNET@CUNYVM.CUNY.EDU

A users' group for the discussion of issues that address end-user support for IBM PC's and similar microcomputers. By providing a central forum for users worldwide, the group will foster the timely communication of solutions to problems with hardware, operating systems, and applications. The group is to include technical support professionals as well as those who find themselves in the role of ad hoc "PC expert". Participants in the group will determine what specific issues are discussed; topics the group is likely to address are:

- Institutional procedures (for example, hard disk backups within departments, software evaluation for institutional support, etc.)
- Exchange of tips and tricks for getting the most from PC's
- Equipment quality and reliability (e.g., which hard disks are most reliable and which are least)
- Differences with new releases of DOS (new commands, changes in command syntax, etc.)
- Comparisons of clones to IBM PC's and PS's in price/performance terms
- Viruses and vaccines

To subscribe send the following command to LISTSERV@YALEVM (non-BitNet users send mail to LISTSERV%YALEVM.BITNET@CUNYVM.CUNY.EDU): SUBSCRIBE PCSUPT-L Your_Full_Name where Your_Full_Name is your real name, not your userid. BitNet VM/CMS users may subscribe by issuing the command: TELL LISTSERV AT YALEVM SUB PCSUPT-L Your_Full_Name To unsubscribe, send the command: UNSUBSCRIBE PCSUPT-L

Coordinator: Bob Boyd <RWBOYD%YALEVM.BITNET@CUNYVM.CUNY.EDU>

PCTECH-L%TREARN.BITNET@VM1.NODAK.EDU
PCTECH-L on LISTSERV@TREARN

The PCTECH-L list has been established as an unedited list for users of MS-DOS PCs. The list is intended for mutual support among users. It may include reviews of software and hardware. The primary difference between PCTECH-L and INFO-PC is that PCTECH-L is not edited.

To subscribe, send: SUB PCTECH-L firstname lastname to LISTSERV@TREARN (LISSTERV%TREARN.BITNET@VM1.NODAK.EDU for Internet users).. Monthly message logs will be kept.

PDP8-LOVERS@AI.MIT.EDU

Mailing list to facilitate communication and cooperation between owners of vintage DEC computers, specifically, but not limited to, the PDP-8 series of minicomputers. Discussions of all manner of hardware, software, programming techniques are invited. Ownership of an 'antique' computer is not required for membership, but flames from people who feel that anything that is not cutting edge technology is worthless are discouraged.

All requests to be added to or deleted from this list, problems, questions, etc., should be sent to PDP8-LOVERS-REQUEST@AI.MIT.EDU.

Coordinator: Robert E. Seastrom <PDP8-LOVERS-REQUEST@AI.MIT.EDU>

PERL-USERS@VIRGINIA.EDU
Perl-Users@UVAARPA.VIRGINIA.EDU
Perl@Virginia (BitNet)
...!uunet!virginia!perl-users (uucp)

For discussion of PERL, Larry Wall's Practical Extraction and Report Language. This list is bidirectionally gatewayed with the USENET newsgroup comp.lang.perl. It is distributed as a digest. A digest is created and distributed at least once per day, more often if traffic warrants.

All requests to be added to or deleted from this list, problems, questions, etc., should be sent to Perl-Users-Request@Virginia.EDU or Perl-Users-Request@uvaarpa.Virginia.EDU (Internet), Perl-Req@Virginia (BitNet), or ...!uunet!virginia!perl-users-request (uucp).

Coordinator: Marc Rouleau <mer6g@VIRGINIA.EDU>

Pharmex@leicester-poly.ac.uk   [Last Updated 12-October-1991]

Pharmacy Mail Exchange is a distribution list for pharmacists and workers in related subjects. To subscribe, or request further details send mail to

Pharmex-request@leicester-poly.ac.uk

Owner: Paul Hodgkinson <phh@leicp.ac.uk> Dept of Pharmacy Leicester Polytechnic

PHIKAP-L@SRU.BITNET   [Last Update 9/92]

This is NOT a LISTSERV list

The purpose of the list is for discussion and communication for chapters of Phi Kappa Theta National Fraternity. Topics for this list are (but are not limited to) rush, new policies, ideas for social activities, and other items related to the fraternity.

This list is NOT a LISTSERV list, so subscription requests may be sent via mail to the List Owner, Michael Hillwig (MLH4125@SRU.BITNET), at PHIKAP-R@SRU.BITNET. In the message, please include: Name, Chapter (both letters and school), Bitnet/Internet Address, and Status (Active Brother, Inactive Brother, Alumni, or Associate/Pledge).

Any questions may be forwarded to the list owner.

Owner: Michael Hillwig <MLH4125@SRU.BITNET>

PHILOS-L%liverpool.ac.uk@NSFNET-RELAY.AC.UK

Mailing list for philosophers (waged or unwaged) in the United Kingdom to discuss matters of mutual concern, and to encourage other such philosophers to meet in the High Country of computer-mail.

Subscribe by sending SUBSCRIBE PHILOS-L [your_name] to LISTSERV@LIVERPOOL.IBM Internet users canjoinby sending the above command to LISTSERV%LIVERPOOL.AC.UK@NSFNET-RELAY.AC.UK.

Coordinator: Stephen Clark <AP01%LIVERPOOL.AC.UK@NSFNET-RELAY.AC.UK>

PHILOSOP%YORKVM1.BITNET@CUNYVM.CUNY.EDU

Academic philosophy mailing list and file server. The files posted by subscribers can be of all sorts: work in progress, comments thereon, advertisements for conferences, newsletters, journals, or associations, job postings, conditional agreements on social action. The items on the board have to have some connection with academic Philosophy; but that's not interpreted narrowly.

To subscribe send the following command to LISTSERV@YORKVM1 (non-BitNet users send mail to LISTSERV%YORKVM1.BITNET@CUNYVM.CUNY.EDU): SUBSCRIBE PHILOSOP Your_Full_Name where Your_Full_Name is your real name, not your userid. To unsubscribe, send the command: UNSUBSCRIBE PHILOSOP

Coordinators: P.A Danielson <CS100046%YUSOL.BITNET@CUNYVM.CUNY.EDU> sol.yorku.CA Nollaig MacKenzie <GL250011%YUVULCAN.BITNET@CUNYVM.CUNY.EDU> vulcan.yorku.CA GL250011@YUORION orion.yorku.CA

PHILRELSOC%HAMPVMS.BITNET@MITVMA.MIT.EDU

A Philosophy, Religion, and Society magazine for intense debate. So far, it has been an Analytic Philosophy debate forum, but philosophically informed articles dealing with society and religion are more than welcome.

All requests to be added to or dropped from the mailing list, as well as all contributions, should be sent to PHILRELSOC@HAMPVMS.BITNET. The editors would appreciate it if all contributions included the following: FROM <name> IN RESPONSE TO: <letter or subject>

PHOTO-L%BUACCA.BITNET@CUNYVM.CUNY.EDU

This list is a forum for discussion of all aspects of photography, including esthetics, equipment, technique, etc.

To subscribe to this list issue the command: TELL LISTSERV AT BUACCA SUB PHOTO-L your_full_name or on VMS systems: SEND LISTSERV@BUACCA SUB PHOTO-L your_full_name Non-BitNet users can subscribe by sending the text: SUB PHOTO-L your_full_name in the body of a message to LISTSERV%BUACCA.BITNET@CUNYVM.CUNY.EDU.

Coordinator: Mark Hayes <MARK@BUIT32.BU.EDU> <CCMLH%BUACCA.BITNET@CUNYVM.CUNY.EDU>

PHYS-L%UWF.BITNET@CUNYVM.CUNY.EDU   [Last Updated 12-October-1991]

This forum is designed for teachers of college and university physics courses. Particular topics of interest include using Bitnet itself as primary medium for the delivery of university courses, innovative teaching laboratory experiments, and the use of micros in the physics classroom The list is open for public subscription.

To subscribe send this command by interactive message to LISTSERV@UWF SUBSCRIBE PHYS-L your-full-name or send mail to LISTSERV@UWF with the above command included as the message body line.

There is no list-specific Internet contact address but, if necessary, can be sent to RSMITH%UWF.BITNET@CUNYVM.CUNY.EDU for subscriptions or

Coordinator: Dick Smith <RSMITH%UWF.BITNET@CUNYVM.CUNY.EDU>

PHYSIC-L <JO%ILNCRD.BITNET@CUNYVM.CUNY.EDU>

A Bitnet newsletter announcing the upcoming weekly colloquia and seminars in Physics at all the Israeli Universities, except the Technion; planned Israeli workshop and conferences in physics are also announced.

To subscribe, send a message to LISTSERV%TAUNIVM.BITNET@CUNYVM.CUNY.EDU with the body of the letter containing the command: SUB PHYSIC-L Your_Full_Name where Your_Full_Name; is your title, first name and last name.

Coordinator: Joseph van Zwaren de Zwarenstein <JO%ILNCRD.BITNET@CUNYVM.CUNY.EDU>

PHYSICS%MARIST.BITNET@cunyvm.cuny.edu

Group for discussion of topics in physics, with some reasonable speculation allowed.

Some archives are maintained on MIT-MC in files:

```
COMAIL;PHYS  FILE    (current messages)
COMAIL;PHYS  FILE00  (oldest archives)
COMAIL;PHYS  FILEnn  (next oldest archives)
COMAIL;PHYS  FILE06  (newest archives)
```

All requests to be added to or deleted from this list, problems, questions, etc., should be sent to PHYSICS-REQUEST@UNIX.SRI.COM (or @MC.LCS.MIT.EDU).

Coordinator: Andrew Knutsen <knutsen@UNIX.SRI.COM>

pinhole@mintir.fidonet.org   [Last Updated 28-January-1992]

This list (pinhole) is an unmoderated list dealing with the discussion of pinhole photography. Camera construction, techniques and style are some of the topics that will be discussed.

To join this list, send a request to: pinhole-request@mintir.fidonet.org

Submissions to the list should be sent to: pinhole@mintir.fidonet.org

This list is being administered by a human being rather than a list server at this time. If you have any questions, feel free to contact the owner of the list:

```
Richard R. Vallon, Jr.        rvallon@mintir.fidonet.org
Photographer                  UUCP: rex!mintir!rvallon
3905 James Drive, Metairie, LA  70003      +1-504-885-7659
```

PJAL on LISTSERV@UTXVM.BITNET or LISTSERV@UTXVM.CC.UTEXAS.EDU

The Progressive Jewish Activism List (PJAL@UTXVM.BITNET) is a forum for organizing and activism-oriented discussion by progressive Jews working for peace and social justice. PJAL is founded on the principles of:

- opposition to discrimination based on race, sex, age, religious belief and practice, and sexuality; support for human rights and freedom of expression

- belief in economic and environmental justice: the right of all people to adequate food, shelter, and quality of life for themselves and their children

- support for individual rights to privacy, including a woman's choice to have an abortion

- support for the resolution of conflict through negotiation; opposition to violence, military culture, and occupation

- support for the self-determination and security of Israelis and Palestinians, including self-determination for Palestinian residents of territories occupied by Israel in 1967, and recognition of the Palestine Liberation Organization as the legitimate representative of the Palestinian people.

PJAL is an outgrowth of the Progressive Jewish Mailing List (PJML), an unmoderated discussion forum for progressive Jews. PJAL is a moderated list, which means that list moderators reserve the right to determine the direction and integrity of submissions posted to PJAL. For unmoderated discussions, subscribers are encouraged to join PJML. Posting and list review on PJAL are restricted to list subscribers.

Let us work together in the tradition of _tikkun olam_, the just repair of the world!

To subscribe to PJAL, please apply to one of the list owners, Steve Carr or Seth Grimes. In your application, please describe your background, state your willingness to adhere to all of the PJAL principles outlined and your acceptance of the moderated format of the list.

List Owners: Steve Carr Seth Grimes Internet: Steven.Carr@UTXVM.CC.UTEXAS.EDU JCIPP@MCIMAIL.COM Bitnet: RTFC507@UTXVM Phone: (512) 453-8540 (h) (202) 547-1861 (512) 471-4071 (o) U.S. Post: 3911-A Ave. F P.O. Box 4991 Austin TX 78751 Washington, DC 20008

PJML on LISTSERV@UTXVM.BITNET or LISTSERV@UTXVM.CC.UTEXAS.EDU

PJML is an educational forum -- a place for sharing information on a variety of Jewish concerns -- aimed at inspiring us to move forward and build a better world. PJML connects activist Jews and our allies across the globe. We come from many traditions but identify ourselves as "progressive"; if we have differences, let us discuss them openly and respectfully. Let us continue in the tradition of _tikkun olam_, the just repair of the world.

PJML is unmoderated, and subscribers are asked to use their best judgment when submitting items that deal with especially emotional issues, such as the Palestinian-Israeli conflict. The list owners reserve the right to take appropriate steps in keeping these discussions constructive and focused.

To subscribe to PJML, send the following message to either LISTSERV@UTXVM.CC.UTEXAS.EDU (Internet) or LISTSERV@UTXVM (Bitnet):

SUB PJML <Your Full Name>

List Owners: Steve Carr   Seth Grimes
Internet: Steven.Carr@UTXVM.CC.UTEXAS.EDU JCIPP@MCIMAIL.COM
Bitnet: RTFC507@UTXVM
Phone: (512) 453-8540 (h)   (202) 547-1861
             (512) 471-4071 (o)
U.S. Post: 3911-A Ave. F   P.O. Box 4991
             Austin TX 78751   Washington, DC 20008

PLEARN-L%UBVM.BITNET@VM1.NODAK.EDU

Mailing list for discussion of possible Poland <-> EARN network traffic.

BitNet users may subscribe by sending the following command to LISTSERV@UBVM via interactive message or e-mail: SUB PLEARN-L Your full name where "Your full name" is your real name, not your login Id. Non-BitNet users can join by sending the above command as the only line in the text/body of a message to LISTSERV%UBVM.BITNET@VM1.NODAK.EDU.

Coordinator: Dave Phillips <DAVEP@ACSU.BUFFALO.EDU>

POET@scruz.ucsc.EDU   [Last Updated 9/92]

Purpose: A workshop/critique forum for poetic works of all descriptions in progress.

Contact: poet-request@scruz.ucsc.EDU (Jon Luini)

Pol-Econ@SHSU.BITNET

Pol-Econ is a list to provide an unmoderated environment where issues, questions, comments, ideas, and uses of Political Economy as a logical framework can be discussed. In a broad sense, this includes virtually anything dealing with economics.

The explicit purpose of Pol-Econ is to provide timely interchange between subscribers, to provide a forum where interesting questions can be addressed within the context of interactive exchange between many individuals, to discuss the evolution and application of Political Economy, to announce professional meetings, calls for papers, etc., and to provide partial tables of contents for current periodicals. As is the case on all unmoderated lists, the discussion and topics are only limited by the participation and interest of its subscribers. Subscribers are welcome to take an active role by posting to Pol-Econ or an inactive role by monitoring the list. Although not necessary for participation, it shall be assumed that subscribers are basically familiar with technical economic jargon.

To subscribe to Pol-Econ, please send a MAIL message to: LISTSERV@SHSU.BITNET

The body of this MAIL message should be one line and contain the words: SUBSCRIBE Pol-Econ

LISTSERV@SHSU.BITNET is not supported by the conventional interactive VM-based LISTSERV, but is instead entirely MAIL oriented.

List owner: George D. Greenwade <BED_GDG@SHSU.BITNET>

POLAND-L%UBVMS.BITNET@VM1.NODAK.EDU

Mailing list devoted to the discussion of Polish culture and events. We are interested in all subjects related to Poland, Polish Americans and Eastern Europe (related to Poland).

POLAND-L is archived weekly. To obtain a list of available files send the following command to LISTSERV@UBVM through e-mail: INDEX POLAND-L

To subscribe to POLAND-L, send the following command to LISTSERV@UBVM via e-mail text: SUBSCRIBE POLAND-L Your_full_name where "Your_full_name" is your real name, not your login Id. We discourage using SEND or similar means, since this sometimes introduces different paths than e-mail and may result in bouncing e-mail. Non-BitNet users can join by sending the above command as the only line in the text/body of a message to LISTSERV%UBVM.BITNET@VM1.NODAK.EDU.

Coordinator: Jerzy Pawlowski <V132NREA%UBVMS.BITNET@VM1.NODAK.EDU>

POLI-SCI@RUTGERS.EDU

POLI-SCI is a spinoff from the HUMAN-NETS discussion list. Shortly after the November 1980 election, HUMAN-NETS began to discuss the impact that electronic communications had on the election. As this discussion continued, it lost its narrow focus on electronic communications and began to consider the election in general, how elections are won and lost, and the nature of the electoral college. The growth of these discussions, and their spawning of related discussions, indicated that a separate discussion list was merited and POLI-SCI was installed. Since then POLI-SCI has begun to consider other topics including the history of the Carter and Nixon presidencies, the Iranian hostage crisis, etc. (with a little less dignity, the list might be characterized as a permanent distributed political bull session).

Archived digest messages are stored on RUTGERS in: <poli-sci>mail.txt and other files in the <poli-sci> directory

All requests to be added to or deleted from this list, problems, questions, etc., should be sent to POLI-SCI-REQUEST@RUTGERS.EDU.

Moderator: JoSH Hall <JoSH@RUTGERS.EDU>

POLITICS@UCF1VM.CC.UCF.EDU   [Last Updated June 1992]

A list for the serious discussion of politics, hosted by the University of Central Florida. Since it is not being moderated, we ask that all users refrain from making attacks or flames of a personal nature.

Log files will be kept on a weekly basis due to their size.

BitNet users can subscribe by sending the following command to LISTSERV@UCF1VM: SUB POLITICS Your_full_name where Your_full_name is your real name, not your userid; for example: SUB POLITICS John Doe Non-BitNet users can subscribe by sending the SUB command as the text/body of a message to LISTSERV@UCF1VM.CC.UCF.EDU

Coordinator: Jim Ennis <JIM@UCF1VM.CC.UCF.EDU>

POLYMERP%RUTVM1.BITNET@CUNYVM.CUNY.EDU

Polymer Physics Discussion. The topics include meetings, articles, software, theories, materials, methods, tools, polymer properties such as solubility, viscosity, self-diffusion, and adsorption.

All requests to be added to or deleted from this list should be sent to the automatic server LISTSERV%RUTVM1.BITNET@CUNYVM.CUNY.EDU as commands (one per line) in the mail body or note. Valid commands are: INFO, HELP, LIST, SUBSCRIBE POLYMERP your_full_name, UNSUBSCRIBE POLYMERP, REVIEW POLYMERP, GET filename filetype.

Archives and data of interest are kept on the same server (GET POLYMERP FILELIST for a list of files).

Coordinator: Jan Scheutjens <SCHEUTJE%HWALHW50.BITNET@CUNYVM.CUNY.EDU>

POPULATION-BIOLOGY <biosci%NET.BIO.NET@VM1.NODAK.EDU>

Population Biology is a synthesis of population ecology and population genetics, pursuing a unified theory to explain the structure, functioning and evolution of populations of living beings. Such populations are very complex systems, exhibiting a variety of phenomena that we stil do not master. Just to quote a famous example, multiannual density cycles (e.g. in lemmings) have not received a satisfactory expalnation, despite of decades of debated studies and speculations. Population Biology is a very active field, encompassing such diverse approaches as tenacious, harsh field work to track long term demographic and genetic fluctuations, or sophisticated conversations with a computer about strange attractors possibly causing chaos in the density fluctuations.

Topics that can be discussed include: ecology, population genetics, systematics, evolution, morphometry, interspecific competition, sociobiology, mathematical modelling, population regulation, pest control, speciation, chromosomal evolution, social behaviour, statistical methodology in population study, population management of endangered species, applications of molecular biology techniques, etc., and, last but not least, your own topic. There is no restriction on the species: viruses, protokaryotes, plants, animals (including man), mythic or extinct species, computer- simulated species... Technical problems, book reviews, meeting annoucements and so on are also welcome.

The BITNET and USENET names of the new group are:

Internet	BITNET	USENET
POPULATION-BIOLOGY	POP-BIO	bionet.population-bio

If you wish to participate in the the group, please send your subscription request to the appropriate BIOSCI node below. More informations on BIOSCI can also be requested at the adresses below:

Address	Location	Network
biosci%NET.BIO.NET@VM1.NODAK.EDU		Internet
biosci@net.bio.net	U.S.A.	BitNet
biosci@irlearn.ucd.ie	Ireland	EARN/BitNet
biosci@uk.ac.daresbury	U.K.	JANET
biosci@bmc.uu.se	Sweden	EARN/Internet

Subscriptions can also be sent to the LISTSERV at IRLEARN by sending a message, note or mail with the line: SUB POP$BIO your_full_name

Moderator: Vincent Bauchau <VINCENT%BUCLLN11.BITNET@VM1.NODAK.EDU>

portmaster-users@msen.com

For users of the Livingston Portmast line of terminal servers and routers, which are in use by several network service providers. The Portmaster series includes a 4-port 56K router (the IR-4) and a 10 port async terminal server (the PM-11) that supports SLIP and PPP.

To join the list send mail to portmaster-users-request@msen.com

To submit messages to the list send to portmaster-users@msen.com

Owner: portmaster-users-request@msen.com

posix-ada@GREBYN.COM
posix-ada%GREBYN.COM@AOS.BRL.MIL

Primarily intended for working group members of IEEE 1003.5, the group that is involved in developing the Ada binding to the IEEE POSIX specification.

All requests to be added to or deleted from this list, problems, questions, etc., should be sent to posix-ada-request@GREBYN.COM (or posix-ada-request%GREBYN.COM@AOS.BRL.MIL).

Coordinator: Karl Nyberg <karl@GREBYN.COM> <karl%GREBYN.COM@AOS.BRL.MIL>

posix-fortran@SANDIA.GOV@Index(posix-fortran)

Mailing list primarily intended for working group members of IEEE 1003.9, the group that is involved in developing the FORTRAN binding to the IEEE POSIX specification.

All requests to be added to or deleted from this list, problems, questions, etc., should be sent to posix-fortran-request@SANDIA.GOV.

Coordinator: Michael J. Hannah <mjhanna@SANDIA.GOV>

POSTCARD on LISTSERV@IDBSU.BITNET

This list is for those interested in exchanging or collecting picture postcards of all types and all eras. Following BITNET policy, it will NOT allow the sales of postcards or any sort of advertising.

Topics for possible discussion include history of picture postcards, finding those who have similar collecting interests, exchanging information on research activities, and so forth. In addition, many members may be interested in exchanging postcards with each other by US/Foreign mail to learn more about one another's environments and cultures.

To subscribe send e-mail to LISTSERV@IDBSU.BITNET with the following command in the BODY of the mail:

SUB POSTCARD your full name Eg. SUB POSTCARD Ansel Adams

Owner: Dan Lester University Library Boise State University Boise, Idaho 83725 ALILESTE@idbsu.Bitnet

POWERH-L on LISTSERV@UNB.CA - PowerHouse 4GL or LISTERV@UNBMVS1.BITNET

POWERH-L list is open to discussion of any topic (vaguely) related to PowerHouse, the 4GL package from COGNOS. Contributions may be anything from tutorials to rampant speculation on issues of technical nature, of administrative procedures and/or of anything else having to do with PowerHouse.

To subscribe to POWERH-L, send the following command to LISTSERV@UNB.CA via mail text (in the BODY) or interactive message:

SUBSCRIBE POWERH-L Your_full_name For example: SUBSCRIBE POWERH-L John Smith.

Contributions are automatically archived, and may be obtained by sending an INDEX POWERH-L command to "LISTSERV@UNB.CA"

Owner: Georges M. Bourgeois <BOURGEG@UMONCTON.CA>

POWER-L%NDSUVM1.BITNET@VM1.NODAK.EDU

Mailing list to discuss the IBM RISC System/6000 family based on the Performance Optimization With Enhanced RISC (POWER) Architecture (also known as RIOS in the rumor mill) announced on February 15, 1990. This includes the POWERstations, POWERservers, Xstation, and related hardware and software.

Archives of the discussions are kept on a weekly basis. Send LISTSERV the commands "INDEX POWER-L" and "INFO DATABASE" for more information (NOTE: the commands are sent to LISTSERV@NDSUVM1 or LISTSERV@VM1.NODAK.EDU and NOT to the list!). The files are also available via ANONYMOUS FTP to VM1.NODAK.EDU (134.129.111.1) by entering CD POWER-L after connecting.

To subscribe to POWER-L send mail (or message on BitNet) to LISTSERV@NDSUVM1 (BitNet), LISTSERV@VM1.NODAK.EDU, or LISTSERV%NDSUVM1.BITNET@VM1.NODAK.EDU with the following command in the body/text of the message: SUB POWER-L your full name where "your full name" is your real name, not your login Id.

Coordinator: Marty Hoag <nu021172@VM1.NODAK.EDU>
<nu021172%NDSUVM1.BITNET@VM1.NODAK.EDU> <nu021172@NDSUVM1> (BitNet)

prion@acc.stolaf.edu

The Prion Digest was formed as a reference point for the discussion and sharring of current research into prion (or slow virus) infection. Common prion related diseases are Creutzfeld-Jakob disease (CJD), Gerstmann-Straussler syndrome (GSS), transmissible mink encephalopathy, bovine spongiform encephalopathy, chronic wasting disease of deer and elk, scrapie, and kuru (from Kingsbury, D.T., "Genetics of Response to Slow Virus {Prion} Infection", Annu. Rev. Genet. 1990._ 24: 115-32).

All comers are welcome, from interested lay people to researchers working with prions and/or prion infections.

This digest is *NOT* on a LISTSERV, administrivia (subscriptions, deletions, changes, etc.) should be addressed to <prion-request@acc.stolaf.edu>

Submissions should be sent to <prion@acc.stolaf.edu>. All submissions are entered into the input for the next digest.

The digest is sent out on a weekly basis (currently at 0330 CST on Sat.).

Back issues are available via anonymous ftp from <beowulf.acc.stolaf.edu> (130.71.192.20) in the pub/prion directory. If you do not have ftp access, send a request to <prion-archive@acc.stolaf.edu> and the requested files will be sent to you.

Prion Digest Moderator: Chris Swanson <swansonc@acc.stolaf.edu>

PROCOM-L%ATSUVAX1.BITNET@VM1.NODAK.EDU

Mailing list dedicated to discussion among users of the ProComm 2.4.2, 2.4.3, and ProComm Plus terminal emulators on PCs and PC clones.

To subscribe, send a message with the text/body containing the line; SUB PROCOM-L your_full_name (where "your_full_name" is your real name, not your login Id) to MAILSERV@ATSUVAX1.BITNET (BitNet) or MAILSERV%ATSUVAX1.BITNET@VM1.NODAK.EDU (Internet).

Coordinator: Bill Bailey <BAILEYB%ATSUVAX1.BITNET@VM1.NODAK.EDU>

PROFSALT on LISTSERV@UCCVMA

PROFSALT@UCCVMA, Profs Alternatives, has been established to discuss tips and techniques for Profs sites who wish to investigate converting to office automation facilities which make more sense given today's network realities.

For instance, tools for converting Profs nickname files to RiceMail compatible Names files could be shared. Alternatives to Profs calendars could be discussed.

To subscribe from a VM system:

tell listserv at uccvma subscribe profsalt firstname lastname

Or, send a mail note to listserv@uccvma with this line of text (not subject):

subscribe profsalt firstname lastname

As always, you will be an item of disdain if you send subscription requests to the list (though I think that with Eric's latest fixes, these may be filtered out).

Owner: Rich Hintz opsrjh@uccvma.bitnet University of California

PROG-PUBS@fuggles.acc.virginia.edu   [Last Updated 28-January-1992]

Contact: PROG-PUBS-request@fuggles.acc.virginia.edu

PROG-PUBS is a mailing list for people interested in progressive and/or alternative publications and other media.

PROG-PUBS was originally created to facilitate and encourage communication among people interested in and active with the "alternative student press" movement. However, the list's scope is now broader than this; we welcome and encourage participation from people involved in all kinds of small-scale, independent, progressive and/or alternative media, including newspapers, newsletters, and radio and video shows, whether campus-based or not.

PROGRESS@THINC.COM   [Last Updated 12-October-1991]

Email User Group devoted exclusively to the discussion of all relevant aspects of the PROGRESS(tm) RDBMS. Discussion may include any topic related to PROGRESS(tm).

To subscribe send Mail to:

To: Progress@THINC.COM
Subject: Add User

Full Real Name : _____
Net Address (From uunet) : _____
Company Name : _____
Voice Phone Number : _____

Coordinator: Ethan A. Lish (Ethan.Lish@THINC.COM)

PROP-L%UTARLVM1.BITNET@VM1.NODAK.EDU
PROP-L on LISTSERV@UTARLVM1

PROP-L is a list for the discussion of problems, suggestions, and helpful information relating to the Programmable Operator component of IBM CMS. Anyone who uses Programmable Operator as part of the operation of their VM system is encouraged to subscribe to this list.

Archives of PROP-L discussions can be listed by sending the command INDEX PROP-L to LISTSERV@UTARLVM1.

To subscribe to PROP-L, send the following command to LISTSERV@UTARLVM1 (LISTSERV%UTARLVM1.BITNET@VM1.NODAK.EDU for INTERNET users) via mail text or interactive message: SUBSCRIBE PROP-L Your_full_name. For example: SUBSCRIBE PROP-L Joe Shmoe.

Owners: Gary Samek <C133GES%UTARLVM1@VM1.NODAK.EDU> David Young <DYOUNG%TRINITY@VM1.NODAK.EDU>

PROTOCOL@VMD.CSO.UIUC.EDU
PROTOCOL@UIUCVMD.BITNET

The PROTOCOL electronic mailing list is a forum for the discussion of all kinds of computer protocols. This includes the format of data when transmitted on communications devices, plus the internal formats used to store data on storage media.

Topics of dicussion will include the formats used by various archiving programs and applications, encodings used to transfer binary files via electronic mail and other text-only media, and networking protocols such as DECNET, UUCP, TCP/IP and OSI. Discussion of file formats are welcome, including UUENCODE, XXENCODE, LCODER, SUPENCOD, ARC, ZIP, ZOO, TAR, COMPRESS, SFIF, GIF, TIFF, PBM, NETDATA, SHAR, and any others. We are interested in contributions toward the development of general-purpose file transfer protocols.

The list has the combined mission of two previous lists called "ProtocolS" and "FFP-L".

The PROTOCOL list is gatewayed to the UseNet list comp.protocols.misc. We welcome free-ranging discussion and product announcements.

The subscription is as for a normal BITNET LISTSERV list. Send a message to LISTSERV@UIUCVMD.BITNET (LISTSERV AT UIUCVMD) or listserv@vmd.cso.uiuc.edu with the contents:

SUBSCRIBE PROTOCOL Your Full Name

The list is unmoderated, open enrollment, and is not digestified. The list coordinators are:

Phil Howard <phil@ux1.cso.uiuc.edu> and David J. Camp <david@wubios.wustl.edu> and David M Katinsky <dmk@pilot.njin.net>

PSI-L%RPIECS.BITNET@CUNYVM.CUNY.EDU

Forum for discussing experiences, questions, ideas, or research having to do with psi (e.g. ESP, out-of-body experiences, dream experiments, and altered states of consciousness). We are especially interested in hearing about personal experiences, and considering why and how these different phenomena happen, the connections between them, how to bring them about, and what psychological or philosophical implications they have.

To subscribe, send mail to the Coordinator.

Coordinator: Ben Geer <BGEER%HAMPVMS.BITNET@CUNYVM.CUNY.EDU>

psion@csd4.csd.uwm.edu

The list is for the discussion and exchange of information and software for Psion computers. This list is for Psion Organiser handheld computers, and Psion laptops (including the MS-DOS models). Non-Psion portable and handheld computer discussion is welcome.

Although this list originates at an Internet site, there are gateways to many other networks and mail systems. Fidonet, Compuserve, MCI and many other systems can also receive this mailing list. Contact the moderator for more information.

There is an archive of Psion software and other information at csd4.csd.uwm.edu in the Psion directory. For users that can't ftp, files can be requested via mail. The archive already contains over 500K, mostly obtained from the PIG (Psion Interest Group) Pen BBS (703-765-6290). The BBS has recently changed formats and will no longer be exclusively Psion oriented but the files and message system will be retained. Any messages or files not already at the archive from the PIG Pen or other source are welcome.

```
mailing list:  psion@csd4.csd.uwm.edu
moderator:     psion-owner@csd4.csd.uwm.edu
subscription/file requests:
        psion-request@csd4.csd.uwm.edu
```

<-:(= Anthony Stieber anthony@csd4.csd.uwm.edu uwm!uwmcsd4!anthony

PSTAT-L%IRLEARN.BITNET@CUNYVM.CUNY.EDU

A forum for the exchange of information about the P-STAT data management and statistics package; code, macros, applications, user news, user group reports etc.

All requests to be added to or deleted from the mailing list, or to have files distributed, should be sent to the Coordinator.

Coordinator: Peter Flynn UCC <CBTS8001%IRUCCVAX.UCC.IE@CUNYVM.CUNY.EDU>

PSRT-L on LISTSERV@UMCVMB

PSRT-L@UMCVMB is a moderated discussion list on Bitnet which deals with issues of interest to professional political scientists, both researchers and teachers. Submissions from all sub-fields of political science as well as related disciplines are encouraged.

The list is not intended to serve as a public forum for debate over current issues in politics, as other lists already fill that niche. Rather it is intended to provide an opportunity for political scientists to present their ideas and ongoing research for discussion, to consider the directions in which the discipline is advancing, and to encourage the dissemination of new concepts in research and teaching. In addition to ongoing discussions, the list editors would like to post announcements of job openings and upcoming conferences.

To subscribe to PSRT-L send mail to LISTSERV@UMCVMB on BITNET with the TEXT or BODY of the mail containing the one line:

SUB PSRT-L yourfirstname yourlastname

Editors of PSRT-L: Michael Malaby Bill Ball <C476721@UMCVMB.Bitnet>

PSYCGRAD@ACADVM1.UOTTAWA.CA   [Last Updated 12-October-1991]

Psychology Graduate Students Discussion Group List

Now graduate students of psychology can communicate among each other efficiently and free of charge because, there is a list on the Listserv called PSYCGRAD (Psychology Graduate Students Discussion Group List). Its main purpose is to provide a medium through which graduate students in the field of psychology can communicate.

If you are a student studying in a graduate-level psychology program, you are invited to join this list. It is asked that conversation topics be relevant to being a graduate student in psychology. As you probably can see, this is a very open category and not too rigorously defined. Virtually, anything goes except junk-mail advertisements. The list will not be moderated and subscriptions are open. (Junk mail has been a terrible problem for many users in the past). Corporations, businesses, agencies, publishers, etc. are not invited to the list.

There are a few ways to subscribe to this list.

1. If your system is part of Bitnet and a VM system, you may do this by using the interactive command by typing at the R; (prompt)- TELL LISTSERV AT UOTTAWA SUB PSYCGRAD Yourfirstname Yourlastname (Don't forget to capitalize and lower case Yourfirstname and Yourlastname).

2. If your system is part of Bitnet and a VAX system, you may do this by using the interactive command by typing this comand. SEND LISTSERV@ACADVM1.UOTTAWA.CA SUB PSYCGRAD Yourfirstname Yourlastname (Don't forget to capitalize and lower case Yourfirstname and Yourlastname).

3. Or, you may mail one single solitary command to Listserv by mailing to LISTSERV AT UOTTAWA, and then make your only line read as follows... SUB PSYCGRAD Yourfirstname Yourlastname.

4. If your system is part of Internet you may mail the same command, as outlined in #3, to LISTSERV@ACADVM1.UOTTAWA.CA

Owner:

Matthew Simpson
BITNET: 054340@UOTTAWA
INTERNET: 054340@ACADVM1.UOTTAWA.CA

PSYCOLOQUY (PSYC@PUCC.PRINCETON.EDU)   [Last Updated 12-October-1991]

PSYCOLOQUY is a refereed electronic journal sponsored by the American Psychological Association. It contains both newsletter-type materials (announcements, conferences, employment notices, abstracts, queries) and short articles refereed by the Editorial Board, as well as refereed interdisciplinary and international commentaries on the articles ("Scholarly Skywriting"). The newsletter sections are not archived but the refereed journal sections are available by anonymous ftp from directory /pub harnad at princeton.edu (128.112.128.1).

To subscribe send to LISTERV@PUCC.BITNET the following one-line message (no subject header): SUBSCRIBE PSYC Youruserid@Yournode.Yourdomain Firstname Lastname If this procedure is unsuccessful, you may write to harnad@princeton.edu to have your name added manually to the list. PSYCOLOQUY is also available as the moderated Usenet newsgroup sci.psychology.digest

Coordinator: Stevan Harnad, PSYCOLOQUY Co-Editor psyc@pucc.bitnet psyc@pucc.princeton.edu

publish@chron.com   [Last Updated 28-January-1992]

The PUBLISH mailing list is for discussion of the role of computers, specifically workstations, in book, magazine, newspaper, and other publishing. It also covers specific publishing-related implementation questions, including, but not limited to:

* Printing and Scanning	* Document management
* Raster Image Processing	* Available Software and Hardware
* Text Tools	* High-Bandwidth Interfaces
* Image Processing	* Integration with Personal Computers

It is NOT a programming or system administration forum, although discussion will sometimes touch on these subjects.

The charter of this list is certainly subject to modification through the general agreement of the members. Other suggested topics are welcome.

Here are the relevant Internet mail addresses for PUBLISH:

publish@chron.com	submissions
publish-request@chron.com	requests to be deleted & added

To join the list, send mail to publish-request@chron.com.

Before sending a request to be deleted from the list, check with your local "postmaster" to see if you are receiving the messages via a local redistribution alias. If you are, then your local postmaster can remove you from the list far more effectively and quickly than I can.

This list is NOT moderated! Anything mailed to the submissions address will be echoed to everyone on the list. Every potential poster is on his or her honor to not abuse this list! Messages sent to this list are archived, but are not yet publically available. Do not ask for old messages - the archive will eventually be made available and an announcement will be made.

Please DO NOT mail "please remove me" requests to the submissions address!

Please publicize this list! The more people that are on it, the more useful it will be.

If you have any questions or corrections about this message, please send them to "sysnmc@chron.com".

PURTOPOI on LISTSERV@PURCCVM

Purdue Rhetoric, Professional Writing, and Language Discussion Group

The PURTOPOI list is a scholarly forum for the discussion of current issues or "topoi" in the fields of rhetoric and composition, professional writing, and language research. While the list began as a list for Purdue only, it became so popular that it has been opened up for general subscriptions.

Previous topics taken up by the group have included:

- the relationship between social construction and ethnographic research in composition.
- the disciplinary relationships between rhetoric, literary criticism, and linguistics.
- the debate between agonistic and rogerian approaches to composition.
- the impact of cultural studies on composition pedagogy and research.
- and the antagonism between post-structuralist and cognitivist approaches to historical, theoretical, and empirical research methods.

Members are encouraged to submit works in progress, reviews of recent publications, reports or announcements of conferences, bibliographies, or questions for group discussion.

Subscription to the list is by listowners. Messages sent to the list are archived and may be retrieved by list members. Also, a filelist containing help files, bibliographies, and papers of interest is available to list members.

For more information on PURTOPOI@PURCCVM, contact Tharon Howard at the addresses below:

Internet: ucc@mace.cc.purdue.edu BITNET: XUCC@PURCCVM

PYNCHON@CC.SFU.CA
PYNCHON%SFU.BITNET@VM1.NODAK.EDU
PYNCHON@SFU (BitNet)

Mailing list for discussion of Thomas Pynchon, a notoriously publicity shy contemporary American novelist with four novels, "V", "Gravity's Rainbow", "The Crying of Lot 49" and "Vineland", and a book of short stories "Slow Learner". The stuff overlaps into several catgories, e.g., post modernism, black humor, conspiracy theory, etc.

To join the list, send a message to the Coordinator; include your name (or a pseudonym) as well as your net address.

Coordinator: Jody Gilbert <USERDOG1%SFU.BITNET@VM1.NODAK.EDU> <USERDOG1@CC.SFU.CA> <USERDOG1@SFU> (BitNet)

Q-METHOD on LISTSERV@KENTVM.BITNET   [Last Updated March 1992]
or LISTSERV@KENTVM.KENT.EDU

Q-Method is an unmoderated list for the discussion of all aspects of Q methodology as innovated and developed by the late William Stephenson (1902-1989). Q methodology is a broad approach to the study of subjectivity, and includes issues of theory, conceptualization, measurement, and analysis. Topics for discussion may therefore range from the Q-sort technique to Q factor analysis to broader concerns about the nature of subjectivity. Q methodology has been applied in psychology, communication, political science, advertising, education, law, health and medicine, and many others fields. Discussion may therefore be expected to be diverse with respect to illustration while unified with respect to methodological principles. (Q-Method began March 1, 1992 and succeeds QTemp@KentVM, which was established as a temporary list on January 14, 1991.)

Archives of Q-Method back issues (including those previously stored under QTemp) can be listed by sending the command INDEX Q-METHOD to LISTSERV@KENTVM or LISTSERV@KENTVM.KENT.EDU in the BODY of e-mail.

To subscribe, send the following command to LISTSERV@KENTVM or LISTSERV@KENTVM.KENT.EDU in the BODY of mail or in an interactive message:

SUB Q-METHOD your full name

where "your full name" is your name. For example:

SUB Q-METHOD Raymond B. Cattell

Owner: Steven R. Brown <SBrown@KentVM> <SBrown@KentVM.Kent.EDU>

QM-L on LISTSERV@YaleVM (BitNet)

or LISTSERV@YaleVM.YCC.Yale.edu (InterNet)

Yale University is currently using CE Software's QuickMail mail package on a campus-wide AppleTalk network. We are attempting to connect as many students, faculty, and staff as possible in order to achieve as close to universal e-mail connectivity as we can. We are interested in talking to other QuickMail users, in order to discuss common experiences, problems, configurations, and the like. We encourage anyone interested in the CE Software QuickMail software to join us on QM-L.

You may subscribe to this list in the usual way you would subscribe to any listserv list. To sign up, send a message or mail to Listserv@YaleVM (BitNet), or mail to Listserv@YaleVM.YCC.Yale.edu (InterNet), with the command:

subscribe qm-l firstname lastname

For MAIL subscriptions this command should appear as the first line of the BODY of the mail message. The subject line is ignored and can be omitted. Obviously, firstname and lastnameare replaced with your first and last name.

Owner:
BITnet: Peter @ YaleVM   InterNet: Peter @ YaleVM.YCC.Yale.edu
Yale University Computer Center   Peter Furmonavicius
175 Whitney Avenue   Senior Research Programmer
P.O. Box 2112
New Haven, CT 06520   (203) 432-6600

qn@queernet.org

qn is a mailing list for Queer Nation activists and for all interested in Queer Nation. The purpose of qn is to network among various Queer Nation chapters, discussion actions and tactics, and for general discussion of how to bring about Queer Liberation.

All mail to be distributed to all list members should go to qn@queernet.org. All administrative information, including requests to join the list, should be directed to qn-request@queernet.org.

Listowner: Roger B.A. Klorese <rogerk@unpc.QueerNet.Org>

QUAKE-L@VM1.NODAK.EDU
QUAKE-L@NDSUVM1.BITNET
QUAKE-L%NDSUVM1.BITNET@VM1.NODAK.EDU

Mailing list for discussion of the ways various national and international computer networks can help in the event of an earthquake, or the help can be enhanced. One of the basic problems discussed might be network reconfigurations which would be temporarily required; others might be in actually putting various groups in electronic contact with each other.

Public notebooks for the list will be available from LISTSERV, can be searched with the LISTSERV database facility (send LISTSERV the command info database for details), and are available via anonymous FTP from VM1.NODAK.EDU (134.129.111.1) after entering CD LISTARCH (use DIR QUAKE-L.* to see any notebooks/archives).

BitNet or Internet users may subscribe to the list by sending a message or e-mail to LISTSERV@NDSUVM1 or LISTSERV@VM1.NODAK.EDU, respectively. On the first line of the text or body of the message enter the command; SUB QUAKE-L your_full_name where your_full_name is your real name, not your login Id.

Coordinator: Marty Hoag <NU021172@VM1.NODAK.EDU> <NU021172@NDSUVM1.BITNET>

Quanta@ANDREW.CMU.EDU

Quanta is the moderated, electronically distributed journal of Science Fiction and Fantasy. As such, each issue contains fiction by amateur authors as well as articles, reviews etc... Quanta is published bi-monthly in two formats, Ascii and PostScript (for PostScript compatible laser-printers).

Back issues are available by anonymous FTP from: fed.expres.cs.cmu.edu (128.2.209.58).

Requests to be added to the distribution list should be sent to either one of the following depending on which version of the magazine you'd like to receive: quanta+request-ascii@ANDREW.CMU.EDU quanta+request-postscript@ANDREW.CMU.EDU

Coordinator: Dan Applequist (da1n@andrew.cmu.edu)

QUILT on listserv@cornell.edu -

The QUILT maillist was formed to discuss quilting: questions, answers, book reports, tips, mail order sources, patterns and favorite stores. This maillist is a general quilting support group. Many of the mailfiles contain questions and answers about quilting; many of the mailfiles are friendly, chatty discussions about quilting, sewing or life in general. The volume of mailfiles ranges from 3-40 per week. Our group includes a mailing list and two quilt block exchanges.

A list of archived files for this mailing list, including archives of the discussion on the list, can be found by sending the command INDEX QUILT in mail to listserv@cornell.edu.

To subscribe to QUILT, send the following command to listserv@cornell.edu via mail text (NB--this server cannot accept interactive messages):

SUBSCRIBE QUILT Your full name.

For example:

SUBSCRIBE QUILT Joe Shmoe.

List Owner: Anne Louise Gockel <alg@cs.cornell.edu>

RACF-L on LISTSERV@UGA.BITNET

This is a list for discussion and questions on the IBM security product, RACF (Resource Access Control Facility.) It is for both the MVS and VM versions of RACF and is open to anyone with an interest in security on IBM mainframe computers. Comparisons between RACF and other IBM mainframe security systems (ACF-2, TOP-SECRET, VM/SECURE) are also welcome. Archives for approximately 6 to 9 months worth of old postings will be available.

To subscribe to RACF-L:

Send the following command to LISTSERV@UGA via mail or interactive message:

SUBSCRIBE RACF-L Your_full_name.

For example: SUBSCRIBE RACF-L John Doe

Owner: Harold Pritchett <HAROLD@UGA>

RAILROAD on LISTSERV@CUNYVM or LISTSERV@CUNYVM.CUNY.EDU   [Last Update 11/92]

The RAILROAD list - for the discussion of anything about railroads, real and model.

To subscribe, you may send an interactive message (from BITNET sites which provide such a facility), or mail (with the command as the body of the mail - *NOT* in the subject field -) to:

LISTSERV@CUNYVM or LISTSERV@CUNYVM.CUNY.EDU

The command should be in the form:

SUB RAILROAD full name

... where "full name" is your full (and correct) name.

To contribute to the list, send your mail messages to:

RAILROAD@CUNYVM or RAILROAD@CUNYVM.CUNY.EDU

For further information, please contact the list owner:

Geert K. Marien - GKMQC@CUNYVM.CUNY.EDU (BITNET node CUNYVM)

ncc1701e!rasi-l@uunet.uu.net   [Last Update 9/92]

This list, RASI-L contains the contents of the Usenet newsgroup rec.arts.startrek.info, a newsgroup dedicated to the dissemination of information about Star Trek.

This is a one-way gateway, from news to mail. Postings sent to the list RASI-L will NOT be gatewayed into the usenet newsgroup rec.arts.startrek.info, but will instead be redistributed to the list, and never make the newsgroup. It is also imperative that you not reply to this list. If you reply to the list, the reply will go to the root account.

There are two addresses that are available for the rec.arts.startrek.info newsgroup, one is trek-info@scam.berkeley.edu, the other is trek-info-request@scam.berkeley.edu. These addresses will appear at the bottom of each posting approved by the moderator, Jim Griffith, "the official scapegoat for rec.arts.startrek.info". If you have questions about the operation of the newsgroup, send mail to trek-info-request@scam.berkeley.edu

You may leave the list RASI-L at any time by sending a "SIGNOFF rasi-l" command to ncc1701!listserv@uunet.uu.net. Please note that this command must NOT be sent to the list address nor moderator's addresses (trek-info@scam.berkeley.edu nor trek-info-request@scam.berkeley.edu), but it MUST be sent to the mail server which handles this mailing list.

Please note that it is presently possible for anybody to determine that you are signed up to the list through the use of the "REVIEW RASI-L" command, which returns the network address of all subscribers.

More information on this mailserver can be found by sending a "HELP" command to ncc1701e!listserv@uunet.uu.net

Owner: ncc1701e!the_sage@uunet.uu.net

REACH on LISTSERV@UCSBVM.BITNET   [Last Update April 1992]

REACH: Research and Educational Applications of Computers in the Humanities, an electronic newsletter

REACH exists solely to provide a means of distributing an electronic version of the paper newsletter of the same name, a publication of the Humanities Computing Facility of the University of California, Santa Barbara. At present, the newsletter is issued four times a year.

Back issues of REACH and related files are stored in the REACH FILELIST. To receive a list of files send the command:

INDEX REACH to LISTSERV@ucsbvm.bitnet

To subscribe to REACH, send the following command to LISTSERV@ucsbvm.bitnet via mail text or interactive message:

SUBSCRIBE REACH Your_full_name

For example: SUBSCRIBE REACH John Doe

Editor: Eric Dahlin
    reach@ucsbuxa.bitnet
    reach@ucsbuxa.ucsb.edu

REGISTRAR-L@CORNELL.EDU   [Last Updated 28-January-1992]

REGISTRAR-L is an unmoderated electronic forum intended to promote sharing of information, experiences, concerns, and advice about issues affecting records & registration professionals. We welcome questions, answers, and discussion about topics of concern, including those subsumed under the following broad areas (but not limited to these areas only):

Academic policy and procedure

Automated records keeping systems
Book reviews (pertaining to the profession)
Calendars and scheduling
Computer systems
Course enrollment
Data collection and interpretation
Degree Audits
Diplomas
Drop/Add
Electronic mail
Enrollment certifications
Enrollment Management
FAX technology
FERPA
IPEDS
Job announcements and descriptions
Meeting and seminar announcements
NCAA certification
Optical Disk technology
Professional Associations
Publications and Forms
Records Office Management
Records Security and Storage
Registration systems and logistics
Software
Transcripts

Humanistic, technical, legal, financial, and administrative viewpoints are encouraged.

Since this forum will not be moderated, at least initially, contibutors should be succinct, should include relevant parts of messages to which they are responding, and should append their names, titles, and institutions to their contribution. Unless otherwise stated, it will be assumed that your contributions represent individual opinion rather than institutional policy.

Please note that this is NOT a LISTSERV list. To subscribe (or unsubscribe) to (from) REGISTRAR-L send your request in mail to

REGISTRAR-L-REQUEST@CORNELL.EDU

Send mail to the list via REGISTRAR-L@CORNELL.EDU

Owner:
Paul Aucoin
Director of Graduate Records
Cornell University
Ithaca, NY 14853-6201
Voice (607) 255-5824
FAX (607) 255-1816
BITNET: P22@CORNELLC
INTERNET: Paul_Aucoin@Cornell.edu

RENAIS-L on LISTSERV@ULKYVM   [Last Updated June 1992]
or LISTSERV@ULKYVM.LOUISVILLE.EDU

RENAIS-L is a forum for debate, discussion, and the exchange of information by students and scholars of the history of the Renaissance. RENAIS-L is ready to distribute newsletters from study groups, and to post announcements of meetings and calls for papers, short scholarly pieces, queries, and other items of interest.

The list currently does not maintain a FTP directory nor is archiving available. Hopefully, this will change in the near future.

RENAIS-L is associated with the general discussion list HISTORY, and co-operates fully with other lists similarly associated.

To subscribe send a message to LISTSERV@ULKYVM or LISTSERV@ULKYVM.LOUISVILLE.EDU. In BODY of the message state: SUB RENAIS-L yourfirstname yourlastname

adding your full name; LISTSERV will accept both BITNET and Internet addresses. Postings should be made to RENAIS-L@ULKYVM.

If you have any questions please contact the owner.

Owner: James A. Cocks BITNET: JACOCK01@ULKYVM Internet: JACOCK01@ULKYVM.LOUISVILLE.EDU

RESEARCH on LISTSERV@TEMPLEVM.BITNET

The RESEARCH list is for those people (primarily at educational institutions) who are interested in applying for outside funding support. That is, support from government agencies, corporations, foundations etc. This list attempts to assist faculty in locating sources of support and also to forward information regarding the latest news from potential sponsors. As an example, National Science Foundation, National Institutes of Health. The list also provides information on upcoming seminars from around the world on various topics from medicine to artificial intelligence.

To subscribe send the following command in an interactive command (TELL or SEND) or in the BODY of mail (NOT the subject) to LISTSERV@TEMPLEVM on BITNET: SUB RESEARCH yourfirstname yourlastname

Owner: Eleanor Cicinsky <V2153A@TEMPLEVM.BITNET>

RESPON-$%UVMVM.BITNET@VM1.NODAK.EDU

Discussion of socially responsible investing by colleges and universities. Particularly for those serving on committees charged with recommending or setting institutional policy on socially responsible investment guidelines, votes on shareholder resolutions, divestment, community investment or other initiatives related to the university's long and short term investments. Internal and external politics. Current issues include South Africa, Northern Ireland, animal testing, environmental protection, corporate PAC's, equal opportunity/affirmative action, and tobacco sales.

BitNet users may subscribe by sending the following command to LISTSERV@UVMVM via interactive message or e-mail: SUBSCRIBE RESPON-$ your full name where "your full name" is your real name, not your login Id. Non-BitNet users can join the list by sending the above command as the only line in the text/body of a message to LISTSERV%UVMVM.BITNET@VM1.NODAK.EDU.

Coordinator: Dayna Flath <DMF%UVMVM.BITNET@VM1.NODAK.EDU>

REVIEW-L on LISTSERV@UOTTAWA.BITNET   [Last Update April 1992]
or LISTSERV@Acadvm1.Uottawa.CA

The CONTENTS project has made available a separate listserv list, REVIEW-L, for those who wish to automatically receive the FULL TEXT of all reviews and book notes published by the RELIGIOUS STUDIES PUBLICATIONS JOURNAL.

Subscribers to REVIEW-L will receive the complete text of any new reviews and book notes published by the CONTENTS project and will also receive any republished reviews or book notes that CONTENTS receives from participating journals. Abstracts of these reviews will be posted to the existing RELIGIOUS STUDIES PUBLICATIONS JOURNAL - CONTENTS (CONTENTS@Uottawa,

CONTENTS@Acadvm1.Uottawa.CA).

TO SUBSCRIBE TO REVIEW-L

Send the e-mail to either

Listserv@Uottawa (BITNET) or
Listserv@Acadvm1.Uottawa.CA (Internet)

with the following command in the BODY of the mail (NOT the subject):

SUB REVIEW-L your full name Eg. SUB REVIEW-L John Calvin

For information on the CONTENTS list see previous announcements or lists of lists.

Inquires regarding the CONTENTS project should be sent to the project director:

Michael Strangelove
Department of Religious Studies
University of Ottawa
177 Waller, Ottawa
K1N 6N5 (FAX 613-564-6641)
<441495@Uottawa> or <441495@Acadvm1.Uottawa.CA>

REXXCOMP@UCF1VM.CC.UCF.EDU

REXXCOMP is a list to discuss all aspects of the CMS REXX Compiler, including installation, maintenance, and use.

Log files will be kept on a monthly basis.

BitNet users can subscribe by sending the following command to LISTSERV@UCF1VM: SUB REXXCOMP Your_full_name where Your_full_name is your real name, not your userid; for example: SUB REXXCOMP John Doe Non-BitNet users can subscribe by sending the SUB command as the text/body of a message to LISTSERV@UCF1VM.CC.UCF.EDU

Coordinator: UCF Postmaster <POSTMAST@UCF1VM.CC.UCF.EDU>

REXXLIST@UCF1VM.CC.UCF.EDU

Discussion of the REXX command language.

Log files will be kept on a monthly basis.

BitNet users can subscribe by sending the following command to LISTSERV@UCF1VM: SUB REXXLIST Your_full_name where Your_full_name is your real name, not your userid; for example: SUB REXXLIST John Doe Non-BitNet users can subscribe by sending the SUB command as the text/body of a message to LISTSERV@UCF1VM.CC.UCF.EDU

Coordinator: UCF Postmaster <POSTMAST@UCF1VM.CC.UCF.EDU>

RFERL-L on LISTSERV@UBVM.BITNET [Last Update 9/92]
or LISTSERV@UBVM.CC.BUFFALO.EDU

This list was formed as a vehicle for distribution of the RFE/RL Research Institute Daily Report. The RFE/RL Daily Report is a digest of the latest developments in the former Soviet Union and Eastern Europe. It is published Monday through Friday (except German holidays) by the RFE/RL Research Institute (a division of Radio Free Europe/Radio Liberty Inc) in Munich.

Archives of list RFERL-L are stored in the RFERL-L FILELIST. To receive a list of the files send the command "INDEX RFERL-L" (without the "") to LISTSERV@UBVM or LISTSERV@UBVM.CC.BUFFALO.EDU in the text of a mail message.

To subscribe, send a mail message containing the following command to LISTSERV@UBVM on BITNET or LISTSERV@UBVM.CC.BUFFALO.EDU (in the BODY of the mail): subscribe rferl-l firstname lastname

For example: subscribe rferl-l Jane Doe

Owner of the list: Dawn Mann <mannd@rferl.org>

RFC Announcements

This list is for distribution of announcements of new Requests for Comments. These are the publications of the Internet protocol development community, and include the specifications of protocol standards for the Internet, as well as policy statements and informational memos.

Requests to be added or deleted should be sent to: RFC-REQUEST@NIC.DDN.MIL

ripe-map@nic.eu.net   [Last Updated 28-January-1992]

This is a mailing list for discussing the issues involved in mapping and visualising computer networks. With the growth in complexity of computer networks, mapping is becoming more important as a visualisation technique and for finding anomalies. There are numerous commericial and public domain tools available but many have serious limitations and are often specific to a single group of protocols. RIPE (Reseau IP Europeen) has set up a working group for studying the problem, this mailing list is intended as a forum for wider discussions.

Some of the issues for discussion are listed here,

- Auto-discovery, automatically discovering the topology of computer networks. How can this be done, what standards need changing to do this efficiently.
- Automatic Layout, Automatically laying out (or untangling) maps so that they look good on in a window or on a piece of paper.
- Features, which feaures of existing tools are the best what else is wanted.
- Formats, in what format should maps be stored and how should they be distributed.
- Model, What database model should be used. Should it be concerned purely with the graphic represention or should it try to model the underlying networks. Different types of map suitable for different purposes, what are the catagories.
- Other Tools and Standards, how can existing tools and protocols be tied in with a mapping database.
- Symbols, Standard symbols for representing network entities. How should the status of such entities be drawn.

To join, send mail to   <ripe-map-request@nic.eu.net>
to contribute send mail to <ripe-map@nic.eu.net>
archives on mcsun.eu.net:~ftp/ripe/archives/ripe-map

Right_Use_of_Will@kether.webo.dg.com   [Last Updated 12-October-1991]
or will@kether.webo.dg.com

This mailing list is for people interested in discussing topics related to the series of books by Ceanne DeRohan, the first of which is called The Right Use of Will, Healing and Evolving the Emotional Body.

These are not ordinary self-help books that show you how to change your life; these books can help you save it.

The understandings given in these four books were received from God in the first person. They are are first so startling, so unlike anything you would expect to hear, that you are apt to become very angry, or flatly incredulous. These understandings have to do with the split that has occurred in each of us between Spirit (male intellect), and Will (female feelings): how this split occurred, and why it has to be healed now, and to go about it. These are not easy books to read, or to fully understand at first reading. But they are very worth your while.

When you have completed the series, you will have some understanding of how the Cosmos came into being, who the four parts of the One God are, who Lucifer is, who the created spirits are and how, why, and when they emerged, where you emerged, what went wrong from the very beginning, the roles played by denial, blame, and guilt, why we and the entire creation, including God, are in peril, and whether you want to heal and remain within God, or not.

Individuals interested in the concepts of Will, emotional healing, Earth's and Creation's current evolutionary track, and the healing of the Divine Feminine and Masculine (within and without) are encouraged to read the books and join in on the discussion.

The service address, to which questions about the list itself and requests to be added to or deleted from it should be directed, are as follows:

Will-Request@kether.webo.dg.com

You can send mail to the entire list via one of these addresses:

Right_Use_of_Will@kether.webo.dg.com Will@kether.webo.dg.com

RISK on LISTSERV@UTXVM.CC.UTEXAS.EDU

RISK is provided as a means of electronically distributing communications related to issues concerning the general topic of risk management and insurance. Although RISK was originally created in order to facilitate discussions amongst academic members of the American Risk and Insurance Association (ARIA), non-ARIA members, including academics, professional risk managers and other interested parties are also invited to subscribe.

To subscribe to RISK, send the following command to LISTSERV@UTXVM.CC.UTEXAS.EDU in the body of a mail message:

SUBSCRIBE RISK your name

For example: subscribe RISK John Doe

To "unsubscribe" to RISK, send the following command to LISTSERV@UTXVM.CC.UTEXAS.EDU in the body of a mail message:

SIGNOFF RISK your name

For example: signoff RISK John Doe

For more information, send the command HELP to LISTSERV@UTXVM.CC.UTEXAS.EDU.

Owner: James R. Garven (Garven@UTXVM.CC.UTEXAS.EDU)

RISKS@CSL.SRI.COM

"RISKS" is a distribution list for discussion of issues related to risks to the public in the use of computer systems. It has sponsorship of the ACM Committee on Computers and Public Policy (Chaired by Peter G. Neumann), but is open to everyone.

Contributions are welcome on a wide range of relevant topics bearing on the stated subject. Contributors are requested to avoid overt political statements, personal attacks, flames, etc. Inappropriate submissions will be rejected.

Back issues may be FTPed from CRVAX.SRI.COM files sys$user:[RISKS]RISKS-vol.no where "vol" and "no" are volume and number. <RISKS>Risks-1.1 was established 1 Aug 85.

All requests to be added to or deleted from this list, problems, questions, etc., should be sent to RISKS-REQUEST@CSL.SRI.COM.

Coordinator: Peter G. Neumann <NEUMANN@CSL.SRI.COM>

ROOTS-L@vm1.nodak.edu
ROOTS-L@NDSUVM1.BITNET
...!psuvax1!NDSUVM1.BITNET!ROOTS-L (UUCP)

Genealogical Issues: Tools, techniques, and requests for information on genealogical research. The list may also be helpful in doing the research by sharing information on specific ancestors, cooperative research, etc. (See also soc.roots on USENET/NETNEWS news). Monthly public notebooks are kept.

All requests to be added to or deleted from this list, problems, questions, etc., should be sent to the Coordinator.

Coordinator: Alf Christophersen <CHRISTOPHE%USE.UIO.UNINETT@NAC.NO>

RNA on LISTSERV@UTFSM.BITNET

RNA is a Neural Net list in Spanish.

Lista de Informacion sobre Redes de Neuronas Artificiales.

RNA es una lista dedicada a todas aquellas personas interesadas en el desarrollo e investigacion en el campo de las Redes de Neuronas Artificiales.

El proposito de esta lista es intercambiar informacion, favorecer el encuentro de personas con intereses afines, promover la formacion de grupos de trabajos y servir de apoyo a quienes se integran al area.

Debido a los objetivos de esta lista, el idioma oficial sera el castellano, aceptandose tambien contribuciones en ingles.

Existe abundante literatura en este campo y se recomienda a los interesados revisar los trabajos del grupo PDP que estan ampliamente difundidos.

Para subscribirse enviar el siguiente comando :

TELL LISTSERV AT UTFSM SUB RNA nombre apellido

en el caso de no poder mensajes interactivos, enviar una nota a LISTSERV@UTFSM.BITNET con el siguiente mensaje en el cuerpo de la nota :

SUB RNA nombre apellido

RRA-L on LISTSERV@KENTVM.BITNET   [Last Updated 28-January-1992]
or LISTSERV@KENTVM.KENT.EDU

RRA-L is a moderated discussion and idea list for lovers of the Romance genre. RRA-L stands for Romance Readers Anonymous. The listowners called it Romance Readers Anonymous knowing that fans of this genre sometimes have trouble admitting their preference for a good juicy love story. We know, we are that way too.

Tenets of RRA-L:

    -Everyone is welcome.
    -Those who wish to adopt the name of a favorite character or
     author may use that name in the postings.
    -The participants WILL have fun.

    Some suitable subjects for posting are:

    -Announcements of forthcoming books and previews.
    -Reviews, criticisms, comments, and appreciations of mysteries
       (books, plays, films).
    -Great bookshops
    -Awards.

Everyone who joins ought to consider contacting her (his) favorite romance author and inviting her (him?) to join this list.

Subscription Instructions:

To subscribe from a Bitnet account send an interactive or e-mail message addressed to Listserv@kentvm . From the Internet send mail to listserv@kentvm.kent.edu .

If you send e-mail leave the subject line blank. The text of the message must be:

Sub RRA-L Yourfirstname Yourlastname

If you have questions please contact the owners. If you need to know how to send e-mail or interactive messages contact your local computer services people for assistance with your local system.

Yours for networked thrills, the Owners:

Jayne A. Krentz (lhaas@kentvm.bitnet)
Onyx Hamilton (krobinso@kentvm.bitnet)

RS1-L%NDSUVM1.BITNET@CUNYVM.CUNY.EDU
...!psuvax1!NDSUVM1.BITNET!RS1-L (UUCP)
RS1-L@NDSUVM1 (BITNET, EARN, NetNorth)

BITNET LISTSERV discussion group for RS/1, BBN Software Products Corporation's research and data analysis system. Topics of interest could include RPL questions, problems/bugs, converting to Release 3, etc.

All requests to be added to or deleted from this list, problems, questions, etc., should be sent to the Coordinator.

Coordinator: User Consultant Coordinator <MCMAHON%GRIN1.BITNET@CUNYVM.CUNY.EDU>

rsaref-users@rsa.com

This mailing list provides a forum for the discussion of topics related to the free reference implementation of RSA public-key cryptography for use in Internet Privacy-Enhanced Mail (PEM). The implementation is called RSAREF and is available from RSA Laboratories, a division of RSA Data Security, Inc. For information about the RSAREF product, send mail to "rsaref-info@rsa.com".

subscription address: rsaref-users-request@rsa.com submission address: rsaref-users@rsa.com owner address (email): rsaref-administrator@rsa.com owner address (snail): RSAREF Administrator RSA Laboratories 10 Twin Dolphin Dr. Redwood City, CA, 94065

RSTRAN-L%YALEVM.BITNET@CUNYVM.CUNY.EDU

Unmoderated mailing list intended for discussion among RSCS systems programmers who are interested in the Yale Transparent linedrivers for RSCS Version 2 on an IBM 7171. The original modifications made at Yale for release 1 of version 2 are available from the list by requesting RSTRAN-L PACKAGE. It is Yale's hope that interested parties who migrate the mods forward for later maintenance levels will send the updated mods to SUSAN@YALEVM so that they can be made available to all.

BitNet users can add themselves to the list by issuing the following command to LISTSERV@YALEVM.BITNET: SUBSCRIBE RSTRAN-L your_full_name where your_full_name is your real name (not your userid). BitNet users can unsubscribe with the command: UNSUBSCRIBE RSTRAN-L

All other requests to be added to or deleted from this list, problems, questions, etc., should be sent to the Coordinator.

Coordinator: Susan Barmhall <SUSAN%YALEVM.BITNET@CUNYVM.CUNY.EDU>

RusHist on LISTSERV@USCVM.BITNET   [Last Updated June 1992]
or LISTSERV@VM.USC.EDU
or LISTSERV@DOSUNI1.BITNET
or LISTSERV@CSEARN

This list will be used as a forum for the reasonable discussion of any aspect of the history of Russia from the reign of Ivan III (1462-1505) to the end of the Romanov dynasty in the person of Nicholas II (1894-1917). Any element of this period is discussable. Any questions about suitable topics should be directed to Valentine Smith, at the Internet address: (cdell@vax1.umkc.edu).

Anyone wishing to participate in this list should send the following command to one of the following Listservs: LISTSERV@USCVM (or LISTSERV@VM.USC.EDU), LISTSERV@DOSUNI1, or LISTSERV@CSEARN via e-mail in the BODY of a mail message (not the "Subject:" line) SUB RusHist your real name

To unsubscribe, send the command UNSUB RusHist . Other Listserv commands can be gotten by sending HELP in the message body to any Listserv.

This is an unmoderated list.

Owner: Valentine Smith (cdell@vax1.umkc.edu)

Russia@IndyCMS.IUPUI.EDU   [Last Updated 12-October-1991]
Russia@IndyCMS.BITNET

Russia (Russia and her neighbors list) is dedicated to the civil and thoughful exchange and analysis of information regarding Russia and her neighbors.

Russia is a moderated list with no gateways to any other ListServ lists or Usenet newsgroups. Russia is archived. To receive a list of files available, send the command INDEX RUSSIA to the ListServ CREN or Internet address below.

To subscribe to the "Russia" list send e-mail to either LISTSERV@INDYCMS.BITNET or LISTSERV@INDCMS.IUPUI.EDU (Internet) with the body (text) of the mail containing the command SUB RUSSIA yourfirstname yourlastname

List owner/coordinator: John B Harlan IJBH200@IndyVAX (CREN) IJBH200@IndyVAX.IUPUI.Edu (Internet)

RUSSIAN on LISTSERV@ASUACAD.BITNET

A ListServ discussion group to discuss Russian Language Issues, preferably in Russian. Topics include but are not limited to Russian language, linguistics, grammar, translations, literature. This list is geared toward students of Russian but, of course, anyone who speaks/reads/writes Russian is invited and encouraged to participate.

To subscribe to this list, send the following command to LISTSERV@ASUACAD on BITNET (in the body of mail or a message):

SUB RUSSIAN your_name

where your_name is your name as you wish it to appear on the subscription list (*not* userid at node). The name must include at the least a "first" and "last" name. For example, SUB RUSSIAN John Q. Public

Thank you. Please direct questions and/or comments to the list owner, Andrew Wollert, at ISPAJW@ASUACAD.BITNET or ISPAJW@ASUVM.INRE.ASU.EDU.

RUSTEX-L@UBVM.CC.BUFFALO.EDU

RusTeX-L was started in September 1989 to facilitate the work on the Russian language version of the TeX typesetting system, but related technical topics are often discussed on the list: other Russian text processing systems, thesauri, spell checkers, Russian keyboard layout, and e-mail to Soviet sites. This list is limited to technical topics only: any articles of political nature (including the discussion of COCOM restrictions on technology transfers) should be directed to another list or newsgroup (e.g., talk.politics.soviet).

A collection of RusTeX-related software (METAFONT sources for Cyrillic fonts, Russian hyphenation patterns, et al) and mailing list archives are kept on UBVM.CC.BUFFALO.EDU.

Coordinator: Dimitri Vulis <DLV%CUNYVMS1.BITNET@CUNYVM.CUNY.EDU>
((rutgers,gatech)!psuvax1,mcsun,unido)!cunyvms1.bitnet!dlv (uucp)

RXIRC-L on Listserv@VMTECQRO or Listserv@vmtecqro.qro.itesm.mx

This is an open forum for discussion of all technical & usage aspects of the rxIRC client software for communicating with Internet Relay Chat servers on the Internet. This software has been created and is maintained by Carl von Loesch (see addresses below).

The intent of the list is to provide rxIRC users a means of communicating amongst themselves, thereby providing each other of support and answers to all the frequently asked questions regarding its installation, setup and use. It will also provide Carl a mechanism for obtaining timely feedback, thus easing further development.

Current (and future) users of rxIRC are encouraged to join this list, by sending the following command in the BODY of an E-Mail letter to LISTSERV@VMTECQRO.QRO.ITESM.MX:

SUBSCRIBE RXIRC-L your-full-name-here

Subscription to this list is recommended only for users who currently have (or will have in the near future) Internet connectivity, as rxIRC is of no use to BITNET-only users.

Owner & editor: Carl von Loesch <Carl.von.Loesch@arbi.informatik.uni-oldenburg.de> or <244661@DOLUNI1>

S-PRESS on LISTSERV@DCZTU1.BITNET   [Last Updated 12-October-1991]
or LISTSERV@ibm.rz.tu-clausthal.de

Attention: list language is German

S-PRESS is designed to foster the communication between the German students press. All folks from other countries' youth-owned press are cordially invited to join the list as guests but should keep in mind, that S-PRESS is performed in German. For subscription please mail to the listowner. For details see German description below.

>>> S-PRESS - Netzwerk der studentischen Presse in Deutschland

S-PRESS ist eine ListServ-Diskussionsliste fuer alle Fachschafts-, Uni-, AStA-,... eben nichtkommerziellen Studenten-Zeitungen oder anderen Publikationen (etwa e-mail-Magazinen, Wandzeitungen, etc.). Ausser dem allgemeinen Informations- und Erfahrungsaustausch (Plausch:) sind uns bisher folgende Dinge eingefallen, fuer die S-PRESS genutzt werden koennte:

- Ueberblick ueber die Szene (Selbstdarstellungen...)
- Artikel-Verbreitung / -Austausch
- Vermitteln von guenstigen Druckereien
- Koordination von ueberregionalen Anzeigen
- Recherche-"Datenbank" (wer hat schon mal ueber XYZ geschrieben?|)
- Adressdatei (wo bekomme ich Infos ueber ...?|)
- Unterkunft bei 'Kollegen' waehrend Messen o.ae.
- Verbreitung hilfreicher PD-Software

Um bei S-PRESS mitzumachen, schickt einfach das uebliche SUB S-PRESS <Name Eurer Zeitung/...> an LISTSERV at DCZTU1 (von BITNET) oder LISTSERV at ibm.rz.tu-clausthal.de (von Internet)

Mit der Bestaetigung erhaltet Ihr einen kleinen Fragebogen und die neuesten Informationen ueber die Handhabung von S-PRESS.

Kommentare, Fragen etc. bitte an den 'Listowner': "Red. Wurzelmaennchen" <PTWURZEL@DCZTU1.BITNET> (bzw. per Internet: PTWURZEL@ibm.rz.tu-clausthal.de)

Vielen Dank an das Rechenzentrum der TU Clausthal fuer die freundliche Bereitstellung der Resourcen fuer diese Liste.

Owner: "Red. Wurzelmaennchen" <PTWURZEL@DCZTU1.BITNET> or
<PTWURZEL@ibm.rz.tu-clausthal.de>

SAFETY%UVMVM.BITNET@VM1.NODAK.EDU

Mailing list for people interested in the various environmental, health and safety issues and problems on college and university campuses. These can include life safety issues (fire protection, trip and fall and other general safety issues), chemical safety issues (waste disposal, laboratory safety, meeting regulations), biological hazards and radiation safety. Both users of hazardous materials and people administering campus safety programs are welcome on the list.

BitNet users can subscribe to the list by issuing the following interactive command on CMS: TELL LISTSERV AT UVMVM SUBSCRIBE SAFETY your_name where "your_name" is your real name, not your login Id. Non-CMS BitNet users can join by sending mail to LISTSERV@UVMVM with the command: SUB SAFETY your_name in the TEXT/BODY of the message. Non-BitNet users can join by sending the above command in the text/body of a message to LISTSERV%UVMVM.BITNET@VM1.NODAK.EDU.

Coordinator: Dayna Flath <DMF%UVMVM.BITNET@VM1.NODAK.EDU>

SAS-L%MARIST.BITNET@CUNYVM.CUNY.EDU
SAS-L%UGA.BITNET@CUNYVM.CUNY.EDU

A Bitnet Listserv discussion group focusing on SAS.

Users can subscribe themselves by sending mail to LISTSERV%MARIST.BITNET@CUNYVM.CUNY.EDU with SUBSCRIBE SAS-L your_full_name as the only line in the message body.

Coordinators: A. Harry Williams <HARRY%MARIST.BITNET@CUNYVM.CUNY.EDU>

sat@mainz-emh2.army.mil   [Last Updated 28-January-1992]

The SAT mail List will be an electronic informational forum to assist USAREUR Supply Support Activities in the sharing of ideas and the soliciting of feedback on problems and concerns. Problems confronting supply personnel are complex and require insight, experience and alternate perspectives to reach realistic solutions. Electronic communications provides a convenient, cost effective, timely method of contacting valuable resources without the restraints of conventional communication.

SAT mail list discussions will be focused around the mission of the SAT which include but is not limited to:

a. Providing on-site logistical assistance to USAREUR Supply Personnel.

b. Conducting surveys/assessments of storage facilities to determine adequacy of facilities, storage aids, space utilization, providing recommendations for modernization of storage aids, source of supply, approximate cost, prepares warehouse planographs, and assist in preparation request.

c. Assisting in evacuation of serviceable/unserviceable major assemblies, turn-in of serviceable to the European Redistribution Facilities (ERF)/

d. Reviewing DSS/ALOC receipt procedures, review/analysis of SSA automated supply process, ASL management, reconciliation, receipt, storage and issue procedures.

e. Scheduling of On-Site Visits.

On-Site visits are at no cost to the unit. If you are interested in the possibilities offered by this mail list then send electronic mail to:

sat-request@mainz-emh2.army.mil

that you be added to the Mainz Army Depot Supply Assistance Team Mail List. Mail for the list can be sent to:

sat@mainz-emh2.army.mil Supply Assistance Team (SAT)

Lists initially will not be moderated nor archived. Comments/recommendations may be addressed to:

List Administrators - rvandunk@mainz-emh2.army.mil
              - jmarton@mainz-emh2.army.mil
Mailing Address: Commander
                Mainz Army Depot
                ATTN: SDSMZ-MS
                APO NY 09185
Commercial Phone (No Autovon or ETS available): 06131-696379
FAX: 06131-696467

SBN on LISTSERV@IndyCMS   [Last Updated 9/92]
or LISTSERV@IndyCMS.IUPUI.EDU

SBNnet is an experiment in human networking for computer users in north central Indiana and southwest lower Michigan USA. (SBN is the standard, three character aviation designation for South Bend, Indiana USA, the area's approximate geographic center.)

The South Bend area community possesses a significant pool of talent in a wide variety of fields and academic disciplines. SBNnet is an attempt to link that talent pool (making it more accessible to the area's computer-using community at large) and to foster a sense of community as electronic neighbors. It is hoped SBNnet will include participants from area business and industry, higher education, non-profit organizations, and private individuals, joining in from home and work, to help their electronically connected neighbors.

SBNnet is a network without dedicated hardware. It uses electronic mail lists to disseminate information of local interest and to facilitate voluntary communication, assistance and cooperation between its participants. Its only requirement for participation is some form of access to e-mail -- connection to academic / research networks such as BITNET / CREN / EARN / NetNorth et al, commercial services such as CompuServe and MCI Mail, uucp mail, etc -- in order to receive and reply to messages from other participants. There is absolutely no cost for participating in SBNnet. The only potential cost is that of an individual's access to electronic mail itself, since that is the medium through which SBNnet operates.

SBNnet presently consists of eight distinct components, each a separate e-mail list available by free subscription from ListServ@IndyCMS / ListServ@IndyCMS.IUPUI.Edu:

- SBNbirds South Bend area birds. SBNbirds is for news and discussion of birds living in and/or flying through our community.
- SBNchat South Bend area conversation. SBNchat is for neighborly conversation about news, sports, weather, etc., of interest in our community.
- SBNevent South Bend area events. SBNevent is for listings and notices of events of interest in our community.
- SBNhelp South Bend area help. SBNhelp is an electronic cross between a library reference desk, a community information and referral center, and a computing center help desk -- with the twist that all SBNnet participants are potential service providers as well as service users (i.e., "from each according to his abilities, to each according to his needs"). SBNhelp is intended to provide a forum for informal information and referral, and reference; it is not limited in subject matter (except that its use for any type of commercial promotion or transaction is strictly prohibited). The modus operandi for the help component is that a participant with a question or need posts an e-mail message to the SBNhelp list (address: SBNhelp@IndyCMS.IUPUI.Edu), which is then automatically redistributed to all other participants. Any participant who has an idea to help answer the question or address the need (or even suggest another possible resource for doing same) then posts an e-mail message back to the SBNhelp list in reply, and that reply is automatically redistributed to the

list. In order to succeed and provide a valuable service to our community's computer users, the help component only needs its participants to read SBNhelp e-mail traffic and to respond to those messages with which they may be able to help.

- SBNjobs South Bend area jobs. SBNjobs is for announcements of positions available in the South Bend area, and for statements of qualifications and interests of those persons seeking employment in our community.
- SBNnews South Bend area news. SBNnews is for the distribution of local and regional news of interest in our community.
- SBNsport South Bend area sports. SBNsport is for the distribution of sports information and scores of interest in our community.
- SBNwx South Bend area weather. SBNwx is for the distribution of weather information of interest in our community.

A ninth list, SBN, is a superlist which automatically adds the subscriber to seven of the eight separate components described above. SBNwx is available only by separate subscription.

A tenth list, SBNnet-L, is used to discuss the design, implementation and management of SBNnet, South Bend's human/e computing network.

SBNnet is a network of good will and neighborliness, a dedicated service for the computer users of our community, computer users from all walks of life, at home and at work. Having dealt with ListServ lists extensively over the past two to three years, I know personally the impact this technology can have on communication on a national and international scale; I believe it can also be applied closer to home to facilitate the dissemination and exchange of information locally.

If you are interested in participating in or observing this project, please contact me at the e-mail address or telephone number below. I hope you will choose to be a part of SBNnet, South Bend's human/e computing network.

John B Harlan
JBHarlan@IndyVAX
JBHarlan@IndyVAX.IUPUI.Edu

SCA@MC.LCS.MIT.EDU

Mailing list for members of, or anyone interested in, the Society for Creative Anachronism. There is also an "alt.sca" Newsgroup gatewayed with the mailing list.

All requests to be added to or deleted from this list, problems, questions, etc., should be sent to SCA-REQUEST@MC.LCS.MIT.EDU.

SCHEME@MC.LCS.MIT.EDU

This mailing list is intended to be a forum for discussing anything related to the Scheme programming language(s), with particular emphasis on the use of Scheme in education. There are over 150 people on the list A/O 15 Nov 85, with more than 80 institutions represented.

The archives are kept on 2 different machines: On MIT-AI: LSPMAI;SCHEME MAIL4 (messages from Sept 85 - 11 July 86) On MIT-MC: LSPMAI;SCHEME MAIL (messages since 11 July 86)

All requests to be added to or deleted from this list, problems, questions, etc., should be sent to Scheme-Request@MC.LCS.MIT.EDU.

Coordinator: Jonathan Rees <JAR@MC.LCS.MIT.EDU>

SCOUTS-L%tcubvm.bitnet@CUNYVM.CUNY.EDU　　　　　　　　　　　[Last Updated 1/92]
SCOUTS-L on LISTSERV@tcubvm

The SCOUTS-L list was formed to provide an opportunity for members of youth groups world-wide to interact, compare notes on their programs, discuss organizational problems, and communicate with members in distant units. The groups discussed may include, but will not be limited to the Boy Scouts,

Girl Scouts, Boys' and Girls' Clubs, etc.

Archives of SCOUTS-L and related files are stored in the SCOUTS-L FILELIST. To receive a list of files send the command INDEX SCOUTS-L to LISTSERV@TCUBVM.

To subscribe to SCOUTS-L, send the following command to LISTSERV@TCUBVM (LISTSERV%TCUBVM.BITNET@CUNYVM.CUNY.EDU for INTERNET users) via mail text or interactive message: SUBSCRIBE SCOUTS-L Your_full_name. For example: SUBSCRIBE SCOUTS-L Joe Scout

Owner: Jon Edison <Edison%TCUBMV.BITNET@CUNYVM.CUNY.EDU>

SCRNWRIT on LISTSERV@TAMVM1   [Last Updated 28-January-1992]

SCRNWRIT is a discussion list of the joy and challenge of screen writing for film and TV. Any topic of interest to writers or potential writers is appropriate (i.e. format, story ideas, dialogue, characters, agents, producers, directors, actors, studios, problems and/or solutions).

To subscribe, send the following command to LISTSERV@TAMVM1 via mail or interactive message:

SUB SCRNWRIT your full name

where "your full name" is your name. For example:

SUB SCRNWRIT Joan Doe

Owner: Jack Stanley <JRS4284@PANAM>

SCRIBE-HACKS@WRL.DEC.COM

Mailing list for Scribe hackers; designed for persons who perform the role of Scribe Database Administrator at their installation. Discussion will be about Scribe features, bugs, enhancements, performance, support, and other topics of interest to Scribe DBAs. The list will NOT be moderated, but will simply consist of a mail "reflector" - ie. if you send a message to the list, it will be rebroadcast to everyone on the list. Discussion at the level of "How do I get a paragraph to indent 5 spaces instead of 3?" is specifically discouraged.

All requests to be added to or deleted from this list, problems, questions, etc., should be sent to SCRIBE-HACKS-REQUEST@WRL.DEC.COM.

Coordinator: Brian Reid <Reid@wrl.dec.com>

SCREEN-L on LISTSERV@UA1VM
or LISTSERV@UA1VM.UA.EDU

SCREEN-L is an unmoderated list for all who study, teach, theorize about or research film and television--mostly in an academic setting, but not necessarily so. SCREEN-L ranges from the abstract (post- post-structuralist theory) to the concrete (roommate match-ups for the next SCS/UFVA conference). Pedagogical, historical, theoretical, and production issues pertaining to film and TV studies are welcomed.

To subscribe to SCREEN-L, send the following command to LISTSERV@UA1VM (or LISTSERV@UA1VM.UA.EDU) via e-mail or interactive message (TELL/SEND):

SUBSCRIBE SCREEN-L <your_full_name>

"<your_full_name>" is your name as you wish it to appear on the list. For example:

SUBSCRIBE SCREEN-L Budd Boetticher

Archives of SCREEN-L and related files are stored in the SCREEN-L FILELIST. To receive a list of files send the command INDEX SCREEN-L to LISTSERV@UA1VM (or LISTSERV@UA1VM.UA.EDU).

Owner: Jeremy Butler JBUTLER@UA1VM JBUTLER@UA1VM.UA.EDU

SCUBA-D@BROWNVM.BROWN.EDU   [Last Updated 12-October-1991]
   BROWNVM.BITNET

SCUBA-D is the digest version of the Usenet rec.scuba list.

To subscribe to SCUBA-D, send a mail message containing the following command to
LISTSERV@BROWNVM.BROWN.EDU or LISTSERV@BROWNVM.BITNET:

SUBSCRIBE SCUBA-D yourfirstname yourlastname

   List owner: Catherine Yang <cyang@brownvm.brown.edu>
   List editors: Catherine Yang <cyang@brownvm.brown.edu>
         Nick Simicich <njs@yktvmh or njs@watson.ibm.com>

SCUBA-L@BROWVM.BITNET   [Last Updated 28-Janaury-1992]

Mailing list for discussion of all aspects of SCUBA diving. Any articles, views, ideas, and opinions
relating to SCUBA diving are welcome. Areas discussed will include, but are not limited to:

Safety/First Aid	Places to Dive
Decompression computation	Best Places to Dive
Decompression Tables	History
New Equipment	Dive Shops
New Technologies	Mail/order Shopping
Diving Science & Technology	Travel
Dive Computers	Tropical Diving
Underwater Photography	Underwater Animal Life
Underwater Vehicles	Questions/Quizzes
PADI certifications	
NAUI certifications	
YMCA certifications	

BitNet users can subscribe by sending the following interactive command to LISTSERV@BROWNVM:
TELL LISTSERV AT BROWNVM SUB SCUBA-L your_full_name (where "your_full_name" is your
real name, not your loginid) or by sending mail to LISTSERV@BROWNVM.BITNET with the first text
line in the BODY of the mail being: SUB SCUBA-L your_full_name Non-BitNet users can subscribe by
sending the above SUB command in the body of a message to
LISTSERV%BROWNVM.BITNET@CUNYVM.CUNY.EDU

Coordinator:Catherine Yang (CYANG@BROWNVM.BITNET)

SCUG-G on LISTSERV@DGOGWDG1
   SCUG-G on LISTSERV@IBM.GWDG.DE (Internet)

Since foundation of list L-VMCTR@AKRONVM we revealed some problems that could not be
discussed in this list, because they are specially related to our situation in the middle of Europe.
Therefore we set up a list, called SCUG-G (Systems Center User Group - German), which is located at
Goettingen (DGOGWDG1.BITNET), Germany.

This new list is concerned to all software components of VMCENTER, VMCENTER II and to
VMSPOOL of Systems Center, Inc., Reston. Topics we want to discuss are:

   legal aspects of Systems Center software
   COCOM restrictions
   difficulties caused by the technical support in Frankfurt/Main et al.
   price policy problems (which usually occur 1 year later than in USA)
   announcements of the german Systems Center User Group

There is no intention to compete with L-VMCTR. Discussion language should be German.

To subscribe, send request to LISTSERV@DGOGWDG1.BITNET using the following message text:

SUB SCUG-G your name

Owner: WGRIEGE@DGOGWDG1 (Wilfried Grieger)
Notebooks: Yes,Private,Monthly
Subscription: Open
Information files: of the User Group available

SEAC-L%UNCVX1.BITNET@CUNYVM.CUNY.EDU

This list is for members of local chapters of SEAC and students interested in forming chapters of SEAC on their campuses. Topics include actions taken by local chapters, coordination of national efforts, conferences, and bulletins of scientific interest on enviromental topics.

To subscribe to SEAC-L, send the command: SUB SEAC-L your_full_name to LISTSERV@UGA e.g. SUB SEAC-L "William H. E. Day"

To have your name removed from the SEAC-L subscriber list, send: SIGNOFF SEAC-L

Commands can be sent to LISTSERV@UGA either as interactive messages or in e-mail (one command per line in the body of the e-mail message). Subscription problems or questions may be directed to the List Coordinator).

Coordinators: UNC SEAC <seac%UNC.BITNET@CUNYVM.CUNY.EDU> Paul Jones
<pjones%UNCVX1.BITNET@CUNYVM.CUNY.EDU>

security@rutgers.edu

Discussion group for all aspects of computer security.

Senior on ListServ@IndyCMS (BITNET/CREN)
or ListServ@IndyCMS.IUPUI.Edu (Internet)

Senior is dedicated to the discussion of all issues relating to the health and lives of senior citizens. It is intended to serve in part as a networking tool to facilitate enhancement of senior health & life by matching senior citizen needs with existing services.

Senior is open to all persons interested in the health and lives of senior citizens, including health care providers, social service providers, gerontologists, and others.

To subscribe to Senior send mail to LISTSERV@INDYCMS.BITNET or LISTSERV@IndyCMS.IUPUI.EDU with the body of the main containing: SUB SENIOR yourfirstname yourlastname

List owner/coordinator: John B Harlan IJBH200@IndyVAX (BITNET/CREN)
IJBH200@IndyVAX.IUPUI.Edu (Internet)

SEMIOS-L on LISTSERV@ULKYVM.BITNET   [Last Update 9/92]
or LISTSERV@ULKYVM.LOUISVILLE.EDU

The list TELESI-L has been changed to SEMIOS-L and the scope of discussion has been expanded. SEMIOS-L is a discussion group for those interested in semiotics, verbal and non-verbal communication, language behavior, visual issues, and linguistics.

To subscribe send the command SUB SEMIOS-L Firstname Lastname

to either LISTSERV@ULKYVM or LISTSERV@ULKYVM.LOUISVILLE.EDU

Owner: Steven Skaggs S0SKAG01@ULKYVM.LOUISVILLE.EDU (same)

SEISM-L%BINGVMA.BITNET@MITVMA.MIT.EDU

Seismological topics of general interest.

To subscribe send the following command to LISTSERV@BINGVMB (non-BitNet users send mail to LISTSERV%BINGVMB.BITNET@MITVMA.MIT.EDU) SUBSCRIBE SEISM-L your_full_name To unsubscribe, send UNSUBSCRIBE SEISM-L

Coordinator: Jim Blake <AS0JEB%BINGVMA.BITNET@MITVMA.MIT.EDU>

serpent-list@sei.cmu.edu

serpent-list@sei.cmu.edu

Primarily intended for technical discussion about Serpent, the user interface management system developed at the Software Engineering Institute.

All requests to be added or deleted from this list, or problems with the mechanics of the list, should be sent to: serpent-list-request@sei.cmu.edu

coordinator: Erik Hardy <erik@sei.cmu.edu>

SF-LOVERS@RUTGERS.EDU

SF-LOVERS has discussed many topics, all of them related in some way to the theme of science fiction or fantasy. The topics have ranged very widely from rewritten stories, SF and fantasy books, SF movies, and SF conventions to reviews of books, movies and television shows. The range of topics is quite wide and anyone is welcome to submit material on these or other topics of interest in this general area.

The digest has a very large number of readers, and trivial messages are strongly discouraged due to the heavy load SF-LOVERS puts on the hosts CPU and disk space. Messages to SF-LOVERS@RUTGERS.EDU are batched and broadcast periodically.

The SF-LOVERS archives are available via anonymous ftp on ELBERETH.RUTGERS.EDU, a unix machine running BSD 4.3. Each volume is contained in its own file, with the contents ordered chronologically. The first archive includes a number of messages from the early days before digests and there is much of "historical" interest.

/u2/ftp/pub/sfl:

2128 sf-lovers.v1	592 sf-lovers.v7	4000 sf-lovers.v12b
1904 sf-lovers.v2	1648 sf-lovers.v8	6000 sf-lovers.v13
1856 sf-lovers.v3	3600 sf-lovers.v9	7568 sf-lovers.v14b
1760 sf-lovers.v4	7472 sf-lovers.v10	4352 sf-lovers.v15a
816 sf-lovers.v5	6752 sf-lovers.v11	3456 sf-lovers.v15b
1744 sf-lovers.v6	4944 sf-lovers.v12a	

For those unfamiliar with unix, the number to the left of the file name is the size of the file in kilobytes. Volume 16 is the current volume. Old issues for the current volume are also available from the archives in the files sf-lovers.xxxyy where "xxx" is the month of publication and "yy" is the current year. BITNET subscribers who currently do not have access to anonymous ftp may send mail to BITFTP@PUCC.BITNET with ftp commands as text of the mail message. Further instructions are available on request.

Also in the archives are some files that may be of interest including episode guides for popular television shows. A partial list as of (May 1 1991) is:

Episode guides:	22 outerlimits.guide
20 blakes7.guide	10 prisoner.guide
18 doctor-who.guide	24 quantam-leap.guide
18 galactica.guide	8 red-dwarf.guide
10 galactica80.guide	14 star-trek-animated.guide
36 lost-in-space.guide	58 star-trek-tng.guide
6 max-headroom.guide	26 star-trek.guide
28 new-twilight-zone.guide	6 tomorrow-people.guide

70 twilight-zone.guide

Text Files:
48 cons.txt
24 down-in-flames.txt
86 hitch-hikers-guide-to-the-net.txt
20 hugos.txt
8 klingonaase.txt
6 nebulas.txt
4 saturn.txt
4 world-fantasy-awards.txt

For INTERNET subscribers, all requests to be added to or deleted from this list should be sent to SF-LOVERS-REQUEST@RUTGERS.EDU. BITNET subscribers may issue the following command:

TELL LISTSERV at RUTVM1 command SFLOVERS "name"

where "command" is either SUBSCRIBE or UNSUBSCRIBE as appropriate. Problems and administrative questions should always be sent to SF-LOVERS-REQUEST@RUTGERS.EDU. Submissions for the digest are to be sent to SF-LOVERS@RUTGERS.EDU only. Unfortunately, due to the large volume of mail that I receive every day, messages sent to the wrong address are very likely to be unprocessed.

Saul Jaffe Moderator SF-LOVERS Digest sf-lovers-request@rutgers.edu

SFER@MTHVAX.CS.MIAMI.EDU

South Florida Environmental Reader - ISSN 1044-3479

The South Florida Environmental Reader is primarily intended for people in South Florida to keep abreast of local environmental issues. The newsletter is published on a monthly basis, and distributed both in electronic and paper formats.

To receive the electronic edition, send a message to sfer-request@MTHVAX.CS.MIAMI.EDU or to SFER@UMIAMI.BITNET.

Coordinator: A.E. Mossberg <aem@MTHVAX.CS.MIAMI.EDU>

SFS-L on LISTSERV@SEARN.BITNET or LISTSERV@SEARN.SUNET.SE

SFS-L; has been opened on SEARN to discuss the VM shared file system. The reason for creating a new list is that the SFS was previously discussed on several lists with a rather small intersection (VMESA-L, VMREL6-L, and occasionally some apparently unrelated lists such as LSTSRV-L or VM-UTIL). In addition, it seems unlikely that a majority of the readers of these lists are interested in long debates about the SFS, which is after all only an optional component of VM. The goal is thus to keep the "mainstream" VM lists for the more general CP and CMS issues, and gather interested parties from all related mailing lists into a new "specialized" list.

The scope of the list is not restricted to any particular version of the SFS (VM/SP 6 vs VM/ESA), nor to any particular topic. We will try to answer technical questions, will debate usability issues, and will gladly welcome installation/configuration hints or even software contributions. Non-technical discussions (company policies, how to deal with workstation users, etc) are welcome, as long as they do not degenerate into pointless religious arguments. In particular, "flames" about the CMS file system will not be tolerated. Intelligent criticism is, of course, allowed.

Subscribing to SFS-L

You will have to send the following command to LISTSERV:

SUBSCRIBE SFS-L My Name

BITNET users can send the command via an interactive message to LISTSERV AT SEARN:

TELL LISTSERV AT SEARN SUB SFS-L John A. Doe

Internet users should send mail to LISTSERV@SEARN.SUNET.SE with the SUBSCRIBE command in the mail BODY.

If you have trouble getting on the list, contact the listowner at:

Internet: sfs-l-request@searn.sunet.se
BITNET: ERIC at SEARN
VNET: ERIC at BITNET

SGANET%VTVM1.BITNET@CUNYVM.CUNY.EDU
SGANET on LISTSERV@VTVM1

SGANet: An International Mailing Network for Student Government Associations

SGANet, developed and implemented at Virginia Polytechnic Institute and State University, is an international mailing network for Student Government Associations, student representative councils, student parliaments, etc. to use in discussing issues faced by such organizations worldwide.

SGANet can be reached through InterNet, an international electronic mail network which links universities and corporations throughout the world. Internet is easy to use and in many cases free of cost. Our operating costs for this network are minimal as should be yours.

SGANet is easy to use and will be the host of many interesting discussions which will be of great interest to your organization. SGANet is open to any student government association at any university worldwide.

SGANet is an automated mailing list located at Virginia Tech. Let's say, for example, that a student government association from a university in Australia wants to share some of the issues it is working on. They would simply write their article and send it via mail to one of the addresses above SGANet then receives their mail and sends copies of it to every organization on the list. There is no limit to mail usage, and any one on the list can submit an article for distribution. It's that simple and it's very low in cost, in many cases FREE.

To become a member of SGANet:

Send the following message to LISTSERV%VTMV1.BITNET@CUNYVM.CUNY.EDU:

subscribe SGANet (Your organization's full name)

{You will receive acknolwedgement and instructions upon receipt of your subscription}

Send articles, comments, anecdotes, etc. to SGANet@VTVM1.BITNET They will be automatically sent to everyone on the list. This allows for really good interactive discussions.

SHADOWRN on LISTSERV@HEARN - Discussion on the Fantasy game ShadowRun

ShadowRn is a list for the discussion of the game ShadowRun. This can be questions, comments, stories (fluff), anything to do with the game ShadowRun. The purpose is to allow players and GMs of ShadowRun to express their opinions, concerns, questions, stories about ShadowRun.

Archives of Shadowrn can be listed by sending the command INDEX SHADOWRN to LISTSERV@HEARN (in the BODY of MAIL or a TELL/SEND).

To subscribe, send the following command to LISTSERV@HEARN.BITNET in the BODY of mail or interactive message:

SUB SHADOWRN your_full_name

where "your_full_name" is your name. For example:

SUB SHADOWRN Brett Barnhart

Owner:Brett Barnhart <BARNHART@KNOX> Any questions can be directed to the owner

SHAKER@UKCC.UKY.EDU

Mailing list for those interested in the history, culture, artifacts, and beliefs of the Shakers (The United Society of Believers). Discussions will cover a broad range of subject matter including, but not limited to: social analysis, history, shaker women's studies, antiques and furniture, and organization.

BitNet users can subscribe by sending the following command via mail text or interactive message to LISTSERV@UKCC: SUBSCRIBE SHAKER your_full_name For Example: SUBSCRIBE SHAKER Jane Doe Internet users can subscribe by sending the SUBSCRIBE command in the text/body of a message to LISTSERV@UKCC.UKY.EDU.

Coordinator: Marc A. Rhorer <RHORER@UKCC.UKY.EDU> {rutgers|uunet}!ukma!rhorer@ukcc (Usenet)

SHAKSPER on LISTSERV@UTORONTO

SHAKSPER is a scholarly BITNET seminar modelled on HUMANIST, currently involving more than ninety Shakespearean researchers, instructors, students, and interested amateurs from seven countries. A number of national and international Shakespeare organizations have expressed an interest in formal involvement, and a number of traditional journals have announced it to their readership.

The SHAKSPER Fileserver offers conference papers and abstracts, an Index to Scholarly Works in Progress, an International Directory of Shakespeare Institutes, a Directory of Shakespearean Conferences and Calls for Papers, biographies of conference members, and reference files on a wide variety of subjects. Members of a number of seminars at the upcoming SAA Conference in Vancouver will find their colleagues ready to share papers, comments, and strategies in advance. SHAKSPEReans also gain indirect access to the SHAKSPER Quarto/Folio Textbase, a 17-megabyte textbase of all 55 authoritative quarto and folio texts of the 38 plays.

The daily SHAKSPER digests offer an opportunity for informal discussion, eavesdropping, peer review, and a fresh sense of worldwide community. Conference announcements, Shakespeare Association bulletins, member notes and queries, book and theatre reviews, textual debate, discussion of lecture strategies -- SHAKSPER has already logged all this and much more.

No academic qualifications are required for membership in SHAKSPER, and anyone interested in English Literature, the Renaissance, or Drama is welcome to join us. Write to the editor, Ken Steele <KSTEELE@vm.epas.utoronto.ca>, or send the command SUB SHAKSPER firstname lastname to LISTSERV@UTORONTO in the body of mail or via an interactive message such as TELL LISTSERV AT UTORONTO SUB SHAKSPER firstname lastname and you will receive a more detailed information file with further instructions for becoming a SHAKSPERean. (SHAKSPER is not open to automatic subscription, but no one is refused.)

Editor: Ken Steele <KSTEELE@vm.epas.utoronto.ca>

(Please consider forwarding this announcement to colleagues who might be interested, whether or not they are currently using Bitnet, or posting a paper copy in your English or Drama department.)

SHARP-L on LISTSERV@IUBVM.BITNET or LISTSERV@IUBVM.UCS.INDIANA.EDU

SHARP-L is a new list devoted to the history of the printed word. In affiliation with the newly-founded Society for the History of Authorship, Reading, and Publishing, SHARP-L means to give all of us who take an interest in this burgeoning field a way of exchanging ideas, information, and inquiries with other scholars in all disciplines all over the world. Whether your interest is incunabula or 20th-century American periodicals, literacy studies or the economics of the book trade, library history or literary theory, this is a list, and an organization, that hopes to bring us all together and get us acquainted. SHARP-L can be a way of bridging the occupational, disciplinary, and geographical differences among students of print culture that have tended to keep us isolated and all-too-ignorant of one another's work and interests.

Subscribing to SHARP-L is easy. Just send an e-mail message to LISTSERV@IUBVM on BITNET or LISTSERV@IUBVM.UCS.INDIANA.EDU and include in the BODY of the message (NOT the subject) the line:

SUBSCRIBE SHARP-L your full name

To post a message to the list, simply address it to either "SHARP-L@IUBVM" (the Binet address) or "SHARP-L@IUBVM.UCS.INDIANA.EDU" (the Internet address.)

Owner: Patrick Leary Department of History Indiana University Bitnet: pleary@iubacs Internet: pleary@ucs.indiana.edu

SHOGI-L%TECHNION.BITNET@CUNYVM.CUNY.EDU
SHOGI-L on LISTSERV@TECHNION

SHOGI-L, the Shogi Discussion List, is a new mailing list started on May 6, 1990 about the strategic board game of Shogi. The list is intended to serve as a discussion point for Shogi-related topics and as a source of information about Shogi tactics and Shogi events. It also offers to Shogi players the possibility to engage in e-mail games in a friendly ladder competition.

Shogi is much like 'western' chess, but has some very interesting differences. One is that almost all pieces can promote to stronger pieces once they reach the opposite side of the board. The second very important difference is that when a piece is captured, it becomes a piece for the capturing side, and can be dropped back onto the board ! This makes for a very exciting game, with an extremely low percentage of draws. Many strong Chess players, such as International Master Larry Kaufman in the US (who is the strongest non-Japanese player outside Japan), have found Shogi to be a great game to play.

Although played by millions in Japan, so far it isn't well known outside Japan. But surely, there are some net-people out there who would like to play or get to know more about it. For Apple Macintosh owners we also have a Hypercard Shogi Stack available, which contains valuable information for every Shogi novice. We would also like to get source or executable code for a program that plays Shogi.

How to subscribe:

Anyone who has direct access to Bitnet can sign on to the list by sending a mail (preferrably), a file or an interactive message to either

LISTSERV AT TECHNION (IBMs) or

LISTSERV@TECHNION (VAXen).

All you have to do to SUBscribe is place the following command into the body of the mail or file or message:

SUB SHOGI-L <your_personal_name>

where <your_personal_name> can be any name by which you want to be known to the list. Quotes around your personal name are not necessary. From the Internet, send mail to LISTSERV%TECHNION.BITNET@CUNYVM.CUNY.EDU with the same text as the body of the message.

List owners: Chris Sterritt chris@adms-rad.unisys.com Pieter Stouten stouten@embl.bitnet Al Hartshorn ccsm1al@technion.bitnet

SHOTHC-L on LISTSERV@SIVM.BITNET   [Last Updated June 1992]

This list provides a forum for scholars and researchers to discuss topics of interest to The Society for History of Technology (SHOT) Special Interest Group on Information, Computing and Society. Subscription is open. The list owner is Dr. Paul Ceruzzi, Dept. of Space History, the National Air & Space Museum.

To subscribe, send the following command to LISTSERV@SIVM.BITNET SUBSCRIBE SHOTHC-L Firstname Lastname

You may send an interactive message to LISTSERV@SIVM. If you choose to subscribe by electronic mail, put the subscribe command in the body of the note; DO NOT put anything in the SUBJECT line.

Mail for the list should be sent to SHOTHC-L@SIVM. Any problems with the list should be reported to NASEM001@SIVM or IRMSS907@SIVM. Monthly log files are kept and publicly available.

SIGMA-NU on LISTSERV@HEARN.BITNET

Discussion on the Sigma Nu Fraternity

Sigma Nu is a list for members of the Sigma Nu fraternity. The purpose is too allow members of Sigma Nu to get together over the network and discuss different issues having to do with the Fraternity. My hope is to allow members around the country to learn about other chapters, events, ideas, problems, anything that deals with Sigma Nu

Archives of Sigma-NU can be listed by sending the command INDEX Sigma-Nu to LISTSERV@HEARN on BITNET.

To subscribe, send the following command to LISTSERV@HEARN via mail or interactive message (in the BODY of the mail):

SUB Sigma-Nu your_full_name

where "your_full_name" is your name. For example:

SUB Sigma-Nu Brett Barnhart

Any questions can be directed to the owner

Owner:Brett Barnhart <BARNHART@KNOX.BITNET>

SIGPAST@List.Kean.EDU [Last Updated 12-October-1991]

SIGPAST is a list devoted to the discussion and research of the history of computers.

Send a message --

To subscribe to the list: SIGPAST-Subscribe@List.Kean.EDU
Questions about list: SIGPAST-Request@List.Kean.EDU
Submissions to the list: SIGPAST@List.Kean.EDU

list-administrator StanL@TURBO.Kean.EDU

SIMULA%BITNIC.BITNET@CUNYVM.CUNY.EDU

A forum for people interested in SIMULA, a language for object-oriented programming and simulation; a member of the ALGOL family. Topics may range from hints on programming techniques to information about available software (both compilers and programs), questions and answers in general, etc. In short, anything that has to do with SIMULA. This group is not restricted to any specific implementation of SIMULA; the exchange of information between users of different implementations is encouraged.

This list is handled by LISTSERV. To add or remove yourself from the list, send a message to LISTSERV%BITNIC.BITNET@CUNYVM.CUNY.EDU. The sender of the message you send must be the name you want to add or remove from the list. The text of the message should be: SUBSCRIBE SIMULA <your name> or SIGNOFF SIMULA Depending on whether you want to add or remove yourself from the list.

Coordinator: Mats Ohlin <MATSO%QZCOM.BITNET@CUNYVM.CUNY.EDU>

simulation@UFL.EDU

comp.simulation (UseNet newsgroup)

All topics connected with simulation are welcome; some sample topics are:

Real time simulation methods

Flight simulation
Parallel architectures for simulation analysis and modeling
Simulation and training
Distributed simulation
Artificial intelligence and simulation
Automatic generation and analysis of models
Analog vs. digital methods, hybrids
Continuous, discrete, and combined methods
Qualitative modeling
Application specific questions
Theory of simulation and systems
Queries and comments about available simulation software
Announcements of simulation-related talks and seminars
Graphics and image processing in simulation

All requests to be added to or deleted from this list, problems, questions, etc., should be sent to simulation-request@UFL.EDU.

Moderator: Paul Fishwick <fishwick@FISH.CIS.UFL.EDU> <fishwick@UFLORIDA.CIS.UFL.EDU>

simulator-users@CS.ROCHESTER.EDU
simulator-bugs@CS.ROCHESTER.EDU

Mailing list to allow users of the Rochester Connectionist Simulator to talk to one another.

Please send BUG REPORTS to simulator-bugs@CS.ROCHESTER.EDU. We are interested in fixing bugs, but can't make any promises! Please make your bug reports as specific as possible.

All requests to be added to or deleted from this list, problems, questions, etc., should be sent to simulator-request@CS.ROCHESTER.EDU.

Coordinator: Liudvikas Bukys <bukys@CS.ROCHESTER.EDU>

SINFONIA@ASUVM.INRE.ASU.EDU
SINFONIA on LISTSERV@ASUACAD

SINFONIA, a ListServ list for Brothers of Phi Mu Alpha Sinfonia, is now up and running. ALL brothers are encouraged to subscribe -- students, faculty, everyone--even if you're not currently affiliated with a chapter.

The list will be moderated and digested (weekly or so) at least in the beginning. Discussions will range from matters pertinent to the Fraternity to most any musical subject people are interested in.

To subscribe, send a piece of mail or an interactive message to LISTSERV@ASUACAD (BITNet) or LISTSERV@ASUVM.INRE.ASU.EDU (Internet) saying:

sub sinfonia <Your full name>

Coordinator: Ben Goren Bitnet: AUBXG AT ASUACAD Internet: AUBXG@ASUVM.INRE.ASU.EDU

Siouxsie@tjhsst.vak12ed.edu

This is an unmoderated mailing list for the discussion of Siouxsie & The Banshees and its offshoots. To subscribe, send mail to:

siouxsie-request@tjhsst.vak12ed.edu

To send mail to the list, the address is:

siouxsie@tjhsst.vak12ed.edu

The list administrator may be reached at the '-request' address above, or failing that:

kdeyoe@tjhsst.vak12ed.edu - or - kdeyoe@vdoe386.vak12ed.edu

SKEPTIC%YORKVM1.BITNET@VM1.NODAK.EDU

Skeptic discussion list for the critical and rigourous exchange of information regarding claims of the paranormal. All topics are welcome, and no one will be refused subscribership due to inclination with respect to these claims. Topics can include, but are not limited to:

Creationism
Bermuda Triangle
Ancient Astronauts(?)
Parapsychological Concerns e.g. Psi, ESP, remote viewing, telekinesis,
    spoon bending, astrology
Trance Channeling
UFOs
Philosophical Ramifications of these claims

The moderator will try to promote inquiry based on the best evidence avaiable whether this evidence be scientific, anecdotal, or otherwise; I wish to be as critical as possible, for if these 'phenomena' are actual, we want to have the best possible understanding of them to continue the investigations. In addition, the list will provide space for the exchange of papers on these subjects for the consideration of those who are interested and those who might be qualified to provide expert critique.

To subscribe to this list issue the command: TELL LISTSERV AT YORKVM1 SUB SKEPTIC your_full_name or on VMS systems: SEND LISTSERV@YORKVM1 SUB SKEPTIC your_full_name

Non-Bitnet users can send mail to LISTSERV%YORKVM1.BITNET@VM1.NODAK.EDU with an empty Subject: and messagebody: SUB SKEPTIC your full name

Moderator: Norman R. Gall <gall@vm1.yorku.ca> <gall@nexus.yorku.ca>

SLART-L%PSUVM.BITNET@VM1.NODAK.EDU

SLART-L is a network for those involved in or interested in second or foreign language acquisition research and/or teaching (SLART). This list is intended as a means of forming a "community of scholars" in SLA. Individuals may choose to discuss research in progress, "publish" papers for feedback, solicit advice on teaching methods, etc. Anyone interested in issues in second or foreign language acquisition is encouraged to join.

Coordinator: Joyce Neu <JN0%PSUVM.BITNET@VM1.NODAK.EDU>

SLOVAK-L%UBVM.BITNET@VM1.NODAK.EDU

Mailing list for discussion of Slovak culture, etc.

BitNet users may subscribe by sending the following command to LISTSERV@UBVM via interactive message or e-mail: SUB SLOVAK-L Your full name where "Your full name" is your real name, not your login Id. Non-BitNet users can join by sending the above command as the only line in the text/body of a message to LISTSERV%UBVM.BITNET@VM1.NODAK.EDU.

Coordinator: Jan George Frajkor <NEWSTV1@CARLETON.CA>

SLUG@AI.SRI.COM

Distribution list to exchange information about the care and feeding, use and abuse, problems and pitfalls, wonders and crocks of the Symbolics Lisp machines. There is also a national users group SLUG, Inc. that is loosely related to, but distinct from, this mailing list. Joining one or the other does not automatically mean you are in both groups.

Mail archives are stored on host WARBUCKS.AI.SRI.COM; some relevant files are:

SLUG.TXT	;the archives
SLUG.*	; more archives

SLUG-INC.INFO   ;Info about SLUG, Inc.

There are other miscellaneous LISPM and SLUG related files in the <ANONYMOUS> directory. WARBUCKS.AI.SRI.COM supports TCP FTP with anonymous login. If anyone else has on-line notes, tips, or tidbits, we will be glad to add them to the SLUG store.

All requests to be added to or deleted from this list, problems, questions, etc., should be sent to SLUG-Request@AI.SRI.COM.

Coordinator: Mabry Tyson <Tyson@AI.SRI.COM>

SMDM-L on LISTSERV@DARTCMS1.BITNET   [Last Updated 28-January-1992]
     or LISTSERV@DARTCMS1.DARTMOUTH.EDU

SMDM-L is a new electronic bulletin board service for members of The Society for Medical Decision Making and others interested in the theory and practice of decision making. The online community draws from a diversified group including physicians and other heath care professionals, students, hospital and health administrators, policy analysts, health economists, educators, computer analysts, psychologists and medical ethicists.

Discussion topics include the analysis of decision making as it applies to clinical practice, to the establishment of health care policies, and to the administration of health care programs. In addition, the service will post announcements of general interest to the decision making community.

SMDM-L is a moderated list with subscription open to all. To subscribe send the command SUB SMDM-L yourfistname yourlastname to LISTSERV@DARTCMS1 or to LISTSERV@DARTCMS1.DARTMOUTH.EDU.

Questions should be directed to the list owner: James Levin, MD PhD <JLEVIN@SIMVAX.BITNET>

sml-list@cs.cmu.edu   [Last Updated 12-October-1991]

a forum for communication among people interested in the Standard ML language and its implementation.

To send a message to the SML-LIST distribution, address it to sml-list@cs.cmu.edu (sites not connected to the Internet may need additional routing). Mail to this address is redistributed to the entire list.

Administrative mail such as requests to add or remove names from the distribution should be addressed to

sml-list-request@cs.cmu.edu

Messages to the list are archived at CMU. The archive can be retrieved by anonymous ftp from internet sites:

    ftp proof.ergo.cs.cmu.edu
    username: anonymous
    password: <empty>
    get /usr/bcp/sml-archive sml-archive

SMOKE-FREE@RA.MSSTATE.EDU   [Last Update 11/92]

SMOKE-FREE is a newly created support list for people recovering from addiction to cigarettes. Anybody with an interest in quitting smoking or in helping others quit is encouraged to join the discussion.

To subscribe to the list, send the following command as the total body of a mail message to LISTSERV@RA.MSSTATE.EDU:

subscribe smoke-free your name

The list is running on UNIX listserv version 5.5, which is similar to but not identical with the LISTSERV program many of you are familiar with. If you subscribe, you will receive more information about listserv commands.

Owner: Natalie Maynor (maynor@ra.msstate.edu) Mississippi State University

SMS-SNUG on LISTSERV@UNVCM1.BITNET
or LISTSERV@UNCVM1.OIT.UNC.EDU

Shared Medical Systems (SMS) National User Group (SNUG) Conference

SMS-SNUG is an electronic conference designed to foster communication concerning technical, operational, and business issues involved in the use of the SMS Inc. products.

Please share your constructive solutions to problems, unresolved 'opportunities,' and thoughts about institutional needs within the product family.

While intended as a forum for SMS users, Shared Medical staff participation is welcomed and solicited.

Subscription is open to anyone interested.

You may subscribe to SMS-SNUG by sending a subscribe command by interactive message or by e-mail. To subscribe by interactive message, send the command: SUB SMS-SNUG YourFirstname YourLastname to LISTSERV@UNCVM1.BITNET. or to LISTSERV@UNCVM1.OIT.UNC.EDU. For example:

IBM VM CMS users would enter tell listserv at uncvm1 sub SMS-SNUG YourFirstname YourLastname
VAX VMS users would enter send listserv@uncvm1 sub SMS-SNUG YourFirstname YourLastname

You may also subscribe by sending an e-mail message to LISTSERV@UNCVM1.BITNET or if your account is on the internet send to LISTSERV@UNCVM1.OIT.UNC.ED, with the following command as the text of the message.

SUB SMS-SNUG YourFirstname YourLastname

This, the 'SUB ...,' must be part of the message; the subject line is ignored.

Additional information in the form of a list of commands for the list server can be obtained by sending the message HELP to the list server (LISTSERV@uncvm1 etc) NOT to the list (SMS-SNUG@uncvm1 etc).

More detailed information is available by sending an information request message to the list server. Use one of the following formats:

INFO ? for a list of topics INFO topic where "topic" is one of the following: GENintro REFcard NEWs KEYwords

Remember two simple rules-of-thumb:

If it's a command (SUBscribe, Help, Info, UNSUBscribe, etc), send it to the list server (LISTSERV@uncvm1...).

If it's a message for general distribution to the members of the list, send it to the list (SMS-SNUG@uncvm1...).

The list is supported by the University of North Carolina Office of Information Technology. Our thanks to their management and staff for permission to use their VM system for the list and for assistance in setting it up. The list is sponsored by the University of North Carolina Hospitals Information Systems Division.

Questions may be directed to Lyman Ripperton or J.P. Kichak.

Lyman A. Ripperton III
Technical Services Manager
Information Services Division
The University of North Carolina Hospitals

Lyman@unchmvs.unch.unc.edu
voice 919/966-3969

Chapel Hill, NC 27514

SNSTCP-L on LISTSERV@NIHLIST (BITNET) LISTSERV@LIST.NIH.GOV (Internet)

SNSTCP-L is for discussion of questions, problems, etc. relating to Interlink's SNS/TCPaccess product for IBM MVS systems. The developers of the product are on the list.

To subscribe to SNSTCP-L, send the following command to LISTSERV@NIHLIST or LISTSERV@LIST.NIH.GOV in the body of an email message or via BITNET interactive message:

SUBSCRIBE SNSTCP-L Your Full Name

For example: SUBSCRIBE SNSTCP-L John Doe

Archives of SNSTCP-L are stored in SNSTCP-L FILELIST. To receive a list of files, send the command INDEX SNSTCP-L to LISTSERV@NIHLIST or LISTSERV@LIST.NIH.GOV.

Owner: Roger Fajman <RAF@NIHCU> (BITNET) <RAF@CU.NIH.GOV> (Internet)

SOC-CULTURE-GREEK <SOC-CULTURE-GREEK-POST@CS.WISC.EDU>

This mailing list relays the soc.culture.greek newsgroup (discussion of Greek society and culture) to/from a group of subscribers, that have NO USENET ACCESS (people overseas, on bitnet, on decnet,etc.). Articles are collected and sent daily in a single mail message; the headers of that message show how to subscribe and how to post something.

All requests to be added to or deleted from this list, problems, questions, etc., should be sent to SOC-CULTURE-GREEK-REQUEST@CS.WISC.EDU.

Coordinator: Manolis Tsangaris <mt@CS.WISC.EDU> ..!uunet!cs.wisc.edu!mt (UUCP)

SOCHIST on LISTSERV@USCVM   [Last Update 9/92] or LISTSERV@VM.USC.EDU

Briefly, this list will address three aspects of what is called the "New Social History":

(1) emphasis on quantitative data rather than an analysis of prose sources.

(2) borrowing of methodologies from the social sciences, such as linguistics, demographics, anthropology, etc.

(3) the examination of groups which have been ignored by traditional disciplines (i.e. the history of women, families, children, labor, etc.)

To subscribe, send e-mail to

LISTSERV@USCVM.BITNET or listserv@vm.usc.edu

with the single line in the BODY of the e-mail:

SUBSCRIBE SOCHIST your full name

for instance, my subscription message would be:

SUBSCRIBE SOCHIST Bob Pasker

Owner: Bob Pasker <bob@halfdome.sf.ca.us>

Societies@athena.mit.edu   [Last update 9/92]

Purpose: Discussion of Greek letter societies of all sorts, primarily those which are at American colleges. Flamage not encouraged by list owners; no affiliation with one is required. Currently unmoderated. Please include your most reliable Internet-accessible address in your subscription request.

Administrative address: societies-request@athena.mit.edu

Owners:
ce202a2@prism.gatech.edu (Peter L. Thomas)
pshuang@athena.mit.edu (Ping-Shun Huang)

SOFT-ENG@MWUNIX.MITRE.ORG

Soft-Eng is a list for discussion of software engineering and related topics, covering such areas as:

Complexity	Productivity	Staffing
Cost estimation	Professional ethics	Systems analysis
Debugging	Quality assurance	Testing
Enhancement	Real-time systems	Verification
Error handling	Reliability	Design
Extensibility	Software: legal issues	Documentation
Hardware/software tradeoffs	Testing Tools	Methodologies
Human factors	Tools	Protection mechanisms
Languages	Training & education	Rapid prototyping
Maintenance	Configuration mgmt.	Specification
Management	Programming Environments	Standards
Modelling	Recovery	Testing
Performance	Requirements	Validation
Portability	Reusable software	Software fault-tolerance
Practices	Software science	

Any and all contributions are welcome (e.g. questions, ideas, "war stories", proposals, humor, abstracts, conference reports, bibliographies, problems, reviews, tutorials, solutions, planned or completed projects). The list is digested.

All requests to be added to or deleted from this list, problems, questions, etc., should be sent to Soft-Eng-Request@MWUNIX.MITRE.ORG.

Moderator: Alok C. Nigam <nigam@MWUNIX.MITRE.ORG>

softpats@uvmvm.uvm.edu

A mailing list for the discussion of software patents and related issues. The mailing list is called softpats@uvmvm.uvm.edu; this list is run by a list server, so to subscribe, send the text "sub softpats your-name" in thr BODY of a message to listserv@uvmvm.uvm.edu.

This mailing list is, for the time being, NOT moderated. Expected topics include legality and desirability of software patents, announcements of new patents granted, and actions taken by various groups for and against the patenting of software. In order to keep noise to a minimum, discussion of look-and-feel issues will NOT be considered acceptable; gnu.misc.discuss is probably a more appropriate vehicle.

List Owner: Garrett A. Wollman - wollman@emily.uvm.edu

softpub@toolz.uucp (Usenet)   [Last Update 28-January-1992]
or softpub%toolz.uucp@mathcs.emory.edu (Internet)

The Software Entrepreneur's Mailing List is devoted to the interests of entrepreneural software publishing, including (but not limited to) shareware. The forum is completely open.

We look forward to your contributions to the list.

Send your mailing list name add/change/deletes to:

UUCP: ...!emory!slammer!toolz!softpub-request Internet: softpub-request%toolz.uucp@mathcs.emory.edu

Send your mailing list postings to:

UUCP: ...!emory!slammer!toolz!softpub Internet: softpub%toolz.uucp@mathcs.emory.edu

Owner: todd@toolz.uucp

SOFTREVU@BrownVM.Brown.EDU (Internet)   [Last Updated 12-October-1991]
    SOFTREVU@BROWNVM.BITNET (BITNET)

Forum for the Discussion of Small Computer Systems Software Reviews and Related Issues

STATEMENT OF PURPOSE: SOFTREVU will provide a forum where users of personal computers and other small computing systems can review, discuss, and examine software products. Cross-platform compatibility issues related to software and hardware, with an emphasis placed on software, are also included in this forum. The relevance, intentions, and uses of various software product categories, such as

* Personal Information Managers (PIMs)
* Utilities
* Graphics (formats, design packages)
* Optical Character Recognition (OCR)
* Multimedia products
* Desktop Publishing (DTP)

* Connectivity (communications)
* Shells and "Front Ends"
* Object-oriented Software
* Programming Language Environments
* Integrated Packages

The three "basics"--Databases, Spreadsheets and Text Managers are also included. Multimedia-based integration of various application categories, discussed from a software perspective, is also encouraged. Software Products include new software packages as well as the latest upgrades/updates to existing software products/packages. Members are encouraged to share knowledge of existing software packages in addition to that of new features being incorporated into upgrades of these products. Members are also encouraged to share knowledge (such as the uses, applications, and features) of recently introduced software products. Therefore, members of the list are encouraged to act as "consultants" and "enquirers" where appropriate.

In accordance with current CREN regulations, commercial activity (such as the selling of software) will be prohibited.

SCOPE: SOFTREVU is intended to cover all microcomputer platforms; such as the Apple Macintosh line, Amigas, IBM PS/2 line, PC compatibles, the NeXT machines, Sun and SPARC workstations, and the like. Within the scope of these computing platforms, a wide range of software products exist. Any and all of these products are viable discussion topics. SOFTREVU does not exist as a topic for issues of ethics in computing - see the ETHICS-L list. However, the merits of software packages, such as their user interface, compatibility across disparate computing platforms, and the like, are acceptable topics. List subscribers are encouraged to ask questions about software, and to offer up their opinions. In keeping with current CREN (Corporation for Research and Educational Networking) and InterNET policies, subscribers are prohibited from attempting to sell software over the network. However, the list moderators cannot be held responsible for the actions of list subscribers.

SOFTREVU does not exist as a forum for the discussion of hardware or programming issues except where the relevance to existing or forthcoming software is explicit. Hardware issues should be directed to the PCTECH-L and PCSUPT-L lists, which are geared toward discussions of that nature. Programming and/or technical issues should be brought up in any of the various lists and special interest groups which are designed for this purpose. Only extremely limited concerns in customization of existing software are included, such as writing simple macros, scripts, and other modest routines. With respect to programming languages, the merits of the environment package - not the actual language - are appropriate for discussion.

MEMBERSHIP: Any person who wishes to share knowledge, answer questions and/or desires to learn and ask questions is welcome. Potential members include users, consultants, programmers, managers, and the like. This list is intended to bring together people from all backgrounds to share information.

GUIDELINES: SOFTREVU is a moderated list. The atmosphere of this list is one of mutual support to all members and advocates cooperation. Members are expected to engage in constructive criticism only. Subscribers are requested to keep personal vendettas off the list. This is not a forum for political or ethical discussions in any capacity; it is a forum for the discussion of software. Problems or complaints should be addressed to the list moderators. Anyone who does not maintain this policy, or is generally disruptive to the harmony of this list, will be removed.

MODERATORS:

Jamie Donnelly IV, ENCSADM1@UCONNVM.BITNET
Elaine Brennan, ELAINE@BrownVM.Brown.EDU
David B. O'Donnell, EL406006@BrownVM.Brown.EDU

ARCHIVING: The list will maintain monthly archives of discussions. These archives will be purged periodically, removing outdated material, and to save system space and overhead. Announcements will be made prior to major purges, but subscribers should expect purges every few months. If necessary, either local or remote filespace may be set aside for the storage of documents of relevance to the list.

ACCESSING THE LIST: To subscribe to SOFTREVU send the command,

SUBSCRIBE SOFTREVU <yourname>

to LISTSERV@BROWNVM (LISTSERV@BrownVM.Brown.EDU). DO NOT SEND LIST COMMANDS TO THE LIST. Send them to the LISTSERV account.

Solaris on LISTSERV@IndyCMS.BITNET or LISTSERV@IndyCMS.IUPUI.Edu

Solaris (Solaris operating environment) is dedicated to discussion of the Solaris operating system produced by SunSoft, a Sun Microsystems company. Solaris (the list) is completely independent of Solaris (the operating environment), SunSoft (the manufacturer) and Sun Microsystems (the parent corporation).

Solaris (the list) is owned and coordinated by a computing professional (Phillip Gross Corporon) and an interested layperson (John B Harlan).

Solaris (the list) is bidirectionally gatewayed to the Inet newsgroup, comp.unix.solaris.

To subscribe to the Solaris e-mail list send mail to LISTSERV@IndyCMS.BITNET or LISTSERV@IndyCMS.IUPUI.Edu the the following command in the BODY of the mail:

SUB SOLARIS yourfirstname yourlastname

List owners/coordinators: Phillip Gross Corporon
phil@CSE.ND.Edu
F3PB88@IrishMVS
F3PB88@IrishMVS.CC.ND.Edu

John B Harlan
JBHarlan@IndyVAX
JBHarlan@IndyVAX.IUPUI.Edu

SovHist on LISTSERV@USCVM.BITNET
or LISTSERV@VM.USC.EDU
or LISTSERV@DOSUNI1.BITNET
or LISTSERV@CSEARN

[Last Updated June 1992]

This list will be used as a forum for the reasonable discussion of any aspect of the history of the Soviet Union from the "February Revolution" of 1917 to the breakup of the USSR that occurred 25 December, 1991.

Any element of this period is discussable. Any questions about suitable topics should be directed to Valentine Smith, at the Internet address: cdell@vax1.umkc.edu.

Anyone wishing to participate in this list should send the following command to one of the following Listservs: LISTSERV@USCVM (or LISTSERV@VM.USC.EDU), LISTSERV@DOSUNI1, or LISTSERV@CSEARN

via e-mail in the BODY of a mail message (not the "Subject:" line) SUB SovHist your real name

To unsubscribe, send the command UNSUB RusHist . Other Listserv commands can be gotten by sending HELP in the message body to any Listserv.

This is an unmoderated list.

Owner: Valentine Smith (cdell@vax1.umkc.edu)

SovNet-L%INDYCMS.BITNET@CUNYVM.CUNY.EDU
SovNet-L on ListServ@IndyCMS

SovNet-L (USSR electronic communication list) is a public discussion and distribution list dedicated to the dissemination and exchange of non-classified information regarding electronic communication to, from and within the Union of Soviet Socialist Republics and its constituent republics. It is intended to treat all forms of electronic communication and to include the Soviet electronic mail discussions begun on RusTeX-L.

SovNet-L is presently unedited and unmoderated.

List owner/coordinator: JBHarlan@IUBACS (John B Harlan)

To subscribe, send request to: ListServ@IndyCMS.BITNET (Internet users send to LISTSERV%INDYCMS.BITNET@CUNYVM.CUNY.EDU)

Using the following message text: Sub SovNet-L Your_full_name

SPACE@ANDREW.CMU.EDU

Discussions (daily digest) on space-related topics.

Archives are not available by ANONYMOUS FTP. Requests for back issues should be directed to SPACE-REQUEST@ANDREW.CMU.EDU.

All requests to be added to or deleted from this list, problems, questions, etc., should be sent to SPACE-REQUEST@ANDREW.CMU.EDU.

There is a BitNet sub-distribution list, SPACE@UGA; BitNet subscribers can join by sending the SUB command with your name. For example, SEND LISTSERV@UGA SUB SPACE Jon Doe To be removed from the list, SEND LISTSERV@UGA SIGNOFF. To make contributions to the list, BitNet subscribers should send mail to the Internet list name, NOT to the BITNET list name.

Coordinator: Owen T. (Ted) Anderson <OTA@ANDREW.CMU.EDU>

SPACE-IL <JO%ILNCRD.BITNET@CUNYVM.CUNY.EDU>

A Bitnet newsletter on space technologies in Israel.

To subscribe, send a message to LISTSERV%TAUNIVM.BITNET@CUNYVM.CUNY.EDU with the body of the letter containing the command: SUB SPACE-IL Your_Full_Name where Your_Full_Name; is your title, first name and last name.

Coordinator: Joseph van Zwaren de Zwarenstein <JO%ILNCRD.BITNET@CUNYVM.CUNY.EDU>

space-investors@cs.cmu.edu

This list is for information relevant to investing in space related companies. Reasonable topics include:

- Results of tests of new space related products
- New product announcements
- Contracts won or lost by space related companies
- Sudden stock price swings
- Space related startups needing venture capital or going public

In general any space related investment opportunities or any events affecting these potential investments are fair game.

To get on this list send mail to: space-investors-request@cs.cmu.edu

Coordinator: Vince Cate vac@cs.cmu.edu

SPORTPSY%TEMPLEVM.BITNET@VM1.NODAK.EDU

Mailing list/bulletin board for exercise and sport psychology.

To subscribe send the command: SUB SPORTPSY firstname lastname in the TEXT of a message or MAIL to LISTSERV@TEMPLEVM.BITNET. Non-BitNet users can send the above command to LISTSERV%TEMPLEVM.BITNET@VM1.NODAK.EDU in the text/body of a message.

Coordinator: Michael Sachs <V5289E%TEMPLEVM.BITNET@VM1.NODAK.EDU>

SPRINT-L%NDSUVM1.BITNET@CUNYVM.CUNY.EDU

Unmoderated mailing list intended to serve as a support group for users of Borland's Sprint word processor and a forum for discussion of problems, solutions, editor macros, configuration, formats, and related whatnot.

All requests to be added to or deleted from this list, problems, questions, etc., should be sent to the Coordinator.

Coordinator: David Dodell <ddodell@stjhmc.fidonet.org>

SQLINFO%UICVM.BITNET@CUNYVM.CUNY.EDU

Mailing list for discussions about SQL/DS and general database topics.

All requests to be added to or deleted from this list, problems, questions, etc., should be sent to INFO%UICVM.BITNET@CUNYVM.CUNY.EDU.

Coordinator: Glori A. Chadwick <GLORI%UMDD.BITNET@CUNYVM.CUNY.EDU>

SRCMSL-L@MCVM1.CIS.MCMASTER.CA

This is a closed list for the Special Resource Committee on Medical School Libraries in Canada.

To subscribe to this list send a mail/note message to FITZ@MCMASTER (on BITNET) requesting a subscription to list SRCMSL-L giving your full name and title.

SRVREQ-L on LISTSERV@INDYCMS.BITNET

A new list has been created to host discussions regarding LAN servers and requesters (workstations), including though not limited to, OS/2 LAN Server, OS/2 LAN Requester, DOS LAN Requester, PC LAN Program, Novell Netware. The initial intent for this list is to provide a forum for discussions related to network programming, installation and configuration of various servers, requesters, and related programs and the underlying protocols-- LAN Support Program, NETBIOS, IPX/SPX, etc..

To subscribe, send the following to LISTSERV AT INDYCMS

SUBSCRIBE SRVREQ-L yourfirstname yourlastname

Owner: Manjit Trehan <ITMS400@INDYCMS>

Stagecraft@Jaguar.cs.utah.edu   [Last Updated 12-October-1991]

Mailing list is for the discussion of all aspects of stage work, including (but not limited to) special effects, sound effects, sound reinforcement, stage management, set design and building, lighting design, company management, hall management, hall design, and show production. This is not a forum for the discussion of various stage productions (unless the discussion pertains to the stagecraft of a production), acting or directing methods (unless you know of ways to get actors to stand in the right spots), film or video production (unless the techniques can be used on the stage). The list will not be moderated unless problems crop up.

Archives will be kept of the discussion (send mail to stagecraft-request for copies).

Requests to be added, problems, questions, etc., should be sent to stagecraft-request@Jaguar.utah.edu

Coordinator: Brad Davis <b-davis%CAI@CS.UTAH.EDU>

STAMPS on LISTSERV@CUNYVM or LISTSERV@CUNYVM.CUNY.EDU

The STAMPS list - for those who collect, or just have a passing interest in, stamps and related items.

To subscribe, you may send an interactive message (from BITNET sites which provide such a facility), or mail (with the command as the body of the mail - *NOT* in the subject field -) to:

LISTSERV@CUNYVM or LISTSERV@CUNYVM.CUNY.EDU

The command should be in the form:

SUB STAMPS full name

... where "full name" is your full (and correct) name.

To contribute to the list, send your mail messages to:

STAMPS@CUNYVM or STAMPS@CUNYVM.CUNY.EDU

For further information, please contact the list owner:

Geert K. Marien - GKMQC@CUNYVM.CUNY.EDU (BITNET node CUNYVM)

STARGAME on LISTSERV@PCCVM.Bitnet

This mailing list is for the Star Trek Role playing game by FASA. There are two main purposes for this list. 1) To discuss the Star Trek Role-playing game and the enhancements that FASA puts out for it 2) to play a game of Star Trek : The Role-playing game.

Some of the topics that could be discussed (besides the playing of the game) could include reviews of new products by FASA, distributing new Starships and different ways to build them, "linking together" the original and the next generation and trying to fill in the history in between the two and lots of other things.

This mailing list is NOT for discussing the Star Trek TV series or movies or talking about rumors and stuff except where they pertain to the Role-playing game.

To subscribe, send the command SUB STARGAME <your full name > to LISTSERV@PCCVM.Bitnet

Logs are kepts and you can obtain an index to them by using the command INDEX STARGAME.

Owner : bh@eng.auburn.edu (Brian Hartsfield)

STARSERVER@ENGR.UKY.EDU

Topic: Discussion of AT&T's StarServer family of computer systems

Audience: Administrators, operators, and/or users of StarServer systems

This list is envisioned as a resource for administrators and operators, as they confront the peculiarities of the StarServer family and its opera- ting system (System V Release 4).

While this list is open to all, it is NOT envisioned as a "Unix Questions and Answers" list; that audience is already served by several mailing lists and Usenet newsgroups.

The list operates through the standard rebroadcast mechanism; any messages sent to the list address are immediately rebroadcast to the list's members. If the list's traffic grows significantly, I will consider moving the list to a digest format.

The list is archived, but the archives are not currently available to the general public. Anonymous FTP of the archives will become available during the summer of 1992.

To subscribe, send an electronic mail message to: starserver-request@engr.uky.edu Postings intended for the distribution list should be sent to: starserver@engr.uky.edu Comments, questions, or suggestions about the list should be directed to: starserver-owner@engr.uky.edu

List Maintainer: Wes Morgan <morgan@engr.uky.edu> or <starserver-owner@engr.uky.edu>

STAT-L%MCGILL1.BITNET@CORNELLC.CCS.CORNELL.EDU

An open discussion group dealing with statistical consulting at university computing centres.

All requests to be added to or deleted from this list, problems, questions, etc., should be sent to one of the Coordinators.

Coordinators: Michael Walsh <CCMW%MCGILLA.BITNET@CORNELLC.CCS.CORNELL.EDU>
CCMW@MUSICA.MCGILL.CA (BitNet)
Sander Wasser <CCSW%MCGILLA.BITNET@CORNELLC.CCS.CORNELL.EDU>
CCSW@MUSICA.MCGILL.CA (BitNet)

STATLG-L%SBCCVM.BITNET@VM1.NODAK.EDU

The Neon-Sign Baseball Statistics League is a BITNET rotisserie league for the ultimate baseball fans. The Neon Sign Stat League (NSSL) is a head-to-head rotisserie league which pits fan against fan in the goal of assembling the best baseball team from among ML players. Weekly performance is determined based upon player performance and wins-losses are determined by comparing two teams which 'play' each other each week. Two or three NSSL seasons are played during each ML season. Choosing lineups and trading players requires strategy and a lot of luck. Users interested in Rotisserie League Baseball are invited to subscribe.

To subscribe to the list send mail (or message) to LISTSERV@SBCCVM with a text of: SUB STATLG-L firstname lastname (in body of mail). For example: SUB STATLG-L Joe Doe Non-BitNet users can subscribe by sending the SUB command in the text body of a message to LISTSERV%SBCCVM.BITNET@VM1.NODAK.EDU.

Coordinator: Kristofer Munn, <KMUNN%SBCCVM.BITNET@VM1.NODAK.EDU>
Commissioner of the NSSL,
Owner of the Terrace Thunderbirds

STD-UNIX@UUNET.UU.NET

List for the discussion of UNIX standards, particularly the IEEE P1003 Portable Operating System Enviroment draft standard. The list is moderated, and corresponds to the newsgroup mod.std.unix on USENET.

Archives may be retrieved from UUNET.UU.NET by anonymous FTP (login anonymous, password guest). The current volume is ~ftp/pub/mod.std.unix, and previous volumes start with ~ftp/pub/mod.std.unix.v1.

All requests to be added to or deleted from this list, problems, questions, etc., should be sent to STD-UNIX-REQUEST@UUNET.UU.NET.

Moderator: John Quarterman <jsq@UUNET.UU.NET> <longway!jsq@CS.UTEXAS.EDU>

STKACS-L%USCVM.BITNET@VM1.NODAK.EDU

Mailing list for discussion of Storage Technology's ACS 4400 system. The ACS 4400 is an automated tape cartridge loading system; the robot in the ACS Library replaces humans for mounting and dismounting tapes in 3480 tape drives. USC runs a single ACS 4400 module shared between USCMVSA and USCVM, and did the beta software work to interface StorTek's robot with Systems Center's VMTAPE software product.

All requests to be added to or deleted from this list, problems, questions, etc., should be sent to the Coordinator.

Coordinator: Karl P. Geiger <KARL%USCVM.BITNET@VM1.NODAK.EDU>

STLHE-L%UNB.CA@CORNELLC.CCS.CORNELL.EDU

The Society of Teaching and Learning in Higher Education (STHLE), Canada, has established an Electronic Mail Forum on the the NETNORTH/BITNET system. The purpose of this Forum is to exchange ideas, views and experiences of importance to STLHE members and others who are interested in the subject of teaching and learning in higher education. The Forum will also post STLHE announcements and news. A periodical summary of the issues discussed in the Forum will be published in the STLHE Newsletter for the benefit of those who do not have access to the electronic mail service.

To subscribe, send the following one-line message to LISTSERV@UNB.BITNET: SUB STLHE-L Your Full Name or send a message to the Coordinator.

Coordinator: Esam Hussein <HUSSEIN%UNB.CA@CORNELLC.CCS.CORNELL.EDU>

STORM-L@VMD.CSO.UIUC.EDU
STORM-L%UIUCVMD.BITNET@CUNYVM.CUNY.EDU

Please see the entry for WX-TALK, STORM-L's new name.

stormcock@cs.qmw.ac.uk

Purpose: For general discussion and news concerning the music of Roy Harper, a folk-rock musician with a conscience. Recommendations and news concerning similar artists are encouraged. The list is set up as a mail reflector.

To join, send mail to: stormcock-request@cs.qmw.ac.uk

To submit, send mail to: stormcock@cs.qmw.ac.uk

NB: Some internet sites may have to route mail through the UK internet gateway, "nsfnet-relay.ac.uk".

STREK-L on LISTSERV@PCCVM.BITNET

STREK-L is a list for the discussion of the many aspects of Star Trek, ranging from discussions about the movies, series, and books; discussions about the characters and/or actors; discussions about Star Trek fan clubs; to anything else dealing with Star Trek. This list is open to anyone with an interest in Star Trek. To subscribe, send the following command to LISTSERV@PCCVM via mail or interactive message:

SUB STREK-L your_full_name

where "your_full_name" is your name. For example:

SUB STREK-L Anthony Giegler

Owner: Anthony Giegler <GIEGLER@USMCP6>
Owner: Iris Jefferson <JEFFERSN@USMCP6>

structure-editors+@andrew.cmu.edu

The structure-editors list was set up as a result of the Workshop on Structure Editors that preceeded CHI'90. The initial list consists of the attendees, but the list is open to all interested in structure editors and the associated technology.

Submission address: structure-editors+@andrew.cmu.edu

Request address: structure-editors-request+@andrew.cmu.edu

Moderator: Ravinder (Rob) Chandhok. chandhok+@andrew.cmu.edu

STUTT-L%TEMPLEVM.BITNET@VM!.NODAK.EDU

Mailing list to facilitate the exchange of information among researchers and clinicians working on the problem of stuttering. Researchers are encouraged to submit descriptions of current projects (purpose, procedures, results if any, current status) and to raise questions that may be of interest to other researchers. Clinicians are encouraged to describe unusual, interesting, or provocative cases and to ask for consultation on particularly difficult cases. Individuals who stutter may also want to get information about therapy, recent research results, etc.

BitNet users may subscribe by sending the following command by interactive message or e-mail to LISTSERV@TEMPLEVM: SUBSCRIBE STUTT-L Your_full_name Where "Your_full_name" is your real name, not your login Id. Non-BitNet users can join by sending the above command in the text/body of a message to LISTSERV%TEMPLEVM.BITNET@VM1.NODAK.EDU.

Coordinator: Woody Starkweather <V5002E%TEMPLEVM.BITNET@VM1.NODAK.EDU>

STUXCH-L@PSUVM.PSU.EDU   [Last Updated 12-October-1991]

STUXCH-L@PSUVM is a list for students in art, architecture, and both visual and basic design. If you are interested in making a student exchange in one of these areas then post your interest to this list. While initially established for Pennsylvania State University the list is open to students in these fields at any institution.

To subscribe to the list send e-mail to LISTSERV@PSUVM.BITNET (or LISTSERV@PSUVM.PSU.EDU on the Internet) with the following command in the body of the mail: SUB STUXCH-L yourfirstname yourlastname

To obtain a list of files available send the following command to LISTSERV@PSUVM: INDEX STUXCH-L

Owner: Harold Ray Lawrence HRL@PSUARCH.BITNET

SUEARN-L on LISTSERV@UBVM (aka LISTSERV@UBVM.CC.BUFFALO.EDU)

The SUEARN-L consists of news items, articles, and how-to questions about the ongoing work on connecting the U.S.S.R. to international computer networks (the internet) contributed by its readers, cross-posted from other mailing lists, and retyped (usually without permission) from the "real" press.

Topics often discussed include directions on reaching Soviet sites by e-mail, discussions of how modems and other equipment work over Soviet phone lines, technology export restrictions, and prospects for connecting more sites to the net.

Submissions for the digest should be mailed to SUEARN-L@UBVM.CC.BUFFALO.EDU. They will be automatically forwarded by the LISTSERV to the editor, who puts together the digest and mails one out every week or so. Questions of the type "Is Soviet site S reachable by e-mail?" may be answered by private e-mail if the editor knows the answer.

The digest is distributed by a LISTSERV mailing list. As with other such lists, one subscribes by sending a NJE interactive message or mail saying in its body

SUB SUEARN-L Your name

to LISTSERV@UBVM.CC.BUFFALO.EDU (or any other LISTSERV). If you try this and fail, ask one of the list owners to help you with your subscription. Many sites channel SUEARN-L digests into NOTES, NEWS, RN, or similar systems that let many users read a single copy of the digest. If you're at such a site, you can save some network bandwidth by reading such a "public" copy, instead of having your personal copy e-mailed to you.

  List Editor/Owner: Mike Meystel MEYSTMA@DUVM.BITNET
  List Owner: Dimitri Vulis DLV@CUNYVMS1.BITNET

Additional Information:

Like most good things on Internet, SUEARN-L free, unless you use a commercial e-mail system, gatewayed to Internet, that charges you for incoming mail. The digest is sent out about once a week, and is typically several hundred lines long.

Please note that the Baltic states aren't considered to be part of USSR by the editors of this digest, and the discussion of e-mail connection to these countires should be sent to BALT-L, not to SUEARN-L; but the discussion of computer network situation in Eastern and Central Europe as a whole (including, but not limited to the USSR) have been posted in the past.

HISTORY: SUEARN-L was split off RusTeX-L in the summer of 1990. (RusTeX-L dealt originally with both quietions of Cyrillic (Russian and other) text processing and Soviet e-mail (the people interested in one are usually interested in the other)). By that time, RusTeX-L traffic dealing with e-mail increased sufficiently to annoy those RusTeX-L readers not interested in the technical aspects of exchanging e-mail with the USSR, so SUEARN-L was born (leaving RusTeX-L for Cyrillic text processing discussions only), and reached its present form (a moderated weekly digest) after months of trial and error.

Sun-386i@RICE.EDU

Mailing list to discuss issues specific to the Sun 386i system.

An archive of previous digests is available by anonymous FTP to MGH-COFFEE.HARVARD.EDU (128.103.80.123). More details concerning this archive and possible future archive services to BitNet and UUCP sites will be announced in upcoming Sun-386i digests.

Requests to be added to or deleted from the list, problems, questions, etc., should be sent to sun-386i-request@RICE.EDU.

Moderator: Mike Cherry <sun-386i-request@RICE.EDU>

Sun-nets@umiacs.UMD.EDU

A mailing list devoted to Sun networking issues. This is an open, unmoderated forum for any questions, issues, or concerns about Sun networking. Some sample topics for discussion include:

    NFS (note that there is a NFS list at, I think, nfs@bmc.com)
    TCP/IP
    RPC/XDR and RPC services
    Sun networking problems
    Sun networking bugs
    Sun network configuration (i.e., how many diskless machines can
       go on one Ethernet)
    Mail
    etc.

As stated above, the list is unmoderated. Archives are available via anonymous FTP on umiacs.umd.edu in the pub directory. Please address all requests for additions, deletions, and whatnot to Sun-Nets-Request@umiacs.umd.edu. Otherwise, everyone on the list will see your junk mail, and many of them will be displeased...

Coordinator: Steve Miller, Networking Special Interest Group Coordinator, SUG
Sun-Nets-Request@umiacs.umd.edu

SUN-SPOTS@RICE.EDU

Newsgroup to discuss software and hardware issues relating to the Sun Workstation. This is an edited list, sent out about once a week.

All requests to be added to or deleted from this list, problems, questions, etc., should go to Sun-Spots-Request@RICE.EDU.

Moderator: Robert Greene (rgreene@ricevm1.rice.edu)

SunFlash <flash@sunvice.East.Sun.COM>

The Florida SunFlash is an electronic news service for Sun Microsystems computer users. It is distributed by more than 90 Sun offices and by about 40 Sun Local Users Groups in more than 35 countries. The Florida SunFlash has a subscription base of more that 50,000 Sun users.

There is a compressed tar file of all of the 1991 articles (291 articles, about 1.25Mb. About 4Mb when uncompressed.) on all of the archive servers. There are compressed tar files for each month as well as the whole year.

paris.cs.miami.edu	pub/sunflash
solar.nova.edu	pub/sunflash
src.doc.ic.ac.uk	sun/sunflash
uunet.uu.net	systems/sun/sunflash

If there are any items that you missed and really want to see, please send the required volume.issue numbers to flash@sunvice.East.Sun.com.

For more information about SunFlash, send mail to info-sunflash@sunvice.East.Sun.COM with a subject of "info" and "info" in the message body.

Coordinator: John J. McLaughlin
System Engineer & SunFlash Editor
Ft. Lauderdale, Florida USA

SUP-COND <JO%ILNCRD.BITNET@CUNYVM.CUNY.EDU>

A Bitnet newsletter on superconductivity in Israel.

To subscribe, send a message to LISTSERV%TAUNIVM.BITNET@CUNYVM.CUNY.EDU with the body of the letter containing the command: SUB SUP-COND Your_Full_Name where Your_Full_Name; is your title, first name and last name.

Coordinator: Joseph van Zwaren de Zwarenstein <JO%ILNCRD.BITNET@CUNYVM.CUNY.EDU>

SUPERGUY on LISTSERV@UCF1VM.BITNET or LISTSERV@UCF1VM.CC.UCF.EDU

Superguy, housed at UCF1VM, is a multi-author world of, mainly, superheroes. There are also alternate universes of SFstory, Neo-Generation and others! Readers are welcome and Authors are begged for! Come on, and check us out.

To subscribe to the list send the following command in the BODY of mail (or an interactive message on BITNET) to LISTSERV@UCF1VM on BITNET or LISTSERV@UCF1VM.CC.UCF.EDU on the Internet:

SUB SUPERGUY yourfirstname yourlastname

Owner: Tad Simmons
SIMMONS@UCF1VM.BITNET
SIMMONS@UCF1VM.CC.UCF.EDU

SUPERIBM on LISTSERV@UKCC (BITNET)   [Last Updated 28-January-1992]
or LISTSERV@UKCC.UKY.EDU

This list is for users of IBM equipment for high performance scientific applications (supercomputing). The anticipated audience will principally be the attendees of SUPER! and other interested users.

If you wish to subscribe to SUPERIBM, send an e-mail message to LISTSERV@UKCC.UKY.EDU, or BITNET nodes can send to LISTSERV@UKCC. The message should contain only the following command (ie. in the body of the mail):

SUBSCRIBE SUPERIBM yourfirstname yourlastname

Owner: Crovo@UKCC (Bob Crovo)
Notebooks: yes public weekly

SWIM-L on LISTSERV@UAFSYSB.BITNET (BITNET)   [Last Updated 28-January-1992]
or LISTSERV@UAFSYSB.UARK.EDU (Internet)

SWIM-L is a list which is dedicated to the discussion of all phases of swimming. To subscribe, send your request to the LISTSERV at UAFSYSB.Bitnet with the following message in the body:

SUB SWIM-L firstname lastname

This should prove to be a fun list for all those who are interested in swimming!

Contact: "L. C. Jones" <LJ27524@UAFSYSB.BITNET>

Symbolic Math <leff%smu.uucp@UUNET.UU.NET>

Mailing list covering symbolic math algorithms, applications and problems relating to the various symbolic math languages. It is primarily the USENET newsgroup sci.math.symbolic; items are forwarded to Internet, BITNET and CSNET from randvax.

Mail to be forwarded to the list should be sent to leff%smu.uucp@UUNET.UU.NET (Internet) or sci.math.symbolic (USENET). Requests to be included on the list should be sent to leff%smu.uucp@UUNET.UU.NET.

Coordinator: Laurence Leff <leff%smu.uucp@UUNET.UU.NET>

SYS7-L on LISTSERV@UAFSYSB or LISTSERV@UAFSYSB.UARK.EDU

SYS7-L is dedicated to the discussion of issues related to the installation, configuration, features and product compatibilities of the Macintosh Operating System version 7.0. Full discussion of all topics related to this subject are appropriate for the list, which will be unmoderated unless moderation becomes necessary to reduce the traffic to a reasonable level. To receive a list of files send the command INDEX LISTNAME to LISTSERV@UAFSYSB.

To subscribe to SYS7-L, send the following command to LISTSERV@UAFSYSB via mail text or interactive message:

SUBSCRIBE SYS7-L Your_full_name For example: SUBSCRIBE SYS7-L Joe Shmoe

Owner: David Remington <DAVIDR@UAFSYSB.BITNET> or <DAVIDR@UAFSYSB.UARK.EDU>

tadream@vacs.uwp.wisc.edu

Purpose: Tadream is a forum for discussions about Tangerine Dream and related artists. The discussions are not moderated, but discussions should have some small relation to Tangerine Dream (solo works and instrumentation discussions are welcome). The list is set up both as a mail relay and a daily digest. (alternate mail-paths: ....uwm!uwpvacs!tadream-request, uwpvacs!tadream-request@uwm.edu)

To join, contact: tadream-request@vacs.uwp.wisc.edu

TAG-L on LISTSERV@NDSUVM1

The TAG-L list is a forum for discussion about Talented and Gifted Education: programs, resources, research, etc. It is hoped that an open and free exchange of ideas will develop from this group.

To subscribe to TAG-L, send the following command to LISTSERV@NDSUVM1 via mail text or interactive message:

SUBSCRIBE TAG-L your-full-name

where "your_full_name" is your name. For example:

SUBSCRIBE TAG-L Bob Smith

Owner: Jolene Richardson <NU172504@NDSUVM1>
Internet: NU172504@VM1.NODAK.EDU

tandem@hobbes.ucsd.edu   [Last Update 9/92]

A mailing list for tandem bicycle enthusiasts. Suitable topics include questions and answers related to tandem componentry, riding technique, brands and equipment selection, prices, clubs, rides and other activities, cooperating on a section on tandems for the rec.bicycles.* FAQ, etc.

This list is not intended to subvert the various rec.bicycles newsgroups, rather to supplement them - items of general interest should be posted to the newsgroups. Faster response to specific questions, a slightly more private forum in which opinions can be expressed with reduced fear of repercussion, and a place to carry on about tandems far beyond what might be considered "polite" in the general purpose newsgroups are some of the anticipated benefits.

To subscribe, send a message to "listserv@hobbes.ucsd.edu" with the line "subscribe tandem firstname lastname" in the message body, where <firstname lastname> is your own name. The list server will deduce your email address. Once subscribed, send messages to the list at "tandem@hobbes.ucsd.edu", and send administrative requests to the listserver "listserv@hobbes.ucsd.edu" or to "tandem-request@hobbes.ucsd.edu"

Coordinator: Wade Blomgren <wade@hobbes.ucsd.edu>

TCP-IP@NIC.DDN.MIL

An unmoderated list for the discussion of topics related to the TCP/IP protocols. It is hoped that this distribution list can aid in the following areas:

- To act as an on-line exchange among TCP developers and maintainers.
- To announce new and expanded services in a timely manner.

All requests to be added to or deleted from this list, problems, questions, etc., should be sent to TCP-IP-REQUEST@NIC.DDN.MIL. Please do not send such requests to TCP-IP@NIC.DDN.MIL, as this address is self forwarding to the entire list membership.

TCPLUS-L@UCF1VM.CC.UCF.EDU   [Last Updated June 1992]

TCPLUS-L is a list intended for discussion of the Borland product Turbo C++.

Log files will be kept on a monthly basis.

BitNet users can subscribe by sending the following command to LISTSERV@UCF1VM: SUB TCPLUS-L Your_full_name where Your_full_name is your real name, not your userid; for example: SUB TCPLUS-L John Doe Non-BitNet users can subscribe by sending the SUB command as the text/body of a message to LISTSERV@UCF1VM.CC.UCF.EDU

Coordinator: UCF Postmaster <POSTMAST@UCF1VM.CC.UCF.EDU>

For information on the content of the list and other non-technical matters, please contact Don Cross at CROSS@UCF1VM.CC.UCF.EDU

Technical Reports Redistribution
E1AR0002%SMUVM1.BITNET@CUNYVM.CUNY.EDU (Internet sites > 10K bytes)
TRLIST@SMU.EDU (Internet sites < 10K bytes)
E1AR0002 @ SMUVM1 (BITNET)
ihnp4!convex!smu!trlist (UUCP)

Redistribution of lists of technical reports from Universities and R&D labs. All technical report lists to be redistributed should include information on ordering the technical reports themselves. We prefer bib or refer format but we would rather a weird format than no list at all.

Administrative matters go to E1AR0002 @ SMUVM1 (BitNet), trlist-request@SMU.EDU or ihnp4!convex!smu!trlist (UUCP)

Coordinator: E1AR0002%SMUVM1.BITNET@CUNYVM.CUNY.EDU

technology-transfer-list@sei.cmu.edu

The Technology Applications group of the Software Engineering Institute is pleased to announce the creation of a new electronic mailing list: technology-transfer-list. This mailing list, focused on technology transfer and related topics, is intended to foster discussion among researchers and practitioners from government and industry who are working on technology transfer and innovation.

Relevant topics include:

- organizational issues (structural and behavioral)
- techno-economic issues
- business and legal issues, such as patents, licensing, copyright, and commercialization
- technology transfer policy
- technology maturation to support technology transition
- lessons learned
- domestic and international technology transfer
- transition of technology from R&D to practice
- planning for technology transition
- models of technology transfer
- studies regarding any of these topics

The technology-transfer-list is currently not moderated, but may be moderated or digested in the future if the volume of submissions warrants. The electronic mail address for submissions is:

technology-transfer-list@sei.cmu.edu

To request to be added to or dropped from the list, please send mail to:

technology-transfer-list-request@sei.cmu.edu

Please include the words "ADD" or "REMOVE" in your subject line.

Other administrative matters or questions should also be addressed to:

technology-transfer-list-request@sei.cmu.edu

TECHSERV@NIST.GOV   [Last Updated June 1992]

The TECHSERV list is a discussion forum about the technology transfer products, programs, resources and services of the Technology Services unit of the National Institute of Standards and Technology (NIST; Technology Administration/U.S. Commerce Department). Fields/topics covered are:

Calibration and Related Measurement Services
Cooperative Research & Development Agreements (CRADA)
Energy-related Inventions
Information Services
Manufacturing Technology Centers
Research and Technology Applications
Standard Reference Materials
Standard Reference Data
Standards and Certification Information
Standards Management
State Technology Outreach
Technology Development and Small Business Innovation
Voluntary Laboratory Accreditation
Weights and Measures

The Director of NIST is Dr. J. W. Lyons. The Director of Technology Services is Dr. D. R. Johnson

Messages to the list will be archived in a file in the anonymous directory on enh.nist.gov <129.6.16.1>; anonymous.archives in techserv.archives. You can access this file via Anonymous FTP. Once you connect via ftp as anonymous enter cd archives .

Messages go to the list with a reply-to address of TECHSERV@NIST.GOV. Thus, a response will automatically go to the list unless you specifically address an individual.

To subscribe (unsubscribe) to TECHSERV, send the following command to TECHSERV-REQUEST@NIST.GOV via mail text: SUBSCRIBE TECHSERV Your_full_name.

UNSUBSCRIBE TECHSERV Your_full_name. For example: SUBSCRIBE TECHSERV Thomas Technology

Owner: johnjohn@micf.nist.gov (John Makulowich)
johnjohn@nbsmicf.BITNET (John Makulowich)

TELECOM@EECS.NWU.EDU

TELECOM@CS.BU.EDU (backup address if EECS lets you down)
TELECOM@HOGBBS.FIDONET.COM (another backup address)
telecom@nuacca.bitnet (BitNet)
Telecom Digest 129/87 (for use from Fido sites; telecom 129/87 also works)
155296378 (ans:ptown) (Telex; slower, but eventually forwards to EECS)

A broad spectrum moderated-digest-format discussion on telecommunictions technology: the telephone system, modems, and other more technical aspects of telecommunications systems. This digest was spun off from HUMAN-NETS.

The Archives are stored on host LCS.MIT.EDU; the usual FTP rules apply: 'ftp lcs.mit.edu' login 'anonymous'; give your name and site as password; i.e. 'name@site.domain' 'cd telecom-archives' 'dir' to see the selections 'get (your selections)' 'bye'

All requests to be added to or deleted from this list, problems, questions, etc., should be sent to TELECOM-REQUEST@EECS.NWU.EDU.

Moderator: Patrick Townson <PTOWNSON@EECS.NWU.EDU> <patrick@chinet.chi.il.us>
TELECOM DIGEST c/o Townson Box 1570, Chicago, IL 60690

TELECOM-PRIV@PICA.ARMY.MIL   [Last Update 28-January-1992]

The telecom-priv digest is a moderated mailing list dedicated to dealing with telecom privacy issues. This forum was spun off of the telecom digest and eventually will deal other aspects of how technology affects privacy. Administrative requests should be sent to telecom-priv-request@pica.army.mil. Back issues are available via anonymous ftp on ftp.pica.army.mil [129.139.160.200].

        moderator: Dennis Rears   <drears@pica.army.mil>
                                     <drears@pilot.njin.net>
                                     P.O. Box 210
                                     Wharton, NJ 07885-0210

TeleUSErs@telesoft.com   [Last Update 9/92]

Purpose: To promote the interchange of technical information, examples, tips, etc., among the users of TeleUSE. The TeleUSErs mailing list is unmoderated. (Mail for TeleSoft TeleUSE Technical Support should NOT be sent to the list, technical support email should be sent to guisupport@telesoft.com)

Contact: TeleUSErs-request@telesoft.com (Charlie Counts)

TeX-Pubs@SHSU.BITNET

A new distribution list for TeX-related electronic form periodicals -- TeX-Pubs -- is being made available in addition to INFO-TeX for your convenience. Initially, the distribution will include TeXhax Digest, UKTeX, and TeXMaG.

The intent of TeX-Pubs is to allow users a single site for delivery of electronic form periodicals, such as TeXhax, UKTeX, and TeXMaG, as well as any others which may be brought to my attention (possibly also including the periodic "frequently asked questions" posts from USENET's comp.text.tex). This list is offered in lieu of directly posting these documents to INFO-TeX. The decision to create a support list is in an effort to provide this information to interested readers, but not replicate it for those who wish to retain their current subscription(s) and not be bothered by extraneous material on INFO-TeX.

There will be no direct archives for TeX-Pubs. Instead, each of the included periodicals will have its own directory available for retrieval at FILESERV@SHSU.BITNET.

If you would like to subscribe to TeX-Pubs, please MAIL the command: SUBSCRIBE TeX-Pubs in the body of a message to LISTSERV@SHSU.BITNET. This LISTSERV is MAIL-oriented only; interactive messages sent to LISTSERV@SHSU.BITNET will be ignored.

Any questions regarding TeX-Pubs or INFO-TeX should be directed to their owner:

George D. Greenwade, Ph.D.   Bitnet: BED_GDG@SHSU
Department of Economics and Business Analysis   THEnet: SHSU::BED_GDG
P. O. Box 2118   Voice: (409) 294-1266
Sam Houston State University   FAX: (409) 294-3612
Huntsville, TX 77341   Internet: bed_gdg%shsu.decnet@relay.the.net

TEXHAX@CS.WASHINGTON.EDU

TeXHAX is for people interested in TeX and Metafont installation and maintanance; it is brought to you as a service of the TeX Users Group in cooperation with the UnixTeX distribution service at the University of Washington. Notices of new versions/bug fixes are sent to this list, and discussion of various CPUs and printers that people are interested in using with TeX is encouraged.

Archives are kept on host JUNE.CS.WASHINGTON.EDU in file: ~ftp/TeXhax

BitNet users can subscribe, unsubscribe, and send address changes by sending a one-line message to LISTSERV@UWAVM.ACS.WASHINGTON.EDU SUBSCRIBE TEXHAX <your name> to subscribe or UNSUBSCRIBE TEXHAX your_full_name to unsubscribe.

All others should send a similar one line mail message to TEXHAX-REQUEST@CS.WASHINGTON.EDU.

Coordinators: Tiina Modisett <modisett@CS.WASHINGTON.EDU> Pierre MacKay <mackay@CS.WASHINGTON.EDU>

TeXMaG <DHOSEK%HMCVAX.BITNET@CUNYVM.CUNY.EDU>

TeXMaG is an electronic magazine published by the Harvey Mudd College Mathematics Department available free of charge to all interested parties reachable by electronic mail. It is published monthly, on the last weekend of each month, except when conditions prevent publication. Article submissions, contributions for the Toolbox, letters to the editor and back-issue requests should be sent to <DHOSEK%HMCVAX.BITNET@CUNYVM.CUNY.EDU>.

BitNet subscription requests should be sent to <DHOSEK@HMCVAX.BITNET> or send the following interactive message to LISTSERV@BYUADMIN: SUBSCRIBE TEXMAG-L Your_Full_Name European users may send the SUBSCRIBE command to LISTSERV@DEARN. On JANET requests should be sent to <ABBOTTP@UK.AC.ASTON.MAIL>, users on CDNnet should send subscription requests to <list-request@ubc.csnet>,and others should send mail to <DHOSEK%HMCVAX.BITNET@CUNYVM.CUNY.EDU>.

Editor: Don Hosek <DHOSEK%HMCVAX.BITNET@CUNYVM.CUNY.EDU>

TEXTILES@TREARN.BITNET   [Last Updated 12-October-1991]

This list is an open forum for the discussion and development of Textiles & Clothing related studies. Interest areas include:

o Textile Science   o Clothing Technology
o Textile Chemistry   o Clothing Engineering
o Textile Engineering   o Textile & Clothing Marketing
o Textile Technology   o Computer Applications to Textiles & Clothing
o Textile Management
o Clothing Science

All academics, industrialists, researchers and students are welcome. To subscribe, send:

SUB TEXTILES YourFirstName YourLastName

to LISTSERV@TREARN.BITNET either as a TELL message, or within the body of a MAIL message.

To submit articles to the discussion list, mail your message to: TEXTILES@TREARN.BITNET

Owner: Haluk Demirbag <TEX5HAD@CMS1.LEEDS.AC.UK>

THEOLOGY <U16481%UICVM.BITNET@VM1.NODAK.EDU>   [Last Updated 12-October-1991]

Mailing list dedicated to the intellectual discussion of religion. Intellectual is stressed as opposed to the "personal", the inspirational, or evangelistic. This does not mean one cannot evangelize, but rather that participants should persuade rather than brow-beat or attack those they disagree with. Arguments are inevitable, but they ultimately should resolve into mutual understanding or at least a truce.

What are the fit subjects? - the Cosmos is the limit; some might be:

- World Religions - Buddhism, Christianity, Hinduism, Islam, Judaism especially inter-religious dialogue.
- Apologetics - How should a religious perspective operate in relation to critical questioning? For example, can you prove God exists if evil also does?
- Conversion - By what means or methods should one faith seek to increase its members? Or is this out-of-bounds in a pluralistic society?
- Dogma - What are the basic tenets of a world religion? Are they coherent? Should they be? What do they derive from, revelation or something else?
- Ethics - Should religious beliefs and values seek to get involved in politics? Should an individual religious person seek to promote their morals apart from their own religious communities?

Coordinator: Charley Earp <U16481@UICVM.UIC.EDU>
                  <U16481%UICVM.BITNET@VM1.NODAK.EDU>
                  <U16481@UICVM> (BitNet)

TheoryNet@IBM.COM
    theorynt@YKTVMZ (BitNet)

Mailing list for theoretical computer science. The TheoryNet list now contains around 200 individuals and some 30 local mailing lists. Messages are mailed to ~90 different institutions in 10 countries.

BITNET, EARN, or NetNorth subscribers can join by sending the SUB command to NDSUVM1 with your name. For example: SEND LISTSERV@NDSUVM1 SUB THEORYNT Jon Doe or TELL LISTSERV AT NDSUVM1 SUB THEORYNT Jon Doe

To be removed from the list, send the SIGNOFF command: SEND LISTSERV@NDSUVM1 SIGNOFF THEORYNT or TELL LISTSERV AT NDSUVM1 SIGNOFF THEORYNT

InterNet users wishing to be added to or deleted from this list should send mail to TheoryNet-Request@IBM.COM (CSNet and internet) or theorynt%YKTVMZ.BITNET@CUNYVM.CUNY.EDU.

To MAKE CONTRIBUTIONS to the list, BitNet, EARN, and Netnorth users may send mail to the list name THEORYNT@NDSUVM1 which will then be forwarded to the Moderator.

All other requests, problems, questions, etc., should be sent to TheoryNet-Request@IBM.COM (CSNet and internet) or theorynt@YKTVMZ (BitNet).

Moderator: Victor Miller
<TheoryNet-Request@IBM.COM> InterNet

<theorynt@YKTVMZ> BitNet/NetNorth/EARN

THETAXI@GITVM1.GATECH.EDU
 THETAXI on LISTSERV@GITVM1

THETAXI, a ListServ list for Brothers of the Theta Xi Fraternity, is now up and running. ALL brothers are encouraged to subscribe -- students, faculty, everyone--even if you're not currently affiliated with a chapter.

The list will be unmoderated and monthly logs will be kept. Discussions will be over matters pertinent to the Fraternity.

To subscribe, send a piece of mail or an interactive message to LISTSERV@GITVM1 (BITNet) or LISTSERV@GITVM1.GATECH.EDU (Internet) saying :

sub thetaxi <Your full name>

TIDBITS on LISTSERV@RICEVM1.BITNET or LISTSERV@RICEVM1.RICE.EDU

The TIDBITS list is a one-way list for receiving the TidBITS weekly electronic newsletter. TidBITS reports on the most interesting events and products of the week in the (micro)computer industry with an emphasis on the world of the Macintosh. Issues are released early each week and are occasionally supplemented by special issues focussing on a single topic or product.

In addition, TidBITS issues are formatted in the straight-text "setext" format which ensures optimal online readability and the ability to decode and import the issues into specially written browsers. These browsers are in progress on several different platforms by various different people around the world. For more information on TidBITS, send email to info@tidbits.halcyon.com and a file will be returned to you promptly.

To subscribe send the following command in an interactive command (TELL or SEND) or in the BODY of mail (NOT the Subject:) to LISTSERV@RICEVM1 on BITNET or LISTSERV@RICEVM1.RICE.EDU:

SUB TIDBITS yourfirstname yourlastname

 Owner: Mark R. Williamson <MARK@RICEVM1.BITNET>
 Editor: Adam C. Engst <ace@tidbits.halcyon.com>

tinymuck-sloggers@ferkel.ucsb.edu   [Last Update 8/92]

Purpose: Discussion of development, programming and technical details of the MUD virtual reality package TinyMUCK.

Contact: tinymuck-sloggers@ferkel.ucsb.edu (Robert Earl)

TIPS on LISTSERV@FRE.FSU.UMD.EDU or LISTSERV%FRE.FSU.UMD.EDU@CUNYVM (BITNET)
 TEACHING IN THE PSYCHOLOGICAL SCIENCES

A forum for the open discussion of all aspects of TEACHING IN PSYCHOLOGY. Though the psychological sciences are the primary content focus of this group, membership is open to all who share an interest in exchanging ideas and information about teaching. The primary goal of this computer conference is to foster growth in teaching by providing a forum for teachers to talk to each other. Topics such as the exchange of experiences, teaching demonstrations, reviews of teaching materials, and the sharing of teaching resources are encouraged. Announcements regarding teaching conferences are welcome as well.

The list is structured so that REPLY's go to the entire list in an effort to stimulate discussion.

To subscribe to TIPS, send e-mail to LISTSERV@FRE.FSU.UMD.EDU on Internet or LISTSERV%FRE.FSU.UMD.EDU@CUNYVM on Bitnet with the following command in the BODY of mail:

SUBSCRIBE TIPS Yourfirstname Yourlastname

For example: SUBSCRIBE TIPS John Doe

To send a message to TIPS, send your e-mail message to TIPS@FRE.FSU.UMD.EDU on Internet or TIPS%FRE.FSU.UMD.EDU@CUNYVM on Bitnet or use the REPLY command if supported by your system.

Owner: Bill Southerly TIPSOWNER@FRE.FSU.UMD.EDU
TIPSOWNER@FRE.TOWSON.EDU

TOLKIE@JHUVM.BITNET   [Last Updated 12-October-1991]
   or LISTSERV@PUCING.BITNET (Chile)

The purpose of this list is to discuss and to exchange information on subjects related to J.R.R. Tolkien's mythological books. Now, TOLKIEN has two peered nodes, which allows me (the current owner of the list) to invite EVERYONE who wishes to chat about TOLKIEN my - thos to enter this List.

For 'Tolkien Lore' reasons, you're expected to have already read the major books, such as the Silmarillion and The Lord of the Rings. If you want to enter the list, just send your request to the owner OR to LISTSERV@JHUVM.BITNET with the body containing:

SUB TOLKIEN yourfirstname yourlastname

A "peer" list is hosted on LISTSERV@PUCING.

Owner: Escuela de Ingenieria <GANDALF@PUCING>

TOOLB-L@AFSYSB.UARK.EDU   [Last Updated 12-October-1991]
   TOOLB-L@UAFSYSB.BITNET

This list provides a discussion of Asymetrix ToolBook software, application development, and it's integration into a multimedia environment. University of Arkansas serves as host to the listserver.

TOOLB-L is a list to provide an unmoderated environment where issues, questions, comments, ideas, and uses of Asymetrix's ToolBook and it's OpenScript language can be freely discussed.

The explicit purpose of TOOLB-L is to provide timely interchange between subscribers, to provide a forum where interesting questions can be addressed within the context of interactive exchange between many individuals, and to discuss the evolution of ToolBook applications. The discussions of TOOLB-L will be archived and available for reference. In the future it is hoped this list will lead to the establishment of public domain toolbook archives. These archives would be very similar to the currently existing archives of hypercard stacks. As is the case on all unmoderated lists, the discussion and topics are only limited by the participation and interest of its subscribers. Subscribers are welcome to take an active role by posting to TOOLB-L or an inactive role by monitoring the list.

To subscribe to TOOLB-L, please send a MAIL message to: LISTSERV@UAFSYSB.UARK.EDU or LISTSERV@UAFSYSB.BITNET

The body of this MAIL message should be one line and contain the words: SUBSCRIBE TOOLB-L your name

Correspondence to the list should be addressed to TOOLB-L@UAFSYSB.

This list is a joint effort between the Kansas University Medical Center and the University of Arkansas. Questions regarding this announcement should be addressed to:

   Ken Schriner
   System Analyst
   University of Arkansas, Computing Services
   KS06054@UAFSYSB or ks06054@uafsysb.uark.edu
 or
   Lee Hancock
   Educational Technologist

University of Kansas Medical Center
LE07144@UKANVM

TOPS20@WSMR-SIMTEL20.ARMY.MIL

Mailing list to discuss DEC's TOPS20 operating system and associated hardware.

The TOPS20 Mailing List Archives are on WSMR-SIMTEL20.ARMY.MIL in yearly mail files named MAIL-yyyy.TXT. Those which would have been too large for MM to read were split into A and B parts. All the files have been moved to PD3:<TOPS20.MAIL-ARCHIVES>.

Moderator: Mark Crispin <MRC@panda.com>

THPHYSIO%FRMOP11.BITNET@VM1.NODAK.EDU

Mailing list for accelerating exchanges of information between scientists working in the field of thermal physiology, such as relevant advices, queries, and ideas. The list is also a good place to ask questions of general interest; stimulating discussion on recent results or publications; and to provide an easy and cheap way to forward general announcements, such as congresses, new journals, administration, relevant news, etc. This is the job of the list moderators. However, anyone who wishes to use the list for announcing interesting scientific events or meetings is invited to do so, or to send the information to the moderators, allowing calls for papers, bibliographies, and reports of lasting interest; obtaining, if possible, the contents pages in electronic format of relevant journals (such as J Thermal Biol, Am J Physiol, J Appl Physiol, Eur J Appl Physiol, etc.) for publication in THPHYSIO.

A side-effect of the list will be that any user can easily access the E-Mail address of colleagues. This may be useful for organizing joint research projects, or for asking advice concerning specific technical problems.

BitNet users may subscribe by sending the following command to LISTSERV@FRMOP11 via interactive message or mail: SUBscribe THPHYSIO Your full name where "Your full name" is your real name, not your login Id. Not-BitNet users can join the list by sending the above command as the only line in the text/body of a message to LISTSERV%FRMOP11.BITNET@VM1.NODAK.EDU.

Coordinator: Michel Jorda <JORDA%FRSUN12.BITNET@VM1.NODAK.EDU>

toaster-list on listserv@karazm.math.uh.edu

Discussion of the NewTek Video Toaster

To subscribe to the toaster-list, send the following command to listserv@karazm.math.uh.edu via mail:

SUBSCRIBE LISTNAME Your_full_name.

Owner: eric townsend <jet@uh.edu>

TPS-L@IndyCMS.IUPUI.EDU

TPS-L (talk.politics.soviet via ListServ) is a ListServ access and distribution point for the Usenet newsgroup, talk.politics.soviet. It is designed to allow network users without Usenet newsgroup feed access to read and contribute to talk.politics.soviet via ListServ.

TPS-L has absorbed the functions of USSR-L (USSR news & information list), USSRecom (USSR means-of-electronic-communication list), and USSR-D (USSR news & information digest), all on ListServ@IndyCMS, which have now been closed. The archives from these lists and SovNet-L, the predecessor to USSRecom and the original dedicated Soviet e-mail list, are in the process of being moved to the new TPS-L FILELIST on ListServ@IndyCMS and should be fully available effective mid- to late February 1991.

To subscribe, send request to: ListServ@IndyCMS.BITNET Using the following message text: Sub TPS-L Your_full_name

List owner/coordinator: John B Harlan IJBH200@IndyVAX (CREN/BITNET)

IJBH200@IndyVAX.IUPUI.Edu (Internet)

TQM-L on LISTSERV@UKANVM.BITNET or LISTSERV@UKANVM.CC.UKANS.EDU

TOTAL QUALITY MANAGEMENT IN HIGHER EDUCATION

A forum for the open discussion of all aspects of TOTAL QUALITY MANAGEMENT concepts and how these concepts can be implemented in institutions of higher education. Case studies and specific examples depicting the application of TQM in controlling/improving processes in an educational environment are most welcome. Discussion of the appropriate "tools" for analysis of processes are certainly appropriate. New ideas and innovations regarding concepts of TQM and how these concepts apply toward quality improvement in the delivery of education/research by Colleges and Universities can be shared by the membership.

The list is structured so that REPLY's go to the entire list in an effort to stimulate discussion. Topics related to both administrative and academic implementation are encouraged.

To subscribe to TQM-L, send the following command to LISTSERV@UKANVM on BITNET or LISTSERV@UKANVM.CC.UKANS.EDU in the BODY of mail text or interactive message:

SUBSCRIBE TQM-L Yourfirstname Yourlastname

For example: SUBSCRIBE LISTNAME Joe Shmoe

Owner: Phil Endacott <ENDACOTT@UKANVAX.BITNET>

TRANSIT on LISTSERV@GITVM1

Transit is an e-mail forum for the discussion of issues related to public transit. Issues such as routing, fares, and safety can be discussed. Feel free to make comments about anything to do with transit.

To subscribe, send the following command to LISTSERV@vm1.gatech.edu

SUB TRANSIT your_full_name

where "your_full_name" is your name. For example:

SUB TRANSIT Im A. Packet

Subscription is open to anyone. Anyone may subscribe to the list.

Once subscribed you may send contributions to TRANSIT@vm1.gatech.edu or TRANSIT@GITVM1 on BITNET. You should use the address corresponding to the LISTSERV address you used to subscribe.

Contributions sent to this list are automatically archived. You can obtain a list of the available archive files by sending an "INDEX TRANSIT" to LISTSERV@vm1.gatech.edu or LISTSERV@GITVM1.Bitnet.

Owner: Nick Donaldson <ndonald@uofmcc.bitnet> <ndonald@ccm.umanitoba.ca>

If you have any questions or problems subscribing to the list, send a message to the list owner (me) and I'll see that you get added or deleted or whatever you wish from the list. Enjoy.

    Nick Donaldson
Bitnet -   Ndonald@UOFMCC or
NetNorth Domain-style - Ndonald@ccm.umanitoba.ca or
On our Unix box -   Ndonald@ccu.umanitoba.ca

transputer@TCGOULD.TN.CORNELL.EDU

The Transputer mailing list was created to enhance the communication among those who are interested in the Transputer and Transputer based systems. Submissions should be of non-proprietary nature and be concerned with, but not limited to:

    Algorithms

Current development efforts (hardware and software)
INMOS and third party systems (Meiko, FPS, etc.)
Interfaces
Dedicated computational resources
Occam and Non-Occam language development

Archives of submissions are available by anonymous FTP from the host
TCGOULD.TN.CORNELL.EDU (userid "anonymous", password is of the form "user@host") and
through uucp on a per-request basis.

All requests to be added to or deleted from this list, problems, questions, etc., should be sent to
transputer-request@TCGOULD.TN.CORNELL.EDU.

Coordinator: Andy Pfiffer <andy@TCGOULD.TN.CORNELL.EDU>

travel-advisories@stolaf.edu

This list distributes US State Department Travel Advisories.

Please send requests for subscription/removal to travel-advisories-request@stolaf.edu

This list is also archived - the form of the archive is yet to be determined, but you can start by looking
(via anonymous FTP) in ftp.stolaf.edu:/pub/travel-advisories/archive and
ftp.stolaf.edu:/pub/travel-advisories/advisories

The latter contains the most recent advisory for a particular country.

The most recent Travel Advisories for each country are also available from St. Olaf's "gopher" server:
gopher.stolaf.edu:/gopher/Databases/US-State-Department-Travel-Advisories

Owner: Craig D. Rice <cdr@stolaf.edu>

TRAVEL-L%TREARN.BITNET@VM1.NODAK.EDU

Mailing list for discussion of tourism.

BitNet users can subscribe by sending the following interactive command to LISTSERV@TREARN:
TELL LISTSERV AT TREARN SUB TRAVEL-L yourfirstname yourlastname or send mail to
LISTSERV@TREARN.BITNET with the command; SUB TRAVEL-L yourfirstname yourlastname in
the first line of the body/text of the mail. Non-BitNet users can subscribe by sending the above SUB
command to LISTSERV%TREARN.BITNET@VM1.NODAK.EDU.

Coordinator: Esra Delen - NAD <ESRA%TREARN.BITNET@VM1.NODAK.EDU>

TRAVELLER@engrg.uwo.ca   [Last Update 11/92]

This mailing list exists to discuss the TRAVELLER Science Fiction Role Playing Game, published by
Game Designers' Workshop. All variants of Traveller (Traveller 2300, MegaTraveller, The New Era),
and Traveller games (Snapshot, Trillion Credit Squadron, etc.) are included, too. Discussion is
unmoderated and open to all facets and levels of Traveller discussion. Listeners as well as contributors
are welcome.

All requests to be added to or deleted from this list, problems, questions, etc., should be sent to
traveller-request@engrg.uwo.ca. Listees can choose to recieve articles immediately or bundled into
twice-weekly digests.

Coordinator: James T Perkins <jamesp@sp-eug.sp-eug.com>

TRDEV-L on LISTSERV@PSUVM.BITNET or LISTSERV@PSUVM.PSU.EDU

TRDEV-L provides a forum for the exchange of information on the training and the development of
human resources. Training is designed to improved human work performance on the job, and
development prepares employees to adjust and grow with the organization. Training and development

plays a strategic role in organization performance, and human resource professionals have a responsibility to explore their field and to expand their knowledge base. Participation in activities such as TRDEV-L assist in accomplishing this task.

The primary focus of this list is to stimulate research collaboration and assistance in training and development for the academic and professional communities. We invite the discussion of policy and practice issues, the posting of position announcements, pre-publication drafts of manuscripts, and news and reports of conferences.

Because of rapid changes in technology, traditional sources of this type of information are no longer adequate. With this in mind, the Institute for Research in Training and Development at Penn State University in cooperation with The University Research Council in Human Resource Development initiated this network for the ongoing and timely exchange of information in this field. This discussion group, managed by the Training and Development Society Graduate Student Organization at Penn State, was developed and field-tested through a grant from the Technical Foundation of America.

We hope that you will actively participate in this network.

You may join the list at any time by sending e-mail to LISTSERV@PSUVM or LISTSERV@PSUVM.PSU.EDU and including the following in the BODY of the mail (NOT the subject):

SUBSCRIBE TRDEV-L yourfirstname yourlastname

Please note that this command must NOT be sent to the list address (TRDEV-L@PSUVM) but to the LISTSERV address (LISTSERV@PSUVM).

Contributions sent to this list are automatically archived. You can obtain a list of the available archive files by sending an "INDEX TRDEV-L" command to LISTSERV@PSUVM. These files can then be retrieved by means of a "GET TRDEV-L filetype" command, or using the database search facilities of LISTSERV. Send an "INFO DATABASE" command for more information on the latter.

Owner: David L. Passmore <DLP@psuvm.psu.edu>

tsig@wdl1.loral.com   [Last Update 8/92]

A group for discussion of the Trusted Systems Interoperability Group (TSIG), its meetings, etc.

Requests for additions, changes and deletions to the list should be sent to tsig-request@wdl1.loral.com.

Owner: Bill Lewandowski <wrl@wdl50.wdl.loral.com>

TSO-REXX@UCF1VM.CC.UCF.EDU

In addition to REXXLIST, the existing VM/SP REXX discussion list, 3 other lists exist to discuss the REXX programming language. They are AREXX-L (for Amiga REXX users), TSO-REXX (for TSO), and PC-REXX (for Personal REXX) users.

Log files will be kept on a monthly basis.

BitNet users can subscribe by sending the following command to LISTSERV@UCF1VM: SUB TSO-REXX Your_full_name where Your_full_name is your real name, not your userid; for example: SUB TSO-REXX John Doe Non-BitNet users can subscribe by sending the SUB command as the text/body of a message to LISTSERV@UCF1VM.CC.UCF.EDU

Coordinator: UCF Postmaster <POSTMAST@UCF1VM.CC.UCF.EDU>

TURBOC-L@UCF1VM.CC.UCF.EDU

The TURBOC-L list is for Turbo C questions, tips, code, bug reports and any other Turbo C related areas of interest.

Log files will be kept on a monthly basis.

BitNet users can subscribe by sending the following command to LISTSERV@UCF1VM: SUB TURBOC-L Your_full_name where Your_full_name is your real name, not your userid; for example: SUB TURBOC-L John Doe Non-BitNet users can subscribe by sending the SUB command as the text/body of a message to LISTSERV@UCF1VM.CC.UCF.EDU

Coordinator: UCF Postmaster <POSTMAST@UCF1VM.CC.UCF.EDU>

TWAIN-L on LISTSERV@YORKVM1 or LISTSERV@VM1.YORKU.CA

The Mark Twain Forum is for persons having a scholarly interest in the life and writings of Mark Twain. Postings may include queries, discussion, conference announcements, calls for papers, information on new publications, or anything else that is related to Mark Twain studies.

The archives of TWAIN-L files are stored in the TWAIN-L FILELIST. To receive a list of files, send the command INDEX TWAIN-L to LISTSERV@YORKVM1 or LISTSERV@VM1.YORKU.CA.

To subscribe to this list, send a mail/note message to LISTSERV@YORKVM1 or LISTSERV@VM1.YORKU.CA with the one-line command in the BODY of the mail:

SUBSCRIBE TWAIN-L your-full-name

For example: SUBSCRIBE TWAIN-L Mulberry Sellers

VM systems may use the interactive command:

TELL LISTSERV at YORKVM1 SUBSCRIBE TWAIN-L your-full-name

Finally, subscribers should be aware that the Forum's database of e-mail addresses will be available to the editor of the _Mark Twain Circular_, James Leonard (leonardj@vax.citadel.edu), when updated lists of Mark Twain Circle of America members' names and postal addresses are prepared for publication. If there is an alternate form of your e-mail address that you think should be published in the _Circular_, please advise the list owner at the address below.

Owner: Taylor Roberts <TROBERTS@YORKVM1> or <TROBERTS@VM1.YORKU.CA>

U2 <metz@jhuvms.hcf.jhu.edu>   [Last Updated 28-January-1992]

Announcing a electronic magazine devoted to the group U2. This will be a very informal forum for discussion about any topic related to U2, from the members, songs, Mother Records, swaps, Propaganda, etc. For a subscription or more info, e-mail:

metz@jhuvms or metz@jhuvms.hcf.jhu.edu

Send contributions to the same address. -Dan Metz (editor)

Ukraine on ListServ@IndyCMS or ListServ@IndyCMS.IUPUI.Edu   [Last Updated 11/92]

Ukraine is dedicated to the civil and thoughtful exchange and analysis of information regarding Ukraine.

Ukraine is archived. To receive a list of files available, send the command INDEX UKRAINE to either of the ListServ addresses below.

To subscribe to UKRAINE send e-mail to LISTSERV@INDYCMS on BITNET or LISTSERV@INDYCMS.IUPUI.EDU on the Internet with the BODY of the mail containing the listserv command:

SUB UKRAINE yourfirstname yourlastname eg. sub ukraine Jane Doe

List owner/coordinator: John B Harlan
JBHarlan@IndyVAX
JBHarlan@IndyVAX.IUPUI.Edu

TV-L on LISTSERV@TREARN

A list for all kinds of TV program discussions. The discussions may be about the TV shows, soap operas or TV films.. The subsciption is open. All you have to do is use the following commands

TELL LISTSERV AT TREARN SUB TV-L your name (for VM users) SEND LISTSERV@TREARN SUB TV-L your name (for VMS users)

Or send MAIL to LISTSERV@TREARN on BITNET/EARN with the BODY/TEXT of:

SUB TV-L yourfirstname yourlastname

Esra (ESRA@TREARN - ListOwner)

UIGIS-L@UBVM.CC.BUFFALO.EDU   [Last Updated 12-October-1991]
UIGIS-L@UBVM.BITNET

This list was formed to serve as a vehicle for discussion of topics related to the design and testing of user interfaces for Geographic Information Systems (GIS) and other geographic software. Related topics on human-computer interaction for spatial information, on spatial cognition related to GIS use, and on the use of geographic information in general, also are welcome. It was established as part of Research Initiative 13 ("User Interfaces for Geographic Information Systems") of the US National Center for Geographic Information and Analysis.

Archives of UIGIS-L and related files are stored in the UIGIS-L FILELIST. To receive a list of files send the command INDEX UIGIS-L to LISTSERV@UBVM or LISTSERV@UBVM.CC.BUFFALO.EDU as the first line in the body of a mail message (NOT the Subject: line).

To subscribe to UIGIS-L, send the command SUB UIGIS-L your name to LISTSERV@UBVM or LISTSERV@UBVM.CC.BUFFALO.EDU via a mail message (again, as the first line in the body of the mail, not the Subject: line).

For example: SUB UIGIS-L William Morris Davis

Owner: David M. Mark <GISMGR@UBVMS>

ULTRALITE-LIST@STARNET.STARCONN.COM   [Last Update 9/92]

An unmoderated list for users of the original NEC UltraLite PC1701 and PC1702 computers (the V30-based notebook computer with a 1MB or 2MB silicon hard disk, not the newer 286- and 386-based models). Topics include general information, tips, techniques, applications, experiences, and sources for hardware, software, accessories, and information.

New subscribers will automatically receive digests of all previous messages from the List, at least until such time that it becomes unwieldy to do so.

To subscribe or unsubscribe to the ultralite-list, send mail to ultralite-list-request@csd.mot.com. At present, requests are handled by a human operator. No particular format for request is required, but please make sure that your full name is included somewhere in the message or header.

Administrative messages other than subscription and unsubscription should be sent to ultralite-list-owner@starnet.starconn.com.

Coordinator: Brian Smithson <brian@starnet.starconn.com>

UN on ListServ@IndyCMS   [Last Updated 28-January-1992]
     or ListServ@IndyCMS.IUPUI.Edu

UN (United Nations) is dedicated to discussion of the United Nations, and is open to all interested persons.

To subscribe send mail to LISTSERV@INDYCMS.BITNET or on the Internet to listserv@IndyCMS.IUPUI.Edu with the following command in the body:

SUB UN yourfirstname yourlastname

List owner/coordinator: John B Harlan IJBH200@IndyVAX IJBH200@IndyVAX.IUPUI.Edu

unisys@TMC.EDU

Mailing list for Unisys related topics. It is currently designed as a mail reflector and does not currently support archive or FTP.

All requests to be added to or deleted from this list, problems, questions, etc., should be sent to unisys-request@TMC.EDU.

Coordinator: Richard H. Miller <rick@SVEDBERG.BCM.TMC.EDU>

UNIX-EMACS@VM.TCS.TULANE.EDU

An unmoderated list for discussion of all EMACS type editors for UNIX. The list is gatewayed both ways to usenet newsgroup comp.emacs.

All requests to be added to or deleted from this list, problems, questions, etc., should be sent to Unix-Emacs-Request@VM.TCS.TULANE.EDU.

Coordinator: John Voigt <sysbjav@vm.tcs.tulane.edu>

UNIX-SOURCES@BRL.MIL

Internet gateway for distribution of the "UUCP net" Unix net.sources newslist. Only ONE person at a site should subscribe, since articles tend to be rather long.

All requests to be added to or deleted from this list, problems, questions, etc., should be sent to UNIX-SOURCES-REQUEST@BRL.MIL. Contributors who wish never to see error messages from the mailer should specify this address as the return-path of their messages.

There is a BITNet/Netnorth/EARN sub-distribution list, UNIX-SRC@NDSUVM1; BNEnet subscribers can join by sending the SUB command with your name. For example, SEND LISTSERV@NDSUVM1 SUB UNIX-SRC Jon Doe To be removed from the list, SEND LISTSERV@NDSUVM1 SIGNOFF. To make contributions to the list, BITNet subscribers should send mail to the Internet list name, NOT to the BITNet list name.

Coordinator: Chuck Kennedy <kermit@BRL.MIL>

UNIX-SW@WSMR-SIMTEL20.ARMY.MIL

UNIX-SW is a vehicle for announcing the availablity of new major packages of UNIX/'C' language software on the WSMR-SIMTEL20.ARMY.MIL repository. This list will also be used to mail periodic updates of the list of all UNIX software held at WSMR-SIMTEL20.ARMY.MIL (probably monthly).

UNIX-SW is not a forum for discussion of this software. Such discussions are more appropriately held with the authors, or in other groups. Rather, we are attempting to make known to the widest possible audience the contents of this large repository of public-domain software.

SIMTEL20 is a DEC-20 machine running the TOPS20 operating system, located at White Sands Missile Range, New Mexico. The machine is a host on the Defense Data Network (DDN), and as such, gives users located on other hosts the capability of directly transferring this software via the FTP (file transfer process) command.

Mail archives are kept on host WSMR-SIMTEL20.ARMY.MIL as TOPS20 mail files named yymm.n-TXT, where n starts with one and increments by one into another file as each file reached 150 disk pages. To conserve disk space, all the mail files in the archive, except for the current year, are individually compressed. The compressed files have the suffix -Z as part of the filetype field; they should be renamed to have the suffix .Z (uppercase Z) when transfered to a Unix system so the uncompress program will find them. The current month's mail is still kept in UNIX-SW-ARCHIV.TXT. The archives are stored in directory: PD2:<ARCHIVES.UNIX-SW> Archive files are available via ANONYMOUS FTP from WSMR-SIMTEL20.ARMY.MIL for those with TCP/IP access to the Internet.

The repository been completely reorganized. The software is now stored in the directory PD2:<UNIX-C> (it used to be stored in PD2:<UNIX>; this directory no longer exists).

All requests to be added to or deleted from this list, problems, questions, etc., should be sent to UNIX-SW-REQUEST@WSMR-SIMTEL20.ARMY.MIL.

Coordinator: Dave Curry <DCURRY@WSMR-SIMTEL20.ARMY.MIL> <davy@INTREPID.ECN.PURDUE.EDU>

UNIX-TeX@MIMSY.UMD.EDU

Discussion of matters involved in porting TeX82 to Unix. Messages sent to the list are directly redistributed without human intervention.

Archives are kept on MIMSY.UMD.EDU in the file: PS:<MAILING-LISTS>UNIX-TEX.ARC

All requests to be added to or deleted from this list, problems, questions, etc., should be sent to UNIX-TeX-REQUEST@MIMSY.UMD.EDU.

Coordinator: Richard Furuta <furuta@TOVE.UMD.EDU>

UNIX-WIZARDS@BRL.MIL

Distribution list for people maintaining machines running the Unix operating system.

All requests to be added to or deleted from this list, problems, questions, etc., should be sent to UNIX-WIZARDS-REQUEST@BRL.MIL.

There is a BITNET/Netnorth/EARN sub-distribution list, UNIX-WIZ@NDSUVM1; BNEnet subscribers can join by sending the SUB command with your name. For example, SEND LISTSERV@NDSUVM1 SUB UNIX-WIZ Jon Doe To be removed from the list, SEND LISTSERV@NDSUVM1 SIGNOFF. To make contributions to the list, BitNet subscribers should send mail to the Internet list name, NOT to the BITNET list name.

Coordinator: Mike Muuss <mike@BRL.MIL>

UPNEWS on LISTSERV@MARIST.BITNET or LISTSERV@VM.MARIST.EDU

[Last Updated 1/92]

"Update-Electronic-Music-News" highlights "underground" music, independent and major label artists and companies, contains record reviews, interviews, perspectives, and a host of other topics that differ from issue to issue. Update is also attempting to close the popular music gap, or mass music gap, by bringing to the forefront those artists and aspects of the music industry that are struggling to make their voice heard. Update is providing artists and other areas of the music industry with an opportunity to have recordings, music products, and/or music services presented directly to a large music audience.

To Subscribe (and you want to!) send a message to LISTSERV@MARIST.BITNET or LISTSERV@VM.MARIST.EDU with the BODY of the mail containing: SUBSCRIBE UPNEWS yourfirstname yourlastname

Editor in chief: Christopher DeRobertis UICD@MARIST.BITNET or UICD@VM.MARIST.EDU

URBAN-L%TREARN.BITNET@VM1.NODAK.EDU

Mailing list for information exchange, ideas, etc. on the science of Urban Planning.

Yearly archives of the list will be maintained.

BitNet users may join the list by sending the following command to LISTSERV@TREARN via interactive message or e-mail: SUB urban-l Your full name where "Your full name" is your real name, not your login Id. Non-BitNet users can join by sending the above command as the only line in the text/body of a message to LISTSERV%TREARN.BITNET@VM1.NODAK.EDU.

URBANITES@PSYCHE.MIT.EDU

The purpose of this mailing list is to discuss and promote self-sufficiency in everyday life in many forms. This includes but is not limited to basic needs such as food, shelter, health, and safety. A unique aspect of this list, however, unlike many others, is that we will concentrate on the city and urban/semi-urbs applications of traditional self-sufficiency technology. Thus, discussions on raising fish in a small backyard pool or in a large aquarium instead of in cage-culture rafts on a farm pond; raising veggies and some small-tree fruits in containers on the patio or under grow-lights at work (a ready source of fluorescent fixtures for most of us!) instead of in a 20 x 40 garden plot "out back".

Certainly folks in a more suburban setting (lucky them!) will find much of the "urbanites" content useful, but the list is here first and foremost for those of us out here in the Concrete Jungle, for whatever reason. Some of us, like myself, are here using the city's resources to learn before setting off for the country or the 'burbs, some are stuck in pay-our-debts jobs here, and some just like the active city environment of places like Harvard Square or Pike's Place. But even though we rent our dwellings and have a postage-stamp size yard, or none at all, we can still get into doing for ourselves in some of the ways our bucolic buddies do.

Send requests to be added directly to urbanites-request@psyche.mit.edu and include "urbanites-request" in your subject line.

Coordinator: sgw@silver.lcs.mit.edu (stephen g. wadlow)

URUSEI-YATSURA@Panda.com   [Last Updated 12-October-1991]

Mailing list for Urusei Yatsura fans.

All requests to be added to or deleted from this list, problems, questions, etc., should be sent to URUSEI-YATSURA-REQUEST@Panda.COM

Coordinator: Mark Crispin <MRC@Panda.COM>

UREXX-L@LIVERPOOL.AC.UK
UREXX-L on LISTSERV@LIVERPOOL.AC.UK

A mailing list for REXX on UNIX. The list has been created in response to the announcement of uni-REXX by the Work Station Group (who also have an XEDIT clone uni-XEDIT).

To join the list include the following line in the body of a mail message:

SUB UREXX-L yourfistname yoursecondname

and send to

LISTSERV@LIVERPOOL.AC.UK (bitnet/internet)

You will receive more information when you subscribe.

Items to be posted to the list itself should be sent to UREXX-L@LIVERPOOL.AC.UK

Note: Please do not use the SIGNON command instead of SUBscribe.

Coordinator: Alan Thew

Bitnet/Earn: QQ11@LIVERPOOL.AC.UK   UUCP: ....!mcsun!ukc!liv!qq11
Internet: QQ11@LIVERPOOL.AC.UK;
             QQ11%LIVERPOOL.AC.UK@NSFNET-RELAY.AC.UK

usenet.hist@ucsd.edu

This list is for the discussion of the socio-cultural, technical and political history of usenet. The list is not moderated and is open to anyone interested in the history of the net.

Coordinator: bjones@ucsd.edu (Bruce Jones)

usml@HC.DSPO.GOV@Index(usml)

Discussion and programs for various universe-generating software (accretion models, Traveller, Other Suns, ...).

Archives are maintained on host HC.DSPO.GOV (192.12.184.4) in directory: pub/usml. ANONYMOUS FTP is supported.

All requests to be added to or deleted from this list, problems, questions, etc., should be sent to usml-request@HC.DSPO.GOV

Coordinator: Josh Siegel <usml-request@HC.DSPO.GOV>

UTS-L@YSUB.YSU.EDU
UTS-L@YSUB (BitNet)

Mailing list for discussion of Amdahl's UTS/580 implementation of Unix and for software running in the UTS environment. Some potential topics for discussion: porting software, integrating with bitnet, internet, and servers, requests for help, using UTS-specific features, hardware issues, and anything else that's UTS-related. Discussion should be limited to the UTS environment (under VM or native),pso this list does not replace info-unix, unix-wiz, aix-l, or any otherpmailing list. Postings not specific to UTS should be posted to one of those lists, instead.

The discussion is not presently moderated, although if message traffic warrants, it may be in the future. All are free to post to the list, with the condition that you must be subscribed to the list to post anything. To help keep the noise down to a reasonable level, we would appreciate if you would contact your site's UTS system administrator (aka "unix guru") for help on your question, before you send it out to everyone.

A monthly notebook of all discussions will be kept online, in files named UTS-L LOGYYMM (UTS-L LOG9001, for example) on the Listserv. To retrieve a notebook, send e-mail or an interactive message to Listserv with a message text/body of GET UTS-L LOGYYMM. Listserv database services are also available - send INFO DATABASE to the list-server for more information. Notebooks will also be available via anonymous FTP to YSUB.YSU.EDU after 1/31/90. More on this later. Sorry, we don't have news (yet, anyway).

BitNet users can subscribe by sending the following command to LISTSERV@YSUB via interactive message or e-mail: SUB UTS-L Your full name where "Your full name" is your real name, not your login Id. Not-BitNet users can join the list by sending the above command as the only line in the text/body of an e-mail message to LISTSERV@YSUB.YSU.EDU.

Administrative questions, problems, etc., should be sent to the Coordinators.

Coordinators:
Doug Sewell <DOUG%YSUB.BITNET@CORNELLC.CIT.CORNELL.EDU>
Lou Anschuetz <TEMNGT23%YSUB.BITNET@CORNELLC.CIT.CORNELL.EDU>

URANTIAL on LISTSERV%UAFSYSB.bitnet@cunyvm.cuny.edu

'URANTIAL' is a forum for the discussion of ideas presented in The URANTIA Book. The perspective of the list is holistic. Contributions are welcomed from the full scope of scientific and theological perspectives as long as they serve to enhance our understanding of ourselves and pertain constructively to the conceptual framework of the URANTIA material. The goal of this list is to utilize The URANTIA Book to gain integration of knowledge and consolidation of worldviews toward an improved life for all on Earth.

Please send subscription requests to LISTSERV@UAFSYSB on BITNET, *not* to the list itself URANTIAL@UAFSYSB. Include the following command in the body or text of the mail:

SUB URANTIAL yourfirstname yourlastname From: "David L. Merrifield"
<DM06900%UAFSYSB.BITNET@VM1.NoDak.EDU>

UUs-L on LISTSERV@ubvm.cc.buffalo.edu   [Last Updated June 1992]

UUs-L is a global meeting place for Unitarian Universalists and anyone going our way. The list's intent is to provide a forum for sharing of UU-related information across district and regional boundaries; to bring into contact people and ideas who normally would never have met; and to foster discussion of functional and structural innovations we can make in our organizations and world.

Electronic conferencing, mail, and the paradigms they encourage are something that most members of this list have a growing familiarity with. These are tools which are already having an impact more profound than the other major influence on human religion and politics; the printing press. The effects these tools can have on an organization are manyfold; better, cheaper, more effective communications; improved dynamics for far-flung groups; and insight into the processes that make up even non-electronic communications.

Subscriptions to UUs-L are obtained by sending the following in the body of a message to LISTSERV@ubvm.cc.buffalo.edu:

SUB UUs-L your full name

UUs-L List Manager: Steve Traugott <uus-lman@TerraLuna.SpaceCoast.Org>

V2LNI-PEOPLE@MC.LCS.MIT.EDU

People using Pronet/V2LNI Ring networks.

[Also see mailing lists INFO-PROTEON (Proteon and Proteon gear in general, with slight leanings toward token ring engineering) and P4200 (Proteon gateway products)]

Coordinator: LWA@MC.LCS.MIT.EDU

VAL-L@UCF1VM.CC.UCF.EDU   [Last Updated June 1992]

Those interested in Soviet news and comment and Gulf war bulletins may wish to subscribe to Val-L (Valentine Michael Smith's commentary) on ListServ@UCF1VM. Many will recognize Valentine as a long-time (and prolific) contributor to such lists as Politics, History, USSR-L and NewsE-L. Valentine's ongoing account of and commentary on world events has now been consolidated on a dedicated list of his own, which promises to be a most valuable addition to the networks.

Log files will be kept on a monthly basis.

BitNet users can subscribe by sending the following command to LISTSERV@UCF1VM: SUB VAL-L Your_full_name where Your_full_name is your real name, not your userid; for example: SUB VAL-L John Doe Non-BitNet users can subscribe by sending the SUB command as the text/body of a message to LISTSERV@UCF1VM.CC.UCF.EDU

Coordinator: UCF Postmaster <POSTMAST@UCF1VM.CC.UCF.EDU>

VAMPYRES on LISTSERV@GUVM.Bitnet

VAMPYRES is for fans of vampiric lore, fact and fiction.

To subscribe, please either SEND the command

SUBSCRIBE VAMPYRES firstname lastname

to LISTSERV@GUVM or, for people who do not have access to BITNET, send MAIL to LISTSERV@GUVM (no subject) that contains one line in the text:

SUBSCRIBE VAMPYRES firstname lastname

Owner: Jim Wilderotter <WILDER@GUVAX.Bitnet>

VETINFO on LISTSERV@UCDCVDLS.BITNET

This list has been created to stimulate discussion in the area of Informatics, with special reference to the field of Veterinary Medicine. Related topics include Clinical decision support systems, laboratory information management, imaging, disease nomenclature and coding systems, expert systems, knowledge bases, etc. Discussions related to specific hardware and software implementations are welcome as well as approaches to specific approaches to challenges in veterinary informatics.

Archives of VETINFO and related files are stored in the VETINFO FILELIST. To receive a list of files, send the command INDEX VETINFO to LISTSERV@UCDCVDLS. To subscribe to the list send the following command to LISTSERV@UCDCVDLS on BITNET via interactive message or in the BODY of e-mail:

SUBSCRIBE VETINFO Your_Full_Name.

LIST Owner: Jim Case DVM,Ph.D (JCASE@UCDCVDLS.BITNET)
James T. Case, Administrator   University of California
Information Systems   School of Veterinary Medicine
California Veterinary Diagnostic P.O. Box 1770
  Laboratory System   Davis, CA 95617
jcase@ucdcvdls.bitnet   (916)752-4408

vhf@w6yx.Stanford.EDU   [Last Update 28-January-1992]

Discussion of Very High Frequency radio propogation, equipment and activity, related to Amateur Radio. Typical topics include equipment reviews, propagation reports, and contest results. Administrivia and subscriptions to: vhf-request@w6yx.Stanford.EDU.

Coordinator: Paul Flaherty, N9FZX (paulf@stanford.edu)

VIDEOTECH@WSMR-SIMTEL20.ARMY.MIL

VideoTech is a combination of the old HOME-SAT, VIDEO-DISC and TELETEXT mailing lists. WSMR-SIMTEL20.ARMY.MIL is the DDN side of this mailing list (which includes a USENET entry); USENET/netnews messages to rec.video will find their way to this list without loops. Appropriate topics for discussion on VideoTech might be, but are not limited to:

Home Satellite (TVRO, DBS)   Teletext
Cable Television   Stereo Television
Video Disc Technology   HighRes Television
Video Tape Recorders (Beta/VHS/UMatic)

Mail archives are kept on host WSMR-SIMTEL20.ARMY.MIL as TOPS20 mail files named · yymm.n-TXT, where n starts with one and increments by one into another file as each file reached 150 disk pages. To conserve disk space, all the mail files in the archive, except for the current year, are individually compressed. The compressed files have the suffix -Z as part of the filetype field; they should be renamed to have the suffix .Z (uppercase Z) when transfered to a Unix system so the uncompress program will find them. The current month's mail is still kept in VIDEOTECH-ARCHIV.TXT. The archives are stored in directory: PD2:<ARCHIVES.VIDEOTECH> Archive files are available via ANONYMOUS FTP for those with TCP/IP access to the Internet.

All requests to be added to or deleted from this list, problems, questions, etc., should be sent to VIDEOTECH-REQUEST@WSMR-SIMTEL20.ARMY.MIL.

BitNet users can subscribe to the list through an automated BitNet mail server. To send a command to the server, simply send the command as the text of a message. Send all command-messages to LISTSERV@UIUCVMD. The command to subscribe yourself is: SUB I-VIDTEK (your personal name) The command to cancel your subscription is: UNSUB I-VIDTEK Substitute your own personal name for the string "(your personal name)" in the example above. If you misspell your name, subscribe again, you do not need to unsubscribe to fix a name spelling error.

Coordinator: Frank J. Wancho <WANCHO@WSMR-SIMTEL20.ARMY.MIL>

VIDNET-L on LISTSERV@UGA

VIDNET-L (Video Network Discussion List) was formed for the discussion of mutual problems and concerns which face all who are involved in the operation of a campus-wide video network. This includes any configuration which may be found in a campus environment-creation, operation, maintenance, programming, teleconferencing, rate structure, videotext are some of the topics expected to be discussed.

To subscribe, send the following command to LISTSERV@UGA on BITNET or listserv@uga.cc.uga.edu on the Internet via mail or interactive message:

SUB VIDNET-L your_full_name

where "your_full_name" is your name. For example:

SUB VIDNET-L John X. Doe

Owner: John R. Stephens, Jr. <JStephen@UGA.BITNET> <JStephen@UGA.CC.UGA.EDU> Internet

VIRTU-L on LISTSERV@UIUCVMD.BITNET [Last Updated 28-January-1992]
or LISTSERV@VMD.CSO.UIUC.EDU

A bi-directional gateway for the Usenet newsgroup sci.virtual-worlds. This is a discussion of all aspects of virtual reality. The mailing list is not moderated. If you have access to the Usenet network of newsgroups, you probably do not need to subscribe to this mailing list. All notes to the mailing list are sent automatically for posting to sci.virtual-worlds, at the discretion of the newsgroup moderators. All sci.virtual-worlds posts are automatically sent to LISTSERV subscribers.

Caution: Traffic on this mailing list is fairly high! Expect about 10-30 messages per day, some of which are lengthy.

To subscribe:

Send email to the Listserv address, either:

LISTSERV@UIUCVMD (for Bitnet) or LISTSERV@VMD.CSO.UIUC.EDU (for Internet)

with the following text:

SUB VIRTU-L <Your full name>

where <Your full name> is your 'True Name,' (NOT your email address!!!)

To unsubscribe:

Send email to the same Listserv address as above, with the text:

UNSUB VIRTU-L

Archives: Listserv does NOT maintain archives of this mailing list. Archives of all posts to sci.virtual-worlds are maintained by the newsgroup sponsors (see below). Archives are available via anonymous FTP to milton.u.washington.edu

Sponsorship: The Usenet newsgroup sci.virtual-worlds is sponsored by the Human Interface Technology Laboratory at the University of Washington, Seattle. Although the Listserv redistribution is sponsored by the University of Illinois and Greg Newby, the HITL crew deserves most of the credit for this important forum.

    The List owner:
      Greg Newby
          Graduate School of Library and Information Science, and
          National Center for Supercomputing Applications, at the
          University of Illinois at Urbana-Champaign
      Email: gbnewby@vmd.cso.uiuc.edu or
          gbnewby@uiucvmd.bitnet
      Phone: 217-333-3280

VIRUS-L%LEHIIBM1.BITNET@CUNYVM.CUNY.EDU

Virus-L is a forum specifically for the discussion of computer virus experiences, protection software, and other virus related topics. The list is currently open to the public and is a non-digest format list. Readers who prefer digest format lists should periodically read the public back logs of submissions, available from the LEHIIBM1 LISTSERV via a GET command (e.g., GET VIRUS-L LOG8806A for the first week of activity during June, 1988). Mail sent to to Virus-L@LEHIIBM1.BITNET will automatically be redistributed to everyone on the mailing list. By default, you will NOT receive a copy of your own letters. If you wish to, send mail to the LISTSERV saying SET VIRUS-L REPRO

Archives are available, as is a file called DIRTY DOZEN which lists a number of viruses, trojan horses, and pirated programs for the IBM PC. All submissions to VIRUS-L are stored in weekly log files which can be downloaded by any user on (or off) the mailing list. There is also a small archive of some of the public anti-virus programs which are currently available. This archive, too, can be accessed by any user. All of this is handled automatically by the LISTSERV.

To find out what files are available on the LISTSERV, send mail to LISTSERV%LEHIIBM1.BITNET@MITVMA.MIT.EDU saying INDEX VIRUS-L Note that filenames/extensions are separated by a space, and not by a period. Once you've decided which file(s) you want, send mail to LISTSERV saying GET filename filetype For example, GET VIRUS-L LOG8804 would get the file called VIRUS-L LOG8804 (which happens to be the monthly log of all messages sent to VIRUS-L during April, 1988). Note that, starting June 6, 1988, the logs are weekly. The new file format is VIRUS-L LOGyymmx where yy is the year (88, 89, etc.), mm is the month, and x is the week (A, B, etc.). Readers who prefer digest format lists should read the weekly logs and sign off of the list itself.

To subscribe send the following command to LISTSERV@LEHIIBM1 (non-BitNet users send mail to LISTSERV%LEHIIBM1.BITNET@MITVMA.MIT.EDU with the command in the message body): SUB VIRUS-L Your_Full_Name where Your_Full_Name is your real name, not your userid. To unsubscribe, send: SIGNOFF VIRUS-L

All other requests, problems, questions, etc., should be sent to the Coordinator.

Coordinator: Kenneth R. van Wyk <LUKEN%LEHIIBM1.BITNET@CUNYVM.CUNY.EDU> <LUKEN@VAX1.CC.LEHIGH.EDU>

VISBAS-L on LISTSERV@TAMVM1.BITNET   [Last Update 9/92]

A list to discuss the Visual Basic software. To subscribe send a message or e-mail to LISTSERV@TAMVM1.BITNET with the following in the BODY:

SUB VISBAS-L yourfirstname yourlastname

Owner: Chris Barnes <x005cb@tamvm1.tamu.edu>

VISION-LIST@ADS.COM

Discussion group for artificial intelligence vision researchers. The list is intended to embrace discussion on a wide range of vision topics, including physiological theory, computer vision, artificial intelligence technology applied to vision research, machine vision algorithms, industrial applications, robotic eyes, implemented systems, ideas, profound thoughts -- anything related to vision and its automation is fair game.

Previous messages are available on request to Vision-List-Request@ADS.COM.

All requests to be added to or deleted from this list, problems, questions, etc., should be sent to Vision-List-Request@ADS.COM.

Moderator: Tod Levitt <levitt@ADS.COM>

VM-UTIL <DYOUNG%TRINITY.BITNET@CUNYVM.CUNY.EDU>

A list for the discussion and redistribution of useful and interesting utilities for use by the VM/SP and CMS operating systems. There is also a FILELIST by the same name which will be used to store some of the utilities collected.

The list is hosted at DEARN, MARIST, TECMTYVM, TREARN, UBVM, UCF1VM, and UTARLVM1. There is also a companion FILELIST available from the LISTSERV's at DEARN, MARIST, UBVM, UCF1VM, and UTARLVM1 which contains a lot of useful VM- and CMS-related utilities that people have contributed. If anyone is interested in contributing a utility to be stored in the FILELIST, they can send a note telling what they wish to contribute along with a description of each utility. Source code is prefered.

To subscribe send the following command to LISTSERV@[one of the above hosts] (non-BitNet users send mail to LISTSERV%[one of the above].BITNET@CUNYVM.CUNY.EDU) SUBSCRIBE VM-UTIL your_full_name To unsubscribe, send UNSUBSCRIBE VM-UTIL

Coordinator: David Young <DYOUNG%TRINITY.BITNET@CUNYVM.CUNY.EDU>

VMVIRUS on LISTSERV@PCCVM

After consulting with the folks 'attached' to VIRUS-L and seeing a void in the area of centralized information about VM, MVS, and VSE viri and worms, I have established a list VMVIRUS at my node. This list is open and public, but as the following text will describe, some files will be restricted. Be aware that a posting to this list will automatically be forwarded to VIRUS-L.

This list has been established to act as a clearing house / archival location for comments and information concerning VM viruses and worms. The logs are public and your comments well be freely available to the network community. I intend to also store samples of source, object, and executable code for examination by selected persons. Commonly these files will only be available to NADs and other selected interested parties. Application may be made for code samples. Userid authenticity WILL BE verified prior to dispersal of infectious programs.

So far the VM community has been spared many of the problems that currently plague the PC, MAC and Unix worlds. Let us hope that it remains that way. This archive is intended as a step in the direction to halt the spread of such malicious programming.

While the name VMVIRUS implies a limitation to the VM environment, this list is open to comments by MVS and VSE users also. I would urge VM, MVS, and VSE sites to send samples of infectious code for storage. The following rules MUST be adhered to in the transmission of potentially harmful programs.

1. Send notification to myself (SYSMAINT@PCCVM) prior to transmission.
2. De-activate the code if possible
3. Transmit the code to SECURE@PCCVM
4. Do not include code in a 'mail-gram'

This site maintains a 'filter' for known infectious materials, hence the required pre-transmission notification. Let all work together to restore the 'clean' computing environment that we used to have and to assist in the eradication / prosecution of offenders.

To subscribe to VMVIRUS send mail or interactive message to LISTSERV@PCCVM on BITNET with the TEXT or BODY of the message containing the command: SUB VMVIRUS yourfirstname yourlastname

Owner:

R N Hathhorn, VM Systems Support   BITNET: SYSMAINT@PCCVM
Portland Community College
P. O. Box 19000
12000 S. W. 49th Ave.
Portland, Oregon 97219-0990
(503) 244-6111 ext. 4705

VMXA-L%UGA.BITNET@MITVMA.MIT.EDU

Discussion of issues in installation, operation and maintenance of VM/XA systems. Included are both the existing VM/XA/SF system as well as the new VM/XA/SP system. Topics include anything related to VM/XA, as well as conversion from VM/SP and VM/SP/HPO to VM/XA.

List archives will be maintained at UGA.BITNET for search via the LISTSERV Database facility.

To subscribe send the following command to LISTSERV@UGA (non-BitNet users send mail to LISTSERV%UGA.BITNET@MITVMA.MIT.EDU) SUBSCRIBE VMXA-L your_full_name To unsubscribe, send UNSUBSCRIBE VMXA-L

Coordinator: Harold C. Pritchett <HAROLD%UGA.BITNET@MITVMA.MIT.EDU>

VPIEJ-L@VTVM1.BITNET VPIEJ-L@VTVM1.CC.VT.EDU

VPIEJ-L is a discussion list for electronic publishing issues, especially those related to Scholarly Electronic Journals. Topics for discussion include SGML, PostScript, and other e-journal formats; as well as software and hardware considerations for creation of, storage, and access to e-journals. Publishers, editors, technical staff, programmers, librarians, and end-users are welcome to join.

One goal of the list is to provide better feedback from users to creators, so we are very interested in receiving and archival issues. This should give those of us involved in publishing an idea as to what distribution methods work and how end-users are accessing and using these publications. Current readers of and contributors to VPIEJ-L have discussed readability and screen display, copyright, and advertising (noncommercial).

Archives of VPIEJ-L are available. A listing may be retrieved by sending a command INDEX VPIEJ-L in the BODY of e-mail or a message to LISTSERV@VTVM1 or LISTSERV@VTVM1.CC.VT.EDU .

To subscribe, send the following command to LISTSERV@VTVM1 or LISTSERV@VTVM1.CC.VT.EDU in the BODY of mail (NOT subject) or in an interactive message:

SUB VPIEJ-L your_full_name

where "your_full_name" is your name. For example: SUB VPIEJ-L Joan Doe

Owner: James Powell <JPOWELL@VTVM1.BITNET> <JPOWELL@VTVM1.CC.VT.EDU>

VSAM-L%TREARN.BITNET@CUNYVM.CUNY.EDU
VSAM-L on LISTSERV@TREARN

A list to discuss issues related to Virtual Storage Access Method has been created at LISTSERV@TREARN.

To Subscribe: issue this command to LISTSERV@TREARN.BITNET: (Internet users mail to LISTSERV%TREARN.BITNET@CUNYVM.CUNY.EDU) SUB VSAM-L myfirstname mylastname

To Post articles: MAIL your article to the addresses above

List owner: Dr. Ozel Ergen <BILMOE@TREARN.BITNET>

VTLSLIST on LISTSERV@VTVM1

VTLSLIST is a discussion list for users of VTLS software. VTLS is the Virginia Tech Library System, an online public access catalog for libraries. Issues affecting all classes of users from patron to manager will be considered. Testing and implementation of modules and PC-based integrated systems such as the VTLS Intelligent Workstation software will also be fair game. Due to our proximity to VTLS, Inc., we hope to have some input from them as well.

VTLSLIST is edited by Buddy Litchfield, Department Head of Database Administration. He oversees the testing, training, and implementation of VTLS software here at University Libraries, Virginia Polytechnic Institute and State University.

To subscribe, send your request along with your BITNET or INTERNET address to:
BUDDYL@VTVM1.Bitnet or JPOWELL@VTVM1.Bitnet.

Owner: Buddy Litchfield <BUDDYL@VTVM1> (on BITNET) Assistant: James Powell
<JPOWELL@VTVM1>

VW5EARN@AWIWUW11.Bitnet

A mailing list about early music. Topics: Anything about early music (medieval, renaissance etc.)
including comments/questions about

1. (new) records
2. books
3. performances
4. song texts & translations
5. encoding early music scores in electronic form
6. etc.

Owner: Gerhard Gonter <GONTER@AWIWUW11.BITNET>

VWAR-L on LISTSERV@UBVM
or LISTSERV@UBVM.CC.BUFFALO.EDU

This list was formed to facilitate communication between scholars, teachers, veterans, and anyone who is
interested in the Vietnam War. Archives of VWAR-L and related files are stored in the VWAR-L
Filelist. To receive a list of files send the command "INDEX VWAR-L" (without the " ") to
LISTSERV@UBVM or LISTSERV@UBVM.CC.BUFFALO.EDU as the first line in the body of a mail
message (not the Subject: line).

To subscribe to VWAR-L, send the command SUB VWAR-L yourfirstname yourlastname
LISTSERV@UBVM on BITNET or LISTSERV@UBVM.CC.BUFFALO.EDU via a mail message
(again, as the first line in the body of the mail, not the Subject: line).

For example: SUB VWAR-L Victor Charles

Owner: Lydia Fish <FISHLM@SNYBUFVA.BITNET>

WAAN@NISC.NYSER.NET

Mailing list is intended to discuss the issues associated with the technology and administration of an
AppleTalk network across the Internet. In addition, the operation of a pilot project network is
occaisionally discussed. This is not intended to be a general AppleTalk discussion list, but is focused on
AppleTalk over IP networks. Most members of the list have a working knowledge of the operations of
either the Kinetics or the GatorBox LocalTalk - Ethernet Gateways.

Requests to be added to or deleted from the list, problems, questions, etc., should be sent to
WAAN-REQUEST@NISC.NYSER.NET.

Coordinator: Craig A. McGowan <MCGOWAN@MAPLE-LEAF.NYSER.NET>

war-worlds@PANARTHEA.EBAY.SUN.COM

Mailing list for discussion of Paramount's syndicated science fiction TV series "War of the Worlds".
Send subscription requests to war-worlds-request@PANARTHEA.EBAY.SUN.COM.

Coordinator: Steven Grimm <sgrimm@SUN.COM>

wefax@IDA.ORG

Mailing list for discussion by users of the APT and HRPT features of TIROS-N and GOES satellites.
Subscribers are primarily amateur radio and academic users; subscription limited to persons actually
involved in use of the satellites and/or development of "homebrew" equipment for this purpose, and
discussion is limited to technical topics related to satellites accessible from continental United States.

Archives of back issues are not currently available due to FTP access restrictions at the host site. All requests to be added to or deleted from this list, questions, comments, etc. should be sent to wefax-request@IDA.ORG.

Coordinator: Dr. Eric Roskos <roskos@IDA.ORG> <roskos@CS.IDA.ORG>

wellfleet-l@nstn.ns.ca

Wellfleet Communications Inc routers user group. Any and all discussion, problems, comments, compliments, complaints are welcome. Wellfleet engineers and users around the world regularly discuss problems of all types, and announcements of interest to users are posted as well. Archives are available by anonymous FTP from nstn.ns.ca in the subdirectory wellfleet-l/archive. All requests to be added to or deleted from the lists should be sent to wellfleet-l-request@nstn.ns.ca. The list is unmoderated.

Coordinator: Daniel MacKay <daniel@nstn.ns.ca>

WEIRD-L%BROWNVM.BITNET@CUNYVM.CUNY.EDU

Mailing list for all manner of weirdness; the local group with which we started concentrates on cutups and short bizarre stories, but anything strange is welcome. As distinguished from the old Bizarre-People list, we're not looking for humor but more for disturbing things. Requests to be put on the mailing list should be addressed to the Moderator, and should be accompanied by a submission.

Moderator: Jeremy Bornstein <JEREMY%BROWNVM.BITNET@CUNYVM.CUNY.EDU>

WELDCOMP@CASCADE.CARLETON.CA

SIG for computer modelling welds, run from CASCADE (Centre for Advanced Studies in Computer Aided Design and Engineering) at Carleton University. Messages related to computer modelling welds and the following topics would be especially welcome; if traffic warrants, anyone of them could become a Special Interest Group (SIG), or distribution list:

Weld pool physics
Weld microstructures
Residual Stress and Distortion
Sensors and Control
Failure Mechanisms and Analysis

All requests to be added to or deleted from this list, problems, questions, etc., should be sent to WELDCOMP-REQUEST@CASCADE.CARLETON.CA

Coordinator: Warren Hik <hik@CASCADE.CARLETON.CA>

WISENET on LISTSERV@UICVM.BITNET or LISTSERV@UICVM.uic.edu

Women in science, mathematics or engineering and students interested in those disciplines are encouraged to join a newly established network to help them progress in their careers. WISENET/Midwest is a Midwest network that promotes women and girls of diverse backgrounds in science, mathematics and engineering.

It's objectives include:

- to improve access to careers and advancement in science and engineering for girls and women of diverse backgrounds
- to support research and analysis of recruitment and retention strategies
- to maintain a database of resources and information about women scientists and engineers in the midwest
- to serve as a communication link among midwest groups and individuals interested in women in science and engineering.

This mail list has been established as one means of communication.

It is available to anyone with access to electronic mail (E-mail). To activate membership, send the following command in the BODY of e-mail to LISTSERV@UICVM on BITNET or LISTSERV@UICVM.UIC.EDU on the Internet:

SUBSCRIBE WISENET your full name

Owner: Dr. Alice Dan, U16715@UICVM.BITNET Notebooks: yes/monthly

whitewater@IUVAX.CS.INDIANA.EDU

Mail.whitewater is devoted to those who enjoy whitewater kayaking, rafting, and canoeing. The list is a forum for the discussion of trips, rivers, equipment, current happenings affecting "river rats", and anything else related to the sport.

Archives are kept on host IUVAX.CS.INDIANA.EDU in directory pub/whitewater, and are available by ANONYMOUS FTP. All requests to be added to or deleted from this list, problems, questions, etc., should be sent to whitewater-request@IUVAX.CS.INDIANA.EDU.

Coordinator: Charles Daffinger <cdaf@IUVAX.CS.INDIANA.EDU>

WIN3-L on LISTSERV@UICVM

The WIN3-L list is a forum for discussion about Microsoft Windows and related issues. It is intended for those who are just starting to use Windows as well as the veterans of the progreSubscribers are encouraged to seek help for problems, share tips and to discuss the good and bad expeiences that they have with Windows. Techical support persons are invited to exchange ideas about how they help others learn and use Windows.

To subscribe to WIN3-L, send the following command to LISTSERV@UICVM via mail text or interactive message:

SUB WIN3-L your_full_name

where "your_full_name" is your name. For example:

SUB WIN3-L Bill Gates

Owner: Tom Cervenka <CTCT100@UICVMC> Internet: ctct100@uicvmc.aiss.uiuc.edu Internet address of LISTSERV: listserv@uicvm.uic.edu

WINTCP-L on LISTSERV@UBVM   [Last Updated 28-January-1992]
    or LISTSERV@UBVM.CC.BUFFALO.EDU

This list was formed to serve as a vehicle for discussion of topics relating to the Wollongong Incorporated TCP/IP products. Archives of WINTCP-L and related files are stored in the WINTCP-L FILELIST. To receive a list of files send the command 'INDEX WINTCP-L' (without the ' ') to LISTSERV@UBVM or LISTSERV@UBVM.CC.BUFFALO.EDU as the first line in the body of a mail message (not the Subject: line).

To subscribe to WINTCP-L, send the command 'SUB WINTCP-L your name' (without the ' ') to LISTSERV@UBVM or LISTSERV@UBVM.CC.BUFFALO.EDU via a mail message (again, as the first line in the body of the mail, not the Subject: line).

For example: SUB WINTCP-L Joe Shmoe

WINTCP-L is also gatewayed into the vmsnet.networks.tcp-ip.wintcp news group of USENET News so if you have access to news reading software, you should read this list there to reduce unnecessary network traffic.

Owner: Jim Gerland <gerland@ubvms>
        Jim Gerland <gerland@ubvms.cc.buffalo.edu>

WITSENDO on LISTSERV@DARTCMS1 or LISTSERV@dartcms1.dartmouth.edu

WITSENDO is a moderated mailing list which discusses all aspects of ENDOMETRIOSIS with particular emphasis on coping with the disease and its treatment. Anyone with an interest in this disease is welcome to participate whether or not they actually suffer from the disease. The list will act as a clearinghouse for information exchange and to promote discussion of current treatments, research and educational literature. Professional (medical) comments are of course, most welcome. However, the list is primarily dedicated to the women who suffer from this painful and often demoralizing disease, therefore any information should be expressed in lay terms and attempt to exclude professional jargon (or at the very least provide adequate references and/or definitions of terms).

To Subscribe to the list, send mail to: LISTSERV@DARTCMS1.BITNET or LISTSERV@dartcms1.dartmouth.edu with the BODY of the mail (NOT subject) containing the command: SUB WITSENDO yourfullname

To post to the list, send mail to: WITSENDO@DARTCMS1.BITNET or WITSENDO@dartcms1.dartmouth.edu

Owner: David Avery <David.Avery@dartmouth.edu>

WMST-L@UMDD

WMST-L@UMDD.UMD.EDU (Internet address)

WMST-L has been formed to facilitate discussion of Women's Studies issues, especially those concerned with research, teaching, and program administration, and to publicize relevant conferences, job announcements, calls for papers, publications, and the like. It is hoped that the list will also serve as a central repository for course materials, curriculum proposals and projects, bibliographies, and other files related to Women's Studies. If you have materials that you'd be willing to put on file, please contact Joan Korenman, Women's Studies Program, U. of Maryland Baltimore County, Baltimore, MD 21228-5398 (KORENMAN@UMBC or KORENMAN@UMBC2.UMBC.EDU).

To subscribe to WMST-L, send the following command via e-mail or interactive message to LISTSERV@UMDD (Bitnet) or LISTSERV@UMDD.UMD.EDU (Internet): Subscribe WMST-L Your_full_name. For example:

Subscribe WMST-L Jane Doe

Messages for distribution on the list should be sent to WMST-L@UMDD or WMST-L@UMDD.UMD.EDU. Please note: only messages for distribution should be sent to WMST-L; all commands (subscribe, signoff, review, etc.) should go to LISTSERV.

Owner: Joan Korenman (KORENMAN@UMBC) [Bitnet]
(KORENMAN@UMBC2.UMBC.EDU) [Internet]

WOODWORK on LISTSERV@IPFWVM.BITNET

WOODWORK is designed to be a forum of discussion of the tools, methods and techniques used in working with wood. If you are a hobbyist or a budding professional, as a member of WOODWORK, please feel free to take part in the ongoing discussions. Without you, WOODWORK can not function. The specific topics to be discussed will be determined by the members of the list.

Subscription requests should be delivered to LISTSERV@IPFWVM.BITNET in a mail message with the first line of the mail message (BODY, not subject) containing the following command:

SUB WOODWORK your given name

If you are on a BITNET system, you can subscribe via an interactive message with the following syntax:

TELL LISTSERV AT IPFWVM SUB WOODWORK your given name

All messages will be logged to a notebook, with a new notebook started each month. Archived notebooks can be searched via LDBASE EXEC (or LDBASE.COM) available from your neighborhood LISTSERV.

Owner: Larry Rondot <RONDOT@IPFWVM.BITNET>

WORD-MAC@alsvid.une.edu.au   [Last Update 11/92]

Mailing list for users of Microsoft Word running on Macintosh computers. It is intended to serve as a forum in which all issues related to MS Word for the Macintosh, technical and non-technical, may be discussed in depth. The list is moderated by Roger Debreceny.

Interested persons may subscribe by sending mail (NOT interactive messages) with a blank subject line and the single command SUBSCRIBE WORD-MAC Your_First_Name Your_Surname to: listserv@alsvid.une.edu.au

Postings to the list may be sent to: word-mac@alsvid.une.edu.au

Administrative questions can be forwarded to: word-mac-request@alsvid.une.edu.au ,or to: mmacword@alsvid.une.edu.au

Moderator of the mailing list is Roger Debreceny, Centre for Accounting and Finance, University of New England-Northern Rivers, Lismore, NSW, Australia (mmacword@alsvid.une.edu.au).

WORD-PC@ufobi1.uni-forst.gwdg.de   [Last Update 9/92]

Mailing list for users of Microsoft Word running under DOS and Windows. It is intended to serve as a forum in which all issues related to MS Word for the PC, technical and non-technical, may be discussed in depth. The list is not currently moderated, but may be at a later date.

Interested persons may subscribe by sending mail (NOT interactive messages) with a blank subject line and the single command SUBSCRIBE WORD-PC to MAILSERV@ufobi1.uni-forst.gwdg.de Unsubscribing is done in the same manner, replacing the SUBSCRIBE command with an UNSUBSCRIBE command. Non-BitNet users can join by sending the above command to WORD-PC%HVRFORD.BITNET@CORNELLC.CIT.CORNELL.EDU.

Coordinator: Reinhold Meyer <rmeyer@ufobi2.uni-forst.gwdg.de>

WORDS-L@UGA.bitnet WORDS-L@UGA.CC.UGA.EDU

WORDS-L is a forum for discussion of the English language. To subscribe, send this message to LISTSERV@YALEVM.BITNET:

sub words-l Your Full Name

  Owners: Al Essa (ESSA@YALEVM.BITNET)
           Natalie Maynor (NM1@RA.MSSTATE.EDU)

WorkS@RUTGERS.EDU

WorkS discusses personal work station computers, such as the Sun2, Sun3, Apollo, Silicon Graphics, and AT&T Workstations. WorkS provides a way for interested members of the Internet community to discuss what is wrong with these machines, compare notes on work in progress, and share useful insights about these kinds of systems.

Archived Digest messages are kept on non-Internet hosts at Rutgers, and must be requested from WorkS-Request@RUTGERS.EDU. All requests to be added to or deleted from this list, problems, questions, etc., should be sent to WorkS-Request@RUTGERS.EDU.

There is a BitNet sub-distribution list, WORKS@RUTVM1; BitNet subscribers can join by sending the SUB command with your name (examples are for the VAX). For example: SEND LISTSERV@RUTVM1 SUB WORKS Jon Doe To be removed from the list: SEND LISTSERV@RUTVM1 SIGNOFF To make contributions to the list, BitNet subscribers should send mail to the Internet list name, NOT to the BITNET list name.

Coordinator: Dave Steiner <STEINER@RUTGERS.EDU>

WORLD-L on LISTSERV@UBVM   [Last Updated 28-January-1992] or LISTSERV@UBVM.CC.BUFFALO.EDU

The WORLD-L is a forum for the discussion of the teaching, methodology, and theory of a scientific and non-Eurocentric world history. It aims to hold regular electronic conferences related to the purpose of the list.

Archives of WORLD-L and related files are stored in the WORLD-L FILELIST. To receive a list of files send the command INDEX WORLD-L to LISTSERV@UBVM or LISTSERV@UBVM.CC.BUFFALO.EDU as the first line in the body of a mail message (not the Subject: line).

To subscribe to WORLD-L, send the command SUB WORLD-L yourfirstname yourlastname to LISTSERV@UBVM or LISTSERV@UBVM.CC.BUFFALO.EDU via a mail message (again, as the first line in the body of the mail, not the Subject: line).

For example: SUB WORLD-L John Doe

Owner: Haines Brown BROWNH@CTSTATEU.BITNET

WRITERS%NDSUVM1.BITNET@VM1.NODAK.EDU

Online discussion group for professional writers and those who aspire to be writers. Discussions center around the art, craft, and business of writing, and also keep members informed about new and varied opportunities for writers. Archives of WRITERS back issues can be Listed by sending the following command to LISTSERV@NDSUVM1 via mail or interactive message: INDEX WRITERS

To subscribe, send the following command to LISTSERV@NDSUVM1 via mail or interactive message: SUB WRITERS your full name where "your full name" is your real name, not your login Id.

Non-BitNet users can access the archives or subscribe by sending the above commands as the only line in the text/body of a message to LISTSERV%NDSUVM1.BITNET@VM1.NODAK.EDU.

Coordinator: Ray Wheeler <DS001451@VM1.NODAK.EDU>
                      <DS001451%NDSUVM1.BITNET@VM1.NODAL.EDU>
                      <DS001451@NDSUVM1> (BitNet)

WWII-L on LISTSERV@UBVM   [Last Updated March 1991]
or LISTSERV@UBVM.CC.BUFFALO.EDU

Topics such as history, strategy, technology, personalities, political issues, general information, and "trivia" are welcome. Announcements of reunions and other items of interest to World War II veterans (and those who still remember and honor them) will also be posted.

The list will be self-moderated by a system of "flags" in the subject line to allow subscribers to skip topics they are not interested in reading. Further information on this will be sent when a subscription is recorded, or you can contact the list-owner.

To subscribe to WWII-L, send the following command to LISTSERV@UBVM (or listserv@ubvm.cc.buffalo.edu) via mail text (BODY) or interactive message:

SUBSCRIBE WWII-L Your_full_name

For example: SUBSCRIBE WWII-L Larry Jewell

Owner: Larry W. Jewell (jewell@mace.cc.purdue.edu)
Co-Owner: Lydia Fish   (fishlm@snybufva)
Co-Owner: Toby Hughes   (thughes@lonestar.utsa.edu)

WX-TALK@UIUCVMD
WX-TALK@UIUCVMD.BITNET@VM1.NODAK.EDU

The list WX-TALK has been created for the purpose of discussing weather-related phenomena such as severe storms, tornadoes, forecasting, interesting local weather events, SKYWARN storm spotter groups, and tornado chasing. The list is not in digested form; a monthly notebook will be maintained.

To subscribe, send the following command to LISTSERV@UIUCVMD via mail or interactive message:

SUB WX-TALK your_full_name

where "your_full_name" is your name. For example: SUB WX-TALK Joan Doe Non-BitNet users can subscribe by sending the text:

SUB WX-TALK your_full_name

in the body of a message to LISTSERV@VMD.CSO.UIUC.EDU or LISTSERV%UIUCVMD.BITNET@CUNYVM.CUNY.EDU. To unsubscribe send the following command: UNSUB WX-TALK

Coordinator: Chris Novy <axvsccn@UICVMC.AISS.UIUC.EDU>
<axvsccn@UICVMC.BITNET>

WXSPOT%UIUCVMD.BITNET@VM1.NODAK.EDU

Mailing list for discussions about severe storm spotter training, spotter networks, training materials, upcoming training, methods of transmitting weather data, and local community programs. The list, although a spin-off of STORM-L, will be used for discussions only and will not carry current weather data. It is hoped that through these discussions better community severe storm spotter training and public awareness programs can be developed.

BitNet users can subscribe by sending the following command via interactive message or as the only line in the text/body of mail to LISTSERV@UIUCVMD (or, if that fails, to LISTSERV@VMD.CSO.UIUC.EDU): SUB WXSPOT your_full_name where "your_full_name" is your real name, not your login Id Example: SUB WXSPOT John Q. Public Non-BitNet users can join the list by sending the above command as the only line in the text/body of a message to LISTSERV%UIUCVMD.BITNET@VM1.NODAK.EDU (or for UUCP sites, to uiucuxc!vmd!listserv).

Coordinator: Chris Novy <AXVSCCN%UICVMC.BITNET@VM1.NODAK.EDU>

X-ADA@EXPO.LCS.MIT.EDU

This list discusses uses of the X Window System with ADA. Also see X11-3D, XIMAGE, XPERT, XVIDEO. All requests to be added to or deleted from this list, problems, questions, etc., should be sent to X-ADA-REQUEST@EXPO.LCS.MIT.EDU.

Coordinator: X Consortium staff <LISTS-REQUEST@EXPO.LCS.MIT.EDU>

X-SERIAL@LLL-CRG.LLNL.GOV@INDEX(X-SERIAL)

Mailing list for discussion on support of X11 across EIA232 (and other low bandwidth media). This list is archived and old messages are available on request. Requests to be added to or deleted from the list, problems, questions, etc., should be sent to X-SERIAL-REQUEST@LLL-CRG.LLNL.GOV.

Coordinator: Casey Leedom <CASEY@GAUSS.LLNL.GOV>

X11-3D@ATHENA.MIT.EDU

This list discusses 3D extensions to the X Window System. Also see X-ADA, X113D, XIMAGE, XPERT, XVIDEO. All requests to be added to or deleted from this list, problems, questions, etc., should be sent to X11-3D-REQUEST@ATHENA.MIT.EDU.

Coordinator: X Consortium staff <LISTS-REQUEST@EXPO.LCS.MIT.EDU>

XCULT-L%PSUVM.BITNET@CUNYVM.CUNY.EDU

An international intercultural newsletter written by undergraduate and graduate students at Penn State University who are enrolled in Speech Communication 497B: Cross-cultural Communication. Each week, students write on a topic being discussed in class. Topics range from non-dominant cultures in the

U.S. to corporate cultures to the use of nonverbal communication in international communication. Participants who receive the newsletter are encouraged to join in the discussions or contribute their own topics and issues.

To subscribe, either send a note to the Editor or subscribe directly by sending a subscribe command to LISTSERV@PSUVM: TELL LISTSERV AT PSUVM SUB XCULT-L Your Full Name

Editor: Joyce Neu <JN0%PSUVM.BITNET@CUNYVM.CUNY.EDU>

XCULT-X on LISTSERV@UMRVMB.BITNET or LISTSERV@UMRVMB.UMR.EDU

The purpose of Xcult-X, Intercultural Communication Practicum, is to foster interdisciplinary discussions of communication philosophy, theory, and practice in the global village through formation of a discussion group via human computer-mediated communication. Xcult-X is a rule-free discussion group open to all. It is sponsored by Lance Haynes who refuses to take any power other than that firmly imposed by the host computer center. Requests for listowner to exert any power whatsoever over the topics or discussion methods on this list will be met with referral to group discussion.

The Intercultural Communication Practicum is a "child" of the International Intercultural Newsletter in that Xcult-X was begun in an effort to house discussion topics and methods that originated on Xcult-L but were not in keeping with its announced purposes.

The list XCULT-X has been created on LISTSERV@UMRVMB. Please send your subscription requests to LISTSERV@UMRVMB or LISTSERV@UMRVMB.UMR.EDU. In the text of the mail include: SUB XCULT-X yourfirstname yourlastname

Sponsor and list owner: Lance Hayes (C0334@UMRVMB.UMR.EDU).

XEDIT-L%UGA.UGA.EDU@VM1.NODAK.EDU

Mailing list for the discussion of the IBM VM System Editor (XEDIT). It is not for discusison of the TSO editor, the PDF editor, QED, KEDIT, QEDIT, EVE, VI, or EMACS. If and when XEDIT is made available under TSO, it will be included here. REXX, as utilized by XEDIT as its macro language is acceptable here also. Peers for this list are located at OHSTVMA, TCSVM, MARIST, and RUTVM1. Monthly notebooks are being maintained at UGA.

To [un]subscribe, send a message to one of the Coordinators.

Coordinators: Harold Pritchett <HAROLD%UGA.UGA.EDU@VM1.NODAK.EDU>
Ross Patterson   <A024012%RUTVM1 .BITNET@VM1.NODAK.EDU>
TCS INFO Account <INFO%TCSVM.BITNET@VM1.NODAK.EDU>
A. Harry Williams <HARRY%MARIST.BITNET@VM1.NODAK.EDU>
Duane Weaver   <TS0007%OHSTVMA.BITNET@VM1.NODAK.EDU>

XIANGQI on LISTSERV@INDYCMS.BITNET or LISTSERV@INDYCMS.IUPUI.EDU

This is an open, unmoderated (read that: uncensored) list for the discussion and opportunity to bring players of Chinese Chess together.

Send your subscription to LISTSERV@INDYCMS.BITNET or LISTSERV@INDYCMS.IUPUI.EDU with the body of the mail containing the command: SUB XIANGQI yourfirstname yourlastname

Archiving of list logs are weekly.

List Owner: Phil Paxton, IQTI400@INDYCMS.BITNET, IQTI400@INDYCMS.IUPUI.EDU 1-800-972-8744 x40836

XIMAGE@EXPO.LCS.MIT.EDU   [Last Updated 8/92]

This list discusses image processing with the X Window System. Also see X-ADA, X11-3D, XPERT, XVIDEO. All requests to be added to or deleted from this list, problems, questions, etc., should be sent to XIMAGE-REQUEST@EXPO.LCS.MIT.EDU.

Coordinator: X Consortium staff <LISTS-REQUEST@EXPO.LCS.MIT.EDU>

XPERT@EXPO.LCS.MIT.EDU   [Last Updated 8/92]

Mailing list for general discussion on the X window system, software running under X, and the like. Also see X-ADA, X11-3D, XIMAGE, XVIDEO. All requests to be added to or deleted from this list, problems, questions, etc., should be sent to XPERT-REQUEST@ATHENA.MIT.EDU.

Coordinator: Keith Packard <keith@EXPO.LCS.MIT.EDU>
X Consortium staff <LISTS-REQUEST@EXPO.LCS.MIT.EDU>

xpilot-list@cs.uit.no   [Last Update 9/92]

XPilot is a multiplayer war gravity game (Gravity Force, Thrust, Asteriods type). Only requirements are that you can access a UNIX box with X and an ANSI compliant compiler. The list's main purpose is to be a channel through which xpilot players can share their experience with others, as well as a way to stay updated with the progress of the game (patches, maps). All submissions should be posted to xpilot-list@cs.uit.no. To subscribe, send a mail with subject "subscribe" to xpilot-request@cs.uit.no.

Coordinator: Bjoern Stabell
University of Tromsoe
(+47) 83 44 053 / 83 75 164
bjoerns@staff.cs.uit.no

XPRESS-LIST@CSD.MOT.COM

An unmoderated list for discussing the X*Change information service that X*Press Information Services Ltd. distributes over some cable television systems. Topics include general information, datastream format, alternate user interfaces, etc.

New subscribers will automatically receive digests of all previous messages from the list, at least until such time that it becomes unwieldy to do so. To subscribe or unsubscribe to the xpress-list, send a request to xpress-list-request@csd.mot.com. At present, requests are handled by a human operator. No particular format for request is required, but please make sure that your full name is included somewhere in the message or header. Administrative messages other than subscription and unsubscription should be sent to xpress-list-owner@csd.mot.com.

Coordinator: Brian Smithson <brian@csd.mot.com>

XVIDEO@EXPO.LCS.MIT.EDU

This list discusses possible extensions for using live and still video within the X Window System. Also see X-ADA, X11-3D, XIMAGE, XPERT. All requests to be added to or deleted from this list, problems, questions, etc., should be sent to XVIDEO-REQUEST@EXPO.LCS.MIT.EDU.

Coordinator: X Consortium staff <LISTS-REQUEST@EXPO.LCS.MIT.EDU>

XVTDEV@qed.cts.com   [Last Updated June 1992]

This is to announce the new XVT Developers' Mailing List. XVT is a multi-platform window environment development tool. Interested parties should send mail with 'HELP XVTDEV' as the body of the letter to: listserv@qed.cts.com

Owner:
Tim Capps   tim@qed.cts.com   or   qed!tim
QED Software   The QED BBS (310)420-9327

XXI@UCHCECVM.BITNET   [Last Updated 12-October-1991]

TITULO: XXI Ciencia & Tecnologia TITLE: XXI Science & Technology

IDIOMAS: Espanol, portugues, ingles. LANGUAGES: Spanish, Portugese, English.

DESCRIPCION: Una plaza publica para conversaciones sobre Ciencia (en el sentido canonico de la palabra) y Tecnologia; abiertas a la posibilidad de ser impresas en un medio de comunicacion masiva.

DESCRIPTION: A public ground for (canonical) Science & Tech conversations. Whoever participates accepts therby that his or her words may be published in a mass media.

The Owner is NLUCO@UCHCECVM. To subscribe send a command or e-mail to LISTSERV@UCHCECVM.BITNET with the command SUB XXI your full name in the body.

OBJETIVO: Enlazar las redes academicas de comunicacion con vias de comunicacion masiva. Se quiere insertar la vida cientifica y tecnologica en la esfera del acontecer reconocido. Se quiere aprovechar para la comunicacion publica el deposito del conocimiento e inteligencia presentes en las redes academicas. Se quiere realzar la nueva realidad que representan las redes de comunicacion electronica en la aldea global y proporcionarles una camara de resonancia en el medio impreso.

OBJECTIVE: To link academic networks with mass media. The idea is to include scientific and technological life in the sphere of acknowledged things-that-happen. The newspaper wants to use for public communication the treasure of knowledge and intelligence residing in academic networks. Therealso is the interest of underlining the importance of this new reality, the global village in electronic networking, by providing an echo chamber to its subtle sounds.

CARACTERISTICA: El administrador de la lista es Nicolas Luco, editor del semanario de Ciencia y Tecnologia "XXI" que circula con "El Mercurio", el diario mas antiguo de habla hispana, de circulacion nacional en Chile.

CHARACTERISTIC: The administrator of the list is Nicolas Luco, editor of the Science & Tech weekly "XXI", a supplement to the "El Mercurio" newspaper, the oldest World Spanish newspaper in print, which circulates in all of Chile, LatinAmerica.

CONTENIDOS: Abiertos a contenidos de caracter cientifico y tecnologica con miras a su comunicacion publica. Se preferiran aquellos que respondan o reaccionen a publicaciones en la revista "XXI". Pero eso no es algo forzoso. Los contenidos pueden ser, por ejemplo:

1) sugerencias	5) debates
2) ensayos breves	6) opiniones
3) hipotesis	7) conversaciones
4) articulos	8) noticias para publicar

No se aceptaran debates de indole politica ni religiosa, salvo que se trate de politica cientifica y tecnologica (p. ej., fondos para la investigacion, patentes y propiedad intelectual, etc.).

CONTENTS: Open to scientific and technological matters to be made public. Those contributions will be preferred which respond or react to matters published in "XXI", the weekly magazine. But this will not be a must. The contents may take the form of :

1) suggestions	5) debates
2) short essays	6) opinions
3) hypothesis	7) conversations
4) articles	8) news to be published

No religious or politica debates will be accepted, except thos about general science and tech. policy, for example: funds for research, or patents and intellectual ownership, etc.)

ALCANCE: Se espera un alcance nacional, especialmente relacionado con los academicos ligados a REUNA, REd Universitaria Nacional, Chile. Pero se desea una interaccin entre academicos y alumnos de otros paises, especialmente de paises del Hemisferio Norte, para un buen intercambio Norte-Sur.

RANGE: The first goal is to be open to REUNA, the Chilean University Network. But this list wants to provide a field for interaction between the faculty an students from different cultures, especially with those from countries of the Northern Hemisphere, in view of a fruitful North-South Exchange.

XYZZY-L%CMUCCVMA.BITNET@CUNYVM.CUNY.EDU

A forum for discussion about Xyzzy, a "Deluxe" chatting exec for VM/CMS Systems, and for Xyzzy-Vax, its counterpart for VAX/VMS systems. The list is for questions and general discussions regarding Xyzzy. All users of either version of Xyzzy are welcome to subscribe and send messages to this list.

To subscribe, issue the command:
TELL LISTSERV AT CMUCCVMA SUBSCRIBE XYZZY-L your_full_name

or send a message to LISTSERV%CMUCCVMA.BITNET@CUNYVM.CUNY.EDU with the above command included as the only message body line. To remove yourself from the list, issue the command: TELL LISTSERV AT CMUCCVMA UNSUBSCRIBE XYZZY-L

or send a message to LISTSERV@CMUCCVMA with that command. For a list of other ListServ commands, use the command HELP instead of SUBSCRIBE or UNSUBSCRIBE.

> Coordinator: Marc Shannon <R602MS5U%CMCCVB.BITNET@VM1.NODAK.EDU>
> XYZZY Developer: David Bolen <DB3L%CMUCCVMA.BITNET@CUNYVM.CUNY.EDU>

Y-RIGHTS@SJUVM.BITNET   [Last Updated 28-January-1992]

As the title suggests, this list is on the discussion of the rights of kids and teenagers (called Y-Rights for "Youth Rights", or "Youngster's Rights" or "Why Rights?" -- whichever strikes your fancy). It's a very open list, and everyone is welcome to participate on it, whether you are a teacher, a professional, a student, or a kid or teenager yourself.

What do I mean when I say "Children's Rights"? Well, I don't necessarily mean the rights for adults to "protect" children, because that "right" seems to be misused and misguided to ends that are, oftentimes, tragic, even with the 'best' intentions. That, of course, is open for discussion on this list, and I'm certain that it will come up at some point.

In my ever changing view of rights for those under the 'age of majority' (which is 18 or 21 in the United States, depending on how you view it, and different in other countries), I am looking more for changes in our judicial system, educational system, and our society, as a whole, to view youth as Human Beings first and foremost, before concerning themselves with the 'correct manners to treat, mold and shape a child', as if s/he is just a ball of clay, and not a human being.

So, with that, I welcome you. Come to talk, or come to listen. Speak up anytime, even if just to say "Hi, I'm still here...."

To add yourself to the list, send an Interactive Message (BITNET) or a Mail message (any system) to LISTSERV@SJUVM with a single line:

SUB Y-RIGHTS Firstname Lastname

This particular LISTSERV takes a minimum of two names, but it can take three, four or more (for example, "J. P. Zelder Hoghorn III" is acceptable. "John" will not work).

Owner:

> Kenneth Udut
> kudut@hamp.hampshire.edu
> kudut@hampvms.bitnet

YACHT-L%GREARN.BITNET@VM1.NODAK.EDU

Yachting, Sailing, Design and amateur BoatBuilding mailing list. The list offers to the people that are interested in these subjects a way to communicate. Discussions about new yachts, designs, construction techniques, races, etc., are welcome.

To subscribe to the list, send the following command to LISTSERV@GREARN:

VM/CMS:
TELL LISTSERV at GREARN SUB YACHT-L Your_Full_Name

VMS:
    SEND LISTSERV@GREARN SUB YACHT-L Your_Full_Name

Non-BitNet users can subscribe by sending a message to
LISTSERV%GREARN.BITNET@VM1.NODAK.EDU with the message text/body: SUB YACHT-L
Your_Full_Name

Coordinator: Kostas Antonopoulos <NETMAINT%GREARN.BITNET@VM1.NODAK.EDU>
<Gandal%GGRCRVAX1.BITNET@VM1.NODAK.EDU>

YTERM-L%YALEVM.BITNET@CUNYVM.CUNY.EDU

Unmoderated mailing list intended for discussion of problems or concerns with the Yale Terminal
Emulation software package. YTERM is a useful VT100 emulator and may be used with the IBM 7171
protocol converter and previous versions of the Yale ASCII terminal communication system. File
transfer with YTERM is accomplished with PCTRANS host software. PC to PC file transfer over an
asynch line is also possible with YTERM.

BitNet users can add themselves to the list by issuing the following command to
LISTSERV@YALEVM.BITNET: SUBSCRIBE YTERM-L your_full_name where your_full_name is
your real name (not your userid). BitNet users can unsubscribe with the command: UNSUBSCRIBE
YTERM-L

All other requests to be added to or deleted from this list, problems, questions, etc., should be sent to the
Coordinator.

Coordinator: Susan Barmhall <SUSAN%YALEVM.BITNET@CUNYVM.CUNY.EDU>

YUNUS on LISTSERV@TRMETU.BITNET

YUNUS is an informal and semi official publication of Turkish TeX Users Group with the purpose: to
discuss, disseminate and exchange information about TeX typesetting system, its variants and especially
Turkish TeX. YUNUS EMRE is a 15'th century Turkish poet and philosopher, who is one of the best
users of turkish language. The list is named after him.

to LISTSERV@TRMETU.bitnet.

There is no language restrictions on the list.

'Owners' of the list: akgul@trbilun.BITNET (Mustafa Akgul) a07820@trmetua.BITNET (Bulent
Karasozen) ZIYA@TRMETU.BITNET (Ziya Karakaya)

List is located at TRMETU.bitnet. So so you can send post files to list by sending them to
YUNUS@TRMETU.bitnet, and subscribe to List via a mail consisting of

SUB YUNUS First_Name Middle_name Last_name

For ordinary mail use:
Mustafa Akgul
Bilkent University
06533 Bilkent
Ankara
Turkey

5 ADDING A LISTING TO THIS GUIDE

If you maintain an Internet mailing list that isn't included this guide, and would like to have your listing included in the next edition please complete the following template, and send it to interest-groups-request@nisc.sri.com.

List Address:

Description:

Archive location and availability:

How to join:

Coordinator/Owner:

Expiration Date[2]:

---

[2]If you only plan to run your list list for a limited time (for example, if your list is for the organization of a one-time activity) please indicate the date at which it will no longer be active.

Index